Understanding Dying, Death, & Bereavement

Fourth Edition

Understanding Dying, Death, & Bereavement

Fourth Edition

Michael R. Leming
St. Olaf College

George E. Dickinson
College of Charleston

Harcourt Brace College Publishers

Fort Worth   Philadelphia   San Diego   New York   Orlando   Austin   San Antonio
Toronto   Montreal   London   Sydney   Tokyo

Publisher:	Earl McPeek
Acquisitions Editor:	Brenda Weeks
Product Manager:	Julie McBurney
Project Editor:	Travis Tyre
Art Director:	Lora Gray
Production Manager:	Kathy Ferguson

Cover image adapted from Corel Corporation image number 138021, © 1996 Corel Corporation.
ISBN: 0-15-505174-1
Library of Congress Catalog Card Number: 97-74390

Address for orders:
Harcourt Brace & Company
6277 Sea Harbor Drive
Orlando, FL 32887-6777
1-800-782-4479

Address for editorial correspondence:
Harcourt Brace College Publishers
301 Commerce Street, Suite 3700
Fort Worth, TX 76102

Web site address:
http://www.hbcollege.com

Harcourt Brace & Company will provide complimentary supplements or supplement packages to those adopters qualified under our adoption policy. Please contact your sales representative to learn how you qualify. If as an adopter or potential user you receive supplements you do not need, please return them to your sales representative or send them to: Attn: Returns Department, Troy Warehouse, 465 South Lincoln Drive, Troy, MO 63379.

Printed in the United States of America

890123456 039 98765432

About the Authors

Michael R. Leming is professor of sociology at St. Olaf College in Minnesota. He holds degrees from Westmont College (B.A.), Marquette University (M.A.), and the University of Utah (Ph.D.) and has completed additional graduate study at the University of California–Santa Barbara. He is the founder and former director of the St. Olaf College Social Research Center and is a former member of the board of directors of the Minnesota Coalition of Terminal Care. He has served as a steering committee member of the Northfield AIDS Response, and as a hospice educator, volunteer, and grief counselor. In 1996, Dr. Leming was a visiting professor of sociology at Chiang Mai University in Thailand. He is author of numerous books on social thanatology and family issues and is presently working on a book based on ethnographic work in a Karen village in northern Thailand.

George E. Dickinson is professor of sociology at the College of Charleston in South Carolina. He holds degrees from Baylor University (B.A. in biology and M.A. in sociology) and Louisiana State University (Ph.D. in sociology). He has completed additional graduate study in gerontology at Pennsylvania State University, in thanatology at the University of Kentucky School of Medicine, and in medical sociology at the University of Connecticut. He has published more than fifty articles in such professional journals as *Social Science and Medicine; Omega; Death Studies; Academic Medicine; Medical Care; Clinical Anatomy; Family Practice Research; Journal of the American Medical Women's Association; Loss, Grief and Care; Journal of Dental Education; Journal of Nursing Education; Journal for the Scientific Study of Religion; Journal of Marriage and the Family; Youth and Society; and Journal of Family Issues*. Dr. Dickinson has been teaching courses on death and dying for twenty-five years and has been actively involved with Hospice of Charleston. He is currently researching physicians' attitudes toward assisted suicide as well as conducting a longitudinal study of medical students' perceptions of "detached concern" toward terminally ill patients.

In addition to *Understanding Dying, Death, & Bereavement* (4th ed.), Michael R. Leming and George E. Dickinson are coauthors of *Understanding Families: Diversity, Continuity, and Change* (Allyn and Bacon, 1990, and Harcourt Brace, 1995), and they are coeditors with Alan C. Mermann of *Annual Editions: Dying, Death, and Bereavement* (Dushkin/McGraw Hill, 1993, 1994, 1995, 1997).

Preface

More than fourteen years ago, we began construction of the first edition of *Understanding Dying, Death, & Bereavement*. At that time, we desired to create a book that was informative and practical, yet theoretical. We visualized a humanistic text that was multidisciplinary in orientation and inclusive of the major foci of the interdisciplinary subject of social thanatology. In 1985 we accomplished those goals. Now in our fourth edition, we continue that tradition of excellence. We have thoroughly revised and updated the text to reflect contemporary developments in thanatology, and we have added new photos and cartoons to help illustrate subjects discussed in the text.

Understanding Dying, Death, & Bereavement (4th ed.) equips the reader with the necessary information to both understand and cope with the social aspects of dying, death, and bereavement. Because both of us have taught courses on thanatology for over twenty-five years, we have come to believe that every student carries both academic and personal agendas when approaching the subject.

Understanding Dying, Death, & Bereavement (4th ed.) will make a significant contribution to your class as it is a proven text informed by fifty years of experience. The book is comprehensive and covers the wide range of topics in social thanatology. It is scholarly and academically sound, and it is practical for students because it addresses personal issues relating to an individual's ability to cope with the social and psychological processes of dying, death, and bereavement. This text appeals to a vast audience, not only because of its wide adaptability on college and university campuses, but also because of its practical implications for all persons who must cope with this topic. Although this text is intended primarily for undergraduate students in sociology, psychology, nursing, social work, kinesiology, religion, gerontology, health science, family studies, philosophy, and education courses, it is also appropriate for professional courses in medicine, nursing, mortuary science, social work, and pastoral counseling.

In an attempt to help our readers increase their understanding of thanatology, we organized *Understanding Dying, Death, & Bereavement* (4th ed.) in four sections. Part One: Understanding Dying and Death addresses the American way of dying and the social meaning of death and dying. Part Two: Understanding Death Attitudes sheds light on death attitudes, developmental perspectives on dying and death, and religion and death attitudes. Part Three: Understanding the Dying Process delves deep into the dying process with discussions of hospice, euthanasia, biomedical issues, and suicide. Finally, Part Four: Understanding the Bereavement Process addresses the anthropology of death rituals, the history of bereavement and burial practices in American culture, funerals, and the bereavement process.

Within each chapter, we include features that we hope will make thanatology more interesting and personally relevant to students and instructors. **Boxed inserts** present timely readings and articles that illustrate issues covered in the text. Chapter **conclusions** and **summaries** serve as study aids to outline the important points of each chapter. **Discussion questions** probe students' understanding of the important issues addressed in each chapter. **Annotated bibliographies** provide information on suggested readings for students who desire further research. **Glossaries** of unfamiliar terms are located at the end of each chapter. And, related **Web sites** provide readers with up-to-the-minute information on the topic of each chapter.

Although collaboration occurred throughout this revision, a division of labor was established from the outset. Michael Leming wrote chapters 2, 5, 7, 8, 12, 13; George Dickinson wrote chapters 1, 3, 4, 6, 9, 10; and James J. Farrell, a colleague from St. Olaf College in Minnesota, wrote chapter 11 (see acknowledgments). Thus, if you occasionally encounter a reference to "I" in a chapter, this first person singular refers to the primary author of that particular chapter. It is our hope that these personal accounts strewn throughout the text will make the reading a little more "real" and a little less "textbookish."

We welcome positive and negative feedback from readers, for we feel such criticism will certainly improve future editions of this book. We would also appreciate correspondence from instructors concerning pedagogy related to the teaching of thanatology. Please write to us at the departments of sociology and anthropology at our respective schools via E-mail Mike at leming@stolaf.edu or George at dickinson@cofc.edu. We also encourage you to look at Mike's Web site and thanatology links at http://www.stolaf.edu/people/leming.

A combined instructor's manual and test bank for *Understanding Dying, Death, & Bereavement* (4th ed.) is available and can be obtained through your local Harcourt Brace representative or by writing to the Sociology Editor, Harcourt Brace College Publishers, 301 Commerce Street, Suite 3700, Fort Worth, TX 76102.

ACKNOWLEDGMENTS

Looking back over the past fourteen years, we are struck by the degree to which this book is the result of a tremendous team effort. In our first edition, we brought together nine national authorities who had extensive academic experience and personal involvement in the topical areas on which they wrote. However, we soon discovered that differences in writing styles and various levels of treatment created problems for our readers. Therefore, with the exception of chapter 11, we have rewritten the chapters previously contributed by our professional colleagues. We are grateful to those first edition contributors and the groundwork they provided. Thank you to Robert Bendiksen, Department of Sociology, University of Wisconsin at La Crosse; Nils C. Fribert, Bethel Theological Seminary, St. Paul, MN; Ann L. Overbeck, School of Social Work, Western Michigan University; Glenn M. Vernon (deceased), Department of Sociology, University of Utah; John W. Abbot, Connecticut Hospice; Robert C. Slater (retired), Department of Mortuary Science, University of Minnesota; and James J. Farrell, History Department, St. Olaf College, MN.

We gratefully acknowledge those who reviewed the third edition and made valuable suggestions incorporated in this fourth edition: Clifton D. Bryant, Virginia Polytechnic Institute and State University; Dennis E. Ferrara, Mott Community

College; Leslie A. Muray, Lansing Community College; James F. Paul, Kankakee Community College; and Alban L. Wheeler, Morehead State University. We are also indebted to all of those at Harcourt Brace College Publishers who devoted a great deal of their time and energies to us and our project: Brenda Weeks, acquisitions editor; Bryan Leake and Janie Pierce-Bratcher, editorial assistants; Kathy Ferguson, production manager; Lora Gray, art director; and Travis Tyre, project editor.

Again, we acknowledge the support of our families during the revision of this book. We appreciate their sharing in our struggle as we "walked in the valley of the shadow of death." They know how much strength we gained from reflecting upon our death-related experiences, and they watched as "our mourning changed into dancing." We hope our readers will experience an appreciation for life as they begin to understand, both intellectually and emotionally, the social-psychological processes of dying, death, and bereavement. Indeed, this book concerns dying and death, but it is really about living and life. May reading this book help make life more meaningful for you.

M.R.L.

G.E.D.

Contents

Chapter 2
Understanding the Social Meaning of Dying and Death   39

Part Two
Understanding Death Attitudes   69

Chapter 3
Children and Death   69

Chapter 4
Developmental Perspective on Dying and Death:
Adolescence Through Older Adulthood 109

Chapter 5
Religion and Death Attitudes 141

Part Three
Understanding the Dying Process   185

Chapter 6
The Dying Process   187

Chapter 7
The Hospice Approach:
Alternative Care for the Dying   231

Chapter 8
Euthanasia and Biomedical Issues   275

Chapter 9
Suicide   307

Part Four
Understanding the Bereavement Process   345

Chapter 12
The Funeral:
Expression of Contemporary American Bereavement   425

Chapter 13
The Bereavement Process   469

Part One
Understanding Dying and Death

Chapter 1

The American Way of Dying

I mourn not those who lose their vital breath
But those who, living, live in fear of death.

—THE ANCIENT GREEK ANTHOLOGY

Death is not the enemy; living in constant fear of it is.

—NORMAN COUSINS

People who relate to any aspect of dying and death are thought by many to be "weird" or "morbid." Note the reactions of others when you tell them that you are taking a course on dying and death. The startled reactions of those when told that we teach courses on dying and death are rather interesting, to say the least. One woman, when informed that I offer a course on dying and death, reacted by saying, "How could you do such a thing?"

Imagine the responses to persons who are funeral directors or who work in a nursing home or on a cancer ward of a hospital. From the reactions that most people have to these death-related issues, it appears that death discussions are considered in bad taste and something to be avoided. **Elderhostel** programs, for example, can present any topic of interest to older persons *except dying and death*. Likewise, according to a recent survey (Hiller, 1996), U.S. high school physical education and health teachers spend less time teaching dying and death than any of the other 21 health topics, and the topic of dying and death is less likely to be required in the 50 states than are any of the other 21 health topics.

Dying in the United States today occurs "offstage," away from the arena of familiar surroundings of kin and friends. Eighty percent of deaths in the United States occur in institutional settings—hospitals and nursing homes (Nuland, 1994, p. 255). The figure has gradually risen since 1949, when it was 50 percent, to 61 percent in 1958, and to 70 percent in 1977, notes Nuland (1994). Grandfather seldom dies at home today, where he has spent most of his life, but instead in a rather impersonal institutional setting. The removal of death from the usual setting prompted Richard Dumont and Dennis Foss (1972, p. 2) to raise the question: "How is the modern American able to cope with his own death when the deaths he experiences are infrequent, highly impersonal, and viewed as virtually abnormal?" Modern-day Americans have been as repressed about death as the Victorians were about sex.

Current Interest in Thanatology

For the past 15 years or so, however, a fascination with dying and death phenomena has been evidenced within much of the U.S. population (Crase, 1994). The fascination has been fueled by print and electronic media, by directives or various legal bodies, and by legal gymnastics surrounding several prolonged and much-observed deaths of individuals. Americans are finally willing to acknowledge that living is the leading cause of death, and they want to talk about it (Foderaro, 1994).

Today's thanatology student is bombarded by pressing issues of the day that involve death and death-related matters: the acquired immunodeficiency syndrome (AIDS) crisis, the prolongation of dying from cancer, the growing incidence of chronic illnesses with uncertain courses, murder, ecological disasters, fetal transplants, and abortion. The topic of death is "alive and well" in today's contemporary society. Let's look at some of the reasons why dying and death as topics of discussion have come into their own in recent years.

WHY THE INCREASED INTEREST?

This increased interest in **thanatology** (the study of dying, death, and bereavement) is due to several reasons.

First, with the majority of Americans dying in hospitals and nursing homes—not the case a century ago—an aura of mystery developed. One is taken to the hospital or nursing home and is brought back dead. Often small children are not allowed to go into certain parts of a hospital; thus the taboo nature of a hospital setting makes one wonder what is going on in there. A desire to examine this "mysterious thing" called death has contributed to a growing interest in thanatology.

Second, with individuals living longer today because of life-support equipment, organ transplants, penicillin, and other antibiotics, an interest has developed in the topic of dying and death. Such prolongation of life has raised ethical issues (e.g., Karen Ann Quinlan and Baby Jane Doe) involving the right to die, causing a furor in philosophy, law, and medicine. With the media highly publicizing these cases, the public was alerted to moral and legal questions on death not previously posed. Whether or not to "pull the plug" and disconnect life-supporting equipment presented questions for which ready answers were not found. An elderly woman recently summed up this dilemma when she spoke to Jinny Tesik of Compassion in Dying (Sturgill, 1995), an organization providing education regarding terminal care: "We used to be afraid to go to the hospital because that's where you went to die; now we're afraid to go because that's where they won't let us die."

The whole issue of when death occurs evolves from these medical developments. The question of who determines when one is alive or dead has been addressed by physicians, lawyers, philosophers, and theologians. These questions, along with the controversy over abortion rights, were a few of the significant ethical issues of the 1970s that provided an open forum for discussion and debate concerning the topic of dying and death.

Third, fewer individuals are raised on farms today than were in the early 20th century. Being brought up in a rural environment gave one direct exposure to birth and death as everyday events. Children were surrounded by the alpha and omega of the life cycle. Kittens, puppies, piglets, calves, chicks, and colts were born—and also died. Thus, it was commonplace to make observations of death and to deal with these situations accordingly. With less than 10 percent of the U.S. population living on farms today, these birth and death scenes have largely been removed from the personal observations of most individuals.

Fourth, the *Challenger* space shuttle disaster in 1986 certainly brought death to the attention of millions of school children around the country. In drawing the attention of children to this topic, it forced adults to deal with the issue. Though the astronauts and the teacher on board were not visible to television viewers, their spaceship was in sight. The live television coverage revealed sudden death on the tube. Death was discussed in the media for weeks following this tragedy.

Fifth, the topic of dying and death continues to maintain a high profile through the 1990s. Extensive media coverage followed Dr. Jack Kevorkian's "suicide machine" in the physician-assisted death of a terminally ill Alzheimer's patient in Michigan in 1990. Subsequent suicide deaths assisted by Dr. Kevorkian through the 1990s (47 by September of 1997) have sparked the fire of this controversy. In addition, the issue of physician-assisted suicide made headlines when voters in Washington, California, and Oregon went to the polls to decide the legality of such action. The voting was followed by court action, and ultimately the Supreme Court.

Operation Desert Storm, during which American troops invaded Iraq in 1991, brought reminders of the Vietnam War to the American public. Though different in many ways from the Vietnam War, nonetheless, Desert Storm brought dying and death to us live through the media. For several weeks this war was the primary focus of the news.

NBA star Earvin "Magic" Johnson's announcement in late 1991 that he had tested positive for the human immunodeficiency virus (HIV) reverberated throughout this country and beyond. This announcement brought the topic of AIDS and death into living rooms and coffee shops everywhere. Because of Johnson's prominence as an athlete, the topic of dying and death was particularly discussed among children and young adults.

Following the failure in 1992 to indict the Los Angeles policemen charged in the beating of Rodney King, riots broke out in Los Angeles and resulted in over 50

THE WIZARD OF ID   Brant parker and Johnny hart

BY PERMISSION OF JOHNNY HART AND CREATORS SYNDICATE, INC.

deaths. The crash of TWA Flight 800 in 1996, soon after the plane took off from New York City, dominated the news for weeks as divers searched for over 200 bodies. Indeed, the deaths of Princess Diana and Mother Teresa in August of 1997 saturated the airways for weeks. Death and destruction continue to maintain a high profile.

Although dying and death have now become issues of intellectual concern and occasional topics of controversy in the media, our society has done little to achieve formal **socialization** of its members to deal with death on the personal and emotional levels. Hospitals have traditionally excluded visitors under the age of 14. Parents have often tried to shield their "innocent" children from death scenes. Medical and theology schools, which train persons who will work with the dying, have not had significant curricular offerings to prepare their students for this death-related work. Overall, our socialization to dying and death situations has been unsystematic and ineffective.

THE MEDIA AND DEATH

As a child growing up in Texas, I have fond memories of spending the night with my grandparents on Fridays and going to the movie with my grandfather. The movie was always a "Western" with basically the same theme—the "good guys" (the cowboys) wore white hats, and the "bad guys" were the Indians. Though toward the end of each movie it appeared that the "good guys" were going to be wiped out, military reinforcements would always come to the rescue just at the last minute. The guys in the white hats would be rescued, and the "bad guys" would receive their "just reward" of death.

In the early 1970s, however, Hollywood began to produce films revolving around the theme of death in which the "good guy" died. For example, in *Love Story* one of the two main characters is dying throughout much of the film and eventually does die during the film. Since that time numerous films have had death as a principal theme. Certainly, Woody Allen films are filled with references to death.

Likewise, many situation comedies on prime time television in the 1970s, 1980s, and 1990s have addressed the topic of death. Some have viewed death in a serious vein, whereas others have taken a humorous approach. Both death and sex are topics about which we joke. They are somewhat uneasy topics, thus to laugh about them is a way to cope.

Numerous television specials in the early 1970s discussed dying and death. "Living With Death" presented various death-related situations observed through the eyes of a CBS reporter. ABC's "The Right to Die" addressed moral questions of mercy killing and suicide. The National Endowment for the Humanities sponsored a program entitled "Dying" in the mid-1970s. For 2 hours this program very sensitively portrayed 4 cancer patients, ranging in age from the late 20s to early 70s, interacting with others. Each died during the course of the filming. A PBS documentary in 1979 showed the last 3 years of Joan Robinson's life. This film revealed the experience of a woman and her husband as they tried to live with her cancer of the breast and uterus.

Death appears to be more abstract for those growing up today than for previous generations. By the age of 15, some media experts say, the average American has seen 13,000 murders on television and has been exposed to an endless stream of war, famine, and holocaust in the daily news (Bordewich, 1988, p. 34). Because we are unlikely to know the deceased individuals, however, the effect of this "death news" upon us is minimal.

Robert Fulton and Greg Owen (1988, p. 381) note that for the Baby Boom generation, which constitutes nearly one third of the American population, the television experience with death revolved around three messages. The first was one of entertainment. Cartoons such as *Tom and Jerry* and *Popeye* presented cartoon characters who systematically annihilated each other in a variety of ways, only to reappear in the next frame or after the commercial break as alive and ready for the next assault. The second message was that life is brutal and often lethal. On shows such as The *Untouchables* and *Miami Vice* young males killed and were killed. This tradition of associating violence and death with the young American male continues in the real world today. The third message conveyed was that death, when it actually occurs, occurs elsewhere and mostly to people alien to ourselves. "Real" death, as depicted on television, usually happened outside the continental limits of the United States, and it was death by violence.

How have the media in the 1980s and 1990s handled AIDS, a disease that has returned premature death to a society that had all but wiped out fatal childhood diseases? Edward Albert (1986) notes that the media portrayals of AIDS reflect the confusion and ambiguity experienced by society at large. He found that media coverage tended to reaffirm the stigmatized status of those at high risk: intravenous drug users and gay men. Reports emphasized deviant lifestyles. For that reason the normally rather private tennis great Arthur Ashe had not revealed that he had AIDS, acquired through a blood transfusion, yet he was forced to make the announcement because the media threatened to leak the information. Prior to his death in 1993, Ashe spent his last months of life working toward reducing this stigma. However, Albert (1987) notes that as the media begin associating the disease with other groups such as college students, heterosexuals, and children, the stigma should diminish to the point that those considered at significant risk belong increasingly to "socially valued groups."

Peter Nardi (1990) analyzed how the media handle AIDS and obituaries. He noted that one of the main issues raised by obituary reporting is personal privacy versus journalistic ethics. Unlike other diseases often unreported in earlier generations such as tuberculosis and cancer, AIDS raises questions of both medical and sexual ethics. The dilemmas faced by the media in AIDS cases draw attention to the continuing stigma attached to AIDS.

Thus, with a flurry of events involving dying and death in recent years and with the tremendous impact of prime time television in disseminating information, our focus on dying and death has been highlighted. However, as Fulton and Owen

(1988, p. 383) note, television only superficially portrays grief and the ruptured lives that death can leave in its wake. Certainly, a need for death education seems apparent in today's society.

THE DISCIPLINE OF THANATOLOGY

The topic of dying and death did not come into its own in recent times until the 1970s. Certainly death, like sex, was not a new event, but both had been rarely discussed openly. Sex, as a subject of discussion, came "out of the closet" in the 1960s, followed by death in the 1970s.

Thanatology flourished in the academic world in the 1970s and continues today. Literally hundreds of courses on dying and death are offered in high schools and colleges. According to Dan Leviton (1977), the number of death education college courses increased from 20 in 1970 to 1,100 in 1974. However, thanatology offerings at the secondary school level seem to have declined in recent years, perhaps because of the pressure to return to the basics (Pine, 1986). V. A. Cummins (1978) in a survey of 1,251 colleges found that 75 percent were offering courses in dying and death and that these courses were offered in many departments. The majority of courses were housed in sociology and social work departments, followed by psychology, religious studies, philosophy, and health education.

Fergus Bordewich (1988) observes that a generation ago death was less likely than sex to be found as a subject in the curricula of American public schools. If death was acknowledged at all, it was usually discussed within the context of literary classics. In the past decade courses treating dying and death far more explicitly have appeared in schools across the country. Though the actual number is not known, thousands of schools are involved, according to groups that either oppose or support death education. Many schools have blended some of the philosophies and techniques of death education into health, social studies, literature, and home economics courses. Others have introduced suicide-prevention programs.

An argument for death education noted by Bordewich (1988, p. 31) from *The School Counselor* in 1977 said:

> An underlying, but seldom spoken, assumption of much of the death-education movement is that Americans handle death and dying poorly and that we ought to be doing better at it. As in the case of many other problems, many Americans believe that education can initiate change. Change is evident, and death education will play as important a part in changing attitudes toward death as sex education played in changing attitudes toward sex information and wider acceptance of various sexual practices.

Death education provides an opportunity to familiarize students and professionals with the needs and issues surrounding dying and death. This is important because of the pervasiveness of formal death institutions, media exposure to death, and haphazard experiences with death professionals, notes Vanderlyn Pine (1986, p. 212). One of the goals of courses on dying and death for all age groups is to increase knowledge about death and about the professions involved with death—funeral directors, medical personnel, and governmental organizations, for example (Gordon & Klass, 1979). Another goal is to help students learn to cope with the death of significant others, deal with one's own mortality, and be more sensitive to the needs of others. A more abstract goal is to understand the social and ethical issues concerning death as well as the value judgments involved with these issues.

What effects do courses on dying and death have on students? As noted in pre- and posttests of the attitudes of 184 students enrolled in a college course on dying and death (Dickinson, 1986), the majority of responses revealed less fear of death and death-related events at the end of the course. These students had higher death anxi- eties on entering the course than did subjects in four similar studies of other popu- lations, including one of coal miners just prior to entering the mines (Dickinson, 1986). After the course, these students revealed death anxieties much lower than those of the other four populations. Perhaps students coming into an elective course in thanatology have a high fear of the topic anyway and enter the course to alleviate their fear. Nonetheless, this study did reveal less anxiety in the students after dis- cussing, reading, seeing films, visiting a funeral home, and going to a cemetery. Re- sults of a similar high school study of pre/post comparisons of adolescents (Rosenthal, 1980) showed that their level of anxiety decreased as a result of an 18-week death education course. Thus, according to these two studies, exposure to dying and death seems to have made the participants less anxious about death-related matters.

In the 1970s Michel Vovelle (1976) published an article entitled "The Rediscov- ery of Death" in which he documented the sudden flurry of publications on the sub- ject of death that appeared in the Western world from the 1950s on. Geoffrey Gorer's 1955 essay on "The Pornography of Death" seemed to open the door for publications on the subject of death. Gorer argued that death had replaced sex as contemporary society's major taboo topic. With death in the community becoming rarer and with individuals actually seeing fewer corpses, a relatively realistic view of death had been replaced by a voyeuristic, adolescent preoccupation with it, observed Gorer. Vovelle argued that the focus of attention represented by these texts amounted to nothing less than the "displacement of a deeply seated taboo on a subject that had lain hidden in the shadows of the western psyche since some unspecified point in the 19th century" (Prior, 1989, p. 4).

One of the early "texts" for thanatology, published in 1959, was an anthology by psychologist Herman Feifel entitled *The Meaning of Death*. Feifel's work was an in- terdisciplinary attempt to restore death to cultural consciousness. In 1963 Jessica Mitford's *The American Way of Death* was very critical of the funeral industry. Elisabeth Kübler-Ross's *On Death and Dying,* published in 1969, advised Americans that they can play a significant role in the lives of the dying. Ernest Becker's *The Denial of Death,* published in 1973, argued that denying death is commonplace in our society. Both Kübler-Ross's and Becker's books became best-sellers. It was Kübler-Ross, a physi- cian, who was a real catalyst in making the medical profession realize that terminally ill patients are more than the cancer patient in Room 713 and are warm, living hu- man beings who have personal needs. Both of these books alerted the public to the issue of dying in America.

Two professional journals on thanatology emerged in the 1970s: *Death Studies* (formerly *Death Education*) and *Omega: The Journal of Death and Dying.* Other related journals that have evolved in recent years are: *The Hospice Journal, Illness, Crises and Loss Journal,* and *Suicide and Life-Threatening Behavior.* The number of articles on death also expanded considerably in journals of education, family, medicine, health, nursing, psychology, social work, and sociology.

THANATOLOGY FOR HEALTH PROFESSIONALS

The emotional conflicts related to dying and death are particularly acute for primary health professionals. Although limited emphasis has historically been placed on death education in schools for health professionals in the United States, the current status of death education offerings in nursing, medicine, paramedicine, pharmacy, dentistry, and social work is somewhat encouraging (Dickinson, Sumner, & Frederick, 1992; Smith & Walz, 1995). Though few schools offer a full course in death education, the majority (with the exception of dentistry) have some emphasis on this topic in their curricula. Most began their offerings since 1975.

As more emphasis is placed on relating to terminally ill patients and their families in the health professions, we would hope that more positive attitudes toward treatment of the dying patient will emerge when these students become practitioners. Helping students deal with their own anxieties about death at the time of actually facing terminally ill patients would seem to be an appropriate time for intervention. Such anxieties are expressed by Dawn McGuire (1988, p. 341), a fourth-year medical student at Columbia Presbyterian Medical Center in New York City:

> I think the proper role for a physician with a dying patient is to enter into a partnership where there is a sense that that partnership is not going to end with the end of medical therapy. But we're not trained for that. Most of us feel totally inadequate and have found our own defenses, including abandoning the patient. It's been confusing to me and a constant source of frustration.

In the end, the young professional, the patient, and the patient's family all should benefit from this emphasis on death education.

Death education should not only prove useful in coping with dying and death situations, but also should actually improve the quality of our living. As Elisabeth Kübler-Ross notes, relating to the dying does not depress her, but rather it makes her both appreciative of each day of life and thankful each morning that she awakes with the potential of another day. Learning more about dying and death should provoke one to strive to make each day count in a positive way. Educating oneself about death will tend to make one "look for the good in others and dwell on it," as the late author Alex Haley suggested on his letterhead stationery.

Defining Death

The "Wizard of Id" defines *death* as a "once in a lifetime experience." Although one cannot refute this definition, it would not suffice in the medical or legal professions. Until the 1960s there was little real controversy about what it means to be dead in the public policy sense (Veatch, 1995, pp. 407–408). Now, for the first time, however, it is a matter of real public policy significance to decide precisely what is meant when someone is labeled "dead." Today, matters have changed because technologies have

greatly extended the capacity to prolong the dying process and the usefulness of human organs and tissues for transplantation or research.

A headline in a newspaper ("Doctors 'kill' patient," 1988) read "Doctors 'Kill' Patient to Save Her Life." The article went on to say that surgeons had put the patient into a coma, stopped her heart, chilled her by 40 degrees, and drained her body of blood for 40 minutes to save her from the aneurysm pressing on her brain. She was placed into a sort of suspended animation that allowed surgeons to cure a hard-to-reach, high-risk aneurysm once considered inoperable. As one surgeon noted, "It may be the surgery of the future in cases where bleeding poses the greatest risk to the operation." Thus, the headline said the physicians "killed" in order to "save" the patient. Defining death is indeed a confusing issue!

The diagnosis of death has vacillated throughout history between the centralist theory and the decentralist theory (Powner, Ackerman, & Grevnik, 1996). The centralist theory proposed that a single organ contains the vital life force and, if it fails, the person would die, a prominent view before the 18th century. Decentralism proposed that the entire body and every organ and cell possesses the life force. This theory gained precedence when physicians discovered that a failed organ could be resuscitated. The modern theory of brain death, however, has resurrected the centralist theory.

The definition of death has changed significantly from the 1960s from strictly physical criteria to a debate about the value of life and the essence of human qualities (Prior, 1989, p. 12). That debate relocated the origin of death in the brain rather than in the respiratory system, and the first test of death became one that questioned the receptivity and awareness of the dying patient (Gervais, 1987). Death, once so clearly defined as a physical fact, became entangled in a discussion about the value of life.

INTERNATIONAL DEFINITIONS OF DEATH

Defining death is a difficult assignment. In the 1950s the United Nations and the World Health Organization proposed the following definition of death: "Death is the permanent disappearance of all evidence of life at any time after birth has taken place" (United Nations, 1953). Thus, as death can take place only after a birth has occurred, any deaths prior to a (live) birth cannot be included in this definition. The latter is called a *fetal death* and is defined in the following way (Stockwell, 1976):

Though some early parish registers did not list the deaths of babies, this early 20th century portrait of an Appalachian family reveals the importance of every member of the family, even the deceased one. This was an obviously sad time for the family, yet the somber expressions on the members' faces were typical of photos from this period.

Death (disappearance of life) prior to the complete expulsion or extraction from its mother or a product of conception irrespective of the duration of pregnancy; the death is indicated by the fact that after such separation the fetus does not breathe or show any other evidence of life, such as beating of the heart, pulsating of the umbilical cord, or definite movement of voluntary muscles.

"Dead" Cancer Patient Awakens in Mortuary

Harare, Zimbabwe—After being pronounced dead in the hospital, a cancer patient later awoke in a mortuary. She said her superstitious relatives were afraid to visit her.

The family of Beauty Shitto had made funeral arrangements to bury her, after doctors at the hospital in Gweru had declared her dead and sent her body to the mortuary.

Adapted from the Charleston, SC, *News and Courier,* Charleston, SC, June 22, 1988, p. 9A.

Not all countries observe the definition of death recommended by the United Nations. In some countries, infants dying within 24 hours after birth are classified as stillbirths rather than as deaths or are disregarded altogether. In some other countries infants born alive who die before the end of the registration period (which may last several months) are considered stillbirths or are excluded from all tabulations. As Robert Hertz (1960) observes, they are considered still a part of the spirit world from which they came, therefore their death is often not accorded ritual recognition, and no funeral is held. Thus, one is not "alive" until officially registered, and one cannot be legally "dead" if never alive!

In the early days of record keeping in the United States (Gottlieb, 1993, p. 134) some parish registers did not list the deaths of babies; babies were remembered as abstractions rather than as persons. In the latter part of the 19th century and early 20th century, however, some families showed that the dead babies were not forgotten and had them appear in the family picture with parents and living children.

For the Kaliai of Papua, New Guinea (Counts & Counts, 1991, p. 193), dying is almost complete "if the breath smells of death, if the person stares without blinking or shame at another person's face, is restless and must be moved frequently, or loses bladder or bowel control." Dying is complete "when breathing stops, when the heart ceases to beat, and when the eyes and mouth hang open." The Kaliai also believe that persons dying or dead may return to life at any time after the dying process begins. The Kaliai have no generic term for *life.* Thus, the whole question of life and death is more complicated than it might initially appear.

AMERICAN DEFINITIONS OF DEATH

By traditional definitions, death is when heartbeat and breathing stop. But medical advances have made this definition of death obsolete. Under this definition many people living today once would have been considered dead because their hearts stopped beating and their breathing stopped as a result of heart attacks. With respirators to artificially breathe for a patient, along with other life-support equipment, many lives are saved. A diagnosis of **brain death** allows respirators to be turned off when the brain is "totally and irreversibly" dead (Cope, 1978).

Leon Kass (1971, p. 699) defines death simply as "the transition from the state of being alive to the state of being dead." Simple enough, yet the issue is clouded by many factors. Traditionally, death has clinically meant "the irreparable cessation of spontaneous cardiac activity and spontaneous respiratory activity" (Ramsey, 1970, p. 59). The functions of heart and lungs must cease before one is pronounced dead by this definition.

In 1968 a committee of the Harvard Medical School (Beecher, 1968) claimed that the ultimate criterion for death is brain activity rather than the functioning of heart and lungs. The Harvard report notes that death should be understood in terms of "a permanently nonfunctioning brain," for which there are many tests. With brain death the body would not be able to breathe on its own because breathing is controlled in the brain. If the brain is dead, any artificially induced heartbeat is merely pumping blood through a dead body.

In 1981 President Ronald Reagan created the President's Commission for the Study of Ethical Problems in Medicine and Biomedical and Behavioral Research to study the ethical and legal implications of the matter of defining death (Crandall, 1991, p. 565). The commission examined three possible ways of determining death: death of part of the brain, death of the whole brain, or nonbrain ways to determine death, such as absence of heartbeat. The commission decided on a definition of death that includes the traditional nonbrain signs of death and a "whole brain" definition. Its proposal to determine death, which was accepted by both the American Bar Association and the American Medical Association, is as follows (Crandall, 1991, p. 565):

> An individual who has sustained either (1) irreversible cessation of circulatory and respiratory functions, or (2) irreversible cessation of all functions of the entire brain, including the brain stem, is dead. A determination of death must be made in accordance with accepted medical standards.

The majority of states have adopted the proposal or one similar in content.

A case in Florida ("Baby born," 1992) involved a baby girl, Theresa Ann Campo Pearson, born without a fully formed brain. She had only a partially formed brain stem, which controls breathing and the heartbeat, and no cortex, the largest part of the brain. Her parents asked the courts to declare her brain dead, but to no avail. The Florida Supreme Court said it did not have the constitutional authority to hear the case. Theresa Ann did not have an "entire brain" and thus did not fit the legal definition for declaring one dead: "irreversible cessation of all functions of the entire brain, including the brain stem." The parents had wanted to donate their daughter's organs, but by the time the 10-day-old girl died, her organs had deteriorated so much that they could not be transplanted.

Various tests can be given to determine any signs of brain activity (Cope, 1978). The determination can be made reliably by competent physicians. They search for any hint of normal brain-controlled reflexes. They turn the head and even put cold water into the ear to look for any sign of movement. They search for any sign of the eye pupils responding to light. One test is to touch the cornea of the eye and see whether this triggers a blink. The respirator is also stopped briefly to look for any sign of spontaneous breathing. Absence of brain activity as signified by a flat electroencephalogram (EEG) is another criterion for brain death. The tests can be repeated 24 hours later to make certain that the absence of these life signs is not temporary. The brain death prognosis is totally predictable and uniform: Brain dead people never regain consciousness, much less any recovery, and suffer cardiovascular failure within a short time (Jasper, 1991, p. 34).

Man Revived After Obituary Published

Cincinnati—A man whose obituary was published after doctors declared him "brain dead" revived and was returned to intensive care in critical condition. Physicians at the University of Cincinnati Hospital declared John Birckhead, 41, of Cincinnati brain dead Wednesday morning.

Funeral arrangements had been made by that evening, and a death notice was purchased for Birckhead, who had been hospitalized in a coma after being found hanging by his T-shirt at a jail. Meanwhile, breathing was detected during a final medical evaluation and Birckhead was returned to intensive care at the hospital.

A misunderstanding between hospital officials and members of Birckhead's family resulted in the publication of John Birckhead's obituary Thursday morning in *The Cincinnati Enquirer.*

The family was told that before a legal declaration of death, a second medical evaluation had to be performed.

Adapted from the Charleston, SC, *News and Courier,* Charleston, SC, September 28, 1985, p. 17A.

According to one neurologist (Cope, 1978), when death is declared on the basis of cessation of breathing and heartbeat, the brain is deprived of blood supply and dies within a matter of minutes. Death of the brain is what is final and absolute. On the other hand, one may lose all brain function, but it is not irreversible. For example, a person having taken an overdose of barbiturates may have a temporary absence of any signs of brain activity, but this is not brain death because it is reversible.

Perhaps as a result of President Reagan's commission, there has come to be increasing acceptance of a brain-oriented criterion for determining death as the "irreversible loss of all brain function" (Youngner et al., 1989, p. 2205). Nonetheless, Raanan Gillon (1990) argues that the criteria for brain death are a compromise between extreme versions of two concerns. On the one hand, the compromise is with a concept of death as complete disintegration of the human organism's biological functioning, with all living components dead or at least totally disintegrated and dissociated from each other. On the other hand, brain death criteria are also a compromise with the concept of death as cessation of personal existence because brain death criteria will classify as alive some humans who are dead as persons. A clinical example is a permanent vegetative state that involves permanent loss of consciousness and of the capacity and potential for consciousness. Because a capacity for consciousness is a necessary condition for being a person, an individual in a permanent vegetative state cannot be a person, yet according to brain death criteria (whether brain-stem death criteria or whole-brain criteria) that same human being is unequivocally alive.

Denying Death

Though some evidence suggests that Americans accept death (the majority have life insurance policies, and approximately one third have wills), it has been suggested that we are a death-denying society (Dumont & Foss, 1972). Such evidence of denying death in the United States includes the following.

First, we prefer to obfuscate the dying process: We do not want to look at death in a point-blank way as an event that will happen to us because it is too frightening, notes John Harvey (1996, p. 181). Therefore, we employ **euphemisms** for death rather than the words *dying, dead,* and *death.* Examples of these euphemisms are: *succumbed, passed away, was taken, went to heaven, departed this life, bit the dust, kicked the bucket, croaked, passed on, was laid to rest, cashed in, expired, ended his/her days, is no more, checked out, signed off, breathed his/her last breath, returned to dust, went out like a light, ran out of time, brought down the curtain, went on to glory, is pushing up daisies, was taken by the Grim Reaper, heard the trumpet call,* and is *six feet under.* It is easier to use euphemisms as buffers than to use the stark words *death, dead,* and *dying.*

Second, we have a taboo on death conversation. A friend recently wrote a two-page letter describing her family's summer activities. She noted that she and her husband were on vacation and that he became ill. He was taken to the hospital for surgery. She said, "He had the best of care. I loved him so." She never said that her husband had died, but it was obvious. It is difficult to say those words—*dead, dying,* and *death.*

Third, **cryonics** (body freezing) suggests a denial of death. In this procedure, the person's body is frozen in dry ice and liquid nitrogen. A very expensive process initially with additional high annual costs, cryonics has not caught on. Cryonics is based on the idea that someday a "cure" will be found for the "deceased" and that he or she can then be treated with the "cure" and thawed out. Thus, one does not die, but rather he or she is put into the cooler and brought back at a later date.

As many as 40 people have had their bodies frozen after death in hopes that new technology would someday be able to restore them to health (Adams, 1988, p. 332). The first was James Bedford, a 73-year-old psychologist from Glendale, California, who was frozen in 1967. Many of the 40 were thawed after their estates ran out of money, and allegedly only 11 are still in "cryonic suspension."

Of 13 cryonics centers in operation a few years ago, only 3 remain open today (Selvin, 1990). Alcor Foundation in Riverside, California, is the largest of the facilities. Options at Alcor include whole-body preservation for $100,000 or just a head for $35,000.

Fourth, we do not die in America, rather we simply take a long nap. Caskets have built-in mattresses, some strawlike and others innerspring, and the head of the deceased person rests on a pillow in the casket. The room in the funeral home where the body is "laid out" is referred to by some as the "slumber room." Certainly, no one ever heard of having pets *killed* by the veterinarian; we have them "put to sleep." As is discussed in chapter 11, the word *cemetery* derives from the Greek word *koimeterion,* which means "sleeping place" (Crissman, 1994, p. 106). Cemetery markers sometimes read "rest in peace" or make other references to sleeping. Some markers for burials from the 19th and early 20th centuries have a crib or bed effect—headboard, footboard, and sideboards, sometimes with a "double bed" for a married couple. Dying does not occur in America; one just goes to sleep.

Fifth, unlike nonliterate societies, we call in a professional when someone does. The funeral director takes the body away, and we do not see it again until it is ready for viewing. When we see the body again, the cosmetic job is such that the person looks

The creation of the Vietnam Veterans Memorial in Washington, DC was the result of a popular movement to recognize the many men and women who lost their lives in a highly unpopular war. This social movement ran contrary to the death denial sentiment typically found in American society.

as "alive" as possible under the circumstances. When viewing a body at a funeral home, I once heard a woman make the comment that the dead person "looks better than I have seen her look for years!" This is the dying of death that is discussed in chapter 11.

Sixth, in many places in the United States, the casket is not lowered into the ground until after the family and friends have left the cemetery. It is not easy to watch a casket lowered into the ground because this reminds the viewers of the finality of death. There are several "bad trips" when a significant other dies—initially being told of the death, seeing the body for the first time, seeing the casket closed for the last time, and seeing the casket lowered into the ground. One can avoid the last "trip" by leaving the cemetery.

Thus, examples of denial of death can be found in the United States. We are not suggesting that this is all bad. It is a way of coping and simply seems to be evident in the American way of dying.

Chilling Answer to Life After Death
Katherine Bishop

San Francisco—Everyone knows that you can't take it with you. But if members of the American Cryonics Society Inc. have their way, they are going to come back and get it.

Last week the organization, which is dedicated to the proposition that death is an imposition on life and ought to be eliminated, celebrated its 20th anniversary here with a $100-a-plate dinner attended by 65 people. The Speaker of the State Assembly, Willie Brown, showed up at the Fairmont Hotel to cut the cake, and Angela Alioto, a newly elected member of the San Francisco Board of Supervisors, made an appearance, testifying to the fact that no group is too eccentric to be ignored here.

Since the term was coined in 1965, cryonics has taken some small steps from the realm of science fiction and has even come up with its own independent religion known as Venturism. Cryonics (derived from the Greek word for cold) refers to the practice of freezing the body of a person after death to preserve it for possible revival in some distant future after a cure has been found for whatever killed the poor soul. Adherents make arrangements to have their bodies placed in cryonic suspension, meaning preservation at extremely low temperatures using liquid nitrogen in stainless steel capsules.

As it turns out, members are planning to come back to a body vastly better than the one they left in. "Usually the body is shot and they don't want to come back in that kind of shape," said H. Jackson Zinn, a San Francisco lawyer who is the organization's president.

Many members believe science will be able to restore their body and build a better one as long as the basic "information" of the person remains properly stored. Thus one popular choice is the "neuro only" option, in which only the head is preserved.

Such practices are not without problems. Last year, six people from Alcor Life Extension Foundation in Riverside, a nonprofit cryonics storage center independent of the Cryonics Society, were handcuffed and taken away for questioning on suspicion of homicide after they removed and froze the head of one client after her heart stopped beating but without having a doctor present at Alcor to pronounce her legally dead.

While criminal charges have not been filed, a grand jury investigation is continuing and Alcor has sued the State Department of Health Services, which believes that cryonics does not qualify as a "scientific" use of human remains and refuses to issue required forms. The lawsuit's outcome will affect the work of all existing storage centers, said Alcor's Manager, Michael Federowicz, who goes by the name Mike Darwin.

(continued)

(continued from previous page)

Should cryonics prove to work, it might lead to a host of social issues, including what is to be done about overpopulation if people continue to be born while others refuse to stay dead. The organization believes that space will be colonized, opening up vast new adventures in living for millions of humans, new or reconstituted.

"To think that we must be confined to this planet is, come on, too parochial," said Jerry White, a founder of the Cryonics Society.

Another problem is where to store all the stainless steel capsules holding the "suspension members," as the frozen bodies are called. Thus far, there are fewer than a half dozen storage centers in the country, with two of them in this state.

Mr. White suggested that there are a number of existing structures that could be adapted for such use, including an abandoned Titan missile site the group has toured in Northern California.

"I was envisioning these big silos just full of liquid nitrogen, the liquid nitrogen generators busy 24 hours a day just spewing stuff in there," he said. "And you could see thousands of patients in there, see them bobbing around."

Cryonics also involves a host of moral and philosophical problems that have not been addressed by society. The most immediate one might be faced by the survivors of the suspended, who might not agree with their loved ones' choice of body preservation and might bring legal challenges to them.

"If I'm frozen, will my wife say, 'Gee, I should have gotten that insurance money,'" mused Irving Rand, a New York City insurance salesman. Mr. Rand is president of Cryonics Coordinators of America, which helps people obtain insurance to cover the cost of freezing and storage.

A more weighty issue to ponder grows out of the fact that if future technology makes it possible to duplicate a person from those parts that have been frozen, it follows that a frozen person could not only be restored, but could also have complete copies made of himself as a sort of human floppy disk.

As Mr. Darwin states the issue, "If you duplicate and store yourself as a backup copy, is that copy you?"

And there is also the question of what the state of the world will have become over time. As Mr. Rand said, "Who knows what the world is going to be like 100 years from now; if it's even worth coming back."

But Mr. Zinn is more upbeat about the prospects. "One hundred years from now, anything that's fun, I don't want to miss it."

K. Bishop, *New York Times,* January 20, 1989, p. 6.

Fearing Death

Lord, If I have to die, Let me die;
  But please, Take away this fear.

KEN WALSH, "SOMETIMES I WEEP," P. 18

In this book the point is made often that death per se has no meaning other than that which people give it. If this is true, why do most of us in America believe that death is something to intrinsically fear? Not everyone, however, seems to have **death anxiety** (used synonymously with *death fear*). For example, B. F. Skinner, the psychologist who popularized behavior modification, approached his death from leukemia with no apparent regrets. The 86-year-old Skinner, just a few weeks before he died, said with a laugh (1990), "I will be dead in a few months, but it hasn't given me the slightest anxiety or worry or anything. I always knew I was going to die." Likewise, 75-year-old psychiatrist Timothy Leary noted a few months before his death from prostate cancer in 1996 that he was "waiting for his graduation." Leary (Mansnerus, 1995) stated that he was "looking forward to the most fascinating experience in life, which is dying." He said that dying must be approached the way that life is lived—with curiosity, hope, fascination, courage, and the help of your friends.

Anthropologists would be quick to respond that not all cultures in the world hold that death is necessarily something to be feared. However, there seems to be a large number of cultures, including our own, that attach fearful meanings to death and death-related situations. Why is it that so many people have less-than-positive views of death?

Death in the United States is viewed as fearful because Americans have been systematically taught to fear it. Horror movies portray death, ghosts, skeletons, goblins, bogeymen, and ghoulish morticians as things to be feared. *Sesame Street* tries to create a more positive view of monsters by showing children being befriended by Grover, Oscar, and Cookie Monster. With the possible exception of Casper "the Friendly Ghost," death-related fantasy figures have not received much in the way of positive press. Instead of providing positive images, our culture has chosen to reinforce fearful meanings of death. Cemeteries are portrayed as eerie, funeral homes are to be avoided, and morgues are scary places where you "wouldn't be caught dead."

The fear of death may be incorporated in the minds of some individuals with the fear of being buried alive. To be taken into the blackness when life is extinct is a dreadful enough prospect, notes Robert Wilkins (1996, p. 15), but for the Grim Reaper to come calling before the "appointed hour" is to condemn the yet-living to a seeming eternity of suffocative horror. Though scattered accounts of individuals being "buried alive" are noted over the past several centuries (Wilkins, 1996), most medical personnel remain skeptical. When the Paris cemetery Les Innocents was moved from the center of the city to the suburbs in the latter part of the 19th century, the number of skeletons found face down in their coffins convinced the lay public that premature burial was common. Skeptics explain such "movement" as being the result of externally imposed movements such as the coffin bumping into walls as it is being negotiated down narrow stairwells or of sudden movements produced by bolting funeral horses. Nonetheless, the fear of being buried alive has persisted over the centuries. Such fear indeed might contribute to the overall fear of death.

One of the reasons why classes in dying and death often incorporate field trips to funeral homes and cemeteries is to confront negative death meanings and fantasies with firsthand, objective observations. The preparation room at the mortuary is a good example. If you have never been to one, think about the mental image that comes to your mind. For many, the preparation room is a place that one approaches with fear and caution-something like Dr. Frankenstein's laboratory, complete with bats, strange lighting, body parts, and naked dead bodies. The great disappointment for most students as they walk through the door is that they find a room that looks somewhat like a physician's examination room. "Is that all there is?" is a comment often heard after visiting the preparation room.

Sociologist Erving Goffman (1959) observed that first impressions are unlikely to change and tend to dominate the meanings related to subsequent social interaction patterns and experiences. Some of us want to retain untrue fearful meanings of death, even when confronted by positive images. On a recent field trip to a funeral home, one student refused to enter the preparation room. While other students were hearing a description of embalming procedures, she discovered a bottle labeled "skin texturizer" and became nauseated. Other students had a difficult time understanding her problem because they had had positive experiences.

Fearful meanings can also be ascribed to death because of a traumatic death-related experience. Being a witness to a fatal auto accident, discovering someone who has committed suicide, or attending a funeral where emotional outbursts create an uncomfortable environment for mourners can increase death anxiety for individuals. However, such occurrences are rather uncommon for most people and do not account for the prevalence of America's preoccupation with death fears.

CONTENT OF DEATH FEARS

When one speaks of death fear or death anxiety, it is assumed that the concept is unidimensional and that there is a consensus about its meaning. Such is not the case, however, because two persons may say that they fear death, and yet the content of their fears may not be shared. Death anxiety is a multidimensional concept and is based upon the following 4 concerns: (a) the death of self, (b) the deaths of significant others, (c) the process of dying, and (d) the state of being dead. This model's more elaborate form (Leming, 1979–1980) shows 8 types of death fears that can be applied to the death of self and the death of others:

1. Dependency
2. The pain in the dying process
3. The indignity in the dying process
4. The isolation, separation, and rejection that can be part of the dying process
5. Leaving loved ones
6. Afterlife concerns
7. The finality of death
8. The fate of the body

Table 1.1

The 8 Dimensions of Death Anxiety as They Relate to the Deaths of Self and Others

Self	Others
Process of Dying	
1. Fear of dependency	Fear of financial burdens
2. Fear of pain in dying process	Fear of going through the painful experience of others
3. Fear of indignity in dying process	Fear of not being able to cope with physical problems of others
4. Fear of loneliness, rejection, and isolation	Fear of being unable to cope emotionally with problems of others
5. Fear of leaving loved ones	Fear of losing loved ones
State of Being Dead	
6. Afterlife concerns	Afterlife concerns
Fear of an unknown situation	Fear of the judgment of others—"What are they thinking?"
Fear of divine judgment	Fear of ghosts, spirits, devils, etc.
Fear of the spirit world	Fear of never seeing the person again
Fear of nothingness	
7. Fear of the finality of death	Fear of the end of a relationship
Fear of not being able to achieve one's goals	Guilt related to not having done enough for the deceased
Fear of the possible end of physical and symbolic identity	Fear of not seeing the person again
Fear of the end of all social relationships	Fear of losing the social relationship
8. Fear of the fate of the body	Fear of death objects
Fear of body decomposition	Fear of dead bodies
Fear of being buried	Fear of being in cemeteries
Fear of not being treated with respect	Fear of not knowing how to act in death-related situations

From Table 1.1 we can see that the content of fear will be influenced by whose death the individual is considering. From a personal death perspective, one may have anxiety over the effect that one's dying (or being dead) will have on others. There might also be private worries about how one might be treated by others. From the perspective of the survivor, the individual may be concerned about the financial, emotional, and social problems related to the death of a significant other.

Because many factors related to the experience of death and death-related situations can engender fear, we would expect to find individual differences in type and intensity of death fear, including social circumstance and past experiences. However, with all of the potential sources for differences, using a death fear scale developed by Dr. Leming, consistently high scores are found for the fears of dependency and pain related to the process of dying, and relatively low anxiety scores are found for the fears related to the afterlife and the fate of the body. Approximately 65 percent of the more than 1,000 individuals surveyed had high anxiety relative to dependency and pain, and only 15 percent had the same high level of anxiety relative to concerns about the afterlife and the fate of the body (Leming, 1979–1980). Thus, it is the process of dying—not the event of death—that causes the most concern.

DEATH FEARS, GENDER, AND AGE

Is there a difference in death fear between males and females? Gender differences in death fear are one of the most frequently noted and poorly understood findings in thanatology (Dattel & Neimeyer, 1990). In a survey of research studies on death fear by gender, Pollak (1979) reported that the majority of findings concluded that women reveal more death fear than men, yet the other studies find virtually no differences between the sexes. Judith Stillion (1985) suggests that the discrepancy in these findings simply reflects the greater tendency of women to admit troubling feelings.

How is age related to death fear? Literature (McMordie & Kumar, 1984) on the relationship between death anxiety and age demonstrates a moderate inverse relationship (i.e., the older the person, the less death anxiety). More recent research (Rasmussen & Brems, 1996) confirmed that age *and* psychosocial maturity are significantly and inversely related to death anxiety. Psychosocial maturity was found to be a stronger predictor than age, perhaps suggesting why previous studies have revealed only moderate correlations between age and death anxiety. Possibly age alone cannot account for the decrease in death anxiety among the elderly; the combination of aging and the achievement of greater psychosocial maturity may serve to decrease death anxiety.

In summary, death fears are not instinctive; they exist because our culture has created and perpetuated fearful meanings and ascribed them to death. They are also a function of the fact that death is not an ordinary experience challenging the order of everyday life in society. They are a function of occasional firsthand encounters with deaths so unusual that they become traumatic.

Mortality Statistics

Ask an individual how he or she wishes to die. With the exception of the comical reply, "When I am 92 and at the hands of a jealous lover," most people will respond, "When I am very old, at home, unexpectedly, in my own bed, while sleeping—and with my full mental and physical capabilities." Unfortunately for most of us, we will not die as we would like. For some, this fact may be a source of apprehension and anxiety.

As noted earlier, most Americans die in institutionalized settings and not at home. According to "Please Notify," we should be more considerate about our dying, whether at home or away.

DEATH ETIOLOGY AND LIFE EXPECTANCY

Whereas in the 19th century the mortality rate was particularly high among children and continued at a high level throughout adult life, the incidence of death is now heavily concentrated among the elderly (Mulkay, 1993). Thus, average life expectancy is now much longer. For most individuals, death approaches slowly over years of

Please Notify

A lecturer was about to address a business association in Los Angeles when the association director reminded its members: "Every week we pay return postage for mail that goes to our members and is not deliverable because you have moved, changed your post office box number, or died without letting us know."

Waynesville, NC, *Mountaineer,* April 11, 1980.

gradual decline. As noted in Table 1.2, the cause of death (etiology) for most of us (65 percent) will be from one of two chronic diseases—heart disease and cancer. With these **chronic diseases,** deaths are usually prolonged and are not sudden and unexpected, as most people might desire.

In the United States, cigarette consumption remains the single most preventable cause of sickness and premature death (Anderson, 1996). American women did not begin smoking in large numbers until after World War II, and their rates of lung cancer are now matching those of men (Cockerham, 1995, p. 43). Indeed, this "preventable" cause of death, cigarette smoking, has increased 75 percent worldwide in the last two decades, according to Robert Anderson (1996, p. 240) and is now responsible on a global basis for about 5 percent (a conservative estimate) of all deaths (approximately 20 percent of all deaths in the United States).

Life expectancy has increased considerably in the past 50 years. Life expectancy for males in the United States has increased from 54 years to over 70 years over the past half century. Females' life expectancy during this same period has increased from 55 to nearly 80 years. Whites live nearly 7 years longer than blacks in the United States. According to a recent study reported in the *New York Times* (1990), however, there may be a limit to how long our bodies can hold out. The study concluded that science and medicine have pushed human life expectancy to its natural limit of about 85 years. The researchers note that even if a cure were found for most fatal diseases such as heart disease and cancer, the natural degeneration of the body puts a cap of about 85 years on the average life span.

White Americans who live to age 80 and over, however, can expect to keep on living longer than octogenarians in other industrialized countries. The United States, which ranks 15th among nations in life expectancy at birth, is having its average life

THE WIZARD OF ID   by Brant parker and Johnny hart

REPRINTED BY PERMISSION OF JOHNNY HART AND NAS, INC.

Table 1.2

10 Leading Causes of Death in the United States, 1900 and 1994 (in Death Rates per 100,000 Population)

Causes of Death	Death Rates Per 100,000 Population	% of All Deaths
		1900★
1. Pneumonia	191.9	12.5
2. Consumption (Tuberculosis)	190.5	12.5
3. Heart Disease	134.0	8.3
4. Diarrheal Diseases	85.1	5.6
5. Diseases of the Kidneys	83.7	5.5
6. All Accidents	72.3	4.7
7. Apoplexy (Stroke)	66.6	4.3
8. Cancer	60.0	3.9
9. Old Age	54.0	3.5
10. Bronchitis	48.3	3.2
		1994
1. Major Cardiovascular Diseases	362.6	41.7
2. Malignancies (Cancer)	206.0	23.4
3. Pulmonary Diseases	39.1	4.5
4. Accidents	34.6	3.9
5. Pneumonia and Influenza	31.5	3.6
6. Diabetes	21.2	2.4
7. Infective Diseases (includes AIDS)	18.6	2.0
8. Suicide	12.4	1.4
9. Chronic Liver Disease	9.9	1.1
10. Homicide	9.1	1.1

★These data are limited to the registration area that included 10 registration states and all cities having at least 8,000 inhabitants. In 1900 this composed 38 percent of the entire population of the continental United States. Since accidents were not reported in the 1900 census, this rate was taken from Lerner (1970).

SOURCES: *Abstract of the Twelfth Census of the United States, 1900.* Table 93. Washington, DC: U.S. Government Printing Office, 1902, and *Statistical Abstract of the United States, 1996.* 116th edition. Table 129. Washington, DC: U.S. Government Printing Office, 1996.

expectancy lowered by a high **infant mortality rate** and higher death rates until middle age (Kolata, 1995). For example, infant mortality rates in Japan and Sweden are half those in the United States. Though the reason is not known for sure, demographers suggest that the reason why the oldest Americans are so long-lived is because their universal health insurance through Medicare may provide better care than old people receive elsewhere. Another factor might be the effect of education. Early in the 20th century, Americans were among the best educated in the world (Kolata, 1995). A more educated society means a higher standard of living which ultimately contributes to longevity.

Though medical and scientific breakthroughs have obviously contributed to an increased life expectancy, the American public has also strived to change its lifestyle and improve its health in recent years. Priorities for health promotion are smoking cessation, physical exercise, nutrition and weight control, stress management, and appropriate use of alcohol and other drugs (Hyner & Melby, 1987). Certainly with the increasing number of AIDS cases, safe sex is also being promoted. Although one cannot change his or her heredity, one can have an impact on life expectancy through exercise, nutrition, and patterns of living. Current statistics on the expectation of life by race, age, and sex are shown in Table 1.3.

GENDER DIFFERENCES IN MORTALITY RATES

Beatrice Gottlieb in *The Family in the Western World: From the Black Death to the Industrial Age* (1993) observes that in spite of childbirth always being risky for women—riskier in the past than now—men do not as a rule outlive women, nor did they in the past.

The only exception worldwide is in south Asia in countries such as Bangladesh, India, Nepal, and Pakistan, where men outlive women (Cockerham, 1991). Nutritional deprivation and lessened access to medical care are among the possible reasons for this reversal of the usual female superiority in life expectancy.

In modern Western countries life expectancy is greater for women than for men, but this is not a new development. Although female infants initially are almost always outnumbered by male infants, a more equal balance is reached now, and also in the past, because male infants had a higher **death rate.** Indeed, the danger of childbirth is an important experience of families in the past, yet whatever is said about women dying in childbirth has to be put into this context of overall female survival (Gottlieb, 1993, p. 128). The notion that women in the Western world ran a disproportionate risk because of childbearing and that they were more likely than men to die in early adulthood turns out to be mistaken, argues Gottlieb (1993).

In 19th-century United States, however, women typically died younger than men, according to Peter Freund and Meredith McGuire (1995, pp. 25–26). Reasons include women incurring risks in pregnancy and childbirth and women often getting what food was left after men and children ate their share. However, by the 1920s the gender patterns in mortality rates in the United States had changed, and women generally were living longer than men, as had seemingly been the case in the rest of the Western world. Today, mortality rates for the two leading causes of death in the United States, heart disease and cancer, are higher for men than for women (Weiss & Lonnquist, 1994, p. 48). Higher death rates from heart disease in men could be contributed to a higher rate of smoking and a harder-driving personality; also, sex hormones secreted by women's ovaries may provide some protection against heart disease. Higher cancer rates in men are likely contributed again to smoking cigarettes, drinking alcohol more excessively, and being exposed to cancer-causing agents in the workplace, according to Weiss and Lonnquist (1994, p. 49). Indeed, men are more likely than women to die from almost all of the most common fatal diseases.

Biological advantages contributing to greater longevity for women may come from hormonal differences. Also, the monthly menstrual cycle of women reduces their iron count, thus women are less likely than men to build up a surplus of iron in their bodies. In addition, the conception ratio, projected to be higher than 120 males per 100 females, favors males in the United States, yet the **sex ratio** at birth is down to 105. Thus, male babies are the "weaker" of the sexes and die off more quickly. In the teens the sex ratio levels off, and after age 80, the ratio is less than 50 males per 100

Table 1.3

Expectation of Life by Race, Age, and Sex, 1993

Expectation of Life in Years

Age (in years)	Total	White		Black	
		Male	Female	Male	Female
At birth	75.5	73.1	79.5	64.6	73.7
5	71.3	68.8	75.1	61.0	70.0
10	66.4	63.8	70.1	56.1	65.1
15	61.5	58.9	65.2	51.2	60.2
20	56.7	54.2	60.3	46.8	55.3
25	52.1	49.6	55.5	42.6	50.6
30	47.3	44.9	50.6	38.3	45.9
35	42.7	40.4	45.8	34.2	41.3
40	38.1	35.9	41.0	30.2	36.9
45	33.6	31.4	36.3	26.4	32.5
50	29.2	27.0	31.7	22.8	28.3
55	24.9	22.8	27.2	19.3	24.3
60	20.9	18.9	23.0	16.2	20.6
65	17.3	15.4	19.0	13.4	17.1
70	14.0	12.3	15.3	10.8	13.9
75	10.9	9.5	12.0	8.7	11.1
80	8.3	7.1	8.9	6.7	8.5
85 and over	6.0	5.2	6.4	5.0	6.3

SOURCE: *Statistical Abstract of the United States, 1996,* (116th ed.). Table 120. Washington DC: U.S. Government Printing Office, 1996.

females. There is evidence that female life expectancy is also higher among many other animal species (Sagan, 1987). Perhaps females simply have better-built bodies. Their bodies have the potential of carrying and supporting a fetus/embryo. Thus, females are the "Porsche" model, whereas males are the more "thrown-together" model.

Regarding cultural differences between the sexes, conceivably females watch their diet more carefully than do males due to their traditional knowledge about food and a special cultural emphasis on weight maintenance. With more current emphasis on diet and exercise for both males and females, however, this difference may diminish.

Anthropologist Ashley Montagu (1968) suggests that women have a superior use of emotions because they are more likely to cry than men. Because it is not "macho" to cry, men generally refrain from such behavior, resulting in more psychosomatic disorders such as peptic ulcers. Montagu asks, "Is this a superior use of emotions?" Perhaps being freer to express themselves through the release of emotional feelings contributes to a decrease of stress for women.

Males have historically been involved in more risk-taking activities, as mentioned earlier, through "masculine" behavior like smoking (the rugged Marlboro man, for example) and drinking. Males have also been more inclined to drive fast cars, live the James Dean devil-may-care life, and participate in violent sports. Accidents cause more deaths among males than among females (Cockerham, 1995, p. 40). Males also have had more dangerous jobs, such as coal mining. Males have been in higher stress-producing positions, such as CEOs and other high-ranking administrative positions, than have females.

Differences in life expectancies for males and females create a situation where there are twice as many females as males at age 80. Is America ready for polygyny as a reward (or punishment) for octo-genarians?

Despite the fact that men die earlier and have more life-threatening illnesses, women have higher **morbidity** (illness) rates than men (Freund & McGuire, 1995). Chronic illnesses are more prevalent among women than men, but they are less severe and life threatening. When sex differences are considered, an inverse relationship appears to exist between mortality and morbidity (Cockerham, 1995, pp. 41-42). Women may be sick more often but live longer. Men may be sick less often but die sooner. Women report more episodes of illness and more contact with physicians. Perhaps women are more willing than "macho" men to report that they are sick. Because illness indicates "weakness," men might be less likely to visit a physician or admit that they are anything less than "healthy."

As sex roles continue to change, as females are found in greater numbers and in a greater variety of nontraditional occupations, as males share more in domestic tasks, and as the sexes come together in more unisex behaviors (more women smoking and drinking, having more stressful jobs, and living the "fast" life), stresses and strains of life should be more equally distributed between men and women. The argument of biology versus culture as influencing life expectancy by sex can then be better addressed.

Coping With the American Way of Dying

Human beings do not respond to all deaths in the same manner. As noted in chapter 2, humans ascribe meanings to death and then respond to these meanings. The American way of dying places higher values on some causes of deaths and ascribes less status to other causes. Likewise, coping with the death of a significant other will be influenced by the cause of the death.

Individual Life Expectancy

The following method for calculating longevity not only points to the inevitability of dying but identifies specific ways of increasing one's chances for longer living. The base number of years of computing life span in the United States is 75.

If you are male, subtract 4; if you are female, add 4: _____

If you plan to live in an urban area for most of your life, subtract 2; if a town or a rural area is planned, add 2: _____

If you anticipate having a desk job for most of your life, subtract 3; if the work requires regular physical labor, add 3; if you anticipate working after 65, add 3: _____

If you anticipate earning over $50,000 or under $10,000 a year, subtract 2: _____

If you exercise vigorously several times weekly, add 3: _____

If you anticipate living with a spouse or friend for most of your life, add 4; if not, subtract 1 for each decade alone after reaching age 30: _____

If you are an extrovert, enjoying the society of others, add 2; if you are an introvert, preferring to be by yourself, subtract 2: _____

If you are intense, aggressive, and easily angered, subtract 3; if you are relaxed, easygoing, and worry little, add 3: _____

If you have been given a ticket for speeding in recent years, subtract 2; if you regularly wear a seat belt while traveling, add 2: _____

If you anticipate finishing, or have finished, college, add 1; for a graduate degree, add 2: _____

If any grandparent lived to 85, add 2; if all four grandparents lived to 73, or are now living, add 3: _____

If either parent died of heart failure before 50, subtract 5; if any parent, brother, or sister under 50 has (or had) a heart condition, or has diabetes, subtract 3: _____

If you get intoxicated at least once a month, subtract 2; if a chronic alcoholic, subtract 8: _____

If you are overweight by more than 50 pounds, subtract 8; by 30–50 pounds, subtract 4; by 10–30, subtract 2: _____

If you smoke more than 2 packs a day, subtract 8; 1 or 2 packs, subtract 6; 1/2 to 1, subtract 3: _____

If you are over 30 make this adjustment: 31–40, add 2; 41–50, add 3; 51–70, add 4; over 70, add 5.: _____

From *Death: Confronting the Reality*, by William E. Phipps, 1987, Atlanta, GA: John Knox Press, 1987.

Although there are some special problems associated with deaths caused by a chronic disease, such as heart disease or cancer, there are some real advantages also. The following is a partial list of the opportunities provided by a slow death caused by a chronic disease:

1. The dying person is given an opportunity to attend to unfinished business—make out a will, complete incomplete projects.
2. The dying person and his or her family can attempt to heal broken family relationships, can say final farewells, and can all participate in constructing a meaningful and dignified death.
3. Funerals and other arrangements can be made with the consent and participation of the dying person.
4. Anticipatory grief on the part of the survivors and dying patient can take place.

Deaths due to **acute diseases** (such as pneumonia), accidents, and suicide also provide special problems as well as advantages to survivors. For all quick deaths there is the problem of being unprepared for the death. The survivors did not have a support group in place and did not have the advantage of having experienced anticipatory grief. Some of the grieving that has preceded the death due to a chronic disease cannot be expressed in deaths of this type. Consequently, grief is usually more intense when the dying takes place in a short period of time. Survivors may also experience more intense guilt: "If only I had done something, she wouldn't have died." Suicide creates special problems for survivors because they can become stigmatized by having a relative commit suicide: "They drove him to it." Finally, when people die without warning, survivors often are troubled because they did not have a chance to mend a broken relationship or say goodbye.

On the other hand, survivors of deaths due to acute diseases, accidents, and suicide are spared the following problems associated with chronic diseases:

1. Dying persons may not be willing to accept death, and when learning of their fates, may act in unacceptable ways.
2. Families may be unwilling to accept the death.
3. The dying process may be a long and painful process, not only for the dying patient, but also for the family.
4. The cost of dying from a chronic disease can be, and usually is, very expensive. The entire assets of a family can be wiped out by the medical bills of a chronically ill patient.

Thus, there seem to be advantages and disadvantages of dying a sudden death and of dying a lingering death. Because we have limited choices in the matter (unless we intervene), we will simply have to take whatever comes along. Who knows? Perhaps death will come when we are very old, at home, unexpectedly, in our own beds, while sleeping—and with our full mental and physical capabilities.

Conclusion

Although the American way of dying is being discussed and researched more today than in previous decades, discussion often poses as many questions as answers.

HI AND LOIS. REPRINTED WITH SPECIAL PERMISSION OF KING FEATURES SYNDICATE, INC.

Aristotle (1941, p. 975) observed long ago that "death is the most terrible of all things," yet it will not go away and, thus, we must learn to cope with it. The following questions do not have simple and straightforward answers: When does death take place? Who should determine the timing of a particular death? Who in society should be responsible for defining the meaning of life and death? When is a death an accident, and when is it a suicide?

Americans have developed a paradoxical relationship with death: We know more about the causes and conditions surrounding death, but we have not equipped ourselves emotionally to cope with dying and death. The American way of dying is such that avoiding direct confrontation with dying and death is a real possibility for many persons. What we need is the ability to both understand and cope with dying and death. The purpose of this book is to provide an understanding of dying, death, and bereavement that will assist individuals to better cope with their own deaths and with the deaths of others. As Rabbi Earl Grollman notes (Foderaro, 1994):

> The important thing about death is the importance of life. Do what you have to do now. Live today meaningfully.

Summary

1. The American way of dying is typically confined to institutional settings and removed from usual patterns of social interaction.
2. American society has done little to formally socialize its members to deal with dying and death on the personal and emotional levels.
3. The "thanatology movement" was a concerted effort in the 1970s to bring about an open discussion and awareness of behaviors and emotions related to dying, death, and bereavement. The movement continues into the 21st century.
4. An increased emphasis on dying and death is reflected in today's media.
5. The issue of when death occurs is a difficult one to resolve because consensus does not exist in America regarding the meaning of life and death.
6. The American way of dying has changed considerably since 1900. Relative to earlier times, Americans are less likely to die of acute diseases. Currently 65 percent of the deaths taking place in the United States can be attributed to two chronic diseases: heart disease and cancer.
7. In the past 50 years, life expectancy has increased approximately 16 years for males and 25 years for females. The increase in life expectancy has had many

Putting a Price on Human Life

Putting a price on human life is a common activity among life insurance companies, airlines, courts, industries, and agencies. Being required by law (Executive Order 12291 issued by President Ronald Reagan in February of 1981), the federal government routinely calculates the value of a life. Ordinary citizens make much the same determination when they choose small cars over larger, take jobs hundreds of feet below the ground for higher pay, or buy inexpensive houses in a flood plain instead of more expensive ones in safer areas.

People have been calculating the worth of their lives and the lives of others for as long as archaeologists, anthropologists, and historians can document human existence. The Aztecs in the 15th century and the Code of Hammurabi of ancient Babylonia created elaborate systems of compensation for injuries and deaths. In both ancient and medieval law a sum of money was paid by a guilty party to satisfy the family of the person injured or killed.

A fundamental difference exists, however, between calculating the value of a life to compensate for its loss, a common practice throughout the centuries, and determining whether it is worth saving, a practice growing more common today. Some philosophers argue that the value of human life

(continued)

effects upon Americans' understanding and ability to cope with dying and death.

8. The manner in which an individual dies will influence the way in which his or her survivors cope with the death. Chronic and acute diseases have advantages and disadvantages for the coping abilities of dying patients and their survivors.

9. The United States is basically a death-denying society.

10. The "value" of human life can be "calculated" in various ways.

11. Death anxiety is a multidimensional concept.

12. Death in the United States is feared because we have been taught to fear it.

Discussion Questions

1. Why did death "come out of the closet" in the 1970s? What events related to the "thanatology movement" helped change the American awareness of dying and death?

2. What factors have contributed to the American avoidance of dying and death?

3. Discuss whether you think the United States is basically a death-denying or a death-accepting society.

4. How has the definition of death changed over the years? What complications has this created for the American way of dying?

(continued from previous page)

is infinite or incalculable. However, insurance agents, economists, legal experts, scientists, and agency administrators are assigning life values ranging from a few dollars to many millions of dollars, depending on the formulas used.

One way of figuring value is to break down the body into chemical elements—5 pounds calcium, 1 and 1/2 pounds phosphorus, 9 ounces potassium, 6 ounces sulfur, 6 ounces sodium, a little more than 1 ounce magnesium, and less than an ounce each of iron, copper, and iodine. On that basis a human life today is worth $8.37, up $1.09 in six years because of inflation.

Another approach is to look at the going price of contract murder. Andreas Santiago Hernandez, 22, recently told the Los Angeles Police Department that he was paid $5,000 to kill Lorraine Keifer, the 67-year-old widow of a San Fernando Valley executive. Lt. Fahey says that in New York City a murder contract can cost nothing, if it is "for practice," or $10,000 and up.

The life insurance industry determines what people would have earned had they lived. It is their earning power over the course of their working life.

Adapted from "Putting a Price on Human Life Is Being Questioned," by W. R. Greer, Louisville, KY, *Courier-Journal,* June 30, 1985, p. 1D.

5. Compare and contrast the relative advantages and disadvantages of dying from acute and chronic diseases. What effect does each of these causes have on the abilities of families to cope with the death of a family member?
6. Discuss why women outlive men in the United States and most countries of the world.
7. What is meant by this statement?:" Death anxiety is a multidimensional concept."?

Glossary

Acute Disease: A communicable disease caused by a number of microorganisms including viruses, fungi, and bacteria. Acute illnesses last for a relatively short period of time and result either in recovery or death. Examples of acute illnesses include the following: smallpox, malaria, cholera, influenza, and pneumonia.

Brain Death: The brain is totally and irreversibly dead. Sometimes referred to as the Harvard definition of death.

Chronic Disease: A noncommunicable self-limiting disease from which the individual rarely recovers, even though the symptoms of the disease can often be alleviated. Chronic illnesses usually result in deterioration of organs and tissues, making the individual vulnerable to other diseases, often leading to serious impairment and even death. Examples of chronic illnesses include cancer, heart disease, arthritis, emphysema, and asthma.

Cryonics: A method of subjecting a corpse to extremely low temperatures through the use of dry ice and liquid nitrogen.

Death Anxiety: A learned emotional response to death-related phenomena characterized by extreme apprehension. Used synonymously with *death fear.*

Death Rate (Mortality Rate):   The number of deaths per 1,000 population.

Elderhostel: Inexpensive short courses, usually 5 days in duration, for older persons on college campuses. Over 160,000 individuals participate annually in a wide variety of courses offered by over 1,000 colleges in the United States and some foreign countries.

Euphemism: A word or phrase that is considered less distasteful than other words or phrases.

Infant Mortality Rate: The number of deaths of children under 1 year of age per 1,000 live births.

Life Expectancy: The number of years that the average newborn in a particular population can expect to live.

Morbidity: The rate of occurrence of a disease.

Sex Ratio: The number of males per 100 females.

Socialization: The social process by which individuals are integrated into a social group by learning its values, goals, norms, and roles. This is a lifelong process that is never completed.

Thanatology: The study of death-related behavior including actions and emotions concerned with dying, death, and bereavement.

References

Adams, C. (1988). *More of the straight dope.* New York: Ballantine Books.

Albert, E. (1986). Illness and deviance: The response of the press to AIDS. In D. A. Feldman & T. M. Johnson (Eds.), *The social dimensions of AIDS: Method and theory.* New York: Praeger.

Albert, E. (1987). *AIDS and the press: The creation and transformation of a social problem.* Unpublished paper presented at the annual meeting of the Society for the Study of Social Problems, Chicago.

Anderson, R. (1996). *Magic, science, and health.* Fort Worth, TX: Harcourt Brace College Publishers.

Aristotle. (1941). Nicomachean ethics III. In R. Mckeon (Ed.), *The basic works of Aristotle.* New York: Random House.

Baby born without brain dies, but legal struggle will continue. (1992, March 31). *New York Times,* p. A8.

Beecher, H. K. (1968, August). A definition of irreversible coma. *Journal of the American Medical Association, 205,* 85–88.

Bordewich, F. M. (1988, February). Mortal fears: Courses in "death education" get mixed reviews. *Atlantic Monthly, 261,* 30–34.

Cockerham, W. C. (1991). *The aging society.* Englewood Cliffs, NJ: Prentice-Hall.

Cockerham, W. C. (1995). *Medical sociology* (6th ed.). Englewood Cliffs, NJ: Prentice-Hall.

Cope, L. (1978, June 22). Is death, like pregnancy, an all-or-nothing thing? *Minneapolis Tribune,* pp. 1, 6A.

Counts, D. A., & Counts, D. R. (1991). Loss and anger: Death and the expression of grief in Kaliai. In D. R. Counts & D. A. Counts (Eds.), *Coping with the final tragedy: Cultural variation in dying and grieving* (pp. 191–212). Amityville, NY: Baywood Publishing.

Cousins, N. (1989). *Head first.* New York: Penguin.

Crandall, Richard C. (1991). *Gerontology: A behavioral science approach.* (2nd ed.). New York: McGraw-Hill.

Crase, D. (1994, Spring). Important consumer issues surrounding death. *Thanatos, 19,* 22–26.

Crissman, J. K. (1994). *Death and dying in central Appalachia: Changing attitudes and practices.* Urbana, IL: University of Illinois Press.

Cummins, V. A. (1978, September). *Death education in four-year colleges and universities in the U.S.* Paper presented at the First National Conference on the Forum for Death Education and Counseling.

Dattel, A. R., & Neimeyer, R. A. (1990). Sex differences in death anxiety: Testing the emotional expressiveness hypothesis. *Death Studies, 14,* 1–11.

Dickinson, G. E. (1986, April 18–20). *Effects of death education on college students' death anxiety.* Unpublished paper presented at the Forum for Death Education and Counseling, Atlanta, GA.

Dickinson, G. E., Sumner, E. D., & Frederick, L. M. (1992, May-June). Death education in selected health professions. *Death Studies, 16,* 281–289.

Doctors "kill" patient to save her life. (1988, September 22). Charleston, SC, *News and Courier,* p. 1A.

Dumont, R. G., & Foss, D. C. (1972). *The American view of death: Acceptance or denial?* Cambridge, MA: Schenkman.

Foderaro, L. W. (1994, April 7). Death no longer a taboo subject. *Palm Beach Post.*

Freund, P. E. S., & McGuire, M. B. (1995). *Health, illness, and the social body: A critical sociology* (2nd ed.). Englewood Cliffs, NJ: Prentice-Hall.

Fulton, R., & Owen, G. (1988). Death and society in twentieth century America. *Omega, 18,* 379–394.

Gervais, K. G. (1987). *Redefining death.* New Haven: Yale University Press.

Gillon, R. (1990). Editorial: Death. *Journal of Medical Ethics, 16,* 3–4.

Goffman, E. (1959). *The presentation of self in everyday life.* New York: Doubleday.

Gordon, A. K., & Klass, D. (1979). *The need to know: How to teach children about death.* Englewood Cliffs, NJ: Prentice-Hall.

Gorer, G. (1955, October). The pornography of death. *Encounter, 5,* 49–53.

Gottlieb, B. (1993). *The family in the Western world: From the Black Death to the Industrial Age.* Oxford: Oxford University Press.

Harvey, J. H. (1996). *Embracing their memory: Loss and the social psychology of storytelling.* Needham Heights, MA: Allyn and Bacon.

Hertz, R. (1960). The collective representation of death. In R. & C. Needham (Trans.), *Death and the right hand* (pp. 84–86). Aberdeen: Cohen and West.

Hiller, M. R. (1996, May 23). Health education lacking. *Post and Courier,* p. 2C. Charleston, SC.

Hyner, G. C., & Melby, C. L. (1987). *Priorities for health promotion and disease prevention.* Dubuque, IA: Eddie Bowers.

Is life expectancy now stretched to its limit? (1990, November 2). *New York Times,* p. A13.

Jasper, J. H., Lee, B. C., & Miller, K. E.. (1991). Organ donation terminology: Are we communicating life or death? *Health Psychology, 10,* 34–41.

Kass, L. R. (1971). Death as an event: A commentary on Robert Morison. *Science, 173,* 698–702.

Kolata, G. (1995, November 2). After 80, Americans live longer than others. *New York Times,* p. A13.

Leming, M. R. (1979-1980). Religion and death: A test of Homans's thesis. *Omega, 10*(4), 347–364.

Leviton, D. (1977). The scope of death education. *Death Education, 1,* 41–56.

Mansnerus, L. (1995, November 26). Dying writer Leary wants creative ending to his story. Charleston, SC, *Post and Courier,* p. 8A.

McGuire, D. (1988). Medical student, fourth year. In I. Yalof (Ed.), *Life and death: The story of a hospital* (pp. 339–344). New York: Random House.

McMordie, W. R., & Kumar, A. (1984). Cross-cultural research on the Templer/McMordie Death Anxiety Scale. *Psychological Reports, 54,* 959–963.

Montagu, A. (1968). *The natural superiority of women* (Rev. ed.). New York: Collier Books.

Mulkay, M. (1993). Social death in Britain. In D. Clark (Ed.), *The sociology of death: Theory, culture, practice* (pp. 31–49). Oxford: Blackwell Publishers.

Nardi, P. (1990). AIDS and obituaries: The perpetuation of stigma in the press. In D. A. Feldman (Ed.), *Culture and AIDS* (pp. 159–168). New York: Praeger.

Nuland, S. B. (1994). *How we die: Reflections on life's final chapter.* New York: Alfred A. Knopf.

Pine, V. R. (1986). The age of maturity for death education: A socio-historical portrait of the era 1976–1985. *Death Studies, 10,* 209–231.

Pollak, J. M. (1979). Correlates of death anxiety: A review of empirical studies. *Omega, 10,* 97–121.

Powner, D. J., Ackerman, B. M., & Grevnik, A. (1996, November 2). Medical diagnosis of death in adults: Historical contributions to current controversies. *The Lancet, 348,* 1219–1224.

Prior, L. (1989). *The social organization of death: Medical discourse and social practices in Belfast.* New York: St. Martin's Press.

Ramsey, P. (1970). *The patient as person: Explorations in medical ethics.* New Haven: Yale University Press.

Rasmussen, C. A., & Brems, C. (1996, March). The relationship of death anxiety with age and psychosocial maturity. *The Journal of Psychology, 130,* 141–144.

Rosenthal, N. R. (1980, Fall). Adolescent death anxiety: The effect of death education. *Education, 101,* 95–101.

Sagan, L. (1987). *The health of nations.* New York: Basic Books.

Selvin, P. (1990, July 17). Cryonics goes cold: People just aren't dying to be frozen. Charleston, SC, *News and Courier,* p. 5C.

Skinner, B. F. (1990, August 7). Skinner to have last word. *Harvest Personnel.*

Smith, T. L., & Walz, B. J. (1995). Death education in paramedic programs: A nationwide assessment. *Death Studies, 19,* 257–267.

Stillion, J. M. (1985). *Death and the sexes.* Washington, DC: Hemisphere/McGraw-Hill.

Stockwell, E. G. (1976). *The methods and materials of demography.* New York: Academic Press.

Sturgill, B. (Producer). (1995). *Death on my terms: Right or privilege* [Videotape]. Chicago: Terra Nova Films.

United Nations. (1953, August). *Principles for a vital statistics system* (Statistical Papers, Series M, No. 19, p. 6).

Veatch, R. M. (1995). The definition of death: Problems for public policy. In H. Wass & R. A. Neimeyer (Eds.), *Dying: Facing the facts* (3rd ed., pp. 405–432). Washington, DC: Taylor and Francis.

Vovelle, M. (1976). La redecouverte de la mort. *Pensee, 189,* 3–18.

Walsh, K. (1974). *Sometimes I weep.* Valley Forge, PA: Judson Press.

Weiss, G. L., & Lonnquist, L. E. (1994). *The sociology of health, healing, and illness.* Englewood Cliffs, NJ: Prentice-Hall.

Wilkins, R. (1996). *Death: A history of man's obsessions and fears.* New York: Barnes and Noble Books.

Youngner, S. J., Landefeld, C. S., Coulton, C. J., Juknialis, B. W., & Leary, M. (1989). "Brain death" and organ retrieval: A cross-sectional survey of knowledge and concepts among health professionals. *Journal of the American Medical Association, 261,* 2206–2210.

Suggested Readings

Anderson, P. (1996). *All of us: Americans talk about the meaning of death.* New York: Dell. Anderson explores American perspectives on death with 60 interviews with Americans ranging from gang kids to moviemakers.

Buckman, R. (1992). *I don't know what to say: How to help and support someone who is dying.* New York: Viking Press. From his own clinical experiences as an oncologist, the author discusses many issues that evolve in the process of watching someone die, including the topic of how to communicate with a dying person.

Dickinson, G. E., Leming, M. R., & Mermann, A. C. (Eds.). (1997). *Annual editions: Dying, death, and bereavement* (4th ed.). Guilford, CT: Dushkin/McGraw Hill. An anthology covering topics on the American way of dying and death, developmental aspects of dying and death, the dying process, ethical issues of dying, death, and suicide, and funeral and burial rites.

Freund, P. S., & McGuire, M. B. (1995). *Health, illness, and the social body: A critical sociology* (2nd ed.). Englewood Cliffs, NJ: Prentice-Hall. This sociological work discusses power issues in health and healing.

Kaizer, B. (1997). *Dancing with Mister D: Notes on life and death.* New York: Doubleday. A Dutch doctor, with training in philosophy as well as medicine, probes the intensity of the American preoccupation with death and dying as he shares his extraordinary experiences among the terminally ill.

Oaks, J., & Ezell, G. (1993). *Dying and death: Coping, caring, understanding* (2nd ed.). Scottsdale, AZ: Gorsuch Scarisbrick, Publishers. A helpful book for teachers, counselors, and health professionals in better understanding dying and death.

Sloan, D. C. (1991). *The last great necessity: Cemeteries in American history.* Baltimore: Johns Hopkins University Press. Changing attitudes and changing landscapes from churchyards to urban cemeteries to suburban parks in the United States are explored in this excellent historical account.

Smith, J. M. (1996). *AIDS and society.* Upper Saddle River, NJ: Prentice-Hall. This well-documented book, written by an attorney with AIDS, is a study of the history of science and medicine, health and illness, sex and death.

Stine, G. J. (1993). *Acquired immune deficiency syndrome: Biological, medical, social, and legal issues.* Englewood Cliffs, NJ: Prentice-Hall. AIDS from numerous academic perspectives.

Subedi, J., & Gallagher, E. B. (1996). *Society, health, and disease: Transcultural perspectives.* Upper Saddle River, NJ: Prentice-Hall. This book presents the interrelationship between health, disease, and different social settings in countries around the world.

Weiss, G. L., & Lonnquist, L. E. (1994). *The sociology of health, healing, and illness.* Englewood Cliffs, NJ: Prentice-Hall. Discusses the influence of the social environment on health and illness, health and illness behaviors, practitioners and their relationship with patients, and the health-care system in the United States and other countries.

Wilkins, R. (1996). *Death: A history of man's obsessions and fears.* New York: Barnes and Noble Books. Examines the lengths to which people throughout history have gone to cope with the five principal fears regarding death: the fear of being buried alive, of our body being defiled in the grave, of disintegrating, of being forgotten, and of suffering an ignominious death.

Related Web Sites

http://www.lsds.com/death/   Thanatolinks contains links to some of the best Internet sites related to death and dying.

http://www.yahoo.com/Society_and_Culture/Death/   The death index of the Yahoo Internet search engine.

http://www.emanon.net/~kcabell/death.html   Contains many World Wide Web links to resources on death and bereavement.

http://www.trinity.edu/~mkearl/b&w-ineq.jpg   Allows one to compare U.S. death rates of different social groups to ascertain social inequalities.

http://coombs.anu.edu.au/ResFacilities/DemographyPage.html   The Internet Guide to Demography and Population Studies.

http://www.cdc.gov/   Home page for the Centers for Disease Control and Prevention.

http://www.ahcpr.gov/   The Agency for Health Care Policy and Research provides information on the dying process in the context of U.S. health policy.

http://www.bardo.org/~bardo/reflects.html   Reflections on Death: A Guest Book/Questionnaire. Copyright 1997 by Jerral Sapienza, curator.

Chapter 2

Understanding the Social
Meaning of Dying and Death

*The symbols of death say what life is and those of life define what death must be.
The meanings of our fate are forever what we make them.*

—LLOYD WARNER, *THE LIVING AND THE DEAD*

This chapter opens with a photograph of Princess Diana and Mother Teresa, two of the world's most famous women of the latter half of the twentieth century. Prior to September of 1997, this picture would evoke a considerably different response than it does today. At that time, these two women died within a week of each other. The mass media coverage was unprecedented. As this chapter expounds on the social meaning of dying, death, and bereavement, consider your reaction to this photo and to the lives of these two women. Social meaning is the most important component of every aspect of dying and death considered in this textbook. If dying is perceived to be primarily a biological process, then defining dying and death simply as biological or physical processes would seem to be appropriate. Most people would likely agree with the "biology-is-primary/social meaning-is-secondary" interpretation. We do not.

Dying, in fact, is much more than a biological process. It is truly one of the most individual things that can happen to the body, and what happens takes place exclusively within the skin of the one person. However, with reference to the *meaning of dying,* the dying process is one of the most social experiences that one can have—all human bodies exist within a social and cultural context. When a person dies, many

---

The Free Fall

When I die, my husband loses his wife, his lover, his confidante. My children lose their mother. Each friend loses me as a friend. But I lose all human relationships. That's the meaning of the free fall. That's the meaning of being alone.

From *Free Fall* (p. 36), by J. K. Smith (a dying person), 1975, Valley Forge, PA: Judson Press.

---

things other than internal biological changes take place. For nearly all human beings, every act of dying influences others. Consequently, the act of dying is a social or shared event.

The sociological perspective emphasizes the social-symbolic nature of human interaction. The key factor that unites biological entities into a social group entity is shared meaning: Many of the goals that one person wants to achieve, and many of the experiences that one person wants to have, require shared and coordinated cultural meanings. Symbols are the means by which socially created meaning is shared in the process of human interaction. Symbols are words or gestures that stand for something else by reason of association.

A specific death has distinct meanings wherever the deceased had meaningful relationships, and the death of one person has extensive social consequences. With a death in a husband-wife **dyad,** one half of that entity dies. If the couple has two children, one fourth of the family dies. One thirty-thousandth of the community dies, and one two-hundred and fifty-millionth of the nation dies.

If a person is identified with many social roles or positions, and that person's death creates a situation where many roles or positions are vacated, then many persons or role occupants die in a single death. Furthermore, we may agree that although one biological body dies, ownership of that body is difficult to determine. "Who owns my body?" is a question often posed by people who are dying. Related to the basic ownership question are "Who is qualified to make decisions about my body?" and "If I am the one who is dying, what right do any others have to tell me what to do with my body?" Because humans are social animals, ownership is a creation of symbol-using people. Joint ownership patterns are created and exist for most people. Therefore, body ownership might be considered shared, and the decisions related to it would be joint decisions.

The elimination or departure of a person from the ranks of "the living" leaves a hole in the midst of the living. Certain meaning is lost, while new meaning is added—behavior that previously involved the dead is literally no longer possible because it also has ceased to exist. Established interaction or behavior patterns are disrupted, an event that demands attention. The funeral process involves activities, rites, and rituals associated with the final disposition of the dead. This process usually reduces the social disruption caused by death insofar as the rituals are acceptable to those involved and are performed according to societal norms. The living are concerned not only with the death of a person, but also with what happens to the living as a result of that death. Although the biological person may be gone, the meaning remains just so long as the

The flowers given in tribute to Diana, Princess of Wales, at Kensington Palace. This image exemplifies the words of the song, "Candle in the Wind" sung by Elton John at her funeral. Rewritten from a song originally composed to commemorate the life of Marilyn Monroe, another star who died tragically at the age of 36, the lyrics include this line, "Goodbye, England's Rose. Your candle burned out long before your legend ever will." More than 2.5 billion people (one third of the world's population) observed the funeral of Princess Diana via television.

living grant the "symboled immortality" or "meaning immortality" to the deceased (Lifton & Olson, 1974).

In the social commentary immediately following the death of Diana, Princess of Wales, a British broadcaster was asked by an American interviewer if the funeral ceremony would be a "royal funeral." He replied,

> Diana is much more than a royal—royals are two a penny. Princess Di is a star the likes of which we have only seen in James Dean, Marilyn Monroe, Elvis Presley, and John Kennedy. Her immortality will transcend the House of Windsor, not because she was born to it, but because it has been bestowed upon her by the British people and the people of the world.

Granting or creating such immortality is one of the things symbol-using beings can do. A person may even be granted considerably greater significance than he or she had while alive, as in the case of Princess Di. For the bereaved, changing the meaning of a lost relationship is essential to the process—and is accomplished with varying degrees of ease—depending on the nature of the relationship. Consider the reaction to the qualitatively different grief expressed by Diana's sons, Princes William and Harry, and her former husband, Prince Charles in the aftermath of the news of her death.

This book will try to counter the widespread tendency to interpret dying as primarily a biological process—something that the body does to the person. We are concerned, rather, with what people *do* about this process. For example, biologists and

This photograph is much more than a man digging a hole in the ground. Consider your emotional response to this photograph.

medical personnel (or anyone else, including social scientists) respond to the meaning of the biology rather than to the biology per se. The physician's decisions are made on the basis of what the biological condition means to that physician. Making a medical diagnosis is the process by which the physician decides the meaning of the biological factors. This diagnosis, then, represents the process of transposing biological factors into meaning factors.

Death-related meaning has changed extensively since the early 1970s. With reference to past knowledge about death, much of what was known was either untrue or incompatible with contemporary knowledge. Although ignorance may cause harm, people's convictions cause greater harm. The sociological statement made popular by W. I. Thomas illustrates this principle—whatever is *defined* as being real to the physician will *become* real in its consequences for diagnoses. Thus, the perspective that "biology is primary" creates a **self-fulfilling prophecy.**

A recurring dramatic illustration of the fact that the behavior of the physician and others stems from the meaning rather than from the biology per se can be seen each time the news media report that a corpse in the morgue has come back to life after being wrongly pronounced dead by the experts. The physician's belief that a body is dead does not guarantee that it is. Behavior follows from the meaning, not from the biological factors per se—a *living* body was sent to the morgue.

Finally, the dying process almost always occurs in a social situation to which meanings are ascribed. Physically, everyone dies in some place, and that place is given symbolic meanings by those involved. Therefore, in this book we will focus on the fact that dying is more than a biological or physical event because it is shared, symboled, and situated.

The Social Nature of Meaning

To understand the role of meaning in death-related behavior, it is necessary to understand the influence of meaning in all human behavior. We use words to tell ourselves and each other what something means. This book consists of words about dying and death. Words are configurations of symbols. The words or symbols are not inherently embedded in the things named—we do not somehow extract words or meaning from the things that we see as meaningful. Rather, we create symbols or words to represent the things named. Symbols re-present (present in a different way) the phenomena of concern. For example, currently the symbol *c-a-s-k-e-t* represents the container into which a dead body is deposited before burial. However, prior to 1850 the primary meaning of *c-a-s-k-e-t* was a case for storing valuable jewelry.

The fact that all symbols are **empirical** means that they can potentially be shared or understood by more than one person. The meaning of a casket can be shared by many—the casket per se cannot. Meaning is created from symbols that are socially constructed, transmitted, and used. However, we must also remember that meaning is always challengeable and changeable because it depends upon group consensus or agreement.

Some symbols have empirical referents. These are the symbols—especially names or labels—that people use to identify, talk, or think about the aspects of the empirical world. Some symbols, however, do not refer to anything empirical. These types of symbols would include the words *beauty, humor, indignity,* and *evil.* Such nonempirically referenced words have an exceptionally meaningful impact upon behavior because they are involved in the human process of making choices. To engage in social behavior, we employ both types of symbols or meanings.

Thus, we have attempted to recognize distinct differences between the empirical world and the meaning world. We have attempted to emancipate the words (symbols or meaning) from the world. Most people do just the reverse: They enslave the words by joining, locking, or laminating them to the empirical world so strongly that the words' separate identity is lost or hardly recognized.

Most discussions of words (symbols or meaning) involve people who think primarily in terms of the world. They have an empirical-world bias, even though they are talking to each other about things that are not physically present and that have no empirical existence. They effectively execute a symbol bypass.

Creating and Changing Meaning

Biological bodies are created; they live, and they die. Bodies of meaning are also created, live, and die. Biological continuity occurs through a process of biological transmission or transference. Meaning (culture) continuity occurs through a process of social-symboled transmission. The socialization process occurs as biological bodies are transformed into social beings and as we teach our children how to behave in what our society considers to be a human way.

Creation of new meaning is always possible. Death-related meaning is no different than any other type of meaning. It is important to remember that this meaning is created by humans, not discovered in the world. All meanings are subject to change.

However, well-established meaning is difficult to change. Meaning, for example, is frequently defined as sacred and, therefore, more likely to be protected and perpetuated than changed. Crises or traumatic conditions may be necessary for change in death-related meaning. As noted in chapter 11, many of the contemporary death-related meanings, including the rituals involved in adjustment, were created by ancestors who experienced dying in quite different social circumstances than those found today. Furthermore, considering the dramatic changes in health, longevity, and health care, our ancestors experienced death in somewhat different biological bodies. Therefore, it is not surprising that discontinuities have developed in American death-related meanings and experiences.

Any aspect of death-related behavior can be changed if there is enough societal (or subsocietal) support. One person can change death-related meaning for himself or herself, but it is difficult to maintain and sustain the new meaning if a **significant other** does not support, legitimate, or validate it.

Like the ripples caused by dropping a stone into a lake, changes in death-related meaning will inevitably have consequences that penetrate other areas of living. Change in the sacred components of dying and death may come in through the back door, so to speak. Cremation may gain increased acceptance, not as a direct result of changes in religion, but rather as a result of the unavailability of space for earth burials. Likewise, changes in life-prolonging, or death-prolonging, procedures may result more from the availability of technological devices than from changes in religion or **mores**—the "must" behaviors that a society believes are for the good of that society.

A Social Science Understanding of Dying and Death

In this book we will present many research findings produced in the social sciences to help provide an understanding of death-related experiences. We will also provide sociological, psychological, religious, historical, and anthropological perspectives for interpreting contemporary American customs dealing with dying, death, and bereavement. Finally, in providing an awareness of the many ways in which humans deal with death-related phenomena, we hope to give the perspective that different does not necessarily mean bad or good but simply different and that death-related behavior can be evaluated only in reference to its social context.

It is our goal to provide multidisciplinary perspectives on dying, death, and bereavement from the bodies of knowledge developed in the social sciences. Chapters 3 and 4 emphasize a psychological viewpoint to understanding death awareness and meanings; chapters 5 and 10 utilize an anthropological or comparative approach in providing a cross-cultural perspective on death rituals; and chapters 11 and 12 review the history of American bereavement and funeral customs. In the remainder of this chapter we will focus on the sociological approach in providing a conceptual understanding of dying and death.

THE SOCIOLOGICAL APPROACH TO UNDERSTANDING DYING AND DEATH

Sociology has been defined in many ways. We define sociology as *the scientific study of human interaction*. We will explore two parts of this definition—sociology as (a) a scientific endeavor with (b) human interaction as the subject of investigation. George C. Homans (1967, p. 7) in *The Nature of Social Science* claims that any science has two basic tasks: to discover and to explain. By the first we judge whether it is a science and by the second, how successful a science it is. The first task is to state and test more or less general relationships between empirical events of nature. The second task is to explain these relationships within a theoretical context. A scientific explanation will tell us why, under a given set of conditions, a particular phenomenon will occur (Homans, 1967, p. 22). In the process of discovery, the scientist is attempting to formulate general statements concerning empirical variables that can be verified by systematic observation.

Even though the claim has often been made that sociology and the other social sciences differ from the natural sciences because they use a radically different technique for doing research, Richard Rudner (1966, p. 5) contends that the differences between the social sciences and the natural sciences are much less fundamental than a difference in methodology. Both the social sciences and the natural sciences use the same empirical methodology. This empirical methodology is based on observation and reasoning, not on supernatural revelation, intuition, appeals to authority, or personal speculation.

Sociology, as a science, aims at both discovering empirical regularities and explaining these regularities by referring to an interrelated set of empirical **propositions.** The goal of sociology is to produce a body of knowledge that not only will provide an understanding of the causal processes influencing human interaction, but that also will enable the sociologist to predict future social behaviors. This is the basis for Homans's contention that sociology is scientific:

> What makes a science are its aims, not its results. If it aims at establishing more or less general relationships between properties of nature, when the test of the truth of a relationship lies finally in the data themselves, and the data are not wholly manufactured—when nature, however stretched out on the rack, still has a chance to say "No!"—then the subject is a science. By these standards all the social sciences qualify. (1967, p. 4)

Sociology shares with the other social sciences the scientific epistemology (study of knowledge) and a concern for understanding human interaction. The success of sociology, like that of any other science, is judged by the explanatory power and predictive ability of the body of knowledge produced by the research efforts within the discipline.

A body of scientific knowledge is a collection of those statements of relationship (or propositions) for which there is empirical evidence. It is organized in two ways. The first way is the unsystematic collection of all research studies dealing with a particular content area published in research periodicals. For example, one might expect to find all social science research investigations that are concerned with death-related behavior to be published in a broad range of sociological and psychological journals. However, one would be more likely to find them in one of the following periodicals: *Omega: The Journal of Death and Dying, Death Studies, The Gerontologist, The American Sociological Review, The American Psychological Review, Human Organization, The Journal of Social Psychology,* and *The Journal of Abnormal and Social Psychology.* The only organization of these findings would be found in the theoretical frameworks of other research investigations and textbooks citing these studies.

The second way by which a body of knowledge is organized is through a theoretical **paradigm.** Research studies sharing general commitments to methodological techniques, research assumptions, and levels of analysis are brought together to form theoretical paradigms. According to George Ritzer:

> A paradigm is a fundamental image of the subject matter within a science. It serves to define what should be studied, what questions should be asked, how they should be asked, and what rules should be followed in interpreting the answers obtained. The paradigm is the broadest unit of consensus within a science and serves to differentiate one scientific community (or sub-community) from another. It subsumes, defines, and interrelates the examples, theories, methods, and instruments that exist within it. (1975, p. 7)

Sociology, like most other scientific disciplines, is a multiparadigm science. There is much debate over the number of paradigms existing within the field of sociology, yet sociologists would agree that no single paradigm is dominant within the discipline. Paradigms are further divided into subparadigms or theoretical orientations. Examples of these theoretical orientations (discussed later in this chapter) are structural-functional theory, conflict theory, social exchange theory, and symbolic interaction theory.

Structural-functional theory and conflict theory are generally concerned with group actions and societal structures and tend to be more macroscopic. Social exchange theory and symbolic interaction theory are the focus of analysis of behavior, attitudes, meanings, and values of individuals and tend to be more microscopic.

Emile Durkheim's work served as the primary foundation for paradigms relating to group actions and societal structures. In attempting to differentiate sociology from social philosophy, Durkheim defined the discipline as the study of social facts. For Durkheim (1964) social facts are "any way of doing things (fixed or not) which are capable of exercising restraint upon the individual." He advocated that sociologists study social facts *as if* they are things. To accomplish this end, Durkheim (1964) formulated the following four guidelines in his *Rules of the Sociological Method* (originally published in 1895):

1. All preconceptions must be eradicated.
2. The subject matter for sociological research must be social facts directly observed.
3. Social facts must be viewed as a product of group experiences and not individual actions.
4. The cause of any given social fact must be sought in its preceding social facts.

Durkheim's (1964) claim that "society is a social system which is composed of parts which, without losing their identity and individuality, constitute a whole which transcends its parts" exemplifies that structural-functional and conflict theories are primarily concerned with group actions and societal structures. From this point of view, social groups or collectivities (e.g., a particular nuclear family) cannot be reduced to merely a collection of individuals, and social phenomena have a reality of their own that transcends the constituting parts.

Therefore, sociological research from this perspective will study group-related phenomena (e.g., death rituals, structures that provide care for dying patients, and professional groups of funeral functionaries) rather than behaviors of particular individuals.

Durkheim advocated the use of historical and comparative methods in sociological research. An example of this type of death-related research might be comparison of the size, structure, and function of colonial funerals in Concord, Massachusetts, with a similar contemporary analysis of funerals in the same city.

Unlike Durkheim, many contemporary theorists employ the survey research questionnaire. The use of the questionnaire creates a problem for some; as George Ritzer (1975, p. 27) says, "How can one study social facts (cultural patterns) by asking individuals questions?" This issue might be more clearly understood by considering the analogy of the relationship between forests and trees. One can study forests in the United States and describe their sizes and distribution, their rates of reproduction, morbidity, and mortality, and the impact of acid rain upon them. However, to adequately understand a forest one must look at a few trees. The same may be true of social patterns and the behaviors of individuals.

Structural-functional theory is concerned with explaining the persistence of social facts, social institutions and structures, and the stability of society. Conflict theory focuses on the competition between the various parts, institutions, and/or structures within a given society and the coercive forces that allow societies to perpetuate themselves at some times and to change at others.

STRUCTURAL-FUNCTIONALIST THEORY

Structural-functionalists view society as a social system of interacting parts in which death-related behavior is analyzed from two perspectives:

1. How do death-related meaning systems and death institutions contribute to the maintenance of the larger social system?
2. In what ways are death-related meaning systems and death institutions affected by their relationships to the larger social system?

Functionalists are interested in positive (eufunctional) and negative (dysfunctional) results of social interaction as well as the intended (manifest) and unintended (latent) consequences of death-related behavior. When family members commit themselves to care for a dying family member, it can be eufunctional for emotional ties within the family; however, it can be dysfunctional (especially if family members must interrupt their employment) for the security of family financial resources. A manifest function of attending a funeral is to support the bereaved as family members attempt to adapt to the loss of a loved one, but a latent function is to strengthen the relationships that exist within social groups.

If structural-functionalist theorists were interested in the funeral rites and rituals, they might investigate one or more of the following research questions:

1. How do funerals help to celebrate and maintain society's most salient social values?
2. How do funerals help to promote relationships within kinship groups (grandparents, parents, aunts and uncles, cousins, brothers, sisters, etc.)?
3. How do funerals contribute to and/or affect the relationships between bereaved families and the larger society?
4. How do funerals facilitate the grieving process as one mourns the death of a loved one?

5. How do death-related rituals help return bereaved persons to their normal social responsibilities?

6. How do differing methods of body disposition and funeral rituals socially differentiate families regarding social status?

The following research example, written by Kathy Charmaz (1980, pp. 183–187), describes the strategies employed by coroner's deputies in maintaining the routine character of their work as they attempt to get surviving family members to take over the responsibility for the care of the dead body and the financial obligations related to final disposition. In this description we can observe that if each party performs his or her socially prescribed role (or social function), the social system runs efficiently and social equilibrium is maintained.

The Announcement of Death by the Coroner's Deputy
Kathy Charmaz

In these coroners' departments, the ways in which deaths are announced to heretofore unsuspecting relatives are strategically constructed with an eye toward accomplishing the objectives of getting the relatives to quietly accept both the burial costs and the death without the deputy's personal involvement. Burial costs are likely to be the "real" issue in countries without access to inexpensive burials. Then, the deputies feel constrained to handle the notification of death strategically in order for the family to readily assume the costs of disposal of the body.

Consequently, the strategies employed in announcing the death to relatives differ according to the necessity of getting them to pay for burial costs. When this is necessary, and therefore an important part of the deputy's work, special techniques are likely to be employed. Notable, strategic control of the encounter is enhanced by making the announcement in person. The deputies then lay the grounds for ensuring that an uneventful and speedy disposition of the body is made at the expense of the family.

The other objective, to induce the relative to accept the death as real, coincides with the deputy's interest in making the announcement of death efficiently without eliciting a subsequent fuss from the bereaved or becoming involved themselves. Part of doing that means constructing situations in which the deputy's sense of self is protected, in addition to his or her control over the encounter in which he or she is engaged. Self-protection strategies are employed to maintain the routine character of the work and to keep the deputies from feeling personally involved in the ongoing scene. Part of the self-protection strategy consists of the effort to remain the polite, sincere, authoritative, but basically disinterested, official.

The strategies for making the announcement help the deputies remain in control of the situation and handle the special problems that emerge in the course of interaction. Not the least of these problems is the necessity of

(continued)

(continued from previous page)

deputies to construct the contextual properties of the announcing scene, besides constructing the announcement itself. In other words, they must create the kind of ambience and interactional circumstances wherein the announcement logically fits so that it is effective and believable; they have no ready-made scene to serve as an official backdrop for their proclamation.

Compared to physicians who announce "bad news" to the relative, deputies have a weighty problem. Besides their much lesser amount of authority and prestige, deputies lack the advantages typically possessed by physicians of a prior relationship with the relative, a fitting organizational setting for giving the news, and a series of prior interactional cues that serve to prepare the relative.

Since deputies have neither the structural supports provided by the hospital situation nor the physician's status, they must devise tactics to get their work done without incident. Typically, their objectives are to announce quickly, to turn the responsibility of the body and its subsequent burial expense over to the family, and to determine that the person who received the news is holding up well or is with someone. But all these tasks may be embellishments to their main task of the disposition of the body and getting the family to assume the expenses, when this is their real objective.

Deputies try to create an authoritative context by rapidly supplying one meaningful cue after another that brings the relatives into interaction as they prepare to move into the announcement. Compared to the medical scene, the cues come much more rapidly and sharply. Thus, the cues cannot be easily dismissed, although the survivor has little time to think about them.

Skillful deputies can be expected to handle the situation in such a way that cues will neither be missed or misinterpreted. The relatives are not permitted enough time to disattend to them and, should they attempt to, the deputies will alter their presentation accordingly. For example, a deputy stated, "Sometimes I'm stern, sometimes I'm sympathetic, sometimes I even shout a little bit louder than they can."

The deputies who telephone find they get a better response when they successively lead the relative into questioning them. By doing so, the officials set the conditions wherein they can impart progressively unpromising news. For example:

> I tell them that he collapsed today while at work. They asked if he is all right now. I say slowly, "Well, no, but they took him to the hospital." . . . They ask if he is there now. I say, "They did all they could do—the doctors tried very hard." They say, "He is dead at the hospital?" Then I tell them he's at the coroner's office.

Most deputies expressly avoid the word "dead" when first imparting the news since they feel it is too harsh. Substitutes are used, such as "fatally injured" and "passed away," if they must refer directly to it at all. A preferred technique is to control the interaction so that the relative refers to the person

(continued)

(continued from previous page)

as "dead." Those making telephone announcements attempt to manipulate the conversation so that the relative says the word "dead." Several deputies remarked that having the survivors themselves say it made the announcement more meaningful to them and the death more "real." Describing a close family member as "dead" becomes symbolic and sets the stage for treating the deceased as such. The deputies then reaffirm the survivor's statements and elaborate on them. Consequently, when the deputies' strategies work, the transition from perceiving one's relative from alive to dead can be made rapidly. The symbolic shift is likely to occur so quickly during the encounter that the relative may remain unaware of how the interaction was managed. Indeed, in an encounter deputies deem successful, the relative is likely to express appreciation for their "sensitivity."

Deputies state that the relatives always ask about the circumstances of dying. The coroners give them what information they have and can release, then turn the situation around by asking about funeral and burial arrangements. To illustrate: "They always ask what happened. Then we reverse it and ask what type of arrangements they are going to make."

Or in the case of the telephone notification, the relative typically inquires, "What can I do [to help]?" The deputies simply state, "All you need to do now is call your family funeral director, and he'll direct you." In both situations, this approach gets the relatives down to business and usually results in their agreement to "help" while in the midst of the initial encounter with the deputies. Likely, the relatives have unwittingly volunteered to underwrite the expenditures before they have any conception of the implications or expense.

Simultaneously, the deputies have played the role of officials who cut through the survivor's grief and shock by pointing to the work that has to be done. Moreover, the deputies have strategically managed the situation in ways that foster the relatives' acceptance of their directives.

CONFLICT THEORY

Whereas structural-functional theory focuses on the issue of societal maintenance and social equilibrium, conflict theory focuses on issues related to social change and disequilibrium. Conflict theorists focus on competition, conflict, and dissension resulting from individuals and groups competing for limited societal resources.

In emphasizing social competition for limited resources, conflict theorists interested in death-related behavior would point out the inequality in the availability and quality of medical care and the differential death rates. For example, the poor are deprived of optimal care, in general, and of life-saving procedures, in particular (Charmaz, 1980, p. 37). Relying on the work of Herbert Marcuse, Allan Kellehear argues that those who control life are the same as those who control death. According to Kellehear (1990, p. 13):

Many sociologists trace the intellectual roots of the conflict theory paradigm to Karl Marx. Marx is buried at Highgate Cemetery in London, England. The epitaph on his tomb reads: "Workers of all lands unite. The philosophers have only interpreted the world in various ways; the point is to change it."

The power elite in any society and that society's politico-economic arrangements—that is class arrangements—determine one's life and death chances. Society determines not only what types of death will occur, but when they occur and to whom and the chances, if any, of doing anything about it.

From a conflict theoretical perspective, Charmaz (1980, p. 39) argues that American society, which has an individualistic perspective on death (as it does on most other social issues), abdicates most of its social responsibilities to the dying and their family members. She asserts that in America we are assured of an inequitable distribution of health care and a lack of social concern for the dying precisely because Americans value individualism and privacy.

Beliefs in individualism, self-reliance, privatism, and stoicism are ideological and justify the ways in which dying is handled. The ideological view of dying as a private affair, something that *should* be the responsibility of the family, relieves other social

THE WIZARD OF ID   Brant parker and Johnny hart

BY PERMISSION OF JOHNNY HART AND CREATORS SYNDICATE, INC.

institutions, notably health and welfare organizations, from the necessity of providing comprehensive services. Such beliefs are justified by ideological views that human beings deserve privacy in their problems, and in order to maintain self-respect, they wish to rely on themselves to handle them whenever possible. When it is not possible, failure may be conferred upon those unable to handle their situations.

What's Fair Is Fair

Even where a will or the law of intestacy calls for equal division of a bequest among a group of beneficiaries and the beneficiaries accept the principle of equal division, conflict may occur. Some possessions are indivisible but desirable to more than one person, such as a prized antique clock. Problems may arise in the attempt to divide valuables equally. Under what circumstances can a treasured rocking chair and a family Bible be divided equally between two or more family members?

If all beneficiaries want fair treatment and a will attempts fair treatment, conflict may occur because beneficiaries have different perceptions of what is fair. Fairness can mean that something is divided equally, but fairness also takes into account various principles of deservingness or right; a division of an estate can be fair without being equal. Because fairness can be determined on many different bases, there may be many competing interpretations on what is fair. The following list, derived from the work of Marvin Sussman et al. (1970) and from interviews carried out during our research, indicates some of the competing principles for determining if the outcome in inheritance is fair.

1. Long residence in a house confers some right to it.
2. Last name identity with the deceased confers some rights to the property of the deceased.
3. Blood relationship confers some rights.
4. High frequency of contact with the deceased confers some rights.
5. Material support of the deceased confers some rights.
6. Correspondence with the deceased confers some rights.

(continued)

If conflict theorists were interested in funeral rites and rituals, they might investigate one or more of the following research questions:

1. What are the dysfunctional consequences of attending funerals?
2. What role conflicts and family disputes arise as a result of planning a funeral for family members?
3. How does not attending a funeral create conflicts between adults in neighborhood, friendship, and occupational groups?
4. What are the problems created by the presence of children at funerals?
5. How do particular family relationships contribute to increased competition for status among family members as they participate in the funeral of a family member?
6. How do methods of planning a funeral and the related expenditures contribute to increased family conflict and competition for scarce financial resources within the family?

(continued from previous page)

7. Having given the deceased a thing confers rights to its return.
8. Need arising from relative poverty, handicap, minorhood, orphan status, or infirmity confers rights.
9. Contribution in building the deceased's estate increases rights.
10. Kinship closeness confers rights.
11. Previous perceived underinheritance increases rights.
12. Overinheritance reduces rights.
13. Hostile relationship with the deceased reduces rights.
14. Congenial relationship increases rights.

In addition to people having discrepant interpretations of what is equal or what is fair, there will be instances where equality and fairness may be competing principles. Some individuals will believe that the estate should be divided equally, while other individuals will believe that it should be divided on the basis of what is fair, though fairness may be perceived differently by different persons.

Because there are so many possible interpretations of what is fair or what is equal and because people often seek fairness or equality, a dispute may not be resolved easily. Disputes over inheritance may be one of the major reasons for adult siblings to break off relationships with each other. In some cases the inheritance dispute may be the final battle between competitive siblings, and in that sense it resembles the "last straw" reported in breakups in other close relationships (Hill, Rubin, & Peplau, 1976; Nevaldine, 1978).

7. In what ways might members of the clergy and funeral directors engage in social conflict due to the fact that family members allocate to each functionary differing amounts of authority and social rewards (money) for conducting the funeral?
8. How is it possible for unethical funeral industry personnel to exploit bereaved survivors during a time of emotional distress?
9. How does the death of a parent create sibling rivalry among the children, and how does the death of a child create marital problems between the parents?

"What's Fair is Fair" is an example of conflict theory applied to family behavior related to the division of family property and the reading of the will.

Theories like social exchange and symbolic interactionism differ from structural-functionalism and conflict theory on two crucial points. The first is that social exchange and symbolic interactionism would contend that the essential feature of society is its subjective character. Social facts do not have any inherent meaning other than what humans attribute to them. W. I. Thomas argues that if people define situations as real, the situations will be real in their consequences. This argument is a basic premise of social exchange and symbolic interactionist paradigms. This principle totally rejects Durkheim's *Rules of the Sociological Method,* which would restrict sociology to the study of objective social facts. Social exchange and symbolic interactionism would contend that all social facts are either intrasubjective or intersubjective.

Words and Meanings
W. A. Armbruster

Blood,
    and Pus . . .
    Entrails,
    Vomit,
    Dung, Spit and Afterbirth.
    Disgusting words.

Love,
    And Soft.
    Mother.
    Kiss, Mood, and Friendship.
    Tender words.

Spring,
    And Smile.
    Dance,
    Play,
    Fun, Sing, and Beachball.
    Happy Words.

(continued)

The second distinguishing feature of the social exchange and symbolic interaction paradigms is the methodological unit of analysis—the individual. These paradigms will emphasize individual behavior over group actions and societal structures.

George Ritzer (1975, pp. 85–86) rightly credits the writings of Max Weber for being the exemplar of the social exchange and symbolic interaction paradigms. The essence of Weber's analysis of social action was the **meaningful action of individuals.** Weber (1966, p. 88) defined *social action* as human behavior to which the acting individual attaches subjective meaning, and that takes into account the behaviors of others.

Weber advocated **interpretative understanding** *(Verstehen)* as the research methodology for investigating social action. The interpretative understanding methodology requires the researcher to develop an empathy for the subjects whom he or she studies. At times this will require the researcher to enter the subjective world of the subject by participating in this person's life experience. A Native American proverb encourages us not to judge the behavior of others until we have walked a mile in their moccasins. In this context, interpretative understanding attempts to describe and explain social behavior from the perspective of the subjective meanings of the actors' intentions for their behavior. Today, contemporary sociologists utilize the Verstehen approach as they employ participant-observation research techniques. We will now consider social exchange theory and symbolic interaction theory.

(continued from previous page)

Death,
    And Fire.
    Pain,
    War,
    Divorce, Poverty, Hospital.
    Sad Words.

No. That's not right at all. You cannot
    String words together
    And say They're bad
    Or good.

Where are the verbs?
    Who are we talking about?
    What are the circumstances?

Vomit is beautiful to a mother whose child
    Had just swallowed a pin.
    Love is pain if you are a third party,
    Outside, looking in.
    Death is very nice for someone very old,
    Very ill, and ready.

(continued)

(continued from previous page)
And surely you've danced with a clod.
   Or had a sad spring.

No, Words aren't sad
   Or glad.

You are.
   Or I am.
   Or he is.

SOCIAL EXCHANGE THEORY

Two traditions are followed by social exchange theorists. The first tradition is consistent with principles of behavioral psychology and stresses psychological reductionism and behavioral reinforcement techniques. The second tradition has been influenced by the work of Peter Blau (1964) and is committed to many of the assumptions held by symbolic interactionists and the social definitionist paradigm. Social exchange theories of this type would contend that human behavior involves a subjective and interpretative interaction with others that attempts to exchange symbolic and nonsymbolic rewards. It is important that such social exchange involves reciprocity so that each interacting individual receives something perceived as equivalent to what is given.

From this perspective, individuals will continue to participate in social situations as long as they perceive that they derive equal benefits from their participation. For example, the social exchange theorist would contend that individuals will attend funerals (even though they tend to feel uncomfortable in such situations and find viewing the body as distasteful and anxiety-producing) because they perceive social benefit in being supportive of bereaved friends.

The following research summary of George C. Homans's work, written by Michael Leming, provides an analysis of human behavior that draws on both types of theoretical traditions found in the social exchange paradigm.

Religious Ritual Observance and Anxiety

George C. Homans (1965, pp. 87–88) concludes his synthesis of the theories of Malinowski and Radcliffe-Brown by citing seven elements related to the study of religious ritual and anxiety.

1. *Primary anxiety.* Whenever individuals desire the accomplishment of certain results and do not possess the techniques that will make for success, they feel sentiments that we call anxiety.

2. *Primary ritual.* Under these circumstances, they tend to perform actions that have no practical result and that we call ritual. But these persons are not simply individuals—they are members of a society with definite traditions. Among other things society determines the form of rituals and expects individuals to perform the rituals on appropriate occasions.

3. *Secondary anxiety.* When these people follow the technical procedures and perform the traditional rituals, their primary anxiety remains latent. We say that the rites give them confidence. Under these circumstances, they will feel anxiety only when the rites themselves are not properly performed. In fact, this attitude becomes generalized, and anxiety is felt whenever any of the traditions of society are not observed. This anxiety may be called secondary or displaced anxiety.

4. *Secondary ritual.* This is the ritual of the purification and expiation that has the function of dispelling secondary anxiety. Its form and performance, like those of primary ritual, may or may not be socially determined.

5. *Rationalization.* This element includes a system of beliefs that is associated with the rituals. The beliefs may be very simple, such statements as that the performance of a certain magic does ensure the catching of fish, or that if an Andaman mother and father do not observe the food taboos they will be sick. The statements may be very elaborate. Such are the statements that accompany the fundamental rituals of any society: the equivalents of the Mass of the Catholic church.

6. *Symbolization.* Because the form of the ritual is not determined by the nature of a practical result to be accomplished, it can be determined by other factors. We say that it is symbolic, and each society has its own vocabulary of symbols. Some of the symbolism is relatively simple; for example, the symbolism of sympathies and antipathies. Some are complicated. In particular, certain of the rituals of a society, and those the most important, make symbolic reference to the fundamental myths of that society just as surely as the Mass makes reference to Christ's sacrifice on Calvary.

(continued)

(continued from previous page)

7. *Function.* Ritual actions do not produce a practical result on the external world-that is one reason why we call them ritual. But to make this statement is not to say that ritual has no function. Its function is not related to the world external to the society but to the internal constitution of the society. It gives the members of the society confidence; it dispels their anxieties; it disciplines the social organization.

In this seven-step conclusion, we can see that Homans has carefully brought together the major points of both Malinowski and Radcliffe-Brown. His basic contention is that when individuals experience anxiety in life-crisis events, such as death, ritual will be instrumental in making sentiment latent. However, the fear of violating ritual obligations will again make anxiety manifest. This new anxiety will call for institutionalized ritual. After individuals have fulfilled these religious magical ceremonies required by society, they will experience a reduction of anxiety.

Having discussed Homans's explicit theory of anxiety and ritual, we shall now turn to his implicit theory of these phenomena. In elaborating upon an implicit theory we must extrapolate Homans's position from his earlier theoretical treatises found in *The Human Group* (1950) and *Social Behavior: Its Elementary Forms* (1961). Although any exegesis adds to the substantive writings of the author, it is believed that our elaboration will not distort Homans's exchange theory (in the tradition of psychological behaviorism), which is predicated upon belief in utilitarian self-interest. Abstracting Skinnerian behaviorism, the basic principle of Homans's theory is that if the individuals have needs they will manifest behaviors that have in the past satisfied these needs. To this basic theorem Homans (cited by Turner, 1974, p. 233) adds the following corollaries:

1. Individuals will avoid unpleasant experiences but will endure limited amounts of them as the cost of emitting these behaviors satisfies overriding needs.

(continued)

If social exchange theorists were interested in funeral rites and rituals, they might investigate one or more of the following research questions:

1. Why do some individuals attend funerals—what are the social rewards acquired by attending?
2. Why do some individuals not attend funerals—what are the social punishments or sanctions acquired by not attending?
3. What are the social and personal costs and benefits for families when they provide wakes, funerals, and other death-related rites of passage?
4. What are the social and personal costs for families when they do not provide wakes, funerals, and other death-related rites of passage?

(continued from previous page)

2. Individuals will continue to perform activities as long as they continue to produce desired and expected effects.
3. As needs are satisfied by particular behaviors, individuals are less likely to emit these behaviors until the needs are again present.

Applying this theorem and its corollaries and Homans's explicit theory to the study of religion and anxiety, we have the following analysis. If individuals encounter an anxiety-producing situation, such as a death of a significant other, and they have utilized religious symbolizing in the past to define death and dispel anxiety, they will engage in religious activity to meet their psychological needs in the present situation. Assuming that their sentiment of anxiety was latent before this present encounter with death, they may have been inactive in religious ritual behavior. The return to religious experience may cause anxiety due to the nonobservance of religious obligations. Although anxiety may be increased at this time (as Radcliffe-Brown would suggest) individuals will continue to perform religious rituals as long as they perceive them as having a potential for anxiety reduction. When the requirements for proper religious observance have been met (as determined by the group), death anxiety will again become latent.

In conclusion, Homans's social exchange theory states that religion functions to relieve anxiety associated with life-crisis situations. Death anxiety calls forth religious activity, which serves to make anxiety latent. However, in order to maintain the external system of religious activity (which eventually becomes institutionalized), the group must continually reaffirm the potential threat of anxiety to unite individuals through a "common concern." This secondary anxiety may be effectively relieved through the group rituals of purification and expiation. However, primary reduction of anxiety is operative within the internal system of individual religion.

"Social Exchange: Providing an Understanding of Religion and Its Function," by M. R. Leming, 1977. In Glenn Vernon (Ed.), *A Time to Die,* Washington, DC: University Press of America.

5. Why would the average American family spend more than $4000 to bury its dead when it could accomplish the same purpose at a fraction of the cost?

SYMBOLIC INTERACTION THEORY

The foundation of symbolic interaction theory is that **symbols** (meaning) are a basic component of human behavior. People interact with each other based on their understanding of the meanings of social situations and their perceptions of what others expect of them within these situations. Stressing the symbolic nature of social interaction, Jonathan Turner (1985, p. 32) says: "Symbols are the medium of our adjustment to the environment, of our interaction with others, of our interpretation of experiences, and of our organizing ourselves into groups."

From the symbolic interactionist perspective, human beings are autonomous agents whose actions are based on their subjective understanding of society as socially constructed reality. Randall Collins (1985, p. 200) makes this point in the following statement:

> Each individual projects himself or herself into various future possibilities; each one takes the role of the other in order to see what kind of reaction there will be to this action; as a result each aligns his or her own action in terms of the consequences he or she foresees in the other person's reactions. Society is not a structure, but a process. Definitions of situations emerge from this continuous negotiation of perspectives. Reality is socially constructed. If it takes on the same form over and over again, it is only because the parties to the negotiation have worked out the same resolution and because there is no guarantee that they cannot do it differently next time.

The symbolic interactionist perspective can be summarized in what some have called the **ISAS** paradigm statement—*individual*-level behavior is in response to *symbols,* relative to the *audience,* and relative to the *situation.* ISAS stands for the initial letter of each of the 4 basic components (see Vernon & Cardwell, 1981). Death-related behavior of the dying person, and of those who care about that person, is in response to meaning, relative to the audience and to the situation. Death-related behavior is shared, symboled (given meaning), and situated. It is socially created and not biologically predetermined.

Symbols

Interaction is a dynamic, flexible, and socially created phenomenon. Meaning is socially created and socially perpetuated; it is preserved in symbols or words. However, preserved words have to be rediscovered and reinterpreted if they are to be continually used in human interaction. Generation after generation repeat the process with a somewhat different content—no book means the same thing to every reader. Similarly, death-related behavior and meanings are dynamic phenomena.

Audience-Related Behavior

As we relate to each other in normal social relationships, talking is the most common form of interaction. Even if we do not convey meaning to others with words, other people understand our meanings with their own words. In making decisions about the meaning of death, one can, in effect, consult established words, other people, the self, or situational conditions. If one is dying, one can make decisions about dying behavior by observing the treatment by others. The audience involved may be family, physicians, clergy, nurses, peers, or even strangers walking down the hall of the hospital. How the patient is treated by these people reveals something about the patient. This treatment includes, but is not limited to, the following:

1. What people are willing to talk about with me—and what they avoid
2. Whether they are willing to touch me, and how they touch me when they do

3. Where I am, or maybe where others have located me—hospital, nursing home, intensive care unit, isolation unit, my room at home
4. Tangible and verbal gifts that others give me
5. What people will let me do, or expect me to do, or will not let me do
6. The tone of voice that people use when they talk to me
7. Frequency and length of visits from others
8. Excuses that these people make for not visiting
9. The reactions of others to my prognosis

Dying with dignity or self-respect does not always happen. Self-meaning can be created and sustained with the help of others. Dying as an unsupported or unloved person, however, makes dying an extremely difficult experience. How you treat another person also influences how that person will treat you. If another person thinks that you are leveling with him or her, he or she will treat you one way. If a person thinks that you want to engage in a game of "let's pretend," that person may be willing to play, as a favor to you. In death-related behavior, as in all behavior, one watches others for cues in deciding how to act.

What Caregivers Should Not Assume about the Dying
Glenn M. Vernon

For the terminally ill person, the significant meaning that is taken into account in decision-making concerning self and others is the meaning she or he realizes. It is suggested that priority attention be given to meaning in any confrontation with death. Likewise the caregiver's behavior is influenced by the meaning the caregiver realizes. The same is also true of all people who are in social situations where dying and death occur.

Working from this perspective, it may be helpful to identify some frequently accepted assumptions that need to be questioned. It is accordingly suggested that those working with the dying and the bereaved should not assume that:

1. Those with whom you work necessarily share your meaning of death.
2. Meanings that were helpful to earlier generations are equally functional today.
3. Meaning remains constant and does not change.
4. Dying biologically is all that is happening.
5. Knowing about the biological aspects of dying will in and of itself provide knowledge about how humans expect to behave in death-related situations.
6. Pretension or deception, which you believe will help you cope with those who are dying, will help those with whom you are working.
7. The terminal patient is the only person who has death adjustment problems.

(continued)

(continued from previous page)

8. Persons facing bereavement have to wait until the death actually occurs before they can start working on their bereavement-meaning adjustment.
9. The person who is dying has somehow stopped meaningful living during the terminal period.
10. A death that is defined as meaningless, from the perspective of the person dying, cannot be given meaning in the last stages.
11. The terminal period without an extended future is necessarily one of no hope.
12. Talking is the only way for the caregiver to communicate "I care."

G. M. Vernon, former professor of sociology, University of Utah

The audience to which the dying person relates may also be supernatural. Symbol users are not restricted to the natural-empirical world. Neither are they restricted to the world of the living. If believers realize that those who have died have an existence in another realm or that there is a life after death, this belief is real to them and has consequences for their behavior.

People who are approaching death may involve themselves in a gradual replacement of a living audience with a supernatural or other-world audience. As we have demonstrated, the dying relate to many audiences.

The Situation

Where a person dies is also given meaning. As patients come to grips with their terminal condition, the manner in which they define the situation (and respond to it) will have a tremendous impact on their dying. Dying in a nursing home or hospital is different than dying in the home, in bed, surrounded by a loving family and feelings of belonging. If patients view the institutional death setting as a supportive environment, their coping behavior may be helped. On the other hand, if they feel all alone, and if they have defined the place of dying as a foreign environment, adjustment will not be facilitated (Leming et al., 1977).

Like other meanings, the definition of the situation is an attempt by the individual to bring meaning to the world. Because the situational definition always involves selective perception, the terminal patient will assign meaning to the environment and will respond to this symbolic reality. The thing to which the patient responds does not have existence independent of his or her definition. Therefore, each terminal patient will interpret the dying environment differently. This accounts for the different experiences of dying patients (Leming et al., 1977). This point will be elaborated upon in chapter 6.

If symbolic interactionists were interested in funeral rites and rituals, they might investigate one or more of the following research questions:

1. What are the social meanings that give rise to the attendance of funerals?
2. How are death-related behaviors influenced by the social audiences of the American funeral?

3. In what ways do families utilize the funeral service to project an image of family value commitments and group cohesiveness?
4. How do families use the funeral to demonstrate status differentiation?
5. What is the influence of location of the funeral upon the meaning of the funeralization process?
6. How does the size of the funeral audience convey meaning to the bereaved and attribute social importance to the life of the deceased?

Conclusion

Why study death from a sociological perspective? The answers are many.

First, although it is not the primary goal of this book to prepare you for your own death or the deaths of loved ones, you may still learn many things that will be personally beneficial. Given the fact that you will have death-related experiences, it might be useful for you to employ a sociological perspective to acquire valuable insights into your own life and the lives of people about whom you care.

Second, as you read about the history of death-related customs in the United States and elsewhere and as you comprehend social class and ethnic variations in bereavement customs, the sociological perspective may provide you with a new appreciation for your own life experiences and family traditions as they relate to issues of dying, death, and bereavement.

Third, as you consider the ways that the family socializes its members to develop death conceptualizations, attitudes, and feelings, the sociological perspective may help you to understand more fully how your own abilities to cope are a function of your upbringing. Furthermore, as you study the material in this book, you may attain a more objective perspective on some of the decisions that may confront you and your family as, one day, you attempt to deal with death-related situations. The sociological perspective, then, can make you more aware of the many options available to you regarding death-related decisions.

Finally, the study of dying, death, and bereavement is an important and interesting area of study to which social and behavioral scientists have much to contribute. A good reason to study dying and death from a sociological perspective is to learn more about the discipline of sociology. Social thanatology provides the student with an opportunity to investigate the meaning and application of many concepts developed in sociology and the other behavioral sciences.

Summary

1. The goal of this chapter is to emphasize the extensive involvement of meaning in what many consider to be primarily a biological process—that is, dying.
2. Meaning consists of symbols that are socially created and socially used. Some symbols refer to something else or have an empirical referent. Some do not. The major function of both types of symbols is to permit humans to relate to each other and thus create shared behavior and meaning.

3. Death-related meaning permits sharing death-related behavior. The death-related behavior of the dying individual and of those who are significant to that individual is in response to meaning, relative to the audience and to the situation. It is a phenomenon that is socially created, not biologically predetermined.

4. Because most people participate in various social groups, they are involved in many different interaction patterns. Consequently, even though it is but one biological body that dies, many "role holes" or vacancies are left by the death of a single individual. Bodies die—so do social relationships and social networks.

5. Death meaning includes evaluations of whatever those involved decide to evaluate. Evaluators may include values believed to be absolute, abstract, and situational. Defining values such as "living is always preferable to dying" as abstract rather than as absolute helps explain the relativity of situational values and is likely to lead to fewer adjustment problems when confronting dying.

6. Dying is a social process. The person who is dying is living and is involved in living experiences with others.

7. Evolving death meanings are part of the general cultural changes taking place in contemporary society. Much of this change is centered around a discounting of biological influences upon social behavior.

8. Research studies that share general commitments to methodological techniques, research assumptions, and levels of analysis are brought together to form theoretical paradigms.

9. Sociology, like most other scientific disciplines, is a multiparadigm science.

10. Structural-functionalists view society as a social system of interacting parts. Structural-functional theory focuses upon the issue of societal maintenance and social equilibrium.

11. Conflict theory is primarily concerned with issues related to social change and disequilibrium. Conflict theorists focus upon competition, conflict, and dissension that result when individuals and groups compete for limited societal resources.

12. Social exchange theory contends that human behavior involves a subjective and interpretative interaction with others that attempts to exchange symbolic and nonsymbolic rewards. Social exchange will always involve reciprocity so that each individual involved in the interaction receives something perceived as equivalent to what is given.

13. From the symbolic interactionist perspective, human beings are autonomous agents whose actions are based on their subjective understanding of society as socially constructed reality.

Discussion Questions

1. Discuss the differences between biological and symbolic death.
2. What arguments are offered in the rejection of this premise: "In death, biology is primary; meaning is peripheral"? Evaluate and discuss.
3. Each act of dying has three interconnected characteristics: shared, symboled, and situated. How does this relate to the statement that more than a biological body dies?
4. Answer this question: "Who or what dies?"
5. Discuss the implications of the following quote: "Even though it is but one biological body that dies, many 'role holes' or vacancies are left by the death of that one person."
6. In making decisions about the death meaning, how does the treatment of the dying patient affect that patient's understanding of death and his or her role in the dying process?
7. As one faces imminent death, one becomes increasingly aware of the social nature of life. This increase in awareness can lead to a life review during which one realizes how extensively one lives with, through, and for others. Speculate as to why this change in perspective takes place.
8. Discuss the implications of the following quote: "I die for whatever it was for which I lived."
9. What are some of the meanings of "not dying"?
10. What are paradigms, and what are their functions for social science research?
11. Compare and contrast the structural-functional and conflict orientations in death-related research.
12. Compare and contrast the symbolic interactionist and exchange orientations in death-related research.

Glossary

Dyad: Two units regarded as a pair (e.g., a husband and a wife).

Empirical: Based on experience, sensory observation, or experimentation.

Interpretive understanding: A methodology for investigating social action that requires the researcher to develop an empathy for his or her subject. In this way, the researcher is able to more fully describe and explain social behavior.

ISAS: A shorthand presentation of the symbolic interactionist's paradigm statement: "Behavior of the individual is in response to symbols, relative to the audience, and relative to the situation."

Meaningful action of individuals: Human behavior(s) to which the acting individual attaches subjective meaning.

Mores: Ways of society that are felt to be for the good of society. "Must" behaviors that have stronger sanctions than a folkway (e.g., eating three meals per day) but that are not as severe as laws.

Paradigm: A set of shared general commitments to methodological techniques, research assumptions, and levels of analysis that unify bodies of knowledge produced by empirical research.

Proposition: A statement of relationship between two or more empirical variables.

Self-Fulfilling Prophecy: When a situation is defined as real, it becomes real in its consequences when individuals act to make it so.

Significant Other: A person to whom special significance is given in the process of reaching decisions.

Symbol: Anything to which socially created meaning is given.

References

Blau, P. M. (1964). *Exchange and power in social life.* New York: Wiley.

Charmaz, K. (1980). *The social reality of death.* Reading, MA: Addison-Wesley.

Collins, R. (1985). *Three sociological traditions.* New York: Oxford University Press.

Durkheim, E. (1964). *The rules of the sociological method.* New York: The Free Press.

Hill, C. T., Rubin, Z., & Peplau, L. A. (1976). Breakups before marriage: The end of 103 affairs. *Journal of Social Issues, 32,* 147–168.

Homans, G. C. (1950). *The human group.* New York: Harcourt Brace Jovanovich.

Homans, G. C. (1961). *Social behavior: Its elementary forms.* New York: Harcourt Brace Jovanovich.

Homans, G. C. (1965). Anxiety and ritual: The theories of B. Malinowski and R. A. Radcliffe-Brown. In W. A. Lessa & E. Z. Vogt (Eds.), *Reader in comparative religion: An anthropological approach.* New York: Harper and Row.

Homans, G. C. (1967). *The nature of social science.* New York: Harcourt Brace and World.

Kellehear, A. (1990). *Dying of cancer: The final year of life.* Chur, Switzerland: Harwood Academic Publishers.

Leming, M. R., Vernon, G. M., & Gray, R. M. (1977, July). The dying patient: A symbolic analysis. *International Journal of Symbology, 8,* 77–86.

Lifton, R. J., & Olson, E. (1974). *Living and dying.* New York: Praeger.

Nevaldine, A. (1978). *Divorce: The leaver and the left.* Unpublished doctoral dissertation, University of Minnesota.

Ritzer, G. (1975). *Sociology: A multiple paradigm science.* Boston: Allyn and Bacon.

Rudner, R. S. (1966). *Philosophy of social science.* Englewood Cliffs, NJ: Prentice-Hall.

Sussman, M. B., Cates, J. N., & Smith, D. T. (1970). *The family and inheritance.* New York: Sage.

Turner, J. H. (1974). *The structure of sociological theory.* Homewood, IL: Dorsey.

Turner, J. H. (1985). *Sociology: A student handbook.* New York: Random House.

Vernon, G. M., & Cardwell, J. D. (1981). *Social psychology: Shared, symboled, and situated behavior.* Washington, DC: University Press of America.

Weber, M. (1966). *The theory of social and economic organization.* New York: The Free Press.

Suggested Readings

Charmaz, K. (1980). *The social reality of death.* Reading, MA: Addison-Wesley. An important book that provides phenomenological, interactionist, conflict, and Marxist interpretations of death-related behavior.

Charmaz, K., Howarth, G., & Kellehear, A. (Eds.). (1997). *The unknown country: Death experiences in Australia, Britain and the USA.* London: Macmillan. This book provides novel portrayals of death experiences in three Western countries that seemingly share cultural roots. However, sociological scrutiny reveals some sharp differences among these countries in cultural beliefs and practices; this book focuses on death within the borders of the heretofore-unknown country.

Clark, D. (Ed.). (1993). *The sociology of death: Theory, culture, and practice.* Oxford: Blackwell Publishers. An anthology of social thanatology articles written from a sociological perspective and offering a range of theoretical and empirical topics, together with a discussion of some of the key methodological questions. The issues covered include the concept of social death; the relationship between death and high modernity; death across the life course; cultural and historical perspectives on death and dying; the social management of death; the meaning of ritual; the role of the caring services; and problems of research, method, and analysis.

Collins, R. (1985). *Three sociological traditions.* New York: Oxford University Press. Ritzer, G. (1975). *Sociology: A multiple paradigm science.* Boston: Allyn and Bacon. Two books on sociological theories that will provide more information and analysis on the four theoretical perspectives discussed in this chapter.

Dickinson, G. E., Leming, M. R., & Mermann, A. C. (Eds.). (1998). *Annual editions: Dying, death, and bereavement.* Guilford, CT: Dushkin McGraw Hill. 43 articles emphasizing the meaning of a wide variety of aspects of death-related behavior.

Fingarette, H. (1996). *Death: Philosophical soundings.* Chicago: Open Court. After an original essay by the author is a collection of 12 classic statements on death written by such individuals as Tolstoy, Schopenhauer, Chuang Tzu, Camus, and Freud.

Frankl, V. (1959). *Man's search for meaning.* Boston: Beacon Press. An outstanding book examining the human desire to find meaning in both life and death.

Fulton, G. B., & Metress, E. K. (1995). *Perspectives on death and dying.* Boston: Jones and Bartlett Publishers. This outstanding discussion of death and dying takes a unique, multidisciplinary approach to the topic. Discussed are not only the traditional subjects of philosophy, psychology, sociology, anthropology, law, and medicine, but also other disciplines that are affected by the rapid changes taking place in the health-care field, such as economics, marketing, and management.

Kellehear, A. (1990). *Dying of cancer: The final year of life.* Chur, Switzerland: Harwood Academic Publishers. Provides a sociological analysis of the process of dying with cancer.

Related Web Sites

http://www.asanet.org/ The home page of the American Sociological Association.

http://www.apa.org/ The home page of the American Psychological Association.

http://www.ameranthassn.org/ The home page of the American Anthropological Association.

http://web.gmu.edu/chnm/aha/index.html The home page of the American Historical Association.

http://www.trinity.edu/~mkearl/death.html Michael Kearl's web site on sociological thanatology. This is the most comprehensive and best resource on the sociology of dying, death, and bereavement.

http://www.lsds.com/death/ Thanatolinks contains Internet links to some of the best web sites related to dying and death.

http://www.yahoo.com/Society_and_Culture/Death/ The death index of the Yahoo Internet search engine.

http://www.emanon.net/~kcabell/death.html Contains many World Wide Web links to resources on death and bereavement.

http://www.adec.org/ Web site of the Association for Death Education and Counseling, an academic resource for researchers and laypersons.

http://rivendell.org/   GriefNet provides many World Wide Web links to web sites on the bereavement process, resources for grievers, and information concerning grief support groups.

http://newciv.org/worldtrans/naturaldeath.html   The Natural Death Centre is a nonprofit charitable project launched in Britain in 1991, with three psychotherapists as directors. It aims to support those dying at home and their caregivers and to help them arrange funerals. It has as a more general aim helping to improve "the quality of dying."

http://www.boston.com/globe/hospice/info.htm   A tremendous resource maintained by the Boston Globe containing articles and information on home care and dying.

http://www.soros.org/death.html   Project on Death in America has the goal of helping people understand and transform the dying experience in America.

http://Axis.LLX.COM:80/~bardo/   Bardo of Death Studies. This site describes itself as: "an eclectic collection site for questions and answers from all cultures and backgrounds about death and dying and their integration with life and living. 'Our purpose for being here is to be of service to those who have curiosities or comments on the subject of Death and Dying, as well as to serve as a Net Memorial for those who have gone before us into this journey called Death.'"

Part Two

Understanding Death Attitudes

Chapter 3

Children and Death

The way I see it, we die in the same order we were born.
It's the only fair way of working it!
> —CHARLES SCHULZ AND KENNETH F. HALL, *TWO-BY-FOURS*

Despite a new openness toward death in the United States, children are still generally not encouraged to express themselves on the topic of dying and death. As Jane Sahler (1978, p. XV) notes in writing about children and death, "One of the fascinating things about children is the naive, simplistic way in which they approach the unknown. Yet it is this very naivete that makes their questions the most difficult to answer." Children usually have no prior experience on which to base their reactions, thus their earliest experiences are unique to each of them.

Children most often confront death at an early age. Their vivid recollections of these first death experiences testify to the impact that such experiences have on these individuals (Hall, 1922; Tobin, 1972; Kastenbaum, 1991). George Dickinson (1992) found in analyzing 440 essays of college students (average age of 24) about their first childhood death experiences that the average age at first experience was 8 years and that the students' recollections were quite clear.

A child's first experience with death is often the death of an animal. In a study of college students' recollection of their first death experiences, Dickinson (1992) found that 28 percent of his subjects' first death experiences involved a pet. From stepping on an ant to seeing a dead animal lying beside the road to the death of a pet, animals are generally involved in children's early death experiences.

A study by Israel Orbach and associates (1985) of 6- to 11-year-old children's concepts of death in humans and animals showed that death in humans is easier to comprehend than death in animals. They note that seemingly the comprehension of animal death is acquired chronologically later than that of human death. Apparently animal death is a more difficult concept than human death. Because animals are a favorite identification object of young children, the death of a pet may be more meaningful and more personal to a child than that of a generalized other human being. Thus, children may erect more defenses against death in animals. Another explanation noted by Orbach is that human and animal deaths can be regarded as two specific examples of the complicated concept of life and death. Although a child may comprehend the meaning of death to a specific example of life, such as humans, he or she may not comprehend it in another sphere of life, such as plants and animals. This reflects a lack of understanding of the broader concepts of life, birth, death, and animate and inanimate objects.

A Burden in Burying the Babies
Douglas Martin

A cold wind whistled across Hart Island the other morning. It bent the leafless trees and swamp grass, and sent whitecaps dancing on Long Island Sound.

Inmates in orange jumpsuits moved briskly, spoke little and didn't smile. In armfuls of three, they unloaded 53 foot-long pine boxes from the rear of a Ford dumptruck onto the muddy ground. For 50 cents an hour, they were burying New York City's poorest infants.

"It's good they're getting buried and not thrown in a garbage pail," said an inmate who is the father of eight children.

"It takes some getting used to," said another inmate. "It takes some getting used to."

Bruce Leggard, a correction officer who lost his daughter when she was 13 years old, groped for meaning. "Everybody dies; you're born to die," he said. "But these babies never had a shot. Whether they would have been strong or weak, they never got much of a chance to be either."

The little coffins had pink labels pasted on them. Some had names. There was a Liz, an Eileen, a Sam. Some were F/C or M/C for female child or male child. Each slip recorded the lifetime of these former residents of Planet Earth—two hours, newborn, five days. On this day, all were from Brooklyn, the biggest source of babies for New York City's potter's field.

(continued)

In a thorough review of literature on children's death concepts, Cotton and Range (1990) concluded that several factors have been shown to influence the development of death concepts. They note that children's death concepts change with age: Older children are considered to have more accurate death concepts; are affected on a cognitive level (those more cognitively mature have relatively more accurate death concepts); and are affected by experience (those having more experience with death are more likely to believe in personal mortality).

There is a need to look more carefully at the dynamics of the young and their families in relating to the concept of death. This chapter will discuss dying children and their parents and siblings and how to explain death to children. In trying to understand children's concepts of death and of their own dying, we must include the involvement of significant others in this relationship. This chapter will also address children's understanding of death from a developmental perspective and will focus on age groups. As with any life cycle approach, the lines of division between ages often overlap rather than serve as clear-cut divisions. However, this is a way to understand children's conceptions of death at various ages of their lives. In addition, the puzzling cause of death among infants which results in sudden, unexplained mortality called sudden infant death syndrome (SIDS) will be presented.

(continued from previous page)

Burials of indigent infants are increasing considerably faster than those of poor adults, also on an upswing. Last year 1,606 babies were buried on Hart Island; in 1986, the number was 1,128.

"There is no question that it is directly linked to the drug epidemic," said Suzanne Halpin, a spokeswoman for the Health and Hospitals Corporation, which first freezes the bodies then delivers them unembalmed to the island off the Bronx.

Infant mortality here has leaped in the last four years, after steadily declining for two decades. The increase coincides with the rise of crack, which causes premature births. Of mothers in the city whose babies died, nearly 32 per 1,000 admitted drug use, up from 7 per 1,000 in 1978, according to city health records.

And Elizabeth Graham, an assistant health commissioner, said the real incidence of narcotics abuse among those mothers might be three times worse because many are reluctant to admit it even on confidential forms.

Further, poor people often don't receive prenatal care. And it doesn't help that the city-owned hospitals are terribly strained: some neonatal intensive care units are operating at 180 percent of capacity.

A few years ago B.C.—before crack—a study by the Coalition for the Homeless showed that 47 percent of children below the poverty level who died before age one were buried on Hart Island. That hasn't declined.

(continued)

(continued from previous page)

And their parents, who can't afford what they were brought up to consider proper burial, face yet another indignity. They fill out a form to reserve a small space on a truck to potter's field. Years later, a tiny handful make arrangements to take a Department of Transportation ferry from City Island to Hart Island to stare at a mass grave.

The potter's field comes from the Bible, Matthew 27:6–7. The chief priests of Jerusalem said that it was wrong to put the 30 pieces of silver that Judas had received for betraying Jesus into the general treasury. So the money was used to buy a field from a potter "to bury strangers in."

Hart Island has had a potter's field since the city bought it from a Bronx family in 1869. Over the years, it has had a variety of uses—as a Civil War prison camp, an amusement park, a nuclear missile launching pad and a final repository for some Ebbets Field bleachers. Its only present residents are 80 inmates who would otherwise be on Rikers Island.

The bodies of New York's poor have never stopped coming. There are now 750,000, making this by far the city's largest cemetery, according to a Correction Department official.

"It's like a never-ending sea," said Al Saunders, who operates a backhoe. "It just keeps going and going."

The holes he digs, about 30 feet across, are extended outward to a final length of 100 feet over a period of several weeks. As the shipments arrive, the coffins are placed length-wise along the width of the hole and stacked four or five high.

A Catholic priest sometimes comes to bless God's little children, en masse. A crumbling monument donated by a tombstone company squats by a derelict road. "Cry not for us," it says. "We are at peace."

The wind blew harder. Inmates moved faster. Some boxes contained twins. A few were broken. An inmate cradled one in his arms, much as if things were different.

"This is a heavy little baby," he said.

"A Burden in Burying the Babies," by D. Martin, *New York Times,* March 28, 1990, p. A14.

The Dying Child

According to Robert Kavanaugh (1972, p. 139), a psychologist and former priest, little people enjoy the same human rights as their bigger counterparts. They have a right to know if they have a fatal condition. When kept in ignorance, children, like adults, will rarely grow beyond the initial stage of denial and isolation. When this occurs, children are robbed of the peace and dignity that can be theirs in the final stage of acceptance and resignation.

KNOWLEDGE IS KINDNESS

The diagnosis of death should be made known to children as soon as the diagnosis is clear and final (Kavanaugh, 1972, pp. 139–140). Physicians, nurses, and family obviously need time to bring their own emotions under control. It is now known how to treat the dying child kindly. Knowledge is kindness, ignorance is cruelty. The child is the patient whose life is being lost and whose concerns are preeminent. Kavanaugh (1972, p. 143) notes that when children have known the truth about their condition and were allowed to talk about it openly, they have been as brave as any adult.

Reasons for the preceding advice given by Kavanaugh (1972, pp. 140–143) are based on the following observations:

First, the dying child is no ordinary child. The ordinary process of maturing quickens through lengthy illness with confinement, suffering, and deprivation. Children ill for a long time usually exhibit a maturity beyond their calendar years.

Second, children's consciences are more tender and concerned than most adults are in a position to know. Deathbed children uninformed of their fate will often have guilt for the sadness and poorly veiled tears that they witness around their bed. They can sense the phoniness around them, and they may believe that they are being punished for something evil that they have done. Their isolation is heightened in their heavy concerns. Nothing is sadder than a dying child learning of his or her fate from playmates.

Finally, moderately aware and normally alert children know what is predicted for them in the signs that they see—recognizing their plight in memories of dying scenes on television. They may ponder why the physician comes so often, why everyone is so nice to them, and why they are receiving all of the gifts. A recent review (O'Halloran & Altmaier, 1996) of studies on death awareness among children who are healthy, chronically ill, and terminally ill reveals that children with life-threatening diseases demonstrate increased understanding of death. In contrast, healthy and chronically ill children appear to require certain age, cognitive development level, or intelligence thresholds to understand these concepts. As anthropologist Myra Bluebond-Langner (1989) observes from her work with dying children, *all* terminally ill children become aware of the fact that they *are dying* before death is imminent. Yet, Bluebond-Langner notes that for these children the acquisition and assimilation of information are a prolonged process. Either a child shares what he or she knows about his or her dying, or the final weeks and months become a lonely vigil, a sentence to fear and guilt, confinement and confusion.

How do we tell a child about his or her dying condition? Kavanaugh (1972, pp. 142–143) notes that to adults brave enough to listen, this is not a valid question. The child will do the telling, if we create an atmosphere in which the child can make all appropriate deductions. The child's talk will flit in and out of the awful revelation.

THE CHILD NEEDS SUPPORT

Who should do the telling or serve as a catalyst for it? Kavanaugh (1972, p. 143) says that anyone strong enough to take the consequences by being a regular visitor, a trusted confidant, and a patient listener can be the catalyst. Many adults cannot qualify.

Woman Sends "Love Letters" to 465 Seriously Ill Children

A woman whose 7-year-old son died of cancer 4 years ago now offers cheer to hundreds of ailing children in a monthly newsletter packed with jokes, puzzles, and stories.

"I can't cure them, but I know how to make them smile while they're here," said Linda Bremner, 40.

Her 10-page newsletters, called Love Letters, go to 465 children with terminal or long-term illnesses in 35 states and 4 other countries. Ms. Bremner said she began writing to seriously ill children in 1984, after the death of her only child, Andy.

"After my son died, I was cleaning out his drawers and I found his address book with the addresses of about 20 children who, like himself, had cancer.

"Remembering how important mail was to Andy, I wrote to them," she said. "What I didn't expect was that they wrote me back and that lit a fire under me," she said.

Stephen Lopez said the newsletter made his 3-week hospital stay "much funner." "I like the dot-to-dots and the mazes most," said the 12-year-old, who suffers from a behavior disorder.

(continued)

From her research with hospitalized terminally ill children between the ages of 6 and 10, Eugenia Waechter (1985) agrees with Kavanaugh's conclusions. Her findings indicate that, despite efforts to shield children from knowledge of the seriousness of their illness, the anxiety of those close to the children is likely to alter the emotional climate in the families. The emotional climate may be altered to such a degree that the children will develop suspicions and fears about their condition. Often they will feel that awareness of their condition is knowledge that they are not supposed to have, so the silence of those nearby isolates children from needed support.

The question of whether children should be told is meaningless, notes Waechter. No curtain of silence should exist around children's most intense fears. Support must especially be made available for them during and following actual encounters with death on pediatric wards. Support is needed to allow introspective examination of attitudes and fears related to death in general and to the death of children in particular.

In working with children with cancer, Yehuda Nir (1987, p. 64) concludes that children's ability to cope with the stress of cancer is important in the way that they deal with the illness itself and with the treatment. Feelings of helplessness and vulnerability dominate, often leading to regressive behavior. Withdrawal and refusal to participate in the treatment are seen almost immediately at the onset of the disease in young children. Because these types of behavior interfere with the medical management of the illness, resistance to treatment is circumvented by such methods as the use of general anesthesia and hypnotic relaxation techniques. Although these interventions are medically justified, they intensify the children's feelings of passivity and helplessness.

(continued from previous page)

"It's the passion of my life. Nothing has ever made me feel this good," said Ms. Bremner.

"When I lose one of my kids I grieve," she said. "But it gives me a fervor, and I sit down and write some more letters."

The newsletters carry games, puzzles, jokes, and "witty and whimsical" stories, said Ms. Bremner, who has made it a rule never to mention diseases or symptoms.

But sometimes her correspondents address serious topics when they write back, and she draws on her experiences with Andy. One 13-year-old girl wrote that she was being teased by classmates because her hair was falling out. "Andy had lost his hair five times and it grew back, so I wrote her and told her it would grow back, too," Ms. Bremner said. When the girl's hair finally grew back, she sent a little lock of blond hair with a note that read, "You were right—it grew back," Ms. Bremner recalled.

In the beginning, she was sending handwritten letters, she said. Now her pen pals get the newsletter, which is drafted on a computer. About a dozen volunteers help design and mail them.

Adapted from an article in the Charleston, SC, *News and Courier*, July 30, 1988, p. 3A.

Nir (1987) further notes that regression can take the form of acute separation anxiety. When the parents are unable to stay overnight in the hospital, they often speak with the children by phone. After talking with their parents, young children sometimes fall asleep with the telephone receiver in their laps, as if to maintain contact with what has become elusive.

Families who seem best equipped to cope are those who develop a therapeutic alliance with the **pediatric oncologist** (Nir, 1987, p. 65). This alliance buffers and protects the child from much of the pain and stress of the daily treatment routines. Other parents who seem successful in reducing stress are those with strong religious beliefs, notes Nir.

By observing and talking to leukemic children ages 3 to 9 in a hospital, anthropologist Myra Bluebond-Langner (1978) concluded that most of them knew not only that they were dying, but also that this was a final and irreversible process. Children may wish and need to be open about their condition, but adults are often traumatized by children's openness and honesty. Bluebond-Langner notes that the age of the children is not as important in their self-awareness of their dying as is their experience with the disease and its treatment.

The founder and executive director of Children's Hospice International, Ann A. Dailey, says (Gamarekian, 1987, p. 19):

Kids intuitively know when they are dying and they tend not to have the fears that adults have. But they want to know what it is going to feel like. Will someone be with them to hold their hand? Will a grandmother who died last year be there to greet him? Families need to cry together, to tell how much they are going to miss each other.

Though one may not know what to say to dying children or may not feel "skilled" in this area, it is imperative that we show support to them and let them know that we care. Support of others is important throughout life, whether relating to a terminally ill person or otherwise. This point is illustrated in the following story told by Rabbi Harold Kushner (1985).

> A little boy had gone to the store, but was late in returning home. His mother asked, "Where were you?" He said, "I found a little boy whose bicycle was broken, and I stopped to help him." "But what do you know about fixing bicycles?" his mother asked. "Nothing," the little boy replied, "I sat down and cried with him."

Many times, we may not know how to "fix the bicycle," but like the little boy in the preceding story, we can give support to the individual in other ways.

Parents of the Dying Child

Although there are many problematic aspects of parenting, none is as devastating to the parents as the loss of a child through death. This was observed by Ronald Knapp (1986, p. 13), based on his interviews with 155 families suffering the loss of a child ranging in age from 1 to 28. Likewise, C. M. Sanders (1980) notes that the death of a child is one of the most grievous of losses, significantly greater, on average, than that of a parent or a spouse. The death of a child represents in a symbolic way the death of the self. Symbolically, a parent will die along with the child, only to survive in a damaged state with little or no desire to live today or to plan for tomorrow. In addition to losing part of themselves, parents lose some of their hope for the future, concludes Reiko Schwab (1992) from a study of 20 couples who had lost children.

Because children are "not supposed to die," especially before their parents do, the death of a child seems more tragic and traumatic than the death of an older person. We often take our children for granted. Although one can *imagine* the loss of a child, how often does one have such thoughts? Even so, such thoughts bear little resemblance to reality. For parents who have lost a child through death, however, the reality of the situation lingers forever. A friend whose son had recently died told me that the stark reality hit him in the face every morning when he woke up and realized that this was not just a bad dream—his son was really dead.

Four years after the death of his son, Eric Wolterstorff said (Buursma, 1987, p. 6):

> We took him too much for granted. Perhaps we all take each other too much for granted. The routines of life distract us; our own pursuits make us oblivious; our anxieties and sorrows, unmindful. The beauties of the familiar go unremarked. We do not treasure each other enough. He was a gift to us. . . . When the gift was finally snatched away, I realized how great it was. Then I could not tell him. . . . The pain of the no more outweighs the gratitude of the once was. Will it always be so?

Though parents can never be really prepared for the end, as the dying child continues to lose ground, they reach a point where resignation begins to replace hope for survival, and the inevitable end slowly comes into focus (Knapp, 1986, p. 62). The character of hope changes from hoping for survival to hoping for a full range of living in the time available and for a comfortable, painfree death. When parents consciously accept the fact that death is imminent, they become totally absorbed in the life of that child and try to make each day a memorable occasion.

Ronald Knapp (1986, p. 67) notes that parents "live" the child's death over and over in their imaginations as the end is near. This imaginary scenario takes them from the moment of death through the funeral of the child. Parents may wish to keep the child at home so that he or she will not die in strange surroundings. When one is able to make the decision to terminate all further treatment and let the disease take its course, a sense of tranquillity results, and parents are ready to release their hold. Sometimes parents must take on the painfully hard task of telling the child that it is all right to let go, it is all right to stop fighting, it is all right to die! Giving permission to die is difficult. Sometimes it takes only gentle encouragement from parents, gentle persuasion that all has been done and that nothing more remains.

Available literature (Schwab, 1992), based on research and clinical observations, indicates that the death of a child strains the parents' marital relationship, sometimes resulting in separation and divorce. One study (Klass, 1987) concluded, however, that marriages did not end because of a child's death but rather because after the child's

The Art of Consoling
Joe Ward

As anyone knows who has ever tried, it is difficult to talk to a parent who has lost a child. Julie McGee, coordinator of the Louisville chapter of The Compassionate Friends—an organization of bereaved parents—says no one who has not lost a child can really understand how it feels.

She says bereaved parents themselves recognize how misguided were their past efforts to console a friend or relative in the same situation. So the organization has compiled the following list of do's and don't's:

Do

Be available to listen, to run errands and to help with housework and other children.

Say you are sorry about what happened to their child and about their pain.

Allow them to express grief without holding back. Listen if they want to talk about the child, as much and as often as they want to.

Encourage them to be patient with themselves, not to expect too much of themselves and not to impose any "shoulds" on themselves.

Talk to them about the special endearing qualities of the child who has died.

Give special attention to the child's brothers and sisters at the funeral and later.

Reassure parents about the care their child received, but be careful not to say anything that is obviously not true.

(continued)

(continued from previous page)

Don't

Avoid them because you are uncomfortable.

Say you know how they feel unless you have lost a child yourself.

Tell them they've grieved long enough and "ought to be feeling better by now." Your guess at an appropriate timetable probably is short. Avoid telling them, in general, what they "should" feel and do.

Change the subject when they mention their dead child.

Worry about mentioning their child's name. You won't make them think of him or her; they probably are doing that anyway.

Try to point out some bright side. They don't want to hear, "At least you have your other children," or "At least you can have another child," or, "At least you had the child for a while."

Try to commiserate with them by saying the child's case was bungled by the doctors or the hospital or someone else involved. They will be plagued by guilt and feelings of inadequacy without any help from you.

"When Death Takes Your Child" by J. Ward, *Louisville Courier-Journal,* July 27, 1980.

death the parents felt that their struggle with marital problems was no longer worth the effort. In a study of 145 bereaved parents, J. A. Cook (1983) concluded that because fathers find it difficult to grieve openly and thus keep their grief to themselves, a barrier is created to their wives' attempts to communicate about their loss. In another article, Cook (1988) noted that men are given little comfort and support in bereavement and are expected to be strong and to provide a source of support for others, yet their nonexpressiveness comes into conflict with their wives' needs for expression. Schwab (1992) concluded in a study of 20 couples who had lost children that husbands and wives appeared generally irritable and less tolerant of their spouses. On the other hand, Schwab noted that husbands and wives with a good marital relationship prior to a child's death appear to have come closer together through the tragedy that shattered their lives. Thus, a weak marriage may collapse with the death of a child, and a strong marriage may indeed be strengthened by the death. Whatever the result, the strain of the death of a child is certainly a test of the marital relationship.

Siblings of the Dying Child

When a newborn comes into the family, siblings of the newborn often feel neglected. Most of the attention seems to go to the baby, therefore the young siblings often have a pity party for themselves. Presents are given to the baby, and adults carry on about how "cute" he or she is. All this time the siblings may be jealous because they no longer seem "special."

A similar situation may occur when a sibling is dying. The energies of parents, grandparents, and significant others seem to be directed toward the dying child. The dying sibling seems to be receiving all of the attention. In her studies of siblings of children dying with cancer and cystic fibrosis, Myra Bluebond-Langner (1989) states that the well siblings live in houses of chronic sorrow. The signs of sorrow, illness, and death are everywhere, whether spoken of or not. Some well siblings see themselves as the less-favored child in the family, and they often feel confused and rejected. Many of the well siblings feel that they cannot express their feelings to their parents because their parents are already too upset, and they do not want to upset them more.

A study of siblings of children with cancer (Sourkes, 1981) notes that parents tend to provide the siblings with less attention, causing them to feel lonely and neglected. Siblings are also distressed by the visibility of the illness and their tendency to identify with it. They are distressed by the treatment process and may feel guilty about being healthy.

Even during remission, siblings are neglected by parents who must catch up on the instrumental tasks of daily living (Spinetta, 1981). Sibling anger begins to surface most clearly during remission when their loss of parental attention becomes even more prominent than at diagnosis.

In a study of 65 children (between the ages of 4 and 16) who were the siblings of deceased children, McCown and Pratt (1985) confirmed previous studies indicating that 30 to 50 percent of surviving children demonstrate increased behavior problems following the death of a sibling. Their studies showed that children in the middle age group, 6 to 11 years, developed more behavior problems than other age groups. Reasons cited for more problems in this age group are that the loss of a sibling at this phase may lead to a sense of self-vulnerability and inferiority and that for the child in this age group who is making the transition to concrete thought, the event and cause of sibling death may evoke confusion. The increased behavior problems may be a reflection of that confusion.

David Adams and Eleanor Deveau (1987, p. 284) note that, after a child's death, many siblings fear minor physical symptoms and worry about death occurring at the same age. Siblings resent parents for their preoccupation with the dead child and blame them for their inability to protect these siblings during illness. Parents are often so consumed by their own grief that they have little energy left to help surviving children. Problems also develop when parents expect surviving siblings to surpass or equal the achievements of a deceased child or to replace the deceased child.

Due to limited resources and energies in the home, peer support and special attention for the siblings of dying children are needed. Teachers in particular need to be alert to the special concerns and needs of these children. The personal worth of surviving siblings needs to be reinforced. As with siblings of a newborn coming into the family, siblings of a dying child have special needs. They, too, wish to be noticed and given some love and care.

Explaining Death to Children

Robert Kavanaugh (1972, p. 126) refers to children as "little people." He sees them as "compact cars instead of Cadillacs," traveling the same roads of life and going the same

Did I Really Love My Brother?
Elizabeth Richter

"Everybody told me to be strong for my parents and to be quiet because I might make them more upset. Everyone told me to put my feelings aside, like my feelings weren't as important as my parents'. I never cried until about a year later, when it hit me that my sister Sandy wasn't around." That's how 18-year-old Lisa describes her own grieving for an older sister who was murdered.

"When I was told my brother had died, I just left the room. I couldn't even cry. My father cried, although he had never cried in his life. Because I couldn't cry, I began to wonder if there was something wrong with me. Did I really love my brother?" That is the way 18-year-old Sharon reacted to her little brother's dying of a brain tumor.

Children are not supposed to die—or so we like to think. But, of course, they do. When a child dies, it means not only the loss of a young life, but also the death of parents' hopes and dreams.

Many professionals believe that schools need to do more to comfort surviving children. Too often, when survivors return to school, there is no acknowledgement of the death of a brother or sister.

Sandra Fox, director of the Good Grief Program at Judge Baker Guidance Center in Boston, says, "Teachers want to avoid the subject of death. It's not malicious. It's just they are afraid to say the wrong things. They tend to err on the side of being supercautious."

Psychologist Gerald Koocher believes that death education classes could be useful in giving young people a chance to think about the issues of dying and death before being confronted with personal loss. We obviously cannot just pat siblings on the head and tell them everything will be okay.

E. Richter, adapted from *U.S. News & World Report*, August 4, 1986.

places as big cars. Although they are more vulnerable and fragile, they have all of the parts and purposes of big people. They are ready and capable to talk about anything within the framework of their own experience. Little people can handle any situation that adults can handle comfortably and should do anything that big people should do as long as they are physically able, notes Kavanaugh (1972, p. 137).

When a child experiences death directly, whether through a pet or a human, it is an emotional time and must be dealt with immediately (Seibert & Drolet, 1993). Adults need to support, comfort, and help the child to express grief. An attempt by adults to protect children from the reality of death reinforces the perception that death is not real or is too frightening to examine or that the ending of life is not worth noting with reverence and respect, observe Seibert and Drolet. Children also have vivid imaginations that may lead to more fear and confusion than reality. Children are "excellent observers" but "poor interpreters," note Seibert and Drolet.

When we "big people" fail to give "little people" credit and try to shield them from information because they are "unable to take it," could it be rather that we "big people" feel uncomfortable talking to children about dying and death and thus avoid the topic altogether? Avoidance is not the best solution, as noted in this example of needless worry and frustration (Dickinson, 1992, p. 174):

> A 4-year-old girl was not told about her puppy's traumatic death by a mowing machine for two or three weeks afterwards. She was allowed to search for him "frantically" every day. She even put out food and would worry at night that he was cold or hungry.

John Bowlby (1980) argues that young children can mourn in a way similar to healthy adults. For this to happen children should participate fully in the awareness of what is taking place during and after the death. Rather than withhold information, questions should be asked and answered. Robert Kavanaugh (1972, p. 132) suggests that we allow the children to talk freely and ask their own questions, without any adult speeches or philosophic nonanswers, let them ramble, talk crudely if they wish, change the subject, or present unanswerable questions without being squelched. The children should always be supported in a "comforting way" with an assurance of a continued relationship. Joy Ufema (1996), a nurse who works with dying patients, observes that children who are afraid of dying can be comforted by a talk on their religion's thoughts on death or on the near-death experiences of others. Their sensitivity on the issue of death comes with growing up as they realize that death is an inevitable part of life.

BE HONEST AND OPEN

Being honest and open with a child in talking about dying and death is a good rule of thumb to follow. If the parent is not honest and open, the child's fantasies may be far worse than the reality. Giving concrete answers, rather than abstract ones, is a realistic way to handle the topic of death. Answer the child's questions as they are asked. If your answer is unsatisfactory, the child will likely ask a follow-up question in a few seconds or a few hours. If the child asks something that you cannot answer, be honest and say that you do not know. If you cannot explain something, find someone who can.

Answer directly, but do not be too detailed with your responses. When a small child asks where he or she came from, you do not go into minute detail about the sperm and the ovum forming a zygote. You state that the child came from his or her mother. If the child is not satisfied, the next question may then be, "How did I get in my mommy?" At this point, I refer the question to the mother!

The same is true if the child asks, "Daddy, what makes the car run?" I respond that the car has an engine. If the follow-up question is, "What makes the engine run?" I refer the child to our local mechanic because my technical skills are severely limited. The point is that the child's questions should be answered *as they occur*, not postponed in the hope that they will be forgotten.

If parents are open to discussing death, opportunities will present themselves—opportunities such as dead flies, mosquitoes, birds, and animals beside the road. When the explanation is postponed until the death of someone or something deeply loved by the child, either the emotional turmoil will complicate the acceptance of the reality of death or the concept of death may preclude for that occasion the appropriate emotional response.

To bury a deceased pet is a positive learning exercise in relating to death. The animal is cold, still, and not alive—it is dead. That is reality. For parents *and* children to conduct the burial together can be a very meaningful experience. When our children were young, they had guinea pigs. These animals have a short life span, thus we held many guinea pig funerals in our backyard, with the entire family participating. For other family members to be present at a time of grief helps an individual to better bear this burden.

AVOID EUPHEMISMS

Try to avoid euphemisms when talking to a child about death. Use words like *dead, stopped working,* and *wore out*—simple words to establish the fact that the body is biologically dead (Schaefer & Lyons, 1986, p. 31). One child was told that Grandfather's heart was bad and stopped working. This seemed to satisfy the child. When the response was couched in different terms, however, another child was told, "Grandfather can breathe easier now," implying that Grandfather is still breathing. This child wanted to join his grandfather because he had asthma and would welcome the chance to "breathe easier." He was told, however, that he was too young to join Grandfather (Dickinson, 1992, pp. 173–174)!

Dead is a difficult word to say, but to use a euphemism like *went to sleep* may make it difficult for the child to go to sleep at night. If Granddad "went to sleep" and was then buried in a box underground or destroyed through cremation, that is likely not what the small child's goals in life are! Thus, the objective is to stay awake and *not go to sleep!* (And parents wonder why the child is still awake at 10 p.m., after having been put to bed at 8!)

To use euphemisms like *went away* or *departed this life* or *passed away* may cause the child to expect the deceased to return. After all, he or she is simply on a trip! Even to suggest that "he's gone to heaven and will live forever" is confusing to a child when this is said through heavy tears and upset emotional feelings.

A 4-year-old was told that her younger sister was "too sick to live with us, so she went to visit Grandmother in heaven and would never come home again." The 4-year-old was frightened for months afterward because "whenever anyone did not feel well, I thought they would go away forever, too" (Dickinson, 1992 p. 173). The father of one 4-year-old girl told her that her kitten "went to heaven to be with God." She responded, "Why does God want a dead kitten?"

For many respondents in Dickinson's study (1992) who recalled childhood memories of death, however, being told that the deceased had "gone to heaven" had been a comforting feeling. They had been told that "heaven was a happy place," thus all was well in the world of fantasy of these children.

Rabbi Harold Kushner (1981) cautions, however, that to try to make a child feel better by stating how beautiful heaven is and how happy the deceased is to be with God may deprive the child of a chance to grieve. By doing such, we ask a child

THE FAMILY CIRCUS
by Bil Keane

"Well, yes — we'll see Granddad someday when we go to heaven."

"Could I just wait in the car?"

REPRINTED WITH SPECIAL PERMISSION OF KING FEATURES SYNDICATE, INC.

to deny and mistrust his or her own feelings, to be happy when sadness is desired. Kushner notes that the child's right to feel upset and angry should be recognized. One should also be cautious that the child not feel that the deceased *chose* to leave and "go to heaven." It should be made clear that the person did not wish to leave or "desert," as the child may feel.

Anthropologist Colin Turnbull (1983) compares the state of being after death with the state of being before birth—a state of nothingness. Ask someone to describe what it was like before birth, and you will probably not receive much of an answer. To suggest that after death there is "no place" to describe—a nothing—would deny children a defined place to imagine. But then, with the vast imagination of children, perhaps this might be more creative for them than a vague description of a "big house in the sky."

After you have made an effort to avoid euphemisms and gotten across the fact that the person is dead, the next step is to explain what is going to happen next. Tell the child about the body being moved from the hospital to the funeral home. Alert the child that funeral arrangements will be made (if that is the case) and that a funeral will follow. Outline the format of a funeral itself, then talk about going to the cemetery (if that is the case) and burying the body in the ground. As the following poem by Edna St. Vincent Millay indicates, however, explaining death (even for "big people") is not always easy.

Lament

Listen children: To save in his bank;
Your father is dead.   Anne shall have the keys
From his old coats   To make a pretty noise with.
I'll make you little jackets;   Life must go on,
I'll make you little trousers   And the dead be forgotten;
From his old pants.   Life must go on,
There'll be in his pockets   Though good men die;
Things he used to put there,   Anne, eat your breakfast;
Keys and pennies   Dan, take your medicine;
Covered with tobacco;   Life must go on;
Dan shall have the pennies   I forget just why.

SHOW EMOTION

It is important that the child knows that it is okay to show emotion when someone dies. Because it is a very sad time, the child should be told that everyone is upset and that many may be crying. If the child feels like crying, he or she should be assured that crying is okay. Crying is normal. It should also be explained that just because some people do not show emotion does not mean that they did not love the dead person (Schaefer & Lyons, 1986, p. 33).

You probably cannot "overhug" a child during these times. It is important to always reassure the child that you care for him or her. Hugs and tears are very compatible expressions. Do not apologize for crying. Your crying in front of the child gives assurance that crying is okay.

Rabbi Earl Grollman (1967) defines crying as the sound of anguish at losing a part of oneself in the death of a person whom one loves. Because children often cry when they get hurt, would it not follow that it would be natural to cry when "losing a part of oneself?" Grollman observes that tears and sorrowful words help the child feel relieved. Displaying emotions makes the dead person or pet seem more worthy. Tears are a natural tribute paid to the deceased. The child misses the one who is gone and wishes that the person were still around.

In recalling their first childhood experiences with death, some individuals indicated that crying was not acceptable and even had negative consequences (Dickinson, 1992, p. 175). A 15-year-old was spanked with a hairbrush for crying over the death of her puppy. A 10-year-old was "smacked" by her uncle to "make her stop crying at the funeral." Some were told that it was not "grown-up" to cry. For many who recalled their first childhood experiences with death, it was the first time that they had seen their fathers cry. No one commented that it was the first time that they had seen their mothers cry.

Several college students, in recalling their first childhood experiences with death (Dickinson, 1992, p. 178), noted that they watched others' reactions, then responded accordingly. Because children are watching adults, a parental role model of expressing one's self in front of children might be very beneficial to the socialization of children. Children then would not feel a need to hide in the closet to cry or cry into their

Adults model appropriate bereavement behavior for their children. The best thing that adults can do for their children is to be well-adjusted, secure, and loving people.

pillow at night, as some reported. One child noted the positive experience of his parents and sibling sitting down together to have a good cry at the death of his pet—this pointed out to him the warmth of the family in sharing this common event. It was not a burden that he carried alone; his family grieved with him. It is comforting to know that others care.

According to the legendary professional football player Rosie Greer, it is okay to cry. He sang a song in which he noted that it was all right for women, men, girls, *and* boys to cry. For little boys to cry is *not* "sissy." If Rosie Greer says that it is okay, it must be okay! Anthropologist Ashley Montagu (1968) agrees with Greer and states that women have a superior use of their emotions because of their ability to express themselves more easily through crying.

Some men feel that "real men" should not cry because it is not macho to cry. Such men will wear dark shades on the cloudiest of days, if they fear that they might cry at a funeral. Several years ago, my teenage daughter and I attended the funeral of a friend. After leaving the cemetery on a very cloudy day, she said to me, "Dad, you were right." I said, "About what?" She said, "Nearly all the men at the graveside services were wearing dark sunglasses to hide the fact that they may be crying." Men hold back the tears and develop psychosomatic disorders like peptic ulcers. "Is this a superior use of emotions?" Montagu would ask.

What favors are we doing for our children by teaching them that it is not okay to cry? It is okay to laugh, so why should it not also be okay to express feelings through crying?

Children's Understanding of Death

A child growing up in the United States today seldom experiences many aspects of the life cycle. People do not live on the farm next to grandparents and other extended family, as was the case earlier in the 20th century; instead, urbanization and mobility have contributed to a separation from this older generation and other extended family. Thus, the child today is often removed from dying grandparents because of distance or because of their dying in the impersonal setting of a hospital or nursing home.

Largely gone are the days when the child lived in the household with a dying grandparent. Death has been removed from the home to more institutionalized settings. This is summed up by the statement of the little boy who said, "I don't want to go to the hospital because that is where you go to die." That is where Grandfather was taken the last time that the little boy saw him alive. After "going to the hospital," Grandfather turned into a cold, stiff corpse. The process of the grandfather's dying was not part of the daily routine in the family's home.

As was pointed out in chapter 1, gone are the days when the majority of children were reared on farms and experienced the life cycle daily—animals were born, and animals died. Birth and death were commonplace in the socialization of children reared on farms. Gone are the days when siblings and relatives were born at home and died at home.

The media expose children to dying and death, but often on television death is viewed as reversible. An individual "dies" on a program this week and reappears in another show the next week. Thus, a child can acquire the idea that death is only temporary and not permanent. For the child growing up today, the media may well be the source of death education. A shortcoming of television when it serves as the "death educator" for children is its inability to respond to questions that children may have. One cannot call into the set and expect to receive an answer. One little boy, reared in the television era, expressed his confusion in this question, "Dad, are we alive or on tape?" Another boy, upon being told that his grandfather had died, asked, "Who shot him?" He was so accustomed to seeing people die on television by the gun that this was his concept of death.

Not being exposed to dying and death today makes this process and event very removed and "foreign" to children. This underscores the natural tendency to deny the facts of death. Just how do children conceptualize death? The following discussion breaks down children into age groups, but one must remember that ages and stages are in no way absolute. Each child must be interpreted with an understanding of his or her experience and the family's cultural heritage.

BIRTH TO AGE 3

By age 6 months an infant perceives differences in caregivers and the degree to which physical and emotional needs are being met. One cannot have a concept of death until the beginning of thought, as evidenced by the emergence of symbolic function between 18 and 24 months. It has been suggested that the origin of death anxiety is in the traumatic separation from mother at the time of birth (Hostler, 1978, p. 7). The delight of playing peek-a-boo lies in the relief of the intermittent terror of separation. Under age 5 death is perceived as separation, but separation from one's caregiver is a terrifying thought.

Erik Erikson (1963) observed that an infant "decides" early in life whether the universe is a warm and loving place to be. Upon this primitive, yet momentous, subconscious decision is based to a large degree the ability to deal with threats and difficulties of later life. We must not assume that the small child has no concept or grasp at all of death, and we must be concerned about the effects of a given death upon his or her life.

A toddler recognizes that a pet is alive and that a table is not. The toddler's vocabulary normally includes "to die" by age 2 1/2 and "to live" by age 3 (Hostler, 1978, p. 7). Although the 2-year-old child dying in a hospital has no real concept of his or her death, the child has a real appreciation of the altered patterns of care and the separation from usual caregivers.

Psychologist Jean Piaget concluded that children progress in stages of **cognitive development** with each stage being qualitatively better than the preceding one (Ginsburg & Opper, 1979). Such an assertion brought about discoveries that small children can grieve over the loss of something only at the point that they have realized that things (and people) are not permanent. This quality, which he called "object constancy," would have to precede any sense of loss. Piaget observed that this happens somewhere around 1 year to 18 months of age.

A critical analysis of the literature concerning the development of the concept of death in early childhood by Stambrook and Parker (1987, p. 137) suggests that some children, under certain conditions (such as experiencing a loss through death), can understand death to be final much earlier than is typically suggested. It has even been hypothesized (Yalom, 1980) that children under 3 years of age "know about but deny death." Perhaps the lack of research consensus found here simply confirms that we cannot depend solely on age categories regarding children's conceptions of death but must also consider individual experiences of the children.

AGES 3 TO 5

The clearest and most consistent observation from the literature on death concepts of children is that children as young as 3 have very definite ideas of what death means, though there is considerable disagreement as to the nature of those ideas, according to Stambrook and Parker (1987, p. 138). Most children 3 to 5 years old lack an appreciation that death is a universal phenomenon and is a final and complete cessation of bodily functions. Though death is seen as temporary and/or partial, Stambrook and Parker (1987, p. 138) note that the child is very curious to know and understand the practical and concrete aspects of all that surrounds death. For some children, death is believed to be life under changed circumstances. For example, the dead in caskets can still sense what is happening in the environment but cannot move.

Maria Nagy (1948) interviewed 378 Hungarian children from 3 to 10 years of age and ranging across a broad spectrum intellectually and being from various religious backgrounds. She asked the younger children to draw pictures concerning death and those older than 7 to write down everything that they could think of about death. Children aged 3 to 5 found death to be reversible and not final. Separation and abandonment are seen as equivalent to death.

Because Nagy's research was conducted in the 1930s in Hungary, one could surmise that many children had heard much about death from relatives and neighbors who had gone through World War I in Europe. Children's deaths were much more common than in the current era.

The permanency of death is not clear in early childhood, as evidenced by this story told to the author about a 3 1/2-year-old whose father had been killed 6 months earlier in an auto accident. One day the little boy's mother came in and said, "I have a surprise for you." The little boy anxiously replied, "Is Daddy coming home?" On another occasion this same little boy was playing with his Legos and built a house. He placed a person inside the house and was asked to identify the individual. He replied, "Oh, that is Daddy. He is asleep for 100 years." Daddy is not dead; he is simply away on a trip or engaged in a deep sleep. Death is not permanent to young children.

When our daughter was 5 years old, she attended the funeral of an elderly friend of ours. After the service and the final viewing, the casket was closed and sealed. At this point Cindy tugged on my coat, and I bent down on my knees to make horizontal eye contact with her (life is a world of knees to small children!). She said to me, "But, Daddy, how is Mrs. Kirby going to breathe in there?" Again, for a 5-year-old it is difficult to grasp a concept of death. Death is not permanent because one still needs to breathe.

The practicality of young children is apparent in this story of a 5-year-old whose mother had died. While waiting in the airport to fly from Kentucky to Texas to bury the child's mother, she looked up at her father and said, "Daddy, can you cook?" This was a traditional family in which the father brought home the bacon, and the mother cooked it. The child's concern was whether or not the father could fill the vacant role.

AGES 6 TO 12

At this age range the child has such motor mastery that he or she can ride a bicycle without holding the handles and can sing a song at the same time (true of better-coordinated children, that is!). The child begins to view the world from an external point of view, and language skills are becoming communicative and less egocentric. The first major separation from home occurs, and the child enters the world of school, where teachers and other adults, other than parents, become the models for

Regardless of how much adults may wish to protect their children from death, it will always be a part of a child's experience.

identification. Although magical thinking persists, the child gains in the ability to test reality (Hostler, 1978, p. 11).

A sense of moral judgment continues to develop in this age group. The child attains an understanding that rules are of human origin and that he or she can participate in their origin and modification. The child is mastering school and social skills and has an interpretation of that experience based on an external point of view—schoolmates, teachers, other adults, readings, and the media.

Between the ages of 6 and 12, the evolution of the concept of death as a permanent cessation of life begins. However, the cognitive obstacles to abstract thought—the persistence of egocentrism, **animism,** and magical thinking—prevent its completion. Psychosocial experiences at home and in one's community influence the development of the death concept (Hostler, 1978, p. 16). Death is linked to forces in the outside world and becomes (Lonetto, 1980):

> Scary, frightening, disturbing, dangerous, unfeeling, unhearing, or silent. Death can be invisible as a ghost, or ugly like a monster, or it can be a skeleton. Death can be a person, a companion of the devil, a giver of illness, or even an angel.

Nagy's research (1948) in Hungary concluded that children aged 5 to 9 personify death, representing death as a live person or some variation such as an angel, a skeleton, or a circus clown. Death is viewed as a *taker,* something violent that comes to get you like a burglar or a ghost or the Grim Reaper. These children felt that they could outmaneuver death, so its universality was supposedly not yet acceptable to them. The children over age 9, however, saw death not only as final, but also as inevitable and universal.

Mother Goose: Teacher of Death

Childhood, a famous poet once wrote, is "the kingdom where nobody dies."

A University of Minnesota psychologist would take issue with that. To illustrate his thesis, Dr. John Brantner tells this story:

A young couple was determined to shield their children from the facts of death. They took extraordinary precautions never to mention the word, or allude to the eventual fate of all men. One day they were at a rented beach house, about ready to romp down to the ocean for a day in the sun, when the father glanced out the window and saw a dead dog in the road they would have to cross. Quickly he drew the blinds and, while his wife distracted the children, called the proper authorities and told them to come and get the carcass.

Within the hour the victim of a speeding motorist had been removed and the father, peeking through the blinds, told his wife it was all right to go to the beach. The family got outside and was about to cross the road separating the beach house from the shore when the little girl looked up at her father and asked, "Daddy, what happened to the dead dog?"

Brantner believes that, by the time children are able to speak, they have some awareness of the reality of death. How do they learn about it?

One way is TV. Brantner cites a recent study which found that, on the average, a child who watches the tube for ten years will see no fewer than 13,500 violent deaths. "And the odds are great that he doesn't see a single natural death," the psychologist adds.   *(continued)*

In analyzing death drawings of 431 children between 9 and 18 years of age in Sweden, Tamm and Granqvist (1995) found that personification of death is present to some extent through all ages, yet more pronounced in boys. There is a fear that death is contagious, something that can be caught like a cold (Schaefer & Lyons, 1986, pp. 20–21). I remember in the early 1950s, as a child of 11 or 12 years of age, that polio was rampant. When two of the children next door were diagnosed with polio, I waited for the "thing" to visit our house next. Though polio usually did not kill the victim, nonetheless, this experience was frightening for a child as "it" weaved throughout the neighborhood.

Swedish researchers Tamm and Granqvist (1995) concluded that children between the ages of 9 and 12 represented death predominantly in biological terms. They were concerned with the physical features of death and the dead and the causes and conditions of death. They were especially concerned with violent death and the rituals of the dead. These 9- to 12-year-olds dealt with death in a realistic and worldly manner, depicting what they knew and perceived daily, largely via television. Besides television, their interest in violent death could be related to the killings of worms and insects by young children or to their playing cops and robbers or other gun-related games involving killing.

(continued from previous page)

Another, surprising teacher of death is that nice little old lady, Mother Goose. Brantner pulls out the comprehensive *Oxford Dictionary of Nursery Rhymes* as evidence. Consider "The Death and Burial of Poor Cock Robin":

Who killed Cock Robin?
"I," said the sparrow,
"With my little bow and arrow, |
I killed Cock Robin."

Who saw him die?
"I," said the fly,
"With my little eye,
I saw him die."

And on it goes, through the funeral, grave digging, burial and final tolling of the bell.

Consider this little ditty:

There was an old woman who had three sons,
Jerry and James and John,
Jerry was hanged, James was drowned,
John was lost and never was found;
And there was an end of her three sons,
Jerry and James and John!

(continued)

Rhymes were a common conveyance of such grim news, Brantner believes, because, back when the classic children's verse came to be, death was much more of an immediate reality for those who recited them. "Until 1900," the professor said, "67 percent of everyone who died was under the age of 15. It was a common part of growing up that you had younger brothers and sisters who died."

Verses not only described peaceful passings. They also were not hesitant to speak of murder, drownings, hangings, and other violent ends, all in light couplet. And death became the ultimate punishment.

Barnaby Bright was a sharp cur,
  He always would bark if a mouse did but stir,
  But now he's grown old, and can no longer bark,
  He's condemned by the parson to be hanged by the clerk.

Or this one:

Little Dicky Dilver
  Had a wife of silver;
  He took a stick and broke her back
  And sold her to the miller;
  The miller wouldn't have her
  So he threw her in the river.

Death was to be mourned, the rhymes told their reciters:

Grandfa' Grig had a pig
  In a field of clover;
  Piggie died, Grandfa' cried
  And all the fun was over.

Fatalism? That can be found, too, as in:

Now I lay me down to sleep,
  I pray the Lord my soul to keep;
  And if I die before I wake,
  I pray the Lord my soul to take.

Nature's destruction of the body comes across grotesquely in this bit of verse:

On looking up, on looking down
  She saw a dead man on the ground;
  And from his nose unto his chin,
  The worms crawled out, the worms crawled in.

(continued)

(continued from previous page)

> Then she unto the parson said,
> Shall I be so when I am dead?
> O yes, O yes, the parson said,
> You will be so when you are dead.

Even pitiful but benign Old Mother Hubbard recounts death, with a magical twist. The second stanza goes like this:

> She went to the baker's
> To buy him some bread;
> But when she came back
> The poor dog was dead.

> She went to the undertaker's
> To buy him a coffin;
> But when she came back
> The poor dog was laughing.

What's a child to make of that? There's little doubt about life's brevity, however, in this well-known rhyme:

> Solomon Grundy,
> Born on a Monday,
> Christened on Tuesday,
> Married on Wednesday,
> Took ill on Thursday
> Worse on Friday,
> Died on Saturday,
> Buried on Sunday,
> This is the end
> Of Solomon Grundy.

Your kids don't hear nursery verse? What about fairy tales? Again, the classics are rife with violence and death. Remember what the giant in "Jack and the Beanstalk" repeated with lust?

> Fee-fi-fo-fum,
> I smell the blood of an Englishman.
> Be he alive, or be he dead, |
> I'll grind his bones to make my bread.

Hansel and Gretel roast the witch in her own oven. Dorothy is trapped in Oz until the wicked witch of the west could be liquidated.

(continued)

(continued from previous page)
And Henny-Penny, the paranoid little chick who thought that the sky was falling down, lead four friends, Turkey-Lurkey, Goosey-Poosey, Duckey-Daddles and Cocky-Locky, to decapitation by the fox.

Bluebeard, a misogynist turned mass murderer, began as a children's story.

Some tales have been changed. In the first version of "The Three Little Bears" there is no Goldilocks, but a little old woman who plays the intruder. Upon being discovered by the Bears she jumps out the window to an uncertain fate. The narrator speculates that she possibly broke her neck.

Before Walt Disney got hold of them, the Three Little Pigs were a morbid bunch. The wolf consumed the first two for lunch, but the third, who declined his invitations to dinner, boiled the beast and ate him for supper. And lived happily ever after.

R. Gibson, *Minneapolis Star,* April 11, 1973, p. 1C.

This sample of Mother Goose nursery rhymes is perhaps cause for concern about childhood readings. In 1937 Allen Abbott urged nursery rhyme reform, as did Geoffrey Hall in 1949. In 1952 Geoffrey Handley-Taylor (Baring-Gould, 1967, p. 20) published a brief biography of the literature of nursery rhyme reform and noted that the average collection of 200 traditional nursery rhymes contains approximately 100 rhymes that "personify all that is glorious and ideal for the child." He noted, however, that the remaining 100 rhymes "harbour unsavory elements." Following is a partial list of Handley-Taylor's findings from Mother Goose:

2 cases of choking to death

1 case of death by devouring

1 case of cutting a human being in half

1 case of decapitation

1 case of death by squeezing

1 case of death by shriveling

1 case of death by starvation

1 case of boiling to death

1 case of death by hanging

1 case of death by drowning

4 cases of killing domestic animals

1 case of body snatching

7 cases relating to the severing of limbs

1 case of the desire to have a limb severed

2 cases of self-inflicted injury

4 cases relating to the breaking of limbs

1 case of devouring human flesh

12 cases of torment and cruelty to human beings and animals

8 cases of whipping and lashing

15 allusions to maimed human beings and animals

Sudden Infant Death Syndrome (SIDS)

Despite a continuing decrease in the rate of infant mortality in the United States, the cause of death known as **sudden infant death syndrome (SIDS)** has not been decreasing and, in fact, has been increasing in many populations. In the Western world, SIDS is the most common cause of death of infants between 1 month and 1 year of age and accounts for approximately 50 percent of deaths of infants between 2 and 4 months of age (Klonoff-Cohen et al., 1995).

Sudden, unexpected infant death is a major cause of death for infants between the ages of 1 week and 1 year in the United States—an estimated 5,000 to 6,000 deaths per year (Willinger, 1995). According to a study by the Foundation for the Study of Infant Deaths, these babies do not cry out as if in pain, but simply die quietly in their sleep, after becoming unconscious. Sudden infant death is usually defined as the sudden, unexplained death of an infant younger than 1 year where no cause is found through a postmortem examination (Willinger, 1995).

Historically, unexpected, unexplainable deaths of infants were routinely attributed to the mothers' lying on them because mothers often slept with infants. If a mother awoke and found her baby dead, she assumed that she had lain on the child, smothering or crushing it. Perhaps the earliest recorded such death is in the Bible in 1 Kings 3:19: "And this woman's child died in the night, because she overlaid it." It is believed that SIDS was occurring long before it was recognized and accepted as a diagnostic label (Beckwith, 1978).

THE ETIOLOGY OF SIDS

SIDS is a distinct medical entity and not just a category of unexplained infant deaths attributed to different causes. Yet, SIDS is difficult to predict or prevent. SIDS is not hereditary and is not suffocation or regurgitation. Though a minor illness such as a common cold may have been present at the time of death, and autopsies reveal inflammation in windpipes in a high number of cases, many SIDS victims are apparently very healthy (DeFrain, Jakub, & Mendoza, 1992).

The **etiology** of SIDS shows that it occurs more often in winter and spring, when respiratory illnesses are frequent. The peak age for death is between 2 and 4 months of age. There is a higher incidence among blacks, poor families, boy babies, premature babies, and babies born to teenage mothers. Deaths are more frequent in infants with low alertness scores at birth and in infants born to mothers who use drugs or who smoke (Cope, 1980; Nam, Eberstein, & Deeb, 1989).

A Swedish study by Haglund and Cnattinguius (1990) highlights the correlation between SIDS and mothers' smoking during pregnancy. They note that smoking is probably the most important preventable risk factor for fetal death. Their findings suggest that if maternal smoking could be eliminated, infants delivered to mothers who gave up smoking would face the same mortality risk as those delivered to nonsmoking mothers, and SIDS death rates would be reduced by 27 percent. Researcher Anne Walling (1996) predicts that SIDS could be reduced by two thirds if parents did not smoke during pregnancy and after birth. Walling reported an independent additional risk if others in the household smoke, thus passive smoke tends to be correlated with SIDS. Another study (Klonoff-Cohen et al., 1995), which compared the smoking habits of 200 mothers of infants who died of SIDS with those of 200 mothers of healthy infants of the same age, race, and sex and with the same smoking habits of fathers and day-care providers, concluded that passive smoke may increase the risk of SIDS.

Support for the preceding findings was found by Southall and associates (1987), who monitored breathing movements of 301 infants who had a sibling who died of SIDS and compared them with a control group of 170 infants, matched by postnatal age. They found that the mothers of the SIDS siblings smoked and consumed alcohol more often during pregnancy than did the mothers of control babies. The siblings had lower Apgar (alertness) scores and were more often breast-fed than were controls.

Evidence (Scragg et al., 1996) suggests a lower risk of SIDS among children who share a room with an adult. Parents are likely to sleep more lightly than children and to have a greater awareness of and concern for their infant's well-being. Parents in developed countries are generally advised that an infant should sleep in a room alone from an early age, yet no epidemiological studies support this advice. Anthropologists have documented that infants in the past were reared in a consistently rich sensory environment and that the solitary sleep environment to which infants in Western societies are exposed is a recent development (Scragg et al., 1996).

Sleep position of the infant appears to be highly correlated with SIDS. A study by Marian Willinger (1995) in Australia found that a decrease in the proportion of infants put to sleep in the prone position (stomach-down) correlated with a decrease in SIDS cases. After critically reviewing epidemiologic studies which found that infants sleeping on their abdomens were at increased risk for SIDS, the American Academy of Pediatrics issued a report in 1992 recommending that healthy infants be placed on their sides or backs (Willinger, 1995). This recommendation was followed in 1994 by the national public education campaign, "Back to Sleep," by several organizations. A concern developed about the onset of flat-headedness in infants placed solely on their backs, but this was found to be easily remedied. Researchers discovered that 69 out of 71 children who developed the condition could be treated simply by alternating head positions during sleep ("Baby Surgery Is Avoidable," 1997).

Most SIDS deaths occur when the baby is sleeping, usually between midnight and 9 a.m., and occur very rapidly with apparently no suffering for the baby. The child turns blue and limp, apparently from lack of oxygen. Clues to SIDS are present in the brain, which should alert the infant to breathe harder, but research is inconclusive on the linkage to brain dysfunction (Cope, 1980).

Natural hormone production in babies could play a significant role in SIDS (King, 1994). Surging hormones (testosterone in males, estradiol in females) could inhibit some babies' breathing during the 2nd through 4th months. If the theory proves true, physicians could measure hormone levels and predict which babies are most at risk for SIDS. Drugs could be used to reduce the levels.

Viral infections have been viewed as a link to SIDS (Valdes-Dapena, 1980). **Viral infections** are evident in autopsies of some babies, but not all. Evidence from postmortem studies showed elevated levels of a thyroid hormone, triiodothyronine (T-3), in 44 out of 50 victims (Rowley, 1981). This may be an important step in determining the cause, and hopefully, the cure for SIDS. It is not clear, however, when the elevation of T-3 occurred—prior to birth or after the death.

If T-3 has an influence on breathing and heartbeat, an infant with an elevated level of T-3 should perhaps be put on a monitor (DeFrain, Taylor, & Ernst, 1982, p. 14). Apparently, all infants experience numerous short periods of not breathing (apnea). A home **apnea monitor** is frequently used in the management of infants at increased risk for SIDS and helps detect the infants' breathing irregularities by sounding an alarm when breathing stops. The effectiveness of home apnea monitoring remains unproven, however, because some infants have died despite evaluation by infant apnea programs (Ward et al., 1986).

Death-scene investigations (Bass, Kravath, & Glass, 1986) of 26 cases of infants brought into an emergency room with presumptive diagnoses of SIDS revealed strong circumstantial evidence of accidental death in 6 cases and found various *possible* causes of death, other than SIDS, in 18 other cases. These researchers suggest that many sudden deaths of infants may have a definable "cause" other than SIDS. They question the extremely high rate of SIDS reported in the population of low socioeconomic status served by their hospital.

Crib Death Tied to Common Bedding

A study suggests that ordinary bedding materials, not just the beanbag cushions already recalled by the government, may have suffocated many babies whose deaths were reported as "crib death," scientists said today.

"Perhaps one in four of sudden, unexplained infant deaths may be attributed to exhaled carbon dioxide being trapped around the baby's face by bedding such as pillows, comforters, and foam beds," said Dr. James Kemp, a pediatrician at Washington University School of Medicine in St. Louis.

Babies whose deaths were ascribed to the mysterious Sudden Infant Death Syndrome, called SIDS or crib death, should be investigated as possible suffocation victims if they were found face down, stated Dr. Bradley Thach, a Washington University pediatrician who conducted the study with Dr. Kemp. Many possible causes have been proposed for SIDS; none has been proved. At least a quarter of all victims are found face down.

In their study, Drs. Kemp and Thach tested rabbits who breathed through a model of an infant airway pressed against the types of bedding materials on which infants died. That test and a new mechanical test

(continued)

(continued from previous page)

suggested five types of bedding that could suffocate infants. These materials caused babies to exhale carbon dioxide, forcing them to rebreathe CO_2 gas without getting enough oxygen. The types tested were an adult pillow filled with synthetically-made material, a three-and-a-half-inch thick foam couch cushion, a three-inch thick foam pad covered with a comforter, a sheepskin-covered infant bed, and a soft bassinet cushion covered by a blanket.

Dr. Henry Krous, a pediatrician-pathologist at the University of California at San Diego, said some of the conclusions were premature, but he added that the researchers were "highly reputable, capable investigators" whose study held some "interesting and provocative" possibilities which could help shed light on the mystery of SIDS.

Adapted from an Associated Press article, New York Times, April 8, 1992, p. B-9.

PARENTS OF SIDS CHILDREN

The majority of SIDS parents see SIDS as the most devastating crisis that they have ever experienced. Approximately one fourth of SIDS parents move from their homes and to other communities in an effort to escape the pain of the baby's death (DeFrain, Jakub, & Mendoza, 1992). A study of 34 pairs of parents bereaved by SIDS (Carroll & Shaefer, 1994) reveals that bereaved parents sought support from within the family most often and from outside resources least often. Parents generally tend to "recover" from the death in approximately 3 years or more.

Some parents "turn to God," whereas others "turn away from God" as a response to their loss (DeFrain, Taylor, & Ernst, 1982). Their reaction may be reflected in church attendance. From 1985 through 1988 a study (Thearle et al., 1995) in Australia examining the emotional health of parents after SIDS, neonatal death, or stillbirth concluded that the bereaved who attend church regularly have less anxiety and depression compared with irregular church attenders and nonchurch attenders. Similarly, in interviews with parents who had lost children to SIDS, researchers Wortman and Silver (1992) found that parents' religious devotion and participation in religious activities were positively related to coping. Among these parents a most important feeling was that they would someday see their children in heaven.

When an infant dies suddenly and unexpectedly, the sense of loss and grief may be overwhelming. When that sudden death is due to a known cause, the concrete character of the event can be incorporated into the normal rationalization of mourning. However, when death is due to an unknown mechanism, as in SIDS, feelings of inadequacy in caring for the child are reinforced for the medical staff and the parents (Mandell, McClain, & Reece, 1987).

Because there are still many unanswered questions about SIDS, parents have a tremendous guilt feeling and shoulder the responsibility for the infant's death. Marital conflict, difficulties with surviving children, and anxiety about future children becoming victims of SIDS are often experienced. With the cause of death in a SIDS case being questionable, the parents are likely to undergo a police interrogation, in addition to the stress of having lost their infant. In an era of child abuse, the parents may be suspected of smothering the child. Being questioned by the police is difficult enough, but the perceived inability of others such as friends and relatives to understand the depth of their despair is also very frustrating to these parents (DeFrain, Jakub, & Mendoza, 1992).

The Centers for Disease Control and Prevention ("Guidelines to Help Discern SIDS from Homicide," 1996) recently issued investigation guidelines to help coroners and police distinguish between SIDS and homicide in infants. The guidelines suggest noting such aspects as the position of the infant's body, any suspected injuries, and any evidence of drug use in the home. The death-scene investigation, the child's medical history, and an autopsy are necessary for a thorough investigation.

Young parents whose baby dies of SIDS have not likely experienced the death of a close relative, thus they are not familiar with the social and emotional aspects of grief and mourning. The death of one's baby is traumatic under any conditions, but the sense of not knowing how to mourn adds to the difficulties of socially adjusting to the loss. The parents and siblings experience "anomic grief"—a grief without the traditional supports of family, church, and community.

A survey of newly trained local SIDS counselors in North Carolina (Kotch & Cohen, 1985) reported that sharing the autopsy report with bereaved parents was a valuable part of the counseling process and removed some of the mystery surrounding the diagnosis of SIDS. The autopsy report, by documenting that the child died a natural death, may relieve some families of the feeling that they were somehow responsible for the death.

My own discussions with parents who have lost a child through SIDS suggest that friends may turn on them as if they are criminals. Parents tend to "blame" each other for the death—"If only you had. . . ." Parents become "victims" because SIDS is both personally traumatic and complicated by problems of social interaction. The uncertainty of the cause of death is frustrating to the parents and medical staff and clouds the whole issue from a societal perspective. A SIDS death must be one of the more traumatic experiences that parents can have in a lifetime.

Conclusion

Rather than try to "protect the young from death talk," we need to have more open communication channels with children on this topic. Children from an early age have a concept of death, and terminally ill children seem to know that they are dying. We need to stop pretending that children cannot handle this topic. It is okay for children (and adults!) to show emotions by crying when they feel so inclined. It is okay to feel the way that one feels—moral judgments should not be attached to feelings. We should try not to be judgmental of others' feelings.

Whoever or whatever (in the case of a pet) has died, children especially need support at this time. One college student recalled to me the occasion of her mother's unexpected death in an accident. The daughter was 5 years old at the time and said that she felt so insecure when she heard the news. She said, "It was like my whole security blanket crumbled." Indeed, her world had collapsed.

We "big people" must be alert to the questions of children about dying and death. When I spoke to a group of 40 fourth graders a few years ago on the topic of dying and death, my frustration was trying to decide whom to call on when a dozen or more students at a time had their hands up, wanting to ask questions. Each student had his or her own concerns, and they were sincere, legitimate concerns. I remember one little boy asking if it is true that one would die from getting embalming fluid on the skin. I tried to assure him that this would not likely be a cause of death, but this was a genuine concern to him. When our son was 6, he asked, "Daddy, do we eat dead people?" Because we eat dead cows and pigs, why not people? We certainly do not eat live cows and pigs. These "little people" have questions, and we "big people" must respond by answering.

Dying children and significant others surrounding these children need a strong support system. It is important to let the children and families know that others care. Though one may not know what to say in such situations, this should not keep one away from the death environs. Go and visit to show that you care. Parents losing a child through SIDS not only have lost their child, but also face a suspicious public questioning the real "cause" of death. Thus, the parents of a child who dies of SIDS receive a double slap.

Summary

1. Due in part to living in an urbanized and industrialized society, children are not exposed to death, other than through the rather artificial means of the media.

2. The permanency of death is unclear to young children, who tend to see death as reversible.

3. Children can take about anything that adults can dish out to them, including the topic of dying and death.

4. Honesty and openness in relating to children about death are very important.

5. Avoid euphemisms when talking to children about death.

6. It is okay to express emotions through crying. Adults can sanction this behavior by not hiding their own tears when they are sorrowful. By seeing big people cry, children can know that crying is normal behavior.

7. Dying children should be told their diagnosis and kept informed of their prognosis. They seem to know when they are dying anyway, so why make them bear this burden all alone? Knowledge is kindness.

8. Dying children and the parents and siblings of dying children need the support of others.

9. Research on sudden infant death syndrome is inclusive as to the causes of SIDS deaths. Research suggests that a defect in the electrical stimulation of the heart, maternal smoking, and sleep position may contribute to SIDS.

Discussion Questions

1. Discuss your first childhood memory of death. How old were you? Who or what died? What do you remember about this event?
2. When you were growing up, how was death talked about in your family?
3. Discuss the various perceptions of death as one goes from birth to age 12. What shortcomings do you find with a life cycle approach?
4. Analyze the Mother Goose rhymes in the chapter. What are some of the themes in these "kiddie" rhymes?
5. Put yourself in the place of a parent with a terminally ill child. How do you think you would relate to this child?
6. List as many euphemisms as you can to identify dying and death. Why do you think euphemisms are used with death?
7. Why is knowledge kindness in relating to a dying child?
8. What is SIDS? Is this a new or an old phenomenon?
9. Discuss why adults tend to avoid talking about death with children.

Glossary

Animism: The tendency (as among young children) to attribute qualities such as motives and feelings to inanimate objects.

Apnea Monitor: A device to detect the temporary stoppage of breathing in infants.

Cognitive Development: Development of processes of knowing, including imagining, perceiving, reasoning, and problem solving.

Etiology: The science of causes or origins.

Pediatric Oncologist: A medical doctor practicing in the field of medicine related to children with tumors (often malignant).

Sudden Infant Death Syndrome (SIDS): The sudden, unexplained death of an infant when no cause is found in postmortem examination.

Viral Infections: Infections caused by viruses.

References

Adams, D. W., & Deveau, E. J. (1987). When a brother or sister is dying of cancer: The vulnerability of the adolescent sibling. *Death Studies,* 11, 279–295.

Baby surgery is avoidable. (1997, February 11). *New York Times,* p. B13.

Baring-Gould, W. S., & Baring-Gould, C. (1967). *The annotated Mother Goose.* New York: World Publishing Company.

Bass, M., Kravath, R. E., & Glass, L. (1986, July 10). Death-scene investigation in sudden infant death. *New England Journal of Medicine,* 315, 100–105.

Beckwith, J. B. (1978). *The sudden infant death syndrome* (DHEW Publication No. HSA 75-5137). Washington, DC: U.S. Government Printing Office.

Bluebond-Langner, M. (1978). *The private worlds of dying children.* Princeton, NJ: Princeton University Press.

Bluebond-Langner, M. (1989). Worlds of dying children and their well siblings. *Death Studies,* 13, 1–16.

Bowlby, J. (1980). *Attachment and loss* (Vol. 3). New York: Basic Books.

Buursma, B. (1987, August 2). Scholar wrestles with son's death. Charleston, SC, *News and Courier,* p. 6D.

Carroll, R. M., & Sarah S. (1994, May). Similarities and differences in spouses coping with SIDS. *Omega, 28,* 273–284.

Cook, J. A. (1983). A death in the family: Parental bereavement in the first year. *Suicide and Life-Threatening Behavior, 13,* 42–61.

Cook, J. A. (1988). Dad's double binds: Rethinking fathers' bereavement from a men's studies perspective. *Journal of Contemporary Ethnography, 17,* 285–308.

Cope, L. (1980, June 4). Research finding clues to crib deaths. *Minneapolis Tribune.*

Cotton, C. R., & Range, L. M. (1990). Children's death concepts: Relationship to cognitive functioning, age, experience with death, fear of death, and hopelessness. *Journal of Clinical Child Psychology, 19,* 123–127.

DeFrain, J. D., Jakub, D. K., & Mendoza, B. L. (1992). The psychological effects of sudden infant death on grandmothers and grandfathers. *Omega, 24,* 165–182.

DeFrain, J., Taylor, J., & Ernst, L. (1982). *Coping with sudden infant death.* Lexington, MA: Lexington Books.

Dickinson, G. E. (1992). First childhood death experiences. *Omega, 25,* 169–182.

Erikson, E. (1963). *Childhood and society.* New York: Norton.

Gamarekian, B. (1987, June 25). A support network for dying children. *New York Times,* pp. 19–20.

Ginsburg, H., & Opper, S. (1979). *Piaget's theory of intellectual development* (2nd ed.). Englewood Cliffs, NJ: Prentice-Hall.

Grollman, E. (1967). *Explaining death to children.* Boston: Beacon Press.

Guidelines to help discern SIDS from homicide. (1996, June 21). Charleston, SC, *Post and Courier,* p. 4A.

Haglund, B., & Cnattinguius, S. (1990). Cigarette smoking as a risk factor for sudden infant death syndrome: A population-based study. *American Journal of Public Health, 80,* 29–33.

Hall, G. S. (1922). *Youth: Its education, regimen and hygiene.* New York: D. Appleton and Company.

Hostler, S. L. (1978). The development of the child's concept of death. In O. J. Z. Sahler (Ed.), *The child and death* (pp. 1–25). St. Louis: C. V. Mosby.

Kastenbaum, R. J. (1991). *Death, society, and human experience* (4th ed.). New York: Macmillan.

Kavanaugh, R. E. (1972). *Facing death.* Baltimore: Penguin Books.

King, W. (1994, May 21). Crib deaths linked to natural hormones. Charleston, SC, *Post and Courier,* p. 7A.

Klass, D. (1987). Marriage and divorce among bereaved parents in a self-help group. *Omega, 17,* 237–249.

Klonoff-Cohen, H., Edelstein, S. L., Lefkowitz, E. S., Srinivasan, I. P., Kaegi, D., Chang, J., & Wiley, K. J. (1995, March 8). The effect of passive smoking and tobacco exposure through breast milk on sudden infant death syndrome. *Journal of the American Medical Association, 273,* 795–798.

Knapp, R. J. (1986). *Beyond endurance: When a child dies.* New York: Schocken Books.

Kotch, J. B., & Cohen, S. R. (1985). SIDS counselors' reports of own and parents' reactions to reviewing the autopsy report. *Omega, 16,* 129–139.

Kushner, H. S. (1981). *When bad things happen to good people.* New York: Schocken Books.

Kushner, H. S. (1985, October). Lecture given in Charleston, SC.

Lonetto, R. (1980). *Children's conceptions of death.* New York: Springer Publishing Company.

Mandell, F., McClain, M., & Reece, R. M. (1987, July). Sudden and unexpected death. *American Journal of Diseases of Children, 141,* 748–750.

Martin, D. (1990, March 28). A burden in burying the babies. *New York Times,* p. A14.

McCown, D. E., & Pratt, C. (1985). Impact of sibling death on children's behavior. *Death Studies, 9,* 323–335.

Montagu, A. (1968). *The natural superiority of women* (Rev. ed.). New York: Collier Books.

Nagy, M. (1948). The child's theories concerning death. *Journal of Genetic Psychology, 73,* 3–27.

Nam, C. B., Eberstein, I. W., & Deeb, L. C. (1989). Sudden infant death syndrome as a socially determined cause of death. *Social Biology, 36,* 1–9.

Nir, Y. (1987). Post-traumatic stress disorder in children with cancer. In J. E. Schowalter et al. (Eds.), *Children and death: Perspectives from birth through adolescence* (pp. 63–72). New York: Praeger.

O'Halloran, C. M., & Altmaier, E. M. (1996). Awareness of death among children: Does a life-threatening illness alter the process of discovery? *Journal of Counseling and Development, 74,* 259–262.

Orbach, I., Gross, Y., Glaubman, H., & Berman, D. (1985). Children's perception of death in humans and animals as a function of age, anxiety and cognitive ability. *Journal of Child Psychology and Psychiatry, 26,* 453–463.

Rowley, J. (1981, November 6). Crib death discovery may lead to simple test for the disease. *Minneapolis Tribune.*

Sahler, O. J. Z. (1978). *The child and death.* St. Louis: C.V. Mosby.

Sanders, C. M. (1980). A comparison of adult bereavement in the death of a spouse, child, and parent. *Omega, 10,* 303–322.

Schaefer, D., & Lyons, C. (1986). How do we tell the children? *A parents' guide to helping children understand and cope when someone dies.* New York: Newmarket Press.

Schulz, C., & Hall, K. F. (1965). *Two-by-fours: A sort of serious book about children.* Anderson, IN: Warner.

Schwab, R. (1992). Effects of a child's death on the marital relationship: A preliminary study. *Death Studies, 16,* 141–154.

Scragg, R. K. R., Mitchell, E. A., Stewart, A. W., Ford, R. P. K., Taylor, B. J., Hassall, I. B., Williams, S. M., & Thompson, J. M. D. (1996, January 6). Infant room-sharing and prone sleeping position in sudden infant death syndrome. *The Lancet, 347,* 7–12.

Seibert, D., & Drolet, J. C. (1993). Death themes in literature for children ages 3-8. *Journal of School Health, 63,* 86–90.

Sourkes, B. (1981). In J. Kellerman (Ed.), *Psychological aspects of childhood cancer.* Springfield, IL: C. C. Thomas.

Southall, D. P., Alexander, J. R., Stebbens, V. A., Taylor, V. G., & Jancaynski, R. E. (1987, July). Cardiorespiratory patterns in siblings of babies with sudden infant death syndrome. *Archives of Disease in Childhood, 62,* 721–726.

Spinetta, J. J. (1981). The siblings of the child with cancer. In J. J. Spinetta & P. Deasy-Spinetta (Eds.), *Living with childhood cancer* (pp. 137-140). St. Louis: C.V. Mosby.

Stambrook, M., & Parker, K. C. H. (1987, April). The development of the concept of death in childhood: A review of the literature. *Merrill-Palmer Quarterly, 33,* 133–157.

Tamm, M. E., & Granqvist, A. (1995). The meaning of death for children and adolescents: A phenomenographic study of drawings. *Death Studies, 19,* 203–222.

Thearle, M. J., Vance, F. C., Najman, J. M., Embelton, G., & Foster, W. J. (1995). Church attendance, religious affiliation and parental responses to sudden infant death, neonatal death and stillbirth. *Omega, 31,* 51–58.

Tobin, S. (1972). The earliest memory as data for research in aging. In D. P. Kent, R. Kastenbaum, & S. Sherwood (Eds.), *Research, planning and action for the elderly.* New York: Behavioral Publications.

Turnbull, C. M. (1983). *The human cycle.* New York: Simon and Schuster.

Ufema, J. (1996, October). Insights on death and dying. *Nursing, 26,* 26–27.

Valdes-Dapena, M. A. (1980). Sudden infant death syndrome: A review of the medical literature, 1974-1979. *Pediatrics, 66,* 597–613.

Waechter, E. H. (1985). Children's awareness of fatal illness. In S. G. Wilcox & M. Sutton (Eds.), *Understanding death and dying* (3rd ed., pp. 299–306). Palo Alto, CA: Mayfield Publishing.

Walling, A. D. (1996, November 1). Risk factors for sudden infant death syndrome. *American Family Physician, 54,* 2099–2100.

Ward, S. L., Keens, T. G., Chan, L. S., Chipps, B. E., Carson, S. H., & Deming, D. D. (1986, April). Sudden infant death syndrome in infants evaluated by apnea programs in California. *Pediatrics, 77,* 451–458.

Willinger, M. (1995). Sleep position and sudden infant death syndrome. *Journal of the American Medical Association, 273,* 818–819.

Wortman, C. B., & Silver, R. C. (1992). Reconsidering assumptions about coping with loss: An overview of current research. In L. Montada, S. Filipp, & M. J. Lerner (Eds.), *Life crises and experiences of loss in adulthood* (pp. 341–365). Hillsdale, NJ: Erlbaum.

Yalom, I. (1980). *Existential psychotherapy.* New York: Basic Books.

Suggested Readings

Bluebond-Langner, M. (1997). In the shadow of illness: Parents and siblings of the chronically ill child. Princeton, NJ: Princeton University Press. From a medical anthropologist perspective, the author looks at the lives of those who live "in the shadow" of chronic illness: parents and well siblings of children who have cystic fibrosis.

Chesler, M. A., & Chesney, B. K. (1995). *Cancer and self-help: Bridging the troubled waters of childhood illness.* Madison, WI: University of Wisconsin Press. Provides good information for parents and professionals who wish to organize and provide leadership or support to local self-help groups. Also an excellent read for students of social science.

Dickinson, G. E., Leming, M. R., & Mermann, A. C. (1998). *Annual editions: Dying, death and bereavement* (4th ed.). Guilford, CT: Dushkin /McGraw Hill. An anthology with several articles relating to children and death.

Doka, K. J. (1995). *Children mourning, mourning children.* Washington, DC: Hospice Foundation of America. An anthology covering these topics: the child's perspective of death, the child's response to life-threatening illness, children mourning and mourning children, and innovative research on children and death.

Edelstein, L. (1984). *Maternal bereavement: Coping with the unexpected death of a child.* New York: Praeger. A book dealing with women and the loss of a child with special emphasis on mourning and bereavement, the mother-child relationship, putting one's life back into order, and emotional and social supports.

Johnson, S. E. (1987). *After a child dies: Counseling bereaved families.* New York: Springer Publishing Company. Though written for practitioners counseling families who have experienced the death of a child, this book could be read by anyone experiencing bereavement following the death of a child.

Knapp, R. (1986). *Beyond endurance: When a child dies.* New York: Schocken Books. An excellent book based on in-depth interviews with 155 families who had lost a child through death.

Rosen, E. J. (1990). *Families facing death: Family dynamics of terminal illness.* New York: Lexington Books. The author blends the fields of family therapy and death and dying.

Schaefer, D., & Lyons, C. (1986). *How do we tell the children? A parents' guide to helping children understand and cope when someone dies.* New York: Newmarket Press. Covers the topics of children's thinking on death, explaining death to children, grief and healing, and children and funerals.

Related Web Sites

http://www.cyberspy.com/~webster/death.html#children   With links to children, neonates, and family support.

http://www.apk.net/ucc/caring/child.htm   The Death of a Child is a resource created by the United Church of Christ.

http://www.legacyatokc.org/   The web site of the Legacy Grief Center for Children.

http://www.circsol.com/SIDS/   The National Sudden Infant Death Syndrome Resource Center (NSRC) provides information services and technical assistance on sudden infant death syndrome (SIDS) and related topics.

http://iul.com/raindrop/   Raindrop is a death education program for children of all ages.

http://www.inforamp.net/~bfo/index.html Bereaved Families of Ontario Support Center. A bereavement self-help resources guide indexes resources of the center along with over 300 listings to other resources and information.

http://www.emanon.net/~kcabell/death.html Contains many World Wide Web links to resources on death and bereavement.

http://www.yahoo.com/Society_and_Culture/Death/ The death index of the Yahoo Internet search engine.

http://rivendell.org/ GriefNet provides many links to World Wide Web resources on the bereavement process and information concerning grief support groups.

http://gladstone.uoregon.edu/~dvb/perrylos.htm These articles provide core principles for helping grieving children.

http://pages.prodigy.com/CA/lycq97a/lycq97tcf.html The Compassionate Friends is a self-help organization for bereaved parents and siblings. There are hundreds of chapters worldwide.

http://www.psych.med.umich.edu/web/aacap/factsFam/grief.htm
The American Academy of Child and Adolescent Psychiatry provides important information to assist parents and families in their most important roles. The article "Children and Grief" is one such resource. Written in English, Spanish, and French.

http://www.aidskids.org/ The Children With Aids Project is an organization whose role is to develop a fuller understanding of children with, and at risk of, AIDS, including the medical, psychosocial, legal, and financial issues. The mission of the organization is to develop local and national adoptive, foster, and family-centered care programs that are both effective and compassionate.

http://www.equip.ac.uk/maag17bereavement.htm The Child Bereavement Trust provides resources for families grieving over miscarriage, stillbirth, neonatal death, and termination for abnormality.

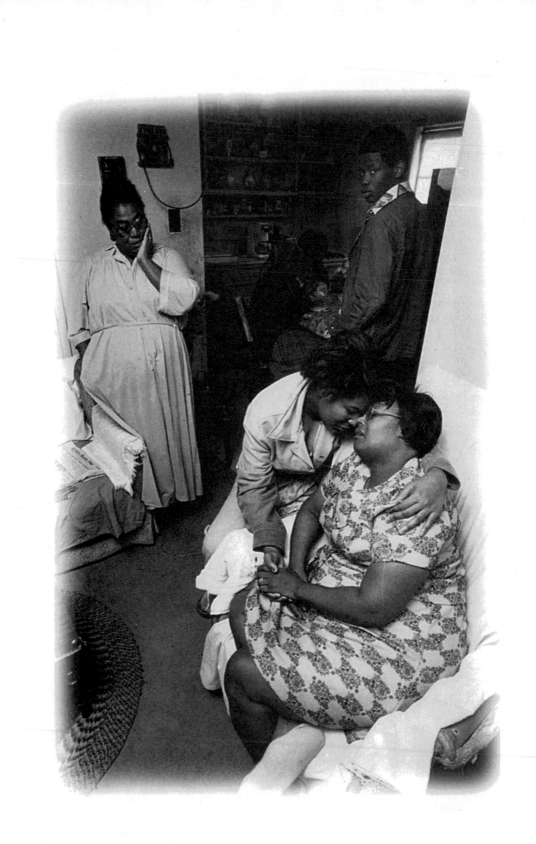

Chapter 4

Developmental Perspective on Dying and Death:
Adolescence Through Older Adulthood

I, too, am trying to find some answers.
I, too, am troubled and sad. Did you know that?
Are you surprised that I don't know all the answers
about death?
Don't be.

Even though no one really understands it,
Death is something we must accept.
We can talk about it.
You can learn something from me.
I can learn something from you.
We can help each other.

—RABBI EARL A. GROLLMAN,
TALKING ABOUT DEATH

In this verse, Rabbi Grollman suggests that, even though no one really understands death, it is something that we must accept. It is something we can, we must, talk about, learn about from each other, and help each other with. In this chapter we will talk about death with the hope that we can "help each other" better understand death conceptualizations at different stages of the life cycle—from adolescence through old age.

Sigmund Freud traced conceptions of death to our earliest feelings concerning sexuality and to our fears of being punished for them. Alfred Adler had several brushes with death himself and, as a child, suffered from a debilitating disease. When Adler formulated his theories concerning the human psyche and its development, he attributed our need to strive and overcome to our early sensitivity to weakness and death.

The **ego psychologists** later departed somewhat from Freud and credited the individual with a greater amount of ability in managing the stresses and problems of life. Yet, they recognized that humans raise a whole set of defenses against the idea of death. Both children and adults have the power to distort their perceptions according to their needs. For example, individuals have ways of denying harsh or painful thoughts, and people often believe and see what they want to believe and see, thus transforming images of their imaginations into reality.

In his Pulitzer Prize-winning book entitled *The Denial of Death,* Ernest Becker (1973) argued that fear and denial of death are basic dynamics for everyone. He asserted that we struggle to find meaning in life through heroic efforts. If we discover that heroic efforts are not possible, the dilemma is avoided by building elaborate systems to explain the dilemma away. Some even flee into neurosis or a psychotic break. Becker felt that the fear of death is a basic problem of meaning with which we all struggle.

Though the subject of death was not a major concern in his writings, Swiss developmental psychologist Jean Piaget was probably instrumental in nudging psychologists to employ better methods of research in the developmental approach toward understanding concepts of death (see Ginsburg & Opper, 1979). Through keen observations of his children and others, Piaget postulated that it is not until the early teen years that one is capable of genuinely abstract thought processes.

Since the publication of Herman Feifel's *The Meaning of Death* in 1959, interest and research on the conceptualization of death have grown. Representing **psychoanalysis, behaviorism, humanism,** and other points of view, much has now been written on a **developmental approach** to death attitudes and awareness.

It is not the intent of this chapter to suggest that age should be seen as the sole determiner of one's death concept. Many other factors influence cognitive development, such as level of intelligence, physical and mental well-being, previous emotional reactions to various life experiences, religious background, other social and cultural forces, personal identity and self-worth appraisals, and exposure to death or threats of death. Though an age-based approach is followed in this chapter, other important factors should not be ignored.

Adolescence

Adolescence is the "training period" between childhood and adulthood in the life experience of humans. Adolescence—from age 12 to age 19—is composed of two significant periods (Gordon, 1986, pp. 17–18). The period from 12 to 15 (with 11 as the threshold) encompasses the acquiring of formal logical thought, the onset of biological sexuality, the growth of the physical structure, and myriad psychosocial tasks. The second period, from 16 to 19, with transition around 15, is characterized by the completion of physical maturation, increasing intimacy with the opposite sex, continued acquisition of adult social skills, clarification of ethics and values, and the ability to

For adolescents, death is an unlikely event. Consequently, when a young person is dying, it is disturbing for all concerned. Death becomes real and must be taken into account.

make long-term commitments to persons and goals. Adolescence is often a time fraught with anxiety, rebellion, and indecision.

Adolescents generally do not think in terms of their distant future. Their struggle with present life experiences, especially the concern with their own identity and anxiety about successes during the immediate future, evidently occupies so much mental energy that thinking about what life will be like at age 45 or 70 is nearly impossible for them.

According to Jean Piaget (1958) and his followers, at about 11 or 12 years of age people are able to move from the use of language and ideation that is concretely oriented to an abstract level of thought. The adolescent can now use conditional statements like "if-then." Ideas can be taken apart and put back together in new ways.

AN IDENTITY CRISIS

Being gripped by questions such as "Who am I?" and "How do I fit into the scheme of things?" the adolescent struggles with good and evil, love and hate, belonging and loneliness, and thoughts of life and death. These can be disturbing issues to the adolescent who is not sure if he or she is a child or an adult because identity signals come from all directions, adding to the confusion of one's self-concept.

The adolescent has a vivid awareness of the dialectic between being and not being, according to psychologist Robert Kastenbaum (1986, p. 11). Daily experience provides occasions for assertions of a new self, of "dyings" of the old self, and of apparent abortions of the new self, notes Kastenbaum. Thus, it is precisely when the adolescent is most endangered by the polarities of being and not being that the concept

Black Adolescents and Death

The black community generally keeps its dying family members at home far more frequently than does the white community, perhaps a reflection of socioeconomic variables as well as a strong tradition of family and religious networking. Thus, black adolescents are typically more socialized at an earlier age to the rituals surrounding death and dying than are most white adolescents. Young black children are routinely taken to funerals and encouraged to interact with family members who are dying in the home. Also, the strong religious background of most black families helps to develop a belief about survival after death that makes death less threatening than it is for the more secularized white middle class.

This is not to suggest that the black culture does not have its fears and superstitions about death. On the whole, however, dying and death are not taboo subjects among black adolescents.

Adapted from "The Tattered Cloak of Immortality" (pp. 16–31), by A. K. Gordon, 1986. In C. A. Corr and J. N. McNeil (Eds.), *Adolescence and Death,* New York: Springer Publishing Company.

of self emerges with singular force. The perception of a self under reconstruction is granted most keenly as one experiences the possibility of failure, loss, catastrophe, and death.

One research study (Koocher et al., 1976) demonstrated that high school students experience much more anxiety, depression, and death fear than do either junior high students or adults. They propose that the "identity crisis" of the adolescent years could be largely responsible for this. Psychiatrist Robert Lifton (1976) also notes that adolescence is the time when a sense of great potential for disintegration, separation, and instability occupies the mind and brings about greater death anxiety.

Sherry Schachter (1991) states that a high percentage of adolescents must adjust to the death of a peer and that this might contribute to the frustration of the teen years. The death of a peer emphasizes the adolescent's own vulnerability and mortality. Because society does not acknowledge the bereaved adolescent in the same manner that it acknowledges the bereaved family, Schachter observes, this experience is compounded for adolescents by isolation, and they become the forgotten mourners. Because adolescents' identity shifts away from parents and family as they tend to see themselves as members of the peer group, the loss of a peer can upset identity formation that may already be unstable (O'Brien, Goodenow, & Espin, 1991).

SOCIALIZATION TO DEATH FEARS

Like masturbation, adolescent **death anxieties and fears** are universally experienced and discussed with equally uninformed peers, notes Audrey Gordon (1986, pp. 20–21). One of the tasks of adolescence is to begin to grapple with the meaning of life and death and to emerge with a philosophical stance that promotes optimism for the future. This is not an easy assignment, especially because one's attitude toward the future may involve more pessimism than optimism.

Our society's discomfort with the process of aging, illness, and death does not contribute positively toward the adolescent's image of a future (Gordon, 1986, p. 22). Because being young is envied and growing old is feared in America, to "grow old along with me" may not mean that "the best is yet to be" in the minds of adolescents. Consequently, a callousness toward physical deterioration and death often develops in adolescence. When the death of a significant other occurs, previous experience has likely not prepared the adolescent for the feelings of rage, loneliness, guilt, and disbelief that accompany a personal loss. If peers have not experienced a similar loss, they may have difficulty being supportive.

Adolescents often see dying and death depicted in the media as excessively "violent, macabre, distant, or unnaturally beautiful" (Gordon, 1986, p. 22). Brutal death results from chain saws (*The Texas Chain Saw Massacre,* 1974), power tools (*The Toolbox Murders,* 1978), or blenders and microwave ovens (*Gremlins,* 1984). *The Big Chill* (1983) opens with the dressing of a body for a funeral as the titles flash past. *Rambo* movies of the 1980s are filled with violence and death. Meaningless deaths were dramatized in the *Halloween* series of films. The *Faces of Death (I, II, and III)* films, allegedly depicting actual human decapitation, autopsies, and executions by injection and electrocution, overflow with bizarre death scenes. With videotapes, adolescents' opportunities to view violence and uncensored death increase.

There seems to be a growing fascination with death among adolescents. One perhaps builds up a sense of invulnerability by seeing other people dead or dying, notes psychologist Fred Hinker ("Death Films Popular," 1985). Hinker says that teenagers watching these movies are like teenagers riding motorcycles at extremely high speeds. They are saying, "It can't happen to me. I'm proving it by flirting with death."

"What prepares the adolescent for an embalmed, cosmeticized body, and how does the teenager learn what to do at the time he or she is gripped by powerful emotions that threaten self-control?" asks Audrey Gordon (1986, p. 24). How embarrassing to lose emotional control and perceive yourself as a child again, rather than a maturing young adult.

Destructive themes in rock music are not unlike many movies viewed by adolescents (in the view of Thomas Attig). According to Wass, Miller, and Redditt (1991, p. 204), however, death themes in rock music might be therapeutic. The themes should be understood metaphorically rather than literally. Rock lyrics may sometimes provide the means for dealing with issues of death and for managing the anxieties created by these themes.

Society is created and held together by **rituals**—morning wake-up rituals, going to school/work rituals, eating rituals, religious rituals, political rituals, and others (Gordon, 1986, p. 23). Ritualization provides sanctioned boundaries within which the self can be safely expressed. Dying, death, and grief all are ritualized by society as a way of containing and giving meaning to feelings of loss. The granting of adult responsibility and privilege to adolescents varies from culture to culture and group to group. Because elders all too often do not teach children the adult rituals for handling dying, death, and grief, it becomes one of the personal tasks of adolescence to acquire this knowledge.

Death Themes in Adolescent Music
Thomas Attig

One key to understanding adolescents is cultivating an understanding of the music that occupies a central place in their lives. Music provides adolescents with mirrors of who they and society are and intimations of what they and society might become.

The stark aversion to old age in some of the music is startling. The lead singer of The Who in "My Generation" (1970) repeatedly asserts a wish to die before becoming old seemingly in part because of a repugnance that is attached to old age itself. Some songs, by contrast, express wonder about what it is like to be old and to see life from its end. The Beatles, for example, in "When I'm Sixty-Four" (1967) wonder about connections with others in old age when they ask whether they will still be needed and cared for as elderly people. Paul Simon in "Old Friends" (1968) sketches a lonely scene of two old friends sitting on a park bench, "winter companions . . . waiting for the sunset."

A theme with the need for continuity is found in Paul Simon's "Flowers Never Bend with the Rainfall" (1966). He offers a song that gives testimony to the extreme difficulty of thinking of oneself as anything but immortal. In "Eleanor Rigby" (1966) the Beatles paint a stark portrait of alienation and meaningless life. The concept of survival after death is treated in Joan Baez' rendition of the folk hymn (1969) "Will the Circle Be Unbroken?" The singer anticipates being reunited with her dead mother in a life to come.

Though a desire for symbolic immortality is noted in Neil Diamond's "Morningside" (1972), apparently the wish was not fulfilled by the survivors. After an account of how an old man spent his last days lovingly making a table so his children would remember him, the song reports that when he did die, no one wept and no one claimed the legacy that he had left behind.

(continued)

HELPING ADOLESCENTS COPE WITH DEATH

Whenever an individual is going through an unstable or stressing period—especially when the stress has to do with basic feelings about self-worth, identity, and capability—the thought of death is particularly difficult to manage. Crucial to positive outcomes is the manner in which parents, friends, peers, teachers, and others enable the adolescent to process positively the ideas of the overwhelming threats of death to self and significant others.

Audrey Gordon (1986, p. 23) notes that adolescents need not stumble around in a darkness that adults have helped to create. With proper preparation and support, younger adolescents can be helped to become aware of death in manageable ways, and older adolescents can be helped to impart a meaning to death and life that transcends everyday events and infuses the future with hope.

(continued from previous page)

The theme of loss and grief is prominent in adolescent music. Songs of tribute are among the best known: countless songs about Elvis Presley have been written and Dion's "Abraham, Martin and John" (1975) refers to Abraham Lincoln, Martin Luther King, Jr., and John F. Kennedy. Also noteworthy is Don McLean's "American Pie" (1972) which views the death of Buddy Holly and other early rockers as a turning point in rock's loss of innocence.

Many songs express alarm over the potentially, sometimes all too real, lethal results of drug use. Lynyrd Skynyrd's "The Smell" (1977) describes the smell of death in the air in the aftermath of the deaths from drug overdoses of many prominent performers including Janis Joplin, Jimi Hendrix, and Jim Morrison. Paul Simon's "Save the Life of My Child" (1968) depicts a scene in which a crowd is gathered beneath a young man perched on a ledge and under the influence of drugs.

Pornographic rock, where fantasy has taken over and death is dehumanized and distorted, is equivalent to the "slasher" movies. Warren Zevon's "Excitable Boy" (1968) describes the rape and killing of "Susie" after a junior prom date and cynically explains that the boy was just "excitable." The Rolling Stones' "The Midnight Rambler" (1969) salutes the Boston Strangler, and Thin Lizzy pays tribute to Jack the Ripper with "Killer on the Loose" (1980).

Death themes in adolescent music afford an opportunity for identification with cultural heroes, values and ideals, hopes and aspirations. It provides communication currency and social connection with peers and provides an alternative frame of reference within which their concerns can be and are addressed.

Adapted from "Death Themes in Adolescent Music: The Classic Years" (pp. 32–56), by T. Attig, 1986. In C. A. Corr and J. N. McNeil (Eds.), *Adolescence and Death*, New York: Springer Publishing Company.

Here are some suggestions from Joan N. McNeil (1986, pp. 197–198) about improving family communication about death:

1. Adults must usually take the lead at least in heightened awareness of the teenager's concerns about death and in openness to discussion of anything that the teenager feels like exploring.
2. Listen actively and perceptively, keeping your attention on the other person and the apparent feelings underlying his or her words.
3. Accept the other's feelings as real, important, and "normal."
4. Use supportive responses that reflect your acceptance and understanding of what the teenager is trying to say.

5. Project a belief in the other person's worth by indicating that you are not attempting to solve his or her problems, but are instead trying to help the adolescent find his or her own solutions.
6. Be willing to take time to enjoy each other's company and to provide frequent opportunities for talking together.

Introduction to Adulthood

We have already observed that one of the main problems with following a developmental scheme in the explanation of how people think, feel, and integrate life's experiences is that there are so many possible combinations of factors in any given life. The longer one lives, the more complex the picture becomes as the probability of additional factors influencing a particular person increases.

Caution is needed when attempting to generalize about what is true concerning any stage of life and especially when looking at people beyond the adolescent stage of life. The premise behind this caution is that research findings describing a particular population, age group, or cross section of people should not be seen as more than a description of that particular sample of people. Research findings are influenced by the theoretical approach of the researcher and limitations of present knowledge, methodologies, and conclusions.

Another implication of this attitude toward understanding adulthood is that accurate conclusions would be drawn concerning any one person at any stage of life if more attention were paid to the many forces and features of that particular person's life history. Other limitations to studying adults' concepts of death include the lack of a satisfactory definition of "maturity" in relation to the concepts of death. There is no way to know when one has arrived at a "mature" concept of death.

Developmental psychologists also are limited in that they have not researched enough in the area of adulthood to draw firm conclusions about the changes in death conceptualization that might develop within an age category. For example, Freud concentrated on infancy and childhood. Erik Erikson was able to move far beyond Freud in describing theoretically how the person develops over the entire life span. Some **longitudinal studies** of men have been published, but few of women. The relationship between these studies and ways of conceiving death is seldom discussed, except in gerontological research. It seems to be assumed that we need to pay attention to only the death concepts of children and the elderly. Less research is taking place in the period of young adulthood to later middle age than in the periods of childhood and old age. The major exceptions to this trend are found in studies of mentally and terminally ill populations.

Finally, a limitation is faced in determining what "adult" actually means. Biologically, though we may stop growing any taller at a certain age, great changes continue in the human body. Psychologically, it is even more difficult to arrive at any definition of adulthood that will be generalizable to a significant percentage of the population. One must conclude that the word *developmental* takes on a more individualistic character. Thus, one should expect that age will be less influential in explaining death conceptualizations for adult populations than for other age groups.

Ecclesiastes 3:1

For everything there is a season,
  and a time for every matter under the heaven,
  a time to be born, and a time to die;
  a time to plant, and a time to pluck up what I planted;
  a time to kill, and a time to heal;
  a time to break down, and a time to build up;
  a time to weep, and a time to laugh;
  a time to mourn, and a time to dance;
  a time to cast away stones, and a time to gather stones together;
  a time to embrace, and a time to refrain from embracing;
  a time to seek, and a time to lose;
  a time to keep, and a time to cast away;
  a time to rend, and a time to sew;
  a time to keep silence, and a time to speak;
  a time to love, and a time to hate;
  a time for war, and a time for peace.

The Holy Bible, Revised Standard Version, 1962, New York: Oxford University Press.

Young Adulthood

From the discussion of the development of the adolescent's intellectual understanding of death, one could expect the young adult, described generously by Strauss and Howe (1991) as encompassing the ages of 22 to 43, to have a good grasp of the universality, inevitability, and finality of death. The young adult should know, at least intellectually, that death is an entirely possible event for anyone at any moment, yet death likely seems far away to most young adults, especially during the early years of young adulthood. Certainly, the untimely death in 1997 of Princess Diana at the age of 36 forced many young adults to think about death, if only for a few days. Unless they are forced to do so, we should not expect that all young adults would normally think of death constantly nor take it into consideration with each decision of importance.

REMEMBER DEATH

In his book entitled *Man's Concern With Death,* historian Arnold Toynbee (1968) wrote:

> From the moment of birth there is the constant possibility that a human being may die at any moment, and inevitably this possibility is going to become an accomplished fact sooner or later. Ideally, every human being ought to live each passing moment of his life as if the next moment were going to be his last. He ought to be able to live in the constant expectation of immediate death and to live like this, not morbidly, but serenely. Perhaps this may be too much to ask of any being.

Members of certain monastic Christian orders have practiced greeting each other daily with the words, "Remember death!" The fact that one tends to recoil from such a practice, however, is evidence that one would rather not take this advice.

The young adult especially would appear to reject the advice to remember death. At this stage of life, one is just entering the arena of a somewhat independent life where capabilities and skills can be tested and pride can be taken in positive results. Hopes, aspirations, challenges, and preparation for success in life are the focus at this age. This means that dealing with dying or death would mean to face rage, disappointment, frustration, and despair (Pattison, 1977).

The 4 types of death most salient for young adults are abortion, the death of a child, death from AIDS, and death by violence, according to Judith Stillion (1995, p. 310). The death of a grandparent is also a common event for young adults, but the deaths of the elderly do not violate young adults' sense of a just world because such deaths are generally viewed as being in the natural order of things. Abortion, however, is a special, very personal, emotional issue. The death of a child after birth seems unjust. AIDS is threatening because it "strikes at the very heart of their ability to work and procreate," primary tasks for this age group (Stillion, 1995, p. 310). Males in this age category are dying by violence, a situation which seems so unnecessary and wasteful.

Young adults struck by serious disability or life-threatening disease have demonstrated that an almost universal sense of injustice and resultant anger exist when a young person is forced to "remember death." Along with all of the international political issues involved, the protests against the Vietnam War in the '60s and '70s probably contained a good deal of repugnance to the idea of risking one's personal future at this stage of life. A walk through the wards of any major veterans' hospital or pediatric oncology floor would soon convince the most stubborn observer that significant physical and mental losses, and death itself, seem most abhorrent when suffered by adolescents or young adults.

THE NOVICE PHASE

Daniel Levinson and colleagues (1978) labeled the young adult stage the "novice phase" because there is a strong sense of the need to learn, practice, and train oneself in the art of reaching one's fullest potential as a person and contributor to self-fulfillment, family, and society. Achieving something worthwhile would be devastatingly contradicted by any thought of serious limitation, sickness, or death.

Lowenthal, Thurnher, and Chiriboga (1975) evaluated 216 people grouped in 4 stages of the life cycle: high school seniors, young newlyweds, middle-aged parents, and an older group about ready to retire. Each person was asked specific questions concerning concepts and thoughts about death. Older people thought of death mainly in connection with specific and personal circumstances, such as the death of a friend, whereas younger people were likely to have death thoughts in response to general events such as accidents, earthquakes, or war.

Again, it is evident that though age may have some influence over the way that one thinks, individual circumstances and external forces have a more powerful influence upon one's thoughts about death. The older that one grows, the more apparent it becomes that one needs to reflect on life as much as one needs to engage in it. Such

Table 4.1

Acquired Immunodeficiency Syndrome (AIDS) Deaths by Age, Sex and Ethnicity: 1982 to 1994

Characteristic	Number		Percent Distribution	
	1982–94*	1994	1994	1982–94
Total**	258,658	31,212	100.0	100.0
Age (in years)				
13–19	850	112	.4	.3
20–29	44,770	4,868	15.6	17.3
30–39	117,759	14,334	45.9	45.5
40–49	64,639	8,396	26.9	25.0
50–59	21,415	2,550	8.2	8.3
60+	9,225	952	3.1	3.6
Sex				
Male	229,450	26,660	85.4	88.7
Female	29,619	4,620	14.8	11.5
Race/Ethnicity				
White	137,602	14,929	47.8	53.2
Black	82,556	11,453	36.7	31.9
Hispanic	36,244	4,488	14.4	14.0
Indian	537	97	.3	.2
Asian	1,750	280	.9	.7

* Includes deaths prior to 1982
**Includes other race/ethnicity groups not shown separately

SOURCE: U.S. Centers for Disease Control, Atlanta, GA. Taken from U.S. Bureau of the Census, *Statistical Abstract of the United States,* 1995 (115th ed.). Table 130. Washington, DC: U.S. Government Printing Office, 1995.

a practice can provide the individual with greater life satisfaction. As one moves into middle adulthood, however, it can have both positive and negative results.

ACQUIRED IMMUNODEFICIENCY SYNDROME (AIDS)

AIDS has become the leading cause of death among Americans aged 25 to 44 (Altman, 1995). One of the biggest difficulties facing the majority of persons with AIDS is the reversal of normal life development (Werth, 1995). Nearly 90 percent of persons with AIDS are between the ages of 20 and 49 (CDC, 1993). Though far more deaths in the Third World are due to diseases of childhood (respiratory disease, diarrhea, and measles), AIDS kills young adults at a high rate (see Table 4.1). These are the people whom a developing economy most needs and for whose training it has already paid ("Poor Man's Plague," 1991). It is sometimes said that AIDS is a disease of the poor, and in the developed world this is becoming the case. In the United States, it is in the inner cities that AIDS is spreading fastest. In poor countries, however, AIDS is often a disease of the relatively rich.

The age group with the greatest percentage of AIDS cases is 30 to 39 years. AIDS is affecting blacks proportionately more than it is affecting whites: Blacks make up 12 percent of the total population of the United States, yet approximately one third of AIDS cases are African Americans (see Table 4.1). Andrew Sullivan (1990, p. 22) noted in talking to minority men with AIDS that it was hard to avoid the impression that the level of denial is measurably greater, the pain more intense, and the isolation more complete than among whites. One gay black man said, "By being black, I'm separated from the white gay community, and by being gay, I'm separated from the African American community."

Not only is AIDS a devastating disease, but for individuals in the gay community, support is literally dying out. At a regional sociology meeting discussing AIDS, one of the other panelists, who happened to be gay and HIV positive, noted that of his immediate group of 40 friends, all but 6 had died of AIDS within a short time. Not only was he saddened, but he had few friends left with whom to share his grief. A similar account is noted in a recent study of the psychosocial impact of multiple deaths from AIDS (Viney et al., 1992, p. 152) by one of the participants:

> I've been counting them up. You know, I've lost 50 people, friends and acquaintances, since this AIDS epidemic started. I've been to that number of funerals in the past few years. And now my lover is ill.

The psychosocial functioning of people who are coping with these problems is similar to that of people who are coping with any severe illness: higher than average levels of anxiety, depression, directly and indirectly expressed anger, and helplessness (Viney et al., 1992, p. 153). Thus, for some young adults today, AIDS is a reckoning force bringing death into focus through personal experience.

Middle-Aged Adulthood

Although there appears to be no agreement among social scientists as to the exact beginning of middle age, most seem to suggest that this period of life starts between ages 40 and 45. The U.S. Census Bureau defines middle age as being ages 45 to 64, whereas Vera in the Broadway play *Mame* describes middle age as being "somewhere between 40 and death." Middle-aged individuals are sometimes referred to as the "sandwich generation" because they may be supporting and/or caring for their own children as well as for their parents. They are "caught between" these two groups.

Carl Jung (1923) suggested that the primary goal of the second half of life is to confront death. Jung (1971) believed that middle adulthood is the time of greatest growth for most people—a time of integration of undeveloped dimensions of personality. He described the major task of the middle years as reassessing and giving up the fantasy of immortality and omnipotence that carries us through earlier years when our own death is incomprehensible. Through the increasing awareness of body changes, loss of significant others, and children moving toward independence, we shift from a future-oriented perspective to an inescapable confrontation—a conscious awareness of death and mortality (Douglas, 1991). Erik Erikson's theory of ego development (1963) in these years suggests a concern for the next generation and an acknowledgment of mortality.

For the person who has lived 40 or 50 years, life brings with it the advantages of experience. Promotion to supervisor, foreman, or analogous status rankings in one's work or social milieu demonstrates that one gains greater political and social power during middle age. Not everyone is promoted, however, and even those who are, as well as their less fortunate colleagues, become gradually aware that physical vitality has now begun to wane.

Robert Fulton and Greg Owen (1988, p. 380) describe this group born after World War II (Baby Boomers) as primarily experiencing death at a distance. Unlike earlier generations, they were likely born in hospitals and no longer likely to die from infectious diseases. Unlike their parents and grandparents, this Baby Boom generation experienced the maximum benefits of an urbanized and technologically advanced society. Fulton and Owen further note that as the commercial meat processing industry removed the slaughtering of animals from the home, so did modern health-care institutions shield this group from general exposure to illness and death. Death became invisible and abstract. This generation was the first in which a person could reach adulthood with only a 5 percent chance that an immediate family member would die.

With an estimated 77 million Baby Boomers reaching the age of 50 between 1996 and 2015 (Cox, 1996), however, a funeral home in Toronto, Ontario, recently held an open house as a marketing ploy aimed at the middle aged (O'Hara, 1996). It is likely that death will become a major topic, perhaps an obsession, with many people of this generation. Hali Weiss (1995) predicts that the Baby Boomers will demand more meaningful deaths and burials in the 2000s, just as they took control of the childbirth experience in the 1970s. With cremation rates rising, a gradual rejection of traditional burial practices is on the horizon, notes Weiss.

Thanks to improved diets, healthier lifestyles, and unprecedented advances in medical care, the Baby Boomers are living longer than their parents did. But even nonsmokers who fasten their seat belts, exercise regularly, and eat plenty of vegetables must die eventually, notes Hank Cox (1996). The images of "being struck down" in one's prime and of the "untimely accident or death" are pervasive for this age group (Purtilo, 1990). Denial, hostility, and depression are factors that often accompany an illness of the middle aged, notes Purtilo.

THE PANIC BEGINS

The "panic" begins when one realizes that the idealized self, with its accomplishments and fulfillments dreamed of for so many years, may not actually come to pass. Gail Sheehy (1976, p. 190) observes that earlier pangs of the panic begin for most men between the ages of 35 and 45 (the "deadline decade") when they confront the certainty of their own death for the first time. Those whose job or self-concept depends upon youthful physical vigor especially suffer from this recognition of possible unfulfilled dreams. No amount of jogging reverses the effects of time. No patent medicine can undo the damage from wear and tear. The only hope is to make the best of what energies and experience remain and to focus on what one does best.

Individuals in the middle years, noting the occasional deaths of their peers, may begin an exercise program to hopefully contribute to longevity. For example, ethicist Ruth Purtilo (1990, p. 251) overheard a middle-aged man, who for years had enjoyed running just for the sport of it, tell his friend, "Yeah, my running will probably guarantee that I live 5 years longer, but I will have spent that 5 years running!" With heredity being a given, an individual can at least try to increase longevity by behavior and eating habits. Exercise, though it takes time, may contribute to a prolongation of life and may indeed help to make the "last of life the best to be."

As noted in chapter 1, cardiovascular disease is the number 1 killer in the United States, and men are especially prone to heart attacks. As individuals, we have some control over heart disease. The probability of a heart attack occurring is associated with the presence of several risk factors (Purtilo, 1990, p. 243): elevated levels of blood lipids (cholesterol, triglycerides), obesity, hypertension, cigarette smoking, family history of heart disease, gout, diabetes, physical inactivity, cardiac type-A personality, and living in an area where the drinking water is soft. Many of these factors can be controlled through behavior and environment.

Those whose strengths lie in intellectual and social skills will be less threatened because there is a cultural-social clock that one is able to impose over the biological clock (Neugarten, 1968). This seems to make more actual difference in the way that one lives and how much satisfaction one is able to derive from life. Jack Riley (1968) found a stronger correlation between education and more positive views concerning death than between age and positive death views. Stated negatively, people with less education appear more often to have more negative views concerning death. One must remember, however, that a correlation does not prove a causal connection. The following reading suggests that education, in particular death education, helped this former student in coping with the death of her husband (she was in her early 60s).

According to developmental theorists, death is a salient issue for midlife adults. Indeed, one of the major midlife tasks to be completed is to accept death as a reality (Waskel, 1995). Failing health, deaths of parents, loss of close friends, and changes in physical appearance contribute to a heightened awareness of death. Midlifers watch

---

Dear Dr. Dickinson,

Recently, I was fortunate enough to be in your death and dying class. On September 14th my husband died unexpectedly of a heart attack. As for the coping, understanding, and emotional humanistic processes I experienced, I'm most grateful for the valuable lessons I learned from both your textbook and class lectures which supported my acceptance of a natural ending phase of life.

Probably the most immediate, meaningful, and personal course of action my spouse and I took after I completed your class was to honestly address our respective concerns regarding procedures to follow after our deaths. However, I did not believe that if I were the one that was left to carry out his wishes for "cremation, no obit, private family-only graveside service" that I could courageously abort religiously ethnic family expectations and ignore the grandiose funeralization steps with which I was more familiar. Yet, it became apparent that after 37 years of confident shared decision-making views, coupled with academic, positive death conceptualization

(continued)

their peers die quick deaths from cardiovascular disease and prolonged deaths from cancer, thus fitness becomes a necessity to help cope with the increasingly familiar threat of death in their own lives (Stillion, 1995, p. 314). As long as one's parents are living, there is a buffer between the person and death—one's parents are "supposed" to die first. After one's parents die, however, this buffer is gone, and one's own generation becomes the genealogical line of descent to die.

The death of a parent can have a profound effect on the ways that adult siblings deal with each other, observes Lawrence Kutner (1990). Adult siblings may experience intense emotions as they reevaluate the meaning of family and their roles within it. The death of a parent, especially the second parent, often accentuates a pattern already existing—as siblings grow older, good relationships become better, and rotten relationships become worse. The death of a second parent often changes the focal point of family rituals such as organizing Thanksgiving or other significant holiday celebrations, notes Kutner. While the parents are alive, the relationships between siblings tend to be balanced as compared with the unbalanced parent-child relationship; yet when parents die, one sibling tends to break out of this balanced relationship (Kutner, 1990).

Joan Douglas (1991, p. 135), in studying reactions of middle-aged persons to the death of their parents, concluded that for many, the integration of the loss of a parent involves confronting the loss of parental power and the reality of one's own mortality as part of the developmental process. The tension created by the need to both sever and maintain the parent-child bond and to face one's own death without giving way to despair forced many to move to a new perspective—a new level of integration.

In analyzing the relationships between death anxiety, age, developmental concerns, and socioeconomic status in a sample of 74 middle-aged women, Richardson and Sands (1987) found that developmental factors were the salient issues with death concern, death as interpersonal loss, and death as a dimension of time. Age was the

(continued from previous page)
factors, that I was able to accomplish my husband's wishes for his last rite of passage. My deepest thanks for being responsible for instilling in me the reality of death which enabled my actions for his wishes to proceed with dignity.

The day after the burial was a beautiful, sunny day. We all went to the beach and carried on like the Patriarch was still with us. We replaced our grief with joy, much the way my husband would have preferred. Unusual it is that a gathering in the name of grief can open a way for a form of guiltless enjoyment as long as the endeared mourners will allow it to happen. You need to know that it's because of people like you and your concern for all humanity in dealing with the final exit that is responsible for empowering me to accept my husband's walkover from a physical to a spiritual world.

Best regards,

Rose Nygren

Extracted from a personal letter to the author, October 26, 1994.

sole predictor of death anticipation, and death denial and income were significant with death as physical. No variable predicted death as depressing. These results revealed the multidimensionality of death attitudes and the significance of considering both developmental and socioeconomic influences in predicting death attitudes.

A MORE PHILOSOPHICAL OUTLOOK DEVELOPS

Elliott Jacques (1965) observed that awareness of death changes people's lives in middle age, causing them to become more philosophical about their lives and to reevaluate values and priorities. In the process of confronting their own mortality, people deepen their capacities for love and enjoyment and ultimately acquire more meaning in their lives. Carl Jung (1933) also believed that adults become more introspective and concerned with meaning during midlife and concluded that they experience an inner transformation after recognizing previously suppressed aspects of their personality. He maintained that those who successfully come to grips with life become more individuated.

Daniel Levinson and colleagues in *The Seasons of a Man's Life* (1978, p. 215) learned from data gathered from men in their study that death for middle-aged men is often contemplated:

> At mid-life, the growing recognition of mortality collides with the powerful wish for immortality and the many illusions that help to maintain it. A man's fear that he is not immortal is expressed in his preoccupation with bodily decline and his fantasies of imminent death. At the most elemental level, he feels that he is fighting for survival. He is terrified at the thought of being dead, of no longer existing as this particular person.

A recent personal correspondence (Dickinson, 1996) in the late autumn from a relative in her 50s reflects on the changing season of the year and, accordingly, on changes in the life cycle with the passing of time:

> When the leaves began falling we covered the pond with latticework and screens on top. . . . The fish seem lively still but soon the cold weather will plunge them into dormancy. I feel fairly dormant myself. I have such trouble getting up early in the morning. I think hibernation is slipping up on me. As I look out the window I realize it has only been a short while since the bright leaves were infant buds and I marveled at spring. Probably the mirror would tell me the same thing.

Age differences in types of death concerns were observed by Stricherz and Cunnington (1982). The middle aged emphasized the pain of dying and dying before being ready. The young adults focused on losing persons they cared for, and the elderly worried about being helpless, taking a long time to die, and having to depend on others. This study found that all age groups consider death, but they do so in different ways and contexts.

Middle-aged adults are aware of getting closer to the "day of reckoning" and will need to evaluate values, meanings, and sense of self-worth in the face of finitude. The individual becomes increasingly conscious of thoughts of painful death, the dying process, and of ceasing to be as a person. An awareness develops of the meaning of absence to significant others—spouse, children, and others.

Thus, death at this point in life often carries with it some of the same sense of injustice and anger that the younger adult experiences with thoughts of death. Now, however, these thoughts are tempered with the recognition that many more forces exist that could bring death "home" to the individual.

PERSONAL GROWTH CONTINUES

Although the mature adult needs to give up fantasies of immortality, omnipotence, and grandiosity, there still needs to be a sense of accomplishment—a fulfillment of oneself and one's plans for family and personal enterprises. Consciousness of time and death, therefore, makes little difference for the middle-aged adult. One strives to put all of one's skills and experiences to the best possible use.

After one is into the decade of the 50s, a turning point is reached at which one's finitude becomes even more evident. One develops an increasing consciousness that one no longer measures time from birth as much as one measures time until death or until the end of one's most productive years. Focusing upon what one wants most to do before retirement or death causes one to avoid those things considered extraneous and/or uninteresting. All of this is not to say that increase in age means cessation of personal growth. To the contrary, as long as there is life, growth can occur for the individual who has the will to live and the will to give of self to others.

However, all is not lost in middle age. Bernice Neugarten (1968) points to evidence that people in their 40s see the world in a more positive way than do those in their 60s. Possibilities for the 60-year-old are more likely to be faced in passive modes of coping than in active modes. She suggests that women tend to cope increasingly in affective and expressive terms, whereas men at this stage increasingly employ abstract and cognitive modes of coping.

Older Adulthood

Death is expected for the elderly person, notes Robert Kastenbaum (1992b). Indeed, in contemporary American society, death is primarily something that happens in old age. Almost two thirds of the 2 million persons who will die in the United States this year will be 65 years of age or older (Morgan, 1995, p. 34). Sweeting and Gilhooly (1991) state that death is seen as appropriate for the very elderly who have lived their allotted span of life. They also note that the elderly are more likely than other members of society to be living alone and are unlikely to be working.

Although some have observed that "growing old is hell," others look forward to the autumn of their lives. As Goethe stated, "To grow old is in itself to enter upon a new venture." An aging professional athlete noted that growing old is really mind over matter—as long as you do not mind, it does not matter. In the movie *Citizen Kane* Mr. Bernstein said to Mr. Thompson, a reporter, "Old age. It's the only disease, Mr. Thompson, that you don't look forward to being cured of." Thus, individuals tend to have different reactions to growing old.

Another division of old age has appeared in recent years—a division between the young-old and the old-old (Neugarten, 1974). The young-old are in the age group of 55 to 75; the old-old are 75 and over. Neugarten pictures the young-old as possessing relatively good health, education, purchasing power, free time, and being politically involved.

The young-old are distinguished from the middle aged primarily by the fact of retirement. Whereas 65 has been the marker of old age since the beginning of the Social Security system, age 55 is becoming a meaningful lower age limit for the young-old because of the lowering age of retirement. Obviously, employment and health status have a tremendous effect upon placement in either category.

Life can be compared with a train traveling through a tunnel. There is a point at which the train is leaving the tunnel rather than entering it. As older relatives and friends die, one cannot help but become aware that he or she is not immune to death. As noted earlier, when no older generation exists, and the members of one's own generation die with increasing frequency, the scarcity of time becomes a reality. Therefore, for the person over the age of 60, the end of the tunnel is in sight.

The following letter, sent to the author and his wife from Lucie Reid, suggests that the "end of the tunnel is in sight" for her. She seems accepting of the fact and ready to die.

The majority of individuals in this age group born in the earlier part of the 20th century were reared on farms or in nonurban environments. For those who lived through the Great Depression, they often had cause to wonder where tomorrow's meal would come from. Robert Fulton and Greg Owen (1988, p. 380) note that illness, dying, and death took place at home and were observed by children and adults alike. Animals were slaughtered for food. Death was visible, immediate, and real. Fulton and Owen observe that to an extent these individuals had lived in terms of the simple round of life known historically to humankind: birth, copulation, and death.

My Dear Children,

This seems a strange gift for this time of the year. This lovely ball was given me by the friend who made it, and I want it to hang for many years on your happy tree. If I live until another Christmas, I would be 97 which is too long to stay in this devastated world which my generation has made. I am ready to depart any time. God has been wonderfully good to me. I have had all any one could ask for-love and care and now every comfort in this shadowing time. I say with Cardinal Newman, "So long thy hand hath led me, sure it will lead me on."

I know that you are leading lives full of meaning, and my blessings go with this bright ball. I believe a circle has no beginning and no end.

Sincerely your friend,

Lucie Reid

After living next door to Lucie Reid for two years in western Pennsylvania, we moved. For several years after that, my wife and I received a beautiful hand-decorated Christmas ball from her. The ball usually arrived in mid-December. One year, however, the ball arrived in mid-July. Her letter was enclosed in the package. Lucie Reid died before "another Christmas."

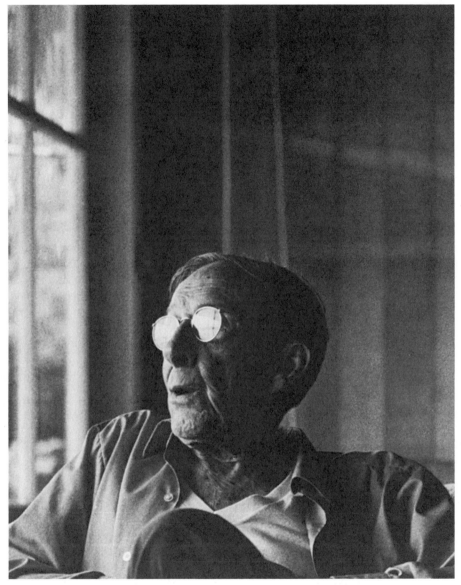

People can and do manage much of what happens within their own minds. The life review is triggered by the realization that one has reached the end of life and that death is near. The life review serves to prepare a person for death; preparation that may decrease fears of dying and death. At any stage of the life cycle, one can be helped to face both life and death more positively.

ERIKSON'S FINAL STAGE OF LIFE

Erik Erikson's theory of human development (1959) divides the life cycle into 8 stages from infancy to old age. Each stage of development presents a crisis in understanding of oneself, of one's purposes, and of relationships with others. The developmental task at each stage is to resolve the crisis successfully; then the person can progress to the next stage of maturity. The 8 stages are infancy, early childhood, play age, school age, adolescence, young adulthood, adulthood, and **senescence.** Erikson argues that a person must have been successful to some degree in resolving the 7 crises that come before in order to resolve the 8th stage—senescence. The task of the final stage of life is to achieve integrity—a conviction that one's life has meaning and purpose and that having lived has made a difference. The following death notice of Mr. William Bradford in 1752 (*Philadelphia Gazette*) suggests that he probably "made a difference" in the lives of many individuals and likely reached senescence.

William Bradford
May 25, 1752

Last Sunday Evening departed this Life, Mr. WILLIAM BRADFORD, Printer, of this City, in the 94th Year of his Age: He came into America upwards of 70 Years ago, and landed at the Place where Philadelphia now stands, before that City was laid out, or a House built there: He was Printer to this Government upwards of 50 Years; and was a Man of great Sobriety and Industry;—a real Friend to the Poor and Needy; and kind and affable to all: His Temperance was exceedingly conspicuous, and he was almost a Stranger to Sickness all his Life: He had left off Business for several Years past, and being quite worn out with old Age and Labour, his Lamp of Life went out for want of Oil.

Philadelphia Gazette archives, CD-ROM edition, Folio II, 1751–1752, Item 1842.

Hannelore Wass (1979, p. 186) observed that the **life review,** a concept advanced by Robert Butler, is in close harmony with Erikson's 8th stage of the life cycle. The life review is triggered by the realization that one has reached the end of life and that death is near. The life review serves to prepare a person for dying—preparation that may decrease the fear of death.

DEATH TABOO AND THE ELDERLY

The death taboo is still practiced with respect to the elderly in the United States (Wass, 1979, p. 190). Many people are reluctant to talk about death with the elderly. As noted in chapter 1, the only taboo topic for elderhostel programs in the United States is dying and death. Because the elderly are nearing the end of their life cycle and dying is in the near future, it is commonly thought that older adults would not want to talk about death. I can remember an undergraduate student of mine in the early 1970s wanting to do a research project on the elderly's attitudes toward dying. Even I thought at the time that the elderly might not wish to talk about death. Was I ever wrong! She had a 100 percent response from those she interviewed.

Hannelore Wass (1979, p. 190) speculates as to why death is avoided with the elderly. Some people believe that younger adults avoid the topic with the elderly because it reminds the young adults too chillingly of their own eventual demise. Others believe that the topic is avoided so as not to upset an older person unduly. Others think that death is avoided with the elderly because of some kind of embarrassment, particularly when an inheritance is involved.

To show how the topic of death is still somewhat elusive to many in our society, several years ago I was invited to speak on dying and death at the annual spring banquet of the local American Association of Retired Persons chapter. As we were sitting at the head table overlooking the 150 members, the moderator for the banquet turned to me just moments before he was to introduce me and said, "I told them you were going to speak on the aging process. Would you mind introducing your topic of death and dying to them?" Apparently, the moderator, who invited me to speak on dying and death, could not bring himself to disclose the topic beforehand. So he had announced my topic to be the aging process. Indeed, the topic of dying and death is still taboo for some individuals.

DEATH FEARS

Like their younger contemporaries, older adults have some anxieties and concerns as they approach death. They fear a long, painful, and disfiguring death, or death in a vegetative state, hooked to sophisticated machines while hospital bills devour their insurance and savings. They fear that their families will be overburdened by their prolonged care and the expense that it involves. And they dread losing control of their lives by consignment to nursing homes (McCarthy, 1991, pp. 505–506). Empirical evidence suggests older persons think of death more often than do younger adults but that older persons appear to have less fear and anxiety concerning death (Bee, 1992; Kalish & Reynolds, 1981; Leming, 1980).

According to Robert Neimeyer and David Brunt (1995, p. 65), several factors account for the elderly's more positive attitude toward dying and death: Their attitude could reflect the diminished quality of elderly persons' health and lives; their greater religiosity; their more extensive experience in having worked through the death of parents, peers, and partners; or the fact that their expectation to live a certain number of years has been met.

Richard Dumont and Dennis Foss (1972) suggest that, because older people are more likely to have fulfilled their goals in life, they are less fearful of death. For others, death might threaten personal achievement. Those older people who have not fulfilled their goals are more likely to have either made their goals more modest or somehow to have rationalized their lack of achievement. It is also possible that older people come from an age cohort whose members were better socialized as children to deal with death. They are more likely to come from rural backgrounds and to have had earlier encounters with deaths of siblings, family members, friends, and animals.

Although the elderly tend to have less fear of death than younger groups, they have had more experience with death (Moss & Moss, 1989, p. 216). They have probably known more people who have died, have been to more funerals, and have visited more cemeteries than have younger persons. Thus, they may have become somewhat more able to imagine a world without them in it as they experience the

> ## Socrates on the Fear of Death
>
> To fear death is nothing other than to think oneself wise when one is not; for it is to think one knows what one does not know. No man knows whether death may not even turn out to be the greatest of blessings for a human being; and yet people fear it as if they knew for certain that it is the greatest of evil.
>
> "The Apology (The Defense of Socrates)" (p. 435), by Socrates, 1971. In W. H. D. Rouse (Trans.), *Great Dialogues of Plato,* Bergenfield, NJ: Mentor Books.

death of others and consider what they will leave behind them. Many older persons have, therefore, in some ways come to terms with their own finitude.

Hannelore Wass (1979, p. 193) reports that few studies have examined sex differences in the fear of death among the elderly. Most studies generally show no sex differences in noninstitutionalized, in institutionalized, and in acute **geriatric** patients. A study by Wass and Sisler (1978) of noninstitutionalized older persons, however, showed significant sex differences that indicated that women have more fear of death than do males. As Judith Stillion (1985) suggested in chapter 1, perhaps women have a greater tendency to admit troubling feelings. In a more recent study by Duff and Hong (1995) of 674 residents from West Coast retirement communities, however, women showed less anxiety than men. A possible explanation is that as the proportion of widows increases in the retirement community, a supportive subculture for widows may emerge that helps buffer them from anxiety over death, note Duff and Hong. In addition, the retirement community may be a very different environment and population, and thus not all observations derived from the outside society are applicable to the retirement community. When only institutionalized versus noninstitutionalized elderly have been studied to determine if death fears vary with these two populations, Wass (1979, p. 193) cites studies that show that the institutionalized elderly in nursing homes tend to be more fearful than those living out in the community in an apartment or house.

Wass (1979, pp. 193–194) further reports that some evidence shows that the widowed tend to be more fearful of death than are the elderly married or remarried. Persons living alone have greater fear of death than those living with a family. As noted earlier in this chapter, education seems to have an impact on views of death: The elderly with only a grade school education have a greater fear of death than do the elderly with a college education. The elderly with low incomes exhibit a greater fear of death than do those with higher incomes. High levels of death anxiety for the elderly seem to be associated with poor physical and mental health.

In a study of terminal cancer patients, Lund and Leming (1975) found that older patients had less anxiety concerning their diseases and terminal conditions than did younger patients. Older patients tended to experience greater depression, however.

There is evidence (Leming, 1980; McKenzie, 1980; Norman & Scaramelli, 1980) that differences in death anxiety and fear appear to be more a function of religiosity than age. Because older persons are more likely to be religious, a sense of comfort should be provided as they approach death. The older person is more likely to believe in an afterlife and to rely on a faith in God as a coping strategy in dealing with death. Duff and Hong's study (1995) of residents in West Coast retirement communities concluded that the ceremonial act of regular attendance at religious services is associated with lower death anxiety, whereas private religious practices such as prayer or scripture reading do not have a significant impact on death anxiety. A longitudinal study of elderly people in New Haven, Connecticut, by Idler and Kasl (1992) also reported that "public religious involvement" has a significant protective effect against functional disability, whereas "private religious involvement" does not. Years ago French sociologist Emile Durkheim in *The Elementary Forms of Religious Life* (1947) argued that it is the ceremonial acts that are mainly responsible for the life-enriching effects of religion.

Despite the preceding concerns of the elderly, many elderly Americans die peaceful and relatively painless deaths. A National Institute of Aging study (McCarthy, 1991, p. 506) of 1,000 persons over age 65 who had died concluded that their health did not deteriorate until fairly near the end in most cases. Over half were in good or excellent health a year before they died. Ten percent were in good health the day before. About one third knew that death was approaching.

Though Robert Kastenbaum (1992a) highlights the diversity of attitudes toward dying and death found in the elderly, he notes certain themes and characteristics found in three studies: Munnichs (1966) in the Netherlands, Weisman and Kastenbaum (1970) in the United States, and Kellehear (1990) in Australia. Munnichs's interviews with 100 men and women over age 70 revealed that fear did not dominate, relatively few were apprehensive about dying, and fewer were obsessed by the idea of death and finitude. Munnichs found that most had worked out some kind of accepting orientation toward death. Death was no longer a threatening stranger or mysterious external force. Kastenbaum (1992a, p. 9) notes that these individuals in Munnichs's study had become "philosophical" about death.

Likewise, in the study of hospitalized geriatric patients in the United States (Weisman & Kastenbaum, 1970), anxiety was not the predominant response to the prospect of dying and death. The ego integration hypothesis of Erikson and the life review theory of Butler were consistent with the pattern of findings. In the Australian study of 100 dying individuals, Kellehear found that most of the terminally ill people engaged in some form of personal preparation for death (funeral arrangements, for example) and seemed to have an implicit conception of the "good death" that emphasized looking after the needs of the survivors in a practical way.

THE PLACE OF DEATH

Death for the older person becomes a normal and expectable event. The crisis for the elderly is not so much death, but how and where the death will take place. The prospect of dying in a foreign place in a dependent and undignified state is a very distressing thought for older adults. They do not wish to be a financial or physical burden on anyone, yet the options of care may be limited.

The question of physically relocating the elderly to another place is a sensitive issue among **gerontologists** (Crandall, 1991, p. 561). Those favoring relocation believe that relocating older persons is often less detrimental than leaving them where they currently live. They believe that moving older persons from substandard facilities, for example, will be beneficial. Those opposed to relocation of the elderly argue that relocating is traumatic and will generally increase their risk of death.

A coroner's office investigator gathers routine information following a death in a nursing home. Approximately 80 percent of all deaths take place in institutional settings.

Although most elderly individuals would prefer to die in their homes in familiar surroundings, the majority continue to die in hospitals and nursing homes (Cox, 1996, p. 271). Marty Zusman and Paul Tschetter (1984) point out that to die at home requires substantial resources, including money, space, and time; thus the well-to-do are sometimes allowed to die at home because of their private control. Many people simply cannot afford the luxury of dying at home. Richard Kalish (1965) notes, however, that institutionalized settings are better equipped to handle dying individuals and that the family is removed from the considerable strain of caring for a dying family member in the home. Thus, although the elderly might prefer to die at home, most are not likely to be allowed to do so.

The elderly are more likely to be separated from family and friends as they die. For them, the dying process may involve a fear of isolation and loneliness. Younger terminally ill patients are usually more concerned about the fears of pain, indignity, and dependency in the dying process, the fear of leaving loved ones, and the fear of not accomplishing their goals (Leming, 1980).

In preparing to grow old, perhaps the words of Jenny Joseph's poem entitled "Warning" provide inspiration (see box on next page).

Conclusion

Psychosocial studies of developmental concepts of death are themselves in a stage of infancy. Significant progress is being made, however, in an understanding of how children and adolescents experience loss at various stages of their development. Adolescence is a particularly vulnerable period with regard to facing death. A strong sense of

Warning
Jenny Joseph

When I am an old woman I shall wear purple
   With a red hat which doesn't go, and doesn't suit me.
   And I shall spend my pension on brandy and summer gloves
   And satin sandals, and say we've no money for butter.
   I shall sit down on the pavement when I'm tired
   And gobble up samples in shops and press alarm bells
   And run my stick along the public railings
   And make up for the sobriety of my youth.
   I shall go out in my slippers in the rain
   And pick the flowers in other people's gardens
   And learn to spit.

You can wear terrible shirts and grow more fat
   And eat three pounds of sausages at a go
   Or only bread and pickle for a week
   And hoard pens and pencils and beermats and things in boxes.

But now we must have clothes that keep us dry
   And pay our rent and not swear in the street
   And set a good example for the children.
   We must have friends to dinner and read the papers.

But maybe I ought to practice a little now?
   So people who know me are not too shocked and surprised
   When suddenly I am old, and start to wear purple.

"Warning," by J. Joseph, 1987. In S. Martz (Ed.), *When I Am an Old Woman I Shall Wear Purple: An Anthology of Short Stories and Poetry,* Watsonville, CA: Papier-Mache Press.

injustice is not uncommon when one dies before reaching the fullest potential and opportunity to experience life.

Concepts of death are powerfully influenced by experience with death or threats of death. Mental health, anxiety management, and meaningfulness in life are the most powerful factors in developing concepts of death. Broad cultural-religious influences also enter significantly into each of these factors.

People can and do manage much of what happens within their minds. One gathers information and insights, helps self to cope, and gives aid to others in need. At whatever stage of the life cycle, one can be helped to face both life and death more positively.

More research is needed to explore the relationships between death conceptualizations, gender differentiation, and place within the adult life cycle. Some stereotypes concerning older men and women are being discredited, but our conclusions are tentative, and more empirical research is needed.

Growing older pushes one to depend more upon educational, intellectual, and social skills than upon physical prowess. Feeling that one is useful and contributes to the well-being of others, as well as having a healthy understanding of death, contributes significantly to meaningful living and dying. As Robert Kavanaugh (1972, p. 226) wrote:

> I am ashamed how little I know about death and dying, but never have I enjoyed life more, dreamed more beautiful dreams each night, than when I began having courage to begin facing death.

Some pessimism can be found in older people, but disengagement from life is not necessarily a universal trait. The fear of death lessens with age, but the thought of death increases. The way that time is used changes, as does the meaning that one finds in life's experiences. Yet, living a happy and meaningful life is one of the ways to develop a positive and healthy view of death. Perhaps Alex Keaton of the television show *Family Ties* best summed up the developmental approach to death when he said, "Children die with opportunities and dreams; old people die with achievements and memories."

Summary

1. An overall psychosocial theory acceptable to a majority of researchers is still lacking.
2. The older the person, the more complex is the task of understanding just what causes the person to think about death in a particular way.
3. During adolescence the sense of personal identity is most vulnerable, and concepts and feelings of death are powerfully influenced by that vulnerability.
4. The young adult stage has been labeled the "novice phase" because a strong sense of need to train oneself in the art of reaching one's fullest potential is contradicted by any thought of death.
5. Not only has AIDS become the major cause of death among 25- to 44-year-olds in the United States, but also for same sex-oriented HIV-positive individuals, their support group is literally dying out.
6. The "panic phase" begins during the middle years when one realizes that the idealized self that one longed to develop may not actually happen.
7. Research concerning the conceptualization of death in middle adulthood is difficult to find.
8. Most people are capable of thinking of death more often and more profoundly than they do, but psychological defenses sometimes prevent this from happening.
9. According to Erik Erikson, the task of the final stage of life, senescence, is to achieve integrity.
10. In the United States discussing death-related topics with the elderly is taboo.
11. The crisis of the elderly is not so much death, but rather how and where the death will take place.

Discussion Questions

1. What are some of the factors, other than age, that influence death conceptualizations? Why are these factors important in understanding the ways that people conceptualize death?
2. Why do high school and college students have a higher level of death anxiety than do junior high school students?
3. Both death education and sex education are viewed by many as problems. Cite any current trends that may suggest that death education and sex education are more in vogue in institutional settings today.
4. In your opinion, have death conceptualizations changed much in the past few decades? Do you see death conceptualizations changing much in the next few decades?
5. What are some of the limitations of the developmental approach to the understanding of death conceptualizations?
6. What are some death themes in contemporary adolescent music? How do you explain death themes in music?
7. How do you explain the popularity of some of the movies with brutal death scenes?
8. Why would young adults appear to reject the admonition to remember death?
9. Why would education tend to reduce one's anxiety about death?
10. Why does the death taboo exist with respect to the elderly in the United States?

Glossary

Adolescence: Stage of life commonly defined as the onset of puberty when sexual maturity or the ability to reproduce is attained.

AIDS: Acronym for *acquired immunodeficiency syndrome,* a lethal syndrome caused by a virus that damages the immune system and weakens the body's ability to fight bacteria.

Behaviorism: A school of psychology that focuses chiefly on overt behavior rather than on inner psychological dynamics that cannot be clearly identified or measured.

Death Anxieties/Death Fears: Learned emotional responses to death-related phenomena that are characterized by extreme apprehension.

Developmental Approach: Branch of social sciences concerned with interaction between physical, psychological, and social processes and with stages of growth from birth to old age.

Ego Psychologists: Theorists and therapists who moved away from Freud toward putting more emphasis in their therapy upon the coping strategies and strengths of the person than upon the more elusive dynamics of the libido and the unconscious.

Geriatrics: The study of the medical aspects of old age.

Gerontology: The study of the biological, psychological, and social aspects of aging.

Humanism: Psychological model that emphasizes an individual's phenomenal world and inherent capacity for making rational choices and developing to maximum potential.

Life Review: Robert Butler's term suggesting a reverence for what one was and for a time for judgment; looking back over one's life and perhaps tracing back one's steps in earlier years; a review of one's life, as death draws near; a therapeutic technique in helping the elderly.

Longitudinal Study: Method of scientific investigation in which selected measurements and observations are taken repeatedly over time in order to determine change, growth, or stability.

Psychoanalysis: A school of theory and therapy that concentrates upon the unconscious forces behind overt behavior, dealing principally with instinctual drives and their dynamics in the individual's inner psyche; uses as principal foci the interplay of transference and resistance between psychoanalyst and client.

Ritual: The symbolic affirmation of values by means of culturally standardized utterances and actions.

Senescence: Erik Erikson's last stage of the life cycle; its task is to achieve integrity, a conviction that one's life has meaning and purpose and that having lived has made a difference.

References

Altman, L. K. (1995, January 31). AIDS is now the leading killer of Americans from 25 to 44. *New York Times,* p. B8.

Becker, E. (1973). *The denial of death.* New York: The Free Press.

Bee, H. L. (1992). *The journey of adulthood.* New York: Macmillan.

Brody, J. A. (1989). Toward quantifying the health of the elderly. *American Journal of Public Health, 79,* 685–686.

Centers for Disease Control and Prevention. (1993, February). *HIV/AIDS Surveillance Report,* 1–23.

Cox, H. (1996, December 30). While the Grim Reaper toils, corporations reap big profits. *Insight,* 42–43.

Cox, H. G. (1996). *Later life: The realities of aging* (4th ed.). Upper Saddle River, NJ: Prentice-Hall.

Crandall, R. C. (1991). *Gerontology: A behavioral approach* (2nd ed.). New York: McGraw-Hill.

Death films popular, store manager says. (1985, December 13). *El Dorado Times,* p. 16.

Dickinson, C. W. (1996, October 19). Personal correspondence to the author.

Douglas, J. D. (1991). Patterns of change following parent death in midlife adults. *Omega, 22,* 123–137.

Duff, R. W., & Hong, L. K. (1995). Age density, religiosity and death anxiety in retirement communities. *Review of Religious Research, 37,* 19–32.

Dumont, R. G., & Foss, D. C. (1972). *The American view of death: Acceptance or denial?* Cambridge, MA: Schenkman Publishing.

Durkheim, E. (1915/1947). *The elementary forms of religious life.* Glencoe, IL: Free Press.

Erikson, E. (1959). Identity and the life cycle: Selected papers. *Psychological Issues, 1,* 1–171.

Erikson, E. (1963). *Childhood and society.* New York: Norton.

Feifel, H. (1959). *The meaning of death.* New York: McGraw-Hill.

Fulton, R., & Owen, G. (1988). Death and society in twentieth century America. *Omega, 18,* 379–394.

Ginsburg, H., & Opper, S. (1979). *Piaget's theory of intellectual development* (2nd ed.). Englewood Cliffs, NJ: Prentice-Hall.

Gordon, A. (1986). The tattered cloak of immortality. In C. A. Corr & J. N. McNeil (Eds.), *Adolescence and death* (pp. 16–29). New York: Springer Publishing Company.

Grollman, E. A. (1970). *Talking about death: A dialogue between parent and child.* Boston: Beacon Press.

Idler, E. L., & Kasl, S. V. (1992). Religion, disability, depression, and the timing of death. *American Journal of Sociology, 97,* 1052–1079.

Jacques, E. (1965). Death and the mid-life crisis. *International Journal of Psychoanalysis, 46,* 502–514.

Jung, C. (1923). *Psychological types.* London: Pantheon Books.

Jung, C. (1933). *Modern man in search of a soul.* New York: Harcourt and Brace.

Jung, C. (1971). The stages of life. In J. Campbell (Ed.), *The Portable Jung.* New York: Viking Press.

Kalish, R. A. (1965). The aged and the dying process: The inevitable decisions. *Journal of Social Issues, 21,* 87–96.

Kalish, R. A., & Reynolds, D. K. (1981). *Death and ethnicity: A psychocultural study.* Farmingdale, NY: Baywood.

Kastenbaum, R. (1986). Death in the world of adolescence. In C. A. Corr & J. N. McNeil (Eds.), *Adolescence and death* (pp. 4–15). New York: Springer Publishing Company.

Kastenbaum, R. (1992a, Spring). Death, suicide and the older adult. *Suicide and Life-Threatening Behavior, 22,* 1–14.

Kastenbaum, R. (1992b). *The psychology of death* (2nd ed.). New York: Springer Publishing Company.

Kavanaugh, R. E. (1972). *Facing death.* Baltimore: Penguin Books.

Kellehear, A. (1990). *Dying of cancer.* London: Harwood.

Koocher, G. P., O'Malley, J. E., Foster, D., & Gogan, J. L. (1976). Death anxiety in normal children and adolescents. *Psychiatric Clinics, 9,* 220–229.

Kutner, L. (1990, December 6). The death of a parent can profoundly alter the relationships of adult siblings. *New York Times,* p. B7.

Leming, M. R. (1980). Religion and death: A test of Homans's thesis. *Omega, 10,* 347–364.

Levinson, D. J., Darrow, C. N., Klein, E. B., Levinson, M. H., & McKee, B. (1978). *The seasons of a man's life.* New York: Alfred A. Knopf.

Lifton, R. J. (1976). The sense of immortality: On death and the continuity of life. In R. Fulton & R. Bendiksen (Eds.), *Death and identity* (Rev. ed.). Bowie, MD: Charles Press Publishers.

Lowenthal, M. F., Thurnher, M., & Chiriboga, D. (1975). *Four stages of life.* San Francisco: Jossey-Bass.

Lund, D. A., & Leming, M. R. (1975, October). *Relationship between age and fear of death: A study of cancer patients.* Paper presented at the Annual Scientific Meeting of the Gerontological Society, Louisville, KY.

McCarthy, A. (1991, September 13). The country of the old. *Commonweal, 118,* 505–506.

McKenzie, S. C. (1980). *Aging and old age.* Glenview, IL: Scott, Foresman, and Company.

McNeil, J. N. (1986). In talking about death: Adolescents, parents, and peers. In C. A. Corr & J. N. McNeil (Eds.), *Adolescence and death* (pp. 185–199). New York: Springer Publishing Company.

Morgan, J. D. (1995). Living our dying and our grieving: Historical and cultural attitudes. In H. Wass & R. A. Neimeyer (Eds.), *Dying: Facing the facts* (3rd ed.). Washington, DC: Taylor and Francis.

Moss, M. S., & Moss, S. Z. (1989). Death of the very old. In K. J. Doka (Ed.), *Disenfranchised grief: Recognizing hidden sorrow* (pp. 213–227). Lexington, MA: Lexington Books.

Munnichs, J. A. A. (1966). *Old age and finitude.* New York: S. Karger.

Neimeyer, R. A., & Brunt, D. V. (1995). Death anxiety. In H. Wass & R. A. Neimeyer (Eds.), *Dying: Facing the facts* (3rd ed., pp. 49–88). Washington, DC: Taylor and Francis.

Neugarten, B. L. (1968). *Middle age and aging: A reader in social psychology.* Chicago: University of Chicago Press.

Neugarten, B. L. (1974). Age groups in American society and the rise of the young-old. *Annals of the American Academy of Political and Social Science, 415,* 187–198.

Norman, W. H., & Scaramelli, T. J. (1980). *Mid-life: Developmental and clinical issues.* New York: Branner/Mazel Publishers.

Nygren, R. (1994, October 26). Personal correspondence to the author.

O'Brien, J. M., Goodenow, C., & Espin, O. (1991, Summer). Adolescents' reactions to the death of a peer. *Adolescence, 26,* 431–440.

O'Hara, J. (1996, July 1). The Baby Boomers confront mortality. *Maclean's, 109,* 64.

Pattison, E. M. (1977). *The experience of dying.* Englewood Cliffs, NJ: Prentice-Hall.

Piaget, J. (1958). *The growth of logical thinking from childhood to adolescence.* New York: Basic Books.

Poor man's plague. (1991, September 21). *The Economist, 320,* 21–23.

Purtilo, R. (1990). *Health professional and patient interaction* (4th ed.). Philadelphia: W. B. Saunders Company.

Richardson, V., & Sands, R. (1987). Death attitudes among mid-life women. *Omega, 17,* 327–341.

Riley, J. W. (1968). Attitudes toward aging. In M. W. Riley et al. (Eds.), *Aging and society: An inventory of research findings.* New York: Russell Sage Foundation.

Schachter, S. (1991). Adolescent experiences with the death of a peer. *Omega, 24,* 1–11.

Sheehy, G. (1976). *Passages: Predictable crises of adult life.* New York: E. P. Dutton.

Stillion, J. M. (1985). *Death and the sexes.* Washington, DC: Hemisphere/McGraw-Hill.

Stillion, J. M. (1995). Death in the lives of adults: Responding to the tolling of the bell. In H. Wass & R. A. Neimeyer (Eds.), *Dying: Facing the facts* (3rd ed., pp. 303–322). Washington, DC: Taylor and Francis.

Strauss, B., & Howe, R. (1991). *Generations: The history of America's future 1584 to 2069.* New York: William Morrow.

Stricherz, M., & Cunnington, L. (1982). Death concerns of students, employed persons, and retired persons. *Omega, 12,* 373–379.

Sullivan, A. (1990, December 17). Gay life, gay death. *The New Republic:* Vol. 210. pp. 19–25.

Sweeting, H. N., & Gilhooly, M. L. M. (1991). Doctor, am I dead? A review of social death in modern societies. *Omega, 24,* 251–269.

Toynbee, A. (1968). *Man's concern with death.* London: Hodder and Stoughton.

Viney, L. L., Henry, R. M., Walker, B. M., & Crooks, L. (1992). The psychosocial impact of multiple deaths from AIDS. *Omega, 24,* 151–163.

Waskel, S. A. (1995, March). Temperament types: Midlife death concerns, demographics and intensity of crisis. *The Journal of Psychology, 129,* 221–234.

Wass, H. (1979). Death and the elderly. In H. Wass (Ed.), *Dying: Facing the facts.* Washington, DC: Hemisphere.

Wass, H. M., Miller, D., & Redditt, C. A. (1991). Adolescents and destructive themes in rock music: A follow-up. *Omega, 23,* 199–206.

Wass, H., & Sisler, S. (1978, January). *Death concern and views on various aspects of dying among elderly persons.* Paper presented at the International Symposium on the Dying Human, Tel Aviv, Israel.

Weisman, A. D., & Kastenbaum, R. (1970). *The psychological autopsy: A study of the terminal phase of life.* New York: Behavioral Publications.

Weiss, H. (1995, September-October). Dust to dust: Transforming the American cemetery. *Tikkun Magazine,* 2–25.

Werth, J. L., Jr. (1995). Rational suicide reconsidered: AIDS as an impetus for change. *Death Studies, 19,* 65–80.

Zusman, M. E., & Tschetter, P. (1984). Selecting whether to die at home or in a hospital setting. *Death Education, 8,* 365–381.

Suggested Readings

Abel, E. K. (1991). *Who cares for the elderly? Public policy and the experiences of adult daughters.* Philadelphia: Temple University Press. Discusses family care for disabled elderly people, with emphasis on the changing role of women's caregiving responsibilities in the future.

Barry, R. L., & Bradley, G.V. (Eds.). (1991). *Set no limits: A rebuttal to Daniel Callahan's proposal to limit health care for the elderly.* A response to Callahan's Setting Limits in which he suggests possible age-based rationing schemes to deny medical care and treatment to the elderly when they reach the end of their "natural life span."

Conner, K. A. (1992). *Aging America: Issues facing an aging society.* Englewood Cliffs, NJ: Prentice-Hall. An exploration of the social challenges and concerns confronting American society.

Corr, C. A., & McNeil, J. N. (1986). *Adolescence and death.* New York: Springer Publishing Company. An excellent anthology composed of 17 chapters ranging from contemporary interactions of adolescents and death; coping with dying, grief, and bereavement; suicide and adolescents; prevention, intervention, and postvention; and annotated resources.

Cox, H. G. (1996). *Later life: The realities of aging* (4th ed.). Upper Saddle River, NJ: Prentice-Hall. An interdisciplinary approach to aging, with discussions of dying and death among the elderly.

Doka, K. J. (Ed.). (1989). *Disenfranchised grief: Recognizing hidden sorrow.* Lexington, MA: Lexington Books. This volume covers death in various stages of the life cycle and is written to help individuals to recognize losses and to better understand the pain that accompanies the loss of a significant other.

Solomon, D. H., Salend, E., Rahman, A. N., Liston, M. B., & Reuben, D. B. (1992). *A consumer's guide to aging.* Baltimore: Johns Hopkins University Press. A practical guide to assist the elderly with staying healthy, maintaining an emotional balance, planning a financial future, changing family roles, and living in the leisure lane.

Szinovacz, M., Ekerdt, D. J., & Vinick, B. H. (Eds.). (1992). *Families and retirement.* Newbury Park, CA: Sage Publications. This book covers such issues as marital relationships in retirement, extended kin relationships in retirement, and the timing of retirement.

Wass, H., & Neimeyer, R. A. (Eds.). (1995). *Dying: Facing the facts* (3rd ed.). Washington, DC: Taylor and Francis. This anthology, with 20 contributors, has especially good discussions of death in different stages of the life cycle.

Young, M., & Cullen, L. (1996). *A good death: Conversations with East Londoners.* London: Routledge. The authors' extensive interviews with cancer patients, diagnosed with only 3 to 4 months to live, are a sensitive, sociological account of what it is like to die of cancer in London today.

Related Web Sites

http://iul.com/raindrop/   Raindrop is a death education program for children of all ages.

http://207.49.29.206/gribin.htm   "What Do Adolescents Worry About: A Quantitative Study." Articles written by Kathy Smith Gribin.

http://www.win.bright.net/~cnelson/Motherloss.htm   Web site for Motherloss, a group started to help with the grieving issues for adult children of mothers who have died.

http://www.unicef.org/pon96/insuicid.htm   UNESCO Web site that provides international suicide rates of young adults.

http://www.paranoia.com/~real/suicide/links.html   Light for Life Foundation Yellow Ribbon Program. A program that provides educational material for American youth to prevent suicide by providing easy access to support services.

http://wonder.cdc.gov   Centers for Disease Control's prevention guidelines. This site has a number of papers on suicide prevention, particularly among American youth. Worth a look if you are an educator or health professional.

Chapter 5

Religion and Death Attitudes

Religion provided me with answers to problems I didn't even know I had.

—St. Olaf College student, 1977

Death radically challenges all socially objectivated definitions of reality—of the world, of others, and of self. . . . Death radically puts in question the taken-for-granted, "business-as-usual" attitude with which one exists in everyday life. . . . Religion maintains the socially defined reality by legitimating marginal situations in terms of an all-encompassing sacred reality.

—Peter Berger, *Sacred Canopy*

When one thinks of **religion** as a cultural system of meaning, an important question becomes relevant: Why did religion come into existence? Because this question attempts to discover the etiology of religious behavior and because we have no scientific record of the first religious activity, any answers must be speculative in nature. They are based on an *ex post facto* analysis in which universal human needs find fulfillment in a transcendent frame of reference. Such answers are also predicated on the assumption that humans have a need for religious expression. Saint Augustine said, "Thou hast made us for thyself, O God, and our hearts are restless until they find their rest in thee." This idea is also reflected in the following statement by Blaise Pascal, the 17th-century French mathematician-philosopher: "There is a God-shaped vacuum in the heart of each man, which cannot be satisfied by any created thing but only by God, the creator, made known through Jesus Christ." Such answers, however, raise another, more fundamental question of why humans have this need.

Death and the Origin of Religion

From a symbolic interactionist perspective (chapter 2), meanings are created and re-produced by humans. These meanings supply a base for activities and actions (behavior is in response to meanings) and provide order for the people who share a given culture. Peter Berger (1969) suggests that the human world has no order other than that created by humans. To live in a world without the order contributed by one's culture would force one to experience a meaningless existence. Sociologists refer to this condition as **anomie**—"without order."

Many situations in life challenge the order on which social life is based. Most of these situations are related to what Thomas O'Dea (1966) refers to as the three fundamental characteristics of human existence: uncertainty, powerlessness, and scarcity.

Uncertainty refers to the fact that human activity does not always lead to predictable outcomes. Even after careful planning, most people recognize that they will not be able to achieve all of their goals. Less optimistically, the 20th century's Murphy's Law states "Anything that can go wrong will go wrong." The human condition is also characterized by powerlessness. We recognize that there are many situations in life, and events in the universe, over which humans have no control—among these situations are death, suffering, coercion, and natural disasters. Finally, in *scarcity*, humans experience inequality with regard to the distribution of wealth, power, prestige, and other things that make a satisfying life. This inequality is the basis for the human experience of relative deprivation and frustration. The three experiences of uncertainty, powerlessness, and scarcity challenge the order of everyday life and are, therefore, marginal to ordinary experiences. According to O'Dea (1966, p. 5), such experiences "raise questions which can find an answer only in some kind of 'beyond' itself." Therefore, **marginal situations,** which are characteristic of the human condition, force individuals to the realm of the transcendent in their search for meaningful answers.

Peter Berger (1969, pp. 23, 43–44) claims that death is the marginal situation *par excellence:*

> Witnessing the death of others and anticipating his own death, the individual is strongly propelled to question the *ad hoc* cognitive and normative operating procedures of "normal" life in society. Death presents society with a formidable problem not only because of its obvious threat to the continuity of human relationships, but because it threatens the basic assumptions of order on which society rests. Death radically puts in question the taken-for-granted, "business-as-usual" attitude in which one exists in everyday life. Insofar as knowledge of death cannot be avoided in any society, legitimations of the reality of the social world *in the face of death* are decisive requirements in any society. The importance of religion in such legitimations is obvious.

It is religion, or a transcendent reference, that helps individuals remain reality-oriented when the order of everyday life is challenged. Contemplating death, we are faced with the fact that we will not be able to accomplish all of our goals in life. We

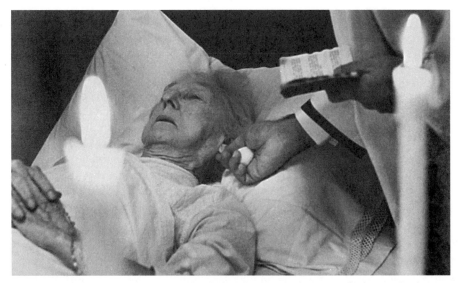

Religious-meaning systems help provide individuals with a transcendent point of reference whereby a loss created by death is compensated for by a system of other-worldly gains.

also realize that we are unable to extend the length of our lives and/or control the circumstances surrounding the experience and cause of our deaths. We are troubled by the fact that some must endure painful, degrading, and meaningless deaths, whereas others find *more* meaning and purpose in the last days of their lives than they experienced in the years preceding "the terminal period." Finally, the relative deprivation created by differential life spans raises questions that are unanswerable from a "this world" perspective.

Religious-meaning systems provide answers to these problems of uncertainty, powerlessness, and scarcity created by death. O'Dea (1966, pp. 6–7) illustrates this function of religion:

> Religion, by its reference to a beyond and its beliefs concerning man's relationship to that beyond, provides a supraempirical view of a larger total reality. In the context of this reality, the disappointments and frustrations inflicted on mankind by uncertainty and impossibility, and by the institutionalized order of human society, may be seen as meaningful in some ultimate sense, and this makes acceptance of and adjustment to them possible. Moreover, by showing the norms and rules of society to be part of a larger supraempirical ethical order, ordained and sanctified by religious belief and practice, religion contributes to their enforcement when adherence to them contradicts the wishes or interests of those affected. Religion answers the problem of meaning. It sanctifies the norms of the established social order at what we have called the "breaking points," by providing a grounding for the beliefs and orientations of men in a view of reality that transcends the empirical here-and-now of daily experience. Thus, not only is cognitive frustration overcome, which is involved in the problem of meaning, but also the emotional adjustments to frustrations and deprivations inherent in human life and human society are facilitated.

Religion as a Means of Providing Understanding of Death

Twenty-five years ago while on a class field trip to a funeral home, I complimented the funeral director on the beautifully painted pastoral scene hanging on a wall. He said it was a very unusual wall hanging, and he took it down to show me the framed, velvet, reverse side, which could also be displayed. He then took out a box containing a cross, a crucifix, and a star of David that could be hung on the velvet backing. The funeral director told the class that he changed the hanging whenever the religious affiliation of the deceased varied. Since the time of that field trip, I have become very conscious of the way that funeral homes extensively employ religious symbols in attempting to create a religious ambience. Consider the following:

1. Within the funeral home, "chapel" is the name given to the room where the funeral is held.
2. Most memorial cards have the 23rd Psalm on them.
3. The music that one hears on the sound systems within most funeral homes is religious in nature.
4. Wall hangings found in most funeral homes usually have religious content.
5. Funeral homes often provide Christmas calendars, complete with Bible verses and religious scenes, for religious groups and other interested members of the community.

Religious systems provide a means to reestablish the social order challenged by death. Our society has institutionalized the continued importance of religion by creating funeral **rituals** that have a religious quality about them.

There have been many attempts to explain the methods by which religion influences death meanings. Most discussion in this area has been strongly influenced by the theoretical writings of Malinowski, Radcliffe-Brown, and Homans.

Stated briefly, anthropologist Bronislaw Malinowski held that religion functions to relieve the anxiety caused by the crisis experiences that people encounter in their lifetimes. Religion has its origin in the crisis experience in death because it provides individuals with a means of dealing with extraordinary phenomena. Religion functions to bring about a restoration of normalcy for the individual.

Malinowski (1965, p. 70) says:

> Every important crisis of human life implies a strong emotional upheaval, mental conflict and possible disintegration. Religion in its ethics sanctifies human life and conduct and becomes perhaps the most powerful force of social control. In its dogmatics it supplies man with strong cohesive forces.

In elaborating on his theory that religion is the "great anxiety reliever," Malinowski (1965, p. 71) claims that "death, which of all human events is the most upsetting and disorganizing to man's calculations, is perhaps the main source of religious belief." From Malinowski's perspective, death is not only the greatest source of anxiety, but also the primary crisis event that calls forth religious behavior. Such theorizing leads us to ask the empirical question: Does religion provide humans with a solace in their attempts to cope with death? From the pragmatic perspective of the funeral industry, the question becomes: Are attempts on the part of the funeral home to merge religious and death meanings necessary and effective in assisting the bereaved?

Anthropologist A. R. Radcliffe-Brown (1965) disagrees with Malinowski's contention that religion functions primarily as an anxiety reliever, and claims, rather, that religion gives people fears and anxieties from which they would otherwise be free— the fear of spirits, God's judgment, the devil, hell. From Radcliffe-Brown's perspective, we would be led to expect that the nonreligious individual would have relatively less death anxiety and would cope better with his or her death and the deaths of others. We might also be led to the conclusion that from the point of reference of personal death anxiety, religious beliefs have **dysfunctional** consequences. George Homans has attempted to resolve this problem by declaring that both Malinowski and Radcliffe-Brown are correct in their theorizing about the role of religion in death anxiety. Rather than pitting Radcliffe-Brown against Malinowski, he argues that Radcliffe-Brown's hypothesis is a supplement to Malinowski's theory. According to Homans (1965), Malinowski is looking at the individual, Radcliffe-Brown at the community. Whereas Malinowski says that the individual tends to feel anxiety on certain occasions, Radcliffe-Brown says that society expects the individual to feel anxiety on certain occasions.

If we start with a psychological frame of reference (as does Malinowski), we focus our attention on the function of religion for the individual. From this perspective, patterns of social integration are contingent upon psychological processes—what works for the individual is functional for society. Therefore, because religious actions and rituals may help some individuals find meaning for death, and consequently dispel anomie in death-related situations, the social function of religion must be anxiety reduction. This point of view is illustrated in the following statement by Malinowski (1965, p. 72):

> Religion in its ethics sanctifies human life and conduct and becomes perhaps the most powerful force of social control. In its dogmatics it supplies man with strong cohesive forces. It grows out of every culture, because lifelong bonds of cooperation and mutual interest create sentiments, and sentiments rebel against death and dissolution. The cultural call for religion is highly derived and indirect but is finally rooted in the way in which the primary needs of man are satisfied in culture.

Turning to the perspective of Radcliffe-Brown, we find the following statement, which poses an alternative to Malinowski's reasoning (Radcliffe-Brown, 1965, p. 81):

> I think that for certain rites it would be easy to maintain with equal plausibility an exactly contrary theory, namely, that if it were not for the existence of the rite and the beliefs associated with it the individual would feel no anxiety, and that the psychological effect of the rite is to create in the individual a sense of insecurity and danger.

In this quotation, Radcliffe-Brown argues that religion might serve to increase anxiety for the individual rather than to reduce it, as Malinowski would contend. Radcliffe-Brown begins with a societal perspective and declares that the function of religion is to create a sense of anxiety that will maintain the social structure of the society:

> Actually in our fears or anxieties, as well as in our hopes, we are conditioned by the community in which we live. And it is largely by the sharing of hopes and fears, by

what I have called *common concern* in events or eventualities, that human beings are linked together in temporary or permanent associations.

George Homans's (1965) thesis is that when individuals encounter death, the anxiety that they experience is basically socially ascribed, or learned. Death fears can be likened to the fears of other things—snakes, electricity, communism, or whatever. If we believe that we are in a dangerous setting, we react accordingly. Religion, with its emphasis on immortality of the soul and its belief in a coming judgment, increases the level of death anxiety for individuals who follow the teachings of the religion. However, after individuals have fulfilled the requisite religious or magical ceremonies, they experience only a moderate amount of anxiety.

Homans brings the perspectives of Malinowski and Radcliffe-Brown together by making 4 conclusions:

1. Religion functions to relieve anxiety associated with death-related situations.
2. Death anxiety calls forth religious activities and rituals.
3. In order to stabilize the group of individuals who perform these rituals, group activities and beliefs provide a potential threat of anxiety in order to unite group members through a "common concern."
4. This secondary anxiety may be effectively removed through the group rituals of purification and expiation.

Summarizing the relationship between **religiosity** and death anxiety, we can arrive at the following theoretical assumptions:

1. The meanings of death are socially ascribed—death per se is neither fearful nor nonfearful.
2. The meanings that are ascribed to death in a given culture are transmitted to individuals in the society through the socialization process.
3. Anxiety reduction may be accomplished through social cooperation and institutional participation.
4. Institutional cohesiveness in religious institutions is fostered by giving participants a sense of anxiety concerning death and uniting them through a common concern.
5. If the religious institutions are to remain viable, they must provide a means for anxiety reduction.
6. Through its promise of a reward in the afterlife, and its redefinition of the negative effects of death upon the **temporal** life of the individual, religion diminishes the fear that it has ascribed to death and reduces anxieties that are ascribed to death by secular society.

In order to test the empirical validity of these assumptions, Michael Leming (1979–1980) surveyed 372 randomly selected residents in Northfield, Minnesota, concerning death anxiety and religious activities, beliefs, and experiences. Subjects were divided into four categories based on a religious commitment scale developed by Charles Glock and Rodney Stark (1966) and Joseph Faulkner and Gordon DeJong (1966). Approximately 25 percent of the respondents were placed into each category—the first consisted of those persons who were the least religious, and the fourth consisted of those persons who were the most religious.

Figure 5.1
Mean Fear of Death Scale Scores by Level of Religious Commitment

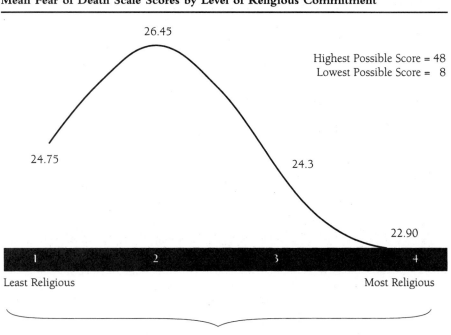

26.45

Highest Possible Score = 48
Lowest Possible Score = 8

24.75

24.3

22.90

| 1 | 2 | 3 | 4 |

Least Religious   Most Religious

Level of Religious Commitment

The graph shown here gives the mean fear of death scores for each of the levels of religious commitment. The relationship between the variables of religiosity and death anxiety is **curvilinear**—persons with a moderate commitment to religion have added to the general anxiety that has been socially ascribed to death from secular sources. The persons with a moderate commitment receive only the negative consequences of religion—what Radcliffe-Brown calls a "common concern." These persons acquire only the anxiety, which religion is capable of producing, and none of the consolation. On the other hand, the highly committed individual has the least anxiety concerning death. Religion, as Malinowski predicts, provides individuals with a solace when they attempt to cope with death attitudes.

In conclusion, religiosity seems to serve the dual function of "afflicting the comforted" and "comforting the afflicted." We have discovered that religion, when accompanied with a high degree of commitment, not only relieves the dread that it engenders, but also dispels much of the anxiety caused by the social effects of death.

At this point we might wonder how religious commitment affects the eight types of death fears discussed in chapter 1. Consistent with what we have seen in the graph, the theoretical model in this chapter suggests a curvilinear relationship between the 2 variables—those persons with moderate religious commitment experience the greatest amount of anxiety in each of the 8 types. In attempting to empirically evaluate this relationship, Leming (1979–1980) found that the theoretical model was supported

> ## Religion and Dying
> ### Robert E. Kavanaugh
>
> My conclusion is that religious faith of itself does little to affect man's peace near death. Worry warts are worry warts no matter their theology. It is not the substance or content of a man's creed that brings peace. It is the firmness and the quality of his act of believing. Firm believers, true believers, will find more peace on their deathbeds than all others, whatever the religious or secular label we place on their creed. The believer, not the belief, brings peace.
>
> *Facing Death* (p. 14), by R. E. Kavanaugh, 1972, Baltimore: Penguin Books.

with only 2 curvilinear trend deviations (see Table 5.1). The deviations were found among people who were the least religious for the fear of dependency in the dying process. It may be that nonreligious individuals are more concerned about being self-sufficient and independent of others and that they find dependency even more distressing than do persons who are more religious. In terms of the fear of isolation, there does not seem to be a relationship between death fear and religious commitment.

Upon further investigation, Leming found that factors of education, age, and even religious preference did not affect the curvilinear relationship. With the exception of the fear of isolation, persons who had the strongest religious commitment were the least fearful with regard to the various types of death concern. Furthermore, in each of the 8 death fear types the strength of commitment was the most significant variable in explaining the relationship between religion and the fear of death. Robert Kavanaugh (1972, p. 14) seems to have empirical support for his statement, "The believer, not the belief, brings peace."

Religious Interpretations of Death

Until this point, we have provided a functional perspective on religion—we have defined religion in terms of what religion does for the individual and society. This perspective focuses on the consequences of religion rather than on the content of religious belief and practice.

We will attempt to provide substantive perspectives on religion and death. The substantive perspective to religion attempts to establish what religion is. Substantive definitions of religion endeavor to distinguish religious behaviors from nonreligious behaviors by providing necessary criteria for inclusion as religious phenomena. The substantive definition of religion that has been used most frequently by sociologists is the one formulated by Emile Durkheim in his *The Elementary Forms of Religious Life,* first published in 1915:

Table 5.2

Mean Scores for the Various Types of Death Fears by Level of Religious Commitment

	Level of Religious Commitment			
	Least Religious			Most Religious
Type of Death Fear*	1	2	3	4
Fear of dependency in dying process Total Mean = 3.9	4.2**	4.10	3.85	3.75
Fear of pain Total Mean = 3.7	3.80	4.00	3.65	3.50
Fear of isolation Total Mean = 3.0	2.80	3.00	2.95	3.0**
Fear of the finality of death Total Mean = 2.9	3.05	3.25	2.80	2.75
Fear of leaving loved ones Total Mean = 2.8	3.05	3.25	2.65	2.60
Fear of the indignity in dying process Total Mean = 2.75	2.55	2.90	2.85	2.55
Fear of afterlife Total Mean = 2.55	2.50	2.95	2.60	2.30
Fear of the fate of the body Total Mean = 2.55	2.50	2.70	2.60	2.40
Combined Leming* Death Fear Score Total Mean = 24.3	24.75	26.45	24.30	22.90

* The possible range for the subscale scores is 1 through 6, with the values of 1 and 6 indicating low and high anxiety, respectively. For the combined death fear score the potential minimum score is 8 and the highest maximum score is 48.
**Curvilinear trend deviation.

> A religion is a unified system of beliefs and practices relative to sacred things, that is to say, things set apart and forbidden—beliefs and practices that unite into one single moral community called a church all of those people who adhere to them.

In this definition, Durkheim designates 4 essential ingredients of religion—a system of beliefs, a set of religious practices or rituals, the sacred or supernatural as the object of worship, and a community or social base. Most substantive definitions of religion employed by contemporary sociologists will incorporate these 4 essential ingredients. However, some sociologists have argued that in order to be inclusive of phenomena that most people consider religious, it might be proper to exclude the necessity of having a sacred point of reference. Buddhism, for example, does not have a supernatural being to which beliefs and rituals are oriented. We will now consider 5 religious traditions and explain how each tradition attempts to interpret the meaning of death-related experiences and provides funeral rites and rituals for the bereaved.

The 5 religious traditions considered are Judaism, Christianity, Islam, Hinduism, and Buddhism.

JUDAISM

Death in the Jewish tradition came into being as a result of Adam and Eve's sin, which caused them to be expelled from the Garden of Eden. When Adam and Eve ate the fruit from the "Tree of Conscience," they received the curse of pain in childbirth, the burden of work, and the loss of physical immortality. According to the biblical account in Genesis (2:4–3:24), although death was a punishment, it also brought the ability to distinguish between good and evil as well as the power and responsibility to make decisions that have a future consequence. According to J. Carse (1981, p. 221):

> Adam and Eve lost their immortality, but acquired consciousness instead. God drove them out of Paradise into death, but also into history. God's design for the people of Israel is not to save them from death, but to save them from their enemies in order that their history might continue.

In this description we gain an understanding of the importance of God's covenant with Abraham—that Abraham would become the father of many nations and that God would have a special relationship with his descendants forever (Gen. 17). Consequently, immortality was to be found in one's identity with the group.

Among contemporary Jews, including those who consider themselves religious, opinion differs regarding personal immortality. Some contend that there is no after-*life,* only an after*death*—the dead go to Sheol, where nothing happens, and the soul eventually slides into oblivion. Other Jews believe in a resurrection of the soul, when individuals are brought to a final judgment (Carse, 1981, p. 221). Still, for others there is a real ambivalence regarding the immortality of the soul. Carse cites the writings of Rabbi Leona Modena (1571–1648), who states:

> It is frightening that we fail to find in all the words of Moses a single indication pointing to man's spiritual immortality after his physical death. Nonetheless, reason compels us to believe that the soul continues.

Regardless of the content of Jewish beliefs regarding the immortality of the soul, Jewish funeral customs and rituals emphasize the point that "God does not save us, as individuals, from death, but saves Israel for history, regardless of death" (Carse, 1981, p. 221).

According to Knobel (1987, p. 396), traditional Jewish burial customs require that the body be cleansed by members of the Jewish burial society (hevra'qaddisha', "holy society") in a washing process called *tahorah,* or "purification." Custom forbids embalming, cremation, and autopsy unless local laws require these procedures. The body is then dressed in plain linen shrouds (*takhrikhim*); men are usually buried with their prayer shawls (*tallit*). The body is then placed into a plain wooden casket and buried before sunset on the day of death, if at all possible. Reform Judaism allows for cremation and entombment, but burial is the most frequent form of body disposition. Throughout this process, it is considered inappropriate to use the funeral as a means for displaying one's social position and wealth.

For the bereaved, the Jewish mourning ritual begins by the rending (tearing) of garments. For some, the ripping of a black ribbon, which is then attached to the clothing, has symbolically replaced the process of rending garments. From the death until burial, mourners are exempt from normal religious obligations (e.g., morning prayers) and must not engage in the following activities: drinking wine, eating meat, attending parties, and engaging in sexual intercourse (Knobel, 1987, p. 396).

The liturgy for the funeral will consist of the recitation of psalms, a eulogy, and the following *El Male' Rahamin* memorial prayer (Knobel, 1987, p. 396):

> O God full of compassion, You who dwell on high! Grant perfect rest beneath the sheltering wings of Your presence, among the holy and pure who shine as the brightness of the heavens, unto the soul of [name of the deceased] who has entered eternity and in whose memory charity is offered. May his/her repose be in the Garden of Eden. May the Lord of Mercy bring him/her under the cover of His wings forever and may his/her soul be bound up in the bond of eternal life. May the Lord be his/her possession and may he/she rest in peace. Amen.

During the interment service the body is lowered into the grave and covered with earth. The interment service consists of an acclamation of God's justice, a memorial prayer, and the recitation of *Qaddish*—a doxology reaffirming the mourner's faith in God despite the fact of death. After the burial service, the people in attendance form two lines between which the primary mourners pass. Those present comfort the mourners as they pass, saying, "May God comfort you among the rest of the mourners of Zion and Jerusalem" (Knobel, 1987, p. 397).

The *shivah* is a period of 7 days following the death in which the mourners act as if they were themselves dead. During this period they are forbidden to engage in work, have sexual intercourse, read the Bible, bathe, shave, or have their hair cut. It is expected that during the *shivah* expressions of emotion and grief are to be of lesser intensity than during the funeral and burial rituals.

After the *shivah*, mourners continue to avoid social gatherings for 30 days after the death. When one is mourning the death of a parent, the restrictions are observed for 1 year. After 1 year, all ritual expressions of grief cease with the exception of the *Yahrzeit*—the yearly commemoration of the person's death. *Yahrzeit* is observed by lighting a memorial light, performing memorial acts of charity, and attending religious services to recite the *Qaddish* prayer (Carse, 1981, p. 221; Knobel, 1987, p. 397).

CHRISTIANITY

Although Christianity shares much of the historical and mythical foundations of Judaism, there are many distinct differences in the Christian approach to death, afterlife, and funeral rituals. For the Christian, death is viewed as the entrance to eternal life and, therefore, preferable to physical life. There is a strong belief in the immortality of the soul, the resurrection of the body, and a divine judgment of one's earthly life after death, resulting in the eternal rewards of heaven or the punishments of hell. For the Roman Catholic there are 4 potential dispositions of the soul after death— heaven, hell, limbo, and purgatory. According to McBrien (1987, p. 443), "some will join God forever in heaven; some may be separated eternally from God in hell; others may find themselves in a state of merely natural happiness in limbo; and others will suffer in purgatory some temporary 'punishment' still required of sins that have already been forgiven."

For the Christian, the teachings of Jesus and the Apostle Paul are the most important sources in arriving at a theology of life after death. Jesus declares to his followers:

> "I am the Resurrection and the Life, he who believes in Me, though he die, yet shall he live, and whoever lives and believes in Me shall never die." (John 11:25, RSV)

In the 15th chapter of the first letter to the Corinthians, the Apostle Paul discusses the significance of Jesus's resurrection for the Christian believer. In this chapter Jesus is portrayed as the "first born from the dead" and as "the one who has destroyed death" (1 Cor. 15:26, RSV). Paul declares (1 Cor. 15:52–58, RSV) that at the end of history,

> The dead will be raised imperishable, and we shall be changed. For this perishable nature must put on the imperishable, and this mortal nature must put on immortality. When the perishable puts on the imperishable, and the mortal puts on immortality, then shall come to pass the saying that is written:
>   Death is swallowed up in victory.

Jewish Group Buries Its Own

When a Jewish congregation here first began the practice of offering simple, inexpensive burials for its dead, some members were upset. But they now increasingly condone it.

Back in 1977, some people had felt it was barbaric when the body of a devout member, Al Sudit, 75, was lowered into his grave in a plain wooden box, with mourners themselves shoveling on the dirt. But recently, when another respected member, Morris Weiner, 81, was given the same sort of elemental funeral, relatives say they neither sensed nor heard any criticism.

Rabbi Arnold M. Goodman, spiritual leader of Adath Jeshurun Congregation, says volunteers of its society to honor the dead—*Chevra Kevod Hamet*—now handle about half the funerals of members.

Goodman, recently elected president of the Rabbinical Assembly, representing the nation's 1,200 Conservative rabbis, regards his congregation as a pioneer in setting up a model for traditional, simplified funerals.

He says congregations in Highland Park, Illinois, Portland, Oregon, and Washington, DC, have adapted the method for their own use. But some other rabbis remain dubious.

The *Chevra* was formed in 1976 after Goodman, in a sermon, dealt with the impact of American values upon the funeral practices of Jewry. He suggested a committee study the requirements of the *Halacha*, or Jewish law, for responding to death.

Months of study convinced committee members that a simple wood coffin should be used, the body should be washed in a ritual process called *tahara*

(continued)

O death, where is thy victory?

O death, where is thy sting?

The sting of death is sin, and the power of sin is the law. But thanks be to God, who gives us the victory through our Lord Jesus Christ.

Christians employ 2 basic, and somewhat paradoxical, perspectives when facing death. The first has just been described—that through faith in Jesus Christ, the Christian has victory over death and gains eternal life with God. The following passage (Rom. 8:31–39, RSV) provides us with an example of this orientation.

What then shall we say to this? If God is for us, who is against us? He who did not spare his own Son but gave him up for us all, will he not also give us all things with him? Who shall bring any charge against God's elect? It is God who justifies; who is to condemn? Is it Christ Jesus, who died, yes, who was raised from the dead, who is at the right hand of God, who indeed intercedes for us? Who shall separate us from the love of Christ? Shall tribulation, or distress, or persecution, or famine, or nakedness, or peril, or sword? As it is written,

"For thy sake we are being killed all the day long; we are regarded as sheep to be slaughtered."

(continued from previous page)

and, because dust is to return to dust as quickly as possible, there should be no formaldehyde in the veins, no nails on the coffin. The society decided to offer traditional funerals free to Adath Jeshurun members. The congregation provided seed money. Memorial donations and voluntary contributions from the bereaved are accepted.

Here's how the *Chevra* functions: A congregation member signs a revokable agreement, asking for the *Chevra's* service when needed. When death occurs, *chaverim* (friends) call on the family, aid in writing the obituary, explain death benefits, aid in other ways and remain available for help.

Chevra Kadisha (sacred society), people of the same sex as the deceased and usually five in number, wash the body at the mortuary while saying prayers. The body is dressed in a shroud sewn by *Chevra* members and placed in a wooden coffin.

Shomrin (guards) watch over the body, in blocks of two hours, until burial. The coffin with rope handles is light enough to be borne by pallbearers, including women. Spurning mechanical contrivances, the pallbearers lower the coffin into the grave. *Chaverim,* the rabbi and cantor shovel in dirt. Family members may participate.

Judaism historically insists that the greatest commandment is to take personal involvement in burying the dead, Goodman says, but affluence enables people to pay surrogates to do it.

Goodman says a funeral costs the Chevra less than $500. A comparable no-frills funeral handled by professionals would cost about $1,500, says Elliot Pinck, a local funeral home director.

Rocky Mountain News, June 25, 1982.

No, in all these things we are more than conquerors through him who loved us. For I am sure that neither death, nor life, nor angels, nor principalities, nor things present, nor things to come, nor powers, nor height, nor depth, nor anything else in all creation, will be able to separate us from the love of God in Christ Jesus our Lord.

The second perspective on death employed by Christians emphasizes the experience of true human loss. This approach is exemplified by Jesus as he responds to the death of his friend Lazarus.

Then Mary, when she came where Jesus was and saw Him, fell at his feet, saying to Him, "Lord, if you had been here, my brother would not have died." When Jesus saw her weeping, and the Jews who came with her also weeping, He was deeply moved in spirit and troubled; and He said, "Where have you laid him?" They said to Him, "Lord, come and see." Jesus wept. So the Jews said, "See how He loved him!" (John 11:32–36, RSV)

"At that time, the disciples came to Jesus saying, 'Who is the greatest in the kingdom of heaven?' And calling to Him a child, He put him in the midst of them, and said, 'Truly, I say to you, unless you turn and become like children, you will never enter the kingdom of heaven. Whoever humbles himself like this child, he is the greatest in the kingdom of heaven.'" (Matthew 18:1–4)

C. S. Lewis, in his book *A Grief Observed* (1961, p. 24), illustrates how Christians utilize this paradoxical double perspective:

> What St. Paul says can comfort only those who love God better than the dead, and the dead better than themselves. If a mother is mourning not for what she has lost but for what her dead child has lost, it is a comfort to believe that the child has not lost the end for which it was created. And it is a comfort to believe that she herself, in losing her chief or only natural happiness, has not lost a greater thing, that she may still hope to "glorify God and enjoy Him forever." A comfort to the God-aimed, eternal spirit within her. But not to her motherhood. The specifically maternal happiness must be written off. Never, in any place or time, will she have her son on her knees, or bathe him, or tell him a story, or plan for his future, or see her grandchild.

The Christian funeral process reflects these themes of victory and loss. The funeral service is primarily a worship service or Mass of Christian burial. During the service, hymns are sung and scriptural passages are read to emphasize the resurrection of the dead and to provide consolation for the bereaved. Occasionally a eulogy or biographical statement concerning the deceased is read.

In the United States, Christian teaching does not discourage the process of embalming, nor does it prohibit the autopsy, cremation, or any other form of final disposition (as is the case among Jews)—provided that such practices do not indicate a rejection of a belief in the resurrection of the body. American Christian funerals are conducted by members of the clergy and funeral directors in a church, funeral chapel, and/or cemetery. Memorial services—religious services in which the dead body is not present—are becoming increasingly popular in many Protestant churches. At the occasion of death, the family of the deceased is expected to disengage from most normal social functioning until after the funeral. Funeral arrangements are typically made with the professional assistance of a funeral director and/or member of the clergy. For most Roman Catholics and many Protestants, on the day before the funeral, a wake or visitation service will be held in the funeral home. During this time (approximately 5 hours in duration), friends may view the body and visit with the family of the deceased. Roman Catholic families may also have a rosary service and/or prayer service during the wake.

The funeral is typically held 2 to 4 days after the death. Occasionally, the funeral is delayed if family members are unable to make travel arrangements on such short notice (this would not be the case for a Jewish funeral). If final disposition involves cremation, the cremation can take place either after the funeral or before the memorial service. Burial and entombment dispositions are usually accompanied by rites of committal. On those occasions when there is no graveside service, words of committal will be read at the conclusion of the funeral service. At the conclusion of the funeral process, family members and others who have attended the services are often invited to share a meal together. This becomes a community rite of reincorporation.

ISLAM

As in Christianity, life after death is also an important focus within the Islamic tradition. Earthly life and the realm of the dead are separated by a bridge that souls must cross on the Day of Judgment. After death, all people face a divine judgment. Then they are assigned eternal dwelling places where they will receive either eternal rewards or punishments, determined by the strengths of their faith in God and the moral quality of their earthly lives. According to the Qur'an, there are seven layers of heaven and seven layers of *alnar* ("Fire of Hell"), and each layer is separated from the layer above by receiving fewer rewards or greater punishments. The fundamental reason why persons might be condemned to a life of torment in the Fire of Hell is a lack of belief in God and in the message of his prophet Muhammad. Other reasons include lying, being corrupt, committing blasphemy, denying the advent of the Judgment Day and the reality of the Fire of Hell, lacking charity, and leading a life of luxury (Long, 1987, p. 132).

Like Jews and Christians, followers of Islam believe that God is fundamentally compassionate and place a similar emphasis on God as just. Therefore, persons are held accountable for moral integrity at the time of their death. The primary expression of the Islamic concern for justice and accountability is found in the belief in assignment to paradise or damnation. Accordingly, the Qur'an provides very vivid sketches of both paradise and hell. However, many Islamic theologians also stress that God's judgment is tempered with mercy, that the angel Gabriel will intercede on behalf of those condemned to punishment, and that they will eventually be pardoned.

The following prayer (the opening of the Surah of the Qur'an) illustrates the Islamic perspective on divine justice and mercy.

> In the name of God, the Merciful, the Compassionate. Praise belongs to God, the Lord of all Being, the All-merciful, the All-compassionate, the Master of the Day of Doom.
>
> Thee only we serve; to Thee alone we pray for succour, Guide us in the straight path, the path of those whom Thou has blessed, not of those against whom Thou art wrathful, nor of those who are astray.

When death comes to the Muslim, it is expected that he or she will be attended by relatives and close friends. Just prior to death the dying person will recite the following Islamic confession of faith: "There is no god but God, and Muhammad is his messenger." The dying person is also encouraged to request forgiveness from anyone whom he or she may have offended because, according to the tradition of Islam, "God will not forgive violation of human rights unless those wronged have forgiven" (Rahman, 1987, p. 128). Islamic tradition forbids embalming and, consequently, it is expected that burial should take place as soon as possible—preferably before sundown. Occasionally, burial is delayed 1 or 2 days to provide out-of-town family members an opportunity to attend. In preparation for burial, the family members will call into their home or the hospital a person of the same gender as the deceased who knows the prescribed ritual for washing and preparing the body. The eyes and mouth of the deceased will be closed, the arms straightened alongside the body, and the body will be washed and wrapped in a white seamless cloth (shroud) similar to that worn for the pilgrimage to Mecca (Eickelman, 1987, p. 401).

When the body has been fully prepared according to the prescribed ritual, it will be placed into a simple wooden coffin. (Occasionally, Muslims will be covered only by the white shroud when they are buried.) During this preparation, prayers and passages from the Qur'an will be recited by a *hoca*—a lay holy man, not a priest—and care will be taken that the body always faces Mecca.

Islamic tradition requires that the funeral service take place without unnecessary delay and that burial rites be simple and austere (Rahman, 1987, p. 128). When it is time for the funeral, the body will be transported from the home or hospital to the mosque on the shoulders of the pallbearers. At the mosque the body will be placed onto a stone bier (*musalla*) in the outer courtyard. The funeral service will be a part of one of the five regular daily religious services (usually the noon service). Because Muslims consider burying the dead a good deed, when worshippers leave the mosque and see the coffin in the courtyard, they will participate in the procession to the cemetery even though they were not acquainted with the deceased (Habenstein & Lamers, 1974, p. 162).

The body is then transported from the mosque to the cemetery on the shoulders of those male mourners in the procession. According to Habenstein and Lamers (1974, p. 163),

> It is customary for every man in good health to carry the coffin on his shoulders for seven steps at least, and for passers-by to accompany the procession for at least seven steps. When a new bearer pushes under the coffin, another steps away so that eight or ten people are always under the load. These customs insure that the remains will have an escort, even though the dead person may have no living relatives. At a pre-arranged spot, hearse and funeral cars await the procession. Where distances to the cemetery are short, the body will be borne to the grave totally on foot.

At the cemetery the body is placed into the grave, and mourners place handfuls of dirt on top of it. The sexton then fills the remainder of the grave using a shovel. At the gravesite, rather than place cut flowers, Muslim mourners plant flowers because they believe that every living plant utters the name of God. During this process prayers are recited, and the service concludes with the preaching of a sermon (Habenstein & Lamers, 1974, p. 163). After returning from the cemetery, all of the participants will partake of a meal that is served at the home of the deceased. Occasionally, some food from this meal is placed over the grave for the first 3 days after the death. Mourning continues for another 3 days, while family members receive social support and consolation from friends and members of the community.

Although Islamic women are allowed to openly express emotion in the bereavement process, Islamic men are encouraged to retain their composure as a sign that they are able to accept the will of Allah. A widow is required by the Qur'an to go into seclusion for 4 months and 10 days before she is allowed to remarry (Eickelman, 1987, pp. 401–402).

HINDUISM

Unlike the religious traditions that we have previously discussed, Hinduism does not have a single religious founder nor a single sacred text. Although the Vedas are recognized by almost all Hindus as an authoritative source of spiritual knowledge, Hinduism is not dogmatic. Many theologies and religious approaches exist within the Hindu tradition. Many gods also exist, each viewed as an aspect or manifestation of a single ultimate reality, but it is *not* essential to believe in the existence of God in order to be a Hindu (Srinivas & Shah, 1968, p. 358). Essentially, Hinduism is a system of social customs imbued with religious significance.

Three concepts are central to an understanding of Hinduism—*karma, dharma,* and *moksha. Karma* refers to a moral law of causation; it suggests that an individual's

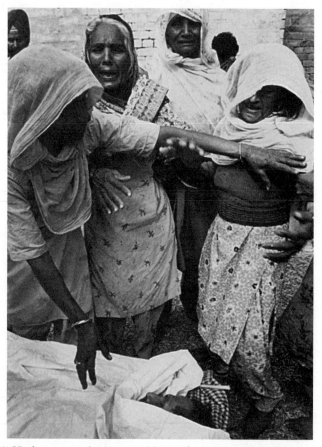

The body of this Hindu woman is being prepared by mourning female family members and friends in her home.

actions produce results for which the individual is responsible. *Karma* also refers to the balance of good and bad deeds performed in previous existences. *Dharma* are the religious duties, requirements, and/or prescriptions. The extent to which one fulfills one's *dharma* determines one's *karma*. In turn, *moksha* is the reward for living a saintly life. The main ways of achieving *moksha* are by acquiring true knowledge, performing good deeds, and living a life of love and devotion to God (Srinivas & Shah, 1968, p. 359).

The central doctrine affecting death-related attitudes and behavior in the Hindu religion is reincarnation and the transmigration of souls (*samsara*). For the Hindu, one's present life is determined by one's actions in a previous life. Furthermore, one's present behavior will shape the future. According to Habenstein and Lamers (1974, p. 116), "The ultimate goal of the soul is liberation from the wheel of rebirth, through reabsorption into or identity with the Oversoul (*Brahma*)—the essence of the universe, immaterial, uncreated, limitless, and timeless."

By way of contrast, whereas Jews, Christians, and Muslims believe in the immortality of the soul and hope for an afterlife, Hindus hope that their soul will be absorbed at death. For the Hindu, the goal is not to experience life after death, but rather to have one's soul united with the Oversoul. Punishment for the devout Hindu might be to *have* "everlasting spiritual rebirth."

Within the Hindu tradition, death brings two possibilities—liberation or transmigration of the soul. Neither is inherently fearful, even though separation from one's friends and loved ones may cause sadness and personal loss. Somewhat analogous to the dual perspectives of Christianity, death for the Hindu individual brings hope of something better but also the human loss of being separated from a dead loved one.

When a death takes place in Hindu society, the body is prepared for viewing by laying it out with the hands across the chest, closing the eyelids, anointing the body with oil, and placing flower garlands around it. This is done by persons of the same gender as the deceased, and this process will be presided over in the home of the deceased by the dead person's successor and heir (Habenstein & Lamers, 1974, pp. 119–120).

Because Hindus believe that cremation is an act of sacrifice, whereby one's body is offered to God through the funeral pyre, cremation is the preferred method of body disposition. In preparation for cremation, family members will construct a bier, consisting of a mat of woven coconut fronds stretched between two poles and supported by pieces of bamboo. The uncasketed body of the deceased will be borne on the bier from the deceased's home to the place of cremation by close relatives. This funeral procession will be led by the chief mourner—usually the eldest son—and will include musicians, drum players, and other mourners. The wife of the deceased will always remain behind in the home (Habenstein & Lamers, 1974, p. 121).

According to Habenstein and Lamers, when the body reaches the place of cremation, usually a platform (*ghat*) located on the banks of a sacred river, the body will be removed from the bier and immersed in the holy waters of the river. During this process a priest will perform a brief disposal ceremony. The body will then be smeared liberally with *ghi* (clarified butter) and placed on the pyre for burning. At this point, the chief mourner, who has brought burning coals from the house of the deceased, lights the pyre, and a priest recites an invocation similar to the following:

> Fire, you were lighted by him, so may he be lighted from you, that he may gain the regions of celestial bliss. May this offering prove auspicious. (Habenstein & Lamers, 1974, p. 123)

After the body has been consumed by the fire, and only fragments of bones remain, the mourners will ritually wash themselves in the river in a rite of purification. They will then make offerings to the ancestral spirits of the deceased. Upon completion of this duty they will recite passages from the sacred texts.

Three days after this ritual, a few relatives of the deceased will return to the cremation site in order to gather the bones. A priest will again read from the sacred texts and sprinkle water onto the *ghat,* while any remains of the deceased will be placed in a vase and given to the chief mourner. It is then the obligation of the chief mourner to cast these remains into the Ganges or another sacred river (Habenstein & Lamers, 1974, p. 124).

Understanding Death in Hinduism
Anant Rambachan

Death and birth are seen by us Hindus as gateways of exit and entry to the stage of this world. This process is described in one of the most striking and famous analogies in the entire Bhagavadgita. It is a verse which we movingly recite when the body is being cremated, and it has given comfort and solace to the grieving Hindu heart for centuries.

> Just as a person casts off worn-out garments and puts on others that are new, even so does the embodied-soul cast off worn-out bodies and take on others that are new.

This analogy is full of suggestions, but I can only briefly draw your attention to a few of these. First, a suit of clothing is not identical with the wearer. Similarly, the body, which is likened here to worn-out garments, is not the true being or identity of the human person. Second, there is the similarity of a continuity of being. When a worn-out suit of clothing is cast off, the wearer continues to be. Similarly, with the disintegration of the physical body, the indweller, that is, the Self, continues to be. Finally, there is the parallel with the timing of the change. A suit of clothing is changed when it no longer serves the purpose for which it was intended. Similarly, the physical body is cast off when it no longer serves the purpose for which it came into existence.

This does not mean that the Hindu is not saddened by death or does not lament the loss it brings. There is a mysterious element in death which will always sadden and hurt. While we ache and long for the beauty, tenderness, and companionship of a dear one, we are deeply comforted in the knowledge that all that is good and true and real in him or her continues to be. What has passed away is what has always been limited by time.

(continued)

Between 10 and 31 days after the cremation, a *Shraddha* (elaborate ritual feast) is prepared for all mourners and priests who have taken part in the funeral rituals. During the *Shraddha*, gifts are given to the guru (religious teacher), the *purohita* (officiating priest), and other Brahmins (religious functionaries). The social status of the family will determine how elaborate the *Shraddha* will be—for the poor this ritual will last 8 to 10 hours, and the wealthy may give a *Shraddha* lasting several days. At the close of the *Shraddha,* the mourning period officially ends, even though later *Shraddhas* may be given as memorial remembrances (Habenstein & Lamers, 1974, pp. 125–126). Although it is believed that these ritual meals provide nourishment to the spirit of the deceased in its celestial abode, from a sociological perspective they serve as rites of family reincorporation and also differentiate the family regarding social status.

According to Habenstein and Lamers (1974, p. 126), next to Hindu wedding ceremonies, funerals are the most important religious ceremonies. Although the funeral

(continued from previous page)

Since death is a necessary condition for rebirth, Hindus also understand it to be a gateway for fresh opportunities. When we look at death from the limited perspective of a single and short life experience, we often see only its tragic side. We must admit, however, that the perspective is different for God—whose vision spans the boundless past and the unending future. Where we only see end and loss, there will be new beginnings and opportunities for a loved one. We need a selfless faith to trust his wisdom and judgment.

Hinduism conceives of life as a continuous chain of existence. In the Hindu view, the word of life is not restricted to describing the span of time between birth and death. While there are some variations in views among the many traditions of Hinduism, we agree that life is a journey toward God—the reality of all that exists. Life is a quest for that which is true and real in the midst of an existence which is so changeful and finite. For Hindus, God, the true and the real, has the highest value and is the source of all joy. We are all seekers and pilgrims, and the sacred journey of life will continue as long as it takes us to discover this final truth of ourselves and the world. As long as we cling to the finite and changeful, and seek comfort and solace in these, our journeys will be never-ending. The mortal and the finite will never satisfy us. The attainment of God is the fulfillment of our pilgrimage. This is moksha, liberation, our home and destination. The longing for it is captured in our daily prayer:

Lead us from untruth to truth
From ignorance to knowledge
From death to immortality.

A. Rambachan, Department of Religion, St. Olaf College. By permission of the author.

process is very costly to families, often resulting in their impoverishment, not providing the *Shraddha* creates more social problems for families than do the financial consequences of these rituals.

BUDDHISM

There are many types of Buddhism, but the most popular are *Theravada, Mahayana,* and *Tantrayana*. According to Peter Pardue (1968, p. 165), *Theravada* Buddhism is the dominant religion in Southeast Asia (Myanmar, Thailand, Laos, Vietnam, Cambodia, and Sri Lanka). *Mahayana* Buddhism is primarily practiced in Korea, China, Japan, and Nepal. *Tantrayana* has traditionally been the dominant form of Buddhism in Tibet, Mongolia, and parts of Siberia. Although there are differences between each of these sects and many others found throughout the world, in general, all Buddhists find a

The Thai Buddhist Funeral

There are three parts of the Thai Buddhist funeral: ceremonies at the *wat*, procession to the site of cremation, and the cremation. When a common person dies, the body is cleaned, dressed, and placed within a casket. The casket is kept either within the home or at the *wat* (temple) for a period of three days. During this period, monks will come every evening to chant the Buddhist scriptures (*Abhidhamma*). Friends will attend these services and will offer gifts of floral tributes. Some of these wreaths will be rented and financial contributions will be made to selected charitable causes (chosen by the family). On the fourth day, the body will be taken to the charnel-ground (cremation site), which is usually a good distance from the *wat*. When a charismatic monk, high governmental official, member of the royalty, or another noble person of high prestige dies, the body will be kept for a longer period of time before final disposition is made. This period of time can vary from a few weeks to a period of many years, determined by the status of the deceased. The fourth lunar month (corresponding to the month of March) is the preferred time for funeral ceremonies.

Bodies of people of high status are embalmed and then bathed and dressed with new clothes. The entire face of the deceased (notably monks) is covered with gold leaves and placed in a casket. Visitors will come to pay respects by offering floral tributes and pouring water on the deceased (*aab nam sob*).

The ceremony prior to cremation will last for several days and will typically be held at the big *vihara* at the *wat* compound. The casketed body will be placed within a larger gilded teak coffin called a *long tong* or outer coffin. The *long tong* will be placed on the right side of the *vihara* and surrounded by many items associated with the deceased (in the case of monks, bronze statues, certificates of title, the deceased's picture decorated with flowers, the honorific fan called a *kruang soong,* and the three-tailed flag which is purported to be the refuge of the dead while traveling in the cycle of death and rebirth).

During these ceremonies held in the *vihara,* monks will chant important sutras from the *Tripitaka*—Buddhist scriptures. At the conclusion of the final service at the *vihara,* there will be a final tribute of flowers and three lighted candles presented to the deceased. The casket will then be removed from the golden case or *long tong* and removed from the *vihara.*

The procession is a significant rite in the Thai Buddhist funeral. The casket is put on a carriage and taken from the *wat* compound to the cremation site. During the procession, a long white cotton cord is attached to the casket and eight (the number is flexible) monks together with lay devotees will carry the cord. In the urban areas the carriage will be motorized, while in traditional funerals and/or funerals in rural areas the carriage will be pulled by walking members of the procession.

The procession is headed by the three-tailed flag and followed by the monk's fan, the title certificate, the set of three yellow monk's robes, the de-

(continued)

(continued from previous page)

ceased's picture, the bronze statue of the deceased, and the coffin, respectively. Upon arrival at the site of the cremation, the casket is carried around the crematorium three times which symbolizes the traveling in the cycle of death and rebirth. After the casket is placed in front of the crematorium, the relatives will pose for pictures around it, after which they will circle it three times.

When the funeral is performed under royal patronage, the *fai phra rajthaan* or the "Royal Fire" is brought in to be used to light the cremation pyre. The royal fire is carried by a group of government officials dressed in the white official uniform, while the orchestra plays the Royal Anthem in salutation to the King of Thailand. During this time all mourners, dressed in black or white, will stand in respect to the King and royal fire.

As a final merit-making rite, five or ten important persons will come forward (one by one) and place a set of yellow robes on the long white cotton cord which is linked to the coffin. High-ranking monks will then be invited to come forward and receive the robes. The final act is when the most important person in the ceremony (e.g., Prime Minister) places the last set of yellow robes on the cotton cord. The most senior monk will collect the robes after "contemplating symbolically the dead." According to religious practice in Buddhism, the contemplation of the corpse by Buddhist monks will bring merit to those who provide such opportunity for the monk to do so. The merit earned can be dedicated further to the dead as well.

The stage is now set for the actual cremation. Just prior to the lighting of the fire, the biography of the deceased is read while *dok mai chan* is distributed to all in attendance. The *dok mai chan* is a sandalwood flower with one incense-stick and two small candles attached. The mourners are all invited to come forward and deposit the *dok mai chan* before the casket. By so doing, mourners are deemed participants in the actual cremation.

The chairman of the ceremony then ignites the fire, and the casket is consumed. The next morning, the ashes (several pieces of bones) are gathered and made into a shape of a human being with the head facing east. Four monks attend this ritual which culminates when the ashes are placed into a receptacle. Afterward, the ashes are enshrined in a reliquary built in the compound of the monastery.

Throughout the funeral ceremony sorrow or lamentation is not emphasized. Rather the focus is upon impermanence of all things. The funeral is primarily a social event that affirms community values and group cohesiveness. Furthermore, it is a time where people are expected to enjoy the fellowship surrounding the rituals. Typically there is entertainment (dancing and musical performances) associated with funeral rituals in order for sorrow and loneliness to dissipate. It is believed that this assists the bereaved to conceptualize a happy and pleasant paradise in which the deceased will reside.

"Funeral Customs in Thailand" (pp. 231–235), by M. R. Leming and S. Premchit, 1993. In J. D. Morgan (Ed.), *Personal Care in an Impersonal World*, New York: Baywood Publishing.

common heritage in the life of Siddhartha Gautama ("The Enlightened One" or "Buddha"). Buddha was born in 563 B.C. as a prince in northern India. When he was a child his thoughts were preoccupied with the finitude of human existence. Unsuccessfully, his family tried to shelter him from human suffering and death. At the age of 29 he left his life of privilege and began to search for personal salvation. After rejecting physical asceticism and abstract philosophy, he attained a state of enlightenment through the process of intense meditation. For the remaining 50 years of his life, he served as a missionary and preached his message of salvation to all people regardless of social position and gender (Pardue, 1968, p. 168).

The Buddhist message of salvation, taught by Buddha in his first sermon, is the "Four Noble Truths." The first of these truths is that all human existence is characterized by pain and suffering in an endless cycle of death and rebirth. The second truth is that the cause of the agony of the human condition is desire for personal satisfaction, which is impossible to obtain. The third truth is that salvation comes by destroying these desires. By completely destroying ignorance, one experiences enlightenment, and the cycle of transmigration of the soul is broken. Finally, in the fourth truth, one can experience perfect peace through the eightfold path to enlightenment. In the words of Pardue (1968, p. 168):

> For this purpose the proper [meditation] is the "eightfold path," an integral combination of ethics (*sila*) and meditation (*samadhi*), which jointly purify the motivations and mind. This leads to the attainment of wisdom (*prajna*), to enlightenment (*bodhi*), and to the ineffable Nirvana ("blowing out"), the final release from the incarnational cycle and mystical transcendence beyond all conceptualization.

Like the Hindu, for the Buddhist the goal is not to experience life after death but rather to experience nirvana—which has the property of neither existence nor nonexistence. According to Margaret Ayer (1964, p. 52), nirvana is the "state of peace and freedom from the miseries of the constantly changing illusion which is existence."

The location of nirvana is to be found in the image of the flame when a candle is "blown out"—it is in a place beyond human understanding. According to Ayer (1964, p. 53), whenever people achieve nirvana "they 'will be seen no more.' It is through loss of desire, selfishness, evil, and illusion that this state of wisdom, holiness, and peace is reached." Buddhism contends that whereas physical death causes one to experience life again in a transmigrated form, "death to this world" (via nirvana) provides the gateway for ultimate happiness, peace, and fulfillment. Unlike Hinduism and the other religious traditions that we have considered, the ultimate goal of Buddhism is a state of consciousness and not a symbolic location for the disembodied soul.

As the religious teachings of Buddha were disseminated throughout Asia, the beliefs and practices were adapted to indigenous cultural traditions dealing with death. Consequently, it is not possible to discuss Buddhist funeral rituals per se. Rather, there are Japanese, Korean, Chinese, and Thai funeral customs practiced within a Buddhist context.

In general, all Buddhist funeral ceremonies have some similarities. At the Buddhist temple, priests assist families as they engage in this important rite of passage. Prayers of the priests illustrate the "lesson of death"—that life is vanity. At funerals, Buddhist priests often read the following words from Buddha (cited by Habenstein & Lamers, 1974, p. 97):

After arriving at the site of cremation, the relatives pose for pictures by the casket. Walking around the casket three times, they then place the casket in front of the crematorium. Many times, young male family members will be ordained as monks for a period of a few days during the funeral ceremonies. The merit earned by these young men can be dedicated to benefit the dead, as well.

The body from which the soul has fled has no worth. Soon it will encumber the earth as a useless thing, like the trunk of a withered tree. Life lasts only for a moment. Birth and death follow one another in inescapable sequence. All that live must die. That man indeed is fortunate who achieves the nothingness of being. All animal creation is dying, or dead, or merits to be dead. All of us are dying. We cannot escape death.

For most Buddhists, cremation is the preferred form of body disposition, but earth burial is also frequently practiced. In Buddhism, unlike Hinduism, there is no "soul"—both the body and the idea of a soul distract from the proper meditation and attainment of nirvana. Cremation serves the function of promoting the process of liberation of the individual from the illusion of the present world. As a reflection of this orientation, Buddhist priests will recite these words prior to the final disposition of the body (cited by Habenstein & Lamers, 1974, pp. 97–98):

O dead one, pursue your destiny. Flee to paradise. You will know rebirth into a better life. Do not linger to haunt those who remain here, and to share this life of invisible darkness which is the lot of the living. Those whom you leave behind reckon accurately your good fortune in your liberation. With happy impatience they await their own turn. You neither want nor need them, and they are happy without you. Now follow your destiny.

During and after the funeral, family members will make offerings through the priests to the spirit of the deceased. They will also give ritual feasts for the priests and

---

Religious and Secular Orientations
Robert E. Kavanaugh

Faith or belief are not the sole privileges of religious people as I once thought. Faith is simply that total commitment of the entire person to an ideal, a way of life, a set of values, to anything or anyone beyond the narrow limitations of myself: God, mankind, the poor, science, human relations, growth and development, anything capable of bringing meaning and purpose to life. . . .

The true believer, after I sort out my personal feelings toward the tenets in his creed, reflects to me a sense of inner worth, a spirit of mission and purpose, a confident conviction and a tranquil assurance. Near death the true believer knows why he lived and can face the unfinished tasks of his life with his vision in clear focus. Because true belief brought perspective into life, so will it endow death with a more satisfying point of view. And no matter how wonderful religion may be for many, it is only one of the many ways to gain this stature of true belief.

Facing Death (pp. 221, 224), by R. E. Kavanaugh, 1972, Baltimore: Penguin Books.

---

other mourners. As in other religious traditions, all of these funeral activities will emphasize the importance of the religious worldview, promote community cohesiveness, and reincorporate chief mourners into routine patterns of social life.

Temporal Interpretations of Death

Even though the funeral industry and most people in the United States tend to merge religious and death meanings, temporal interpretations of death also provide a means for protecting social order in the face of death. Such interpretations tend to emphasize the empirical, natural, and "this world" view of death.

According to Glenn M. Vernon (1970, p. 33), "when death is given a temporal interpretation and is seen as the loss of consciousness, self-control, and identity, the individual may conclude that he or she can avoid social isolation in eternity by identifying him or herself with specific values, including religious ones." If we define religion as a system of beliefs and practices related to high-intensity value meanings and/or meanings of the supernatural (Vernon, 1970), then it is possible for individuals with temporal orientations to be "religious" in their outlook without affirming an afterlife. Furthermore, because any death has many consequences for the persons on whom it impinges, we would expect that even religious persons would assign some temporal meanings to death.

Vernon has pointed out that individuals whose interpretations are primarily temporal share the following beliefs and attitudes:

1. They tend to reject or deemphasize a belief in the afterlife.
2. They tend to believe that death is the end of the individual.

3. They tend to focus upon the needs and concerns of the survivors.
4. They tend to be present-oriented for themselves, but present-and future-oriented for those who will continue after them.
5. Any belief in immortality is related to the activities and accomplishments of the individual during his or her lifetime-including biological offspring and social relationships that the individual has created.

There is a strong temptation to view the person who has a temporal orientation as being very different than the person who finds comfort in a religious interpretation of death. In fact, both will attempt to restore the order in their personal lives, and that found in society, by placing death into the context of a "higher" order.

For the individual with religious commitments, protection from anomie and comfort for anxiety are to be found by being in relationship with the supernatural. For the person with a secular or temporal orientation, these same benefits are found in becoming involved with other people, projects, and causes. These involvements, although not pertaining to the supernatural, still provide a frame of reference that transcends the finite individual—a person may die, but his or her concerns will continue after death.

The Fading of Immortality

In quantitative terms, the twentieth century seems more death ridden than any other. Yet mass death is strangely impersonal; an eighteenth-century hanging at Tyburn probably had more immediate impact on the watching crowd than the almost incomprehensible statistics of modern war and calculated terror have today. In the last century, Byron, Shelley, Keats, and a whole generation of young poets haunted by romanticism and tuberculosis could be "half in love with easeful Death," wooing it as they would woo a woman. Even before World War I, German poet Rainer Maria Rilke could still yearn for "the great death" for which a man prepares himself, rather than the "little" death for which he is unprepared.

In today's literature there are few "great deaths." Tolstoy, Thomas Mann, and Conrad gave death a tragic dimension. Hemingway was among the last to try; his heroes died stoically, with style, like matadors. Nowadays, death tends to be presented as a banal accident in an indifferent universe. Much of the Theater of the Absurd ridicules both death and modern man's inability to cope with it. In Ionesco's *Amedee, or How to Get Rid of It,* the plot concerns a corpse that grows and grows until it floats away in the shape of a balloon—a balloon, that is, on the way to nowhere.

"If there is no immortality, I shall hurl myself into the sea," wrote Tennyson. Bismarck was calmer. "Without the hope of an afterlife," he said, "this life is not even worth the effort of getting dressed in the morning." Freud called the belief that death is the door to a better life "the oldest, strongest, and most insistent wish of mankind." But now death is steadily becoming

(continued)

(continued from previous page)

more of a wall and less of a door. . . . The Christian view of eternity is not merely endless time, and it need not involve the old physical concept of heaven and hell. It does involve the survival of some essence of self and an encounter with God. "Life after death," said theologian Karl Barth, "should not be regarded like a butterfly"—he might have said a balloon—"that flutters away above the grave and is preserved somewhere. Resurrection means not the continuation of life, but life's completion. The Christian hope is the conquest of death, not a flight into the Beyond."

The Fear of Nothingness

Admittedly, this hope so stated is more abstract than the fading pictures of sky-born glory, of hallelujah choruses and throngs of waiting loved ones. "People today could be described as more realistic about death," says one psychiatrist. "But inside I think they are more afraid. Those old religious assurances that there would be a gathering-in some day have largely been discarded, and I see examples all the time of neuroses caused by the fear of death." Harvard theologian Krister Stendahl agrees. "Socrates," he points out, "died in good cheer and in control, unlike the agony of Jesus with his deep human cry of desertion and loneliness. Americans tend to behave as Socrates did. But there is more of what Jesus stands for lurking in our unconsciousness."

Alone with his elemental fear of death, modern man is especially troubled by the prospect of a meaningless death and a meaningless life—the bleak offering of existentialism. "There is but one truly serious philosophical problem," wrote Albert Camus, "and that is suicide." In other words, why stay alive in a meaningless universe? The existentialist replies that man must live for the sake of living, for the things he is free to accomplish. But despite volumes of argumentation, existentialism never seems quite able to justify this conviction on the brink of a death that is only a trap door to nothingness.

There are surrogate forms of immortality: the continuity of history, the permanence of art, the biological force of sex. These can serve well enough to give life a purpose and a sense of fulfillment. But they cannot outwit death, and they are hardly satisfactory substitutes for the still persistent human hope that what happens here in three score years and ten is not the whole story.

"On Death as a Constant Companion," November 12, 1965, *Time Magazine.* Copyright 1965 Time, Inc. Reprinted by permission.

SYMBOLIC IMMORTALITY

Symbolic immortality (Lifton & Olson, 1974) refers to the belief that the meaning of the person can continue after he or she has died. For the religious, symbolic immortality is often related to the concept of soul, which either returns to its preex-

> I am assured of immortality, not by anything I do, but by not dying.
> —*Woody Allen*

istent state, goes to an afterlife, is reincarnated in another body, or is united with the cosmos. For the person whose primary orientation is temporal, symbolic immortality is achieved by being remembered by others, by creating something that remains useful or interesting to others, or by being part of a cause or social movement that continues after the individual's death.

One of the reasons that many parents give for deciding to have children is the need for an heir—someone to carry on the family name. Research has demonstrated that in the United States, families with only female children are more likely to continue having children (in hopes of producing a male offspring) than are families with only male children. For the ancient Hebrews, the cultural institution of the **levirate marriage** required that a relative of the deceased husband have sexual intercourse with his dead relative's widow in order to provide a male heir. If it is possible to pass on something of oneself to one's children, then children are one method of providing symbolic immortality.

Investing oneself in relationships with others also ensures that one will be remembered after death. Damon Runyon said as he was dying, "You can keep your things of bronze and stone, just give me one person who will remember me once a year." Some will argue that if we have influenced the lives of others, something of us will continue in their lives after we die. Organ donations supply a tangible method for providing this type of symbolic immortality. In this way, one can even ensure that a part of his or her physical self can continue in another person. Currently there is an increasing tendency for individuals to donate their organs and tissues upon death to the living (see chapter 8). In many urban areas, kidney foundations, eye banks, and transplant centers will supply donor cards and, when death occurs, will arrange for transplants. Currently, many kinds of tissues or organs are used for transplantation, including eye, skin, bone, tendon, bone marrow, kidney, liver, pancreas, blood vessel, lung, and heart.

One of the reasons why people write books, especially books on dying and death, is to promote their own symbolic immortality. As long as their books can be read, their influence will outlive their biological body. The same is true for television and motion picture stars. Each year the youthful Judy Garland is resurrected from the dead as *The Wizard of Oz* is shown on television.

Great inventors, political leaders, and athletic "hall of famers" are also given immortality when we use their products, remember their accomplishments, and celebrate their achievements. In the case of medical practitioners and bionic inventors, not only do the living remember their accomplishments, but also these accomplishments extend the lives of those who provide the dead with immortality.

RELATIVE DEATH MEANINGS IN SOCIETY

One of the most feared, distressing, and anxiety-producing deaths is a death that is perceived as being relatively meaningless. A lifetime is spent searching for and

Ozymandias
Percy Bysshe Shelley

I met a traveler from an antique land
    Who said: Two vast and trunkless legs of stone
    Stand in the desert . . . Near them, on the sand,
    Half sunk, a shattered visage lies, whose frown,
    And wrinkled lip, and sneer of cold command,
    Tell that its sculptor well those passions read
    Which yet survive, stamped on these lifeless things,
    The hand that mocked them, and the heart that fed;
    And on the pedestal these words appear:

"My name is Ozymandias, king of kings:
    Look on my works, ye Mighty, and despair!"

Nothing beside remains. Round the decay
    Of that colossal wreck, boundless and bare
    The lone and level sands stretch far away.

creating meaning. The search for meaning is a task that all people share. Furthermore, significant others are involved as individuals try to create meaning for themselves. In many respects, the meaning created turns out to be meaning for the group or society.

As the dying of martyrs dramatically illustrates, a death may be willingly entered into if it is meaningful. Given the right configuration of meaning components (see chapter 2), not to die would be more difficult. For example, dying may be preferable to defining oneself, and being defined by others, as a coward or a traitor.

Dying is acceptable if it furthers "the cause." People may, in fact, literally work themselves to death in order to obtain a promotion, an artistic achievement, or public recognition. Whatever the specific content, the key factor of concern is the meaning involved. If the meaning is right, dying may be evaluated as a worthwhile thing.

Within a given society there are high-status and low-status types of death. Giving one's life in defense of family or country is generally conceived as being of the high-status type. In times past, dying in childbirth was considered to be a high-status death for females.

The person's finite identity is protected by the group's permanence. Just as Standard Oil is the legacy of John D. Rockefeller, John H. Leming and Son's Insurance Agency will remain even after John H. Leming and his sons are dead (providing that the new owners feel that it is in their business interest not to change the name of the company).

The same can be said for people who give themselves to political movements and causes. Marx, Lenin, Stalin, and Mao—as leaders of communism—will be remembered by future communists, despite the efforts by present officials to accomplish the contrary. We even provide infamous immortality to villains, murderers, and traitors. It

The body of Mother Teresa, "the once and future saint" lying in state prior to her funeral.

seems ironic that most of us spend a lifetime working for immortality, when the guns of John Wilkes Booth, Lee Harvey Oswald, Sirhan Sirhan, and James Earl Ray supply their owners with our everlasting remembrance.

SOCIETY'S HEROES

The death of an individual brings about a change in influence over the members of his or her group or society. Heroes are more likely to come from the ranks of the dead than of the living.

Hero meaning is a symboled-meaning component. One cannot attain the status of hero by oneself. Society bestows this rank only upon certain of its members, one type of symboled immortality. Death is often a part of the process by which heroes are made. When something dies, something else is born or created. The death of Jesus Christ has expanded in significance over time. It is likely that Christ's death has had a greater impact upon humanity than did His life. The Roman Catholic Church grants sainthood only to persons who have been dead for many years. For that reason Mother Teresa, undoubtedly destined for sainthood, could only be given a funeral "fit for the best of mortals." Conversely, governments may grant pardons to convicted persons years after their deaths. Meaning is a flexible, yet powerful thing.

A number of interesting speculative questions arise. If there is an afterlife (in which those who are dead are "alive"), and if all of the heroes will become our contemporaries (assuming that we make it, too), what would this do to their hero status? In such a situation, would the hero status be retained? Would this person have to meet new hero qualifications? Would everyone in that "kingdom" be a hero? What would a society of heroes be like? Would the hero status be meaningful?

In conclusion, symbolic immortality is something that only the living can give the dead. Yet people live with the faith that their survivors will remember them and perpetuate the meaning of their lives after they die. Like religious interpretations of death, temporal meanings enable individuals to protect themselves and their social order from death. One problem remains, however, for those whose immortality depends upon others: What would happen if a nuclear holocaust were to occur, and there were no survivors?

Afterlife Experiences by the Clinically Dead

EMPIRICAL EVIDENCE FOR AFTERLIFE BELIEFS?

In the past, one of the assumptions that most people made about the field of thanatology was that the real "experts" were not among us—they were dead. With the publication of Raymond Moody's *Life After Life* (1975), many people have stepped forward to challenge this assumption. Having been near death, or having been declared clinically dead by medical authorities, a number of survivors from these experiences have "returned from the dead" to tell us that they now know what it is like to be dead and that they possess empirical evidence to support a rational belief in the afterlife.

A 1981 Gallup poll reported that 8 million (1 in 19) Americans had experienced the near-death phenomenon (Peay, 1991). If this ratio were applied to today's population there would be approximately 13 million people in the United States with near-death experiences (NDE). Barbara Walker (1989) claims that one adult in five within the United States has undergone a near-death experience. It is not surprising that scholars have organized the International Association for Near-Death Studies (IANDS), which publishes the *Journal of Near-Death Studies.*

The description in *Life After Life* (p. 193), developed by Raymond Moody, is a composite of the many accounts by individuals who have survived the experience of being near death or being declared clinically dead. This ideal model was constructed by interviewing more than 150 people who had had these experiences. Moody reports, and other scientists support (Noyes & Kletti, 1977; Rawlings, 1978; Ring, 1980; Flynn, 1986; Johnson, 1990), the similarity of most of these "life after death" accounts in which nine traits (Perry, 1988) define the near-death experience (even though it is rare for anyone to experience all nine). According to Moody (cited by Perry, 1988), at least one of the following 9 traits is enough to constitute a near-death experience.

1. *A sense of being dead.* At first many people don't realize that the experience that they are having has anything to do with being near death. They find themselves floating above their body and feeling confused. They wonder, "How can I be up here, looking at myself down there?"

2. *Peace and painlessness.* An illness or accident is frequently accompanied by intense pain, but suddenly during a near-death experience the pain vanishes. According to research by psychologist Kenneth Ring, 60 percent of people who have had a near-death experience report peace and painlessness.

3. *Out-of-body experience.* Frequently people feel themselves rising up and viewing their own bodies below. Most say that they are not simply a point of consciousness but seem to be in some kind of body. Ring says that 37 percent have out-of-body experiences.

4. *The tunnel experience.* This generally occurs after an out-of-body experience. For many a portal or tunnel opens, and they are propelled into darkness. Some hear a "whoosh" as they go into the tunnel, or they hear an electric vibration or humming sound. The descriptions are many, but the sense of heading toward an intense light is common to almost all tunnel experiences. Twenty-three percent of Ring's subjects reported entering darkness, which some described as entering a tunnel.

5. *People of light.* After people pass through the tunnel, they usually meet beings of intense light that permeate everything as these beings fill the people with feelings of love. As one person said, "I could describe this as 'light' or 'love,' and it would mean the same thing." They frequently meet with friends and relatives who have died, though the glowing beings can't always be identified. In Ring's research, 16 percent saw the light.

6. *Being of Light.* After meeting several beings of light, there is usually a meeting with a Supreme Being of Light. To some this is God or Allah, to others simply a holy presence. Most want to stay with him forever.

7. *The life review.* The Being of Light frequently takes the person on a life review, during which his or her life is viewed from a third-person perspective, almost as though watching a movie. Unlike watching a movie, however, the person not only sees every action, but also its effect on people in his or her life. The Being of Light helps put the events of life into perspective.

8. *Rising rapidly into the heavens.* Some people report a "floating experience," in which they rise rapidly into the heavens, seeing the universe from a perspective normally reserved for satellites and astronauts.

9. *Reluctance to return.* Many find their unearthly surroundings so pleasant that they don't want to return. Some even express anger at their doctors for bringing them back.

As we consider near-death experiences, the following 3 questions become relevant as we contemplate the relationship between these experiences and other material presented in this chapter.

1. Are NDEs real, and what do they tell us about the dying process and/or being dead?
2. Can afterlife beliefs be empirically supported by these NDE accounts?
3. How do religious beliefs affect the content of near-death or clinical death experiences?

To all of our questions, we must temper our responses by saying that if not real, these experiences are very real to those who have experienced them. Not unlike being in love, NDE phenomena are extremely subjective and do not lend themselves to verification by others. Research by Stevenson, Cook, and McClean-Rice (1989) has discovered that of those claiming the near-death experience only 45 percent were judged by medical experts to have had serious, life-threatening illnesses or injuries; the rest were judged to have had no life-threatening condition. It is difficult to doubt that the individual has experienced something; however, we are unable to prove, or disprove, that the individual has died. All that we can say scientifically is that the individual claims to have had the experience of "being dead."

Life After Life
Raymond A. Moody, Jr.

A man is dying and, as he reaches the point of greatest physical distress, he hears himself pronounced dead by his doctor. He begins to hear an uncomfortable noise, a loud ringing or buzzing, and at the same time feels himself moving very rapidly through a long dark tunnel. After this he suddenly finds himself outside of his own physical body, but still in the immediate physical environment, and he sees his own body from a distance, as though he is a spectator. He watches the resuscitation attempt from his unusual vantage point and is in a state of emotional upheaval.

After a while, he collects himself and becomes more accustomed to his body with very different powers from the physical body he has left behind. Soon other things begin to happen. Others come to meet and to help him. He glimpses the spirits of relatives and friends who have already died, and a loving, warm spirit of a kind he has never encountered before—a being of light— appears before him. This being asks him a question, nonverbally, to make him evaluate his life and helps him along by showing him a panoramic, instantaneous playback of the major events of his life. At some point he finds himself approaching some sort of barrier or border, apparently representing the limit between earthly life and the next life. Yet, he finds that he must go back to earth, that the time for his death has not yet come. At this point he resists, for by now he is taken up with his experiences in the afterlife and does not want to return. He is overwhelmed by intense feelings of joy, love, and peace. Despite his attitude, though, he somehow reunites with his physical body and lives.

Later he tries to tell others, but he has trouble doing so. In the first place, he can find no human words adequate to describe these unearthly episodes. He also finds that others scoff, so he stops telling other people. Still, the experience affects his life profoundly, especially his views about death and its relationship to life.

Life After Life: The Investigation of a Phenomenon—Survival of Bodily Death, by R. A. Moody, Jr., 1975, Boston: G. K. Hall. Reprinted by permission of LAL, Inc.

Returning to our analogy of being in love, all that can be known is that a person says that he or she is in love. Whether or not the person really is cannot be determined empirically. From the perspective of the individual, it does not really matter because a situation that has been defined as real will have very real behavioral consequences.

Barbara Walker claims that many NDE experients have post-NDE depression due to the fact that health-care providers and family members often deny the validity of the NDE experience. It is not uncommon for NDE experients to tell a nurse or psychiatrist about their near-death event, only to be told that they were hallucinating (Walker, 1989, p. 64). Ring (cited by Walker, 1989, p. 64) has noted a considerable number of divorces resulting from a spouse's inability to relate to the NDE.

If we try to determine the validity of a belief in an afterlife, we are confronted with problems similar to those encountered in the near-death experience. What can science say about beliefs in the afterlife? Scientifically, afterlife beliefs cannot be proved, or disproved, with NDE evidence. **Science** is based upon the principle of **intersubjectivity.** This means that independent observers, with different subjective orientations, must agree that something is "true" based upon their separate investigations. Unfortunately, the opportunity to experience the afterlife (and to return) is not uniformly available to all observers. Research by Tillman Rodabough (1985) gives many metaphysical, physiological, and social-psychological alternative explanations to account for the near-death experience. Therefore, although those who have had these experiences may feel rationally justified in their beliefs, the evidence that they use is not scientifically based. Science, at this point, can neither verify nor falsify afterlife beliefs.

In responding to our last question concerning the effects of religious beliefs on the content of near-death or clinical death experiences, there is some scientific evidence that can provide limited answers. According to Moody (1975) and Canning (1965), the content of afterlife experiences is largely a function of the religious background, training, and beliefs of the individuals involved. Only Roman Catholics see the Virgin Mary and the host of Catholic saints, whereas encounters with Joseph Smith are reserved for Mormon believers. Like dreams, continuity exists between experiences in "this world" and experiences in the "afterlife." For example, personages in the afterlife are dressed in an attire that would conform to the individual's cultural customs and beliefs. Also, relatives appear to be at the same age that they were when they were last seen. In fact, there is so much continuity between this world and the "other world" that persons with afterlife experiences report few, if any surprises. In response to this evidence, Kathy Charmaz (1980) raises the following question: Is the consciousness reported in these near-death experiences a reflection of a shared myth or evidence for it?

What we do know is that near-death experiences have profound effects upon the lives of most experients. According to P. M. Atwater (Johnson, 1990), 65 percent of NDE experients make significant changes in their lives, and 10 percent make radical changes. According to Skip Johnson (1990), people with a near-death experience have the following aftereffects as a result of the phenomenon:

Loss of fear of death. People report that they no longer fear the obliteration of consciousness of self.

Sense of the importance of love. A near-death experience can radically change peoples' value structure. They see the importance of brotherly love.

Sense of cosmic connection—feeling that everything in the universe is connected. Many have a new-found respect for nature and the world around them.

An appreciation of learning. People gain a newfound respect for knowledge, but not self-gain. Many often will embark on new careers or take up serious courses of study.

A new feeling of control. People feel that they have more responsibility for the course of their lives.

A sense of urgency. Some realize the shortness and fragility of their lives.

A better-developed spiritual side. This leads to spiritual curiosity and abandoning of religious doctrine purely for sake of doctrine.

While on the operating table my heart stopped beating and I died. At that moment, Merv, I learned that there was life after life and a chance for a best selling book based on this discovery, and a hit movie based on the book, and TV guest shots to plug the movie, and commercials generated by TV appearances and . . .

Reduction in worries. Some people feel more in control of life's stresses and are able to be more forgiving and patient.

Reentry syndrome. Some have difficulty in adjusting to normal life, especially those who undergo intensive changes in values that disrupt their former lifestyle. Some people report developing psychic abilities that can be scary to them and/or family and friends.

Finally, there is evidence that individuals (even attempted suicides) who have had near-death experiences do not try to bring about an end to their lives in order to return to the "life beyond." In fact, most individuals find new reasons for living as a result of these experiences (Flynn, 1986).

Conclusion

Religion is a system of beliefs and practices related to the sacred—to what is considered to be of ultimate significance. The cultural practice of religion continues because it meets basic social needs of individuals within a given society. A major function of religion, in this regard, is to explain the unexplainable.

For most "primitive," or less-complex societies, events are explained by a supernatural rather than rational or empirical means. Thus, an eclipse of the sun or moon was said to be a sign that the gods had a message for humankind. These supernatural explanations were needed, in part, because there were no competing rational or scientific explanations. Technologically and scientifically advanced societies tend to be less dependent upon supernatural explanations. Yet such explanations are still important, especially when scientific explanations are incomplete. It is not uncommon to hear a physician say, "Medical science is unable to cure this patient; it's now in God's hands." Or, a physician might say, "It's a miracle that the patient survived this illness; I can't explain the recovery." Thus, one might suggest that religion takes over where science and rationality leave off. We depend less on religious or supernatural explanations than do nonliterate societies, but nonetheless we rely on them when knowledge is incomplete.

Religion plays a significant role in societies by helping individuals cope with extraordinary events—especially death. Not only does religion help restore the normative order challenged by death, but also strong religious commitments can enable individuals to cope better with their own dying and the deaths of their loved ones. For others, strong commitments to a temporal orientation may fulfill many of the functions provided by a religious worldview.

Summary

1. Religion helps individuals, when the order of everyday life is challenged, by providing answers to problems of uncertainty, powerlessness, and scarcity created by death.
2. Religious systems provide a means to reestablish the social order challenged by death.
3. When one encounters death, the anxiety experienced is basically socially ascribed.
4. Religion provides individuals with solace when they attempt to cope with death.
5. Temporal interpretations of death provide a means for protecting the social order by emphasizing the empirical, natural, and "this worldly" view of death.
6. Symbolic immortality is evidenced by offspring carrying on the family name, by donating body organs, and by having accomplishments or achievements (positive and negative) remembered by others.
7. Near-death or afterlife experiences are influenced by the individual's religious background, cultural beliefs, and prior social experiences.
8. The strength of one's religious commitment is a significant variable in explaining the relationship between religion and the fear of death.

Discussion Questions

1. How does religion function to provide a restoration of the order challenged by the event of death?
2. What is the relationship between religious commitment and death fear?

3. Explain the following statement: "Religion afflicts the comforted and comforts the afflicted."
4. With regard to death anxiety, why does the believer, not the belief, bring peace?
5. How can symbolic immortality and temporal interpretations of death provide a source of anxiety reduction for those who face death?
6. How can organ donations provide symbolic immortality for donors and their loved ones?
7. Do accounts of near-death experiences provide empirical evidence for afterlife beliefs? Why or why not?
8. What are the similarities and differences in Jewish, Christian, Islamic, Hindu, and Buddhist beliefs about death and funeral practices?

Glossary

Anomie: A condition characterized by the relative absence or confusion of values within a group or society.

Curvilinear: Referring to a type of nonlinear relationship between two variables where at a certain point, associated with the increasing values in the independent variable, the relationship with the dependent variable changes. A scattergram graph of this relationship will look like either a U or an inverted U.

Dysfunctional: Referring to any consequence of a social system that is judged to be a disturbance to the adjustment, stability, or integration of the group or the members of that group.

Intersubjectivity: A property of science whereby two or more scientists, studying the same phenomenon, can reach the same conclusion.

Levirate Marriage: An institution typified by the Hebrew requirement that a relative of the deceased husband must have sexual intercourse with the deceased's widow in order to provide a male heir.

Marginal Situations: Unusual events or social circumstances that do not occur in normal patterns of social interaction.

Religion: A system of beliefs and practices related to the sacred, the supernatural, and/or a set of values to which the individual is very committed.

Religiosity: The extent of interest, commitment, or participation in religious values, beliefs, and activities.

Rituals: A set of culturally prescribed actions or behaviors.

Science: A body of knowledge based upon sensory evidence or empirical observations.

Symbolic Immortality: The ascription of immortality to the individual by perpetuating the meaning of the person (the self).

Temporal: Referring to a "here and now" or "this worldly" orientation that does not take into account the afterlife or a supernatural existence.

References

Ayer, M. (1964). *Made in Thailand.* New York: Knopf.

Berger, P. L. (1969). *Sacred canopy: Elements of a sociological theory of religion.* New York: Doubleday.

Canning, R. R. (1965). Mormon return-from-the-dead stories: Fact or folklore? *Utah Academy Proceedings, 42,* 1.

Carse, J. (1981). Death. In K. Crim, R. A. Bullard, & L. D. Shinn (Eds.), *Abingdon dictionary of living religions* Nashville: Abingdon Press.

Charmaz, K. (1980). *The social reality of death.* Reading, MA: Addison-Wesley.

Durkheim, E. (1915). *The elementary forms of religious life.* New York: George Allen and Unwin.

Eickelman, D. F. (1987). Rites of passage: Muslim rites. In M. Eliade (Ed.), *The encyclopedia of religion* (12th ed.). New York: Macmillan.

Faulkner, J., & DeJong, G. F. (1966). Religiosity in 5-D: An empirical analysis. *Social Forces, 45,* 246–254.

Flynn, C. P. (1986). *After the beyond: Human transformation and the near-death experience.* Englewood Cliffs, NJ: Prentice-Hall.

Glock, C., & Stark, R. (1966). *Christian beliefs and anti-Semitism.* New York: Harper and Row.

Habenstein, R. W., & Lamers, W. M. (1974). *Funeral customs the world over.* Milwaukee: Bulfin Printers.

The Holy Bible (Revised Standard Version). (1962). New York: Oxford University Press.

Homans, G. C. (1965). Anxiety and ritual: The theories of Malinowski and Radcliffe-Brown. In W. A. Lessa & E. Z. Vogt (Eds.), *Reader in comparative religion: An anthropological approach.* New York: Harper and Row.

Johnson, S. (1990, August 26). Near-death experiences almost always change lives. Charleston, SC, *News and Courier/The Evening Post,* p. 13I.

Kavanaugh, R. E. (1972). *Facing death.* Baltimore: Penguin Books.

Knobel, P. S. (1987). Rites of passage: Jewish rites. In M. Eliade (Ed.), *The encyclopedia of religion* (12th ed.). New York: Macmillan.

Leming, M. R. (1979–1980). Religion and death: A test of Homans's thesis. *Omega, 10*(4), 347–364.

Lewis, C. S. (1961). *A grief observed.* London: Faber and Faber.

Lifton, R., & Olson, E. (1974). *Living and dying.* New York: Praeger.

Long, J. B. (1987). Underworld. In M. Eliade (Ed.), *The encyclopedia of religion* (12th ed.). New York: Macmillan.

Malinowski, B. (1965). The role of magic and religion. In W. A. Lessa & E. Z. Vogt (Eds.), *Reader in comparative religion: An anthropological approach.* New York: Harper and Row.

McBrien, R. P. (1987). Roman Catholicism. In M. Eliade (Ed.), *The encyclopedia of religion* (12th ed.). New York: Macmillan.

Moody, R. A., Jr. (1975). *Life after life: The investigation of a phenomenon—Survival of bodily death.* Boston: G. K. Hall.

Noyes, R., Jr., & Kletti, R. (1977). Panoramic memory. *Omega, 8,* 181–193.

O'Dea, T. (1966). *The sociology of religion.* Englewood Cliffs, NJ: Prentice-Hall.

Pardue, P. (1968). Buddhism. In *International encyclopedia of the social sciences* (2nd ed., pp. 165–184). New York: Macmillan.

Peay, P. (1991, September-October). Back from the grave. *Utne Reader, 47,* 72–73.

Perry, P. (1988, September). Brushes with death. *Psychology Today, 22,* 14–17.

Radcliffe-Brown, A. R. (1965). Taboo. In W. A. Lessa & E. Z. Vogt (Eds.), *Reader in comparative religion: An anthropological approach.* New York: Harper and Row.

Rahman, F. (1987). *Health and medicine in the Islamic tradition.* New York: Crossroad Press.

Rawlings, M. (1978). *Beyond death's door.* Nashville: Thomas Nelson.

Ring, K. (1980). *Life at death: A scientific investigation of the near-death experience.* New York: Coward, McCann and Geoghegan.

Rodabough, T. (1985). Near-death experiences: An examination of the supporting data and alternative explanations. *Death Studies, 9,* 95–113.

Srinivas, M. N., & Shah, A. M. (1968). Hinduism. In *International encyclopedia of the social sciences* (Vol. 6., pp. 358–366). New York: Macmillan.

Stevenson, I., Cook, E. W., & McClean-Rice, N. (1989). Are persons reporting "near-death experiences" really near death? A study of medical records. *Omega, 20*(4), 45–54.

Vernon, G. M. (1970). *Sociology of death: An analysis of death-related behavior.* New York: Ronald Press.

Walker, B. A. (1989). Health care professionals and the near-death experience. *Death Studies, 13,* 63–71.

Suggested Readings

Berger, P. L. (1969). *Sacred canopy: Elements of a sociological theory of religion.* New York: Double-day. Excellent treatment of the role of religious worldviews as they relate to life crises. Death is discussed as the ultimate marginal situation to normal social functioning that calls forth religious meaning systems.

Eliade, M. (Ed.). (1987). *The encyclopedia of religion.* New York: Macmillan. Tremendous academic resource on religious rites, beliefs, and traditions. This reference tool is written from an interdisciplinary perspective by international scholars of religion.

Flynn, C. P. (1986). *After the beyond: Human transformation and the near-death experience.* Englewood Cliffs, NJ: Prentice-Hall. Rodabough, T. (1985). Near-death experiences: An examination of the supporting data and alternative explanations. *Death Studies, 9,* 5–113. Walker, B. A. (1989). Health care professionals and the near-death experience. *Death Studies, 13,* 63–71. A book and two articles that provide a background for dealing with persons who claim to have had the near-death experience.

Homans, G. C. (1965). Anxiety and ritual: The theories of Malinowski and Radcliffe-Brown. In W. A. Lessa & E. Z. Vogt (Eds.), *Reader in comparative religion: An anthropological approach* (pp. 83–88). New York: Harper and Row. Leming, M. R. (1979–1980). Religion and death: A test of Homans's thesis. *Omega, 10*(4), 347–364. Two articles that review the theoretical and empirical evidence regarding the relation between religion and death anxiety.

Kavanaugh, R. E. (1972). *Facing death.* Baltimore: Penguin Books. A former Roman Catholic priest, Kavanaugh reflects on his experiences with death in the context of his religious background. He discusses the role of religion in the adjustment process to dying and death.

Moody, R. A., Jr. (1975). *Life after life: The investigation of a phenomenon—Survival of bodily death.* Boston: G. K. Hall. Ring, K. (1980). *Life at death: A scientific investigation of the near-death experience.* New York: Coward, McCann and Geoghegan. Two books that provide an understanding of the near-death experience.

Parry, J. K., & Ryan, A. S. (Eds.). (1995). *A cross-cultural look at death, dying, and religion.* Chicago: Nelson-Hall Publishers. Religion and death are discussed in this anthology. Groups included are African Americans, Buddhists, Roman Catholics and other Christians, Chinese, Dominicans, Filipinos, Christian fundamentalists, gays, Muslims, Jews, Koreans, lesbians, Mexican Americans, and women.

Spiro, H. M., Curnen, M. G. M., & Wandel, L. P. (Eds.). (1996). *Facing death: Where culture, religion, and medicine meet.* New Haven, CT: Yale University Press. Christian, Judaic, Islamic, Hindu, and Chinese perspectives on death and rituals of mourning are discussed.

Young, M., & Cullen, L. (1996). A good death: Conversations with East Londoners. New York: Routledge. This book takes 4 approaches to death: The rational, the spiritual, the humorous, and the poetic.

Related Web Sites

http://scholar.cc.emory.edu/scripts/AAR/AAR-MENU.html   The home page of the American Academy of Religion.

http://www.evansville.edu/~philweb/relinks.html   World Wide Web links to Judaism, Christianity, Buddhism, Hinduism, and Islam.

http://www.bates.edu/Faculty/Philosophy%20and%20Religion/Religion_Resources.html   Internet resources for the study of religion.

http://www.gasou.edu/psychweb/psyrelig/links.html   Psychology links to religion sites, including Judaism, Christianity, Buddhism, Hinduism, and Islam.

http://www.realtime.net/~rlp/dwp/mystic/ Mysticism in World Religions is a web site that presents the mystical traditions of Judaism, Christianity, Islam, Buddhism, Hinduism, and Taoism. It allows one to compare and contrast these six religions, or one can go to a religion's particular index.

http://www.asanet.org/ The home page of the American Sociological Association.

http://www.apa.org/ The home page of the American Psychological Association.

http://www.ameranthassn.org/ The home page of the American Anthropological Association.

http://www.trinity.edu/~mkearl/death-4.html#us Michael Kearl provides a religious perspective on death as he discusses the uniqueness of humans in their needs for order and meaningfulness.

http://www.wwdc.com/death/quest.html "The Quest for Meaning" is an article written by John Morgan dealing with spiritual meanings and interpretations of death.

http://www.shemayisrael.co.il/burial/index.htm Web site of the International Jewish Burial Society.

http://uscj.org/michigan/s-fielcs/bergde.html A very comprehensive bereavement guide for Judaism.

http://ucsu.colorado.edu/~jsu/launcher.html The ultimate Jewish/Israel link launcher with 6,000 World Wide Web links.

http://www.apk.net/ucc/caring/death.htm Resources on death and dying provided by Curt Ackley of the United Church of Christ Council for Health and Human Service Ministries.

http://www.cin.org/cinmateo.html The web site of the Catholic Information Network. Many of the topics are death-related.

http://www.webdesk.com:80/catholic/prayers/prayers.html A web site of Roman Catholic prayers.

http://www2.hawaii.edu/uhpress/Journals/BC/BCArts.html The home page of the *Journal of Buddhist-Christian Studies.*

http://www.realtime.net/~rlp/dwp/mystic/Buddhist/Sogyal/book.html Web site dedicated to the topic of the *Tibetan Book of Living and Dying.*

http://www.sisfotel.net.id/htm/dsi/ngaben.htm An article that describes a cremation ceremony in Bali.

http://hyperlink.com/weaver/95/25_5/newcon/sikh/death/sikhdeth.htm Death from the point of view of the Sikh religion.

http://www.wam.umd.edu/~ibrahim/ World Wide Web Islamic page with links to Islamic sites.

http://www.vt.edu:10021/org/islam_sa/death.txt A web site concerned with Islamic views of dying and death.

http://www.eas.asu.edu/~voegele/bioarchy/said.html An article on death and burial in Islamic societies.

http://www.vmedia.com/shannon/voodoo/death.html Web site dedicated to the topics of voodoo and death.

http://www.sisfotel.net.id/htm/dsi/ngaben.htm A web site dedicated to the celebration of Day of the Dead (*Dia de los Muertos*).

http://www.cts.com/~rosfshp/pla/plaeng01.html   "The Passing—And Life Afterward" is a Rosicrucian perspective on death.

http://www.csulb.edu:80/~persepha/death.html   A "new age" goddess worshipper resource on death.

http://www.codesh.org/articles/flynn_04_96.html   A web site that provides a secular humanist perspective on death and dying.

http://134.184.35.101/IMMORT.html   "The Will for Immortality," written by C. Joslyn and V. Turchin and published on the Principia Cybernetica web site.

http://www.dircon.co.uk/reincarn/   Reincarnation International home page, a web site that puts soul into your life; from the publishers of the only magazine in the world devoted to the exploration of reincarnation and its implications.

http://www.spiritweb.org/Spirit/reincarnation.html   Web site concerning thoughts about reincarnation and alternative forms of spirituality.

http://www.tiac.net/users/smurungu/shona_religion.html   Shona religion and beliefs; an article about an African tribal religion.

http://www.critpath.org/newsletters/wtp/0196/spiritl.htm   "Spiritual Support at the End of Life" is an article written from a Christian perspective for patients dying with AIDS.

http://www.thebody.com/anin/aninpage.html   AIDS National Interfaith Network (ANIN) is a private, nonprofit organization founded in 1988. ANIN was created to ensure that individuals with HIV and AIDS receive compassionate and nonjudgmental support, care, and assistance. ANIN coordinates a network of nearly 2,000 AIDS ministries. ANIN works with national faith-based, AIDS-specific networks; supports community-based AIDS ministries; and educates AIDS service organizations, the religious community at large, and the general public about AIDS ministries.

http://www.coredcs.com/~sbro/hpdying.htm   Christian prayers for the dying.

http://www.execpc.com/~careres/   This is a collection of articles, books, seminars, and a newsletter for pastors and other Christian counselors who are looking for helpful materials for the people whom they counsel. The subject matter covered includes such typical issues as guilt and shame, grief and trauma, and other topics that come up in pastoral and Christian counseling.

http://www.trinity.edu/~mkearl/death-3.html#hf   Web site dealing with symbolic immortality and memorialization.

http://www.alcor.org/   Web site of Alcor, the world's largest cryonics organization.

http://www.cryocare.org/cryocare/   A web site dealing with cryonics.

http://204.127.237.11/   The web site of the United Network for Organ Sharing Transplantation Information.

http://www.transweb.org/   TransWeb is a web site all about transplantation and organ donation.

http://www.ca-probate.com/wills.htm   Mark Welch's wills and testaments of the famous and not-so-famous on the World Wide Web.

http://www.iands.org/iands/   Home page for the International Association for Near-Death Studies (IANDS).

http://odin.community.net:80/~timlig/afterdth.html   "Can There Really Be a Life After Death?" is an article written by Reverend Donald K. Rogers.

http://www.trinity.edu/~mkearl/never.html   "You Never Have to Die: On Mormons, NDEs, Cryonics, and the American Immortalist Ethos," written by Michael Kearl, forthcoming in Kathy Charmaz, Glennys Howarth, and Allan Kellehear (Eds.), *The Unknown Country: Experiences of Death in Australia, Britain and the USA* (London: Macmillan).

http://gaia.ecs.csus.edu/~williamk/   A web site with many NDE accounts that is updated regularly.

http://www.mindspring.com/~scottr/end.html   This web site provides links to most of the near-death experience (NDE) information on the Internet.

Part Three

Understanding the

Dying Process

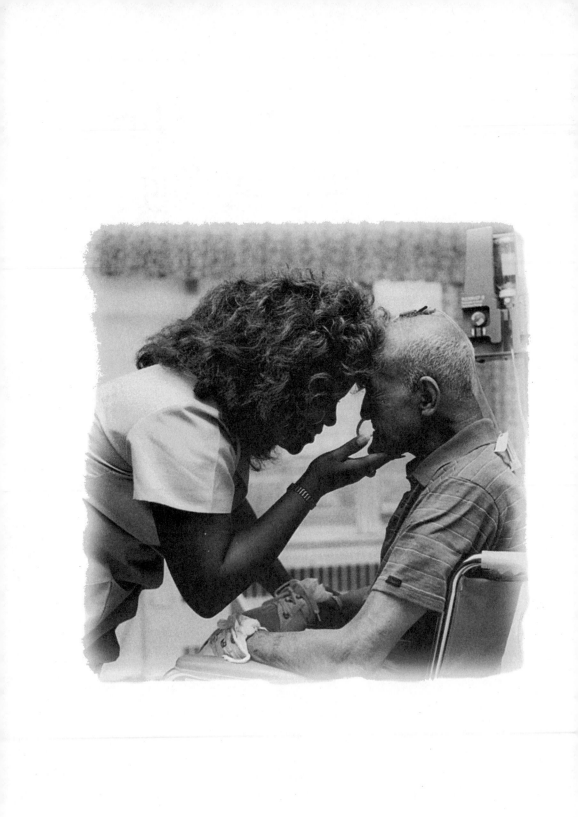

Chapter 6

The Dying Process

After the death of his wife, Jenny, Forrest Gump stated, "Mamma always said that dying is a part of life. I sure wish it wasn't."

—FORREST GUMP

I'm not afraid of dying. I just don't want to be there when it happens.

—WOODY ALLEN

Of all of the events in life, dying can be the most stressful. Most of us would probably agree with both Forrest Gump's and Woody Allen's observations on dying: We wish that dying did not have to occur and would really prefer to not be there when it happens. As discussed in chapter 1, people tend to fear the process of dying more than the event of death itself. Many factors will contribute to and alleviate the stress related to the dying process. In this chapter, we are primarily concerned with the physical and social factors.

Among other things, dying is a process that happens to the physical body of the individual. Although the determination of the timing of death is problematic, there is a qualitative difference between a live and a dead human being. For the most part, the cause of death is ultimately attributed to physiological factors. However, the biological aspect of dying means less to us than the meaning we place upon the events that take place during the dying process.

Death Meanings and Their Effects Upon the Dying Process

The meaning of our dying will depend to a great extent upon the social context in which the dying occurs. As discussed in chapter 2, meanings are the basic component of human behavior because individuals respond to the meanings of phenomena rather than to the phenomena themselves. Meanings are both socially created and socially perpetuated (Leming, Vernon, & Gray, 1977).

Sociologist Robert Merton, in a classic article written in 1949 entitled "The Bearing of Sociological Theory on Empirical Research," illustrates the idea of responding to the conceptual situation or meaning, rather than to the physical object or phenomenon itself, with "gasoline drums." Objects conceptually described as "gasoline drums" will produce behavior of great care in people. But, if people are confronted with "empty gasoline drums," behavior is different: A smoker, for example, will not likely be very cautious around an "empty" drum. Yet, the "empty" drum is more hazardous because it contains explosive vapor. We respond, not to the physical object, but to the conceptualized situation or meaning of the phenomenon or object. "Empty" here is a synonym for "null and void or inert," without regard to vapor in the drum. Thus, empty gasoline drums become the occasion for fires. Clarification of the meaning of "empty" would have a profound effect upon our behavior.

The major types of meanings to which individuals respond in death-related situations are the following: time meanings, space meanings, norm and role meanings, value meanings, object and self meanings, and social situation meanings (Vernon, 1972). We will now look at each of these types of meanings and their effects upon the dying process.

TIME MEANINGS

As anthropologist Colin Turnbull once told the author, "Americans want to live forever. If you ask individuals how long they wish to live, they will probably say somewhere in the upper 90s because they do not suspect they will reach 100. But if they reach 100, then they will aim for 101, 102, etc." Turnbull says that African groups know when it is time to die, and they accept this. Perhaps Richard Pryor summed it up well when he said, "Even if I live for 100 years, I'll be dead a lot longer." Thus, one is dead longer than alive.

In thinking about the dying process, the first thing that comes to our awareness is the concept of time. We are confronted with the fact that time, for the terminally ill patient, is running out. Yet, when does the dying process begin? Are we all not dying, with some reaching the state of being dead before others? From the moment of our births, we are approaching the end of our lives. We assume that terminally ill patients will experience death before other individuals, but this is not always the case.

Because it is possible to diagnose diseases from which most people die, we can assume that patients with these diseases are "more terminal" than individuals without them. The terminally ill patient is very much concerned with the time dimension of his or her physical existence. Many surveys (see Glaser & Strauss, 1965) have demonstrated that as many as 80 percent of patients want to be told if their illness is

---

Guest Lecturer

I invited to class a woman who had been diagnosed as a terminal cancer patient. Deeply impressed by the visitor's positive outlook on the time left to her, one student on the following day noted, "When I came into the session I expected to meet someone who was dying. Instead, I realize that woman is more alive than I am. The discussion wasn't about dying at all, it was about living."

"Dialectic on Dying" (pp. 182–189), by J. M. Boyle. In M. M. Newell et al. (Eds.), *The Role of the Volunteer in the Care of the Terminal Patient and the Family*, New York: The Foundation of Thanatology/Arno Press, 1981.

---

terminal. However, physicians traditionally may have felt unprepared to tell their patients of a terminal diagnosis.

With more emphasis on consumer rights today, physicians are more likely to tell patients of their diagnosis than was the case in the early 1960s. In a 1961 survey of physicians (Oken, 1961), only 10 percent favored telling a cancer patient his/her diagnosis, whereas in 1994, 95 percent of physicians surveyed self-reported that they always disclose the diagnosis (Holland, 1994). This change could reflect the American Medical Association's shift in policy in 1980 (Dickinson & Tournier, 1994) of encouraging physicians to tell the patient his/her prognosis:

> The physician must properly inform the patient of the diagnosis and of the nature and purpose of the treatment undertaken or prescribed. The physician must not refuse to so inform the patient. Previously, the AMA had left the decision to the discretion of the physician. Additionally, under the Federal Patient Self-Determination Act of 1991, hospitals must inform patients of their rights to make their own decisions about their medical care (Blackhall et al., 1995); physicians today commonly tell their patients their diagnoses, no matter how dire.

A recent study by Dickinson and Tournier (1994) of physicians' attitudes toward terminally ill patients revealed more of an openness toward informing the patient of his or her prognosis after 10 years of practicing medicine than soon after graduation from medical school. A study by Seale (1991) in England suggests a general preference for more openness between physicians, dying patients, and their families about illness and death. This openness should be tempered by the consideration that bad news needs to be broken slowly in a context of support while recognizing that not everyone wishes to know all. Suggestions for breaking bad news to patients by Sean Morrison and Jane Morris (1995; adapted from R. Buckman, 1992) follow a 6-step protocol:

1. Arrange to meet in a private setting, where you will not be interrupted.
2. Establish what the patient (and/or family) already knows.
3. Identify how much the patient (and/or family) wants to know.
4. Share the diagnosis and prognosis with the patient (and/or family). Present the various treatment options available and provide a realistic appraisal of the benefits and burdens of each.

5. Respond to the patient's (and/or family's) feelings, and identify and acknowledge their reactions.

6. Formulate a plan of care and establish a contract for the future.

Kerry Gasperson (1996), in her recent study of first-year medical students' attitudes toward delivering bad news in a clinical context, observes that a prominent concern of these students is the choice of specific words to use and to avoid. The professionals seem to differ regarding the use of euphemisms when delivering bad news, notes Gasperson. Maguire and Faulkner (1992) endorse the use of euphemisms to ease the patient into the truth, whereas Timothy Quill (1991) strongly advises against using euphemisms when communicating a diagnosis to the patient. When the message is not clear, some clinicians think, communication difficulties may result. For example, stories are abundant about patients, when told that they have a malignancy, being relieved to know that it is not cancer (Sell et al., 1993).

Some ethnic groups in the United States prefer that the patient not be told the prognosis. A study of 800 elderly patients in California (Blackhall et al., 1995) found that immigrants from South Korea and Mexico were far less willing to let terminally ill patients make decisions about medical care than were either black or white Americans. For immigrants from those countries, the role of the family was larger and that of the individual was smaller than is generally the case in the United States. As to whether a terminally ill patient should be told the truth, black and white respondents were about twice as likely as Korean Americans to say yes and about one and a half times as likely as Mexican Americans. In Japan a similar situation exists as doctors rarely tell dying patients that they are terminally ill (Kristof, 1996).

Though many physicians in the past have not favored telling their patients, Elisabeth Kübler-Ross (1969) claims that it is not a question of whether the patient should be told, but rather of *how* the patient is told. Should patients be told the amount of time that they have left? Specifying an amount of time dispels hope and serves no function other than telling the patient that the condition is very serious and life threatening, advises Kübler-Ross (1969). If the patient presses for time specificity, a range of time should be given, such as: "Sixty percent of the patients with your disease live as long as 3 to 5 years." This statement provides hope without deluding the patient. Also, it is honest. Medical science cannot say with any certainty that a person will live 1 year—some die sooner, and others live longer (some even outlive the physician!).

The doctor's informing the patient that he or she will do everything possible to help the patient and make the illness as painless as possible is certainly reassuring to the patient. I had an acquaintance who was told by his neurologist that he had a malignant tumor on the brain. The patient immediately said, "That means I will die, doesn't it, Doctor?" The physician replied, "Not necessarily. We have chemotherapy, radiation, and surgery that we can try." Immediately, this news gave the patient the zest to try to overcome the disease and not give up. He would not have to fight the battle alone; the physician was fighting with him.

An important aspect of communication between physician and patient is that the doctor should be clear in giving information to the patient and should avoid gobbledygook terminology, whether relating to a terminal condition or otherwise. When I was a graduate student, several hours after I had had surgery a nurse came into my room and asked, "Have you voided?" I had no idea what "voided" meant. I'm sure that

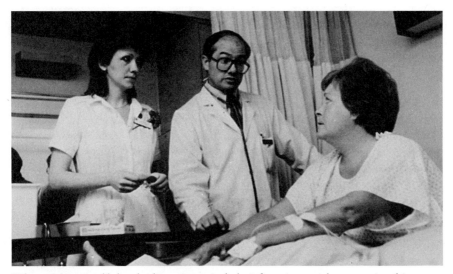

When a patient is told that the disease is terminal, the information must be communicated in a manner that is honest but does not rob the patient of a sense of hopefulness.

I had a blank look on my face and made no response. After a few seconds, she told me that if I did not void within the next 2 hours, a catheter would have to be inserted. Knowing what a catheter was, I almost voided on the spot! Indeed, had she used layperson's language and said "urinated," that would have been clear to me.

Thus, after the physician has given the news to a patient, there is no wonder that when the physician asks the patient if there are any questions the patient often has none. Many times the patient is not clear about what the doctor said. Indeed, as patients we need to be more assertive and to inquire because it is our lives and our right to know that are at stake.

SPACE MEANINGS

Even when the patient has not been told of a terminal condition, he or she will eventually become aware of it. Many times factors related to social space will give the patient clues that the condition is terminal. As E. P. Seravalli (1988, p. 1729) notes, "The dying usually come to know when the end is near by observing themselves and the people around them." Within the hospital, there are areas where the very ill are treated. When one is placed into the intensive care unit or onto an oncology ward, it becomes obvious that all is not well and that death is a real possibility. When being moved from a double room to a single-patient room, 17-year-old Tom Nelson, who was dying of cancer (as seen on CBS's "Living With Death"), said, "Isn't this what they do to you when you are about to die?"

Confinement to a health-care institution conveys a tremendous amount of meaning to the patient. For the most part, the patient is alone. Through spatial meanings the individual is "informed" that he or she is removed from those things that give life

---

Sharing the Experience of Dying

Some of the most beautiful human interactions I have witnessed have occurred between dying patients and supportive families. Sometimes the quality of human interactions in the terminal phase far exceeds anything the patient or family experienced prior to diagnosis.

I strongly feel the dying patient should be told as much as he or she wants to know. The family should also be encouraged to share feelings with the patient in an open manner. Nothing is worse than dying alone. The terminal patient whose family won't broach the subject, or who is afraid to upset his or her family or doctors with fears and feelings, does die alone.

A physician's comment from a survey of 1,093 physicians conducted by Dickinson and Pearson, 1980–1981.

---

meaning and purpose—family, friends, and job. For the terminally ill patient this is the first stage of **societal disengagement**—the process by which society withdraws from, or no longer seeks, the individual's efforts.

The following statement (Hale, 1971) demonstrates the significance of space when applied to the dying patient:

> As for the patient himself, he faces his life's ultimate crisis in a foreign place—the hospital. Usually, he dies alone, not in the presence of anyone who cares. Often the family is allowed to visit even the dying only during the hours set by the hospital. And since hospital visits usually lack privacy, they are of little comfort either to the patient or to the relatives who are entering the period of "anticipatory grief." There is little room or opportunity for sharing that most poignant moment of a lifetime—death! There is little opportunity for dignity in those settings.

Though many institutional settings have liberalized their visitation policies somewhat since the early 1970s, unfortunately the preceding statement by Hale still basically holds.

Within any health-care setting, the patient's confinement serves to diminish his or her social and personal power. According to Rodney Coe (1970), three processes occur within the institution to accomplish this—"stripping," controlling resources, and restricting mobility. The process of stripping takes place when the patient is issued a hospital gown and stripped of any valuables for safe keeping. When this is done, the patient's identity is also stripped. Most factors that differentiate patients with regard to status in the larger society are taken from the patients and create the primary status of patients—all patients look alike. According to Coe (1970, p. 300), "Every distinctly personalizing symbol, material or otherwise, is taken away, thus reducing the patient to the status of just one of many." Perhaps this helps to explain why physicians are known to be such bad patients—they are forced to relinquish their physician status when they are admitted to the hospital.

The second process is *controlling resources*. When the patient is denied access to medical records and important information about the events of the hospital, personal power is greatly diminished. Personal power is the ability to make decisions that determine the direction of one's own life. Without all of the information concerning one's situation and the place of one's confinement, it may not be possible to make important decisions. One method used by hospitals in controlling resources is to deny all patients and their families access to medical charts and records—an "ignorance is bliss" mentality.

The third process is *restricting mobility.* Not being able to leave one's room or bed further reduces the patient's personal power. The patient is put into a position of dependency upon others. Confinement of this type greatly affects the patient's autonomy. It also makes it possible for others to withdraw from the patient.

Social space is very important in the process of patient disengagement. This disengagement can be accomplished by two methods—the patient can withdraw from others, and others can withdraw from the patient. If the patient is debilitated by illness, energy may not be abundant enough to continue normal patterns of social interaction. The loss of physical attractiveness can also cause the patient to withdraw. Some patients, knowing that their condition is terminal, may disengage as a coping strategy to avoid having to see all that their death will take from them. They may disengage as a sign of their acceptance of social death—"I'm as good as dead" (anticipatory death).

When significant others withdraw from the patient, patient disengagement will take place. In this situation the process of disengagement is something beyond the patient's control. Family members and friends can refrain from visiting the patient as a sign of their acceptance of social death. The terminal label can stigmatize the patient, and others may treat the individual differently.

Orville Kelly, founder of Make Each Day Count (a support group for persons with cancer), tells the story of being invited by a friend to dinner. The table was set with the finest china and silverware—with one exception. Orville's place setting consisted of a paper plate and plastic fork, spoon, and knife. Mr. Kelly was the guest but he had cancer so he was supposed to use disposables so no one would be contaminated!

Randall Wagner, an active volunteer with the American Cancer Society, recalls a situation at a high school football game when his leukemia was in a state of remission. A friend had a Thermos of hot chocolate but had only two cups. The first cup was given to Randall. After he had finished drinking, he returned the cup to be filled for someone else. Nobody would drink out of Randall's cup, however. He was told to "just keep it."

Many individuals are afraid of "catching" cancer. One does not "catch" cancer. Likewise, many individuals are afraid to be physically near someone with AIDS for fear of acquiring the disease. Because AIDS is primarily passed through sexual intercourse, intravenous drug needles, blood transfusions, and from the mother to the fetus/embryo, one is not going to acquire AIDS by sitting next to someone or by physically being in the room with an AIDS victim. Because many do not know how to relate to persons with cancer or AIDS or to the terminally ill in general, they withdraw as a method of coping with their inadequacy.

NORM AND ROLE MEANINGS

Norms are plans of action or expected behavior patterns felt to be appropriate for a particular situation. **Roles** are plans of action or expected behavior patterns specifying what should be done by persons who occupy particular social positions. Applied to the death-related behavior of the dying patient, norm definitions would involve the general expectation that the dying patient should be brave and accept the fact that life will soon end. The patient is not supposed to cry or become verbal in regard to feelings about his or her death. Nurses often sanction such behavior by giving less attention to patients who deviate from this norm. Elisabeth Kübler-Ross (1969, pp. 56–57) gives the following example of one such deviant:

> The patient would stand in front of the nurses' desk and demand attention for herself and other terminally ill patients, which the nurses resented as interference and inappropriate behavior. Since she was quite sick, they did not confront her with her unacceptable behavior, but expressed their resentment by making shorter visits to her room, by avoiding contact, and by the briefness of their encounters.

Role meanings differ from norm meanings in that they specify, in a detailed fashion, what behavior is expected of persons who occupy specific social positions. For example, if a wife/mother who is a principal provider in the family is dying, it is expected that she do all that she can before death to provide for the financial needs of her family. It would probably be expected that she make arrangements for her funeral, ensure that her bills are paid, finalize her will, and establish a trust fund for her children.

One of the important aspects of norm and role meanings is their relationship to the process of societal disengagement by which society withdraws from the individual (Atchley, 1994). The individual can also withdraw from societal participation and choose not to perform the roles that he or she performed before the terminal diagnosis. This type of disengagement goes beyond withdrawing from interaction patterns with others and refers to a withdrawal from the social structure (such as quitting one's job and taking a trip around the world).

Role disengagement has many consequences for the patient and his or her family members. N. J. Gaspard (1970, p. 78) notes the following about a family with traditional gender roles:

> If the father is ill, the mother must generally become the breadwinner, and children who are able often must take over household tasks sooner than they otherwise might. Each person in such a situation may feel both guilt and resentment at such a change whereby they can no longer adequately fulfill the expectations they have had of themselves. Conversely, if the mother is ill, household help may be hired, and problems may arise with regard to the mother's maintaining, in so far as is possible, her self-image in relation to caring for her family.

In addition to the disengagement process, patients are expected to acquire the **sick role** (Parsons, 1951). They are expected to want to get better and to want to seek more treatment even though everyone realizes that such treatment only prolongs death and not life. This role disengagement can create conflict within the family, especially when the patient has accepted his or her death (and even longs for it), whereas family members are unwilling to let the patient go. As Kübler-Ross (1969) documents, families many times cannot comprehend that a patient reaches a point when death comes as a great relief and that patients die easier if they are allowed and helped to detach themselves slowly from all of the responsibilities and meaningful relationships in their lives. John Harvey (1996, p. 173) states:

There is a kind of freedom that comes with a recognition that your time is limited. Long-term consequences seem less important. A certain kind of fearless authenticity often comes from a confrontation with one's mortality.

Often, we the survivors are the stumbling blocks for dying persons. We do not want the dying person to die, thus we will not "let go" and allow her or him to say good-bye and break away.

VALUE MEANINGS

Values, like all other meaning systems, are socially created. They are not inherent in the phenomena, but rather they are applied by humans to the phenomena. Death per se is neither good nor evil. Humans do ascribe value, however, to the different types of deaths. Each of these value meanings has important behavioral consequences.

Most people in our society view death as being intrinsically evil and, therefore, something to fear. We tend to see death as an intruder—the spoiler of our best plans. Thus, in the past the medical profession has attempted to delay death in favor of life. People are kept on machines to prolong life, even if death is inevitable. We assume that people wishing to die are mentally ill or irrational because we see death as something to be avoided. Yet, the terminally ill eventually come to view death as a great blessing, when they have finally accepted the fact that they are going to die. This is possible because humans are able to create hierarchies of values in which value meanings take on relative meanings. To the terminally ill patient, dignity is more highly valued than is life with pain, indignity, and suffering. Consequently, death may be ascribed positive value for the dying patient who has accepted the inevitability of his or her death.

Daniel Goleman (1989) cites research that shows that confronting individuals with the fact that they will die makes them cling tenaciously to their deepest moral values. They tend to become more moralistic and judgmental. They are harsher toward those who violate their moral standards and kinder toward those who uphold them. Open-minded persons, however, become even more tolerant of those whose values differ from theirs. Researchers (Goleman, 1989) note that these findings give the fear of death a central role in psychological life and that a culture's model of "the good life" and its moral codes all are intended to protect people from the terror of death. Cultures prescribe what one must do to lead a "good life," and if one leads a "good life," he or she will be protected from a tragic fate at death.

OBJECT AND SELF MEANINGS

The previous discussion focused on meanings that have been applied to an object— the dying patient. From a biological perspective the person is a living organism—a physical object. From a social-psychological perspective, the patient is a social object—a self.

Many patients who are defined as having a terminal condition begin to view themselves as being "as good as dead." As discussed in chapter 4, perhaps the dying person has reached Erik Erikson's eighth stage of the life cycle—senescence. This feeling of integrity that one's life has meaning and purpose and that having lived made a difference is a final stage of life from which the person is ready to break away. Life is over, and the dying patient is accepting of that. The patient has accepted the terminal

Dying with dignity or self-respect does not always happen. Positive self-meanings can be created and sustained with the help of others. These others, who become the social audience for dying-related behaviors of the patient, include family, physicians, clergy, nurses, peers, or even strangers walking down the hall of the hospital. How the patient is treated by these people reveals something about the patient.

label, has applied it to a personal understanding of who she or he is, and has experienced anticipatory death. Families tend to see their loved ones as being in bereavement. This symbolic definition of the patient is reinforced by the role disengagement process, the spatial isolation of the dying patient, and the terminal label placed upon the patient by the physician and other medical personnel. The patient seems to take on a status somewhere between the living and the dead.

As death draws near, individuals may speak of preparation for travel, often recognizing one who has already died coming for them (Callanan & Kelley, 1992). Occasionally, angels or religious figures are mentioned as beckoning to them. A friend, who works with chronically ill children in a hospital setting, told me about a child who said that the pretty woman with flowers standing in the corner of the room was calling the child to come with her to play with the children. "I am not ready to go yet," the little girl replied. A couple of days later, the child again said that the woman "in the corner of the room" was signaling for her to come and play with the children, who were laughing and having a good time. The child said to my friend, "I am now

---

Don't Abandon the Patient

When I say I feel as comfortable with a dying patient as with any other, and that I do not find treating a dying patient unpleasant, I do not mean that I am anaesthetized to the fact that they are dying, and do not have feelings about the patient which are different from my feelings about a patient whom I know will get well. Anesthetizing of feeling is the method which we physicians employ initially in dealing with the pain—ours and theirs—involved in treating a dying patient. But this passes, and when one accepts the patient as part of life, and not someone who is no longer a real part of the world (or a frightening part of the world), then caring for the dying patient becomes (though often sad) neither unpleasant nor something one wishes to avoid. To abandon the dying patient is the worst thing that can be done—both for the patient and the doctor.

A physician's comment from a survey of 1,093 physicians by Dickinson and Pearson, 1976.

---

ready to go with them." She died an hour later. Thus, there is a connection between the living and the dead as one prepares for "the journey."

The dying person needs to feel that meaning for significant others has not been lost. With death close, dying patients may still want to express what they experience and to convey their fantasies about death (Seravalli, 1988). The presence of the physician in this last phase of life may be crucial for a peaceful death. Such a presence may allow the patient not only to die with self-respect, but also to feel less lonely. Arthur Frank (1991, p. 4), who himself had two serious illnesses by the age of 40, believes that too many ill individuals are deprived of conversation. He notes that too many believe that they cannot talk about their illness: They simply repeat what they know from the medical staff. When ill persons try to talk in medical language, they deny themselves the drama of their personal experience. Frank notes that sick persons need to talk about their hopes and fears and the prospect of death. But because such talk embarrasses us, we do not have practice with it, and lacking practice, we find such talk difficult.

Elisabeth Kübler-Ross (1969, p. 116) states that in the end the terminally ill have a need to detach themselves from the living to make dying easier. The following example illustrates this point:

> She asked to be allowed to die in peace, wished to be left alone—even asked for less involvement on the part of her husband. She said that the only reason that kept her still alive was her husband's inability to accept the fact that she had to die. She was angry at him for not facing it and for so desperately clinging on to something that she was willing and ready to give up. I translated to her that she wished to detach herself from this world, and she nodded gratefully as I left her alone.

When an individual's condition has been defined by self and others as terminal, all other self-meanings take on less importance. Although a given patient may be an attorney, a Democrat, mother, wife, or Presbyterian, she tends to think of herself primarily as a terminally ill patient. The terminal label becomes her **master status** because it dominates all other status indicators. Consequently, most of the symbolic meanings previously discussed become incorporated into the individual's self-meaning.

Acquiring the terminal label as part of the self definition is not an easy task for the individual. In her best-selling book *On Death and Dying* (1969), Elisabeth Kübler-Ross delineated the following 5 stages that patients go through in accepting their terminal self-meaning: denial, anger, bargaining, depression, and acceptance.

In the first stage, *denial,* the patient attempts to deny that the condition is fatal. This is a period of shock and disbelief (for example, the patient wants to believe that the physician must have read the wrong X-ray). The patient wants to believe that a mistake has been made. One may seek additional medical advice, hoping that the terminal diagnosis will be proven false. When the diagnosis is verified, the patient may often retreat into self-imposed isolation.

The second stage, *anger,* is a natural reaction for most patients. The patient may vent anger at a number of individuals—at the physician for not doing enough, at relatives for outliving the patient, at other patients for not having a terminal condition, and at God for allowing the patient to die. In other words, a scapegoat is sought—the patient seeks someone or something on which the blame can be placed.

When one has incorporated the terminal label into self-meaning, an attempt to bargain for a little more time may result. This third stage, *bargaining,* may include promises to God in exchange for an extension of life, followed by the wish for a few days without pain or physical discomfort. For example, in the movie *The End,* Burt Reynolds decides to commit suicide by drowning. He swims far out into the ocean but begins to change his mind about wanting to die. He bargains with God and prays to God to make him the best swimmer in the world so that he can swim *back* to shore. In return for God's granting his wish, Reynolds promises to give most of his income for the rest of his life to the church. As he draws nearer to shore and realizes that he is going to survive, his "promises" to God are reduced to 50 percent of his income, then 40, and downward, until he reaches the shore and reduces his promise to almost nothing. Bargaining generally includes an implicit promise that the patient will not ask for more if the request to postpone death is granted. The promise is rarely kept, however, notes Kübler-Ross (1969, p. 84).

In the fourth stage, *depression,* the patient begins to realize that a mistake was not made, the X-rays were correctly read, and the prognosis is not good. The patient realizes that meaningful things of life—family, physical appearance, personal accomplishments, and often a sense of dignity—will be lost as death approaches. This is a time to "get one's house in order" and to begin breaking away.

In the fifth stage, *acceptance,* the patient accepts death as a sure outcome. Although not happy, this acceptance is not terribly sad, either. The patient is able to say, "I have said all the words I have to say and am ready to go."

Kübler-Ross's stage theory of dying is not without its critics (see Kellehear, 1990; Charmaz, 1980; Garfield, 1978; Pattison, 1977; Kaufmann, 1976). Some reject the developmental nature of the sequential stage approach because it lacks universality—not all patients manifest all five stages of behaviors. Others have noted that the stages are not mutually exclusive—some patients may bargain, be depressed, and angry at the

---

The Care of the Dying Patient

No matter how we measure his worth, a dying human being deserves more than efficient care from strangers, more than machines and septic hands, more than a mouth full of pills, arms full of tubes and a rump full of needles. His simple dignity as man should merit more than furtive eyes, reluctant hugs, medical jargon, ritual sacraments or tired Bible quotes, more than all the phony promises for a tomorrow that will never come. Man has become lost in the jungle of ritual surrounding death.

Facing Death (p. 6), by R. E. Kavanaugh, 1972, Baltimore: Penguin Books.

---

same time. Finally, others have observed that the order of the stages is more arbitrary than Kübler-Ross would have us believe—dying patients may go from denial to acceptance, followed by depression and anger.

Kathy Charmaz (1980, p. 153) argues that the stages emanate from preconceived psychiatric categories imposed upon the experiences rather than from the data. She notes that what originated as *description* of a reality often becomes *prescription* for reality.

The stages also do not adequately take into consideration the perspective of the patient. Anger, for example, may be vented at others because they have withdrawn from the patient as their attempt to cope with the loss of someone for whom they care. The bargaining behavior of the patient may be motivated by a need for moral and social support from caregivers, rather than by a hope for an extension of time (Gustafson, 1972). Depression may be a function of the severity of the physical condition of the patient rather than an emotional response to the terminal condition (Charmaz, 1980). As the disease progresses, the strength of the patient will diminish and be evaluated by others as psychological depression. In actuality, the patient may be depressed not by dying, but rather by the physical effects of the illness.

In a chapter entitled "On Death and Lying," Kaufmann (1976) identifies a contradiction between Kübler-Ross's perspective and her actual findings. He notes that in the introduction to her work she suggests that the denial of death is psychologically inevitable and yet she goes on to record interviews with literally hundreds of dying people who were not apparently "inevitably" and uniformly denying death.

With regard to the stages of dying, we must conclude that dying behavior is more complex than 5 universal, mutually exclusive, and linear stages. Kübler-Ross has helped us, however, in understanding that each of the five behaviors is a "normal" coping strategy employed by dying patients. It may be that it is the social situation that accounts for the similar coping strategies of dying patients and that in other cultural settings different patterns of behavior will be found.

SOCIAL SITUATION MEANINGS

As the dying person comes to grips with a terminal condition, the way in which the social situation is defined will have a tremendous impact upon the process of dying.

If the hospital is viewed as a supportive environment, patient coping may be facilitated. However, if the patient feels all alone in the place of confinement, and if the hospital is defined as a foreign place, personal adjustment to dying and death will be hindered.

Like all other meaning systems, the definition of the social situation is an attempt by the individual to bring order to one's world. Because situational meaning always involves selective perception, the terminal patient will create the meaning for the social environment and will respond to this meaning and not to the environment itself. Each terminal patient will not only experience death in a different environment, but also will have a unique interpretation of the social situation. This accounts for the different experiences of dying patients. The hospice movement (see chapter 7) is an attempt to create a more positive and supportive social situation in which dying can take place.

Physicians and the Dying Patient

Physicians may have a greater need than others to reject death. Some physicians may compensate for their unconscious personal fear of illness and death by distancing themselves from dying patients (Black, Hardoff, & Nelki, 1989). American medicine is often indicted because physicians are educated to treat diseases rather than people and to deal with patients impersonally rather than holistically. Yet, Michael Bell (1996), in the latter stages of a fight against terminal cancer, observed that this priority of technical skills over bedside mannerisms may be exactly what we prefer that our doctors develop because one's very life may depend on such skills and knowledge. The death of a patient may be viewed by the physician as a professional failure and thus generate guilt. Therefore, it is important for medical students to develop technical skills necessary to deal efficiently with terminally ill patients and their families.

Surgeon Sherwin Nuland in his book *How We Die* (1994) shares the story of one of his patients, a 92-year-old woman with heart disease, who was being treated for an acute digestive tract disorder. Dr. Nuland persuaded the patient to have an operation for the disorder, though she argued that she had lived long enough and did not want any further intrusions into her body. The young doctor was following the medical code to "prolong life and relieve suffering." Yet, he was not listening to the patient's system of logic to use this sudden illness as a gracious way to die. The patient survived the operation, yet died 2 weeks later of a stroke. She told Dr. Nuland that he had let her down by not allowing her to die in due course without the pain and complications experienced from the operation. Dr. Nuland said he learned from this experience that for dying patients "the hope of cure will always be shown to be ultimately false." He learned that he needs to listen to the logic of his patients and not rely solely on his own medical code of logic.

Americans are poorly socialized with regard to issues of dying and death, as noted in chapter 1. One might expect that the early socialization experiences of physicians would be similar to that of other members of society. This is exemplified by the following story told to the author by the late Dr. Charles B. Huggins, Nobel recipient for cancer research and professor at the University of Chicago School of Medicine, about his first day as a student in medical school:

At one time in the United States, long before Dr. Huggin's time, acquiring a corpse to dissect for medical purposes was not an easy task. Corpse snatching and grave robbing was known to be performed by students desiring to learn about human anatomy. Medical societies, formed in the late 1700s and early 1800s, became active in attempting to force legislation to permit legal dissection for medical study (Coffin, 1976, p. 194). In 1824, Connecticut passed a law allowing medical schools to take possession of unclaimed corpses from its prisons, and in 1831 a Massachusetts law made human dissection legal. These pioneer acts served as models for other states, and soon there was no more reason for grave *robbing* in the name of science.

After the gross anatomy professor finished the initial lecture, the class went to the laboratory to begin work on the cadavers. My cadaver was a female. After taking one look at the body (having never seen either a dead woman or a naked woman), I said to myself, "I should have gone to law school after all."

Even though this Nobel recipient entered Harvard Medical School in 1920 (at the age of 18), many 1st-year medical students today have had similar experiences and feelings and find that their first exposure to death is an impersonal experience in an anatomy lab. Human dissection in gross anatomy lab, typically taken during the first semester, is a rite of passage for all future medical doctors (Dickinson et al., 1997). The students must deal with the psychological and social aspects of cutting and touching a dead body and must struggle with questions of her or his own and others' mortality (Evans & Fitzgibbon, 1992). In addition to their own anxieties about death, students in gross anatomy are subjected to horror stories from upperclassmen and classmates. **Cadaver** stories portray, and thus help create, a world of outsiders and insiders and emotionally weak or strong medical students (Hafferty, 1991). A norm within medicine is that one must have emotional strength to survive the mental stress brought on by practicing medicine; strength begins and must be displayed in gross anatomy.

Entry into medical school involves movement from a largely lay to a largely medical culture, notes Frederic Hafferty (1991, p. 178) in his study of the socialization of first-year medical students. Experiences such as the dissection of human cadavers in anatomy lab provide students with opportunities to internalize a variety of attitudes, values, motives, and rationales with respect to both their current role as student and their future role as physician. These experiences give students an opportunity to assess their progress in identity transformation and skill building (Hafferty, 1991).

Students entering the medical profession come in with certain attitudes and feelings toward patients that will be shaped and continually processed until their attitudes comply with those of the medical profession itself. Howard Becker (1964, pp. 44–46) refers to this "molding" as **situational adjustment.** As one moves in and out of social situations, the requirement for continuing in a situation for success in it are learned. With a strong desire to deliver the required performance, the individual becomes the kind of person that the situation demands. Thus, the medical student is "molded" into the medical profession by learning what is expected and then "doing it." Becker notes that much of the change in an individual is a function of the interpretive response made by the entire group—the consensus that the group reaches with respect to its problems.

The process of situational adjustment accounts for changes that people undergo, but people also exhibit some consistency as they move from situation to situation. Howard Becker (1964, pp. 49–51) refers to this consistent line of activity in a sequence of varied situations as "commitment." A variety of commitments constrains one to follow a consistent pattern of behavior in many areas of life.

Whether one's medical socialization took place many decades ago, as for Dr. Huggins, or whether it takes place in the 1990s, medical training is a pathway by which laypersons are transformed into something else—physicians (Hafferty, 1991). Merton, Reader, and Kendall (1957, p. 287) noted that socialization is the collection of "processes by which people acquire the values and attitudes, the interests, skills, and knowledge—in short, the culture—current in the groups of which they are, or seek to become, a member." When we speak of socialization (Hafferty, 1991, p. 3), we are talking about the structure, the method, and the route by which initiates move from one status to another and acquire the technical skills, knowledge, values, and attitudes associated with the new position or group. Thus, one must attain a new cultural base but must also facilitate movement away from the old status.

DEATH EDUCATION IN MEDICAL SCHOOLS

As noted in chapter 1, medical education has historically offered only limited assistance to the medical student encountering death for the first time (Dickinson, 1985). From 1975 to 1985 the number of full-term death and dying courses in medical school in the United States increased from only 7 to 14 (out of a total of 113 and 128 medical schools, respectively). By 1990 the number of courses had increased to 18 (Mermann, Gunn, & Dickinson, 1991, p. 36); yet by 1995 the number had dropped to 9 (Dickinson & Mermann, 1996). Eighty percent of the medical schools in 1975 and 1985 offered death education in the form of an occasional lecture or minicourse; however, this number had increased to 90 percent by 1995 (Dickinson & Mermann, 1996). The average number of years of these offerings in 1985 was 8. Thus, an emphasis on dying and death in medical schools has a brief history and remains somewhat limited today, although the exposure for students is increasing.

The dilemma faced by Dr. Huggins on his first day in gross anatomy lab would have been addressed by the current offering at the University of Massachusetts Medical School. According to S. C. Marks and S. L. Bertman (1980), sessions on dying and death are integrated into the anatomy course before dissection begins. Some of the objectives are to identify and articulate feelings about death in general and to assist students in identifying and talking about their feelings about death and dissection. Unfortunately, this course is unique, and most medical schools today are like that experienced by Dr. Huggins in 1920.

Because gross anatomy is required in all medical schools, this exposure to death may be the first experience for some students. In a study (Dickinson et al., 1997) of 1st-year medical students in gross anatomy lab, a pre- and postsurvey of the 84 students revealed that 54 percent showed less death anxiety after completing gross anatomy, 29 percent had increased fear of death, and 17 percent experienced no change. Thus, the gross anatomy course may help desensitize students to death, whether or not there is a conscious effort toward this desensitization, as at the University of Massachusetts Medical School. In addition, to show more sensitivity in the lab, at the end of the gross anatomy course some medical schools, such as the University of California at Berkeley, are holding a memorial service for the cadavers that are dissected (Durbin, 1996). Through such a dedication service the students give thanks to those who in death taught them about life.

Perhaps physicians are expected to be all things to all people. Certainly the death of a patient runs counter to what medicine is all about because the graduate of medical school takes an oath to "prolong life." From the point of view that the physician is the defender of life, sworn to use his or her best judgment in protecting the patient, death is the enemy, and the dying patient is a lost cause from the beginning.

The medical training of most physicians historically seems to be primarily concerned with the patient's physical state rather than with the patient's social-psychological needs. Some changes are occurring though, as noted by Dartmouth Medical School's interest in "facilitating the medical students' understanding of the patient as a bio-social-psychological being" (Nelson, 1980). The medical students are to learn from the terminally ill patient what it is like to be dying. Thus, the patient is used as "teacher." The inclusion of a humanistic emphasis in death education should help both the dying patients and the medical students.

At the Yale School of Medicine Alan Mermann (Mermann, Gunn, & Dickinson, 1991) offers a seminar for first- and second-year medical students on problems in communicating with dying and seriously ill patients. Professor Mermann also uses very sick patients as teachers. Approximately one third of the first-year students take this elective course. Goals for students in the course are to: (a) learn to talk with, and listen to, sick persons; (b) learn to establish a professional relationship without the intrusion of friendship; (c) ascertain the meaning of compassion without sentimentality and the need for humility before the physician's ignorance; (d) learn of our common frailty as human beings, the finality of death, and the need that we all have for companionship when death is near; and (e) enrich the students' understanding of those in their care.

Professor Mermann's goals do not differ significantly from those of Black, Hardoff, and Nelki (1989, p. 752) in teaching medical students to better relate to dying patients and their families. Each course has the following objectives:

1. To identify the dying patient's needs and wishes
2. To understand the family's needs
3. To recognize the phases of normal grief and mourning
4. To be aware of cultural and religious aspects with regard to death and the roles of other people, such as chaplains, in caring for the patient and the family
5. To clear away the barriers that have been erected around the subject
6. To make the student appreciate his or her own death, thus contributing to his or her emotional development
7. To appreciate the need to relieve the physical and emotional distress of the dying patient
8. To consider ethical issues such as euthanasia, abortion, organ transplantation, and so on

The care of the dying is an art that should have its fullest expression in helping patients cope with the technologically complicated medical environment surrounding them at the end of life, note Sidney Wanzer and his medical associates (1989, p. 846). The concept of a good death requires the art of deliberately creating a medical milieu that allows a peaceful death. The physician must seek a level of care that optimizes comfort and dignity and needs to formulate a flexible care plan, tailoring treatment to the patient's changing needs as the disease progresses.

Pain control must be a top priority of physicians, observe Wanzer and associates (1989, p. 847), because one of the major causes of anxiety among patients and their families is the perception that physicians' efforts to relieve pain are badly deficient. As sickness progresses toward death, dying patients may require **palliative care** of an intensity that rivals even that of curative efforts. Indeed, death education in medical schools must strive to help the student know how to make the dying patient's last few days more comfortable. As in natural childbirth—the other occasion on which the role of the physician and nurse is not to cure but to make the patient comfortable—natural death involves demedicalization to the extent that death is defined as a natural rather than a medical event (Walter, 1995). Nurses and doctors cannot conquer death, but they can become "midwives of the dying," assisting through this natural transition (Albery, Elliot, & Elliot, 1993).

MORE DEATH EDUCATION NEEDED IN MEDICAL SCHOOLS

A survey of over 600 physicians (Dickinson, 1988) in 1986 revealed that the majority (78 percent) agree that more emphasis in medical school should be placed on communication skills with terminally ill patients and their families. A study of medical students in England (Field & Howells, 1986) found that, of the 77 percent of students expressing worries about the prospect of interacting with dying patients, communicating with such patients was their most frequent concern. Results from another study of 350 family physicians in South Carolina (Dickinson, 1988) in 1987 reveal that the majority felt that their medical education was inadequate in helping them relate to terminally ill patients and their families.

In a recent Harris survey (Richardson, 1992), 91 percent of 1,501 practicing dentists, nurses, pharmacists, physicians, and veterinarians said that teaching students how to communicate effectively with patients and their families is very important, yet 36 percent gave their schools a poor rating in this area. Seeing the need for better communication skills with patients, the Association of American Medical Colleges in 1991 added two 30-minute essays to the admission test to help medical schools evaluate communication skills (Altman, 1989). Similarly, the American Medical Association (Montgomery, 1996) announced in 1996 a major effort, beginning in 1997, to teach doctors how to aid the dying by helping patients and their families plan for dying, by providing effective ways to reduce suffering, and by treating psychiatric complications.

In a study of 441 family medicine practitioners in South Carolina (Durand, Dickinson, Sumner, & Lancaster, 1990), those who reported having been taught concepts concerning terminally ill patients and their families while in medical school had a more "positive" attitude toward death than did those who received no instruction. Other studies (Bugen, 1980; Dickinson & Pearson, 1980–1981; Leviton, 1977; Miles,

1980) have reported attitudes that are more favorable, less fearful, and less avoiding with respect to dying and death as a result of death education.

Good rapport with dying patients might be an intrinsic quality of certain medical students that is reinforced by experience, or it might be something in which medical students are given instruction. Though values, ethics, and communication skills may be presented and "learned" in medical school, there is no guarantee that they will be carried over into clinical practice. Perhaps the results would be known if only the majority of medical schools in the United States offered a course on relating to terminally ill patients and their families. With the current curricula trend since 1975, however, this is not likely to occur in the near future.

Relating to Dying Patients

Richard Kalish's study of college students' attitudes toward the dying (1966) perhaps reflects society's reactions to the dying in general. He found that one third of the respondents would not willingly allow a dying person to "live within a few doors" of them. Only half of the sample would willingly become close friends with a dying person. Kalish notes that if these college students' reactions are in any way typical, then most people would avoid the dying, as they do the grieving, often noting that they do not know what to say.

Physicians likely are no better off than others in the population in their attitudes toward the dying. Physicians' unwillingness to deal with death and terminally ill patients is cited frequently in the literature (see Kane & Hogan, 1986, p. 12). Physicians as a group tend to express more conscious death anxiety than do groups of individuals who are physically ill. Anne Kane and John Hogan (1986, p. 20) note that death anxiety is significantly linked with both age and experience for physicians as a whole. The older a physician becomes, the lower the death anxiety. Likewise, the longer a physician has practiced medicine, the less death anxiety he or she has. As noted earlier in this chapter, similar findings were noted by Dickinson and Tournier (1994) in a 10-year follow-up of a study of physicians soon after they graduated from medical school. The younger, less-experienced physicians reported higher levels of death anxiety and felt less comfortable with dying patients.

In a study of 1,012 physicians, Dickinson and Pearson (1979a) concluded that those physicians with a high probability of dealing with dying patients (such as oncologists) were more open with their patients than were physicians who practiced medicine in areas where there was a lower probability of dealing with death (for example, obstetricians and gynecologists). Because this study suggests that differences exist among medical specialties in relating to dying patients, it is possible that one factor influencing the selection of a medical specialty is the medical student's personal understanding and feelings concerning dying and death issues.

GENDER VERSUS PROFESSIONAL ROLE

Prior to the 18th century the care and control of the dying and of the corpse were substantially in the hands of women (James, 1992). Since that time, however, the

Am I Dead?

Once upon a time a patient died and went to heaven, but was not certain where he was. Puzzled, he asked a nurse who was standing nearby, "Nurse, am I dead?" The answer she gave was, "Have you asked your doctor?"
Anonymous, circa 1961.

medicalization of death has involved the increasing power of male doctors over the female bedside carers of the dying. This defeminization of the power to define and control the management of death, although leaving women with much of the dirty work, is currently being challenged and is shifting somewhat in professional circles, notes James (1992).

Physicians and nurses are intricately entwined in dealing with dying patients (Pine, 1975). It is the physician who defines when the patient is "dying" or "dead," and the nurse must wait for this "official message." The patient may then be treated as if there were little chance for recovery. This alteration in treatment is predicated by the physician's decision but is not carried out until he or she communicates it.

A study by Thomas Campbell and colleagues (1984) comparing the attitudes of physicians and nurses toward death found differences that were tied to professional roles, not to gender. Nurses tended to see a more positive meaning in death than did physicians—death as rebirth rather than as abandonment and as tranquil rather than as frightening. Because physicians make the crucial decisions, whereas nurses carry out the orders, the implication of patient death as professional failure is reduced for nurses.

Howard Becker's emphasis on situational adjustment (1964), followed by a commitment of consistency, seems to suggest that socialization to occupational role overcomes earlier gender role socialization. This is the conclusion of Dickinson and Ashley-Cameron (1986) in explaining the different attitudes of female nurses and physicians regarding dying patients. Even if women have traditionally been socialized to be the more nurturant gender, more sensitive and responsive to the needs of others, female physicians tend to be less sensitive and responsive than female nurses. Thus, the differences between physicians and nurses regarding death and terminally ill patients tend to be more a function of the role expectations of the particular medical occupation than of gender.

Jack Kamerman (1988, p. 62) cautions, however, that as nurses are given greater responsibility in diagnosis and treatment, their attitudes toward death may move closer to those of physicians. In addition, as nurses become more susceptible to the strains that physicians experience at a patient's death, it is possible that they will retreat further behind the shield of professional detachment, particularly if nursing follows the medical model of professional status.

By contrast, a study by Martin, Arnold, and Parker (1988, p. 340) shows that gender differences do play a role in how male and female doctors communicate with patients. Perhaps this is because medical schools do not place heavy emphasis on patient interviewing, and female patients therefore default to the less-directed communication style that is used predominately by females in American society. Women's styles of speech are typically less obtrusive; men are more likely to interrupt women than vice versa, and women are more likely to allow such interruptions. The conflicting paradigm to this less-directed communication style of women is that physicians are socialized to dominate the physician-patient interaction. The physician is to control the flow and topics of conversation. Female physicians tend to integrate these two models of communication by being more egalitarian in their relationships with patients, more respectful, and more responsive to patients' psychosocial issues (Martin, Arnold, & Parker, 1988).

The successful communication skills of female physicians are supported by Dickinson and Pearson (1979b). In their 1976 study of over 1,000 physicians they found that female physicians related better to dying patients and their families than did male physicians. A 1986 follow-up of this study (Dickinson & Tournier, 1993) showed even more striking differences between males and females after a decade of practicing medicine. Perhaps the traditional "feminine characteristics" of gentleness, expressiveness, responsiveness, and kindness help to explain these differences.

Martin, Arnold, and Parker (1988), in studying gender and medical socialization, reported that medical students regard female faculty physicians with clinical responsibility for patients to be "more sensitive, more altruistic, and less egoistic" than males; nurses believe that female physicians are more "humanistic" and have greater "technical" skill in communicating with patients; and patients also perceive female physicians as more humanistic, more empathic, and better listeners. If more physicians and other medical personnel were to display these "human qualities" with a greater frequency, patients might receive more help and support in their dying.

AWARENESS CONTEXTS OF DYING

Whether medical personnel are male or female, nurse or physician, communication with terminally ill patients is of utmost importance. Barney Glaser and Anselm Strauss (1965) present 4 awareness contexts in interacting with a dying patient. These researchers define the **awareness context** as what an interacting person knows of the patient's defined status, and his or her recognition of the patient's awareness of a personal definition. The awareness contexts are: closed, suspicion, mutual pretense, and open.

Closed awareness is usually the first context. In order to maintain the patient's trust, and yet to keep him or her unaware of the terminal condition, the staff may construct a fictional future biography. If the patient has not been told "the truth," or has been "told" but did not want to hear, this often places an additional burden on the nursing staff in working with the patient on an 8-hour shift. Because the physician often directs the medical team, nurses are sometimes forced to work in a closed awareness context regardless of their own view. Because most patients are able to recognize death-related situational and spatial clues, this context tends to be unstable, and the patient usually moves to the suspicion or full awareness contexts.

Suspicion awareness is a contest for control between the patient and the medical staff. The patient suspects that he or she is dying but receives no verification from the staff. Nurses must use teamwork to refute this challenge.

Mutual pretense often follows and requires subtle interaction with both patient and staff "acting correctly" to maintain the pretense that the patient is not approaching death. A game continues to be played whereby all concerned "act" as if they know nothing about the terminal condition of the patient.

If mutual pretense is not sustained, *open awareness* follows in which the patient and everyone else knows that the patient is dying. This is the context found in hospice programs (see chapter 7). Ambiguities may develop in this context, however. The patient is obligated not to commit suicide and to die "properly." Dying "properly" is difficult, however. Nurses and other medical staff expect "proper" dying, but the patient usually knows no model to follow, notes Robert Blauner (1966). If the patient is dying in an unacceptable manner, then difficulties are faced when trying to negotiate for things from the staff.

Ashley-Cameron and Dickinson (1979) found that nurses working with dying patients seem to be comfortable in a closed awareness context. Because nurses spend more time with patients in the hospital than do physicians, a closed awareness context may produce a more comfortable setting for the nurse. A recent study in England, however, produced a very different finding regarding awareness contexts. Open awareness was preferred in a study of 548 physicians and nurses (Seale, 1991). Eighty-one percent of these British practitioners said that they found it easier to work with dying patients if the patients were aware of their terminal condition. Perhaps the openness of the 1990s and/or the difference in cultures is reflected in these seemingly contradictory findings over different time periods.

John Stephenson (1985, p. 78) states that dying is a human activity that is carried out in a normative manner. The individual learns from society the meaning of death and what are considered to be proper or "good" ways of dying. One hopes to die what one's society considers to be a good death.

Anthropologist Margaret Mead seemed to close out her life in the way that she had lived it. A recorded interview with her on public television a few months prior to her death revealed a woman who gave the last moments of her life as energetically, as intelligently, and as openly as she had given the early years of her life (Cuzzort & King, 1995, p. 204). Her conversation was animated—no brooding soul turned inward by the thoughts of impending death. At the end of the program she briefly revealed her attitude toward life and work and death. Then she arose and began to walk backward slowly, into the shadowy and dark recesses of the stage setting, still facing the camera. She smiled a charming smile, waved her cane, and said, "Goodbye, goodbye, goodbye"—knowing that it was the final farewell as she stepped into the darkness. As Cuzzort and King (1995) note, it was an act, yet a wonderful act. It summed up the way that she lived, wrote, and felt about people.

Though there is no good role model to follow in dying, perhaps the late Senator Hubert H. Humphrey of Minnesota came close by maintaining some control over final events in his life. Even in his dying, he kept a most positive attitude and frequently made telephone calls to individuals to wish them well. Calling former President Richard M. Nixon, for whom many in Humphrey's position would have had limited affection, to wish him a happy birthday epitomizes Humphrey's behavior during the final days of his illness. Because an **appropriate death** is generally consistent with past personality patterns, Senator Humphrey died as he had lived. Likewise, Jacqueline Kennedy Onassis spent her last few days of life as she had lived, with poise and dignity.

THE FAMILY CIRCUS   **By Bil Keane**

10-4
© 1996 Bil Keane, Inc.
Dist. by Cowles Synd., Inc.

"If somebody dies in the hospital,
angels move them to the
eternity ward."

The concept of an appropriate death has been suggested as an alternative goal for those working with the dying (Hooyman & Kiyak, 1988, p. 449). An appropriate death means that the individual dies as he or she wishes to die. The individual maintains as much control over dying as possible in order to make it meaningful. Although an appropriate death is usually only partially achieved, those working with the dying can assist them in exerting such control.

Anne Hawkins (1990), in an article on pathographies about dying, notes various "constructions of death" in the literature, including de Beauvoir, Conley, and Wertenbaker. Simone de Beauvoir's model of death (1965) describes her mother's death from cancer as "an easy death," one in which suffering is avoided. Herbert Conley (1979) describes death as one's "finest hour," when death is accepted as a part of life with avoidance of self-pity, concentrating on the needs of others and maintaining dignity and self-composure. Conley's description of death fits Elisabeth Kübler-Ross's concept in *Death: The Final Stage of Growth* (1975). Lael Wertenbaker (1957) offers the model of a "heroic death," a "manly" death in which pain is endured as a test of bravery, courage, and heroism.

Whether a person is a nurse or a physician, the ability to cope with terminally ill patients does not come easily. Society has not prepared one for such interaction. Some obviously react better than others. Working with AIDS patients may be especially difficult due to the fear of acquiring AIDS. The key to good relations with dying patients is personally coming to grips with death. One should also have good communication

Making Out a Will to Provide for Dependents and to Dispose of Property

In order to personally determine who receives one's property after death, it is important to have a **will.** To die without a will (**intestate**) means that important decisions like who gets your assets and raises your kids may be made by a state judge in ways that you might not like. Indeed, only about 30 percent of Americans have a will (Tyson, 1997, p. 22).

Real property, which includes land and what is attached to it, such as a house (as opposed to personal property such as clothes or cars), is transferred in three ways—through a deed, a will, or inheritance. The latter two deal with property transfer at death. Thus, a will is important if one wishes to have any say in the transfer. Each of the 50 states has its own laws regarding wills, thus what is true of one state may not necessarily be true of the others.

If one dies intestate, classes of heirs are established by the various states to determine how the property passes. Typically, if one is married at the time of death, the spouse receives the inheritance. If one has children, they also take from the inheritance (if minors, to be held in a trust until they reach a certain age). If the **decedent** (the deceased person) was single, the parents usually inherit. If the parents are dead, brothers and sisters are usually next in line to inherit, followed by grandparents, and then aunts and uncles. If one dies intestate and without heirs, one's property goes to the state (the legal term for this is **escheat**).

A will is therefore essential if one does not want the state to determine the distribution of his or her property. Thus, a well-executed will can provide an

(continued)

---

skills. If only the dying patient could be viewed as a person, not as the "lung cancer" case in Room 314, and treated as a human being, certainly the trauma of the dying process could be eased. In the end medical personnel, the patient, and the family would benefit.

Living With Dying

Many individuals today are living for years with a serious illness. Chances of an illness going into remission or even "going away" are more likely this year than last, and the same will be true of next year over this year because of scientific and medical advancements each year.

The workforce today is filled with individuals who experience chronic and serious illnesses. "Life goes on," even though one may have been diagnosed with heart

(continued from previous page)

orderly distribution of property, get the decedent's assets to the people to whom he or she wants them to go, can reduce the expense in probate court, and allows the **testator** (the one making the will) to name an individual of his or her choosing to administer the estate and someone to be legally responsible for young children rather than have the court appoint an administrator and place minor children (in the event of a single parent).

In order to make out a will, the following criteria generally apply, though this may vary by states:

1. The person must be at least 18 years of age.
2. The person must be of sound mind (know the nature of the document).
3. The will must be in writing.
4. The will must be signed by the testator.
5. The will must have two witnesses to the signing.
6. The will must be dated.

A will can be changed by adding an amendment called a **codicil**—made at a later date in accordance with the same formalities required for the validity of the original will. A codicil allows one to amend the will by adding new provisions without having to rewrite it entirely. The will should be kept in a safe place, and family members should be notified as to its whereabouts.

Though legal in only about half of the states (Wolf, 1995, p. 166), a **holographic will** is one written wholly in one's own handwriting and does not generally require witnesses. A holographic will also must be signed by the testator.

G. E. Dickinson.

disease or cancer. In situations where one is asymptomatic or experiences minor symptoms and little pain, it may be possible to continue to maintain a good quality of life, even one that approaches the standard of life prior to the diagnosis (Doka, 1993, p. 89). With a population better educated on health issues, the stigma of cancer (the "big C" disease) has diminished considerably in recent years. Unlike cancer, heart disease did not seem to ever have the stigma that patients had to be "avoided" for fear of "catching" the disease. Likewise, AIDS has been viewed as a "contagious" disease, though this stigmatization has decreased significantly in the 1990s.

In the early phases of a disease, or in periods of remission, the nature of life may not change dramatically from earlier times (Doka, 1993). This lack of change can be reassuring to the patients and families, suggesting that a good quality of life can be maintained, even in the face of a life-threatening disease. Hope may appear at this phase. Some individuals may plan for forthcoming events likely to occur as the illness progresses. The individuals may be forced to make financial arrangements and should complete a will, if they do not already have one.

A person may suffer various setbacks with the illness and may have to return to the clinic for treatment or try different medications that may or may not have side effects. Assuming that the person is basically feeling okay, however, she or he should be able to return to a normal routine. For others, if increasing dependency follows, psychological distress and crisis may follow.

Sociologist Arthur Frank (1991, p. 3), who had a heart attack and cancer before reaching middle age, observed that, to seize the opportunities offered by illness, we must live illness actively. We must think and talk about it. In that way, as individuals and as a society, we can then begin to accept illness fully. Only then can we learn that it is nothing special, notes Frank. Do not curse your fate, but rather count your possibilities, advises Frank (1991, p. 7). Being ill is just another way of living, but by the time we have lived through illness, we are living differently. As a friend who was dying of lung cancer recently told me, "I look at a sunrise and sunset and watch the tide come in and go out in a different way than before my illness." Indeed, in dying one is living differently; dying changes the perspective on events in life.

I continue to be amazed at how upbeat many individuals living with life-threatening diseases are. Many of them continue to hold down jobs, go to and from

"And my newish Cadillac, with no equity and only 57 more payments, goes to my trusted banker."

treatments, and basically live life to the fullest. Simply because an illness, such as cancer, is diagnosed does not necessarily mean a death sentence. Life goes on, and the person continues to function. Granted, the person's priorities may shift, and happenings in life that previously could have been bothersome will likely no longer seem important.

A recent colleague, who continued to teach though "dying of cancer," sent a letter to friends inviting us to come see him ("keep me company," as he put it). He noted that if "you don't know what to say," come anyway. He further said, "You don't have to avoid talking about health matters: My situation is real, and I'm not ignoring it. But I *am* determined to be upbeat and positive." Many individuals avoid visiting someone who is seriously ill for fear that they will not know "what to say" or, worse yet, will say the wrong thing. However, it is very important that you make contact with a significant other who is seriously ill. Even if you do not know what to say, go anyway to let the person know that you care. Go to be with him or her; that is what is important. Communication does not have to be verbal. Your sheer presence is sending a very positive message: You care. You are "keeping me company."

Recently I was asked to visit a 76-year-old woman who was in the latter stages of cancer. She wanted me to assist in planning her funeral and writing her obituary. The day I met this delightful individual, Dorothy Sutch, her mobility had decreased to the point that she was confined to a wheelchair. Her breast cancer had spread throughout her body, and the prognosis was not good. Mrs. Sutch was a chipper individual with a most positive outlook. She desired to "get her house in order" before she died. She wanted the details of the funeral completed and her obituary in place so that her adult children would not have to "worry themselves" with these matters. We talked for about an hour. When the assignments were completed, she threw her arms into the air and, with a smile on her face, said, "Now, I'm ready!" Her preparation for death was then complete. She then talked about how dying was "like a journey." "It's happening so fast," she said, "it's exciting, unfolding before my eyes." I visited her two more times that week. Her condition was deteriorating rapidly. By the second meeting, she had gone from the wheelchair, just 2 days before, to the bed. By the end of the week, she was dead. Indeed, it happened so fast.

Though I had not previously had the pleasure of knowing Mrs. Sutch, I later learned from her many friends that she was always going about doing good for others. She had lived as one who cared and tried to make life enjoyable for those around her. In her dying, she again had been upbeat and pleasant. Generally, we die as we lived. One who is amiable and congenial while living a healthy life will tend to be the same in dying; likewise, the pity-party-for-self, poor-little-old-me type person in life will likely be the same in dying—a real pain to be around.

We can learn much from persons with life-threatening diseases. As noted in chapter 1, physician Elisabeth Kübler-Ross says that working with the terminally ill has made her appreciative of life. Each day that she awakens she is thankful for the potential of another day of life. I learned much about living and dying from my one week's acquaintance with Dorothy Sutch.

In dying, one often lives life to the fullest. It has been said that some individuals live more in their final months of life, knowing that the end is near, than they had lived in their previous years. Living with dying can be a most meaningful experience, both for the patient and for those with whom she or he comes into contact.

Dying as a Normal State

Dying must be considered as a normal state in and of itself. The process of dying is not extraordinarily different than the process of healthy normal living, for they coexist in the same world. It is the world of patienthood which is artificial. Modern medicine with its technology has created industrial complexes called hospitals. That environment is so artificial that creating normalization is essential.

Normalization of the life of the dying person is not the same as is normalization of the life of a patient. To be dying is normal and that is determined by the patient. In attempting normalization for the patient the staff tries to keep the patient from slipping into an exaggerated state of patienthood. In normalization for the dying, the dying person must teach the staff that there is a normal process going on.

Hospitals are places in which dying could be allowed. There are many things patients need at times of their dying to make their time left more tolerable. There is room in hospitals to allow for the dying. Normalization is not really based on ethnic preferences, social patterns, and familial behavior. Normalization targets self-esteem, goal orientation, and abatement of loneliness. It generates a community that allows patients to continue to have full participation in human commerce.

The dying person redefines his or her community. The dying person is the high priest of his or her own temple. It is as if life has a holy of holies where only those initiated into that inner sanctum are allowed. It transcends the human construct of hospital and the secular state of patienthood. Hospitals will be able to accommodate dying persons only if the staff recognizes this transcendent element of the dying process. The current view of the human body as a machine that can be fixed without the spirit leaving the driver's seat makes it difficult to accommodate dying.

Adapted from "In My Opinion . . . Normalization While Dying" (pp. 18–21), by J. van Eys, Summer 1988. In *Children's Health Care, 17.*

Dying as Deviance in the Medical Setting

Medical personnel's treatment of the terminally ill patient may well be a product of socialization into the medical profession. The medical profession's attitudes toward patients, in particular dying patients, are functional to the reinforcement of the view of "the physician as healer" and functional with respect to maintenance of order in the medical subculture.

The dying patient is a deviant in the medical subculture because death poses a threat to the image of the "physician as healer" (see Alban L. Wheeler, 1973, for an excellent discussion of dying as deviance—the source from which much of this section was taken). I remember submitting a manuscript on physicians' attitudes toward terminally ill patients to a medical journal a few years ago and the editor writing back, stating that dying patients cannot be called "deviants."

Death also creates embarrassing and emotionally upsetting disruptions in the scientific objectivity of the medical social system. Thus, the disruption caused by death in the medical social system, if not controlled, could lead to a great deal of conflict.

LABELING THEORY

A major school of thought explaining deviance is **labeling theory.** The perspective of this school of thought does not focus on the act or the actor, but rather on the audience observing. When a person is labeled deviant, that person is stigmatized. Erving Goffman (1963) describes the stigmatized person as one who is reduced in the minds of others from a "whole and usual" person to a "tainted and discounted" one. Therefore, the key to the identification of deviance is found in the audiences labeling the individual or act as deviant. Thus, in analyzing the dying patient as deviant in the medical subculture, the medical audiences who interact with and participate in the labeling of the patient must be examined.

Regardless of whether or not the individual is responsible for the deviant label, the label-stigmatized individual is still discredited and is treated with less respect than other people. With such labeling, an entire interactional framework is created within which the "normals" relate to the "deviant." If indeed the dying patient is labeled "deviant," an individual with AIDS has a double deviant label—*dying* with *AIDS.*

Jerome Schofferman (1988) states that AIDS may be considered a socially unacceptable disease because common routes of infection are gay sexual activity and intravenous drug use. A former student of mine, currently suffering from AIDS, desired volunteer work at a funeral home because of his fascination with death. His request was denied. He later, rather jokingly, told me that he did not know if the refusal came because he is gay or because he has AIDS. As Earl, Martindale, and Cohn (1992, p. 36) report from their study of coping with HIV infection, how individuals become infected is frequently of more concern in the evaluation of positive adaptation than is the stage or progress of the ailment. Thus, whether the AIDS patient acquired the disease through sexual activity or intravenous drug use or through some other means, the stigma of deviance tends to apply.

According to Elliot Freidson (1972, p. 236), when a person is labeled deviant, the stigma interferes with normal interaction. Although other individuals may not hold the deviant responsible for his or her stigma, they are nonetheless "embarrassed, upset or even revolted by it," says Freidson. Therefore, the assumption can be made that the deviant person elicits certain aversive attitudes from the audience with whom interaction occurs. These aversive attitudes may be of sufficient strength to elicit attempts to manage them and to decrease aversion through avoidance behavior.

DEVIANCE RESULTS IN PUNISHMENT

The primary reaction to deviance of any type is punishment of some sort. French sociologist Emile Durkheim (1961) observed that the primary purpose of punishment is not to punish the deviant himself or herself, but rather to affirm in the face of the offense the rule that the offense would deny. Thus, one could suggest that illness is a rejection of the societal value of health or that the terminally ill patient to the physician is the antithesis of healing and getting well taught in medical school. For the AIDS patient, homophobia may be present in the community (Schofferman, 1988). The patient may feel extreme guilt or shame for being ill or may blame himself or herself for "getting what was deserved."

Robert Kavanaugh (1972, p. 8) characterizes American deification of physical health, the hospital, and the physician in the following way:

> Our universal deity, Physical Health, is the major god currently worshipped. His demands for untold dollars in tribute are incessant. Every day it costs more to worship at his shrine (the hospital), yet the devout seem only too willing to scrape and to pay. They sit uncomplaining for endless hours in the offices of His high priests (physicians), and will purchase any drug or pill or lotion the priests prescribe, in any combination. In His shrine, the dying are excommunicated, the dead are damned.

The dying person can seldom assume normal role functioning, although he or she views the illness as undesirable and has tried to cooperate with medical personnel to get well. The dying person, therefore, is permanently cast into a deviant role due to the inability to respond to treatment and get well.

The Autopsy

A dissection and examination of a just-deceased patient is an **autopsy** (Clark & Springen, 1986). The **pathologist** performing the autopsy assumes a mechanical, physical cause for the death. A *complete autopsy* refers to an examination of the organs of the three major cavities of the body—the abdomen, chest, and the head. The pathologist makes a Y-shaped incision extending from each armpit to the center of the lower abdomen. Various internal organs are removed and weighed, and blood, urine, and other fluids are sampled. Much can be told from the size, color, and feel of various body parts. For example, an alcoholic's liver may be pale and shriveled, and a diseased heart is likely to be flabby and grossly enlarged.

Autopsies for natural deaths or deaths occurring among patients under the care of a physician are usually performed at the hospital where the death occurred and with the permission of the next of kin ("Autopsy Frequency," 1988). Local statutes may require an autopsy for traumatic or sudden, unexpected deaths or for deaths due to external causes. Such an autopsy is requested by either a coroner or a medical examiner.

"Doctor," complained the patient, "all of the other physicians called in on my case seem to disagree with your diagnosis."

"Yes, I know they do," said the doctor, "but the autopsy will prove that I'm right."

An autopsy is performed whenever the cause of death is uncertain. Although the process is a mechanical procedure, the dignity of the patient should always be respected.

The purposes of an autopsy are noted by W. C. Roberts (1978):

1. Serves as a check on the accuracy of the clinical diagnoses and historical data
2. Can be a check on the appropriateness of medical and surgical therapy
3. Helps gather data on new and old diseases and surgical procedures
4. Obtains information beneficial to the deceased's family
5. Clarifies real or potential medicolegal deaths

The autopsy has ancient roots and has produced countless medical advances over time (Clark & Springen, 1986). The cumulative data gathered through autopsies have enabled physicians to treat or prevent a number of diseases. Postmortems confirmed the link between cigarette smoking and lung cancer. They helped discover abnormalities involved in congenital heart defects, multiple sclerosis, Alzheimer's disease, and viral infections in the brain that may cause dementia shown by some victims of AIDS. Perhaps the purpose of an autopsy is summed up by the statement on the entrance to

An Autopsy Observed and Experienced
Elizabeth Maxwell

We stepped into the autopsy room wondering what to expect. I was nervous for we had just been told that we might feel sick, and if we did we should leave the room so we would not faint and hurt ourselves. The sights and smells overwhelmed my senses. The mixed odors were of formaldehyde and old blood, and the air was thick with that scent. I was wondering how long I would last in this environment when we were offered surgical masks to wear. "I nearly fainted from the smell when I watched my first autopsy. Those masks help a little," said the resident who was working on the case. She was right about that.

The room was lined with stainless steel shelves and drawers. These contained countless preserved specimens from "interesting or unusual cases" to be studied in the future or used as references for curious medical students. Two large rectangular steel tables were in the center of the room. Each table had a gutter and tilted into a draining area leading to a sink. The water was always running to wash down the blood.

If what I've described so far is all there was, the room itself would not have been too bad. But there was more to the scene. On the top of one of the steel tables lay a large, naked, old, male body. That was my second shock (after the smell) and the major cause for my alarm. Fearing that I would pass out, I stood as far away from the tables and other people as I could. I took deep breaths and I stood with my legs spread apart for better balance, but I did not faint.

This man on the table seemed so vulnerable. I tried to think of him as only a body. Despite my efforts I began imagining myself in his position—a resident, a medical student, and an autopsy specialist cutting, probing, and making comments about my physical condition; other interested people coming into the room now and then to check out the progress; and six more students curiously watching the whole procedure. I did not like this situation, and I felt sympathy for the autopsy victim. Yet I was curious enough to stay and try to survive the whole autopsy.

When we had become accustomed to our surroundings, the resident told us about the "patient." This fifty-five-year-old white male had come to the hospital to get his foot treated. He had an ulcer (an open sore common to diabetics like himself) on his foot. "He was very lucky to have come in when he did, his foot ulcer was getting bad and it could have led to gangrene," said the resident. His accident happened as he was dressing to leave the hospital after getting treatment for the ulcer. He fell and broke his hip. His surgeon operated, making a large incision from the upper thigh to his waist. He replaced the joint and sent him into recovery. The surgeons thought he was doing well, but he died the next day (Hip operations are not usually life-threatening.).

(continued)

(continued from previous page)

This man had a good heart and did not smoke. He was not fat and he seemed to be in good health. What went wrong? The autopsy team was instructed to look for possible blood clots or other problems in the internal organ system.

When we began observing, the autopsy specialist was finishing the job of resuturing the long incision in the victim's hip. A blood clot the size of a big potato had been extracted. It was soft and jello-like and looked like a raw liver. When I asked, they told me that it was a small clot and that it was not the main reason for this poor man's death.

The next part of the autopsy process again unnerved me—and again I did not faint though I thought I would. The autopsy specialist made a huge Y-shaped incision from the lower abdomen to the lower chest branching out to the shoulders. The layer just below his skin was yellow and fatty, and the strong muscle layer was dark red. The upper layer peeled away from the muscle, but the muscle stuck tight to the ribs. The specialist then hacked through the muscle and ribs around the outside of the chest cavity with a curved pruning shears that had long handles for good leverage. Then he pulled away that layer to expose the heart and lungs.

The centrally located heart was at least as big as two of my fists. The lungs were located high in the chest region, starting at the top of the shoulders and going down only halfway to the lower ribs. They were pink and porous, and I wondered how such small organs could take in enough air for a man his size.

The heart, lungs, liver, and the rest of the smaller organs were then removed and put aside to be studied by the resident medical student, Kris. While Kris "breadsliced" (cut lengthwise at one-inch intervals to study the inside of the organ) the liver, lungs, and digestive system, the autopsy specialist started his electric saw; I wondered what he was planning to do with it. The noise was alarming. He cut a one-foot segment of the backbone out of the man's back and then cut that lengthwise down the middle. Then he extracted the spinal cord and laid it on the table for us to see. I touched it. The finger-thick cord was made up of hundreds of tiny nerves. To see and touch all of these incredible impulse messengers awed me.

The specialist was not done with the saw. While we were watching the dissection of the organs, the patient's scalp lay inside out over his face. I was glad that I could not see his face. The saw started again and cut away a portion of his skull at the back of his head. I looked inside the hole at the body's mastermind—the brain. The resident told me that the brain was too soft to cut right then, so they would store it in formaldehyde for several days until it "firmed up."

As we were examining the organs on another table, two more male medical students arrived. They planned to practice inserting a vein catheter. To practice they used our patient's leg veins. They worked at cutting a small hole

(continued)

(continued from previous page)

and inserting the catheter tube (which drains out blood). They saw that there were some young, female observers in our group so they wanted to be noticed. They joked about how they were going to save him now. I was appalled at this crude behavior. I wondered how anyone could joke in a situation like this one. I tried to remind myself that it was a horrible place to work and that these students used humor to relieve their tensions and make their work more manageable.

We had to leave soon after that incident. We thanked the resident and autopsy specialist and left the room. It was nice to take off the gloves, masks and aprons we had been wearing. Fresh air was welcome, too. But I began thinking about what I had seen that morning. I was upset by the whole situation: an innocent, older man suddenly dies, and with the loss of his life, he loses his identity and dignity. He was just a body for anatomical study. He was not a person, though he was still wearing his wedding ring.

As I contemplated this paradox, I thought again of the whole autopsy process, and was dismayed again. It had been so brutal. It was nothing like the delicate surgery I had expected. Since an autopsy must show every detail, huge incisions must be made. Nothing needs replacement, so little care is taken to keep the parts intact. This carelessness upset me.

I tried to sort everything out in my mind—the patient, the tragic accident, the brutal procedure, the stoic autopsy specialist, the helpful and concerned medical student (Kris), and the joking male medical students. All of this was too much for me to comprehend.

All that day and night, I kept smelling the autopsy odor in various places I went; I could not escape it! The next morning I wrote down my feelings in my journal concerning what I had seen and felt. I also talked with people about my frustrated emotions for several weeks. With the passing of time I can now talk about it, but sometimes I think about that old man.

E. Maxwell, a college sophomore at St. Olaf College, after visiting a medical center during a health science internship experience.

the autopsy room at the Medical University of South Carolina: "This place is where death rejoices to come to the aid of life."

Despite the usefulness of autopsies, there has been a sharp decline in the number of autopsies performed in the United States in recent years (Altman, 1988). In the mid-1940s half the patients who died in a hospital were dissected, whereas today only 13 percent are subjected to postmortems (Clark & Springen, 1986). Autopsy findings are believed to increase the reliability of death certificate data and therefore to provide an essential check on the accuracy of diagnoses—although there may be legitimate disagreement between the attending physician and the pathologist as to precisely what killed the patient.

Physicians, hospital administrators, and families of the deceased have shown reduced interest in autopsies. Physicians in particular fear that an autopsy will uncover an error and thus spur malpractice suits (Clark & Springen, 1986). High-tech methods of diagnosis such as CAT scans have made some believe that postmortems are not necessary. Autopsies also cost hospitals $1,000 to $3,000 each and must be subsidized by general charges because they are not directly covered by health insurance. In addition, physicians are reluctant to ask bereaved next of kin for permission to perform a procedure that many regard as upsetting and an invasion of privacy.

In the previous reading, a college student discusses her observations of an autopsy and her emotional reactions to it. Although it is difficult to generalize from one experience, it is possible that her first encounter with the autopsy is not unlike that of many first-year medical students.

Conclusion

Because the thought of dying is stressful, it seems appropriate that we be aware of dying and death. With more awareness, hopefully a greater acceptance of dying and death will result. Through a better understanding of death meanings, our coping with dying and death should be enhanced. It is difficult to relate to the dying if we ourselves have not been sensitized to our own death.

Traditionally, medical schools have had very limited offerings in death education. On-the-job training may only enforce one's anxieties about the dying. It is encouraging, however, that medical schools seem more concerned about the social and psychological aspects of their patients today. Although death education does not constitute a significant part in current medical curricula, the situation is nonetheless improving.

With dying patients being viewed as deviants in the medical subculture, the treatment of the dying is not always the most humane. After all, death is counter to what physicians learn in medical school. They take an oath to prolong life and to relieve suffering—sometimes contradictory situations. To lose a patient is a failure.

Individuals with life-threatening diseases often continue their daily routines, with few interruptions. We can learn about living from relating to those who are dying.

We often play games in communicating with a dying patient. We know, the physician and nurse know, and the patient knows (probably whether told or not) when the condition is terminal, but we often exist in anything but an open awareness context. No one lets the other know that he or she knows. Death talk remains taboo.

Summary

1. The meaning of dying is dependent upon the social context in which it takes place.
2. Time, space, norm, role, value, self, and situation are important components of the meaning of our dying.
3. One may go through stages in accepting his or her terminal self-meaning.
4. Physicians have limited education concerning issues of dying and death.
5. The dying patient is *viewed* as a deviant in the medical setting, thus the dying patient is *treated* accordingly.

6. Different awareness contexts exist between medical personnel, patients, and the patients' families.
7. Living with dying can be a most meaningful experience for both the patient and significant others.
8. Autopsies are sometimes performed after death to aid in determining the cause of death.

Discussion Questions

1. What does it mean that the meaning of dying will depend upon the social context in which the dying takes place?
2. Would you prefer to live with a person with a terminal disease or a person who is chemically dependent? Discuss the advantages and disadvantages of each.
3. How could steps be taken to overcome the diminished social and personal power of the hospital patient? Are such limitations on patients necessary for an orderly hospital?
4. Discuss this statement: The terminally ill eventually come to view death as a blessing.
5. You have just been told that you have inoperable cancer. Discuss how you think you would react. In what ways would you change your life?
6. If a patient's death represents a failure to a physician, how can medical schools assist in creating an attitude of acceptance of death as the final stage of growth?
7. List as many types of deviant individuals as you can. Do you include the dying patient as deviant? Why or why not?
8. What is meant by this statement: "Deviance may vary with time and place"?
9. Discuss Glaser and Strauss's 4 awareness contexts. Which do you think most often exists in a medical setting with a dying patient?

Glossary

Appropriate Death: This means that the person has died as he or she wished to die and that the death is generally consistent with past personality patterns.

Autopsy: A pathologist's medical examination of the organs of the dead body to determine the cause of death.

Awareness Context: What each interacting person knows of the patient's defined status and his or her recognition of the others' awareness of a personal definition.

Cadaver: A dead body. Human cadavers are used in medical schools for the purpose of dissection to learn the parts of the body.

Codicil: An addition or supplement to a will made at a later date in accordance with the same formalities required for the validity of the will.

Decedent: A deceased person.

Escheat: The fact that property of a decedent goes to the state if not disposed of by a will and if the decedent has no heirs.

Holographic Will: A will written wholly in one's own handwriting and generally requiring no witnesses; not recognized in all states.

Intestate: Describing a person who dies without a will.

Labeling Theory: The theory that the significance of how an act is viewed is on the audience observing rather than on the act itself or the actor.

Master Status: The status (position) most important in establishing an individual's social identity.

Norm: A plan of action or expected behavior pattern thought to be appropriate for a particular situation.

Palliative Care: Care designed to give the patient as painfree a condition as possible.

Pathologist: A physician who deals with the nature of disease, especially with the structural and functional changes caused by disease.

Role: Specified behavior expected for persons occupying specific social positions.

Sick Role: A set of characteristic behaviors that a sick person adopts in accordance with the normative demands of the situation.

Situational Adjustment: The process by which an individual is "molded" by the group into which he or she is seeking acceptance; the person learns from the group how to continue successfully in a situation.

Societal Disengagement: A process whereby society withdraws from or no longer seeks the individual's efforts, as distinguished from *social disengagement* in which the individual withdraws from society.

Testator: A person who makes a will.

Will: A legal document in which a person states how he or she wants property and possessions distributed after death.

References

Albery, N., Elliot, G., & Elliot, J. (Eds.). (1993). *The natural death handbook.* London: Virgin.

Altman, L. K. (1988, October 18). U.S. moves to improve death certificates. *New York Times,* p. 25.

Altman, L. K. (1989, November 14). Physicians endorse more humanities for premed students. *New York Times,* p. 22.

Ashley-Cameron, S., & Dickinson, G. E. (1979, February). Nurses' attitudes toward working with dying patients. Unpublished paper presented at the Alpha Kappa Delta Research Symposium, Richmond, VA.

Atchley, R. C. (1994). *Social forces and aging* (7th ed.). Belmont, CA: Wadsworth.

Autopsy frequency—United States, 1980–1985. (1988, April 22). *Journal of the American Medical Association, 259,* 2357–2362.

Becker, H. (1964, March). Personal change in adult life. *Sociometry, 27,* 40–53.

Bell, M. D. (1996, December). Magic time: Observations of a cancer casualty. *The Atlantic Monthly, 278,* 40–43.

Black, D., Hardoff, D., & Nelki, J. (1989). Educating medical students about death and dying. *Archives of Disease in Childhood, 64,* 750–753.

Blackhall, L. J., Murphy, S. T., Frank, G., Michel, V., & Azen, S. (1995). Ethnicity and attitudes toward patient autonomy. *Journal of the American Medical Association, 274,* 820–825.

Blauner, R. (1966). Death and social structure. *Psychiatry, 29,* 378–394.

Buckman, R. (1992). *How to break bad news: A guide for health care professionals.* Baltimore: Johns Hopkins University Press.

Bugen, L. A. (1980). Coping: Effects of death education. *Omega, 11,* 175–183.

Callanan, M., & Kelley, P. (1992). *Final gifts: Understanding the special awareness, needs, and communications of the dying.* New York: Poseidon Press.

Campbell, T. W., Abernethy, V., & Waterhouse, G. J. (1984). Do death attitudes of nurses and physicians differ? *Omega, 14,* 43–49.

Charmaz, K. (1980). *The social reality of death.* Reading, MA: Addison-Wesley.

Clark, M., & Springen, K. (1986, November 17). The demise of autopsies. *Newsweek,* p. 61.

Coe, R. M. (1970). *Sociology of medicine.* New York: McGraw-Hill.

Coffin, M. M. (1976). *Death in early America.* New York: Elsevier/Nelson Books.

Conley, H. N. (1979). *Living and dying gracefully.* New York: Paulist Press.

Cuzzort, R. P., & King, E. W. (1995). *Twentieth-century social thought.* Fort Worth, TX: Harcourt Brace College Publishers.

de Beauvoir, S. (1965). *A very easy death* (P. O'Brien, Trans.). New York: G. P. Putnam.

Dickinson, G. E. (1985, December). Changes in death education in U.S. medical schools during 1975–1985. *Journal of Medical Education, 60,* 942–943.

Dickinson, G. E. (1988, January). Death education for physicians. *Journal of Medical Education, 63,* 412.

Dickinson, G. E., & Ashley-Cameron, S. (1986, April 4–6). *Sex role socialization versus occupational role socialization: A comparison of female physicians' and female nurses' attitudes toward dying patients.* Unpublished paper presented at the Eastern Sociological Society's Annual Meeting, New York City.

Dickinson, G. E., Lancaster, C. J., Winfield, I. C., Reece, E. F., & Colthorpe, C. A. (1997). Detached concern and death anxiety of first-year medical students: Before and after the gross anatomy course. *Clinical Anatomy, 10* (Vol. 3.), 201–207.

Dickinson, G. E., & Mermann, A. C. (1996, December). Death education in U.S. medical schools, 1975–1995. *Academic Medicine, 71,* 1348–1349.

Dickinson, G. E., & Pearson, A. A. (1979a.) Differences in attitudes toward terminal patients among selected medical specialties of physicians. *Medical Care, 17,* 682–685.

Dickinson, G. E., & Pearson, A. A. (1979b.) Sex differences of physicians in relating to dying patients. *Journal of the American Medical Women's Association, 34,* 45–47.

Dickinson, G. E., & Pearson, A. A. (1980-1981). Death education and physicians' attitudes toward dying patients. *Omega, 11,* 167–174.

Dickinson, G. E., & Tournier, R. E. (1993, January-February). A longitudinal study of sex differences in how physicians relate to dying patients. *Journal of the American Medical Women's Association, 48,* 19–22.

Dickinson, G. E., & Tournier, R. E. (1994). A decade beyond medical school: A longitudinal study of physicians' attitudes toward death and terminally-ill patients. *Social Science and Medicine, 38,* 1397–1400.

Doka, K. J. (1993). *Living with life-threatening illness: A guide for patients, their families, and caregivers*. New York: Lexington Books.

Durand, R. P., Dickinson, G. E., Sumner, E. D., & Lancaster, C. J. (1990, Spring-Summer). Family physicians' attitudes toward death and the terminally-ill patient. *Family Practice Research Journal, 9*, 123–129.

Durbin, D. (1996, August 16). Med students reach out to dead. New Orleans *Times-Picayune*, p. A5.

Durkheim, E. (1961). *Moral education*. Glencoe, IL: The Free Press.

Earl, W. L., Martindale, C. J., & Cohn, D. (1992). Adjustment: Denial in the styles of coping with HIV infection. *Omega, 24*, 35–47.

Evans, E. J., & Fitzgibbon, G. H. (1992). The dissecting room: Reactions of first year medical students. *Clinical Anatomy, 5*, 311–320.

Field, D., & Howells, K. (1986). Medical students' self-reported worries about aspects of death and dying. *Death Studies, 10*, 147–154.

Frank, A. W. (1991). *At the will of the body: Reflections on illness*. Boston: Houghton Mifflin.

Freidson, E. (1972). *Profession of medicine*. New York: Dodd Mead.

Garfield, C. A. (1978). *Psychosocial care of the dying patient*. New York: McGraw-Hill.

Gaspard, N. J. 1970. The family of the patient with long-term illness, *Nursing Clinics of North America, 5*: 77–84.

Gasperson, K. R. (1996). *Delivering bad news in the clinical context: Current recommendations and student perspectives*. Unpublished master's thesis, University of Kentucky, Lexington.

Glaser, B., & Strauss, A. (1965). *Awareness of dying*. Chicago: Aldine.

Goffman, E. (1963). *Stigma*. Englewood Cliffs, NJ: Prentice-Hall.

Goleman, D. (1989, December 5). Fear of death intensifies moral code, scientists find. *New York Times*, p. 19.

Gustafson, E. (1972). Dying: The career of the nursing home patient. *Journal of Health and Social Behavior, 13*, 226–235.

Hafferty, F. W. (1991). *Into the valley: Death and the socialization of medical students*. New Haven: Yale University Press.

Hale, R. (1971, September). Some lessons on dying. *Christian Century* (Vol. 88), 1076–1079.

Harvey, J. H. (1996). *Embracing their memory: Loss and the social psychology of storytelling*. Needham Heights, MA: Allyn and Bacon.

Hawkins, A. H. (1990). Constructing death: Three pathographies about dying. *Omega, 22*, 301–317.

Holland, J. C. (1994). Now we tell—But how well? *Journal of Clinical Oncology, 7*, 557–559.

Hooyman, N. R., & Kiyak, H. A. (1988). *Social gerontology: A multidisciplinary perspective*. Boston: Allyn and Bacon.

James, N. (1992). Care = organization + physical labor + emotional labor. *Sociology of Health and Illness, 14*, 488–509.

Kalish, R. A. (1966). Social distance and the dying. *Community Mental Health, 11*, 152–155.

Kamerman, J. B. (1988). *Death in the midst of life: Social and cultural influences on death, grief and mourning*. Englewood Cliffs, NJ: Prentice-Hall.

Kane, A. C., & Hogan, J. D. (1986). Death anxiety in physicians: Defensive style, medical specialty, and exposure to death. *Omega, 16*, 11–22.

Kaufmann, W. (1976). *Existentialism, religion and death*. London: New English Library.

Kavanaugh, R. E. (1972). *Facing death*. Baltimore: Penguin Books.

Kellehear, A. (1990). *Dying of cancer: The final year of life*. Chur, Switzerland: Harwood Academic Publishers.

Kristof, N. D. (1996, September 29). For rural Japanese, death doesn't break family ties. *New York Times*, p. 10.

Kübler-Ross, E. (1969). *On death and dying*. New York: Macmillan.

Kübler-Ross, E. (1975). *Death: The final stage of growth*. Englewood Cliffs, NJ: Prentice-Hall.

Leming, M. R., Vernon, G. M., & Gray, R. M. (1977, July). The dying patient: A symbolic analysis. *International Journal of Symbology, 8*, 77–86.

Leviton, D. (1977). The scope of death education. *Death Education, 1*, 41–56.

Maguire, P., & Faulkner, A. (1992). Communicating with cancer patients: Handling bad news and difficult questions. *British Medical Journal, 297*, 907–909.

Marks, S. C., & Bertman, S. L. (1980). Experiences with learning about death and dying in the undergraduate anatomy curriculum. *Journal of Medical Education, 55*, 844–850.

Martin, S. C., Arnold, R. M., & Parker, R. M. (1988, December). Gender and socialization. *Journal of Health and Social Behavior, 29*, 333–343.

Mermann, A. C., Gunn, D. B., & Dickinson, G. E. (1991, January). Learning to care for the dying: A survey of medical schools and a model course. *Academic Medicine, 66,* 35–38.

Merton, R. K. (1949). The bearing of sociological theory on empirical research. In *Social structure and social theory.* New York: The Free Press.

Merton, R. K., Reader, G. G., & Kendall, P. L. (Eds.). (1957). *The student-physician: Introductory studies in the sociology of medical education.* Cambridge: Harvard University Press.

Miles, M. S. (1980). The effects of a course on death and grief on nurses' attitudes toward dying patients and death. *Death Education, 4,* 245–251.

Montgomery, L. (1996, December 12). AMA to teach physicians how to aid the dying patient. Charleston, SC, *Post and Courier,* p. 4A.

Morrison, R. S., & Morris, J. (1995, July). When there is no cure: Palliative care for the dying patient. *Geriatrics, 50,* 45–50.

Nelson, W. A. (1980). Clinical teaching of care for terminally ill in a psychiatry clerkship. *Journal of Medical Education, 55,* 610–615.

Nuland, S. B. (1994). *How we die.* New York: Knopf.

Oken, D. (1961). What to tell cancer patients. *Journal of the American Medical Association, 175,* 1120–1128.

Parsons, T. (1951). *The social system.* New York: The Free Press.

Pattison, E. M. (1977). *The experience of dying.* Englewood Cliffs, NJ: Prentice-Hall.

Pine, V. (1975). Institutionalized communication about death and dying. *Journal of Thanatology, 3,* 1–12.

Quill, T. E. (1991). Bad news: Delivery, dialogue, and dilemmas. *Archives of Internal Medicine, 151,* 463–468.

Richardson, W. C. (1992, June 3). Educating leaders who can resolve the health-care crisis. *The Chronicle of Higher Education* (Vol. 39), p. B1.

Roberts, W. C. (1978, August 17). The autopsy: Its decline and a suggestion for its revival. *The New England Journal of Medicine, 299,* 332–338.

Schofferman, J. (1988). Care of the AIDS patient, *Death Studies, 12,* 433–449.

Seale, C. (1991). Communication and awareness about death: A study of a random sample of dying people. *Social Science and Medicine, 32,* 943–952.

Sell, L., Devlin, B., Bourke, S. J., Munro, N. C., Corris, P. A., & Gibson, G. J. (1993). Communicating the diagnosis of lung cancer. *Respiratory Medicine, 87,* 61–63.

Seravalli, E. P. (1988). The dying patient, the physician, and the fear of death. *The New England Journal of Medicine, 319,* 1728–1730.

Stephenson, J. S. (1985). *Death, grief, and mourning.* New York: The Free Press.

Tyson, E. (1997, February). Save thousands on wills and trusts with computerized legal programs. *Money, 22.*

Vernon, G. M. (1972). *Human interaction.* New York: Ronald Press.

Walter, T. (1995). Natural death and the noble savage. *Omega, 30*(4), 237–248.

Wanzer, S. H., et al. (1989). The physician's responsibility toward hopelessly ill patients. *The New England Journal of Medicine, 320,* 844–849.

Wertenbaker, L. T. (1957). *The death of a man.* New York: Random House.

Wheeler, A. L. (1973, April). *The dying person: A deviant in the medical subculture.* Unpublished paper presented at the Southern Sociological Society Annual Meeting, Atlanta, GA.

Wolf, S. S. (1995). Legal perspectives on planning for death. In H. W. Wass & R. A. Neimeyer (Eds.), *Dying: Facing the facts* (3rd ed., pp. 163–184). Washington, DC: Taylor and Francis.

Suggested Readings

Bethel, E. R. (1995). *AIDS: Readings on a global crisis.* Boston: Allyn and Bacon. Discusses the ecology of AIDS, the epidemics of AIDS in the United States, Africa, Latin America, Great Britain, and Asia, and programs for behavioral change.

Buckman, R. (1992). *I don't know what to say: How to help and support someone who is dying.* New York: Viking Press. From his own clinical experiences as an oncologist, the author discusses many issues that evolve in the process of watching someone die, including the topic of how to communicate with a dying person.

Charmaz, K. (1991). *Good days, bad days: The self in chronic illness and time.* Rutgers, NJ: Rutgers University Press. Sociologist Charmaz describes three stages through which chronic illness can progress: The illness disrupts life; it intrudes nearly every day and holds no promise of abating; and it engulfs the individual, becoming the paramount feature of life.

Doka, K. J. (1993). *Living with life-threatening illness.* New York: Lexington Books. A book to help patients, families, and caregivers in relating to a life-threatening illness.

Field, D., Hockey, J. and Small, N. (1997). *Death, Gender and Ethnicity.* New York: Routledge. Examines ways in which gender and ethnicity shape the experiences of dying and bereavement.

Frank, A. (1991). *At the will of the body: Reflections on illness.* Boston: Houghton Mifflin. Written by a medical sociologist who had a heart attack at age 39 and cancer at age 40, this book tells us how illness affects us and what it can teach us about life.

George, R., & Houghton, P. 1997. *Healthy Dying.* Bristol, PA: Taylor & Francis. Examines a wide range of issues surrounding the terminally ill, including difficulties faced by caregivers.

Hafferty, F. W. (1991). *Into the valley: Death and the socialization of medical students.* New Haven: Yale University Press. A sociologist using participant observation describes the experiences of a class of 1st-year medical students as they are exposed to dying patients and gross anatomy lab.

Keizer, B. (1997). *Dancing with Mister D: Notes on life and death.* New York: Doubleday. A Dutch doctor, with training in philosophy as well as medicine, probes the intensity of the American preoccupation with dying and death as he shares his extraordinary experiences among the terminally ill.

Kellehear, A. (1990). *Dying of cancer: The final year of life.* Chur, Switzerland: Harwood Academic Publishers. A sociological account of the social behavior and experiences of 100 individuals who were dying of cancer.

Konner, M. (1987). *Becoming a doctor: A journey of initiation in medical school.* New York: Penguin Books. An anthropologist and physician, Konner takes the reader through hospital rounds, in various specialty areas, and discusses encounters with death and with dying patients.

Nuland, S. B. (1994). *How we die: Reflections on life's final chapter.* New York: Alfred A. Knopf. The author, a surgeon and professor at Yale, shares accounts of dying that reveal not only why someone dies but also how.

Riska, E., & Wegar, K. (1993). *Gender Work and Medicine.* London: Sage Publications. This collection of articles provides a critical assessment of the division of labor in medicine, setting current practice in its historical context.

R.N. Proctor (1995). *Cancer wars: How politics shapes what we know & don't know about cancer.* New York: Basic Books. Discuss how government regulatory agencies, scientists, trade associations, and environmentalists have managed to obscure the issues and prevent concerted action around the fight against cancer.

Rosen, E. J. (1990). *Families facing death: Family dynamics of terminal illness.* New York: Lexington Books. A family therapist provides guidance to the wide range of disciplines that interact with families facing death.

Smith, J. M. (1996). *AIDS and society.* Upper Saddle River, NJ: Prentice-Hall. Discusses various aspects of AIDS: demographics, prejudice, discrimination, morality, institutional barriers, and economic and international issues.

Spiro, H. M., Curnen, M. G. M., & Wandel, L. P. (Eds.). (1996). *Facing death: Where culture, religion, and medicine meet.* New Haven, CT: Yale University Press. Physicians discuss the current clinical setting for dying. Also, Christian, Judaic, Islamic, Hindu, and Chinese perspectives on death and mourning rituals are presented.

Related Web Sites

http://www.lsds.com/death/   Thanatolinks contains links to some of the best Internet sites related to dying and death.

http://www.emanon.net/~kcabell/death.html   Contains many World Wide Web links to resources on death and bereavement.

http://www.yahoo.com/Society_and_Culture/Death/   The death index of the Yahoo Internet search engine.

http://www.cdc.gov/   Home page of the Centers for Disease Control and Prevention.

http://www.ahcpr.gov/   The Agency for Health Care Policy and Research provides information on the dying process in the context of U.S. health policy.

http://newciv.org/worldtrans/naturaldeath.html   The Natural Death Centre is a nonprofit charitable project launched in Britain in 1991 with three psychotherapists as directors. It aims to support those dying at home and their caregivers and to help them arrange funerals. It has as a more general aim that of helping improve "the quality of dying."

http://www.boston.com/globe/hospice/info.htm   A tremendous resource maintained by the *Boston Globe* and containing articles and information on home care and dying.

http://www.soros.org/death.html   The Project on Death in America has the goal of helping people understand and transform the dying experience in America.

http://www.trinity.edu/~mkearl/paradigm.html   Paradigm does not suggest that there is one particular way of dying well. However, it is possible to identify some general developmental tasks that the dying person can accomplish if dying well is the goal. (Paradigm, P.O. Box 14061, San Francisco, CA 94114; phone 415 522-9192)

http://www.coredcs.com/~sbro/hpdying.htm   Christian prayers for the dying.

http://www.well.com/user/suscon/esalen/participants/Halifax/dying.html   "Being With Dying," written by Joan Halifax, is concerned with providing contemplative approaches to working with dying people for the Death in America Project.

http://www.aidskids.org/   Children With Aids Project is an organization whose role is to develop a fuller understanding of children with, and at risk of, AIDS, including the medical, psychosocial, legal, and financial issues. The mission of the organization is to develop local and national adoptive, foster, and family-centered care programs that are both effective and compassionate.

http://www.netlink.co.uk/users/vess/lwvh.html   Living wills (advance directives) help medical staff and others to make decisions about care and treatment of the seriously ill who are unable to speak for themselves. In some circumstances, living wills may become legally binding on health-care staff. The Living Will and Values History Project was set up in response to an alarming growth of living will documents that bore little correlations to academic and empirical data on their usefulness or effectiveness. It works on a nonprofit basis and attempts to collate, analyze, and apply research in this area, acting as an adviser and resource base, as well as publishing its own document.

http://aps.cnidr.org/   AIDS Patents Project provides access to the full text and images of international patents relating to acquired immunodeficiency syndrome (AIDS).

gopher://gopher.niaid.nih.gov:70/11/aids/cdcds   The CDC AIDS gopher network with articles on AIDS.

http://www..hivatis.org/   The HIV/AIDS Treatment Information Service (ATIS) provides information about federally approved treatment guidelines for HIV and AIDS.

http://www.thebody.com/anin/aninpage.html   AIDS National Interfaith Network (ANIN) is a private, nonprofit organization founded in 1988. ANIN was created to ensure that individuals with HIV and AIDS receive compassionate and nonjudgmental support, care, and assistance. ANIN coordinates a network of nearly 2,000 AIDS ministries. ANIN works with national faith-based, AIDS-specific networks; supports community-based AIDS ministries; and educates AIDS service organizations, the religious community at large, and the general public about AIDS ministries. ANIN's programs include networking/collaborating and referral activities, as well as public education and federal AIDS policy advocacy.

http://www.nih.gov/od/oar/   Home page of the Office of AIDS Research for the National Institutes of Health.

http://www.viaticus.com/   A resource for families who wish to buy life insurance for the terminally ill.

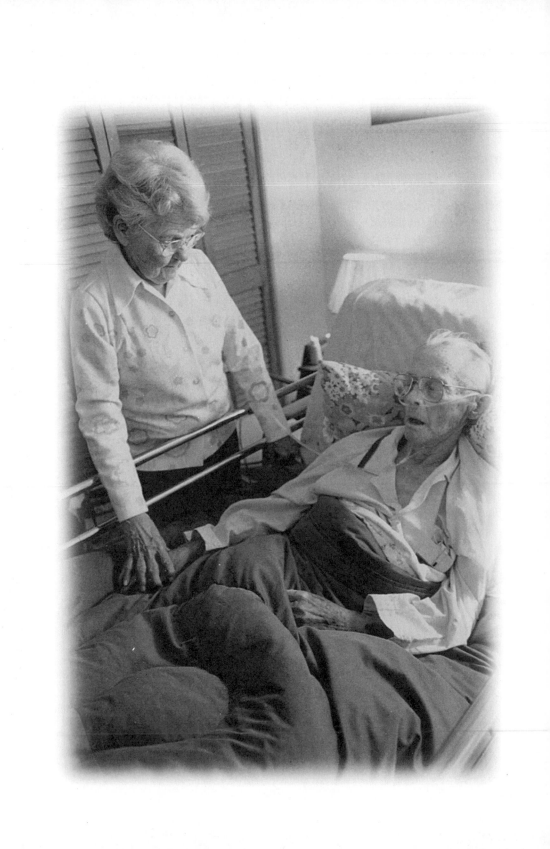

Chapter 7

The Hospice Approach:
Alternative Care for the Dying

"I'm afraid of the pain."
"I don't want to be alone when I'm dying."
"I'm afraid of a long, protracted period of suffering."
"I don't want to die in a hospital. Let me die at home."
"I'm not afraid for myself, but I am worried about the effect of my death on those I love."

—FREQUENT RESPONSES TO THE QUESTION: DOES DYING FRIGHTEN YOU?

In chapter 1 we discovered that of the 8 types of death fears, the 3 that elicit the highest anxiety are the fear of pain, the fear of dependency, and the fear of isolation (Leming, 1979–1980). As the opening responses reflect, it is the *process* of dying and not the *event* of death that causes the most concern for people in this country.

This chapter is about the worldwide **hospice movement** that has developed as a response to fears related to the dying process and the institutionalized ways in which death is typically handled in institutional settings. The 3 primary patient concerns that hospice care directly addresses are the problems related to symptom and pain control, the apprehension caused by having others in control of one's life, and the anxiety about being alone at the time of death (Magno, 1990).

The History of the Hospice Movement

Hospice should be thought of primarily as a concept of care—a way to provide humane and supportive care for dying patients and their families (Burns et al., 1989, p. 65). Its philosophical approach is derived from the teachings of Jesus found in the 25th chapter of Matthew when He encourages His followers with the following words:

> Then I, the King, shall say to those at my right, "Come, blessed of my Father, into the Kingdom prepared for you from the founding of the world. For I was hungry and you fed me; I was thirsty and you gave me water; I was a stranger and you invited me into your homes; naked and you clothed me; sick and in prison, and you visited me." ... "Whenever you did these things for the least of these my brothers, you were doing them for me!" (Matt. 25:34–36, 40)

The words *hospice, hospital, hostel,* and *hotel* all are derived from the same Latin root *spitium*—which means "host" or "guest." According to Kenneth Cohen (1979, p. 15), "the first hospitals were actually an outgrowth of religion rather than of medicine." As early as the 4th century, Roman Emperor Julian expressed his concern about the emergence of the Christian movement. As a response to the Christian emphasis upon humanitarianism, Julian encouraged the priests of the Roman religion to "establish hospices (*xenodochia*) in every city and thereby not permit others to excel us in good deeds" (Phipps, 1988).

In medieval times, the word *hospice* referred to a way station for travelers needing assistance. Sandol Stoddard (1978) and William Phipps (1988) describe some of the early medieval hospices. Probably the most famous hospice in the world is the Hospice of Great Saint Bernard in the Alps. This hospice, founded over 1,000 years ago, trains dogs to rescue travelers lost on the Alpine slopes. With the passing of time, the word *hospice* came to encompass houses maintained for the sick as well as for the traveler.

As time and the secularization of the modern age evolved, hospitals have come to be dominated by secular administrators and medical practitioners who have established the priority of providing medical cures for the acutely ill rather than caring for those who are incurable. In 1905 the Irish Sisters of Charity established St. Joseph's Hospice in Hackney (near London) to provide patient-centered care for the terminally ill. One third of St. Joseph's Hospice's beds are for patients with a prognosis for living 3 months or less (Phipps, 1988, p. 96). According to the medical director of St. Joseph's Hospice, J. F. Hanratty, M.D., physicians find it difficult to care for patients whom they cannot cure and accept palliative medical skills and treatments as authentic medical protocol. It has not been uncommon to hear medical practitioners telling terminal patients, "There is nothing more I can do."

> At St. Joseph's "more" is done, and the "more" is sophisticated therapies to control, as much as possible, all of the patient's distressing symptoms. The practice at St. Joseph's Hospice is, first of all, to establish that the diagnosis is accurate and that death is not far distant. The management of terminal illness then requires a change of roles and attitude on the part of those caring for the patient. (Hanratty, cited by Carr, 1989, p. 266)

The Universal Prayer of Pope Clement XI

Teach me to realize that this world is passing,
    that my true future is the happiness of heaven,
    that life on earth is short,
    and that life to come eternal.

Help me to prepare for death
    with a proper fear of judgment,
    but a greater trust in Your goodness.

Lead me safely through death
    to the endless joy of heaven.

Found in the sacramentary and used by priests after they say Mass at St. Joseph's Hospice (cited by Carr, 1989, p. 267).

St. Christopher's Hospice in London played a pivotal role in the global development of the modern hospice movement by actively disseminating the hospice concept of care and ministering to the spiritual and physical needs of dying patients. Having opened in 1967, St. Christopher's was founded by Dr. Cicely Saunders, who had begun her career as a nurse and subsequently became a social worker. However, it was not until Dr. Saunders became a physician and obtained a grant to work with the Sisters of Charity at St. Joseph's Hospice that she was able to provide international influence on institutionalized health care for dying patients. Her achievements were recognized in 1981 when Queen Elizabeth II granted her the status of Dame.

In the United States, the first modern hospice program was the Connecticut Hospice, whose origin was directly linked to that of St. Christopher's in London. In 1963 Dr. Saunders was invited to lecture in New Haven at the Yale University School of Medicine. Over the next several years, contacts between Dr. Saunders and personnel from the Yale Nursing and Medical Schools were frequent. Local leaders from various disciplines became involved in the development of a hospice in Connecticut, and their planning resulted in the establishment in 1971 of Hospice, Inc., later changed to the Connecticut Hospice.

The original intent of the planning group was to build an inpatient facility similar to St. Christopher's. Funding proved to be a problem, however, and the group decided to inaugurate its home care program in 1974. To test the viability of home care, the National Cancer Institute provided funds for a 3-year demonstration project. As a result, an inpatient facility was eventually built with the help of both federal and state funds and opened in 1980 in New Branford, Connecticut.

After the inpatient facility was completed, the Connecticut Hospice, with the help of a foundation grant, organized a separate corporation—the Connecticut Hospice Institute for Education, Training, and Research. The institute offered special help to health care leaders desiring to improve the quality of care given to the terminally ill and their families. In 1981 the institute was merged with its founder and continues its educational work as the John D. Thompson Hospice Institute for Education, Training, and Research, the teaching arm of the Connecticut Hospice. The purpose of this institute is to "share the hospice philosophy, experience and skills with students, caregivers, administrators, the lay community and all those who desire to improve the quality of care for patients and their families enduring irreversible illness" (the Connecticut Hospice, 1997).

Since that beginning, the number of hospice programs throughout the United States has increased to over 2,800 serving more than 400,000 patients annually. In 1978 the National Hospice Organization (NHO) was formed to provide coordination of hospice activities and to ensure that quality standards of care would always be demonstrated by any program calling itself a hospice. Instrumental in working toward an accreditation procedure, the NHO also provides educational programs, technical assistance, publications, advocacy, and referral services to the general public. Although it serves most of the nation's hospices and over 4,200 professional members (National Hospice Organization, 1997), every state now has its own hospice organization to promote education and standards of quality.

In 1997 the National Hospice Organization estimated that more than 25,000 people are employed in hospice care across the country. On average the 2,800 hospice programs serve 140 patient-families per year, and in serving these patients, more than 96,000 volunteers contribute more than 5.25 million hours of their time each year.

The Nature of the Contemporary Hospice

Although different types of hospice institutions exist, all hospice programs are unified by the general philosophy of patient care. **Hospice** is a specialized health care program that serves patients with life-threatening illnesses. In 1996 approximately 78 percent of hospice patients in the United States had cancer, 10 percent had cardiovascular diseases, 4 percent had AIDS, 1 percent had renal or kidney disease, 1 percent had Alzheimer's disease, and the remaining 6 percent had a variety of other diseases (National Hospice Organization, 1997). Nationally, in 1992 the average hospice patient spent 64 days in hospice care (National Hospice Organization, 1997). More than 90 percent of hospice care hours are provided in patients' homes, with inpatient care available as needed. In hospice, the patient-family is the unit of care. The primary goals of hospice care are to promote patient-family autonomy, to assist patients in obtaining pain control and real quality of life before they die, and to enable families of patients to receive supportive help during the dying process and the bereavement period.

PAIN MANAGEMENT

A hospice program is basically a medical program with physician direction and nurse coordination. Hospice leaders have discovered that patients cannot achieve quality of life unless physical pain and symptoms such as nausea, vomiting, dizziness, constipation, and shortness of breath are under control. A major emphasis of hospice, therefore, is pain and symptom management.

Traditional medical care is often based upon a **PRN** (for the Latin *pro re nata*) approach, which means that medication is given "as the situation demands." In practice, this means that often a person must first hurt and ask for relief before pain management can be administered. This approach is responsible for much of the suffering endured by the terminally ill.

But, when Cicely Saunders began working at St. Joseph's Hospice in 1958, she developed an alternative method of pain control that has become the standard of hospice care. She writes:

> Here at St. Joseph's, as elsewhere at that time, one saw people "earning their morphine," and it was wonderfully rewarding to introduce the simple and really obvious system of giving drugs to prevent pain happening—rather than to wait and give them once it had occurred. Here too there was the potential for developing ideas about the control of other symptoms, and also for looking at the other components of pain. But first of all I must salute the Sisters of St. Joseph's and the compassionate matter-of-factness of their dedicated care. Together we began to develop the appropriate way of caring, showing that there could be a place for scientific medicine and nursing. We could illustrate an alternative approach to the contrast between active treatment for an illness (as if to cure it were still possible) or some form of legalized euthanasia. (Saunders, 1992, p. 20)

Hospice physicians believe that a patient should not hurt at all. Regular medication is, therefore, given before the pain begins. The aim is to erase the memory of the pain that has been experienced and to deal with the fear of pain in the future. Pain medications are standardized to the needs of the patient. The aim is to control the pain and other symptoms without sedating the patient. Every symptom is treated as a separate illness because only when each symptom is under control can a patient begin to find fullness and quality of life.

The hospice concept includes both home care and inpatient care. Ideally, hospice care represents a continuum that includes both forms of care when each is necessary. However, the major emphasis of hospice treatment is home care.

HOME AND INPATIENT CARE

Inpatient care usually becomes necessary for 1 of 3 reasons. The first is that in order to bring the patient's pain and symptoms under control, a stay of a few days in an inpatient facility may be necessary or helpful. The second is that the family taking care of the patient at home may become exhausted and need a few days, rest while the patient is cared for elsewhere. The third reason is that home care may be inappropriate at a given stage of the illness due to the patient's condition or home situation. It is hoped that upon admission to an inpatient facility, patients will be able to move back and forth from home care to inpatient care at various stages of the illness.

THE HOSPICE TEAM

Hospice care is provided by an interdisciplinary **hospice team,** with each discipline having something to contribute to the whole. All disciplines work together, each in its own area of expertise, and each interdisciplinary team includes several layers or levels of care. At the center of the team is the *patient and his or her family.* The hospice movement emphasizes the need for people to make their own decisions with the supportive help of health care professionals and other trained persons. A vital part of the process is the *patient's own physician*—the professional who will continue to be in charge of the care of the patient and write medical orders when necessary.

The next layer of the team includes the hospice's professional caregiving staff. This consists first of *physicians,* required to direct medical care. *Nurses* comprise the next layer. Registered nurses are responsible for coordinating the patient's care. Licensed practical nurses and nurse's aides are also included—especially in inpatient settings.

The *hospice social worker* constitutes an important part of the team. The social worker spends considerable time working with families, thus enabling family members to communicate with each other. Although family members may be aware that the patient is dying, they may never have discussed it with each other or with the patient. The social worker also spends time dealing with social problems, such as alcoholism and marriage problems, and working with the children or grandchildren of patients. All too often in modern society children have been shielded from participating in events focused on the death of a family member.

Pastoral care is also a basic part of the team. A larger hospice may employ a *chaplain,* who will direct pastoral care to patients and their families, counsel other members of the caregiving team on spiritual issues, and try to involve clergy of the community in the care of their own people. In smaller hospice programs all of the care may be provided by local clergy who work closely with the hospice staff.

Financial counseling is a significant aspect of the hospice team. Because patients and families have often exhausted their financial resources at the time of care, attention is given to forms of third-party reimbursement, such as those provided by Medicare or private insurance companies, and to seeking other programs for which the patient may be eligible.

The next layer of the hospice team includes a variety of health-care professionals or other key leaders in the community whose help may be called upon during the illness. A *psychiatrist* or *psychologist* may be needed to provide expert counseling help. *Nurses, home health aides,* and *homemakers* employed by public health nursing agencies—such as visiting nurse associations—may be needed to provide special continuing health care or to share in the provision of patient care. Physical and/or *occupational therapists* may be needed to work with the patient to ensure maximum daily functioning. Finally, the services of a *lawyer* and/or *funeral director* may be required to help the patient settle personal affairs and provide the needs of survivors after the death.

Artists are increasingly recognized as important members of the hospice team. The Connecticut Hospice pioneered the development of an arts program that considers the arts as a means to help patients find meaningful fulfillment during their last days. In many programs artists in such areas as metalwork, photography, pottery, drama, dance, and music work with patients interested in such self-expression.

Trained *volunteers* comprise an essential part of the hospice team. Medicare reimbursement is predicated on the requirement that volunteer time represent 5 percent of all patient care—no hospice can exist for long without a strong volunteer component. NHO-affiliated programs recruit their volunteers from many sources: churches

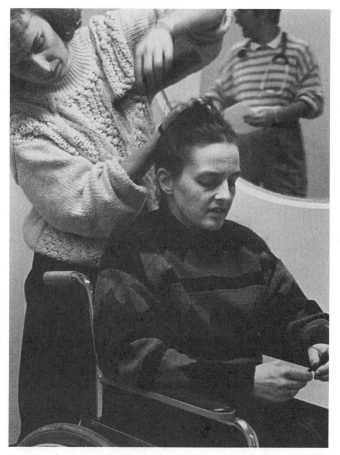

For many hospice patients, just having a volunteer attend to their physical appearance is an important aspect of patient-centered care.

(94 percent recruit in churches), civic groups (80 percent), social groups (70 percent), professional organizations (65 percent), business and industry (47 percent), colleges (34 percent), and secondary schools (12 percent).

Hospice volunteers include people from the following groups: housewives, students, retired persons, and professionals such as social workers, psychologists, teachers, gerontologists, members of the clergy, and architects (Chng & Ramsey, 1984–1985, p. 240). Many volunteers have lost loved ones and find that this experience provides them with an opportunity to serve others. Some volunteers are retired health care professionals such as physicians or nurses. Others are nonprofessionals who are deeply interested in the needs of dying patients and their families. Each volunteer has skills and experiences that can greatly enhance the life of the terminal patient (Chng & Ramsey, 1984–1985, p. 240).

Before volunteers begin a hospice program's extensive training program, they are interviewed by the volunteer coordinator and may be asked to complete specially designed questionnaires that assess their feelings and sensitivity toward dying persons.

The National Hospice Organization (1997) claims that on average hospices require 22 hours of training prior to the time that a volunteer is allowed to work directly with a patient or family.

In addition to the initial volunteer training program, every hospice program has regular in-service training to maintain and update the volunteers' skills. The average volunteer provides services for 3 years, and 50 percent of hospice volunteers stay 6 or more years (National Hospice Organization, 1997).

Some volunteers work in patient care tasks such as providing transportation, sitting with a patient to free family members to get out of the house for a while, carrying equipment, or providing bereavement counseling to family members after the death of the patient. However, according to Chng and Ramsey (1984–1985), hospice volunteers perform primarily 3 roles: companion/friend, advocate, and educator. In 1992 the average hospice received 3,300 hours of service from volunteers. Nationwide, that translates into more than 5.25 million hospice volunteer hours—approximately two thirds of which pertain directly to patient care (National Hospice Organization, 1997).

A 1992 national study of volunteers by the NHO determined that 87 percent of volunteers were female and that 58 percent of these were 60 years of age or younger, compared with 53 percent of male volunteers. The vast majority of these volunteers had experienced the death of a significant other-most of whom were parents in hospice programs (National Hospice Organization, 1993).

In a study of volunteers at the Mercy Hospital Hospice Care Program of Urbana, Illinois, Michael Patchner and Mark Finn (1987–1988) discovered that 86 percent of the hospice volunteers felt capable of performing all of their duties involved in hospice work and that they were very satisfied with volunteering but were most satisfied with assignments that involved direct contact with patients and families and palliative care work within the hospital. Volunteers were least satisfied with the following instrumental tasks: completing forms, attending volunteer meetings, and performing clerical duties. These volunteers were involved in hospice work primarily because they felt that they had something to offer others and wished to be of service to others (Patchner & Finn, 1987–1988, pp. 135–142).

The unpaid volunteer has the double benefit of being identified by the patient and family as being knowledgeable but not having the professional status that can create a social distance. In the hospice program where I volunteer, we refer to the companion/friend role as being a "competent presence" or "safe place." By being a stranger who provides a "listening ear," without emotional involvements or professional entanglements, the volunteer can support the patient and family members as can no other participant in the social network of dying.

The volunteer also functions in an advocate role by acting on behalf of the dying patient and family. Sometimes patients and their loved ones are afraid to challenge or ask questions of physicians and other medical personnel. The volunteer, who has become a trusted friend and confidant, can often speak up for patients and their families and make their needs known to those responsible for their care. I once served as the primary volunteer for a male patient who was undermedicated. When the patient complained to his nurse regarding his pain, he was told to "brave it out." Knowing the medical system, I was able to contact the appropriate individuals, who were, indeed, able to have his pain medications reevaluated. The words of Chng and Ramsey (1984–1985, p. 240) are good advice at this point:

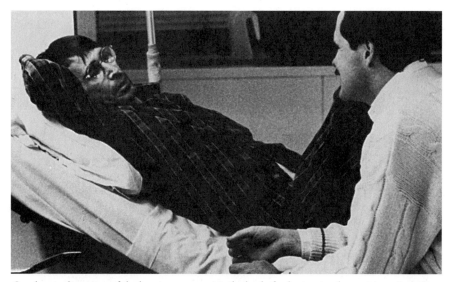

One key to the success of the hospice movement is the level of volunteer involvement in patient care. In this photograph, a hospice volunteer offers the patient friendship, companionship, and the competent presence of a nonjudgmental listener.

To be truly effective, the suggestions of the volunteer have to stem from knowledge and understanding of the intricate patient-family-institutional configurations. Under the careful guidance of professionals, the volunteer can serve a significant role as ancillary to professionals.

The final role served by volunteers is that of educator. Most individuals in our society have not had many personal experiences with death. The hospice volunteer

Sharing the Journey: A Ministry in Hospice
Janet White

As a trained hospice volunteer, I provided vital non-clinical services such as transportation, companionship, respite care, and light housekeeping. My weekly visits also kept the patient and family in contact with the world beyond their own home, preserving the tie between them and the community, and preventing further isolation during the last phases of illness.

My first patient was like a grandfather to me. When I took my weekly turn in caring for Tom, I always received more than I gave. His attitude reflected an inner joy and peace, even though his frail body was wrecked by the perpetual coughing and shortness of breath that left him weaker every day.

"Please open the curtains," he would whisper first thing in the morning. "I want to see the sunshine."

(continued)

(continued from previous page)

His reply was always the same when I accomplished the task. "Thank you, my dear, that's grand." Oh, how he loved the sunshine. He reveled in each warming ray.

Although other family members, as well as doctors and nurses, did their best in taking care of his physical needs, the Lord knew he needed someone like me. I could listen and hold his almost transparent hand.

I often read the Bible to Tom, and we prayed together. We talked about heaven, where all sickness and pain, heartache and sorrow would no longer be our constant companion. This gave him courage and hope—something to look forward to beyond his feeble earthly existence. He knew his pain was only temporary and would end soon.

Tom loved music, and had sung in the church choir for most of his eighty-nine years. Sometimes I brought him Christian cassettes to listen to in the long hours alone. He played the "Hallelujah Chorus" again and again.

"Soon I'll be singing Hallelujah right to Jesus," he struggled to say with a weak smile. "I'll have a new voice and plenty of breath to praise the Lord."

After his funeral, I cried every time I heard that beloved classic, as I thought of Tom lying in the hospital bed in his living room. The brevity of

(continued)

can learn from each experience in working with dying patients and pass on insights that may be helpful to patients and families. The volunteer can help the dying and their loved ones understand that the dying process is usually complex, stressful, and disordered. In addition, most patients and families have a strong need to have their feelings and experiences validated. Patients and families who have a difficult time understanding their feelings, emotions, and experiences during the dying process should be assured that they are "quite normal."

Within the community at large, a number of influences either assist with patient care or help to make it possible. Family members or friends are urged to participate in the patient's care as much as possible. When family members cannot provide as much care as may be needed at certain times, hospice personnel will try to meet the patient's needs by exploring all possible options to do so (National Hospice Organization, 1988). The patient-family support system is the most significant factor in the dying process for many patients, but elements of the system also include numerous close or distant relatives, friends, neighbors, members of local churches, and/or other civic groups.

Hospice programs are dependent on a high degree of community interest and support. Bringing this about requires a planned program of public information. The concept of hospice must be sold to the medical community and to members of the larger community. Specific activities require not only financial support (especially while the hospice program is developing), but also a willingness to testify before regulatory agencies about the granting of hospice accreditation, Medicare certification, and/or approval to begin offering services to the people of the area.

(continued from previous page)

life had helped both of us focus on what was truly important and of eternal value. I had shared Christ's love in a tangible way to a hurting person, acting as His hands extended to a dying world.

Working as a hospice volunteer, I gained a sense of mission and fulfillment of God's purpose for my life. I now see care-giving and servanthood as a way of life for every Christian.

This verse became my daily prayer: "Lord make me to know my end, And what is the extent of my days, Let me know how transient I am" (Psalms 39:4).

Each Christian is God's gift to humankind, a treasure to be shared. We are blessed to be a blessing. We have a hope beyond death that we can share with others.

Jesus came not to be served, but to serve others. Sharing the journey of a dying man was how I followed my Lord's example of ministering to "one of the least of these."

J. White, 1992, *The Lutheran Journal*, 60(3), pp. 24–25.

PATIENT-CENTERED CARE

One of the distinguishing features of the hospice concept of care is that, whenever possible, hospice enables patients to make decisions about how and where they want to live their lives. **Patient-centered care** is nonjudgmental, unconditional, and empowering.

One of the patients of the hospice program where I volunteer provides an example of this philosophy of care. This patient had adult children in town but lived as a single person with his dog. He had lung cancer and desired to die at home alone. He was also a smoker and heavy alcohol drinker. Our hospice program agreed to honor the patient's desires whenever it was possible. Therefore, a hospice nurse visited his house every 4 hours, and members of the police department checked in on him every hour from 10 p.m. to 7 a.m. The patient's pain was kept under control without sedation. A hospice volunteer (who also happened to be a licensed vocational nurse) visited the patient 2 to 3 times each day, and she, along with friends and family members, met the patient's requests for liquor and cigarettes. Visits from all members of the hospice team never lasted longer than 10 minutes. The patient died as he wanted—in his home, free from pain, and in control of his own care.

Although not every member of the hospice team, or the patient's family, would have chosen to die as this patient did, everyone respected his right to make decisions regarding his care. The hospice philosophy states that patients and their families have the right to participate in decisions concerning their care and that they should not be judged because their decisions are contrary to the beliefs of their caregivers.

The Dying Person's Bill of Rights

I have the right to be treated as a living human being until I die.

I have the right to maintain a sense of hopefulness, however changing its focus may be.

I have the right to be cared for by those who can maintain a sense of hopefulness, however challenging this might be.

I have the right to express my feelings and emotions about approaching death in my own way.

I have the right to participate in decisions concerning my care.

I have the right to expect continuing medical and nursing attention even though "cure" goals must be changed to "comfort" goals.

I have the right not to die alone.

I have the right to be free from pain.

I have the right to have my questions answered honestly.

I have the right not to be deceived.

I have the right to have help from and for my family in accepting my death.

I have the right to die in peace and dignity.

I have the right to retain my individuality and not be judged for my decisions which may be contrary to the beliefs of others.

I have the right to expect that the sanctity of the human body will be respected after my death.

I have the right to be cared for by caring, sensitive, and knowledgeable people who will attempt to understand my needs and will be able to gain some satisfaction in helping me face my death.

Cancer Care Nursing (p. 33), by M. Donovan and S. Pierce, 1976, New York: Appleton-Century-Crofts.

BEREAVEMENT CARE

Because the family is part of the unit of care, the responsibility of the caregiving organization cannot arbitrarily stop when the patient dies. Hospice programs offer continuing bereavement follow-up to members of the patient's family for as long as may be appropriate, and 69 percent of hospice patients and families accept these bereavement services.

Eighty-one percent of hospice programs have a **bereavement team,** consisting primarily of interdisciplinary volunteers, which follows up on all of the family members after the patient dies or on those family members who are at risk of developing serious problems later. Often these bereavement services are also offered to the community at large, not just to those families served directly by hospice.

Hospices work with a wide variety of community organizations (e.g., churches, hospitals, nursing homes, and community mental health agencies) in providing bereavement support. For NHO-affiliated programs, 80 percent provide support group services; 67 percent offer memorial services; 63 percent provide educational programs to the community; 60 percent provide individual/family counseling; 43 percent pro-vide crisis counseling; 35 percent provide specific services for children; and 15 per-cent provide emergency room support (National Hospice Organization, 1997).

The bereavement team of the Connecticut Hospice illustrates this continued follow-up. The team consists of a number of persons who have previously served as volunteers within the organization. A considerable amount of time was spent by the team studying grief and how the team could best aid people in the grieving process. When members feel that bereavement follow-up would be helpful to a family, a re-ferral is made to the team. The team has found that many family members appreciate and need the opportunity to tell the story of the patient's illness to someone who has not previously heard it. Occasionally, a bereavement team member enters the picture while the patient is still alive.

After the referral has been made, the team works out a care plan for the family, and a team member accepts the family as his or her own responsibility. The objective of bereavement care is to encourage the family to carry on its grieving process in an open and helpful manner. Hospice bereavement care has several goals (Boulder County Hospice, 1985):

1. To assess the normal grief response
2. To assess individual coping mechanisms and stress levels
3. To assess support systems
4. To set up additional support (groups, individual therapy, visits by team mem-bers) when needed
5. To identify individuals at high risk and make appropriate interventions
6. To make referrals for financial problems and medical care

Here, too, as in other aspects of hospice care, the art of listening is emphasized. Family members need someone willing to listen while they discuss their feelings. Be-reavement team support may last for a year or more, although the team tries to en-courage family members to stand on their own feet as soon as possible.

PERSONS SERVED BY THE HOSPICE

Hospice care knows no age restrictions, though 70 percent of the patients tend to be persons over 65 years of age. Of the remaining, 29 percent are adults, and 1 percent are children (National Hospice Organization, 1997). Most hospices provide care for patients suffering from any illness with a time-limited prognosis. According to David Bass, Neal Garland, and Melinda Otto (1985–1986, p. 67):

> The "average" hospice patient is white, in his or her middle sixties, . . . is afflicted with a form of cancer and . . . is being taken care of by his or her spouse. The patients re-main in the program for an average (mean) of forty-seven days. The profile of the "av-erage" patient, while helpful in a number of ways, also conceals as much as it reveals. For example, while it is true that the average hospice patient is sixty-two years of age, there is a substantial segment of patients who are either much younger or older than this average. Further, evidence presented in our research suggests that younger-than-average patients have different experiences with hospice care (i.e., they remain in the program for a shorter period, receive fewer staff visits, and are more likely to die in a facility).

With End in Sight, Daniel Rasmussen Chose How to Die
Ann Nordby

In the spring of 1990, Daniel was diagnosed with astrocytoma grade 3, a deadly form of brain cancer. Surgeons removed most of the tumor right away, but because of the disease's characteristic offshoots into other parts of the brain, surgery was only a defensive measure to reduce pressure inside Daniel's head. Chemotherapy and radiation would only keep him comfortable and keep the disease from spreading quickly into other parts of his body.

Gordon Rasmussen remembers that the day his 36-year-old son was diagnosed, the doctor had trouble spitting out the words he wanted to say, that Daniel would die, probably within the next year or two. He kept talking about lifestyle.

"Daniel helped him," Gordon Rasmussen remembered. "He asked the doctor, 'What do you mean, lifestyle?'" When the doctor hesitated again, Daniel phrased the question differently.

"Have you ever had a patient with this disease before?" he asked. The doctor answered readily that he had. "What do they do?", Daniel probed further. The doctor responded that some patients continued working as long as they felt comfortable doing so. Others just gathered their assets and went on a world tour. Daniel then knew, his father remembered, that the doctor was telling him he was going to die.

During the next 66 weeks, the Rasmussens many times encountered people who were uncomfortable with the concept of death and its social side effects. They encountered others who enabled Daniel and the entire family to be together until the end, and to make choices about his treatment, death and funeral that made everyone as comfortable as possible.

Surgery enabled Daniel to stay in his south Minneapolis house through that first summer. But doctors found a second tumor in his brain that fall, just days before he was scheduled to leave on his fourth overseas USO tour, playing with a band called "Wizard."

Daniel's radiologist, the Rasmussens remembered, wanted him to start treatment on the tumor right away. Daniel asked whether his chances of survival would improve. When the doctor admitted they would remain the same, he decided there was no question that he would go on the tour.

Although the tumor was beginning to affect his left hand (the hand with which he made chord changes on the guitar), Daniel performed with the band throughout Greece, Turkey and Sicily. It was in Naples that he gave up and went home, this time to his parents' home on Manitou Street.

By December, Daniel was beginning to have seizures. A Christmas Eve episode left him in a coma. A doctor presented the Rasmussens with a choice: an experimental drug that would either bring Daniel back to life or

(continued)

(continued from previous page)

kill him. The family chose to take the risk, but only after making sure the comeback would be complete, and not just a life-prolonging measure. "If you can bring him back to be a vegetable, we don't want it," Gordon said they told the doctor.

The experimental injection worked a miracle, and Daniel was himself again, almost to the end.

During the winter and spring, Daniel lived with his parents. He periodically made trips to Fairview Southdale Hospital for chemotherapy and radiation, and to Northfield Hospital as needed. In between, local caregivers came and went from the house, making sure Daniel was bathed, fed and comfortable.

Home health aides cared for his physical needs. Physical Therapist Paul Prefontaine took a personal interest in Daniel, taking him for walks and pizza, and keeping Daniel mobile until June. "He is a magician," Gordon said.

Hospice workers cared more for the family's emotional needs. They spent time with Daniel and each of the family members talking about their feelings, plans and fears. They became friends, and supported the family in all their choices. Gordon said they not only responded well, but anticipated most problems before they happened. "I never felt intruded upon. We looked forward to seeing them. They were just good friends," Gordon said.

The Rasmussens say they were lucky in many ways. Daniel and the rest of the family were in agreement that his life would not be extended artificially. And they had the support of hospice workers and others as they made their non-traditional choices.

As the time of Daniel's death grew nearer, Gordon said, a couple of his older children came to him and suggested they take care of Daniel to the very end, not just in life, but in death, too.

At first, this idea was disturbing, even to Gordon, who as a retired minister, has seen death come many times. He said his children couldn't know that in death, the body's muscles let go, necessitating cleanup that isn't very pleasant. Most families today choose to leave that work to hospitals and funeral directors. "It's not like in the old movies, where the lady has the long, flowing blond hair," Gordon said.

But the siblings persisted, and Gordon and Charlotte eventually warmed to the idea. Gordon began building the box that would carry Daniel from his bed to the funeral home where he would be cremated. Gordon made the box from the tabletop on which Daniel's toy train set had been mounted and the handles from old hockey sticks.

He began visiting funeral directors to ask how to get a death certificate, how to transport the body and what equipment would be needed. Unfamiliar with the family's strong commitment and with Gordon's

(continued)

(continued from previous page)

previous experience with dying and death, all but one discouraged him from what he was proposing. But that one gave Gordon the information he needed and became very helpful. The Rasmussens were able to borrow his covered pickup truck, as well as fill out much of the death certificate themselves.

When Daniel died on Aug. 26, 1991, his family cleaned him and dressed him in the running shorts he wore on a jog around Lake Harriet the night before he was diagnosed. Pastor Morris Wee presided over a private service. The only non-family member attending was Daniel's physical therapist and friend, Paul Prefontaine.

Daniel's family said goodbye to him individually and together. They laid him in the box and by chance, it was the grandchildren who fitted the screws into the box's lid. Around midnight, everyone drove to the funeral home.

Still feeling their task was unfinished, they hesitated to leave. Sensing their feeling, the funeral director offered to let them carry the box to the cremation oven. "We had been with him while he was suffering, so being with him now was not unusual," Gordon said.

Together, the entire family lifted the box and slid it into the steel door on the end of the fire brick oven. Their task accomplished, the Rasmussens got in their cars and went home.

Charlotte and Gordon say they realize the choices their family made during Daniel's illness are not for everyone. "I would never urge you to do it," Gordon said.

Charlotte added, "This is the way we wanted to do it, don't feel you have to handle it the same way."

In fact, Charlotte said, she isn't sure she would choose the same route if Gordon died. But the large family, the unanimity of their feelings, the

(continued)

Patient eligibility criteria usually include a diagnosis of a terminal illness, a prognosis of 6 months or less, consent and cooperation of the patient's own physician, and a willingness to deal with the dying process in an open awareness context. Ninety-eight percent of hospices require signed, informed consent for all patients, but only 40 percent require **DNR** ("do not resuscitate") orders (National Hospice Organization, 1997). This order will enable workers to withhold resuscitation measures.

Home care is often more viable when a relative (or friend) can be a primary caregiver in the home and can assume responsibility for patient care when the patient is unable to provide care for himself or herself. Inpatient care usually requires that help is needed with pain or symptom control. For these reasons only 45 percent of hospices admit patients without primary caregivers, even though another 31 percent admit patients without caregivers on a case-by-case basis (National Hospice Organization, 1997).

(continued from previous page)

support of Daniel's friends and professionals from Northfield Hospice and health care workers made it right for Daniel.

Charlotte's biggest concern was how Daniel's dying would affect the grandchildren, aged 11 through 18. Neither Charlotte and Gordon nor any of their children ever pushed the younger family members to be there when Daniel died or for the family service. They told them they could leave or stay away whenever they felt uncomfortable. But they never shied away from participating. "I thought, fine. They need to know that, too," Charlotte said.

Charlotte is on the board of Northfield Hospice. The local organization is one of more than 1,800 in the country. They provide support groups, medical care, psychological help and bereavement services. They are Medicare-certified and most of them are non-profit.

In Northfield, Hospice Director Kathie Harrington said about 9–10 patients are being served at any one time, the majority of them over age 65.

This is the tenth year of hospice in Northfield and during that time, Harrington said, the program has grown in numbers and in professional involvement. Rather than relying on volunteers as it did in the beginning, it has a paid staff. Dr. Robert Shannon is the hospice physician.

Although the Rasmussens' choices seem unusual, Charlotte notes, "This is nothing new." For hundreds of years, human beings have taken care of their own sick family members. It is only in the past two or three generations that we have removed ourselves from it. The Rasmussens said the support of hospice made it possible not only to keep Daniel at home during his illness, but for Daniel and the others to choose how and where he would die.

A. Nordby, *Northfield News,* November 27, 1992, pp. 1A, 5A.

SPECIAL ASPECTS OF HOME CARE

Because 77 percent of American hospice patients die at home (National Hospice Organization, 1997), one of the questions frequently raised by family members is what to do if an emergency develops in the middle of the night or on a holiday. Although many physicians and other health care professionals do not make house calls, hospice personnel do. Home care for hospice patients is made viable by the fact that a physician and a nurse are on call 24 hours a day, 7 days a week. This gives patients and families confidence that they can manage at home.

Community physicians continue to be involved in the care of their patients, and usually remain primary caregivers, while the patient is receiving home care. Such community involvement relates the hospice program to the area in which it is located and tends to give hospice care greater visibility than is sometimes true of health care programs.

Signs of Approaching Death and What to Do to Add Comfort

Hospice exists to support the family's desire to aid a dying loved one in familiar surroundings. This time period is a very difficult one for families. The following was devised to help alleviate some of the fears of the unknown. The information may help caregivers prepare for, anticipate, and understand symptoms as patients approach the final stages of life. It is important to note that some symptoms may appear at the same time and some may never appear.

Symptom: The hospice patient will tend to sleep more and more and may be difficult to awaken.

Action: Plan activities and communication at times when he or she seems more alert.

Symptom: You may notice your loved one experiencing confusion about time, place, and identity of people.

Action: Remind your family member of the time, day, and who is with him or her.

Symptom: Loss of control of bowel and bladder may occur as death approaches, as the nervous system changes.

Action: Ask the hospice nurse for pads to place under the patient and for information on skin hygiene. Explore the possibility of a catheter for urine drainage.

Symptom: Arms and legs may become cool to the touch, and the underside of the body may become darker as circulation slows down.

Action: Use warm blankets to protect the patient from feeling cold. Do not use electric blankets since tissue integrity is changing and there is danger of burns.

Symptom: Due to a decrease in oral intake, your loved one may not be able to cough up secretions. These secretions may collect in the back of

(continued)

In inpatient care the patient's own physician turns over the care of the patient to a hospice physician but must be willing to resume care if the patient is able to return home. Whereas traditional medical care in recent years has tended to concentrate care in specialized hospitals or in nursing homes, hospice care returns the focus to the family.

SPECIAL ASPECTS OF INPATIENT CARE

Because the family is the unit of care within the inpatient hospice facility, sufficient space must exist for a large number of family members to congregate. In addition,

(continued from previous page)

the throat causing noisy breathing. This has been referred to as the "death rattle."

Action: Elevate the head of the bed (if using a hospital bed) or add extra pillows. Ice chips (if the patient can swallow) or a cool, moist washcloth to the mouth can relieve feeling of thirst. Positioning patient on his or her side may help.

Symptom: Hearing and vision responses may lessen as the nervous system slows.

Action: Never assume the patient cannot hear you. Always talk to the patient as if he or she could hear you.

Symptom: There may be restlessness, pulling at bed linens, having visions you cannot see.

Action: Stay calm, speak slowly and assuredly. Do not agree with inaccuracy to reality, but comfort with gentle reminders to time, place, and person.

Symptom: Your loved one will not take foods or fluids as the need for these decreases.

Action: Moisten mouth with a moist cloth. Clean oral cavity frequently. Keep lips wet with a lip moisturizer.

Symptom: You may notice irregular breathing patterns, and there may be spaces of time when no breathing occurs.

Action: Elevate the head by raising the bed or using pillows.

Symptom: If your loved one has a bladder catheter in place, you may notice a decreased amount of urine as kidney function slows.

Action: You may need to irrigate the tube to prevent blockage. If you have not been taught to do this, contact the hospice nurse.

Source: Hospice in the Home Program, Visiting Nurse Association of Los Angeles.

such care requires a homelike environment—the aim is to make the facility as much like a home away from home as is possible. Patients are encouraged to bring with them favorite possessions such as pictures, a favorite chair, or plants.

No arbitrary visiting restrictions are placed on those wishing to see hospice patients. One may visit at any time of day or night. Visitors of any age, including young children, are not restricted in their visitation. Furthermore, family pets, such as dogs or cats, may come as well. The goal of an inpatient hospice facility is to provide a homelike environment where the patient and his or her family can appreciate the joys of social relationships.

The goal of an inpatient hospice facility is to provide a homelike environment where the patient and his or her family can appreciate the joys of social relationships.

The inpatient facility of the Connecticut Hospice in Branford illustrates the preceding principles. The family room is off limits to staff and provided solely for the comfort of family members. Hospice care places considerable emphasis on the tastiness, attractiveness, and nutritional value of food prepared for patients. The Connecticut Hospice employs a gourmet chef with training in Paris to supervise its food preparation. Kitchens containing a refrigerator, a microwave oven, a stove, and a sink are also available for use by families. Washing machines are likewise maintained for their use. Large living rooms with fireplaces are available. Twelve rooms with 4 beds in each help patients develop social support systems among family groups. There are 4 single bedrooms, also. Spacious corridors next to patient rooms contain plants and areas for family gatherings. Beds may be moved around as desired—on a nice day these beds are often outside on patios. A common room and chapel are used not only for religious services but also for presentations by various kinds of artists. Operated by volunteers, a beauty parlor is available to help patients feel better about themselves. A preschool exists for 3- and 4-year-old children of staff, volunteers, and people in the community. When the patient dies—14 percent of all hospice deaths in America occur within inpatient facilities (National Hospice Organization, 1997)—he or she is taken to a viewing room for the family members.

Models of Inpatient Hospice Care

There are approximately 100 hospice inpatient facilities with 1,200 beds. Approximately 72 percent of these are nonprofit, 4 percent are government organizations, 15 percent are for-profit, and 9 percent are "other" or unidentified, according to the National Hospice Organization (1997). Organizationally, inpatient facilities fall into the following categories—30 percent of hospices are independent community-based institutions; 51 percent are divisions of hospitals, nursing homes, or home health agencies, 5 percent are divisions of hospice corporations; and the remaining fall into the "other" or "not identified" category.

The first model, the *freestanding hospice,* is entirely independent—it works closely with other components of the health care system but employs its own staff and raises its own funds. Thirty percent of hospices in America are of this type. An example of the independent community-based hospice is the Connecticut Hospice. This 52-bed, freestanding inpatient facility and home care program offers palliative care for those needing to have pain and symptoms brought under control before returning home as well as intensive round-the-clock medical and nursing care for those who cannot be cared for at home.

The second model of inpatient hospice care is based in a *hospital, nursing home,* or *home health agency.* Fifty-one percent of all NHO-affiliated hospice programs were of this type in 1997 (National Hospice Organization, 1997). This inpatient model provides inpatient care within the physical plant of a hospital, nursing home, or home health agency. It also provides home care through its own home care department, through arrangements with a local public health nursing agency, or through its own staff employed for that purpose. The Northfield Hospice in Minnesota, where I have served as a volunteer, is an example of a hospital-based program.

The third model of inpatient care is the *hospice corporation,* which provides inpatient care for profit with its affiliated local and regional hospice agencies. The largest and best known of this type is the VITAS Healthcare Corporation, which has its headquarters in Miami, Florida, providing palliative hospice care since 1982. VITAS has 25 affiliated programs in 9 states (Florida, California, Texas, Illinois, Pennsylvania, Ohio, Indiana, New Jersey, and Wisconsin). All VITAS hospice patients must have a prognosis of 6 months or less and agree to a care plan that is palliative rather than curative. The VITAS palliative care plan involves aggressive treatment of physical and emotional pain and symptoms. All such treatments focus on enhancing a patient's comfort and quality of life. Like other hospice programs VITAS employs a team approach of health-care professionals and volunteers. Although VITAS is a for-profit corporation, it accepts Medicare and Medicaid as 100 percent coverage for its services, and patients have no additional out-of-pocket expenses. VITAS services are also paid by private insurance plans.

Annually VITAS serves 25,000 patients and their families with approximately 3,200 employees. (The average daily census is nearly 5,000 patients.) Five percent of all hospice programs in the United States are affiliated with proprietary hospice corporations (National Hospice Organization, 1997).

Hospice planning groups exist in most large, and many smaller, cities across the United States. They range from discussion groups of interested citizens to fully developed freestanding hospice programs. As mentioned, there are more than 2,800 hospice programs in the United States. In the 1990s the annual growth of hospices has averaged approximately 8 percent, and growth of patients served by all hospices has averaged 17 percent (National Hospice Organization, 1997).

Hospice Issues

Some have called the development of hospices a "people's movement." If the existing health-care programs in the community had been meeting the needs of the dying and

The Connecticut Hospice in Branford, Connecticut—the first hospice in the United States—is a facility for the terminally ill in their last few weeks of life. The emphasis is on care, not on cure.

had been supporting their families throughout the period of the illness and bereavement, hospices would not have been necessary. They originated in local communities, however, as the result of the desire of health care professionals and civic leaders to provide better care. Many hospice leaders consider their role to be to eventually work themselves out of their jobs as the principles of hospice care are absorbed by the health care system. In the meantime, however, hospices pose a number of critical issues for health care in America. We will now examine some of them: the quality of life, the patient-family as the unit of care, cost, the training of professionals, and public attitudes.

QUALITY OF LIFE

The hospice movement proclaims that every human being has an inherent right to live as fully and completely as possible up to the moment of death. Some traditional health care, emphasizing the curing of the patient at any cost, has ignored that right.

Many physicians have been trained, for example, to emphasize restoring the patient to health. Accordingly, many patients are subjected to a series of operations designed to prolong life, even though a cure is sometimes impossible, as in the case of a rapidly progressing cancer. Most hospice patients have had some surgery, chemotherapy, or radiation treatments. Some continue these even while they are hospice patients because of the pain-relieving nature of the treatments (radiation may reduce the size of a tumor and, therefore, reduce the discomfort). There comes a point, however, if quality of life is a goal, when one should refuse further surgery, seek ease of pain without curing, and attempt to live qualitatively rather than quantitatively. In hospice, cure goals for patients are changed to comfort goals, and every patient has a significant role in all health care decisions.

Because of the emphasis on quality of life, hospices pay attention to many facets of pain reduction, including but not limited to physical pain. Hospice medical professionals have spent considerable time in developing a variety of methods of pain control that subdue not only what the patient describes as pain, but also the symptoms related to the illness.

Much of this emphasis on pain control has developed despite the practice by some professionals of sedating patients in pain. Quality of life cannot be achieved if the patient is "knocked out" or has become a "zombie." Physicians try to find the point at which the pain is managed but sedation has not occurred. Such pain management has necessitated considerable retraining of health care leaders.

Hospice people also deal with social, psychological, financial, and spiritual pain. Terminally ill patients may experience social abandonment or personal isolation that comes when friends and acquaintances stop visiting them because of an inability to cope with issues of death, a lack of knowledge about what to say or do, or simply a lack of awareness of what the patients are experiencing. According to Chng and Ramsey (1984–1985), "in too many cases family members may inadvertently 'reject' the patient when confronted with the reality of death, while the professional staff may distance itself to avoid becoming too emotionally involved." It is ironic that the dying patient's need for social support and companionship comes at a time when he or she may often be more alienated than at any other time in life.

Financial problems are also experienced by patients and their families, who face large hospital and medical bills at a time when family income may also be diminished. Finally, there is a spiritual pain that people experience when they seek answers to existential questions and ultimate meaning and purpose in the face of suffering. "Why did God allow this to happen to me?" and "Why do bad things happen to good people?" are questions frequently asked by patients and their families.

Hospice care makes the meeting of social, psychological, financial, and spiritual needs a major priority in patient care. By doing this, hospice provides an alternative to the health care found in most medical treatment centers. However, none of the social, psychological, financial, or spiritual needs of patients (or their families) can be met until all health care professionals are comfortable with discussing death-related issues. If a physician, for example, is afraid of death or chooses to ignore it, it will be difficult for him or her to enable the patient to deal with the issues involved.

On another scale, the hospice movement emphasizes the importance of the environment in which quality of life can be experienced. The term *environment* refers to the home setting where provisions are made for the patient's needs. Much of the architecture, decor, and furnishings of most health care facilities has been provided for the convenience of staff rather than for the needs of patients.

A critical question is: What constitutes quality of life? What do people most want to accomplish before they die? What do they most want to do? When one of my hospice patients in Northfield, Minnesota, was asked that question, he said that he had always wanted to take a helicopter ride. With the help of the local NBC television station, we made this dream a reality. Like this patient, almost everyone has unfinished business in life. Some may wish to renew relationships with friends or family members. Others may desire to put their own affairs in order, to write their memoirs, to plant a garden, to watch the sunset, or to plan their own funeral service.

The Meaning of Pain
Sylvia A. Lack

Anxiety and depression are part of the chronic nature of pain. The patient is anxious about the pain returning; he or she is anxious because of the meaning of the pain. This is not the acute pain doctors are trained to deal with. It is not like the pain of a toothache or childbirth or appendicitis— pains which have a foreseeable end. Acute pain may serve a purpose by warning of a malfunction. Pain for the cancer patient has a sinister meaning. If I wake up in the morning with a stiff neck I assume I slept in a draft. The cancer patient wakes up in the morning with a stiff neck and assumes she has metastases. The degree of perceived pain is totally different in these two situations. One must take into account the anxiety with which these patients suffer, along with the chronic depression caused by chronic pain.

"Hospice: A Concept of Care in the Final Stage of Life," by S. A. Lack, 1979, *Connecticut Medicine*, 43(6), pp. 369–370.

Robert Kavanaugh (1972) tells the story of Elaine, who, in her last months of life, studied for her real estate license examination, passed the test, and with the help of her husband sold 2 houses. Thus, at age 37, Elaine found her first job while dying.

THE PATIENT-FAMILY AS THE UNIT OF CARE

Traditional health care has concentrated on the patient and ignored the family. Perhaps many health care workers would say, if given an opportunity to state their opinions confidentially, that they would prefer family members to stay away. Traditional ratios of physicians, nurses, social workers, or chaplains to those needing care have been based on an assumption that only the patients need attention. Although hospice staff, to be sure, are not given the responsibility to meet physical needs of family members, they do have tremendous concern for the social, psychological, and spiritual needs of the family.

Hospices challenge the health care system to provide an adequate ratio of professional staff members to patients. For example, in the state of Connecticut the public health code, in its regulations for hospice licensure, stipulates that at all hours of the day or night there must be at least 1 registered nurse for every 6 patients and at least 1 nursing staff member (licensed practical nurse or nurse's aide and a registered nurse) for every 3 patients.

Family care, however, involves much more than numbers of staff. It requires that health-care workers know how to cope with the fears, worries, tears, and turmoil of family members and when to speak, when not to speak, and what to say. It requires that they take time to listen, to determine how they may be most helpful.

Hospice care is costly care due to the number of staff people involved. It challenges society as a whole to give priority to such care because of the right of the dying to quality of life. A harried nurse in a traditional hospital setting, trying to meet

How to Live With a Life-Threatening Illness

With the help of hospice you can:

1. Talk about the illness. If it is cancer, call it cancer. You can't make life normal again by trying to hide what is wrong.
2. Accept death as a part of life. It is.
3. Consider each day as another day of life, a gift from God to be enjoyed as fully as possible.
4. Realize that life never is going to be perfect. It wasn't before, and it won't be now.
5. Pray, if you wish. It isn't a sign of weakness, it is your strength.
6. Learn to live with your illness instead of considering yourself dying from it. We are all dying in some manner.
7. Put your friends and relatives at ease. If you don't want pity don't ask for it.
8. Make all practical arrangements for funeral, will, etc., and make certain your family understands them.
9. Set new goals; realize your limitations. Sometimes the simple things of life become the most enjoyable.
10. Discuss your problems with your family, including your children if possible. After all, your problems are not individual ones.

O. Kelly, *Make Each Day Count* newsletter.

the needs of perhaps a floor of patients at night, is not being granted the time required to sit with a dying patient for whom night is especially fearful. Neither does this nurse have the time to be of assistance to husbands, wives, or children struggling with grief.

The interdisciplinary team supports the staff person within each discipline by enabling resources of the entire team to come into play in meeting family needs. For example, a night-shift nurse who is asked questions relating to spiritual care might wish to give an answer at the time that the question is asked. This nurse will, however, also have the resources of the chaplain to determine the best methods to meet patient needs. In hospice care the patient-family unit is involved in decision making. This poses crucial questions to caregivers who may be accustomed to making decisions and having everyone go along with what they have decided.

COST OF HOSPICE CARE

Even though hospice care is personalized to meet the needs of each of its patients (involving an entire team of professional and volunteer caregivers) it is also very cost effective because more than 90 percent of hospice care hours are provided in patients' homes, thus substituting for more expensive multiple hospitalizations. A study released in 1995 by Lewin-VHI and commissioned by the NHO (1997) showed that for every dollar that Medicare spent on hospice, it saved $1.52 in expenditures. Furthermore, during the last year of life, hospice patients incurred $1,786 less in costs than those not in hospice care. These savings totaled $3,192 in the last month of life as hospice home care days often substituted for expensive hospitalizations.

Ideally, no prospective hospice patient may be turned away because of lack of money. Even though only 15 percent of all hospice programs are for-profit organizations, each year these programs provide some care for those patients who cannot afford to pay, and most poor, underinsured, and uninsured families do receive some financial assistance. According to the National Hospice Organization (1997), sources of payment for hospice services are as follows: Medicare, 66.8 percent; private insurance, 14.6 percent; Medicaid, 9.1 percent; indigent (nonreimbursed) care, 6.3 percent; and other, 3.2 percent.

Hospice care is insured by the Medicare Hospice Benefit enacted in 1982, provided that the hospice is Medicare certified. A hospice program must undergo a vigorous evaluation of the services that it provides to become Medicare certified and must agree to directly provide the following services: nursing care, medical social services, physician services, counseling, and volunteer services. As of 1997, 77 percent of all hospices were Medicare certified and 3 percent had pending applications (National Hospice Organization, 1997). According to the National Hospice Organization, the daily, per-patient payment rates in 1997 made to Medicare-certified hospices (before local wage adjustments) are:

Routine home care	$94.17
Continuous home care	$549.65
Inpatient respite care	$97.41
General inpatient care	$418.93

To the preceding payments there is an $13,974 annual per-patient program cap (this cap is computed on an aggregate basis for all Medicare patients in the hospice program). Furthermore, Medicare specifies that not more than 20 percent of hospice care provided by a certified hospice program may be provided within inpatient facilities (National Hospice Organization, 1997). In 1994 Medicare spent $1.2 billion on hospice services. Additionally, hospice became an optional benefit under state Medicaid in 1986. In 1997 state Medicaid hospice benefits were available in 40 of the 50 states (National Hospice Organization, 1997), and annual payments exceed $150 million for hospice services.

The General Electric Company was the first major employer in the United States to provide a hospice benefit for its employees. Presently coverage for hospice is provided to more than 80 percent of employees in medium and large businesses. Furthermore, the majority of private insurance companies offer a comprehensive hospice care benefit plan, and major medical insurance policies, provided through insurance companies and offered to employees as part of a benefit package, also underwrite hospice coverage in most instances. However, many hospice programs still rely on grants, donations, and memorials to meet the needs of their patients and families that are not covered by Medicare, Medicaid, and insurance reimbursements (National Hospice Organization, 1997).

Hospice leaders hope to make it possible for any person of any age suffering from a terminal illness to be eligible for the coverage of costs related to hospice care. They are also firm in their conviction that such care saves considerable money in the long run. Many patients currently hospitalized would not need hospitalization if hospice services were available for patients and families. A basic societal question is whether as Americans we believe enough in quality of life for the dying to be willing to make it possible.

Though hospice care requires a higher ratio of staff to patients than that usually provided in health-care programs, it should be remembered that the cost is nonetheless lower than other forms of care. Because the majority of hospice patients are able to remain at home for much, if not all, of the illness, the costs of patient home care, when compared with any forms of inpatient care, are proportionately low. Due to the level of services provided, hospice inpatient care, however, will normally be higher than that provided in a nursing home, but lower than inpatient care in a general hospital setting.

TRAINING PROFESSIONALS

Most physicians, nurses, social workers, and clergy were trained in their respective fields of work without special attention to the needs of the dying. To rectify this problem, hospice programs in most states provide seminars and workshops that deal with the basic principles of hospice care. These programs not only train hospice leaders and volunteers in the specifics of hospice care, but also provide other health-care workers with the knowledge and skills to do a better job in their own settings regardless of whether they work in a hospice program.

Health-care decision makers need to be encouraged to invest the time and money required for their staffs to better cope with the terminally ill and their families. Likewise, the curricula of schools of medicine, nursing, social work, and theology need to be revised to provide specialized training along the lines outlined in this chapter. (See chapter 6 for a discussion of the status of thanatology curricula in health care schools.)

PUBLIC ATTITUDES

The hospice movement began at a time when public consciousness of dying and death issues had reached an all-time high. It afforded an opportunity to do something tangible for other people, and many took advantage of the chance to volunteer for an active role. At the same time, increasing public awareness of dying and death gave rise to considerable publicity in the media. This helped provide public support when regulatory agencies held hearings on granting approval for hospice services.

Public attitudes toward care of the terminally ill and their families will play an increasingly important role in the future. These attitudes will help to determine whether health care professionals will, in fact, broaden the scope of care to encompass the family and strengthen their skills in dealing with dying patients. Patients and families are, after all, consumers. In this age of consumer awareness it is becoming increasingly evident that those who purchase services can control to some extent the types of services available. Health care professionals are increasingly responsible to desires of their clients. The most important factors causing caregivers to seek improvement of skills will be the desires of those they serve. At the same time, especially in areas of competition among hospitals, consumer awareness will play an important part in encouraging such institutions to humanize the care that they give.

Many physicians, nurses, social workers, clergy, and other personnel at hospitals and nursing homes have heard about hospice care and have taken the initiative to secure specialized training and to incorporate the hospice philosophy into routine treatment of their patients. When any people's movement arises, an immediate question is whether it will become institutionalized to such an extent that the original spirit will be lost as it adjusts to the reality of regulation, control, and payments of costs. The hospice movement is currently at that juncture. There is every cause for hope that one of two things will happen: Either hospices will continue to provide the specialized care for dying patients, or the health care system itself will change to incorporate many of the improvements represented by the hospice movement. Either outcome should result in the betterment of medical care for patients and their families.

Evaluation of Hospice Programs

Although evaluations of hospice programs have not flooded the literature, some studies have taken a look at the hospice approach. An in-house evaluation of the Connecticut Hospice (Lack & Buckingham, 1978) reported less depression, anxiety, and hostility among terminally ill patients receiving home care as compared with others not receiving these services. In addition, it was found that the overall social adjustment of family members was improved—individuals were better able to express thoughts and feelings with less distress.

Colin M. Parkes (1978) reports that only 8 percent of those who died at St. Christopher's Hospice in London suffered unrelieved pain; this compares with 20 percent who died in hospitals and 28 percent who died at home. John Hinton (1979), in comparing the attitudes of terminally ill patients at a British hospice with those in hospital wards, noted that hospice patients appeared less depressed and anxious while preferring the more open type of communication environment available to them.

Janet Labus and Faye Dambrot (1985–1986) compared the experience of 28 cancer patients who died in an independent, voluntary, community-based hospice program with 29 nonhospice cancer patients who were treated in a small community hospital in northeastern Ohio. Whereas all of the nonhospice patients died in the hospital, 50 percent of the hospice patients died at home.

Furthermore, hospice patients at the time of admission were less likely to be ambulatory than hospital patients. According to Labus and Dambrot:

> The hospice group was younger, had more people living with them, and had been ill for a shorter period of time prior to hospice admission than the hospital group. Hospice patients spent more time in the hospice program after admission prior to death. The hospital patients spent fewer days in the hospital prior to death. Hospice patients were referred to other agencies significantly less frequently than hospital patients.

Labus and Dambrot concluded that this hospice program was succeeding in fulfilling the needs of its patients and in containing health care costs through the multidisciplinary team—only one outside referral had to be made, and 50 percent of the patients died at home. They argue that because the hospice group was, on average, 7 years younger (due to the requirement that a primary caregiver be available in the home), the hospice movement ought to consider ways in which its programs might be extended to groups presently excluded: some very elderly, even though spouses are not able to be caregivers, and single people who do not have live-in caregivers.

In the evaluation of hospice programs, another important concern is the effect of these programs upon professional caregivers. A study of hospice nurses conducted by Pamela Gray-Toft and James Anderson (1986–1987) sought to explain burnout and rapid turnover in the nursing staff. They found that hospice caregiving is significantly more stressful for nurses for the following reasons:

1. Traditional nurses often resent the special roles and treatment received by hospice nurses within institutional settings. Many hospital-based hospice nurses report feeling socially isolated from other hospital nurses.
2. Hospice nurses are often regarded by others as being "weird" or "different" because they choose to work with the dying.
3. The hospice concept of care creates increased (and often unrealistic) patient expectations; consequently, hospice nurses experience inordinate demands placed upon them by the patients and families with whom they work.
4. Because hospice often creates long-term relationships between dying patients, families, and nurses, nurses often experience strong feelings of loss and grief after the death of their patients. Many times hospice nurses are not given an opportunity to grieve after a patient's death because of the demands of their other duties.
5. Hospice nurses are overexposed to death, which can sometimes contribute to a morbid view of life.

As a result of these findings Gray-Toft and Anderson created an experimental staff-support program for hospice nurses. Based on the initial success of this experiment, the group-support program has now expanded to include the professional contributions of a chaplain and medical social worker.

A prominent figure in the thanatology movement, Robert Kastenbaum (1981), notes that although hospice program evaluations tend to be encouraging, methodological flaws and limitations are difficult to avoid. He notes 3 primary limitations to such evaluations: (a) High-quality research is difficult to conduct in such settings where the sensitivities of so many people must be considered; (b) techniques for effective research into care of the terminally ill are at an infant stage of development; (c) research and evaluation priorities generally fall way down on the list—improved care is the primary objective.

Although Kastenbaum notes that many emerging reports on hospice are emphasizing the cost of hospice care as compared with that of traditional hospitalization, he hopes that the question of cost does not gain undue prominence. He is concerned that financial issues may warp our expectations and affect our ability to concentrate on the caring process itself.

It is the conclusion of Edward Crowther (1980) that the United States is not ready for the hospice. He notes that it is not a problem of training or funding, but more a problem of being unable or unwilling to change our attitudes toward proper care for a dying patient.

Crowther cites typical hospice development committee problems as power struggles, personal conflicts, and different opinions on approaches to take. The biggest

A Few Reservations Concerning the Hospice Movement
Constance Holden

Some American doctors are cautious about the hospice idea. John C. Hisserich of the Cancer Center at the University of Southern California is eager to see the idea tried, but he warns that no scientific evaluation has been made of hospice care and that evidence of success is largely anecdotal. He also believes that hospice enthusiasts sometimes exhibit "a certain zealotry about the thing that may be necessary but that has the effect of turning off physicians who might otherwise be interested. . . ."

Perhaps the most serious reservations about efforts to sprout hospices in America come from Mel Krant, director of cancer programs at the new University of Massachusetts School of Medicine in Worcester. "My first reaction," he says, "is it's going to fail as an American idea. It will get into operation, but its intent will fail." The reason, he feels, is that hospices will simply add to the excessive fragmentation, overspecialization, and discontinuity in American medicine. A hospice will be the incarnation of yet another specialty—care of the dying—and will become "another discontinuous phenomenon" when what is needed is integration. Krant has high regard for the English hospices, but he fears that without the spirit of voluntarism and community feeling that exists in England, and without leaders as "utterly devoted" as Cicely Saunders, hospices will turn out looking like nursing homes. He also thinks hospices would help relieve hospitals and physicians of their true responsibilities, which should include more community involvement. Krant thinks it better that Americans develop their own indigenous models for incorporating hospice concepts.
C. Holden, July 1976, *Science,* 193.

problem, however, seems to be attitudinal. He notes that the medical community remains to be convinced that current methods of treating the terminally ill must be changed. The dying cannot be treated in the same way as those who can expect to be cured. Physicians must learn the difference between the hospice goal of "care" and the traditional goal of "cure." The care concept admits that the patient is dying. Medical personnel must put their knowledge and efforts into relief of distressing symptoms and into human understanding. If this change in attitude does occur, Crowther believes, terminal care consistent with the ideals of the hospice movement can be provided in the United States.

This notion is supported by Dr. Josefina Magno (1990, p. 117), the first executive director of the National Hospice Organization, when she claims that the biggest problem of the hospice movement in the 1990s is the lack of involvement of the medical profession. Physicians are most likely to wait to refer a patient to hospice during the last few days of life when they are absolutely sure that the patient is dying, rather than at the time of the terminal diagnosis, when the hospice concept of care would be more beneficial to the patient-family.

Creating a Pleasant Stop on the Journey to Death
Timothy Egan

For the last four years, the designers of the Bailey-Boushay House have been wondering precisely how to create a large home in which somebody was going to die about every 30 hours.

Of course, it would need emergency equipment and the tools of hospitals and hospices, as well as places to cry and to say goodbye. But the designers wanted something more.

The Bailey-Boushay House represented one of the first opportunities in the country for people with the virus that causes AIDS to create a residence from the ground up. What emerged from hundreds of interviews was a single overwhelming sentiment: The place should be life-affirming, not reeking of death.

So when Seattle officials gave a tour of the $7 million residential complex today to the news media, they acted as if they were showing off a new museum or garden.

"Some Saving Grace"

It may very well turn out to be a model, not only for AIDS patients, but for chronically ill elderly people, said Dr. June Osborn, the chairwoman of the National Commission on AIDS.

"I've always said that if we do something like this right, we may be able to find some saving grace in this awful epidemic," said Dr. Osborn. "Our geriatric population is about to explode in the next few years, and housing is going to be the most critical need, as it is now for AIDS patients."

From the outside, the Bailey-Boushay House, named after two Seattle AIDS activists, looks more like a small European spa than an institution. Inside, there is a greenhouse on the third floor and solariums at the end of every hallway, and in every room there are wood armoires as well as a sofa for friends or relatives to stay overnight. Sun decks provide views of the Cascade Mountains, and artwork, some of it stunningly modern and bold, hangs from walls. There are beds for 35 residents, and day care space for another 35 adults. For most of them, it will be the last place they call home.

"What this says to me is that I'm not going to end up on the street or in some sterile hospital room," said Kazas Jones, a founding board member of the Bailey-Boushay House who has AIDS.

Lower Costs, Too

But for all its gilded touches, the Bailey-Boushay House has attracted as much attention in the medical community for its costs as for its looks. Administrators say they can care for a patient for $200 a day—about one

(continued)

(continued from previous page)

third the cost of similar care in a regular nursing home or hospital. The extraneous costs of caring for people with a variety of illnesses are eliminated in the Bailey-Boushay House, where every chair, dinner table or bathing room was designed for the needs of AIDS patients.

"You can save a tremendous amount of money when you remove the diagnostic superstructure of a hospital," said Dr. Wayne C. McCormick, the associate medical director of the house.

Seattle does not have a big AIDS population; with 2,000 cases since the outbreak of the disease, Seattle has about 1 percent of the nation's total number of AIDS cases. But with the number of cases here expected to double by 1995, city officials say they are determined to get ahead of the disease.

Although there are numerous community homes for AIDS patients nationwide, officials here say the Bailey-Boushay House is the only newly built licensed care center in the United States designed for people with AIDS. Most of the building costs were paid for by private donors, more than 5,000 individuals and corporations, with city taxes contributing a portion. The residence will be run by Virginia Mason Medical Center, a nonprofit group with a hospital and clinics in the Pacific Northwest.

When plans to build the center were announced, neighboring residents and businesses were sharply opposed. The Madison Valley neighborhood is an older one, with expensive single-family homes, boutiques, small retail shops, restaurants, and one of the city's most exclusive private schools all nearby.

Some residents of the neighborhood filed a lawsuit, trying to stop the project. But the suit has long since been dropped, and some of those homeowners who initially opposed the project have become silent donors.

As construction got underway, a huge banner was hung from a neighboring house, reading: "Welcome to my backyard."

(continued)

AIDS: Hospice Challenge for the New Century

The health care challenge of the new century will be the increasing numbers of patients with AIDS and AIDS-related complex (ARC). Unlike other terminal illnesses, AIDS is a communicable disease involving extremely labor-intensive care for patients who are often without family support systems. Furthermore, the physical, psychosocial, and emotional complexities of AIDS often require especially sensitive and humane approaches by health care providers of every community. Even though AIDS accounts for only 4 percent of hospice patient deaths, in 1996 NHO-affiliated hospices provided terminal care for one third of all AIDS deaths in America (National Hospice Organization, 1997).

(continued from previous page)

"Part of what changed many peoples' minds was when they realized this was not going to look like a hospital wing, but that it would be more like the bagel and latte places in this neighborhood," said Bill Block, a resident who favored construction of the house.

The doors will open to the first residents some time in the spring, officials say. The center, which will be open to any AIDS patient in Seattle, is intended for someone who does not require intensive care, but has fully developed the symptoms of AIDS. Health insurance or Social Security benefits will cover patients' expenses.

Patients' Requests

In its small and big touches, the Bailey-Boushay House reflects the collective requests of AIDS patients who were interviewed in focus groups. For instance, chairs of solid maple frames and soft cushions meet all the regulations of nursing homes, and they are very easy to get in and out of. The meditation room is nondenominational, but has stained glass windows and broad, hand-carved wood benches.

In the greenhouse, patients can grow flowers, vegetables or other plants, just a few doors down from their rooms. "The greenhouse reflects the dream of horticultural therapy, the belief in the healing power of making things grow," said Christine Hurley, who is the administrator of the residence.

But growing plants may be offset by a more telling statistic: Officials say the average stay of a patient will be about 45 days.

"Somebody is going to die in this place every 30 hours," said Betsy Lieberman, an official with the project. "So much money is spent on things like birthing rooms in hospitals, so we thought, 'Why not make it as nice as possible for a place where somebody will spend the last hours of life?'"

T. Egan, *New York Times,* January 8, 1992, p. A10.

Jeannee Parker Martin (1988), a member of a health care team of the Visiting Nurses and Hospice of San Francisco, has written a significant article describing her hospice's treatment of AIDS/ARC patients in which she presents the special challenge to the hospice movement by the AIDS epidemic. In this article she exalts the appropriateness of the interdisciplinary team approach. Yet it is crucial that professional caregivers and volunteers in hospice be trained to deal with the special needs of AIDS/ARC patients. Furthermore, hospice programs must review all policies and procedures, such as admission criteria and infection-control policies, as they reach out to those infected with the AIDS virus. Finally, Martin concludes that from a societal point of view it is imperative that "home care and hospice services are available to all persons with AIDS/ARC and that when home care is no longer a viable alternative, other long-term care options are available."

Hope at the Hospice
Reverend A. Stephen Pieters

In spite of the fact that many people today are living long and well with HIV and AIDS, people still die from the complications of AIDS. As Christians, we are called to bring hope not only to persons who are newly diagnosed or living with HIV/AIDS, but to people who are dying. As a volunteer chaplain at an AIDS hospice, I have seen many people face death with hope, and this hope comes primarily from faith. As a person living with AIDS, I have been very close to death myself, and I have found that faith gives us everything we need to live with hope, even as we die.

One recent resident of the hospice slowly hemorrhaged to death. As his young life literally dripped away, all I could do was sit with him, holding tissues to his bleeding nose, and soothing him with talking, reading, and praying. His hope at this point came from his strong Christian background, and he reclaimed and grabbed onto his faith with grateful strength. And it worked: he met his death with a peace that would surprise many people.

As different residents of the hospice approach their death, I find myself asking again and again, what does it mean to have hope when facing death? For some, it means clinging to the promises of their faith. For others, it means an end to pain and struggle, and the coming of peace. For still others, it means living in blissful denial.

One resident talked about moving to the Midwest to be with his lover. One of the first things he told me when I introduced myself was, "I'm not here to die." But objectively, he was dying. He refused all food (he said he couldn't keep anything down anymore), and he was no longer ambulatory when he arrived at the hospice. He was badly wasted, and in a great deal of pain. But he was "not here to die." He had plans! I believe he knew on some level that he was dying. But something in him could not accept this, and his hope lay in dreaming of his new home with his lover. Who am I or anyone to take away that hope? Aren't we entitled to live with hope as we die, even if that hope comes from denial, or from flights of dementia?

Another man's legs have been so badly swollen and disfigured by Kaposi's Sarcoma that they look and smell as if they're rotting. The hospice staff have kept him as comfortable as possible, but his hope lies literally in leaving his body. That moment will be an end to his suffering. And in that belief, he finds hope.

Some people die without feeling any hope. I've seen people approach their deaths with enormous fear which no amount of either intellectual or spiritual discussion can relieve. My urge is to try and rescue them from this fear by nurturing some belief that their suffering will be over. But oftentimes, they cling to their fear as if that will defend them from the inevitable. It doesn't. And all any of us can do is to be with them in as loving a way as possible.

(continued)

(continued from previous page)

When I see a person die without any sense of hope, it makes me very grateful for my faith. I have seen over and over again how faith gives people hope and life, even in facing death.

Jesus says in John 11:25–26, "I am the resurrection and the life; those who believe in me, even though they die, they shall live; and whoever lives and believes in me shall never die." Through our faith in Jesus Christ, we are guaranteed eternal life. There is life after death. Our bodies may die, but through our faith in Jesus Christ, we believe that the essence of who we are will live forever.

I used to have a hard time believing this, even though I professed to be a Christian. My skeptical, 20th-century mind, accustomed to a culture of investigative reporting and scientific inquiry, could not buy the concept. If there really is life after death, why isn't there concrete evidence? As a result of my skepticism, death was the single thing I feared most about life.

Then God gave me an opportunity to face that fear. In October, 1985, I had been treated for six months with suramin, the first anti-viral tried against HIV. My KS and lymphoma were in complete remission, thanks to the suramin, but I was wasting away. I had no appetite. I lost about 25% of my body weight. I had no energy. I was sleeping uncomfortably about 20 hours a day. I couldn't stand up without blacking out. My whole body ached all the time.

The doctor finally figured out that I was suffering from adrenal insufficiency caused by the suramin. She called at 7:30 one evening after she'd seen me, and said I had to come into the emergency room immediately. "You're likely to be dead by morning. You need cortisone NOW!" I had my neighbor drive me in, and she dropped me at the emergency room door.

I was eventually put in triage, where all my valuables were taken away and I was hooked up to monitors. I remember being vividly conscious of everything that was going on around me, even though I had no ability to do more than blink my eyes.

The ER staff took vial after vial of blood, but kept delaying the cortisone my own doctor had ordered. One resident thought he saw a shadow in my lung x-ray, and wanted me tested for PCP. A doctor told him the shadow was my heart.

A nurse took my blood pressure, and told me it was 50 over 30. She suggested I say my prayers. I prayed with every breath.

As they were taking one more vial of blood, my blood stopped flowing, and someone said, "Pump your hand." I remember thinking, "Why isn't he doing what they're telling him to?"

Then I didn't care anymore. I was floating free of my body, and for the first time in a long time, I felt no pain. I felt perfect peace, the "peace that passes all understanding." I felt whole in a way I'd never felt before: I finally

(continued)

(continued from previous page)

understood all those things I'd never understood about myself. I felt completely surrounded by love, just as if every person who had ever loved me was right there with me, holding me, and caring for me. I had been terrified of dying alone, and I discovered that fear is totally irrelevant. We are not alone, even in dying.

Then I was conscious of being back in my body, and I was angry. It had been so restful, so perfect, and now I was in pain again.

I came away from this experience no longer afraid of dying or of death. I know now that what awaits us after we leave our bodies is perfect peace, understanding, and love. There is nothing to be afraid of.

This is why I believe hope is possible even at the hospice. It is through faith, but also through experience, that I know hope can be a reality for people who are dying. Hope is theologically correct, even in facing death. Faith gives us the hope we need to live, even as we die.

"Spirituality Column for the Body," by Reverend A. S. Pieters, March 15, 1996, Web site http://www.thebody.com/pieters/mar1596.html.

Conclusion

As the American way of life has changed from a primary group orientation to a more secondary, impersonalized orientation, so has dying shifted from the home to the hospital or nursing home setting—away from kin and friends to a bureaucratized setting. The birth of the hospice movement in the United States might be considered a countermovement to this shift. As we seek out primary group relations in our secondary-oriented society, we seek to die in the setting of a familiar home rather than in the sterile environment of a hospital. Perhaps we are evidencing a return to a concern for each other—a dignity to dying may be on the horizon.

Hospice is a return to showing care and compassion. It is a revival of neighbors helping neighbors—a concept so often lost in our urbanized society. Hospice consists of professionals literally going the extra mile and coming to one's home when needed—medical personnel actually making house calls. Hospice, for example, encourages children under the age of 14 to be present with the terminally ill person rather than making them wait in the hospital lobby. Hospice is a grass-roots movement springing up in small communities, as well as in larger urban settings, to provide better health care. To paraphrase the words of Robert Kavanaugh (1972, p. 19), the hospice concept of care helps us to unearth, face, understand, and accept our true feelings about death and provides us with the opportunity to live joyfully and die as we choose. In short, hospice is a movement that transforms our awkwardness in death situations into a celebration of life.

With federal money now covering most hospice expenses and with rigid government requirements for approval of hospice programs, it is important that every effort be made to prevent hospice programs from being strangled by the bureaucracy from which they receive financial assistance. Hospice programs must also continue to make the patient-family unit the focus of its care and treat these clients in a nonjudgmental and unconditional manner, thus empowering them as autonomous human beings. Finally, because 55 percent of all hospice programs do not admit patients who do not have primary caregivers, it is imperative that in the future hospice programs do more to extend services to patients who are without this resource. These are the dying patients to whom Jesus (Matt. 25:40) was referring when he said, "Whenever you did these things for the least of these my brothers, you were doing them for me."

Summary

1. Hospice is a specialized health care program that serves patients with illnesses such as cancer during the last days of their lives.
2. Hospice care includes both home care and inpatient care.
3. The hospice interdisciplinary team includes the patient, family, physician, nurse, social worker, chaplain, trained volunteer, psychologist, physical therapist, and lawyer.
4. A homelike environment is provided for hospice inpatient care.
5. The first hospice program in the United States was the Connecticut Hospice, modeled after St. Christopher's in London.
6. The hospice movement demonstrates that every human being has an inherent right to live as fully and completely as possible up to the moment of death.
7. Hospice care emphasizes relief from physical, social, psychological, and spiritual pain.
8. Much of the cost of hospice care is covered by third-party reimbursements, Medicare, and/or Medicaid; no prospective hospice patient is turned away because of lack of money.
9. Presently 4 percent of hospice patients have AIDS, and one in three AIDS patients dies in hospice programs. Hospice programs are attractive to patients with AIDS because they provide a unique opportunity for patients to be cared for humanistically and because the special needs for individualization often required by AIDS patients can be addressed within the hospice concept of care. However, AIDS also presents special challenges for hospice programs.

Discussion Questions

1. What is hospice care? How does it differ from the treatment given by most acute-care hospitals? Identify the major functions of a hospice program.
2. Trace the history of the hospice movement in the United States.
3. Discuss issues related to the family as the unit of care in hospice programs. How do hospices try to achieve quality of life for each of the "patients" they serve? How does the interdisciplinary hospice team concept help achieve this?
4. What are some of the special aspects of inpatient and home care in hospice programs? What are some of the advantages of each of these approaches?
5. What, in your opinion, are the negative aspects of hospice care? How would you suggest that they be rectified?
6. Do you feel that bereavement care should be offered to the families of the terminally ill even after their loved ones have died? Justify your answer in terms of medical, emotional, and financial considerations.
7. If you were terminally ill, would you consider entering a hospice? Explain your answer and refer to specific reasons such as cost, family burden, and imminent death.
8. Discuss the special opportunities and challenges in providing hospice services to AIDS patients.

Glossary

Bereavement Team: An interdisciplinary group made up primarily of volunteers who follow up on families after patients die in order to encourage healthy grieving.

DNR, or *do not resuscitate*: A controversial order required by some hospices in order for heroic care or other resuscitative measures to be withheld.

Hospice: A specialized health care program that serves patients with life-threatening illnesses, such as cancer, during the last days of their lives.

Hospice Movement: A response to fears related to the dying process and the institutionalized ways in which death is typically handled in institutional settings.

Hospice Team: An interdisciplinary team of professionals and volunteers who work together to contribute their expertise to the quality of patient care.

Inpatient Care: The type of institutionalized care that is required, for example, as an illness progresses and that may be provided in a hospice facility.

Patient-centered Care: A distinguishing feature of the hospice approach which enables patients to make decisions about how and where they want to live their lives. Patient-centered care is nonjudgmental, unconditional, and empowering.

PRN, or *pro re nata*: A traditional medical approach which means that medication is to be given "as the situation demands." In practice, it means that patients must first hurt and ask for relief before pain management can be administered.

References

Bass, D. M., Garland, T. N., & Otto, M. E. (1985–1986). Characteristics of hospice patients and their caregivers. *Omega, 16*(1), 51–68.

Boulder County Hospice. (1985). *Bereavement care manual.* Boulder, CO: Author.

Burns, N., Carney, K., & Brobst, B. (1989). Hospice: A design for home care for the terminally ill. *Holistic Nursing Practice, 3*(2), 65–76.

Carr, W. F. (1989). Lead me safely through death. *America, 160*(11), 264–267.

Chng, C. L., & Ramsey, M. K. (1984–1985). Volunteers and the care of the terminal patient. *Omega, 15*(3), 237–244.

Cohen, K. (1979). *Hospice, prescription for terminal care.* Germantown, MD: Aspens Systems.

The Connecticut Hospice. (1997, January 12). *About hospice* (On-line). Available: Web site http://www.hospice.com/about.html.

Crowther, C. E. (1980). The stalled hospice movement. *The New Physician,* 26–28.

Gray-Toft, P. A., & Anderson, J. G. (1986–1987). Sources of stress in nursing terminal patients in a hospice. *Omega, 17*(1), 27–38.

Hinton, J. (1979). Comparison of places and policies for terminal care. *Lancet,* vol. 1, 29–32.

Kastenbaum, R. J. (1981). *Death, society, and human experience* (2nd ed.). St. Louis: C.V Mosby.

Kavanaugh, R. E. (1972). *Facing death.* Baltimore: Penguin Books.

Labus, J. G., & Dambrot, F. H. (1985–1986). Comparative study of terminally ill hospice and hospital patients. *Omega, 16*(3), 225–232.

Lack, S. A., & Buckingham, R. (1978). *First American hospice: Three years of care.* New Haven, CT: Hospice, Inc.

Leming, M. R. (1979–1980). Religion and death: A test of Homans's thesis. *Omega, 10*(4), 347–364.

Magno, J. B. (1990). The hospice concept of care: Facing the 1990s. *Death Studies, 14,* 3109–3119.

Martin, J. P. (1988). Hospice and home care for persons with AIDS/ARC: Meeting the challenges and ensuring quality. *Death Studies, 12,* 463–480.

National Hospice Organization. (1988). *The basics of hospice.* Arlington, VA: Author.

National Hospice Organization. (1993). *1992 annual report.* Arlington, VA: Author.

National Hospice Organization. (1997). *Hospice fact sheet.* Arlington, VA: Author.

Parkes, C. M. (1978). Home or hospital? Terminal care as seen by surviving spouses. *Journal of the Royal College of General Practice, 28,* 19–30.

Patchner, M., & Finn, M. (1987–1988). Volunteers: The life-line of hospice. *Omega, 18*(2), 135–143.

Phipps, W. E. (1988). The origin of hospices/hospitals. *Death Studies, 12,* 91–99.

Saunders, C. (1992, Winter). The evolution of the hospices. *Free Inquiry,* 19–23.

Stoddard, S. (1978). *The hospice movement: A better way of caring for the dying.* New York: Vintage.

Suggested Readings

Burns, N., Carney, K., & Brobst, B. (1989). Hospice: A design for home care for the terminally ill. *Holistic Nursing Practice, 3*(2), 65–76. Carr, W. F. (1989). Lead me safely through death. *America, 160*(11), 264–267. Phipps, W. E. (1988). The origin of hospices/hospitals. *Death Studies, 12,* 91–99. Saunders, C. (1992, Winter). The evolution of the hospices. *Free Inquiry,* 19–23. Stoddard, S. (1978). *The hospice movement: A better way of caring for the dying.* New York: Vintage. Five great resources on the history of the hospice concept of care. They also provide a vivid description of the workings of the hospice programs, emphasizing how the patients and their families begin to help others.

Connor, S. R. (1997). *Hospice: practice, pitfalls, promise.* Bristol, PA: Taylor & Francis. Describes hospice operations and problems; examines the goals of hospice; and also looks at the business side of hospice.

Death Education, 2(1, 2), 1978. Special issue on the hospice movement covering six models of hospice care found in the United States, England, and Canada.

Lamberton, R. (1973). *Care of the dying.* London: Priory Press, Ltd. Saunders, C. (1959). *Care of the dying.* London: Macmillan. Two early, influential works that explain the hospice philosophy and care for dying patients and their families.

National Hospice Organization. (1997). *1996 annual report.* Arlington, VA: Author. National Hospice Organization. (1997). *Hospice fact sheet.* Arlington, VA: Author. National Hospice Organization. (1997). *The basics of hospice.* Arlington, VA: Author. These pamphlets, along with other information regarding the hospice concept of care, are valuable resources that can be obtained without charge by contacting the National Hospice Organization, 1901 North Moore Street, Suite 901, Arlington, VA 22209; phone (703) 243-5900; fax (703) 525-5762; E-mail drs.nho@www.nho.org.

Ray, M. C. (1997). *I'm here to help: A guide for caregivers, hospice workers, and volunteers.* New York: Bantam Books. Discusses and delineates the communication skills that are necessary in the hospice environment to keep it peaceful and comfortable. Presents new ideas on how to facilitate communication between hospice workers and their patients and among all of those involved in the process.

Related Web Sites

GENERAL HOSPICE ISSUES

http://www.nerdworld.com   Nerd World has a large index of home care- and hospice-related Internet resources created by Nerd World Media.

http://www.boston.com/globe/hospice/info.htm   A tremendous resource maintained by the Boston Globe containing articles and information on the hospice movement.

http://www.rbvdnr.com/health/hospice/hos-main.htm   Hospice   Manager's Monograph provides a number of hospice articles of interest.

http://www.hospicefoundation.org Hospice Foundation of America has general information about hospice and specific information on the foundation.

http://www.roxane.com/HNA Hospice Nurses Association is an international professional association with the mission of promoting excellence in hospice nursing.

http://www.npha.org National Prison Hospice Association promotes hospice care for terminally ill inmates and those facing the prospect of dying in prison. The goal of the association is to assist corrections professionals in their efforts to develop high-quality patient care procedures and management programs.

http://www-acc.scu.edu/~dlarson/hhp.htmlx The Hospice home page is Dale Larson's compilation of great ideas submitted from a wide variety of sources.

http://hospice-cares.com Hospice Hands has an extensive collection of links to hospice resources.

http://www.aahpm.org American Academy of Hospice and Palliative Medicine is the only organization in the United States for physicians dedicated to the advancement of hospice/palliative medicine and its practice, research, and education.

http://pages.prodigy.com/caregiving *Grief and Healing Caregiving* newsletter contains useful information about topics pertinent to hospice patient lifestyle: setting and keeping priorities, hiring home health help, purchasing home medical equipment supplies, and finding time for your own interests and hobbies.

http://www.trinity.edu/~mkearl/paradigm.html Paradigm does not suggest that there is one particular way of dying well. However, it is possible to identify some general developmental tasks that the dying person can accomplish if dying well is the goal. (Paradigm, P.O. Box 14061, San Francisco, CA 94114; phone 415 522-9192)

BEREAVEMENT ISSUES

http://rivendell.org/ GriefNet provides many links to World Wide Web resources on the bereavement process, resources for grievers, and information concerning grief support groups.

http://ube.ubalt.edu/www/bereavement Bereavement and Hospice Support Netline is an on-line directory of bereavement support groups and services and hospice bereavement programs from across the United States that will provide information to locate support in coping with issues of loss and grief.

http://www.growthhouse.org Growth House is a nonprofit organization working with grief, bereavement, hospice, and end-of-life issues.

http://www.readersndex.com/admpub National Directory of Bereavement Support Groups examines many issues that are often hard to discuss and provides help for the bereaved individual.

http://www.inforamp.net/~bfo/index.html   The Web site of Bereaved Families of Ontario Support Center contains an expanding information section that includes highlights from its newsletter as well as a monthly column. The Bereavement Self-Help Resources Guide indexes the center's resources along with over 300 listings to other resources and information.

REGIONAL HOSPICE ORGANIZATIONS

http://www.zenhospice.org   The Zen Hospice Project organizes programs dedicated to caring for people approaching death and to increasing the understanding of impermanence. The Zen Hospice Project also runs a small hospice in a restored Victorian house near the San Francisco Zen Center.

http://www.vnahv.com/   The Visiting Nurse Association of Hudson Valley (VNAHV), New York, provides quality health care to all people in their communities regardless of ability to pay in a manner that recognizes the whole person and the person's environment. A primary focus is to maximize resources for the organization for the benefit of the patient. The VNAHV strives to foster independence and choice for all individuals with the overall goal of improving the quality of life by assuming a proactive advocate role.

http://www.hospice.com   The Connecticut Hospice was founded in 1974 as the nation's first hospice. Today it offers a statewide hospice home care program and the state's only 52-bed inpatient hospice care center that accepts referrals from throughout the United States and the world. Being a leader in palliative medicine, the Connecticut Hospice became the first and only accredited teaching hospice offering training and consultation to professionals from around the world through its teaching arm, the John D. Thompson Hospice Institute for Education, Training, and Research.

http://www.radix.net/~tangsolo/gallery/hhospice.htm   Houston Hospice provides, regardless of ability to pay, the highest quality of care for patients with life-threatening illnesses and their families through a well-qualified interdisciplinary team of professionals and volunteers.

http://www.silcom.com/~campbell/hospice   Hospice Service of Santa Barbara is a program of the Santa Barbara Visiting Nurse Association.

http://www.hospice.org   Hospice of Southern Illinois is a physician-directed, nurse-coordinated Medicare/Medicaid-certified program serving 27 counties in southern Illinois.

http://www.shopthenet.net/hospice_gso/index.html   The Hospice at Greensboro, North Carolina, is a not-for-profit specialized health-care agency that provides physical, emotional, and spiritual support for persons with a life-limiting illness and those who care for them.

http://www.holyname.org/brochure/hospice.htm   The hospice program at Holy Name Hospital in Teaneck, New Jersey, is designed to provide physical, psychological, social, and spiritual care for the terminally ill and their families. This concept of caring enables the patient to live each day as fully as possible and involves the entire family in providing care, usually in the patient's home.

http://www2.southwind.net/~hospice   Hospice Incorporated of Kansas offers a comprehensive, coordinated program of services to terminally ill patients and their families in private residences, nursing homes, and inpatient settings. Physical, emotional, social, and spiritual care are available from an interdisciplinary team under the direction of the patient's physician. Hospice Incorporated team members include a medical director, registered nurse, home health aide, social worker, pastoral counselor, and volunteer. Their focus is to provide quality care that exceeds National Hospice Organization standards.

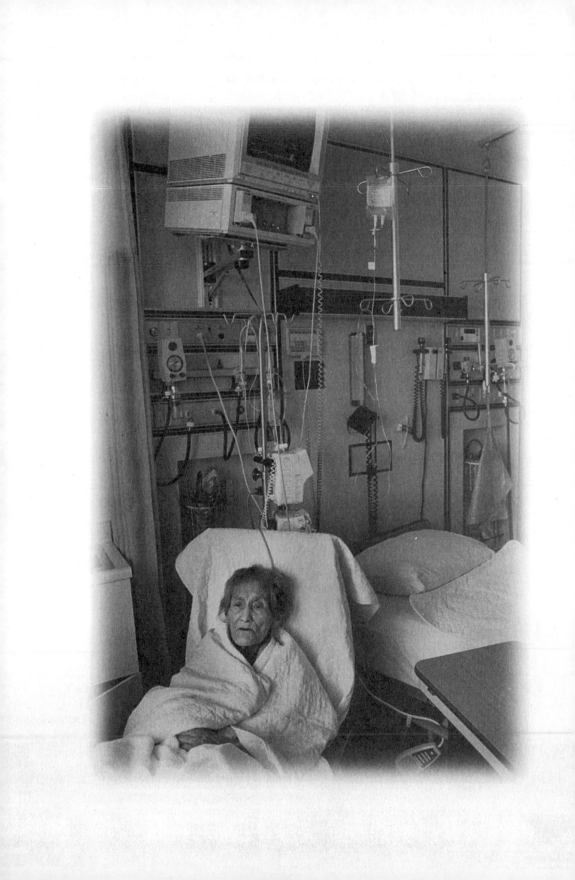

Chapter 8

Euthanasia and Biomedical Issues

It is silliness to live when to live is torment;
And then have we a prescription to die when death is our physician?

—WILLIAM SHAKESPEARE, OTHELLO

All substances are poisons; there is none which is not a poison.
The right dose differentiates a poison and a remedy.

—PARACELSUS

What is euthanasia? For many it means mercy killing; for others it means natural death without the so-called benefit of technologies related to life-extending, death-prolonging medical interventions. However, the etymology of the term reveals that **euthanasia** literally means "good death." Both of the preceding definitions, then, may qualify.

Sanctity and Quality of Life

When most people think about a "good death," they usually do so within the context of their understanding of the meaning of life. What is life? When does life begin?

When does life end? Is there a difference between biological life and human life as they are socially defined?

Occasionally you may read that the survivor of a serious automobile accident is in a vegetative state. Has the patient died? Is the patient no longer human? Now consider the situation in which an individual is assaulted and put into an irreversible coma. Has the assailant committed murder or assault and battery? If this same patient is disconnected from life support or **intubation** (tube feeding) and dies, who caused the death—the person who committed the crime or the medical personnel who withdrew the life support or feeding device?

In general, people respond to such questions about medical conditions from one of two orientations concerning the meaning of life. The first orientation would emphasize the **sanctity of life,** whereas the second would emphasize a **quality of life.** Euthanasia from a sanctity-of-life orientation would contend that all "natural" life has intrinsic meaning and should be appreciated as a divine gift. As a consequence, human beings have the obligation to enhance the quality of life as it may exist.

Hessel Bouma, et al. note that the Hippocratic tradition in the medical profession recognizes that physicians' responsibility to terminally ill patients is to simply "mitigate their suffering while allowing them to die." Furthermore, the Hippocratic Oath, reacting against an earlier practice of actively and intentionally hastening the deaths of terminal patients, forbids the giving of "a deadly drug" to dying patients (Bouma, Diekema, Langerak, Rottman, & Verhey, 1989, pp. 267–268).

The following two quotations illustrate the *sanctity-of-life* orientation:

> The sanctity of life approach is concerned about the quality of human life. The quality of all our lives suffers, it insists, unless every human life is considered inviolable because of the very fact of its existence. A dying patient's relationship to those about him or her symbolizes the relationship of all individuals to one another. To practice direct euthanasia, even at the request of the patient, is to weaken the claim of each one of us to the right to have others respect and not violate us. (Weber, 1981, p. 49)
>
> No horror against life is impossible once we have allowed anyone but the Creator to usurp sovereignty over life. Whom the gods would destroy they first make mad. Legalized euthanasia (mercy killing) is such madness. (Morriss, 1987, p. 149)

The *quality-of-life* orientation holds that when life no longer has quality or meaning, death is preferable to life. The following statements by Claire Harrison, the central character in Brian Clark's play *Whose Life Is It Anyway?* (1981, pp. 73–74), illustrate this orientation:

> Any reasonable definition of life must include the idea of its being self-supporting. I will spend the rest of my life in a hospital, but while I am there, everything is geared just to keeping my brain active, with no possibility of it ever being able to direct anything. As far as I can see, that is an act of deliberate cruelty . . .
>
> The best part of my life was, I suppose, my work. The most valuable asset that I had for that was my imagination. It's just a shame that my mind wasn't paralyzed along with my body. Because my imagination—which was my most precious possession—has become my enemy. And it tortures me with thoughts of what might have been and of what might be to come. I can feel my mind slowly breaking up . . .

I am filled with absolute outrage that you, who have no connection with me whatever, have the right to condemn me to a life of torment because you can't see the pain. There's no blood and there's no screaming so you can't see it. But if you saw a mutilated animal on the side of the road, you'd shoot it. Well, I'm only asking that you show me the same mercy you'd show an animal. But I'm not asking you to commit an act of violence, just take me somewhere and leave me. And if you don't, then, you come back here in five years and see what a piece of work you did today...

Both sanctity-of-life and quality-of-life perspectives introduce ambiguous terms for those who must decide appropriate criteria for a "good death." Those who have a sanctity-of-life perspective must adequately define "natural" life. Should biological life, sustained by a respirator, be considered "natural?" How about life sustained by a feeding tube or intravenous glucose solution? When is it appropriate to reject medical intervention, and how can we determine when a "natural" death has taken place? Ivan Illich (1976, pp. 207–208) illustrates this problem:

Today, the man best protected against setting the stage for his own dying is the sick person in critical condition. Society, acting through the medical system, decides when and after what indignities and mutilations he shall die. The medicalization of society has brought the epoch of natural death to an end. Western man has lost the right to preside at his act of dying. Health, or the autonomous power to cope, has been expropriated down to the last breath. Technical death has won its victory over dying. Mechanical death has conquered and destroyed all other deaths.

From a quality-of-life perspective, the concept of "quality" is even more difficult to define. Who should decide when life has quality? *Quality* is a relative term, and its meaning often changes as one progresses through his or her life cycle and as a result of social circumstance. I have little doubt that the quality of my life would diminish if I became paralyzed, blind, and/or deaf. However, many people with these disabilities experience a life of quality filled with purpose and meaning.

Passive and Active Euthanasia

Individuals try to facilitate a "good death" by 2 methods—passive and active euthanasia. **Passive euthanasia** involves a protocol whereby no action or medical intervention hastens death. It usually involves removing medical technology or withholding medical intervention and is supported by people who affirm both sanctity-of-life and quality-of-life perspectives. In a 1985 Harris poll, 85 percent of respondents endorsed a terminally ill patient's right to tell the doctor to stop trying to extend life. Although not legally binding in some states, living wills provide a vehicle by which individuals make their intentions known concerning the withholding of medical treatment. Later in this chapter we will discuss the legal steps involved in the creation of living wills that assist family members in making decisions regarding the medical treatment of terminally ill patients.

Some people have the false impression that passive euthanasia is incompatible with a belief in the sanctity of life. The following statement by Pope Pius XII (1977,

Routine CPR Can Abuse the Old and Sick
Fazlur Rahman

Since cardiopulmonary resuscitation was introduced in 1960, it has saved countless lives. But we are in danger today of abusing this procedure. At some point, we must stop adding to the suffering of dying patients by pounding on their chests, possibly breaking bones, just to extend their lives by a few days or weeks.

CPR is performed routinely in hospitals, without regard to patients' chances of recovering to lead normal lives. Why try to revive with CPR a patient who has been sick for years with diabetes, hypertension, heart disease and kidney failure, and who has just had an operation for a perforated intestine? Why batter the sternum of a drastically debilitated, 85-year-old woman who is suffering from pneumonia? In terminal cases like these, the idea of beating on the chest of an old and sick person is morally and physically repugnant. Yet, for the lack of prior understandings between patients, families, and physicians, the procedure continues to be used indiscriminately.

Although some people will refuse as long as possible to let a loved one die, most families will abide by the medical decision on CPR. Trouble arises, however, when neither the terminal patient nor the doctor raises the subject of CPR soon enough. There is a vague hope that the problem may not have to be faced soon. Then, under the duress of the moment, it is hard for families to make a quick decision. So, the physician simply follows the routine of CPR.

What can we do to avoid this predicament?

(continued)

pp. 283–284, 286) illustrates the Roman Catholic church's belief in maintaining sanctity of life while affirming passive euthanasia:

> Natural reason and Christian morals say that man (and whoever is entrusted with the task of taking care of his fellow man) has the right and the duty in case of serious illness to take the necessary treatment for the preservation of life and health. This duty that one has toward himself, toward God, toward the human community, and in most cases toward certain determined persons, derives from well ordered charity, from strict justice, as well as from devotion toward one's family.
>
> But normally one is held using only *ordinary* means—according to circumstances of persons, places, times, and culture—that is to say, means that do not involve any grave burden for oneself or another. A more strict obligation would be too burdensome for most men and would render the attainment of the higher, more important good too difficult. Life, health, all temporal activities are in fact subordinated to spiritual ends. Consequently, if it appears that the attempt to resuscitate constitutes in reality such a burden for the family that one cannot in all conscience impose it upon them, they can lawfully insist that the doctor should discontinue these attempts, and the doctor can lawfully comply.

(continued from previous page)

First, we have to educate the public and professionals. An increasing number of patients are asking for a peaceful death. In time, I hope that this demand will become universally accepted. Medical and nursing schools need to teach more about accepting death and dying.

Second, patients should sign living wills. Many states have enacted laws that recognize the terminally ill patient's right to refuse life-sustaining treatment. By court decisions, 12 states have acknowledged such a right.

Third, patients with incurable diseases should be tactfully approached by their families and physicians about the use of aggressive measures. While discussing the subject, one should not convey hopelessness; hope is an important part of medical care.

If the patient is opposed to resuscitation, the primary physician must write clearly on a patient's chart, "No CPR." Simply having an understanding with the nurses on the floor will not work. When a CPR code is activated by hospital monitors, doctors and nurses will rush to the victim. If the attending physician is not around and there are no instructions on the patient's record, confusion arises about what to do. In our lawyer-dominated society, hospitals have been forced to devise bureaucratic rules that may not have the patients' welfare foremost in mind. Moreover, once a patient is on the life-support system it is not easy to "pull the plug." Legal complexities will override ethical justifications. Thus, it is all the more important to decide ahead of time what steps are appropriate to take when considering reviving incurable patients.

F. Rahman, *Minneapolis Star and Tribune,* February 27, 1989, p. 9A. (Originally written for the *New York Times.*) Copyright 1989 by the New York Times Company. Reprinted by permission.

LIVING WILLS

A **living will** is a document that states that one does not want medical intervention if the technology or treatment that keeps one alive cannot offer a reasonable quality of life or hope for recovery (see "A Living Will" box that follows).

All states have legislation authorizing the use of legal documents such as living wills and durable powers of attorney for health care (sometimes referred to as health-care proxy, surrogate, agent, or attorney-in-fact), which together are known as *advance directives.* Forty-eight states recognize durable power of attorney, 47 states recognize living wills, and 23 states have statutes for surrogate decision making. It is thought that between 12 percent and 20 percent of the population have completed living wills or durable powers of attorney for health care (Maddox, 1995, p. 26.)

Despite a growing acceptance of living wills, the issue is still complicated by emotion and questions of when a will should be invoked. Many persons are reluctant to take steps leading to a patient's death, and some are willing to withhold further medical treatment but do not want to disconnect existing life support. Others cannot even distinguish living wills from "do not resuscitate" (DNR) orders—a situation that has

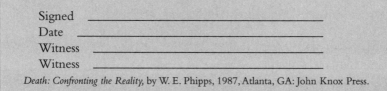

A Living Will

To my family, my physician, my lawyer and all others whom it may concern:

Death is as much a reality as birth, growth, maturity, and old age. Death is the one certainty of life. If the time comes when I can no longer take part in decisions for my own future, let this statement stand as an expression of my wishes and directions, while I am still of sound mind.

If at such a time the situation should arise in which there is no reasonable expectation of my recovery from extreme physical or mental disability, I direct that I be allowed to die and not be kept alive by medications, artificial means or "heroic measures." I do, however, ask that medication be mercifully administered to me to alleviate suffering even though this may shorten my remaining life.

This statement is made after careful consideration and is in accordance with my strong convictions and beliefs. I want the wishes and directions here expressed carried out to the extent permitted by law. Insofar as they are not legally enforceable, I hope that those to whom this will is addressed will regard themselves as morally bound by these provisions.

Signed   _____

Date   _____

Witness   _____

Witness   _____

Death: Confronting the Reality, by W. E. Phipps, 1987, Atlanta, GA: John Knox Press.

caused the deaths of healthy and alert people who have not suffered cardiac or pulmonary arrest (Stone, 1994).

In 1994 Cugliari and Miller determined that 29 percent of New York state hospitals would not honor a patient's request to withdraw or withhold treatment (Cugliari & Miller, 1994). In another study by Almgren (1993) in which 140 nursing home directors of nursing were interviewed, it was discovered that the competency of the patient and type of nursing home ownership were the primary factors influencing decisions to withdraw nutrition from terminal patients—the fact that a patient had signed a living will had little influence on these decisions. Furthermore, Miles and August (1990) have demonstrated that the courts have a gender bias in the forced implementation of living wills. Because men were perceived as more rational and women as more unreflective, emotional, and immature, the courts accepted the treatment preference of 75 percent of the men but only 14 percent of the women. This pattern of bias had been discovered in many states and remains unchanged when one controls for the patient's age, condition, and treatment modality (Miles & August, 1990). Consistent with the research findings just cited, Donald Dilworth (1996, p. 79) conducted his own research in 5 hospitals and reached the following conclusion:

Living wills do virtually nothing to reduce patient suffering, because doctors and hospitals ignore them. Some 80% of doctors either misunderstood or set aside the dying requests, and a program to help patients avoid painful life-prolonging treatments had no effect at any of five hospitals I studied. The cause of the problem is the medical culture that rejects death and promotes technology.

If you are considering a living will, you should make certain that such a will is legal in your state of residence. After the will is drawn up, make several copies of it and share it with physicians and other health care providers, family members, and friends. A copy of the will should also be given to your attorney to be kept in his or her office. This is not something that you should limit to a single copy, lock up in a safe deposit box, and keep as a big secret. Share the news!

In December 1991 the federal government created the Patient Self-Determination Act, which requires most hospitals, nursing facilities, hospices, home health-care programs, and health maintenance organizations (HMOs) to inform patients at admission of their right to create advance directives relating to their care (see sample "Directive to Physicians" on pp. 285–287). According to Ken Wibecan (1992), the two most common of these directives for health care are the living will and the **durable power of attorney**. The latter names a surrogate decision maker who has legal authority to give consent (or to refuse consent) for medical treatment should the patient lack competency to make such decisions.

If one accepts the legitimacy of passive euthanasia as set forth in the living will, it is clear that the use of extraordinary measures is not required of terminal patients, members of their family, or attending physicians. However, differentiating between ordinary and extraordinary measures is not easy. Gerald Kelly (cited by Bouma et al., 1989, pp. 274–275) defines these terms in the following manner: *Ordinary means* of preserving life are all those medicines, treatments, and operations that offer a reasonable hope of benefit for the patient and that can be obtained and used without excessive expense, pain, and other inconvenience.

Extraordinary means of preserving life are all those medicines, treatments, and operations that cannot be obtained without excessive expense, pain, or other inconvenience or that, if used, would not offer a reasonable hope of benefit.

These definitions introduce other ambiguous terms—"reasonable hope," "excessive expense," "excessive pain," and "excessive inconvenience." What is reasonable and excessive? Who among us can make decisions employing these highly relative concepts? Which of the following groups should society allow to determine these matters: politicians, physicians, lawyers, judges, members of the community at large, and/or patients and their families?

Many within the medical community have operationalized **ordinary measures** to be any procedures that are "usual and customary" medical practice and **extraordinary measures** to be any procedures that are exotic, innovative, and medically experimental. However, it is clear that this distinction provides us with little help because (a) technology has a way of imposing itself upon modern society in an amoral fashion and (b) what has been considered innovative and experimental becomes usual and customary with time. Consider the situation in which a Down's syndrome infant starves to death because parents will not permit a physician to perform a simple operation that would allow food to be digested by the child. The fate of this Down's

Bioethicists and the Medical System
Raymond DeVries

Bioethics and bioethicists are recent additions to the world of medicine. Hired by hospitals and academic medical centers, bioethicists are called on to bring their philosophical and legal expertise to bear on difficult decisions about medical treatments and end-of-life care. Many people hope this new bioethical presence in health care settings will make medicine more humane, more ethical. But is this, in fact, the case? A sociological view suggests that bioethicists might begin with good motives, but their position in the structure of health care may come to color their decisions.

Consider for a moment the interests of those who are represented by bioethicists. Most bioethicists claim that they represent the patient, protecting his or her autonomy against the power of medicine. A more cynical view of bioethics—represented by Ruth Shalit's journalistic account of the new profession—comes to quite a different conclusion. In answer to her question, "...just whom...[are] the ethicists really serving?", Shalit★ asserts: *"A swelling corps of HMO utilitarians are cashing in on their ethical expertise, marketing their services to managed care executives eager to dress up cost-cutting decisions in Latinate labels and lofty principles."*

Is Shalit's observation correct? Look at the organizational location of bioethics. The presence of bioethicists in medical institutions leads to an affinity between bioethicists and other professionals there. In fact, the role of a bioethicist is not unlike that of a public defender in the American legal system. The formal role of each is to represent the interests of a client in a large and confusing bureaucracy, but, like public defenders, bioethicists must maintain good relationships with other members of that bureaucracy, many of whom are working against the interest of their clients. Given this organizational situation, bioethicists will be inclined to represent the interests of medical professionals and medical institutions over those who are merely passing through—the patients and their families.

★Ruth Shalit. 1997. "When We Were Philosopher Kings." The New Republic. 216 (17): 24–28. Raymond DeVries is Associate Professor of Sociology at St. Olaf College and co-editor (with Janardan Subedi) of Bioethics and Society: Constructing the Ethical Enterprise, Prentice-Hall, 1998.

syndrome infant is a classic example of what sociologists call **cultural lag**—a condition created by rapid medical technological development and relatively static definitions of biological life and death. Medical practice today can prolong life (or postpone death) without having precise definitions of a point at which meaningful living has stopped and death has occurred. This condition would be of little significance if medical science were unable to maintain some biological functioning of the individual by artificial means, but such is not the case. As Joseph Fletcher (1977, p. 355) said, when the terminal patient "contemplates modern medicine's ability to prolong life, death itself is welcomed compared to the terrors of senility and protracted terminal treatment."

1989 Supreme Court Decision: Cruzan v. Director, Missouri Department of Health

Nancy Cruzan, the victim of a car crash, had been in a "persistent vegetative state" for six years. Her parents went to the Missouri state court to seek permission to have her feeding tube removed; the court refused. Missouri law required "clear and convincing" evidence of the patient's own wishes. Cruzan had told friends, in casual college chats, that she did not want to live "like a vegetable," but Missouri did not think that convincing enough.

The state, citing its "unqualified interest in life," set itself up as Cruzan's proxy and protector, deciding on her behalf that her best interest would be served by continuing to live. The U.S. Supreme Court narrowly ruled in Missouri's favor, and Cruzan lived until a county court judge ruled in December of 1990 (on new evidence of her wishes) that the tube should be disconnected.

Between 5,000 and 10,000 Americans are now being kept alive in circumstances, and with prognoses, much like Cruzan's.

The Economist, July 20, 1991, pp. 21–24. Copyright © 1991 The Economist Newspaper Group, Inc. Reprinted with permission.

Furthermore, even if one were able to distinguish between ordinary and extraordinary measures, would it be acceptable for patients (or someone acting on their behalf) to request the withdrawal of ordinary life support such as food and water? This is an issue that tends to divide persons who affirm a sanctity-of-life perspective and favor passive euthanasia.

If one can accept the legitimacy of passive euthanasia, Lowell Erdahl (1987, p. 143) raises the following questions:

> There are circumstances in which active euthanasia is more compassionate than passive. Is it, for example, more kind to cause death by dehydration and starvation than it is to kill the patient by lethal injection? In both cases the motive and effect are exactly the same; only the method is different. Is it possible that in some cases the sin of omission (permitting death by dehydration and starvation) may be greater than the sin of commission (causing death by lethal injection)?

Active euthanasia requires a direct action to bring about death. There are 2 types of active euthanasia: **suicide** and **mercy killing.** Suicide is the voluntary act of taking one's own life. Those who favor active euthanasia prefer to use the term **self-deliverance** when the life of a terminally ill patient is terminated. However, they would reject the legitimacy of suicide for persons with clinical depression or other forms of psychological pain.

In a study conducted in Cleveland in 1977 by Mostafa Nagi and associates concerning the attitudes of Protestant and Roman Catholic clergy toward euthanasia (1977–1978, p. 159), it was discovered that 73 percent and 69 percent of Protestant and Roman Catholic clergy, respectively, found passive euthanasia acceptable for patients who wanted to go home and, surrounded by family members, to die in peace.

However, only 18 percent of Protestant clergy and 2 percent of Catholic clergy found active euthanasia acceptable.

Although it may be possible to distinguish analytically between active and passive euthanasia, a number of studies (Winkler, 1995; Logue, 1994; Quill, 1994; Curzer, 1994; Brody, 1993; Potter, 1993) have demonstrated that after one accepts the legitimacy of letting people die by terminating life-sustaining treatment, it is impossible to convincingly explain why it is wrong to assist terminal patients wishing to commit suicide or to perform active euthanasia. A 1992 telephone survey conducted by Ruth Huber, Virginia Meade-Cox, and William Edelen determined that 90 percent of the 200 midwestern respondents favored some kind of personal control over death circumstances (mercy killing and passive and active euthanasia). With the exception of physician-assisted suicide, respondents accepted as equally viable the legalization of many forms of personal control over death.

In the United States, the Hemlock Society, founded in 1980, assists terminally ill individuals in the act of self-deliverance. In 1981 the Hemlock Society published a book written by its cofounder and director, Derek Humphry, entitled *Let Me Die Before I Wake: Hemlock's Book of Self-Deliverance for the Dying.* The first 10 chapters of this book provide detailed case studies of individuals who chose self-deliverance as an alternative to passive euthanasia (often with the assistance of family members and friends). The remainder of the book provides a bibliography and an extended discussion of personal and legal issues related to the decision to take one's life.

A year earlier, the English counterpart of the Hemlock Society—**EXIT** (founded in 1935 as the British Voluntary Euthanasia Society)—published *A Guide to Self-Deliverance* (1980). This book was unique because it provided the reader with detailed instructions to successfully and painlessly commit suicide. In the United States this book would have been construed as an attempt to intentionally aid and/or solicit another to commit suicide—a felony in most states. Until 1991, when Derek Humphry published *Final Exit,* the Hemlock Society had not been willing to be explicit in providing such information to its members. However, with public sentiment turning more favorably toward active euthanasia, the Hemlock Society began to take a more active role in promoting self-deliverance. In 1991 the Hemlock Society became a strong advocate of Washington state's Initiative 119, which would have legalized physician-assisted suicide, contributing $313,000 in support of the bill, which narrowly failed (Gabriel, 1991, p. 46).

After Humphry retired as executive director of the Hemlock Society in 1992, he created the Euthanasia Research and Guidance Organization (known as ERGO!). This nonprofit educational corporation sought to improve the quality of background research in physician-assisted deliverance for persons who are terminally or hopelessly ill and who wish to end their suffering. As well as conducting opinion polls, ERGO! develops and publishes guidelines—ethical, psychological, and legal—for patients and physicians to better prepare them to make life-ending decisions. The organization supplies literature to, and does research for, other right-to-die groups worldwide and also briefs journalists, authors, and graduate students who are interested in right-to-die issues. ERGO! is also willing to counsel dying patients (and their families) provided that they are competent adults and are at the end stage of a terminal illness. Persons suffering from unbearable mental illness are referred by ERGO! to alternative forms of skilled help. The Internet Web site of the Euthanasia Research and Guidance Organization is http://www.islandnet.com/~deathnet/ergo.html.

The Hemlock Society and ERGO! have been careful to differentiate suicide from self-deliverance and self-deliverance from mercy killing. Suicide is often condemned socially and religiously as a selfish act or as an "overreaction of a disturbed mind." Suicide is considered by many to be an irrational act that is a permanent solution to what is often a temporary problem. In contrast, self-deliverance should be considered a positive action taken to provide a permanent solution to long-term pain and suffering for the individual and his or her loved ones faced with a terminal condition. (Chapter 9 provides an extended treatment of suicide.)

Self-deliverance is a completely voluntary act on the part of the patient, whereas mercy killing involves other people's behavior that may or may not be sanctioned by the patient. In a 1985 Harris poll, 61 percent of the respondents favored a patient's right to ask the doctor to "put him out of his misery." U.S. laws do not distinguish between murder and mercy killing, and therefore mercy killing is predominantly treated as a criminal offense regardless of the motivations of individuals involved.

The Hemlock Society, ERGO!, and EXIT wish to eliminate the stigma attached to self-killing and to extend to all individuals the right of active, rational, and voluntary euthanasia whenever the dying process promises only unrelieved pain and a life devoid of dignity, meaning, and purpose.

Directive to Physicians

This directive is made this _____ day of _____ (month) _____ (year).

I, _____, being of sound mind, willfully and voluntarily make known my desire

____(a) That my life shall not be artificially prolonged and

____(b) That my life shall be ended with the aid of a physician under the circumstances set forth below, and I do hereby declare:

1. If at any time I should have a terminal condition or illness certified to be terminal by two physicians, and they determine that my death will occur within six months,

   ____(a) I direct that life-sustaining procedures be withheld or withdrawn, and

   ____(b) I direct that my physician administer aid-in-dying in a humane and dignified manner. (You must initial (a) or (b) or both.)

   ____(c) I have attached Special Instructions on a separate page to the directive. (Initial if you have attached a separate page.)

The action taken under this paragraph shall be at the time of my own choosing if I am competent.

(continued)

(continued from previous page)

2. In the absence of my ability to give directions regarding the termination of my life, it is my intention that this directive shall be honored by my family, agent (described in paragraph 4), and physician(s) as the final expression of my legal right to

____ (a) Refuse medical or surgical treatment, and

____ (b) To choose to die in a humane and dignified manner.

(You must initial (a) or (b) or both, and you must initial one box below.)

____ If I am unable to give directions, I do not want my attorney-in-fact to request aid-in-dying.

____ If I am unable to give directions, I do want my attorney-in-fact to ask my physician for aid-in-dying.

3. I understand that a terminal condition is one in which I am not likely to live for more than six months.

4. (a) I, _____ do hereby designate and appoint _____ as my attorney-in-fact (agent) to make health care decisions for me if I am in a coma or otherwise unable to decide for myself as authorized in this document. For the purpose of this document, "health care decision" means consent, refusal of consent, or withdrawal of consent to any care, treatment, service, or procedure to maintain, diagnose, or treat an individual's physical or mental condition, or to administer aid-in-dying.

(b) By this document I intend to create a Durable Power of Attorney for Health Care under The Oregon Death With Dignity Act and ORS Section 126.407. This power of attorney shall not be affected by my subsequent incapacity, except by revocation.

(c) Subject to any limitations in this document, I hereby grant to my agent full power and authority to make health care decisions for me to the same extent that I could make these decisions for myself if I had the capacity to do so. In exercising this authority, my agent shall make health care decisions that are consistent with my desires as stated in this document or otherwise made known to my agent, including, but not limited to, my desires concerning obtaining, refusing, or withdrawing life-prolonging care, treatment, services and procedures, and administration of aid-in-dying.

(continued)

THE SLIPPERY-SLOPE ARGUMENT

Persons who oppose active euthanasia often do so on the grounds of what they call the **slippery-slope-to-Auschwitz argument** (see Wilkinson, 1995; Potter, 1993). They allege that the justification for withholding some treatments also applies to withholding any and all treatments from those whom society considers

(continued from previous page)

5. This directive shall have no force or effect seven years from the date filled in above, unless I am incompetent to act on my own behalf and then it shall remain valid until my competency is restored.

6. I recognize that a physician's judgment is not always certain, and that medical science continues to make progress in extending life, but in spite of these facts, I nevertheless wish aid-in-dying rather than letting my terminal condition take its natural course.

7. My family has been informed of my request to die, their opinions have been taken into consideration, but the final decision remains mine, so long as I am competent.

8. The exact time of my death will be determined by me and my physician with my desire or my attorney-in-fact's instructions paramount.

I have given full consideration and understand the full import of this directive, and I am emotionally and mentally competent to make this directive. I accept the moral and legal responsibility for receiving aid-in-dying.

This directive will not be valid unless it is signed by two qualified witnesses who are present when you sign or acknowledge your signature. The witnesses must not be related to you by blood, marriage, or adoption; he or she must not be entitled to any part of your estate; and he or she must not include a physician or other person responsible for, or employed by anyone responsible for, your health care. If you have attached any additional pages to this form, you must date and sign each of the additional pages at the same time you date and sign this power of attorney.

Signed: _____

City, County, and State of Residence _____

(This document must be witnessed by two qualified adult witnesses. None of the following persons may be engaged as witnesses: (1) a health care provider who is involved in any way with the treatment of the declarant, (2) an employee of a health care provider who is involved in any way with the treatment of the declarant, (3) the operator of a community care facility where the declarant resides, (4) an employee of an operator of a community care facility who is involved in any way with the treatment of the declarant.)

The Oregon Death With Dignity Act, Oregon Revised Statutes, Chapter 97, 1990.

unworthy. It is further argued that if a society wishes to extend to any of its members the right to active euthanasia, none of its members is protected from being killed. Such was the case under Hitler when German society's "unproductive," "defective," and "morally and mentally unfit"—Jews, homosexuals, and handicapped—were sent to Auschwitz and other places of confinement to be "euthanized" (murdered).

Jack Kevorkian poses with Marcella Lawrence and Marguerite Tate at his attorney's office follow-ing a press conference concerning the passage of Michigan's law banning assisted suicides. Both women took their lives with Kevorkian present just hours before Michigan's governor signed the bill into law.

The slippery-slope argument alleges that society moves toward a disregard for human life in predictable steps. The first step is the acceptance of passive euthanasia when medical technology and surgical procedures are withheld from (or rejected by) chronically and/or terminally ill patients. The second step occurs when ordinary or customary procedures are withdrawn—such procedures would include food and water. We arrive at the third step when society accepts the legitimacy of suicide (self-deliverance). The fourth step is when these "rights" are extended to nonterminal pa-tients such as quadriplegics. In the fifth step, the medical system will assist patients in self-deliverance or active euthanasia (as is presently the situation in Holland), believ-ing that the incurably ill deserve the same "humane" treatment as that accorded to a beloved animal that is "put to sleep." In the sixth step all of these provisions are ex-tended to the nonterminally ill and/or persons acting on their behalf. Finally, we ar-rive at the seventh step—"Auschwitz"—when society is willing to accord these "privileges" to the unwilling, incompetent, and/or undesirable.

To prevent society from reaching such a level of desensitization, people who em-brace the slippery-slope argument argue that no type of euthanasia should be consid-ered socially acceptable—in other words, to be safe, society should "stay off the slope entirely!" However, other biomedical scholars who favor active euthanasia and physi-cian-assisted suicide (Ogden, 1995; Weijer, 1995; Logue, 1994; Hill, 1992) argue that if patients *voluntarily* permit and/or cooperate with their physicians to cause a prema-ture death, their rights and dignity as persons will be enhanced, and a Nazi–like pro-gram of extermination will be unlikely.

Although one might doubt that these steps inevitably lead to a rejection of the sanctity of human life, one might acknowledge that the noble intentions of those who favor active euthanasia do not in themselves justify a public policy allowing mercy killing, nor will they counteract the potential abuse to which euthanasia can be put by those whose motives may be self-serving (Bouma et al., 1989, p. 301).

Without a doubt, even so-called voluntary actions can be unduly influenced by social pressures. Consider the case of an elderly nursing home resident who realizes that the cost of her care depletes financial resources that might be used to support an able-bodied spouse or other family members. When one defines oneself as a burden to society, is euthanasia (even self-deliverance) truly a voluntary choice? Erdahl responds this way (1987, p. 145):

> As costs of care increase, individuals in specific circumstances and society as a whole will be strongly tempted to sell out both compassion and responsible reverence for life in exchange for economic considerations. If the day comes when euthanasia is established as an economic policy, we will have ceased to be either fully moral or fully human.

Donation of Organs Is Unusual in China
Seth Faison

BEIJING, February 23, 1997—In a country that savors ceremony and invests great symbolism in public events, China's formal farewell to its paramount leader, Deng Xiaoping, is a big deal.

So it attracted a fair amount of attention last week, when the authorities announced that Mr. Deng would be cremated a day prior to the memorial service. That precludes the usual practice of displaying the deceased in a bed of flowers, to be encircled by those who come to say a final goodbye.

Even more surprising, the announcement specified that the Deng family wanted to respect the patriarch's wishes—to have his corneas donated to an eye bank and body parts offered for medical research.

That may have shocked the Confucian faithful, who hold that the body should remain intact, even after death. Yet combining cremation and organ donation was a double attack on the old way of doing things, which was exactly how the authorities wanted to make it look: Mr. Deng, known for his bold strokes in life, would be fighting tradition in the name of selflessness and science, even in death.

"Deng is setting an example with his own action, and challenging old customs," said Li Weiye—though as director of ophthalmology and the cornea bank at Xiehe Hospital here, he is hardly a disinterested party. "When I heard that he is donating his corneas and body," he said, "I felt he really is a great man."

Inevitably, however, in a society where information is controlled and conspiratory theories are rife, the decision to cremate Mr. Deng's body—

(continued)

(continued from previous page)

before it could be publicly seen—has fed suspicion that he actually died some time ago. Mr. Deng had not appeared in public for three years before he died Wednesday night, assuming that the official time of death was correct.

"It's like, can't see the person when he's alive, and can't see the body when he's dead?" said a taxi driver in Beijing. "For a long time there were no reports on him, no appearance on TV. And now suddenly we are told he is dead? It's hard to judge."

China's Communist leaders have been trying to eradicate traditions they deem superstitious, but with only mixed success. So it is understandable that cremation is still met with suspicion.

In 1956, Mao called on all Chinese to forgo traditional burials for cremation—sensible in a land with so many people and not enough land—and he and Prime Minister Zhou Enlai and Mr. Deng all pledged that they themselves would be cremated.

Of course, Mao himself lived outside the rules that governed ordinary senior leaders, and was later embalmed and put on display in a glass sarcophagus that rests in Tiananmen Square, where tens of thousands of people see him each week.

And only about 30 percent of the seven million people who died in China last year were cremated, though the percentage is higher in large cities, and reached 95 percent in Beijing.

Even fewer make organ donations, although human rights groups have charged that organs are removed from death-row prisoners for medical transplants. Dr. Li said his hospital's cornea bank, prepared so that transplants can be made to needy patients, had not done very well because Chinese tradition works against making such gifts.

"In China, not only corneas, but also other organs, are all in short supply," Dr. Li said. Part of the problem lies beyond the Confucian bias against dismemberment. Because Chinese society is so grounded in personal relations with family and close friends, and highly mistrustful of strangers, the idea of voluntarily donating one's body to be used by a person one will never know is anathema to many Chinese.

But not, at least, to Mr. Deng.

S. Faison, *New York Times International,* February 24, 1997, p. A6.

Organ Donations

Human organ transplants have long been cloaked in a special aura of mystery. Sometimes, it is fear linked to religious concerns about the sanctity of the body. Other times, it is linked to frightening fictional stories like Frankenstein (Malcolm, 1986, p. 8). Because of the sensitive nature of the topic, human organ transplants have not been widely discussed by society.

In many urban areas today kidney foundations, eye banks, and transplant centers supply donor cards and arrange for transplants when Death occurs. Many kinds of tissues and organs are used for transplantation, including eyes, skin, bones, tendons, bone marrow, kidneys, livers, pancreases, blood vessels, lungs, and hearts. Although some of these transplant operations are still involved in the areas of research, techniques are constantly improving.

The first modern human organ transplant was a kidney transplant in 1950 which took place in Chicago (Cooper & Lanza, 1984, p. 1). The first liver transplant was performed in 1963 in Denver (Ezell, Anspaugh, & Oaks, 1987, p. 178). Transplantation received especially wide coverage in the media with the first transplantation of a human heart by Dr. Christiaan Barnard in South Africa in 1967.

Currently, it is possible to successfully perform approximately 25 different organ and tissue transplantations, including bone and cartilage, bone marrow, cornea, heart, lung, kidney, liver, and pancreas. Acceptable organ donors range from newborns to senior citizens and are people in good health but who have died suddenly or who have been declared "brain dead." With advances in medical technology and preservation techniques, vital organs may be procured and transported hundreds of miles to a

ONE KIDNEY, TWO HEARTS AND A PANCREAS! COMING RIGHT UP, DOC!

PARTS DEPT.

©1982 MIAMI NEWS

SOURCE: Don Wright/The Miami News

The Recycled Man
Joel L. Swerdlow

Consider this scenario: Dan Smith is injured in a boating accident. Physicians certify that his brain has quit functioning. Although medical equipment can maintain his heartbeat, he is dead. A nurse enters his Social Security number into a computer and the screen flashes "Universal Donor." The display notes that Dan's wife had approved his decision (and signed up herself).

The hospital calls the local organ and tissue center, and late that evening doctors remove Dan's pancreas, liver, kidneys, lungs, and heart. They also take more than 70 kinds of tissue—corneas, skin, bones, ligaments and tendons, veins and middle ears—with procedures so careful that the family can still have an open-casket funeral the next day.

Within 24 hours, elements of Dan's body are used to release two kidney patients from the rigors of dialysis. His heart saves a 40-year-old father of two. His lungs give life to a steelworker and a grandmother. His liver saves a college student and his pancreas is transplanted to a young diabetic.

In the next few days, he gives hearing to one child and eyesight to two others. His skin helps two burned firefighters. Other tissues aid in reconstructive surgery. Some of his bones are freeze-dried for dental and other use; some tissues are assigned to research labs.

Computer networks help allocate the material, allowing physicians to find a proper match (hip and knee bones, for example, are cut to fit specific patients) and all transplant results are fed into a data bank shared by clinicians and researchers.

The collective value of these procedures runs to millions of dollars. The lives saved and suffering relieved are priceless. Yet the cost of Dan's tissues and organs is zero. All were donated.

This is no futuristic daydream. Each of the medical techniques and communication technologies described above exists today.

J. L. Swerdlow, *Washington Post,* June 25, 1989, p. 3B. Excerpted from *Matching Needs, Saving Lives,* published by the Annenberg Washington Program of Northwestern University.

recipient center for transplantation. Hearts and lungs can be preserved for up to 6 hours before transplantation, and kidneys can be preserved up to 72 hours (United Network for Organ Sharing, 1997).

There is an increasing tendency today for individuals to donate upon their deaths their organs and tissues to the living. By 1996 there were a total of 16,845 transplants from living (2,789) and recently-deceased donors (14,056). This includes approximately 10,000 kidneys, 3,500 livers, 2,000 hearts, 1,000 pancreases, and 700 lungs (United Network for Organ Sharing, 1997).

The National Conference on Uniform Laws developed the Uniform Anatomical Gift Act to help answer questions concerning transplantations, and by 1971 all

---

Uniform Donor Card

UNIFORM DONOR CARD of (name of donor). In the hope that I may help others, I hereby make this anatomical gift, if medically acceptable, to take effect upon my death. The words and marks below indicate my desires.
I give:

a. _____ any needed organs or parts

b. _____ only the following organs or parts—specify the organs(s) or parts(s)—for the purposes of transplantation, therapy, medical research, or education:

c. _____ my body for anatomical study if needed

Signed by the donor and the following two witnesses in the presence of each other:

Signature of donor	Date of birth of donor
Date signed	City and state
Witness	Witness

---

50 states had adopted the act with only minor variations (Ezell, Anspaugh, & Oaks, 1987, p. 181). The act permits a person over 18 years of age to donate part or all of his or her body upon death. If the body or body part has not been donated prior to death, a family member may agree to do so, with permission based on the priority of the relationship. The priority is as follows: spouse, adult son or daughter, parents, adult sibling, legal guardian, or other party responsible, for disposition of the body.

Various problems affect human transplantations. Whether or not the donor and donee tissues are compatible can be a problem. There is often a shortage of donors, thus producing a difficult decision in selecting among potential recipients. A lack of a legal definition of death in some states prevents surgeons from removing healthy organs when brain activity has stopped but the heart and lungs are still functioning. The lack of a nationwide communications network to coordinate information presents another problem for human transplantations.

Other problems include the question of who will pay for expensive transplantation procedures. A few public insurers have recently decided in favor of coverage for heart and liver transplants. Kidney transplants have been covered since 1973 under Medicare's end-stage renal disease program. Though the costs of solid organ transplants are high, the benefits are substantial when one considers that they may be life-saving. Estimated average total first-year costs of solid organ transplant procedures are $95,000 for a heart transplant, $35,000 for a kidney transplant, $130,000 for a liver transplant, and $35,000 for a pancreas transplant (Ezell, Anspaugh, & Oaks, 1987, p. 185).

As medical technology has progressed and transplantations have become more successful, the demand for transplantation has greatly increased. In 1996 more than

Baby Without Brain Dies; Organs No Longer Fit to Transplant

The short life of Theresa Ann Campo Pearson ended Monday, just 10 days after she was born without a fully formed brain. But the troubling issues raised by the tiny anencephalic infant's life live on.

By the time of her death, her major organs had deteriorated and were no longer viable for transplants, said Les Olson, director of organ procurement for the University of Miami. The corneas of her eyes were saved and will be given "to another tiny baby," Olson said.

The 4-pound baby girl died Monday afternoon at Broward General Medical Center in Fort Lauderdale, Fla., about 19 hours after she was removed from a ventilator that had briefly sustained her when her vital organs began to fail. Her parents, Laura Campo and Justin Pearson, were at her side, doctors said. The cause of death was listed as cardiac and respiratory failure.

"It was very peaceful; the baby just sort of slipped away," said Dr. Brian Udell, director of the medical center's neonatology unit. "At the end, they got to hold her and kiss her."

Since the infant's birth by Caesarean section March 21, her parents had been battling for legal permission to have her heart, lungs, kidneys and liver removed so they could be transplanted to other children who might need them. But 2 state courts ruled that state law prevented the taking of vital organs from anyone who was not brain dead.

Attorney Scott Mager had argued the law didn't apply.

"How can you have cessation of brain activity when you don't have a brain?" he asked.

(continued)

50,000 patients were waiting for organ transplants, and even after nearly 17,000 successful transplants were performed, 4,000 Americans died while waiting for organs to be donated (United Network for Organ Sharing, 1997). If we add to this problem the fact that increasingly HMOs, insurance companies, and other third-party providers will not pay for transplantation procedures, we face a situation in which those who receive organ and tissue transplantations are primarily those who can afford such surgeries.

The sensitive issue of who receives donor organs becomes even more problematic when considering a future where the rich have the ability to secure organs from the poor. If poor people do not have enough money to feed themselves, and they need only one kidney to survive, what would prevent a poor person from selling a kidney for $50,000 to a dying rich person? Presently this is not possible in the United States (even though some recipients are giving financial consideration to the survivors of donors for "funeral expenses"), but this ethical nightmare is a reality in other nations of the world, and with a global economy, wealthy Americans may well become involved.

(continued from previous page)

Late Monday the Florida Supreme Court agreed to hear the couple's appeal. But by then, it was too late.

In fact, doctors said, it was too late for Theresa Ann within days of conception. She was anencephalic, born with nothing but the nub of a brain stem—enough to provide her only with breath and a heartbeat. She had no brain, no top to her skull, no feeling or cognition, and no hope, said Udell.

Most anencephalics are stillborn. Of those born alive, the vast majority die within minutes. But Theresa Ann lived unaided by mechanical support for 8 days.

"Theresa's legacy is that now, hopefully, people in this country will understand what brain death is," Olson said. "Organ donation is the only loving thing to come out of the death. But the only candidates for organ donation are those patients who are kept alive artificially. She was not a suitable donor."

Anti-abortion activists, who opposed efforts to take vital organs before the baby died, staged a demonstration outside the hospital Monday.

"We are not here to point accusatory fingers of judgment," said the Rev. Patrick Mahoney. "We are here to reach out with hands of hope."

"Baby Theresa was a gift from God...She was not created by God for spare parts," said one demonstrator, Eddie Soblotne of Coral Springs.

Susan Clarke, the baby's maternal grandmother, saw it differently.

"Taking one and helping two, three, five—that's pro-life," she said.

She said the family would continue to press for a change in the law.

"We will go on from here to help the children ... the families. You don't stop in midstream," she said hours before the baby died.

Dr. Wayne DiGiacomo who delivered the baby praised Laura Campo. "She's a brave woman to make the decision to carry the fight to this level, to have her child live on through other children," he said.

St. Paul Pioneer Press, March 31, 1991, pp. 1A, 8A.

Public Policy

Until this section we have primarily taken a social exchange perspective on biomedical issues. We have analyzed euthanasia and organ transplants from a cost-benefit point of view and assumed that the individual (or small group of people) is the appropriate unit of analysis. In this final section of the chapter we will analyze American public policy in dealing with the health needs of critically ill persons.

Many Americans assume that health care should be a guaranteed right of all citizens who desire and can afford to pay for it. For those unable to pay, the government provides basic health care through Medicaid. Although passive euthanasia would affirm the right of those who choose to reject medical intervention, many believe that those who wish to live have a legitimate claim to the resources of society in providing the medical assistance necessary for living. According to *The Economist* ("Euthanasia," 1991):

Egypt's Doctors Impose Kidney Transplant Curbs
Chris Hedges

CAIRO—In an effort to end the sale of human organs by the country's poor, Egyptian doctors have announced a ban on all kidney transplants from living donors that are not done between relatives. The ban, to take effect in July, was established by the Egyptian society of kidney specialists. It applies to all of Egypt's doctors. The society is moving to set up an organ bank and for the first time begin to transplant kidneys from cadavers, rather than live donors.

"By July we want to replace this kidney trade with a kidney bank," said Dr. Rashad Barsoum, Secretary General of the Egyptian society of kidney specialists.

Egypt, like India and other third-world countries, does a brisk business in the sale of organs, primarily kidneys, especially to wealthy Persian Gulf Arabs who come to one of Cairo's six kidney transplant centers. The transplant centers do about 350 operations a year.

Foreigners who want to buy Egyptian kidneys must come to Egypt because there are no provisions here for the preservation of transplant organs. Patients and donors are wheeled into the operating theater at the same time.

While other countries in the Arab world have transplant centers, few have the vast numbers of poor who are willing to sell their organs.

Private laboratories often act as brokerage houses, sending out recruiters to the slums of Cairo to entice prospective donors in for tissue tests. Patients needing kidneys go to the laboratories, where they are matched with a donor and sold an organ. Kidneys sell for $10,000 to $15,000. Dr. Barsoum said he has even heard of auctions with the organ going to the highest bidder.

(continued)

The terminally ill now account for 20 to 30 percent of hospital expenditures, yet no amount of money is going to make them better. Doctors tend to shy away from principles of "utility" and cost worthiness. Instead, they argue a principle of "justice."

Yet, with annual medical care costing more than $1 trillion and with heightened concerns for government fiscal responsibility and cost containment, Americans are beginning to reevaluate universal access to health care. This reevaluation of public policy is motivated by a utilitarian concern for distributive justice.

Utilitarianism is the belief that social policy should be directed at providing the greatest good (maximum benefits) for the greatest number of people. If providing an artificial heart for 1 patient who will live 3 months inside a hospital costs more than a million dollars, utilitarians believe that the same amount of money might be more appropriately spent on prenatal care for 10,000 women. Furthermore, in the United States approximately 50 percent of the medical expenditures that an individual will incur during his or her lifetime will be for medical services delivered in the final 6 months of life. Because all of us are involved to some extent in paying for these

(continued from previous page)

"We have stooped to a low point with this business," Dr. Barsoum said. The sale of organs evolved into an organized business in 1987, 11 years after the first kidney transplant took place in Egypt, medical authorities say. Doctors, too, have been criticized for profiting from the buying and selling of organs.

The doctors' union banned live-donor transplants from Egyptians to foreigners in 1987 and prohibited newspaper advertisements in which kidneys were sought.

But the moves did little to affect the trade, which seemed to grow as the country's medical establishment was able to handle more patients.

"I could foresee an international market developing in this area," Dr. Barsoum said.

The ban will put more pressure on the country's medical centers, which already cannot cope with the large numbers of kidney failures. About 10,000 of the 56 million Egyptians suffer kidney failure annually, three times the rate in the West. Only 2,000 of those patients are able to receive kidney dialysis treatment because of the high cost and the shortage of equipment.

Setting up an organ bank will also take time, since it can only be accomplished through an act of Parliament. While medical authorities have managed to get the backing of Muslim leaders, and even the head of the Coptic Christian community, they must change the Constitution, which stipulated that the dead must be buried immediately, in accordance with Islamic law.

Muslim authorities, while allowing the procedure, insist that organs can only be taken from cadavers if the deceased agreed in advance to the donation. The clerics have long held that the sale of organs violates Islamic law.

C. Hedges, *New York Times International,* January 23, 1992.

medical costs (either through government subsidy or health insurance premiums), it is easy to question whether or not these expenditures are a worthwhile investment for such a limited return.

These types of cost-benefit analyses deemphasize the health needs of particular individuals in favor of the health needs of the entire society. Garrett Hardin (1985, p. 21), a professor of ecology at the University of California at Santa Barbara, presents this argument with the following statement: "Easy access to health care is exhausting America's medical resources." According to Hardin, whenever meeting medical needs becomes an obligation of the entire community, utilization will always benefit individuals, whereas costs will be shared by all members of the system. Therefore, individuals can never be expected to limit their use, and health care costs will naturally rise to such a level that the system will collapse—the end of health care to all. He asks:

> Should the artificial heart be considered an inalienable right of any needy patient? Should the public at large pay the extra cost of saving premature babies? What is to be gained by extending the lives of comatose patients a few more years? It is clear

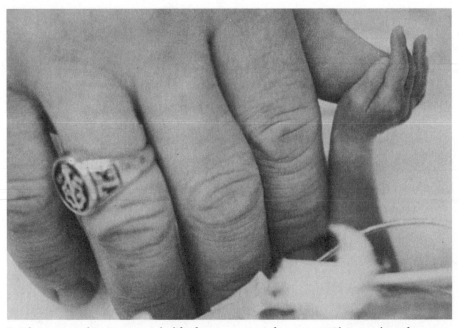

Is it better to spend money to save the life of one premature infant or to provide prenatal care for 10,000 women?

that our society faces a grave danger: as medical technology advances and we spend more and more for less and less, we edge ever closer to what might be called the tragedy of the medical commons. . . . A tragic end can be prevented only by saying NO! But what should we limit? The kinds of defects and malfunctions eligible for treatment? The age beyond which a patient may not be treated with heroic medicine? These are good candidates. Every point in our medical and legal systems seems to be biased in favor of compassion. At some point compassion must yield to principle.

A recent survey (Jankel, Wolfgang, & Hoff, 1994) of Georgia state legislators asked the respondents to rank the importance of funding for specific health care services. The legislators assigned the highest priority score to providing care to pregnant women and their unborn children, and the lowest score to organ transplants. It seems that, for at least some elected officials, in the allocation of government health care dollars the goal is to maximize the state's return on its investment.

This sentiment is reflected in a statement by Dr. John Kitzhaber (cited by Robinson, 1989, pp. 4–5), a physician and president of the Oregon State Senate:

We spend over $50 billion a year on people in the last 6 months of their lives, while closing pediatric clinics. We spend over $3 billion a year on intensive care for newborn babies, while denying prenatal care to hundreds of thousands of expectant women. Every dollar spent on health care is one that can't be spent on schools, roads, or a cleaner environment. In the last 10 years many states have changed eligibility requirements that have removed more than 800,000 American women and children from Medicaid. Presently Medicaid covers only 38 percent of the nation's poor, while 10 years ago it provided benefits for 64 percent.

Dr. Daniel Callahan, director of the Hastings Center, has advocated that persons over 80 be ineligible for Medicare reimbursements for cancer surgery, intensive care, and heart bypass surgery. Callahan (cited by Robinson, 1989, p. 5) says:

> As a nation, we must set a hard line against the endless prolongation of life. We must direct our medical energies only to the relief of pain and suffering in the elderly, and to help them prepare for a graceful death after a full life.

Yet, there are more radical proposals that even the most utilitarian of persons would have a difficult time accepting. Professor Fung (1993) of Memphis State University has proposed that the hopelessly ill voluntarily elect physician-assisted death and thereby, save society's resources. To ensure that the saved resources would not be rechanneled to additionally futile treatments for other terminally ill patients, those who chose active euthanasia would be allowed to determine how the saved resources would be redeployed. A related, but significantly more modest, proposal by Howard Curzer (1994) argues that justice sometimes requires increasing a patient's risk of death by shifting scarce health and financial resources to patients who need them more. Although these decisions are very difficult, the cost and availability of life-extending medical procedures financed primarily by the government and third-party providers force us to admit that there cannot be a guaranteed right to health care in the United States.

Conclusion

As a society we are confronting difficult decisions and problems caused by modern medicine's successes, not failures. One of those problems is that when we are faced with medical decisions for ourselves and for those who are significant to us, we may act in ways that when applied to an entire society would be imprudent or counterproductive. Yet, to allow the making of these decisions to become a matter of personal choice determined solely in terms of financial resources would be unjust from a societal (or global) point of view.

We have obviously come to a point where very tough health care decisions must be made. Many of these are personal and family decisions—for how long do we wish to extend the dying process for ourselves and those we love? Other decisions will involve the welfare of the entire society and will require us to make choices between extending terminal care to those whose time is diminished and investing resources to prevent the more able-bodied from becoming ill. From a personal perspective, we will always find it difficult to withhold treatment from anyone. From a national perspective, we must always support health care policies that will benefit most of our citizens without inflicting pain and suffering on any.

Summary

1. Euthanasia, or "good death," must be defined within the context of one's understanding of the meaning of life.

2. The sanctity-of-life perspective of euthanasia contends that all "natural" life has intrinsic meaning and should be appreciated as a divine gift. As a consequence, human beings have the obligation to enhance the quality of life as it may exist.

3. The quality-of-life perspective of euthanasia contends that when life no longer has "quality," death is preferable to living a life devoid of meaning.

4. Individuals try to facilitate a "good death" by two methods—passive and active euthanasia. Passive euthanasia involves a protocol whereby no action or medical intervention hastens death. Passive euthanasia usually involves the removal of medical technology or the refusal of medical intervention. Passive euthanasia is supported by people who affirm both sanctity-of-life and quality-of-life perspectives.

5. Active euthanasia requires a direct action to bring about death. There are two types of active euthanasia: suicide and mercy killing.

6. Suicide is the voluntary act of taking one's own life. Those who favor active euthanasia prefer to use the term *self-deliverance* when the life of a terminally ill patient is terminated. Self-deliverance should be considered a positive action taken to provide a permanent solution to the long-term pain and suffering of the individual and his or her loved ones who are faced with a terminal condition.

7. Self-deliverance is a completely voluntary act on the part of the patient; mercy killing involves other people's behavior, which may or may not be sanctioned by the patient. At present both suicide (self-deliverance) and mercy killing are illegal in the United States.

8. Persons opposing active euthanasia often do so with the "slippery-slope-to-Auschwitz" argument. They allege that the justification for withholding some treatments also applies to withholding any and all treatments from those whom society considers unworthy. The slippery-slope argument asserts that society moves toward a disregard for human life in predictable steps.

9. Because of the sensitive nature of the issue, human organ transplantation has not been widely discussed in society. Difficult decisions need to be made about what qualifies a person to be eligible for a transplant.

Discussion Questions

1. Compare and contrast the sanctity-of-life and quality-of-life perspectives on euthanasia. What are the limitations of each perspective?

2. Compare and contrast passive and active euthanasia. What difficulties does implementing each of these approaches have for current social policy dealing with health care for the terminally ill?

3. What are the difficulties in defining the following terms?
   a. Natural death
   b. Quality of life
   c. Ordinary and extraordinary medical interventions
   d. Usual and customary medical procedures
   e. Excessive expense and reasonable benefit

4. If your parent were dying from an extremely painful and incurable form of cancer and decided that life was not worth living, what role would you be willing to play in assisting him or her in self-deliverance? Would you be unwilling to assist your parent? If not, what actions would you take in discouraging your parent's action?

5. Provide arguments for and against the removal of food and water from a terminal patient in a coma.

6. What are a living will and a durable power of attorney? How do they differ? What is the benefit of having one over the other?

7. Discuss some of the problems affecting human organ transplantations from both a societal and a personal point of view.

8. Should the society make eligible for a transplant only those persons who can afford it, or should the potential societal contribution of the individual be taken into account? Are there some medical procedures that should never be financed by insurance benefits or government funds because they are too expensive?

Glossary

Active Euthanasia: A direct action that causes death in accordance with the stated or implied wishes of the terminal patient. There are two types of active euthanasia: suicide and mercy killing.

Cultural Lag: A situation in which some parts of culture change more slowly than others. A typical situation occurs when technology changes faster than the values of the culture.

Durable Power of Attorney: A document that ascribes to a surrogate decision-maker the legal authority to consent (or refuse to consent) to medical treatment should the patient lack competency for making such decisions.

Euthanasia: Literally, a "good death."

EXIT: A British society that promotes euthanasia.

Extraordinary Measures: All of those medicines, treatments, and operations that cannot be obtained without excessive expense, pain, or other inconvenience or that, if used, would not offer a reasonable hope of benefit.

Intubation: A medical procedure whereby the patient is fed through a tube placed in the stomach.

Living Will: A document that states that one does not want medical intervention if the technology or treatment that keeps one alive cannot offer a reasonable quality of life or hope for recovery.

Mercy Killing: Ending the life of a terminal patient in accordance with that person's stated or implied wishes.

Ordinary Measures: All of those medicines, treatments, and operations that offer a reasonable hope of benefit to the patient and that can be obtained and used without excessive expense, pain, or other inconvenience.

Passive Euthanasia: The withholding of treatment, which, in effect, hastens death.

Quality of Life: The perspective that when life no longer has quality, death is preferable to living a life devoid of meaning.

Sanctity of Life: The perspective that all natural life has intrinsic meaning and should be appreciated as a divine gift. As a consequence, human beings have the obligation to enhance the quality of life as it may exist.

Self-Deliverance: A rational and voluntary act of taking one's life; an alternative to the terms *suicide* and *mercy killing*.

Slippery-Slope-to-Auschwitz Argument:
The belief that if a society extends to any of its members the right to active euthanasia, none of its members is protected from being killed. Auschwitz was a German concentration camp where people were killed during World War II.

Suicide: The voluntary act of taking one's life.

Utilitarianism: The principle of evaluation based upon the goal of providing the greatest good (maximum benefits) for the greatest number of people.

References

Almgren, G. (1993). Living will legislation, nursing home care, and the rejection of artificial nutrition and hydration: An analysis of bedside decision-making in three states. *Journal of Health and Social Policy, 4*(3), 43–63.

Bouma, H., Diekema, D., Langerak, E., Rottman, T., & Verhey, A. (1989). *Christian faith, health, and medical practice.* Grand Rapids, MI: Eerdmans.

Brody, H. (1993, Summer). Causing, intending, and assisting death. *Journal of Clinical Ethics, 4*(2), 112–117.

Clark, B. (1981). *Whose life is it anyway?* Chicago: Dramatic Publishing Company.

Cooper, D. K., & Lanza, R. T. (1984). *Heart transplants: The present status of orthotopic and heterotopic health transportation.* Boston: MTP Press.

Cugliari, A. M., & Miller, T. E. (1994, April). Moral and religious objections by hospitals to withholding and withdrawing life-sustaining treatment. *Journal of Community Health, 19*(2), 87–100.

Curzer, H. J. (1994, Winter). Withdrawal of life-support: Four problems in medical ethics. *Journal of Medical Humanities, 15*(4), 233–241.

Diekstra, R. F. W. (1987). Suicide should not always be prevented. In J. Rohr (Ed.), *Death and dying: Opposing viewpoints.* St. Paul, MN: Greenhaven Press.

Dilworth, D. C. (1996, February). Dying wishes are ignored by hospitals and doctors. *Trial, 32*(2), 79–81.

Erdahl, L. (1987). Euthanasia is sometimes justified. In J. Rohr (Ed.), *Death and dying: Opposing viewpoints.* St. Paul, MN: Greenhaven Press.

Euthanasia: What is the "good death"? (1991, July 20). *The Economist,* pp. 21–24.

EXIT. (1980). *A guide to self-deliverance.* London: Author.

Ezell, G., Anspaugh, D. J., & Oaks, J. (1987). *Dying and death: From a health and sociological perspective.* Scottsdale, AZ: Gorsuch Scarisbrick Publishers.

Fletcher, J. (1977). Ethics and euthanasia. In D. J. Horan & D. Mall (Eds.), *Death, dying, and euthanasia.* Washington, DC: University Publications of America.

Fung, K. K. (1993). Wealth transfer through voluntary death. *Journal of Health and Social Policy, 5*(2), 77–86.

Gabriel, T. (1991, December 8). A fight to the death. *New York Times Magazine,* pp. 46–88.

Hardin, G. (1985, September-October). Crisis on the commons. *The Sciences,* 21–25.

Hemlock Society. (1981). *The hemlock manifesto.* Los Angeles: Author.

Hill, P. T. (1992). Individual rights vs. state interests: Ethical concerns in thanatology. *Loss, Grief and Care, 6*(1), 51–59.

Huber, R., Meade-Cox, V., & Edelen, W. B. (1992). Right to die responses from a random sample of 200. *Hospice Journal, 8*(3), 1–19.

Humphry, D. (1981). *Let me die before I wake: Hemlock's book of self-deliverance for the dying.* Los Angeles: the Hemlock Society.

Jankel, C. A., Wolfgang, A. P., & Hoff, M. J. (1994, March-April). Health care priorities: Opinions of one state's citizens and legislators. *Health Values, 18*(2), 7–14.

Illich, I. (1976). *Medical nemesis: The expropriation of health.* New York: Pantheon.

Logue, B. J. (1994). When hospice fails: The limits of palliative care. *Omega, 29*(4), 291–301.

Maddox, G. (1995). Advanced directives in health care: Living wills and durable power of attorney. In *The Encyclopedia of Aging.* New York: Springer.

Malcolm, A. H. (1986, February 15). Taboo to commonplace: Transplants now routine. *New York Times,* p. 8.

Maples, P. (1991). Washington to vote on legalizing suicide. *Hartford Courant,* p. A17.

Miles, S. H., & August, A. (1990, Spring-Summer).

Courts, gender and "the right to die." *Law, Medicine and Health Care, 18*(1, 2), 85–95.

Montgomery, P. (1987, September 2). In Holland, the promise of an easy death. *Minneapolis Star and Tribune,* p. 15A.

Morriss, F. (1987). Euthanasia is never justified. In J. Rohr (Ed.), *Death and dying: Opposing viewpoints.* St. Paul, MN: Greenhaven Press.

Nagi, M. H., Puch, M. D., & Lazerine, N. G. (1977–1978). Attitudes of Catholic and Protestant clergy toward euthanasia. *Omega, 8*(2), 153–164.

Ogden, R. D. (1995, December). The right to die: A rejoinder to Bruce Wilkinson's critique. *Canadian Public Policy, 21*(4), 456–460.

Pope Pius XII. (1977). The prolongation of life: An address of Pope Pius XII to an international congress of anesthesiologists. In D. J. Horan & D. Mall (Eds.), *Death, dying, and euthanasia.* Washington, DC: University Publications of America.

Potter, A. C. (1993). Will the "right to die" become a license to kill? The growth of euthanasia in America. *Journal of Legislation, 19*(1), 31–62.

Quill, T. E. (1994, Winter). Physician-assisted death: Progress or peril? *Suicide and Life-Threatening Behavior, 24*(4), 315–325.

Robinson, D. (1989, May 28). Who should receive medical aid? *Parade Magazine,* pp. 4–5.

Stone, J. (1994, July). Advance directives, autonomy and unintended death. *Bioethics, 8*(3), 223–246.

United Network for Organ Sharing. (1997, March 4). UNOS facts and statistics about transplantations (On-line). Available: website http://204.127.237.11/stats.htm.

Weber, L. J. (1981). The case against euthanasia. In D. Bender (Ed.), *Problems of death: Opposing viewpoints.* St. Paul, MN: Greenhaven Press.

Weijer, C. (1995, Spring). Learning from the Dutch: Physician-assisted death, slippery slopes and the Nazi analogy. *Health Law Review, 4*(1), 23–29.

Wibecan, K. (1992, August-September). How can I be sure my living will is honored? *Modern Maturity, 35,* 73.

Wilkinson, B. W. (1995, December). The "right to die" by Russell Ogden: A commentary. *Canadian Public Policy, 21*(4), 449–455.

Winkler, E. (1995, July). Reflections on the state of current debate over physician-assisted suicide and euthanasia. *Bioethics, 9*(3, 4), 313–326.

Suggested Readings

Bouma, H., Diekema, D., Langerak, E., Rottman, T., & Verhey, A. (1989). *Christian faith, health, and medical practice.* Grand Rapids, MI: Eerdmans. This book deals with biomedical issues from multidisciplinary and Christian points of view.

Callahan, D. (1987). *Setting limits: Medical goals in an aging society.* New York: Simon and Schuster. Interesting food for thought about decisions regarding the elderly when financial resources are limited.

Chambliss, D. F. (1996). *Beyond caring: Hospitals, nurses, and the social organization of ethics.* Chicago: University of Chicago Press. Based on 10 years of field research, a sociologist gives eyewitness accounts and personal stories demonstrating how nurses turn the awesome into the routine. *Beyond Caring* shows how patients often become objects of the bureaucratic machinery of the health-care system and how ethics decisions, once the dilemma of troubled individuals, become the setting for political turf battles between occupational interest groups.

DeVries, R. A., & Subedi, J. (Eds.). (1998). *Bioethics and society: Constructing the ethical enterprise.* Prentice Hall. An anthology of sociological articles concerned with biomedical and bioethical issues.

Dickinson, G. E., Leming, M. R., & Mermann, A. C. (Eds.). (1997). *Annual editions: Dying, death, and bereavement.* Guilford, CT: Dushkin Publishing Group. This reader contains a section dealing with ethical issues related to dying and death with seven articles on the following topics: euthanasia, the right-to-die controversy, physician-assisted dying, active euthanasia, natural death, and organ transplantation.

Hoefler, J. M. (1997). *Managing death*. Boulder, CO: Westview Press. Examines the medical, legal, ethical, and clinical aspects of right-to-die issues that arise over decisions about life-sustaining medical treatment.

Horan, D. J., & Mall, D. (Eds.). (1977). *Death, dying, and euthanasia*. Washington, DC: University Publications of America. Rohr, J. (Ed.). (1987). *Death and dying: Opposing viewpoints*. St. Paul, MN: Greenhaven Press. Weir, R. F. (Ed.). (1986). *Ethical issues in death and dying*. New York: Columbia University Press. Three excellent anthologies on biomedical issues.

Humphry, D. (1991). *Final exit: The practicalities of self-deliverance and assisted suicide for the dying*. Eugene, OR: the Hemlock Society. Humphry, D. (1981). *Let me die before I wake: Hemlock's book of self-deliverance for the dying*. Los Angeles: the Hemlock Society. These books published by the Hemlock Society present a number of case studies of terminally ill individuals who chose self-deliverance as an alternative to passive euthanasia (often with the assistance of family members and friends). These books also provide methods for self-deliverance, a bibliography, and an extended discussion of personal and legal issues related to the decision to take one's life.

Tong, R. (1996). *Feminist approaches to bioethics: Theoretical reflections and practical applications*. Boulder, CO: Westview Press. Confronts the moral diversity that reveals feminism in bioethical issues.

Related Web Sites

http://www.trinity.edu/~mkearl/death-5.html#eu   An Internet resource on biomedical issues.

http://www.acusd.edu/ethics/euthanasia.html   Recent articles dealing with euthanasia and biomedical ethics (including legal and legislative summaries).

http://www.acusd.edu/~hinman/euthanasia.html   A Web site dedicated to biomedical ethics and issues of euthanasia.

http://www.yahoo.com/Society_and_Culture/Death/Euthanasia/   Yahoo's Internet euthanasia links and listings.

http://www.islandnet.com/~deathnet/open.html   DeathNET is an Internet searchable Web site containing links to many biomedical topics, including living wills, "how to" suicide, euthanasia, mercy killing, and legislation regulating care for the terminally ill.

http://www.lsds.com/death/   Thanatolinks contains links to some of the best Web sites related to dying and death.

http://www.mindspring.com/~scottr/will.html   This Web site contains the largest collection of links to living wills and other information on advance directives and living wills.

http://www.netlink.co.uk/users/vess/lwvh.html   Living wills (advance directives) and values histories help medical staff and others to make decisions about care and treatment of the seriously ill who are unable to speak for themselves. In some circumstances, living wills may become legally binding on health-care staff. The Living Will and Values History Project was set up in response to an alarming growth of living wills that bore little correlation to academic and empirical data on their usefulness or effectiveness. It works on a nonprofit basis and attempts to collate, analyze, and apply research in this area, acting as an adviser and resource base, as well as publishing its own document.

http://www.euthanasia.org/lwpdf.html On this Web site, the Living Will and Values History Project provides a free living will package that can be downloaded.

http://www.netlink.co.uk/users/vess/wfmap.html An Internet resource that provides links to right-to-die organizations worldwide.

http://www.rights.org/deathnet/KevorkianFile.html An Internet resource archive devoted to Dr. Jack Kevorkian.

http://www.islandnet.com/~deathnet/ergo.html Web site for Derek Humphry's Euthanasia Research & Guidance Organization.

http://www.netlink.co.uk/users/vess/dutch.html Web site dedicated to the issue of euthanasia as practiced in the Netherlands.

http://www.choices.org/ The Choice in Dying organization provides information to patients interested in active and passive euthanasia.

http://www.islandnet.com/~deathnet/lr_journal.html The Last Rights organization publishes electronically the complete texts of many of the key legal documents concerning the dying patient's right to die.

http://www.mcgill.pvt.k12.al.us/jerryd/cm/euthan.htm Contains euthanasia links and listings from a Roman Catholic perspective.

http://acils.com/NotDeadYet/ Americans with disabilities have a Web site to mobilize Americans against euthanasia and mercy killing. They say, "We don't want your pity or your lethal mercy."

http://www.awinc.com/partners/bc/commpass/lifenet/euthan1.htm LifeWeb provides links to Internet resources that oppose euthanasia.

http://www.iaetf.org/ International Anti-Euthanasia Task Force provides more links to Internet resources that oppose euthanasia.

http://198.68.36.114/GIB/reinv/RIS-222.html An article on the "good death" written by Allan Kellehear, School of Sociology, La Trobe University in Australia.

http://204.127.237.11/ The Web site of the United Network for Organ Sharing.

http://www.transweb.org/ TransWeb is a Web site all about transplantation and organ donation.

Chapter 9

Suicide

Suicide is a permanent answer to a temporary set of problems.
—*NBC Evening News*, March 12, 1987

There are times in life when we would like to die temporarily.
—Mark Twain

Though suicide has been around for as long as recorded history, the word suicide is of relatively recent origin. The word *suicide* is not in the Bible—or in the pamphlet by John Donne (1644) on self-homicide. The *Oxford Dictionary* states that suicide was first used in English in 1651 and is derived from the modern Latin *suicidium,* which stems from the Latin pronoun for "self" and the verb "to kill" (Farberow, 1975). Though the word *suicide* was not used, the earliest recorded suicides known to Western culture were the deaths of Samson and Saul around 1000 B.C. (Stillion & McDowell, 1991, p. 327). Two other Old Testament individuals who took their own lives were Abimilech and Achitophel. Probably one of the more famous suicides was that of Socrates by drinking hemlock.

Historically, attitudes toward suicide have been somewhat mixed. Early societies sometimes forced certain members to commit suicide for ritual purposes: Suicide was occasionally expected of the wives and slaves of husbands or masters who had died as an expression of fidelity and duty. In the ancient Roman empire, suicide was socially acceptable until slaves started to practice it. Because the suicide of slaves caused a severe financial loss, however, suicide was declared a crime against the state (McGuire & Ely, 1984). Modern Judaism, although officially regarding suicide as a sin, rests upon a long tradition of honoring "heroic" suicides to avoid being raped or forced into slavery or idol worship (Curran, 1987). From early times to the present, the Roman Catholic church has denied Catholic ritual and burial to those who take their own lives (*Codex Juris Canonici,* 1918). For Japanese kamikaze pilots in World War II, suicide represented the "great death." The Chinese regarded suicide as acceptable and honorable, particularly for defeated generals or deposed rulers (Ingram & Ellis, 1992). The New Testament records only the suicide of Judas Iscariot, but in no way is the act of taking one's own life condemned in the scriptures (Alvarez, 1971).

Attitudes toward suicide changed radically when St. Augustine, drawing heavily from the philosophy of Plato and Aristotle, laid down rules against suicide that became the basis for Christian doctrine throughout the succeeding centuries. Societal opposition to suicide in Christian communities continued throughout the Middle Ages, until the Renaissance broadened thinking on the subject. Public and private opinion, however, remained far from unanimous. Even today in the United States, attempted suicide is considered a felony in 9 states: Alabama, Kentucky, New Jersey, North and South Carolina, North and South Dakota, Oklahoma, and Washington (Curran, 1987).

Traditionally, suicide has been morally proscribed by Western culture. Calhoun and Allen (1991) note that surveys have suggested that the families in which a suicide has occurred are expected to feel shame and that individuals who commit suicide have been viewed as "crazy," mentally ill, and psychologically stressed. Yet when respondents were asked to evaluate individuals whom they knew had been bereaved by suicide, the negative stigma was less. Knowing the individual may buffer the degree of negative social reactions. In addition to the negative feelings, surviving relatives of suicide victims are thought to be more grief stricken because their loved ones willfully took their own lives (Ingram & Ellis, 1992). Calhoun and Allen (1991) conclude that although recent data indicate that society rejects suicide less today under some specific conditions, such as a terminal illness, suicide continues to be viewed as an undesirable and abnormal act. The traditional idea in the United States is that the only legally, ethically, and morally correct response to suicide is intervention, with such ethical codes being found in many helping professions and their organizations, such as the American Psychological Association (1992). Action to prevent a suicide is expected and required, based on the assumption that anyone who considers suicide is suffering from some sort of mental problem (Werth, 1995). Because suicide is still socially unacceptable, the family may lack the support systems normally available to those grieving other kinds of death—a traumatic loss is suffered, and the taboo act generates feelings of disapproval and shame (Dunn & Morrish-Vidners, 1987).

The difficulty of the stigma attached to a suicide for family members is pointed out in a study by Gibson, Range, and Anderson (1987). A vignette about the death (from either suicide or a rare disease) of an 11-year-old boy who came from either a single-parent home or a two-parent home was provided to 120 high school juniors and seniors. The suicide victim and his family were perceived more negatively than their rare disease counterparts, but knowledge that the parents were divorced

Doonesbury

BY GARRY TRUDEAU

did not interact with the cause of death to affect the respondents' impressions. A study by Range and Goggin (1990) also found that people respond more negatively to the victim and the bereaved family if the death is by suicide rather than by viral illness.

The general attitude of the public toward suicide remains confused and sometimes contradictory (Ingram & Ellis, 1992, p. 33). Extreme views on suicide range from total acceptance to total rejection of the right of an individual to commit suicide. At the heart of the debate is the question of whether people should be allowed to die without interference.

The meaning of suicide continues to be problematic. If we accept the definition of suicide as "any death resulting either from a deliberate act of self-destruction or from inaction when it is known that inaction will have fatal consequences" (Theodorson & Theodorson, 1969, p. 427), we could possibly classify the following persons as engaging in suicidal behavior:

1. A person who smokes cigarettes, knowing that the surgeon general has determined that smoking is a major cause of lung cancer
2. A race car driver who races even though he or she knows that in any given race there is a good chance that someone will be killed
3. A person who takes a bottle of sleeping pills, hoping to call attention to self as one who has personal needs that are not being met
4. A person who mistakenly takes an overdose of a prescribed drug
5. A person who continues to eat fatty foods after having suffered a heart attack
6. A person in the advanced stages of cancer who refuses chemotherapy or surgery
7. A person who overeats (or undereats) to the extreme that his or her health is directly affected
8. A person with high blood pressure who refuses to take medication to control blood pressure or fails to control food intake or to exercise
9. A person who mixes alcohol and drugs

Probably most of us would not consider the preceding list of persons as suicidal. Rather, we would be concerned with whether the person in question was intentionally trying to kill himself or herself. In classifying deaths as suicides, it is difficult to determine the motivations of a person no longer living.

There is a qualitative difference between a "suicide gesture" and a "completed suicide." Suicide gestures are motivated by a need for aid and support from others, whereas completed suicides are acts of resignation. At this point, we have a problem of tautology—suicide gestures that mistakenly end in death are classified as intentional suicides, and unsuccessful suicide attempts are considered "suicide gestures." In addition, suicides are sometimes classified as accidents or natural deaths as a favor to family members or as a method of "providing a more positive view" of the deceased. Thus, there are deaths resulting from intentional acts of self-destruction that are recorded as "natural deaths," and there are suicidal gestures accidentally ending in death that are recorded as suicide. Obviously, there are problems in compiling suicide statistics!

In recent years suicide has attracted increasing interest as a large-scale social phenomenon (Battin, 1982). Awareness of the problem of suicide has caused both increased scrutiny of the phenomenon by sociologists, psychologists, and researchers in other disciplines and increased efforts to reduce its frequency by physicians, counselors, social workers, and the police. In fact Lindsay Prior (1989, p. 11) notes that during most of this century, the study of death was the study of suicide, and that in turn was the study of social causation. Efforts to seek causes and to reduce the frequency of suicide work together. Suicide research centers and suicide prevention services have developed in recent years, and the literature on suicide has increased significantly. Even a "cookbook" on ways to commit suicide, entitled *Suicide, Its Use, History, Technique and Current Interest* by Guillon and LeBonniec, came out in France in 1982 and soon worked its way to the United States. In 1991 Derek Humphry's *Final Exit,* which tells people how to commit suicide, rose to number 1 on the *New York Times* best-sellers list. And throughout the 1990s physician-assisted suicide (discussed later in this chapter) has been a major topic of the media, an issue at the ballot boxes, and a concern in the courts.

In the United States, nearly 30,000 individuals commit suicide each year—one person every 20 minutes (Marrone, 1997, p. 60). The number of reported suicides represents only 10 or 15 percent of the people attempting suicide. Typically, the suicide rate for males peaks during adolescence and especially the elderly years, whereas the rate for females shows a gradual increase from young ages until ages 45 to 50, after which the rate gradually declines (McCall, 1991, p. 43). Suicide obviously is a major concern in the United States today.

Theoretical Perspectives on Suicide

SOCIOLOGICAL PERSPECTIVE

The most significant contribution of sociologists to the study of suicide has been the sociological perspective itself—the insistence on seeing suicidal actions as in some way the result of social factors (Douglas, 1967, p. 158). Suicidal persons construct their meanings of suicide and motivations for committing it out of collective values upon which the social structure rests. What constitutes suicide and why it happens at all are both understood through the meanings conferred on it by various persons. Thus, meanings of suicide arise out of what people think, feel, and do about it rather than out of what is simply given in the act. What people think, feel, and do about acts defined as suicide are intertwined with larger social values and meanings (Charmaz, 1980, p. 234).

A comprehensive sociological theory of self-destruction was proposed in 1897 by the noted French sociologist Emile Durkheim in his book entitled *Suicide: A Study in Sociology* (1951). The most frequent interpretation of Durkheim's *Suicide* by American sociologists involves the following propositions (Douglas, 1967, pp. 39–40):

1. The structural factors cause certain degrees and certain patterns of social interaction.
2. The degrees and patterns of social interaction then cause a certain degree of "social integration."
3. "Social integration," defined as either states of individuals or as a state of the society, is then defined as the "strength of the individual's ties to society."
4. The "strength of ties" is then defined either in terms of egoism, altruism, and anomie, or else the "strength of ties" is hypothesized to be the cause of the given degrees of egoism, altruism, and anomie.
5. "Egoism" is defined as a relative lack of social or collective activity that gives meaning and object to life; "altruism" is defined as a relatively great amount of social activity; and "anomie" is defined as a relative lack of social activity that acts to constrain the individual's passions, which, without constraint, increase "infinitely."
6. And, finally, the given balance of the degrees of egoism, altruism, and anomie is hypothesized to be the cause of the given suicide rate of the given society.

Thus, the 3 types of Durkheim's suicide just noted are related to his conception of social integration. Two recent time-series analyses of sociological and economic variables accounting for suicide rates in the United States give somewhat mixed findings to Durkheim's theory. One study of the United States from 1940 to 1984 by Bijou Yang (1992) concluded that economic growth seemed to have a beneficial impact on male suicide rates, yet a detrimental impact on female suicide rates. This means that the suicide rates did not increase during the economic booms and busts as predicted by Durkheim. The impact depended on the social group involved. Durkheim had posited that because economic prosperity and depression bring about less social integration and less social regulation than do normal economic situations, the suicide rate rises accordingly. Another time-series study by Yang, Lester, and Yang (1992) of the United States from 1952 to 1984 revealed that the economic variables of gross national product per capita and the unemployment rate contributed significantly to the suicide rate, as did the social variables of divorce rate and female participation in the labor force. Thus, social processes that have been presumed to decrease social integration appear to be associated with a higher suicide rate.

Durkheim's main point was that, although we think of suicide as a supremely individual and personal act, it also has a social and nonindividual aspect. For example, different types of society produce different rates of suicide. **Egoistic suicide** occurs when persons are inadequately integrated into the society, such as intellectuals or persons whose talents or stations in life place them into a special category (celebrities or stars) and who therefore are less likely to be linked to society in conventional ways.

Altruistic suicide happens when individuals are overly integrated into the society (an exaggerated concern for the community) and are willing to die for the group, like kamikaze pilots of World War II or terrorists of today. **Anomic suicide** results from the lack of regulation of individuals when the norms governing existence no longer control those individuals (feel let down by the failure of social institutions), such as business people who commit suicide after a stock market crash or middle-aged individuals who kill themselves after suddenly losing their jobs because of downsizing.

As Talcott Parsons (1949) interpreted *Suicide,* Durkheim considered altruistic suicide to be largely the result of the external forces of group structure. Egoistic suicide was seen to be more a result of the internal forces of the "collective conscience." Anomic suicide was seen as almost entirely the result of the internal forces of the "collective conscience."

A fourth type, called **fatalistic suicide,** was introduced by Durkheim and has recently received more attention. This type suggests that a person may receive too much control by society and feel oppressed under extremely strict rules. In fatalistic suicide, one dies in despair of being able to make it in a society allowing little opportunity for satisfaction or individual fulfillment. Both the altruistic and the fatalistic suicide involve excessive control of the individual by society (Kastenbaum, 1995, p. 244). Extreme examples of such control would be living in slavery or under totalitarian rule.

DRAMATURGICAL PERSPECTIVE

Derived from the general approach of symbolic interactionism, the **dramaturgical perspective** highlights the construction of action and its context by using the metaphor of the drama to explain behavior. Such a perspective is not unlike the "psychological autopsy," which is a procedure for the reconstruction of suicidal death through interviews with survivors (Beskow & Asgard, 1990, p. 307). Rather than inquire into the definition of the situation, the dramaturgical analyst emphasizes the definition of the situation that seems apparent in the event. When someone commits suicide, this approach would look at how family members acted afterward and would assess the meaning of the death to the family members as it is visible in what they actually do, rather than what they might say about it to an interviewer. This approach tends to take nonverbal behavior into account.

A dramaturgical approach does not accept the social determinist view that social forces motivate the individual to act, but rather it believes that motives are invoked by social actors as a way of explaining or accounting for past actions (Charmaz, 1980, pp. 26–31). Behavior is analyzed from the standpoint of the observer (**etic approach**) rather than from the subjective meanings of participants (**emic approach**). Whereas the dramaturgical analyst emphasizes action, the symbolic interactionist emphasizes intention. Both perspectives lead to an examination of meanings derived from interaction.

A good example of the dramaturgical approach is the film entitled *But Jack Was a Good Driver.* In this film Jack, a high school student, has died in a single-car accident. As his two friends walk away from the cemetery, they begin to recall recent events involving Jack. As they describe the actions of Jack in recent weeks, he had flunked a chemistry exam, broken up with his girlfriend, given away his CD collection, and acted in ways out of the ordinary for Jack. They conclude that Jack's "accident" was more likely a suicide (Jack was a good driver and could have negotiated that curve had he so desired) because his actions of recent weeks showed some signs of suicide. The observers (Jack's friends) viewed the actions of the actor (Jack)—the dramaturgical approach.

EXISTENTIALIST PERSPECTIVE

Existentialist philosophy acknowledges that human existence is finite and that we all must face death. One must assume responsibility for his or her own actions and must be responsible for moral choices and actions. An emphasis is placed on the anticipation of death and the effects of that anticipation on everyday life, thus causing one to come to an understanding of how death and life are linked. From an existentialist view, it is conceivable that the confrontation with death during a suicidal crisis may cause suicidal individuals to sense their aloneness and personal responsibility for their experience. Thus, the choice of death may be fully akin to the choice of life—both the result of reflection. Death through suicide or any other means is not the enemy that it is in other perspectives (Charmaz, 1980, p. 242).

Existentialism is linked with the phenomenological method of inquiry. This method starts with an examination of the point of view of the experiencing person—from an emic perspective. Experience is studied from the inside—from what it appears to be to the involved person. What is dying to those who are experiencing it? This method tries to study the phenomenon directly and to discover how it is constituted. In studying attempted suicide, one would conduct interviews with persons having attempted suicide to determine what they were thinking during their crisis. By comparing patterns one can determine parallels between the suicidal experiences of these individuals (Charmaz, 1980, pp. 51–56).

ALIENATION

An individual may feel alienated if he or she does not feel in control of a situation. **Alienation** is a state of consciousness resulting from a concrete relationship between human beings and their products. Karl Marx noted that laborers are separated or alienated from nature itself, capitalism separates workers from each other, and capitalism produces a separation of the workers from their work. The realization of human potential and creativity is prevented, according to Marx. Thus, alienation results in a loss of self or a lack of self-realization.

A sense of powerlessness may result, leading to hopelessness over time, then a feeling of helplessness (Charmaz, 1980, p. 260). Individuals may not be wholly aware of their alienation and may feel frustrated, worthless, dependent, and powerless without connecting their feeling to the social structure. A worker on an assembly line, for example, performing the same task over and over again for 8 hours, is more likely to feel alienated than would a craftsperson who takes a raw material in hand and creates a finished product. Such feelings are likely to be intensified by the individuals' acceptance that their feelings reflect who they are and what they may become. Such assessments may lead to feelings of hopelessness. Alienation may, therefore, lead to suicide.

This woman contemplates suicide as a solution to her feelings of alienation and social isolation. Her suicide gesture elicits a response from another to indicate the meaningfulness of her life.

As noted from the preceding theoretical perspectives on suicide, the "whys" of suicide are not always easy to explain. For the survivors of a completed suicide, guilt is often associated with the event. The survivors may feel that they have contributed to the suicide and that "if only" they had acted differently, it might not have happened.

Social Factors, Signs, and Methods of Suicide

SOCIAL FACTORS OF SUICIDE

The relationship between suicide and variables associated with suicide is not simple and easily understood. Nonetheless, some of the variables associated with suicide include age, gender, marital status, and socioeconomic level (Kastenbaum & Aisenberg, 1976, pp. 252–271). As noted elsewhere in this chapter, suicide is rare in childhood, rises sharply during adolescence and early adulthood, and peaks with elderly persons. Suicide could be described as a masculine type of behavior because males have a higher rate of completed suicides than females. A study (Taylor, 1990) conducted by Cornell University Medical School revealed that men infected with AIDS were 36 times more likely than average males to commit suicide. The same study also found that AIDS patients were far more likely to choose to end their lives than were men with other fatal diseases. Elisabeth Kübler-Ross (1987) suggested that the motivation of many people with AIDS to consider suicide is to avoid enduring their painful feelings of despair, isolation, and discrimination and the ravaging deterioration that they have seen among their friends. Indeed, a study of 44 terminally ill patients (Brown et al., 1986) concluded that patients with a terminal illness who are not mentally ill are no more likely than the general population to wish for premature death.

Regarding marital status, the suicide rate is lower for the married than for those never married, and highest for the widowed, divorced, and separated. Individuals with children commit suicide less than childless individuals. These data on marital and parental status fit Durkheim's theory that suicide is a function of social integration.

Suicide rates tend to be highest at both extremes of the socioeconomic ladder. Certain professions such as physicians, dentists, and lawyers tend to be particularly suicide prone, whereas the suicide rates of teachers and clergy are rather low.

There is also a difference in suicide rates between blacks and whites in the United States. Suicide rates among blacks are substantially lower than among whites—9 blacks versus 16.7 whites per 100,000 population annually (McIntosh, 1995). The suicide rate for Native Americans has been reported to be greater than the national average, 18.1 per 100,000 (McIntosh, 1995); however, rates have been found to vary greatly from reservation to reservation (Ellis & Range, 1989). Suicide among Native Americans tends to be more frequently alcohol related, and violent methods (firearms and hanging) are more commonly used than in the mainstream U.S. population (May, 1990, p. 200).

More suicides occur in heterogeneous urban areas than in more homogeneous rural areas. Though nostalgic times like the latter part of December are thought to have high suicide rates, the "renewal of life" times like spring have consistently had the highest rates for suicide. Autumn has the second most suicides, followed by winter and then summer. Monday and Tuesday are nearly always the highest days for suicides, with Wednesday, Thursday, Friday, and Sunday lower. The lowest risk of all is on Saturdays (McIntosh, 1995, pp. 339–340). The highest rate of suicide is found in the Jewish faith; Protestant faiths have higher rates than Catholics (Oaks & Ezell, 1993, p. 217). Contrary to popular belief, suicide occurrence does not vary by lunar phase (Maldonado & Kraus, 1991, p. 186).

SIGNS OF SUICIDE

People who commit suicide tend to talk about their attempt prior to the act. A person should be taken seriously if he or she repeatedly talks of suicide. Other than outright stating, "I am going to kill myself," more subtle verbal clues might include such statements as, "I'm not the person I used to be," "You would be better off without me," "I can't stand it anymore," "Life has lost its meaning for me," and "Nobody needs me anymore."

Behavioral clues might include giving away valued personal possessions, getting one's house in order as if ready for departure, crying frequently without explanation, changing daily behavior, such as beginning to take long walks at night, having poor sleeping habits, having loss of appetite, not being able to concentrate, making a sudden change in appearance, showing a sudden shift in the quality of school work, and suddenly withdrawing from various organizations. The following factors tend to describe an individual at high risk of committing suicide: lethal weapon readily available, history of prior suicide attempts, detailed suicide plan, feelings of hopelessness and helplessness, severe personal loss such as health problems or bereavement, alcohol or drug abuse, and problems at school, work, in relationships, or with finances (Oaks & Ezell, 1993, p. 215).

METHODS OF COMMITTING SUICIDE

Listed in decreasing order of frequency are the ways of committing suicide in the United States: shooting with firearms (especially handguns), overdosing on drugs (most often those prescribed by physicians), cutting and stabbing, jumping from high places, inhaling toxic gas, hanging, and drowning (Oaks & Ezell, 1993, p. 218). Whereas women *attempt* suicide more often, men more often *complete* suicide. Because men are more likely to use firearms in suicide attempts and women more likely to use drugs, this obviously contributes to the higher "success" rate of males in suicide.

Childhood Suicidal Behavior

Suicidal deaths are virtually nonexistent before age 5 and are rare in the age group of 5 to 9 years. Indeed, very little research on suicidal children under the age of 5 can be found, perhaps because early infancy research does not focus, in the main, on suicide (McGuire & Ely, 1984, p. 21). The policy of the U.S. Division of Vital Statistics is to not even report the deaths of children under age 8 as suicides, regardless of what data may have been entered on a given death certificate—"other and unknown and unspecified causes" are the classifications used for these deaths. Suicide is similarly uncommon in the cohort of children between the ages of 10 and 14 (Smith, 1985, p. 103).

Adults prefer to believe that children do not commit suicide, notes Israel Orbach (1988). It seems inconceivable that children could become so desperate at their young age that they could choose death over life. Adults may also have the false perception that childhood is a carefree, happy time. Perhaps these perceptions account for the unique conclusion of a U.S. county coroner who stated that any death of a child under 14 should be regarded as accidental, even when a suicide note is left behind (Orbach, 1988, p. 23).

As with many other suicides, child suicides are easily mistaken for accidents. The causes of death themselves involve an element of chance: traffic accidents (sometimes running into traffic), falls (jumping?) from high places, fatalities in handling guns, or drowning (Orbach, 1988, p. 25). The fact that young children do not write suicide notes compounds this difficulty because notes are a chief category of evidence that coroners use to verify suicide (McGuire & Ely, 1984, p. 19).

The role of family seems to play a major part in suicide attempts of children. A study of 8- to 13-year-old psychiatric inpatients and suicide attempts (Asarnow & Carlson, 1988) found strong support for a link between suicide attempts in children and perceptions of low family support. Likewise, another study (Garfinkel, Froese, & Hood, 1982) of 505 children and adolescents who made 605 attempts to commit suicide and were admitted to an emergency room (as compared with a control group of another 505 persons admitted and matched by sex and similar age) concluded that

How You Can Help in a Suicidal Crisis

1. *Recognize the clues to suicide.* Look for signs of hopelessness and helplessness. Listen for suicide threats and words of warning. Notice if the person becomes withdrawn and isolated.
2. *Trust your own judgment.* If you believe that someone is in danger of suicide, act on your beliefs. Don't ignore the signs of suicide.
3. *Tell others.* Share knowledge with parents, friends, teachers, employers, or other people who might help. If you have to betray a secret to save a life, do it. Don't worry about breaking a confidence if someone's suicidal plans are revealed to you.
4. *Stay with a suicidal person.* Don't leave a suicidal person alone if you think there is immediate danger. Stay until help arrives or the crisis has passed.
5. *Listen.* Encourage a suicidal person to talk. Don't give false reassurances that "everything will be okay." Listen and sympathize with what the person says.
6. *Urge professional help.* Offer to make an appointment for and go with the person for professional help, if that is what it takes. Call your community hotline or crisis number for suggestions.
7. *Be supportive.* Show the person that you care. Help to make the person feel worthwhile and wanted.

Adapted from *Youth and Suicide* (p. 96), by F. Klagsbrun, 1976, New York: Pocket Books.

family disintegration played a significant part in these families where suicides were attempted. Children with one or more family members who have committed suicide are at higher risk of attempting suicide than are children who do not have this family history; this is true regardless of the degree of closeness that the children had with the suicidal family members (Gutierrez, King, & Ghaziuddin, 1996).

Though the suicide rate among children is not high, a study of junior high school children (Domino, Domino, & Berry, 1987) indicates that over 20 percent have "seriously thought about suicide" and that a slightly higher percentage have personally known someone who committed suicide. The Suicide Prevention Center of Los Angeles, in its work with children and adolescents in crisis (Peck, 1980), estimates that 50 percent of the deaths reported as accidents in the groups they studied are, in reality, unreported suicides. Thus, the state of reporting suicides and attempts of children and adolescents is filled with inconsistencies, confusion, and concealment.

Adolescent Suicidal Behavior

The age group beginning with age 15, however, marks a noticeable shift in suicide rates. For example, every 90 minutes one teenager in the United States will take his or her own life, and every 9 minutes a teenager will attempt to kill himself or herself

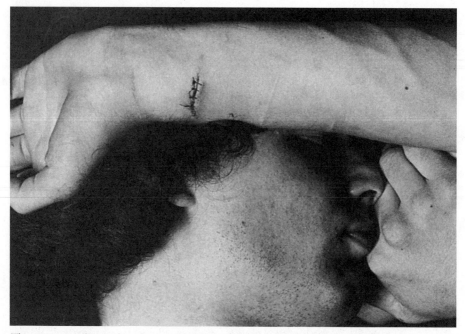

This young man has cut his wrist in a suicide gesture. His problems are now compounded by the fact that he must live with the stigma of a failed suicide attempt.

(Coleman, 1987, p. 1). Adolescent and young adult suicide is not unique to contemporary times, but the significance of the problem has recently emerged in the United States, especially since 1950. In recent years, cluster suicides (discussed later in this chapter) have certainly called attention of the media to suicide and have caused parents and educational personnel to be even more aware of suicides.

The suicide rates for adolescents and young adults between the ages of 15 and 24 increased approximately 250 percent from 1950 to 1980 (Osgood & McIntosh, 1986). The suicide rate for this age group in 1950 was 4.5 per 100,000; by the end of the 1980s, however, the rate was 12.9 (Fulton & Metress, 1995). These numbers could reflect a greater willingness today to report a death as a suicide. The "taboo" nature of identifying suicide is not as significant today as in 1950. Suicide is now the third-leading cause of death in this age group (following accidents and homicides) (McIntosh, 1995, p. 336). Since 1980, however, the number of deaths by suicide among teenagers has begun to level off, possibly because of a decline in the use of mind-altering drugs and an increase in attention given to children at risk of taking their own lives (Brody, 1987, p. 16).

Accidents and homicides are viewed by many researchers as disguised suicides (Coleman, 1987, p. 1). Many drug overdoses, fatal automobile accidents, and related self-destructive food and alcohol disorders are likely uncounted teen suicides. Thus, the total number of adolescent suicides may be greater than reported. The most commonly identified correlates of suicidal behaviors are depressive symptoms, social problems, family disorganization and problems, life stress, and poor problem-solving skills, notes Carol Garrison (1989, p. 129). Overall, identity crises and mood fluctuations are significant psychological risk factors for suicide among adolescents, according to Stillion and McDowell (1991, p. 343). In Conrad's study (1992) comparing 11th and 12th graders who reported suicidal behavior with those who did not, 93 percent of those who reported suicidal behavior also knew a friend, family member, or acquaintance who had attempted suicide. On the other hand, only 50 percent of the students in the sample who did not report suicidal behavior knew someone who had attempted suicide. Likewise, Gutierrez, King, and Ghaziuddin (1996), in a study of adolescent attitudes about death in relation to suicide, concluded that adolescents experiencing the suicide of a friend or immediate family member or exposed to attempted suicide reported a weaker attraction to life and a stronger attraction to death than did adolescents lacking this experience.

Geographically, Nevada is first in youth suicides, and New Mexico is second. In taking their own lives, boys tend to use violent means such as shooting and hanging, though girls seem to be turning to violent means also (Brozan, 1986). Perhaps by using violent means these adolescents are suggesting that they indeed are serious about their "attempts." It is more than a "cry for help." Warning signs of suicide in adolescence include self-mutilation (for example, tattooing oneself with a penknife), changes in habits, truancy, behavior that implies preparation for death (for example, giving away valuable possessions), and poor school performance (Stillion & McDowell, 1991, p. 345).

Suicides of young individuals are especially difficult to understand because these people are just "growing up" and beginning to launch out into the world. On the other hand, with the frustrations of adolescence and growing up and making the transitions to adulthood, often being expected to "act like an adult" and at times being "not old enough" for certain behaviors, it is no wonder that the suicide rate in this age group is so high. Suicide becomes an available solution to one's problems. When stress is experienced, a constricted view of future possibilities and a momentary fix on present escapes may hold sway. Impulsive action and limited alternative problem solving may turn suicidal fantasies into suicidal behaviors. As noted at the beginning of this chapter, suicide is an answer (though permanent) to a set of temporary problems. The problem is gone, but so is life.

The following letter (Berman, 1986, p. 151), written by a 17-year-old who took his life, apparently indicates that death was "the solution" to this adolescent's dilemmas of life. He lived with various problems but tended to keep his pain mostly to himself.

> Dear Mom, Dad, and everyone else,
>
> I'm sorry for what I've done, but I love you all and I always will, for eternity. Please, please, please don't blame it on yourselves. It was all my fault and not yours or anyone else's. If I didn't do this now, I would have done it later anyway. We all die some day, I just died sooner.
>
> Love,
> John

After John's body was found, people began to piece together his life and were filled with the inevitable "if onlys." This reconstruction of an interpretation after the event of suicide follows the dramaturgical approach, as discussed earlier.

Heaven's Gate: An Example of Mass Suicide
Ernest G. Rigney

The suicide of an individual can have a devastating effect on his or her immediate family or friends. Psychiatrists and clinical psychologists can, quite appropriately, attempt to understand an individual's self-inflicted demise. However, as Durkheim (1951) cogently demonstrated, suicide rates, cluster suicides, and mass suicides have their unfortunate provenance in sociology—not psychiatry or psychology.

On the morning of March 25, 1997, an on-again-off-again member of the Heaven's Gate "UFO cult" discovered the bodies of 39 former congregants elaborately entombed in a mansion located at Rancho Santa Fe, San Diego, California. In the aftermath of this discovery, the most pressing questions were: Who were these people? Who or what led them to do this? The most obvious and quickest answers were provided courtesy of the Internet, television, and the print medium: "Charismatic leader(s) and a bunch of losers—each and every one."

However, upon closer "sociological" scrutiny, the "loser" designation appears to fit uneasily. The median age of the suicide victims was 40. They were adults; that is, the "victims" were not impressionable young people—most of the members of Heaven's Gate had families and were pursuing

(continued)

Daniel Bell (1977) found that college students in the mid-1970s viewed suicidal peers as "cowardly, sick, unpleasant, and disreputable" and were much more negative in their attitudes toward peers who attempted suicide and lived than toward those who completed suicide. Thus, in the eyes of one's college-aged peers, at least over 2 decades ago, the individual is better off to not fail in his or her efforts to commit suicide.

Because adolescents are caught between childhood and adulthood, the often intense and conflictual task of separating from the world of family can be more difficult when family dynamics interfere with children's move toward self-sufficiency (Berman, 1986, p. 157). Parents of suicidal adolescents have been found to experience more overt conflict, threats of separation and divorce, and loss of a parent occurring prior to the children's twelfth year. Suicidal adolescents report receiving little affection, hold negative views of their parents, describe time spent in their family as unenjoyable, have deficient problem-solving skills, tend to have more prevalent use of drugs and alcohol, and see themselves as different than their parents. Results of a study of 8- to 13-year-old psychiatric inpatients (Asarnow & Carlson, 1988) provide strong support for a link between suicide attempts in children and perceptions of low family support. Suicidal behavior in childhood appears to be more closely associated with family turmoil and stress than is suicidal behavior in later life.

Active peer involvement may be the support that one needs to discourage suicidal behavior. Being involved with peers is negatively correlated with a depressive mood in adolescence. Suicidal adolescents tend to show greater withdrawal from, and less involvement with, the school milieu. On the other hand, suicidal adolescents tend

(continued from previous page)
productive and useful jobs or careers. Heaven's Gate was not a new organization. The putative leaders—Marshall Applewhite and Bonnie Nettles—had been recruiting followers since the 1970s. Their message was an eclectic syncretism of Christian apocalypticism, New Age mysticism, and science fiction. Apparently this brew whetted the appetites of certain people—especially "baby boomers" who were endlessly searching for some sort of spiritual ballast in the wake of the 1960s. An organization that promised androgynous members a space ride to heaven may have been appealing; but, and this is an important question: Was Heaven's Gate all that strange?

Despite their rather diverse menagerie with diverse motivations, Applewhite and Nettles presented a twisted, yet seemingly coherent, "Christian" message: namely, by maintaining strong beliefs in an afterlife; by refraining from indulgences in tobacco, alcohol, and sex; then, and only then, would they inherit the "Kingdom of Heaven." Is this truly a strange or aberrant theology? Granted, those who believe in a "God" may not think of resurrection in terms of a ride in a "spaceship," or they may question the "spiritual" appropriateness of suicide; but, was Heaven's Gate so radically different from mainstream religious denominations? If so, how?

E. G. Rigney is associate professor of sociology at the College of Charleston in Charleston, SC.

to have more frequent and serious problems with peers, to be more interpersonally sensitive, and to be less likely to have a close confidant (Berman, 1986, p. 159). Adolescents are especially vulnerable to rejections from their peer group (Rich et al., 1991). Because adolescents are highly suggestible individuals, suicidal adolescents are highly vulnerable to influence because they often lack reinforcing role models and may be low in self-esteem and ego strength. Thus, suicidal behavior by one may lead to an epidemic of followers.

THE MEDIA AND SUICIDE CLUSTERS

A **suicide cluster** is an excessive number of suicides occurring in close temporal and geographical proximity and most closely approximates the concept of an "outbreak" in a particular community (Gould, Wallenstein, & Davidson, 1989, p. 17). Philip May (1990), in compiling a bibliography on suicide among American Indians, concluded that suicide clusters among particular groups of youths tend to take on epidemic form in many Indian communities. Suicide clusters among teenagers have been noted in the media, and imitation is generally cited as the "cause." Cluster suicides account for between 1 and 5 percent of all youth suicides in the United States (Fulton & Metress, 1995, p. 414).

Madelyn Gould and David Shaffer (1986) studied the variation in the numbers of suicides and attempted suicides by teenagers in the greater New York area 2 weeks before and 2 weeks after 4 fictional films were broadcast on television in the autumn and winter of 1984 and 1985. The number of suicide attempts in the period after the broadcasts was significantly greater than the number before the broadcasts, leading the researchers to conclude that some teenage suicides are imitative.

Another study, by David Phillips and Lundie Carstensen (1986), examined the relation between 38 nationally televised news or feature stories about suicide from 1973 to 1979 and the fluctuation of the rate of suicide among American teenagers before and after these broadcasts. The observed number of suicides by teenagers within 7 days after these broadcasts was significantly greater than the number expected. The more networks carrying a story on suicide, the greater was the increase in suicides thereafter. Teenage suicides increased more than adult suicides after stories about suicide. An extensive review of suicide clusters by Gould, Wallenstein, and Davidson (1989) confirms that temporal and geographical clusters of suicides occur, that they appear to be multidetermined, and that they appear to be primarily a phenomenon of youth. Imitation and identification are factors hypothesized to increase the likelihood of cluster suicides.

With the suicide of Kurt Cobain, some individuals feared that large numbers of copycat teen suicides would occur (Waters, 1994). However, it was noted that those apt to copy the rock star are those who already have significant emotional problems. Those individuals with low self-esteem and self-identify tend to get hooked on heroes and are more likely to fall into the same self-destructive behavior.

Though the preceding findings certainly suggest a correlation between media broadcasts on suicide and increased suicide clusters among adolescents, this is not to suggest that such media exposure "causes" an overall increased rate of suicides. Indeed, viewers previously thinking of suicide might be persuaded one way or the other after watching television programs on suicide. Those who do kill themselves are more likely to have made a previous attempt at suicide, to have lost a close friend or relative to violent death, or to have suffered a recent breakup with a girlfriend or boyfriend (Fulton & Metress, 1995, p. 414).

For nonsuicidal persons as a group, however, the impact may be somewhat different. For example, in exposing university students to films on suicide and violence, 1 study (Biblarz et al., 1991, p. 382) concluded that there was no reason to believe that nonsuicidal young people as a group will view suicide in a more positive light as a result of watching movies with suicidal or violent content. However, exposure to suicide films appears to have increased viewers' arousal levels significantly, if only temporarily.

Studies of the effect of the media on suicide have neglected the audience receptivity to suicide stories, notes Steven Stack (1992). Thus, Stack set out to test the thesis from symbolic interaction theory that the degree of media influence is contingent on audience receptivity. He developed a taxonomy of stories from the Great Depression using the years 1933–1939 (1933 being the first year for which suicide data were collected for the nation as a whole). Stack hypothesized that the economic context of the nation's worst economic depression of the 20th century would increase the effect of the media on suicide—the economic collapse would promote a suicidal mood of depression, disrupted family organization, and other psychosocial processes thought to underlie suicide risk. However, there was no overall impact of suicide stories on suicide. The only significant relationship found by Stack to be associated with increases in the suicide rate was publicized stories about suicides by political heroes.

Suicide and the Elderly

Throughout the rest of the world (Moscicki, 1995), as well as in the United States, a much greater percentage of elderly people commit suicide than of any other age group (Brown, 1996). It is estimated that 15 percent of the general population in Western societies are 65 and older, yet this group commits up to 30 percent of all known suicides (Adamek & Kaplan, 1996).

Suicide in the elderly may be even more prevalent than the statistics suggest, note researchers Butler, Lewis, and Sunderland (1991), because: (a) Intentional overdoses of prescribed medications may go unrecognized or unreported. (b) Older persons may commit "chronic" or "passive" suicide whereby they lose the will to live and simply stop caring for themselves. (c) They may cease taking medications, take increased health risks, or delay treatment for medical conditions. (d) They may slowly stop drinking and eating until they become sick and die.

The suicide rate of persons aged 65 and over rose 8.5 percent from 1980 to 1992, according to the *Morbidity and Mortality Weekly Report's* "Suicide Among Older Persons" (1996). In the 3 decades before 1980, the elderly suicide rate exhibited a decreasing trend and decreased 42 percent between 1950 and 1980 (Osgood & McIntosh, 1986). Some sociologists and psychologists have proposed that the increased suicide rate among the elderly may be due to technological advances that extend the lives of the elderly and result in intolerable quality of life and/or medical treatments of ailing older patients that result in the depletion of family savings (Tolchin, 1989). In addition, the increased suicide rate among the elderly may result from social isolation and society's growing acceptance of suicide ("Suicide Rate," 1996). Our society also places great value on youth, health, and beauty; this ageist view adds to the sense of worthlessness that some elderly persons experience (Devons, 1996).

Age by itself does not cause suicidality. The person statistically most likely to commit suicide in the United States, however, is the white male over the age of 85 (Devons, 1996). The traditional, assertive, achievement-oriented, middle-aged male may not be as adaptable to the retirement situation as the traditionally more passive, nurturant, middle-aged woman. Thus, the greater change in behavior and self-esteem necessitated in the older man may create more stress and depression if he is unable to find satisfaction in this new situation. A greater potential for suicidal behavior results (Aiken, 1991, p. 72).

GENDER AND SUICIDE IN THE ELDERLY

In the United States, men commit 81 percent of suicides among the elderly ("Suicide Rate," 1996). Because gender is one of the most important predictors of suicide in the elderly, Silvia Canetto (1992) has addressed the question of why older women are less suicidal than older men. She suggests that women are less likely to die of suicide because they are more likely to seek professional help. Suicidal behavior in the elderly has been attributed to poverty, yet older women are more likely to be poor but less likely to be suicidal than older men. Canetto surmises that for many women, limited access to financial resources has been a long-standing problem, whereas for many men limited access to financial resources is less common until retirement. Thus, financial difficulties for older men may be a new experience.

Though living alone is frequently assumed to be a precipitant of suicidal behavior among the elderly, older women are more likely to live alone than older men. However, living alone may be more normative for older women, and older men living alone tend to be more isolated than older women living alone, concludes Canetto.

Though widowhood is a predictor of suicide in both women and men, the effect seems to be stronger for men than for women. Canetto observes that older men are more likely to depend on their wives for emotional support than vice versa because older women appear to have more emotional connections with friends than do older men. Older men depend on their wives for their personal care and the running of the home. Losing a spouse may thus disrupt social support and emotional functioning more for a man than for a woman.

Although older men have a much higher suicide rate than older women, between 1979 and 1992 data from the National Center for Health Statistics revealed an increasing trend in rates of suicide for women over the age of 65 (Adamek & Kaplan, 1996). During this period of time, shooting replaced poisoning as the most prevalent method of suicide by women 65 and over.

DANGER SIGNALS AND METHODS OF SUICIDE

The *threat* of suicide is uncommon in the elderly—they simply kill themselves, and their attempts rarely fail. When an elderly person makes an attempt at suicide, he or she usually has a profound death wish and thus selects ways that are likely to fulfill that wish. Recent studies have revealed that suicide is rarely an impulsive act unheralded by any warning signs but rather as a rule is an act that can be anticipated. It has been estimated that 75 percent of elderly individuals contemplating suicide consult their physicians only shortly before committing the act (Achte, 1988, p. 63). However, physicians apparently do not typically bring up suicide with the elderly, as noted by a recent Gallup survey (1993). In a survey of 802 Americans age 60 and older who lived independently Gallup found that, during their last physical examination, only 6 percent had been asked about depressed, suicidal thoughts.

Kalle Achte (1988) states that loneliness is the great tragedy of aging. Old age has been called "the era of losses" (Achte, 1988, p. 58). After each loss, an elderly person has to try to pull himself or herself together and to adjust in order to be able to retain psychological equilibrium. Losses for the elderly may include jobs, social status, health, independence, friends, and family (Osgood, Brant, & Lipman, 1991). These losses may result in stress at a time when the individual is least able to cope. If there is no possibility of communication with other people, loneliness can become extremely distressing for the older individual.

Robert Kastenbaum (1992, p. 2) agrees that the reduced likelihood of open and substantive communication contributes to the possibility of suicide in the elderly. Kastenbaum notes that the following tend to reduce communication channels for the elderly: (a) Living alone reduces the opportunities to express and explain suicidal intent to a caring person; (b) residing in a low-income, transient urban area tends to make a person socially invisible; (c) the depressive state often associated with suicidality frequently has the effect of reducing communication; and (d) the fact that most suicides in old age are committed by men suggests that reluctance to seek help may be strongest among those elderly who are at greatest risk.

Though some danger signals for suicide among the elderly have already been noted, a list of all such signals would include depression, withdrawal, bereavement (especially within the last year), isolation, expectation of death from some cause, retirement, loss of independence, physical illness, desire and rational decision to protect survivors from financial disaster, philosophical decision (no more pleasure or purpose in life), decreased self-esteem, and organic mental deterioration (Eddy & Alles, 1983, pp. 169–171).

The elderly employ the same methods of suicide as do other age groups: shooting, taking drugs, hanging, and jumping are the most common methods. Subtler means such as not eating, not taking medication, drinking too much, delaying medical treatment, or taking physical risks are also used (Oaks & Ezell, 1993, p. 226). Sometimes the elderly will "give up" psychologically, and this triggers biological changes that increase potential for disease.

A recent National Institutes of Mental Health study (Hohmann & Larson, 1993) found that an elderly person with a severe mental health problem is more likely to seek the help of clergy than the aid of a mental health specialist. Because 80 percent of the elderly are members of a church or synagogue and over half (52 percent) worship at least once a week (Gallup, 1994), both clergy and the larger religious community may have an effective means to help those elderly in distress (Weaver & Koenig, 1996). More than 50 studies in the past 15 years demonstrate a strong association between faith practices (for example, regular church attendance, Bible reading, and prayer) and mental health among older persons, according to Andrew Weaver and Harold Koenig (1996). Older persons who practice their faith frequently have lower rates of depression, alcoholism, and hopelessness (Koenig, 1994).

Joseph Richman (1992) says that there is a great publicity campaign in favor of the view that suicide is a rational response to growing old. Though many elderly suicidal persons have severe problems in accepting their age, many of them have revealed similar problems in self-acceptance throughout their lives, and many felt "old" at age 15, notes Richman. The decision to commit suicide does not arise overnight, but rather is part of a lengthy process during which the significance of the individual's entire existence has been called into question. In working with over 800 suicidal persons, many of whom were elderly, ill, or terminal, Richman (1992, p. 134) says, "I can state unequivocally that suicide is not a rational response to aging."

Physician-Assisted Suicide

As previously noted, the issue of active euthanasia and **physician-assisted suicide** has been highlighted in the media during the 1990s. Dr. Jack Kevorkian's "death machine" in Michigan has received numerous headlines. In 1991 the voters of Washington state defeated Initiative 119 (54 percent to 46 percent), which would have legalized physician-assisted suicide. Also in 1991, as noted earlier, Derek Humphry's *Final Exit,* providing detailed information on how to "self-deliver," went on the market and became a best-seller. The *New England Journal of Medicine* published Dr. Timothy Quill's experience of assisting his patient "Diane" by prescribing barbiturates after she refused treatment options for leukemia in 1991 (see abridged version following).

My Patient's Suicide
Dr. Timothy Quill

Diane was feeling tired and had a rash. Her hematocrit was 22, and her white-cell count was 4.3 with some metamyelocytes and unusual white cells. I called Diane and told her it might be serious. When she pressed for the possibilities, I reluctantly opened the door to leukemia. Hearing the word seemed to make it exist. "Oh, shit!" she said. "Don't tell me that." I thought, I wish I didn't have to.

Diane was raised in an alcoholic family and had felt alone for much of her life. She had vaginal cancer as a young woman, and had struggled with depression, and her own alcoholism for most of her adult life. I had come to know, respect, and admire her over the previous 8 years as she confronted and gradually overcame these problems. During the previous three and a half years, she had abstained from alcohol and had established much deeper connections with her husband, her college-age son, and several friends. Her business and artistic work were blossoming. She felt she was living fully for the first time.

Unfortunately, a bone-marrow biopsy confirmed the worst: acute myelomonocytic leukemia. In the face of this tragedy, I looked for signs of hope. This is an area of medicine in which technological intervention has been successful, with long-term cures occurring 25 percent of the time. As I probed the costs of these cures, I learned about induction chemotherapy (3 weeks in the hospital with probable infections and hair loss; 75 percent of patients respond and 25 percent do not). Those who respond are then given consolidation chemotherapy (with similar side effects; another 25 percent die, thus a net of 50 percent survive). For those still alive to have a reasonable chance of long-term survival, they must undergo bone-marrow transplants (hospitalization for 2 months, a whole-body irradiation—with complete killing of the bone marrow—infectious complications; 50 percent of this group survive, or 25 percent of the original group). Though hematologists may argue over the exact percentage of people who will benefit from therapy, they don't argue about the outcome of not having any treatment—certain death in days, weeks, or months.

Believing that delay was dangerous, the hospital's oncologist broke that news to Diane and made plans to begin induction chemotherapy that afternoon. When I saw her soon after, she was enraged at his presumption that she would want treatment and devastated by the finality of the diagnosis. All she wanted to do was go home and be with her family. She had no further questions about treatment and, in fact, had decided that she wanted none. Together we lamented her tragedy. I felt the need to make sure that she and her husband understood that there was some risk in delaying, that the problem would not go away, and that we needed to keep considering the options over the next several days.

(continued)

(continued from previous page)

Two days later Diane, her husband, and her son came to see me. They had talked at length about the problem and the options. She remained very clear about her wish not to undergo chemotherapy and to live whatever time she had left outside of the hospital. Her family wished she would choose treatment but accepted her decision. She articulated very clearly that it was she who would be experiencing all the side effects of treatment and that one-in-four odds were not good enough for her to undergo so toxic a course of therapy. I had her repeat her understanding of the treatment, the odds, and the consequences of foregoing treatment. I clarified a few misunderstandings, but she had remarkable grasp of the options and implications.

I have long been an advocate of the idea that an informed patient should have the right to choose or refuse treatment, and to die with as much control and dignity as possible. Yet there was something that disturbed me about Diane's decision to give up a 25 percent chance of long-term survival in favor of almost certain death. Diane and I met several times that week to discuss her situation, and I gradually came to understand the decision from her perspective. We arranged for home hospice care, and left the door open for her to change her mind.

Just as I was adjusting to her decision, she opened up another area that further complicated my feelings. It was extraordinarily important to Diane to maintain her dignity during the time remaining to her. When this was no longer possible, she clearly wanted to die. She had known of people lingering in what was called "relative comfort," and she wanted no part of it. We spoke at length about her wish. Though I felt it was perfectly legitimate, I also knew that it was outside of the realm of currently accepted medical practice and that it was more than I could offer or promise. I told Diane that information that might be helpful was available from the Hemlock Society.

A week later she phoned me with a request for barbiturates for sleep. Since I knew that this was an essential ingredient in a Hemlock Society suicide, I asked her to come to the office to talk things over. She was more than willing to protect me by participating in a superficial conversation about her insomnia, but it was also evident that the security of having enough barbiturates available to commit suicide, if and when the time came, would give her the peace of mind she needed to live fully in the present. She was not despondent and, in fact, was making deep, personal connections with her family and close friends. I made sure that she knew how to use the barbiturates for sleep, and how to use them to commit suicide. We agreed to meet regularly, and she promised to meet with me before taking her life. I wrote the prescriptions with an uneasy feeling about the boundaries I was exploring—spiritual, legal, professional, and personal. Yet I also felt strongly that I was making it possible for her to get the most out of the time she had left.

(continued)

(continued from previous page)

The next several months were very intense and important for Diane. Her son did not return to college, and the two were able to say much that had not been said earlier. Her husband worked at home so that he and Diane could spend more time together. Unfortunately, bone weakness, fatigue, and fevers began to dominate Diane's life. Although the hospice workers, family members, and I tried our best to minimize her suffering and promote comfort, it was clear that the end was approaching. Diane's immediate future held what she feared the most: increasing discomfort, dependence, and hard choices between pain and sedation. She called her closest friends and asked them to visit her to say good-bye, telling them that she was leaving soon. As we had agreed, she let me know as well. When we met, it was clear that she knew what she was doing, that she was sad and frightened to be leaving but that she would be even more terrified to stay and suffer.

Two days later her husband called to say that Diane had died. She had said her final good-byes to her husband and her son that morning, and had asked them to leave her alone for an hour. After an hour, which must have seemed like an eternity, they found her on the couch, very still and covered by her favorite shawl. They called me for advice about how to proceed. When I arrived at their house we talked about what a remarkable person she had been. They seemed to have no doubts about the course she had chosen,

(continued)

In 1992 California voters chose not to pass Proposition 161, an initiative similar to Washington state's Initiative 119. In 1993 active euthanasia was decriminalized in the Netherlands, and physicians are now allowed to help patients take their own lives under certain circumstances (Switzerland allows physician-assisted suicide in carefully controlled situations.). The Supreme Court of Canada, also in 1993, refused (by a vote of 5 to 4) to allow a woman with ALS to have her physician legally assist her death. In 1994 Measure 16 passed (51 percent to 49 percent) in Oregon, legally allowing physicians to hasten death for the terminally ill; the results, however, were tied up in court, and Oregon plans to have the voters again take up the issue in November of 1997.

In March of 1996 the Ninth Circuit Court of Appeals in Washington state ruled that the Washington statute prohibiting physicians from prescribing life-ending medication for use by terminally ill, competent adults who wish to hasten their own deaths is unconstitutional because it violates the Due Process Clause of the 14th Amendment of the U.S. Constitution. Then in April of 1996 the Second Circuit Court of Appeals in New York reached a similar ruling that expanded on the Ninth Circuit Court's ruling in also finding that allowing terminally ill patients to die through physician removal of life-sustaining treatments, such as mechanical ventilators or artificial hydration and nutrition while not allowing such patients to die by taking physician-prescribed medication, is a violation of the equal protection guarantee of

(continued from previous page)

or about their cooperation, although the unfairness of her illness and the death were overwhelming to us all.

I called the medical examiner to inform him that a hospice patient had died. When asked about the cause of death, I said acute leukemia. He said that was fine and that we should call a funeral director. Although acute leukemia was the truth, it was not the whole story. But any mention of suicide would probably have brought an ambulance, efforts at resuscitation, and a police investigation. Diane would have become a "coroner's case," and the decision to perform an autopsy would have been made at the discretion of the medical examiner. The family or I could have been subjected to criminal prosecution; I could have been subjected to a professional review. Although I truly believe that the family and I gave her the best care possible, allowing her to define her limits and directions, I am not sure the law, society, or the medical profession would agree.

Diane taught me about the range of help I can provide people if I know them well and if I allow them to express what they really want. She taught me about taking charge and facing tragedy squarely when it strikes. She taught me about life, death, and honesty, and that I can take small risks for people I really know and care about.

"Death and Dignity: A Case of Individualized Decision Making," by T. Quill, May 1991, *Harper's Magazine*, pp. 32–34. Originally published in the *New England Journal of Medicine*, 324, March 7, 1991.

the 14th Amendment. The Supreme Court of the United States agreed to take up this issue in January of 1997, based on cases in Washington state and New York. The Supreme Court ruling in June of 1997 failed to uphold the two lower courts, thus the matter was thrown back to the states.

In the Northern Territory of Australia in September of 1996 the world's first law permitting voluntary euthanasia was tested when the first person died under it. In March of 1997 however, after 4 acts of voluntary euthanasia were reported, the law was revoked. The 1990s has certainly been a decade filled with issues of euthanasia and physician-assisted suicide.

Both U.S. medical ethics literature and U.S. medical associations have traditionally condemned physician-assisted death (Jecker, 1994). The AMA Council on Ethical and Judicial Affairs stated that, although life-prolonging medical treatment may be withheld, "the physician should not intentionally cause death" (1992). In addition, the American Geriatrics Society (1994) has stated that physicians should not provide interventions that will intentionally cause the death of patients.

Though there is opposition to physician-assisted suicide, acceptance among health professionals is beginning to occur (Dickinson et al., 1997). For example, few people publicly criticized the case in which Dr. Timothy Quill assisted "Diane" in ending her life in 1991. In December of 1996 the 30,000-member American Medical Student Association filed a brief before the Supreme Court supporting physician-assisted suicide.

Public opinion of physician-assisted suicide is also becoming more accepting. In 1950 only 34 percent of people in the United States supported active euthanasia for incurably ill patients if they and their families requested it (Blendon, Szalay, & Knox, 1992). By 1973, however, a Gallup poll in the United States found that 53 percent of those interviewed said that physicians should have the legal right to painlessly end the life of a person with a terminal illness if the patient and family request it (Nagi, Puch, & Lazerine, 1978). In 1977, as many as 60 percent supported active euthanasia. By 1991, 63 percent of the U.S. population supported active euthanasia, and a majority (64 percent) favored allowing physician-assisted suicide (Blendon et al., 1992).

Because physicians would be involved with active euthanasia, we must wonder about their views on this topic. A comprehensive survey in 1993 of 938 Washington state physicians indicated that they are polarized: A slight majority favor legalizing physician-assisted suicide and euthanasia in at least some situations, but most would be unwilling to participate in these practices themselves (Cohen et al., 1994). In a **replication** study of the Washington state survey, George Dickinson and colleagues (1997) found that 587 South Carolina physicians had attitudes remarkably similar to those of the physicians in Washington state: Their attitudes were sharply polarized, with fewer than 15 percent neutral on the questions of euthanasia and assisted suicide. Another survey (Watts, Howell, & Priefer, 1992) of 727 geriatricians on their attitudes toward assisted suicide among dementia patients found that 21 percent would consider assisting in the suicides of competent, nondepressed patients. H. G. Koenig (1993) states that increasing support within the medical community for physician-assisted suicide comes from a recent decision by Michigan physicians to reverse their stand against the practice, preferring that it not be considered a felony.

In the Netherlands, where active euthanasia has been decriminalized, the physician, when following prescribed guidelines, can actually administer a lethal injection

Assisted Suicide: Australia Faces a Grim Reality
Seth Mydans

The last meal of sandwiches and beer seems to have been more agonizing for Dr. Philip Nitschke than for the cancer-ridden patient whose life he was about to take.

"I just about choked on my ham sandwich," the doctor said. "I was very, very anxious to the point where I was sweating. He spent a lot of time trying to calm me down, and I thought: 'Great. You spend your last meal trying to pacify the doctor.'"

Then the 66-year-old patient, Robert Dent, said, "You've got a job to do; get on with it." And Dr. Nitschke inserted into Mr. Dent's arm an intravenous needle connected to the doctor's battered gray laptop computer.

Without another word, the doctor recalled, Mr. Dent punched in a series of commands, and a lethal dose of barbiturates began flowing into his veins. Moments later, he was dead—the first person to die under a landmark law allowing doctors to assist patients who want to end their lives.

Adapted from S. Mydans, *New York Times,* February 2, 1997, p. 3.

to the patient. But in the United States, if physician-assisted suicide (limited to prescription of medication or the counseling of an ill patient so that she or he may use an overdose to end her or his life) is legalized, as it was in 1994 by Oregon voters, it will likely follow these conditions:

1. The patient must request a physician's assistance in suicide 3 times, the last in writing, with the statement dated and signed by the patient in the presence of two witnesses.
2. Two physicians must determine that the patient has a life expectancy of 6 months or less.
3. The physician must wait at least 15 days after the initial request, and at least 2 days after the final request, before writing the prescription for the lethal drugs.
4. The physician must determine that the patient is not suffering from a psychiatric or psychological disorder or depression causing impaired judgment.
5. At least 1 of the 2 witnesses to the patient's written request for the lethal prescription must be a person who is not a relative of the patient, does not stand to benefit from the estate of the patient, and is not an employee of the institution where the patient is being treated.

With wide public interest in assisted suicide and euthanasia, whether legalized or not, the medical profession should work to improve the care of terminally ill patients through more effective control of pain and other symptoms. As the next section of the book discusses, however, whether patients are terminally ill, pain-free, or not, rational suicide may be the answer for some individuals.

Specific Problems Associated With Physician-Assisted Suicide

There is a likelihood of serious accidents inherent in the patient giving an overdose in the physician's absence. Vomiting may occur as the patient slips into a coma, with aspiration of the vomitus. Should isolated patients change their minds, they may nevertheless choke to death in a panic, or, if rescued, die of pneumonia. Since morphine, barbiturates, or other compounds can produce states of confusion, such patients may experience terror, panic, or become assaultive, if someone else is in the room.

If a physician is present, and if the physician is prepared to intervene to bring about the patient's death in the event that a self-administered dose is insufficient or results in vomiting, panic, or assault, there is little moral difference for the physician between actively providing euthanasia or assisting at a suicide.

Providing a patient a lethal prescription and then absenting oneself from the bedside thrusts inappropriate responsibility on the untrained friends or family who may be present when the patient attempts to die. The emotional impact on those who witness the suicide must be taken into account.

Others argue that the presence of a physician would put pressure on the patient to end her or his life. If no physician is present, it is easier to change one's mind. Ambivalence is inevitably present in such situations.

Taken from "Report of the Committee on Physician-Assisted Suicide and Euthanasia," 1996, *Supplement to Suicide and Life-Threatening Behavior, 26*, pp. 1–19.

Rational Suicide

There have been times in history when misery was so common and the outlook so bleak that suicide probably seemed a serious option. The Mark Twain quote at the beginning of the chapter suggests that there are times in life when we would like to die temporarily. The Judeo-Christian tradition, however, has generally advocated life and strongly urged that life not be disposed of no matter what the temptations. For the elderly, taking one's life tends to be a more rational or philosophical decision. Elderly individuals and others today seem to be asking if life is to be valued under all conditions because it has intrinsic value or if the value of life is relative to the circumstances. The following reading, describing Mr. and Mrs. Saunders' final days, suggests that the value of life for them was relative to the circumstances.

Although suicide is usually treated as the product of mental illness or as a desperate cry for help used by someone who does not really want to die, suicide can be considered a rational act. **Rational suicide** is suicide in which the individual is presumably not insane, in which the decision is reached in unimpaired, undeceived fashion, and in which the choice made is not a bad thing for that individual to do (Battin, 1982). James Werth (1995) describes rational suicide as having 5 components: (a) The person has a realistic assessment of the situation. (b) The person's mental processes are unimpaired

After 60 Years of Marriage, Couple Decides to Leave World Together

Julia Saunders, 81, had her hair done. Her husband, Cecil, 85, collected the mail one final time and paused to chat with a neighbor. Inside their mobile home, they carefully laid out a navy blazer and a powder-blue dress.

After lunch, the Saunderses drove to a rural corner of Lee County and parked. As cows grazed in the summer heat, the couple talked. Then Cecil Saunders shot his wife of 60 years in the heart and turned the gun on himself.

Near the clothes they had chosen to be buried in, the couple had left a note:

"Dear children, this we know will be a terrible shock and embarrassment. But as we see it, it is one solution to the problem of growing old. We greatly appreciate your willingness to try to take care of us.

After being married for 60 years, it only makes sense for us to leave this world together because we loved each other so much."

On the floorboard of the car, Cecil and Julia Saunders had placed typewritten funeral instructions and the telephone numbers of their son and daughter.

Then they consummated their suicide pact, becoming 2 of the more than 4,000 elderly Americans authorities say will commit suicide this year.

"What struck all of us was how considerate, how thoughtful they were to all concerned about killing themselves," said Sheriff's Sergeant Richard Chard, who investigated the August 19 murder-suicide. "They didn't want to impose or be a bother to anyone. Not even in dying."

Julia's dimming eyesight, heart congestion and a stroke had driven Cecil to place his wife in a nursing home earlier this year. But she became hysterical over what she said was poor care there, and Cecil brought her home, said neighbors at the mobile home park where the couple had lived since 1974.

"You never saw him without her," said Vera Whittimore, 67. "If there ever was true love, they had it. I think they were just tired of living and couldn't wait for God to take them."

The Saunderses had hot dogs and beans for lunch, then drove their Caprice to pastureland 5 1/2 miles from their mobile home, parking on the grassy shoulder.

As thunderstorms rumbled in the distance, they talked.

"I can picture in my mind them sitting there," Chard said. "Maybe they spoke about how things were when they were young. Then he leaned over and gave her a farewell kiss."

The bodies were found by workers from nearby Owl Creek Boat Works, who called police.

(continued)

(continued from previous page)

In Philadelphia, a police officer stood by as the Saunderses' son, Robert, 57, was told of his parents' death. His parents wanted no tears shed over their decision to die. The note they left for Robert and his sister, Evelyn, 51, ended with a wish:

"Don't grieve because we had a very good life and saw our 2 children turn out to be such fine persons. Love, Mother and Father."

Minneapolis Star and Tribune, October 4, 1983, p. 12A.

by psychological illness or severe emotional distress. (c) The person has a motivation that would be understandable to a majority of uninvolved community members. (d) The decision is deliberated and reiterated over a period of time. (e) If at all possible, the decision-making process should involve the suicidal person's significant others.

Certainly one could argue that the Saunderses' act in the preceding reading was a rational homicide/suicide. Jacques Choron's assertion (1972, pp. 96–97) that "rational" implies "not only that there is no psychiatric disorder but also that the reasoning of the suicidal person is in no way impaired and that his motives would seem justifiable, or at least 'understandable,' by the majority of his contemporaries in the same culture or social group" seems to "fit" the case of the Saunderses.

Richard Brandt (1986, p. 339) states that the person contemplating suicide is obviously making a choice between future world courses—the future world course that includes his or her demise an hour or so from now and several possible courses that include his or her demise at a later point. Although one cannot have precise knowledge about many features of the latter courses, it is certain that they all will end with death sooner or later. The basic question for the person to answer to determine the best (or rational) choice is which course would be chosen under conditions of optimal use of information, when all personal desires are taken into account. It is not a question just of what is preferred now.

Certainly one's desires, aversions, and preferences may change after a short while. When one is in a state of despair, nothing but the thing that he or she cannot have— a love that has been rejected or a job that has been lost—may seem desirable. The passage of time is likely to reverse all of this. So if one acts on the preferences of today alone, when the emotion of despair seems more than one can stand, death might seem preferable to life. But if one allows for the preferences of the weeks and years ahead, when many goals might be enjoyable and attractive, life might be found to be preferable to death. Thus, Brandt is suggesting that a future world course might well be different than that of the present.

Brandt further suggests that one must take into account the infirmities of one's "sensing" machinery. Knowing that the machinery is out of order will not tell one what results it would give if it were working, thus the best recourse might be to refrain from making any decision in a stressful frame of mind. If decisions have to be made, one must recall past reactions, in a normal frame of mind, to outcomes like those under assessment. The future world course obviously did not look to be "enjoyable and attractive" to the Saunderses after 80 years of life.

A Few Words on Suicide: Don't Try It!

A few months ago, I tried to commit suicide. The reason I did this was that I could no longer find happiness within me. I know that sorrow and pain are parts of life, but so are joy and laughter. I wasn't getting enough of the happiness that should be in everyone's life. I felt that, no matter how hard I tried to be a good, kind, thoughtful person, I failed. My best just wasn't good enough for people. This was making me miserable, and a miserable person is a burden to others. I didn't want to live the rest of my life feeling the way I was feeling, so I decided to end it all and find out what my Lord thought of me. It was wrong. I know that society thinks it's wrong. That's why, when I made the decision to commit suicide, I really wanted to die. Having to survive and face the music, so to speak, seemed worse than death itself.

I'm hoping now, though, that you won't make me feel as though I should be ashamed of myself. You see, I'm really glad to be alive, and I even believe I have a bright future. Someday I might even have children, and I don't want them to think badly of me. I know they won't if you don't.

I've learned to be stronger: I've done this by becoming a little more selfish. But that is necessary, or else you'll lose yourself to others and become their puppet. I've learned to make demands of others. The big one I'm making now is that you just keep giving me affection.

Sincerely,

Don't Try Suicide

Boston Globe, July 7, 1981, p. B13.

Individuals opposed to suicide outright would argue that a person does not have the right to commit suicide regardless of the circumstances. Others believe that circumstances may be so unbearable that suicide is understandable but that this should be an individual act and not one encouraged by society or the legal system, note Ellen Ingram and John Ellis (1992, p. 35) in their review of literature on suicidal behavior. Opponents with extreme views argue that life should be preserved regardless of circumstances even in the case of a terminal illness. They would argue that suicide is an ambivalent act and that every person who wants to die also wants to live. Such a view suggests that suicidal thoughts are only temporary and that through intervention the crisis often passes (Ingram & Ellis, 1992). Not only may the thoughts be temporary, but also the quote at the beginning of the chapter reminds us that "suicide is a *permanent answer* to a *temporary* set of problems."

Conclusion

Just what constitutes a suicide is not clear today. Many persons display "suicidal behavior" by constantly taking risks and gambling with their lives; yet if death results from such behavior, it is often classified as "accidental" or "natural." Sociologists argue that suicidal persons construct their meanings of suicide and motivations for committing it out of collective values upon which the social structure rests. Meanings of suicide arise out of what people think, feel, and do.

Persons bereaved by a suicide may have a longer and more difficult grieving process due to their perceiving less social support than other bereaved individuals (Thompson & Range, 1992–1993). Some grief reactions, such as shame or rejection, may account for this lack of support. Shame may occur because of the stigma surrounding death by suicide (Silverman, Range, & Overholser, 1994–1995). Rejection may result because suicide implies that the deceased rejected not only life but also family and friends. Suicide survivors may also have more difficulties discussing the death with others, thus they may try to deny the cause of death.

Suicidal persons are more likely to be adolescents or very elderly, male, and not married. Though age by itself does not cause suicidality, the person most vulnerable to suicide is a white male over the age of 85. Suicidal persons tend to talk about suicide prior to the act and often display observable signs of suicide. Males are perhaps more "successful" at completing suicide than are females because males tend to use a more lethal weapon—firearms. For suicidal persons, this act becomes an easy "solution" to their problems—a permanent answer to a temporary set of problems. Suicide can be a rational act, and one does not have to be "insane" to take one's own life.

In the event that someone does not take the advice of the preceding letter, and suicide is completed, here are some suggestions for dealing with the aftermath of suicide:

1. Be available to the survivors by taking the initiative to help. Do not hesitate to visit them, even if you do not know what to say. Just being present shows that you care.
2. Discourage guilt feelings. Suicide tends to result from long-term feelings, thus the grievers should not blame themselves with "if only" feelings.
3. Be truthful and honest at all times.
4. Discourage self-pity and encourage the individual to become involved in activities.
5. Encourage the griever to express his or her real feelings. Help guide the individual toward thinking ahead to the future.

Summary

1. Suicide has been around for as long as recorded history.
2. Suicide has historically been viewed in different ways in different places. Even today the general attitude toward suicide remains confused and sometimes contradictory.
3. The meaning of suicide is problematic. Suicide research centers have evolved in recent years to address the complex issues of suicide.
4. In the late 1800s French sociologist Emile Durkheim noted that suicide is related to one's degree of social integration. Different types of society produce different suicide types: egoistic, altruistic, anomic, and fatalistic.

5. The dramaturgical approach to suicide study uses the drama or action to explain the behavior.

6. The existentialist perspective on suicide may view the choice of death as it views the choice of life—both the result of reflection—and not view death as "the enemy."

7. If one feels alienated and powerless, suicide may appear to be a solution.

8. Though age by itself does not cause suicidality, elderly males are most vulnerable to suicide in the United States.

9. People who commit suicide tend to talk about their attempt prior to the act.

10. The most frequent method of completed suicide is by firearm.

11. The concept of rational suicide suggests that a person does not have to be mentally ill to take his or her own life.

12. The media have contributed to clusters of suicides by teenagers, according to some researchers.

13. Suicidal deaths are virtually nonexistent prior to age 5 and are rare between 5 and 9 years. Adults prefer to believe that children do not commit suicide.

14. Social factors tend to be associated with suicide: age, gender, marital status, and socioeconomic level.

15. Physician-assisted suicide has been a major issue in the United States and throughout the rest of the world in the 1990s.

Discussion Questions

1. Discuss why the meaning of suicide continues to be problematic today.

2. Give examples of Durkheim's 4 types of suicide.

3. How does the dramaturgical approach view suicide?

4. How does an existentialist perspective "explain" suicide?

5. Describe signs of suicide. What should you do if you observe some of these signs in a friend?

6. Discuss why the suicide rate tends to be high among adolescents and the elderly.

7. The concept of rational suicide implies that one does not have to be mentally ill to take his or her own life. Discuss whether you feel that one can be "sane" and take his or her own life.

8. Discuss your reaction to the deaths of Julia and Cecil Saunders.

9. Discuss your reaction to Dr. Timothy Quill's assisting his leukemic patient, "Diane," with her death.

10. Physicians are sworn to "prolong life and relieve suffering," yet physician-assisted suicide is counter to "prolonging life." The majority of people in the United States favor physician-assisted suicide. Discuss the pros and cons of physician-assisted suicide.

Glossary

Alienation: One does not feel in control and does not feel a part of a situation, often resulting in a lack of self-realization and a feeling of powerlessness and hopelessness.

Altruistic Suicide: The individual is overly integrated into society and willing to die for the group.

Anomic Suicide: Results from a lack of regulation of the individual when the norms governing existence no longer control that individual.

Dramaturgical Perspective: Highlights the construction of action by using the metaphor of the drama to explain behavior.

Egoistic Suicide: Occurs when the person is inadequately integrated into the society.

Emic Approach: An analysis of behavior from the perspective of the participant (the one being studied). If, for example, one is studying suicide, one would be an individual who has attempted suicide. What was this experience like from her or his point of view?

Etic Approach: An analysis of behavior from the perspective of the observer (the one doing the study, not the participant).

Existentialist Philosophy: The choice of death may be like the choice of life; death is not the enemy as viewed by other perspectives.

Fatalistic Suicide: Too much control over a person by society may lead to feelings of oppression under extremely strict rules.

Physician–Assisted Suicide: When a physician prescribes medication and/or counsels an ill patient so that the patient can overdose to end his or her own life.

Rational Suicide: Suicide in which the individual is not insane and is aware of what he or she is doing.

Replication: The repetition or duplication of the procedures followed in a particular study in order to determine whether or not the same findings are obtained at another time and/or place.

Suicide Cluster: An excessive number of suicides occurring in close temporal and geographical proximity.

References

Achte, K. (1988, Spring). Suicidal tendencies in the elderly. *Suicide and Life-Threatening Behavior, 18,* 55–65.

Adamek, M. E., & Kaplan, M. S. (1996). The growing use of firearms by suicidal older women, 1979–1992: A research note. *Suicide and Life-Threatening Behavior, 26,* 71–78.

Aiken, L. R. (1991). *Dying, death, and bereavement* (2nd ed.). Boston: Allyn and Bacon.

Alvarez, A. (1971). *The savage god: A study of suicide.* London: Weidenfeld and Nicolson.

American Geriatrics Society, Public Policy Committee, Voluntary Active Euthanasia. (1994). *Journal of the American Geriatrics Society, 39,* 826. American Medical Association's Council on Ethical and Judicial Affairs. (1992). Current opinions. Chicago: American Medical Association.

American Psychological Association. (1992). Ethical principles of psychologists and code of conduct. *American Psychologist, 47,* 1597–1611.

Asarnow, J. R., & Carlson, G. (1988, Summer). Suicide attempts in preadolescent child inpatients. *Suicide and Life-Threatening Behavior, 18,* 129–136.

Battin, M. P. (1982). *Ethical issues in suicide.* Englewood Cliffs, NJ: Prentice-Hall.

Bell, D. (1977). Sex and chronicity as variables affecting attitudes of undergraduates towards peers with suicidal behaviors. *Dissertation Abstracts International, 38,* 3380B.

Berman, A. L. (1986). Helping suicidal adolescents: Needs and responses. In C. A. (microfilm) Corr & J. N. McNeil (Eds.), *Adolescence and death* (pp. 151–166). New York: Springer Publishing.

Beskow, J., & Asgard, U. (1990, Winter). Psychological autopsies: Methods and ethics. *Suicide and Life-Threatening Behavior, 20,* 307–323.

Biblarz, A., Biblarz, D. N., Pilgrim, M., & Baldree, B. F. (1991, Winter). Media influence on attitudes toward suicide. *Suicide and Life-Threatening Behavior, 21,* 374–384.

Blendon, R. J., Szalay, U. S., & Knox, R. A. (1992). Should physicians aid their patients in dying? The public perspective. *Journal of the American Medical Association, 267,* 2658–2662.

Brandt, R. B. (1986). The morality and rationality of suicide. In R. F. Weir (Ed.), *Ethical issues in death and dying* (2nd ed., pp. 330–344). New York: Columbia University Press.

Brody, J. E. (1987, March 3). Child suicides: Common causes. *New York Times,* p. 16.

Brown, A. S. (1996). *The social processes of aging and old age.* Upper Saddle River, NJ: Prentice Hall.

Brown, J. H., Henteleff, P., Barakat, S., & Rowe, C. J. (1986, February). Is it normal for terminally ill patients to desire death? *American Journal of Psychiatry, 143,* 208–211.

Brozan, N. (1986, January 13). Adolescent suicides: The grim statistics. *New York Times,* p. 16.

Butler, R. N., Lewis, M. I., & Sunderland, T. (1991). *Aging and mental health: Positive psychosocial and biomedical approaches* (4th ed.). New York: Macmillan.

Calhoun, L. G., & Allen, B. G. (1991). Social reactions to the survivor of a suicide in the family: A review of the literature. *Omega, 23,* 95–107.

Canetto, S. S. (1992, Spring). Gender and suicide in the elderly. *Suicide and Life-Threatening Behavior, 22,* 80–97.

Charmaz, K. (1980). *The social reality of death.* Reading, MA: Addison-Wesley.

Choron, J. (1972). *Suicide.* New York: Charles Scribner's Sons.

Codex juris canonici. (1918). Rome, Italy: Polyglot Press.

Cohen, J. S., Fihn, S. D., Boyko, E. J., Jonsen, A. R., & Wood, R. W. (1994). Attitudes toward assisted suicide and euthanasia among physicians in Washington state. *New England Journal of Medicine, 331,* 89–94.

Coleman, L. (1987). *Suicide clusters.* Boston: Faber and Faber.

Conrad, N. (1992). Stress and knowledge of suicidal others as factors in suicidal behavior

of high school adolescents. Issues in *Mental Health Nursing, 13,* 95–104.

Curran, D. K. (1987). *Adolescent suicidal behavior.* Washington, DC: Hemisphere Publishing.

Dickinson, G. E., Lancaster, C. J., Sumner, E. D., & Cohen, J. S. (in press). Attitudes toward assisted suicide and euthanasia among physicians in South Carolina and Washington. *Omega.*

Devons, C. A. J. (1996, March). Suicide in the elderly: How to identify and treat patients at risk. *Geriatrics, 51,* 67–71.

Domino, G., Domino, V., & Berry, T. (1987). Children's attitudes toward suicide. *Omega, 17,* 279–287.

Donne, J. (1930). *Biathanatos.* New York: Facsimile Text Society. (Original work published 1644)

Douglas, J. D. (1967). *The social meanings of suicide.* Princeton, NJ: Princeton University Press.

Dunn, R. G., & Morrish-Vidners, D. (1987). The psychological and social experience of suicide survivors. *Omega, 18,* 175–186.

Durkheim, E. (1951). *Suicide: A study in sociology.* New York: The Free Press. (Original work published 1897)

Eddy, J. M., & Alles, W. F. (1983). *Death education.* St. Louis: C. V. Mosby.

Ellis, J. B., & Range, L. M. (1989). Characteristics of suicidal individuals: A review. *Death Studies, 13,* 485–500.

Farberow, N. L. (1975). *Suicide in different cultures.* Baltimore: University Park Press.

Fulton, G. B., & Metress, E. K. (1995). *Perspectives on death and dying.* Boston: Jones and Bartlett Publishers.

Gallup, G. H. (1994). *Religion in America: 1994* (Suppl.). Princeton, NJ: Gallup Poll.

Gallup Survey. (1993, April). Physicians need to detect suicide warning signs. *Geriatrics, 48,* 16.

Garfinkel, B. D., Froese, A., & Hood, J. (1982, October). Suicide attempts in children and adolescents. *American Journal of Psychiatry, 139,* 1257–1261.

Garrison, C. Z. (1989, Spring). The study of suicidal behavior in the schools. *Suicide and Life-Threatening Behavior, 19,* 120–130.

Gibson, J. A., Range, L. M., & Anderson, H. N. (1987). Adolescents' attitudes toward suicide: Does knowledge that the parents are divorced make a difference? *Journal of Divorce,* 163–167.

Gould, M. S., & Shaffer, D. (1986, September 11). The impact of suicide in television movies. *New England Journal of Medicine, 315,* 690–694.

Gould, M. S., Wallenstein, S., & Davidson, L. (1989, Spring). Suicide clusters: A critical review. *Suicide and Life-Threatening Behavior, 19*, 17–29.

Guillon, C., & LeBonniec, Y. (1982). *Suicide, its use, history, technique and current interest.* Paris: Editions Alain Moreais.

Gutierrez, P., King, C. A., & Ghaziuddin, N. (1996). Adolescent attitudes about death in relation to suicidality. *Suicide and Life-Threatening Behavior, 26,* 8–18.

Hohmann, A. A., & Larson, D. B. (1993). Psychiatric factors predicting use of clergy. In E. L. Worthington, Jr. (Ed.), *Psychotherapy and religious values* (pp. 71–84). Grand Rapids, MI: Baker Book House.

Ingram, E., & Ellis, J. B. (1992). Attitudes toward suicidal behavior: A review of the literature. *Death Studies, 16,* 31–43.

Jecker, N. S. (1994). Physician-assisted death in the Netherlands and the United States: Ethical and cultural aspects of health policy development. *Journal of the American Geriatric Society, 42,* 672–678.

Kastenbaum, R. (1992, Spring). Death, suicide and the older adult. *Suicide and Life-Threatening Behavior, 22,* 1–14.

Kastenbaum, R. J. (1995). *Death, society and human experience* (5th ed.). Columbus, OH: Charles E. Merrill.

Kastenbaum, R., & Aisenberg, R. (1976). *The psychology of death.* New York: Springer Publishing.

Koenig, H. G. (1993). Legalizing physician-assisted suicide: Some thoughts and concerns. *Journal of Family Practice, 37,* 171–179.

Koenig, H. G. (1994). *Aging and god.* New York: Haworth Press.

Kübler-Ross, E. (1987). *AIDS: The ultimate challenge.* New York: Macmillan.

Maldonado, G., & Kraus, J. F. (1991). Variation in suicide occurrence by time of day, day of the week, month, and lunar phase. *Suicide and Life-Threatening Behavior, 21,* 174–187.

Marrone, R. (1997). *Death, mourning, and caring.* Pacific Grove, CA: Brooks/Cole.

May, P. A. (1990). A bibliography on suicide and suicide attempts among American Indians and Alaska natives. *Omega, 21,* 199–214.

McCall, P. L. (1991). Adolescent and elderly white male suicide trends: Evidence of changing well-being? *Journal of Gerontology, 46*(1), 43–51.

McGuire, D. J., & Ely, M. (1984, January–February). Childhood suicide. *Child Welfare, 63,* 17–26.

McIntosh, J. (1995). Epidemiology of suicide in the United States. In J. B. Williamson & E. S. Shneidman (Eds.), *Death: Current Perspectives* (4th ed., pp. 330–344). Mountain View, CA: Mayfield.

Moscicki, E. K. (1995, Summer). Epidemiology of suicide. *International Psychogeriatrics, 7,* 137–148.

Nagi, M. H., Puch, M. D., & Lazerine, N. G. (1978). Attitudes of Catholic and Protestant clergy toward euthanasia. *Omega, 8,* 153–164.

Oaks, J., & Ezell, G. (1993). *Dying and death: Coping, caring, understanding* (2nd ed.). Scottsdale, AZ: Gorsuch Scarisbrick Publishers.

Orbach, I. (1988). *Children who don't want to live: Understanding and treating the suicidal child.* San Francisco: Jossey-Bass.

Osgood, N. J., Brant, B. A., & Lipman, A. (1991). *Suicide among the elderly in long-term care facilities.* New York: Greenwood Press.

Osgood, N. J., & McIntosh, J. L. (1986). *Suicide and the elderly: An annotated bibliography and review.* New York: Greenwood Press.

Parsons, T. (1949). *The structure of social action.* New York: The Free Press.

Peck, M. (1980). *Recent trends in suicide among young people.* Los Angeles: Institute for Studies of Destructive Behaviors.

Phillips, D. P., & Carstensen, L. L. (1986, September 11). Clustering of teenage suicides after television news stories about suicide. *New England Journal of Medicine, 315,* 685–689.

Prior, L. (1989). *The social organization of death: Medical discourse and social practices in Belfast.* New York: St. Martin's Press.

Range, L. M., & Goggin, W. C. (1990). Reactions to suicide: Does age of the victim make a difference? *Death Studies, 14,* 269–275.

Rich, C. L., Warsradt, G. M., Nemiroff, R. A., Fowler, R. C., & Young, D. (1991, April). Suicide, stressors, and the life cycle. *American Journal of Psychiatry, 148,* 524–527.

Richman, J. (1992, Spring). A rational approach to suicide. *Suicide and Life-Threatening Behavior, 22,* 130–141.

Silverman, E., Range, L., & Overholser, J. (1994–1995). Bereavement from suicide as compared to other forms of bereavement. *Omega, 30,* 41–51.

Smith, W. J. (1985). *Dying in the human life cycle.* New York: Holt, Rinehart and Winston.

Stack, S. (1992, Summer). The effect of the media on suicide: The great depression. *Suicide and Life-Threatening Behavior, 22,* 255–267.

Stillion, J. M., & McDowell, E. E. (1991). Examining suicide from a life span perspective. *Death Studies, 15,* 327–354.

Suicide among older persons in the United States, 1980–1992. (1996, January 12). *Morbidity and Mortality Weekly Report, 45,* 3–6.

Suicide rate among elderly climbs by 9% over 12 years. (1996, January 12). *New York Times,* p. A11.

Taylor, G. W. (1990, July 16). AIDS mercy killings. *Maclean's, 103,* 14.

Theodorson, G. A., & Theodorson, A. G. (1969). *Modern dictionary of sociology.* New York: Thomas Y. Crowell.

Thompson, K. E., & Range, L. M. (1992–1993). Bereavement following suicide and other deaths: Why support attempts fail. *Omega, 26,* 61–70.

Tolchin, M. (1989, July 19). When long life is too much: Suicide rises among elderly. *New York Times,* p. 1.

Waters, H. F. (1994, April 18). Teenage suicide: One act not to follow. *Newsweek,* p. 49.

Watts, D. T., Howell, T., & Priefer, B. A. (1992). Geriatricians' attitudes toward assisting suicide of dementia patients. *Journal of the American Geriatrics Society, 40,* 878–885.

Weaver, A. J., & Koenig, H. G. (1996). Elderly suicide, mental health professionals, and the clergy: A need for clinical collaboration, training, and research. *Death Studies, 20,* 495–508.

Werth, J. L., Jr. (1995). Rational suicide reconsidered: AIDS as an impetus for change. *Death Studies, 19,* 65–80.

Yang, B. (1992, January). The economy and suicide: A time-series study of the U.S.A. *American Journal of Economics and Sociology, 51,* 87–99.

Yang, B., Lester, D., & Yang, C. (1992). Sociological and economic theories of suicide: A comparison of the U.S.A. and Taiwan. *Social Science and Medicine, 34,* 333–334.

Suggested Readings

Holinger, P. C., Offer, D., Barter, J. T., & Bell, C. C. (1994). *Suicide and homicide among adolescents.* New York: Guilford Publications. An examination of suicide and homicide in terms of the similarities and differences in the two forms of adolescent wastage. Offers a comprehensive approach to adolescent violence with an emphasis on a public health approach.

Kennedy, G. J. (Ed.). (1996). *Suicide and depression in late life.* New York: John Wiley and Sons. Written from a psychiatric perspective, this anthology is divided into three parts: critical issues in clinical science, therapeutic approaches, and toward a more informed public policy.

Laufer, M. (Ed.). (1995). *The suicidal adolescent.* Madison, CT: International Universities Press. An easy-to-read work written primarily from a psychodynamic perspective toward suicidal attempts.

Levine, C. (1993). *Taking sides: Clashing views on controversial bioethical issues* (5th ed.). Guilford, CT: Dushkin Publishing Group. Presents material on decisions about death and discusses public policy and bioethics.

Orbach, I. (1988). *Children who don't want to live: Understanding and treating the suicidal child.* San Francisco: Jossey-Bass. Integrates current theoretical, empirical, and clinical knowledge about different manifestations of child suicide and uses case histories of suicidal children and their families as illustrations.

Smolin, A., & Guinan, J. (1993). *Healing after the suicide of a loved one.* New York: Simon and Schuster. This book is directed toward the lay public and individuals suffering from the loss of a significant other by suicide.

Stilling, J. M., and McDowell, E. E. 1996. *Suicide across the life span*. Bristol, PA: Taylor & Francis. A thorough review of suicide literature from a developmental psychology perspective.

Werth, J. 1996. *Rational Suicide?* Bristol, PA: Taylor & Francis. Presents rational suicide as a legitimate option for some individuals. Has implications for mental health professionals.

Zimmerman, J. K., & Asnis, G. M. (Eds.). (1995). *Treatment approaches with suicidal adolescents*. New York: John Wiley and Sons. A comprehensive and sophisticated program of suicide assessment, treatment interventions, and preventive programs for work with suicidal adolescents.

Related Web Sites

http://www.lsds.com/death/   Thanatolinks contains links to some of the best Internet sites related to dying and death.

http://www.yahoo.com/Society_and_Culture/Death/   The death index of the Yahoo Internet search engine.

http://www.io.com/~sheol/suicide.html   A Web site that raises questions and provides some answers about suicide.

http://www.unicef.org/pon96/insuicid.htm   UNESCO Web site that provides international suicide rates of young adults.

http://www.paranoia.com/~real/suicide/   This Web site provides information about suicide and its prevention and includes frequently asked questions, statistics, international crisis resources, and annotated links to other suicide sites.

http://www.geocities.com/RainForest/1801/suicide1.htm   If you are thinking about suicide, read this first: a Web site dedicated to suicide prevention providing resources for people who are considering suicide. Based on the premise that suicide is not chosen; it happens when pain exceeds resources for coping with pain.

http://www.save.org/   Suicide Awareness—Voices of Education is the most popular suicide site on the Internet. A well-kept and thorough site, with material on dealing with suicide both before and after, along with material from many education sessions.

http://www.paranoia.com/~real/suicide/links.html   The Light for Life Foundation Yellow Ribbon Program provides educational material for American youth aimed at preventing suicide by providing easy access to support services.

http://www.cyberspy.com/~webster/death.html#depressed   A Web site on depression, anxiety, and suicide to help us learn more about how depression and suicide can affect our lives.

http://wonder.cdc.gov   The Centers for Disease Control's Prevention Guidelines. This site has a number of papers on suicide prevention, particularly among American youth. Worth a look for educators and health professionals.

http://ourworld.compuserve.com/home pages/span   This is a more political site of Suicide Prevention Advocacy Network, a nonprofit organization whose aim is to have suicide treated as a national (and global) problem that must be solved as a priority.

http://web.idirect.com/~casp   A simple Web site of the Canadian Association for Suicide Prevention has details on the organization, current suicide prevention research, electronic brochures, and upcoming conferences.

http://www.sfsuicide.org   San Francisco Suicide Prevention has a well-presented Web site with some interesting facts and details on local prevention programs. Worth a look for similar organizations.

http://www.4-lane.com/supportchat/pages/suicidechat.html   Interactive chat system for Suicide Chat. As is becoming more common these days, Internet chat is moving to the Web. This interactive support system has a lot of potential, if only because it is more accessible (and reliable) than IRC (Internet relay chat).

http://www.rights.org/deathnet/KevorkianFile.html   An Internet resource archive devoted to Dr. Jack Kevorkian.

http://www.netlink.co.uk/users/vess/wfmap.html   An Internet resource that provides links to right-to-die organizations worldwide.

http://www.islandnet.com/~deathnet/ergo.html   Web site for Derek Humphry's Euthanasia Research and Guidance Organization.

Part Four
Understanding the Bereavement Process

Chapter 10

The Anthropology of Death Ritual

Some children love to watch the cremations. The skull is usually the last thing to be burned. Sometimes it collapses with a loud pop, like a balloon bursting. When that happens, the children clap their hands.

—ALEXANDER CAMPBELL, *THE HEART OF INDIA*

Death occurs in all societies, yet it evokes an incredible variety of responses. At the moment of death, survivors in some societies remain rather calm, others cry, and still others mutilate their bodies. Members of some societies officially mourn for months, while others complete the ritual within hours. In many societies families are involved in preparing the corpse for the funeral ritual; in others, families engage professional funeral directors to handle the job.

The variety of responses to death is further noted by Richard Huntington and Peter Metcalf in *Celebrations of Death: The Anthropology of Mortuary Ritual* (1992). They state that corpses are burned or buried, with or without animal or human sacrifice; they are preserved by smoking, embalming, or pickling; they are eaten—raw, cooked, or rotten; they are ritually exposed as dead or decaying flesh or simply abandoned; or they are dismembered and treated in a variety of these ways. Funerals are times for avoiding people or holding parties, for weeping or laughing, or for fighting or participating in sexual orgies.

In most non-Western societies, death is not seen as one event, but rather as a process whereby the deceased is slowly transferred from the land of the living to the land of the dead (Helman, 1985). The process is illustrated by rituals marking biological death, followed by rituals of mourning, and then by rituals of social death. The deceased person is often viewed as a soul in limbo during rituals of mourning, though he or she is still a partial member of the society (Sweeting & Gilhooly, 1992). For the Kota people of south India, for example, a person is not socially dead until after the dry funeral—the second funeral for the deceased held annually and lasting 11 days (Mandelbaum, 1959).

The structural-functionalist perspective of sociologist Emile Durkheim (1915/1954) and anthropologists Bronislaw Malinowski (1948) and A. R. Radcliffe-Brown (1964) reduces the ritual process into an equilibrium-producing system. Death rituals are emphasized as mechanisms that re-create social solidarity. Because society is assumed to be a smoothly running machine, death "disrupts" a society's assumed smooth operation. Rituals of death help to restore order to that that has been disrupted. Individuals gain strength from the ritual affirmations of the community, and they are then able to continue their lives with the restoration of a smoothly running society. Thus, functionalists deduce that ritual is the key to a stable society living in equilibrium (Kozak, 1991).

For some, the burial ground can serve as a symbolic representation of the social order (Bloch & Parry, 1982, p. 34). Among the Merina of central Madagascar, for example, after death one returns "home" to the tomb, representing a regrouping of the dead—a central symbol of the culture and an underlying joy of the second funeral. By the entry of the new corpses into the collective mausoleum, the tomb and the reunited dead within it represent the undivided and enduring descent group and become the source of blessings and the fertility of the future. The force of this symbol of the tomb as the representation of the eternal undivided group can be sustained only by downplaying the individuality of the corpses that enter it.

Societal Management of Death-Related Emotions

Though they vary significantly, all societies seem to have some customs for managing death-related emotions and reconstructing family interaction patterns modified by death. These customs are passed down from generation to generation and are an integral part of a society's way of coping with a major event like death.

The study of death rituals is a positive endeavor. Regardless of whether societal customs call for festive or restrained behavior, the issue of death throws into relief the most important cultural values by which people live their lives and evaluate their experiences (Huntington & Metcalf, 1992). Life becomes transparent against the background of death, and fundamental social and cultural issues are revealed.

Anthropologists do not claim to have a special understanding of the mystery of death, but they can recount the collective wisdom of many cultures. The entire web of human social interrelations is founded on many invisible and indirect meanings that are bestowed onto various individuals (Cuzzort & King, 1995, p. 18). Although we cannot actually see a mourner or a mortician, we can observe those who occupy such statuses. Until we are informed that they occupy such statuses (and are expected to behave accordingly), however, we cannot respond in an appropriate way.

As a scientist the anthropologist is concerned with the meanings that different events have for different societies. As Kellehear (1990, p. 10) notes, anthropology has given modern sociological analysis a rich source of **ethnographic** description for comparative purposes, thus providing some basis for a general, cross-cultural analysis of the multifaceted and complex responses to death. A true understanding of various rituals and activities results from an "immersion" in the culture. Although the anthropologist cannot determine what is in the mind of the person acting, similar events observed over time can result in some understanding of the behavior within that context. Marvin Harris (1974, p. 4) states that human life is not merely random or capricious. Just as one does not expect dreamers to explain their dreams, one should not expect lifestylers to explain their lifestyles. Through careful observation over time, however, one can come to a better understanding of why people do what they do.

The Ritual Solution
Kenneth L. Woodward With Anne Underwood

I was introduced to death early in life. In the Roman Catholic grade schools of my youth, funerals were part of the informal curriculum. When a classmate's parent died, we all assembled for the funeral mass, passing by the (usually) open casket and sharing—as best we could—the sorrow of the grieving family. Occasionally, it was a fellow pupil lying in the casket, snatched from life by an accident or—like my closest fifth-grade friend—from an illness, in his case a fatal epileptic seizure. What brought us together, young and old, was sacred ritual.

The liturgy that gathered and directed our emotions was familiar and color-coded. For funerals, the priest wore black vestments symbolizing death, just as he wore red for feast days of the martyrs and—on ordinary Sundays—green for the hope that all Christians have of life eternal. The music varied, too. Long before I learned a modern language, I knew by heart the somber Latin funeral hymn "Dies Irae" ("Day of Wrath"). I knew, too, that the clouds of incense billowing around the body were meant to honor flesh that was soon to turn to dust. By such appeals to the senses we children were inducted into the abstract mystery of death—our own as well as that of others. Sad? Yes. But never morbid. Death is real, the liturgy instructed us. But so is the promise of Resurrection.

Grief demands ritual. To die alone is bad enough, but to grieve without rituals that lift the broken heart is worse. Those whose grief is affirmed within a larger community of faith are fortunate. But not everyone is religious. And even those who claim to be often find God's dominion harder to acknowledge—especially when a child dies or a young parent is taken

(continued)

(continued from previous page)

from them—than that of death itself. There is, in short, no single way to grieve, any more than there is a uniform "American way of death."

Jewish mourning rituals focus more on the bereaved than on the body. By custom, Jews bury their dead within 24 hours—if possible, without embalming—in a plain, wooden coffin. Traditional Jews never put the body on view or have it cremated. "After the Holocaust, any Jew who opts for cremation is obscene," says Professor Neil Gillman of the Jewish Theological Seminary in New York.

Among observant Jews, mourning proceeds in stages and centers on sitting *shiva* in the home. At death or at the funeral, survivors cut their clothing with a razor—on the left for a parent; on the right for a spouse, child, or sibling—to symbolize the tear in life that death has produced. After a ritual healing meal, shiva begins. For the first week, men don't shave; survivors are not supposed to wash their whole bodies; and the entire family receives visitors while sitting on the floor or on low chairs. "The idea is to be uncomfortable," says Gillman. "It's a statement that you are experiencing pain." Formal mourning may continue for 80 days—and for nearly a year if the deceased is a parent.

Muslims mourn their dead in mosques, never at funeral parlors. The body is washed in a special room (men prepare males; women females) while the family and friends recite *suras* from the Koran as blessings for the deceased. Within hours of death, the body is buried—just as Dodi Fayed, Princess Diana's companion—was. In most Islamic traditions, all the male members of the community walk in a procession to the gravesite; women visit later during a 40-day mourning period. A close friend of the deceased climbs into the grave to read final instructions to the dead in preparation for his or her meeting with Allah. Then, according to Islamic belief, the angels

(continued)

Why Study Cross-Cultural Death Rituals?

Why should a student of dying and death become familiar with the death customs of other cultures? Our culture is characterized all too often by **ethnocentrism**—we tend to think that our way is the superior way. Just because another society's customs differ from our own does not mean that they are wrong. In comparing different death-related customs, the similarities between cultures are often greater than the differences. As you read this chapter, note the many parallels between our death customs and those of others.

Being familiar with cross-cultural death customs should help you to better understand the American concept of death. To blame a supernatural entity or a physician or someone else for another's death is functional in both literate and nonliterate

(continued from previous page)

who accompany every believer in life enter the grave to question the departed soul on matters of faith and life: "Who is your Lord? Who is your prophet? What book do you follow?" "If the person was pious" says Abdulaziz Sachedina, professor of religious studies at the University of Virginia, "the grave is broadened and there is room for a garden inside. If the person was not so good in life, the grave becomes a very narrow place."

Whatever their differences, religious rituals for the dead are always communal events. Feeding the survivors cuts across all traditions, and so does the telling of stories. "Grief is an isolating emotion," observes James Campbell, professor of philosophy at the Rochester Institute of Technology. "When we grieve, we want to run away and hide, and that's not a good way to handle grief."

But, as funeral directors are the first to notice, an increasing number of Americans confront death with no inherited faith or liturgy for support. As a result, the funeral director has become by default the weaver of instant rituals. One approach is to have the survivors recreate the life story of the deceased. "I help them write things they never got to say to the person and put them in letters and place them in the casket," says Bruce Conley, a funeral director in Elburn, Illinois. Another ritual that some of Conley's customers like is tucking the body into the casket before the final closing, as a mother does with a child at night. "When we put the two together," Conley finds, "when we approach sorrow with celebration, it purges the emotions."

Even so, the rituals that possess the greatest healing power are those not solely of our own invention. When death is absorbed into a liturgy that affirms transcendent life, something more than grief finds expression. The experience is called *communion*.

"The Ritual Solution," by Kenneth L. Woodward with Anne Underwood, September 18, 1997, *Newsweek,* p.62.

societies—an "explanation" for the death and a scapegoat to relieve one's guilt feelings. Although some nonliterate groups might attribute a death to the ghost of a deceased ancestor, a literate group might blame medical personnel.

We should also study death cross-culturally because of linkages with diseases around the world. AIDS, for example, in less than 2 decades has become globally pandemic (Feldman, 1990, p. 2). Though the origin of AIDS is unknown, we do know that AIDS is rapidly emerging with major implications for the future vitality of humanity. In southwestern and northern Uganda in Africa, half of all adults under 50 are HIV positive. In Zambia in Africa one fourth of adult men and women between 20 and 50 years of age are HIV positive (Feldman, 1990, p. 3). In the United States, AIDS is as devastating as it has become in parts of Europe, Africa, Asia, and Latin America. For students considering work in the health professions, a combination of respectful

The American Wake of Ireland

Nineteenth-century Irish immigrants to the United States were mainly peasants who lived a harsh life. Coming to America between 1820 and 1920 represented hope for the Irish but was also viewed as a symbolic form of death: Families were separated temporarily and permanently. Like when someone died, when one left for America, the Irish held a wake for the individual—sometimes called a live wake, parting spree, convoy, or farewell supper. The American wake, referred to as early as 1830, was recognized throughout Ireland by the end of 1850, but it almost completely disappeared by the decade after World War I.

Much overlap existed in rituals between an actual wake for the dead and the American wake. Both involved public participation and allowing the family and community to grieve over their loss. Attendance reaffirmed family and group ties and was a mixture of grief and gaiety. Both an Irish funeral and an American wake drew very large crowds (in the Irish language the same word can be used interchangeably for both funeral and multitude). Though sad, one could actually rejoice at the departed's rebirth to a new state: death and immigration freed one forever from the stark hopelessness of poverty. Music, singing, dancing, and wake games were usually a part of the affair. Gifts were often brought to the wake, except for the years following the Great Famine, when offerings were meager.

Though the merriment at wakes for the dead or for the immigrant may seem disrespectful, they actually demonstrated the strong belief that the physically or symbolically dead would continue to exist more happily elsewhere. The American wake, like the Irish funeral, reiterated the significance of transitional times for the Irish, whether changes in the seasons or major life changes such as birth, death, and immigration. Public involvement in funerary rituals avows the passing from one status to another. A funeral also mirrors the values and expectations of a group. The Irish wake, reflecting Irish life and Irish death customs, was unique to Ireland.

Adapted from "The American Wake of Ireland: Symbolic Death Ritual," by E. Metress, 1990, *Omega, 21*, pp. 147–153.

behavior and a conscientious effort to understand individuals from another culture will go far in enabling clinicians to work well with dying patients from many backgrounds (Hallenbeck, Goldstein, & Mebane, 1996).

Cross-cultural studies of death reveal that most societies seem to have a concept of soul and immortality. For some, a belief in a soul concept explains what happens in sleep and after death. For others, a belief in souls explains how the supernatural world becomes populated (Tylor, 1873). Much of the death ritual performed is related to the soul and is often an appeasement of the beings in the spiritual world. This spiritual dimension of death plays a significant role in the social structure of societies that hold such beliefs.

Death and Dying in African American Traditions

The African American contemporary reactions to death are closely connected and deeply rooted in the African tradition, yet are tempered by the American sociocultural experience. Funeral customs have evolved over centuries and now reflect a tradition rich in cultural symbolism. To be an African American in the United States is to be part of a history told in terms of contact with death. For in the era of slavery, death or other forms of personal loss could come at any time or age and often at the whim of someone else. This history is reflected in artistic expression in music, spirituals, poetry, novels, drama, and visual arts. These various art forms mirror the attitudes of African Americans toward death. A consistent theme of death is often connected to a sense of solace in a theology and a belief in an afterlife and promise of a better life.

Not unlike other Protestant groups in the United States, most African American Protestant churches have no formally prescribed funeral ritual dictated by church hierarchy. Local church custom is followed. African American funerals represent an attempt toward dignity and esteem often denied in the dominant culture. Mourners are likely to depend upon the church and the community for support during bereavement. The African American funeral is indeed a primary ritual and a focal occasion with a big social gathering after the funeral and the closest thing to a family reunion that might ever take place; a latent function of funerals.

Adapted from "Psychocultural Influences on African-American Attitudes Toward Death, Dying and Funeral Rites," by R. K. Barrett, 1992. In J. Morgan (Ed.), *Personal Care in an Impersonal World*, Amityville: NY, Baywood Publishing.

In studying death cross-culturally we are reminded of other similarities such as beliefs in ghosts. For many groups, souls of the dead become ghosts. Ghosts may take up residence. After a short period of wandering, ghosts may cease to exist. Some people converse with ghosts and make offerings to them. This is sometimes referred to as the "cult of the dead" (Taylor, 1988). These ghosts are not worshiped but simply maintain a relationship with a person. They act as a guide and protector. They also confer power. In some societies, to have a guardian spirit is a positive experience. For others, like Navajo and Apache Native Americans, ghosts are responsible for sickness and death and are to be avoided (Cox & Fundis, 1992). Ghosts are not unique to nonliterate cultures, however, but seem to also "exist" in literate societies. Many sane, sober individuals in the United States have had "encounters" with ghosts.

This chapter will present various death rituals and discuss the functions of such activities. In no way are these various cultures representative of all. Some examples may appear bizarre to the reader, but keep in mind that our own death rituals may appear equally strange to persons from other cultures.

Death as a Rite of Passage

Death is a transition, but only the last in a long chain of transitions, according to Richard Huntington and Peter Metcalf (1992). The moment of death is related not only to the process of afterlife, but also to the process of living, aging, and producing progeny. Death relates to life—to the recent life of the deceased and to the lives that he or she has procreated and now leaves behind. There is an eternity of sorts on either side of the line that divides the quick from the dead. Life continues generation after generation, and in many societies it is this continuity that is focused upon and enhanced during the rituals surrounding a death. To ease this continuity and "soften" the shock of death, euphemisms are often used, as discussed in previous chapters. Traditional African customs, for example, regard it as impolite to state bluntly that someone is dead. "Good breeding" is reflected by referring to the death of someone in euphemistic terms (Barrett, 1992).

One of the best-known accounts of death as one of a series of such **rites of passage** through the life cycle comes from Van Gennep (1909/1960) in his treatment of funerals. He had expected that the element of separation would be more marked in funerals than in other rites of passage, but his evidence demonstrated that it is the transitional or the liminal that dominates mortuary ritual and symbolism. Van Gennep (1909/1960, p. 164) noted social status aspects of ritual and mourning:

> The length of the period (of mourning) increases with the closeness of the social tie to the deceased and with higher social standing of the dead person. If the dead man was a chief, the suspension affects the entire society.

However, persons for whom no rites are performed (Van Gennep, 1909/1960, p. 160)

> ... are the most dangerous dead. They would like to be reincorporated into the world of the living and since they cannot be, they behave like hostile strangers toward it. They lack the means of subsistence which the other dead find in their own world, and consequently must obtain them at the expense of the living.

Individuals are often considered to be composed of several elements, each of which may have a different fate after death (Palgi & Abramovitch, 1984, p. 117). The purpose of destroying the corpse, whether through cremation, burial, or decomposition, is to separate the elements—the various bodies and souls. For example, in India, when a son breaks the skull of his father on the funeral **pyre** (a combustible pile for burning a corpse), he is demonstrating that the body no longer has any value—because it is worn out—but the soul lives on (Tully, 1994).

For the Lugbara of Uganda (Middleton, 1965) when people die, they cease to be "people of the world outside" and become "people who have died" or "people in the earth." Death marks the beginning of an elaborate rite of passage as a dead person has relations with both living and dead kin.

The Ritual of Mourning at Death

Ritual can be defined as the symbolic affirmation of values by means of culturally standardized utterances and actions (Taylor, 1988). People in all societies are inclined

This Japanese funeral emphasizes the social status of the man who has died. The living honor the dead and thereby create a symbolic community consisting of their ancestors and living members of their families.

to symbolize culturally defined feelings in conventional ways. Ritual behavior is an effective means of expressing or reinforcing these important sentiments, and it helps make death less socially disruptive and less difficult for individuals to bear (Haviland, 1991, p. 577).

Rituals differ from other behaviors in that they are formal—stylized, repetitive, and stereotyped (Rappaport, 1974). Rituals are performed in special places, occur at set times, and include liturgical orders—words and actions set forth previously by someone.

Functions of rituals include validating and reinforcing values, providing reassurance and feelings of security in the face of psychological disturbances, reinforcing group ties, aiding status change by acquainting persons with their new roles, relieving psychological tensions, and restabilizing patterns of interaction disturbed by a crisis (Taylor, 1988). Such functions can be noted in Ireland, where the dead have a special place in life through dialogue (Enright, 1994): The dead are called upon to cure the afflicted and to comfort the lonely. Thus, at funerals in Ireland people never say farewell because they fully expect to hear from their friends and loved ones again. Likewise, in rural Mexico it is important that the dead leave the world happily because many older people talk unashamedly to the spirits of their dead relatives, with no one considering this strange (Caistor, 1994). Anthropologist Karl Heider (1991) observes that mourning is functional for the Dani in western New Guinea in giving those affected by the loss an opportunity to come together to reaffirm their ties and to begin restoring the social network that has been torn by the death. Though many are functional in a positive way, death rituals do not always have positive consequences. Ritual can also have negative functions by causing tensions, observes Robert Taylor (1988).

Cuttin' the Body Loose: Dancing in Defiance of Death in New Orleans

"They gon cut the body loose!"

One short brother with a mustache was running up and down the funeral procession explaining that they wasn't going to have to go all the way to the cemetery on account of they was going to cut the body loose. This meant that the hearse would keep on going and the band and the second liners and the rest of the procession was going to dance on back to some tavern not too far away.

"They gon cut the body loose, y'all."

The marshal, out in front of the hearse, was draped in a blue-black suit that was a little too big and too long but was all the better to dance with. He wore yellow socks and brown shoes as a crazy combination of his own. After the body was cut loose, the steps he invented were amazing contortions of knees, shins, and flying feet. He executed those moves with the straightest, most nonchalant, don't-give-a-damn look I have ever seen on anybody's face what was doing as much work as he was doing under this merciless hot sun. He had somebody by him fanning and wiping his face after every series of grief-inspired movements. He looked so sad to be dancing so hard and making so many others of us smile as we watched him. We tried to imitate some of his easier and more obvious moves but couldn't. He was the coolest person in that street marching toward a tavern two or three blocks away under a 2:30 p.m. New Orleans summer sun. The coolest.

So we stood in a line and the second liners were shouting, "open it up, open it up," meaning for the people in front to get out the way so the hearse could pass with the body. After the hearse was gone we turned the corner and danced down to the bar.

Like a sudden urge to regurgitate and with the intensity of an ejaculation, an explosive sound erupted from the crowd under the hot New

(continued)

Whereas death rituals in the United States are generally subdued and rather gloomy affairs, some societies engage in rather spirited activities. The Bara of Madagascar, for example, engage in "drunken revelry" at a funeral—rum is consumed, sexual activities occur, dancing takes place, and contests involving cattle occur (Huntington & Metcalf, 1992). Among the Cubeo of South America, simulated and actual ritual coitus is part of the mourning ritual (Goldman, 1979). The dances, ritual, dramatic performances, and the sexual license have the purpose of transforming grief and anger over a death into joy.

THE DISPLAY OF EMOTIONS

A study of ethnographic data from 78 societies (Rosenblatt, Walsh, & Jackson, 1976) to identify the essence of universal grief behavior showed that death is nearly

(continued from previous page)

Orleans sun. People spontaneously answered the traditional call of the second line trumpet.

"Are you still alive?"

"YEAH!"

"Do we like to live?"

"YEAH!"

"Do you want to dance?"

"YEAH!"

"Well damn it, let's go!"

The trumpeter was taunting us now, and the older people were jumping from their front porches as we passed them, and they were answering that blaring hot high taunt with unmistakable fires blazing in their 60-year-old black eyes. They too danced as we passed them. They did the dances of their lives, the dances they used to celebrate how old they had become and what they had seen getting to their whatever number years. The dances they used to defy death.

Nowhere else in this country do people dance in the streets after someone has died. Nowhere else is the warm smell of cold beer on tap a fitting conclusion for the funeral of a friend. Nowhere else is death so pointedly belittled. One of us dying is only a small matter, an occasion for the rest of us to make music and dance. Nothing keeps us contained. With this spirit and this music in us, black people will never die, never die, never.

We were all ecstatic. We could see the bar. We knew it was ending, we knew we were almost there and defiantly we danced harder anyway. We hollered back even that much louder at the trumpeter as he squeezed out the last brassy blasts his lungs could throw forth. The end of the funeral was near, just as the end of life was near for some of us but it did not matter. When we get there, we'll get there.

Taken from "Cuttin' the Body Loose: Dancing in Defiance of Death in New Orleans," by K. Salaam, September-October 1991, *Utne Reader,* pp. 78–79.

universally associated with emotionality and that the most usual expression among the bereaved is crying. The study further concluded that, if there are gender differences in emotions during bereavement, the women tend to cry and self-mutilate more than men. The men tend to direct anger and aggression away from self. One of the traditional theories suggested to explain gender differences in emotional expression was that it may be easier to socialize women than men to be overtly nonaggressive; thus crying may represent a female expression of aggression. Another theory was that women will be more affected by the loss from a death because of their stronger attachments through their role as mothers. On the other hand, women may not experience death more strongly, but they may simply be used as the persons symbolizing publicly, in burdensome or self-injuring ways, the loss that all experience. The analysis of data from these 78 societies concludes that the kind of data needed to "explain" the emotional difference by gender is lacking.

Paul Rosenblatt and colleagues (1976) note that most societies have developed mechanisms to control the anger of the bereaved and channel it along nondestructive paths. Ritual specialists help to minimize anger that leads to disruptive social behavior. In a country so deritualized as the United States, funeral directors may provide a positive role in developing sets of norms for mourning behavior.

The expression of emotions ranges from complete abstinence of emotion to amplified wailing, notes Effie Bendann's *Death Customs: An Analytical Study of Burial Rites* (1930). She states that after a death the aborigines of Australia and Melanesia indulge in the most exaggerated forms of weeping and wailing. They display other manifestations of emotional excitement seemingly because of grief for the departed. At the end of a certain designated time period, however, they cease with metronomic precision, and the would-be mourners indulge in laughter and other forms of amusement. Likewise, Hindus in India are encouraged to express their grief openly, even sometimes extravagantly, through shrieks of women mourners and floods of tears, yet no weeping is to occur during the cremation ceremony (Tully, 1994).

An outgoing display of emotions is found among the Kapauku Papuans of west New Guinea (Pospisil, 1963). Their ritual at death requires the relatives of the deceased to give a formal expression of their grief as soon as the soul leaves the body. They weep, eat ashes, cut off their fingers, tear their garments and net carrying bags, and smear their faces and bodies with mud, ashes, or yellow clay. A loud singsong lamentation follows.

As just noted, mourning often falls most heavily upon the women. For example, women among the Cheyenne Indians cut off their long hair and gash their foreheads as the blood flows (Hoebel, 1960). If the deceased was killed by enemies, they slash their legs until caked with dried blood. Mourning gives the women their own masochistic outlet. Cheyenne men, on the other hand, simply let down their hair in mourning and do not bother to lacerate themselves. In traditional African funerals (Barrett, 1992) women tend to wail, whereas men sing and dance; men are not to cry in front of women because they would appear weak before the very group that they are to protect.

The Dinka women of the Sudan (Deng, 1972) cut their leather skirts and cover their bodies with dirt and ashes for as long as a year. Widows among the Swazi in Africa (Kuper, 1963) shave their heads and remain "in darkness" for 3 years before given the duty of continuing the **lineage** for the deceased through the **levirate**—required marriage to her dead husband's brother. Mourning imposed on the Swazi husband is less conspicuous and shorter than that imposed on the wife.

Somewhat less dramatic than the previous examples, the Huicholes of Mexico (Weigand & Weigand, 1991, pp. 62–65) display a "great deal of crying and wailing" at the actual moment of death. This subsides during the preparation of the corpse but resumes again at the funeral site. However, Huichol women who have suffered the death of a mother or a child often express their loss by suicidal gestures—the stated goal of such behavior is to accompany the deceased. In reality, however, these gestures seldom result in suicide, according to Weigand and Weigand (1991).

In the United States some funeral directors have noted that occasionally individuals "carry on to the point of fainting" but catch themselves before completely passing out. If such behavior is expected within a subculture, some will comply. However, a more stoic approach appears to be normative in the United States. For example,

Jacqueline Kennedy, when President John F. Kennedy was assassinated in Dallas in 1963, was praised by the media for "holding up well." Her reaction was probably one of shock more than of bravery. In the 19th century, Italian immigrants to the United States actually hired mourners for funerals—a custom from the Old World (Cowell, 1986, p. 79).

TYPES OF WEEPING

One could argue that people display the outward emotion of crying at the time of death because they are sad. Perhaps it is not as simple as that. Anthropologist A. R. Radcliffe-Brown (1964) notes two types of weeping. There is reciprocal ritual weeping to affirm the existence of a social bond between two or more persons. It is an occasion for affirming social ties. Although participants may not actually feel these sentiments that bind them, participation in various rites will strengthen whatever positive feelings they do have. The second type of weeping—weeping over the remains of a significant other—expresses the continued sentiment of attachment despite the severing of this social bond.

Richard Huntington and Peter Metcalf (1992) observe that Radcliffe-Brown was strongly influenced by the French sociologist Emile Durkheim. Durkheim (1915/1954) argued that the emotions developed are feelings of sorrow and anger and are made stronger by participation in the burial rite, whereas Radcliffe-Brown argued that those participating in ceremonial weeping come to feel emotion that is not sorrow but rather togetherness. What Durkheim finds significant is the way that other members of society feel moral pressure to put their behavior into harmony with the feelings of the truly bereaved. Even if one feels no direct sorrow, weeping and suffering may result. Thus, to say that one weeps because of sadness may be too simplistic.

In conclusion, cross-cultural studies of the ritual of mourning at death reveal that a double standard prevails among some cultures—different "scripts" for different genders. Women in many societies, including the United States, are expected to display more of their emotions than are men. Mourning rituals also tend to last for a set period of time in many societies.

Attitudes Toward Death

In some societies death is viewed as a continuation of life, simply in a different form. For example, the traditional African attitude toward death is "positive and accepting and comprehensively integrated into the totality of life"; death becomes a prolongation of life (Barrett, 1992). Death may be accepted by some as a natural part of life— the "final stage of growth," as Elisabeth Kübler-Ross notes. Yet for others, death is the end of everything. For example, the Navajo Indians (Habenstein & Lamers, 1974) have no belief in a glorious immortality for the soul and believe that death is the end of everything good. Likewise, the Semai of Malaya (Dentan, 1968) talk about life after death, but most admit that they do not believe in it. Thus, attitudes toward death are partly reflected in beliefs about what happens after death.

In our own culture, a popular belief is that the dead and the living are separated from each other. Yet, like many cultures, we periodically pay respect to the dead

The Feast of the Dead in Peru demonstrates the belief in the continuity of relationships between the living and the dead.

through All Saints Day and Memorial Day (Decoration Day). For example, people in New Orleans still throng cemeteries on All Saints Day (Marcus, 1988). Burial places bloom with white and yellow chrysanthemums, and family tombs are scrubbed and whitewashed as in the past. A century ago in New Orleans on All Saints Day crowds poured into cemeteries from dawn to dusk. Families gathered for picnics, entertained friends, and told stories about the dead. Even today, All Saints Day remains a holiday for New Orleans municipal employees.

In other regions of the United States, however, at the traditional celebrations of All Saints Day and All Souls Day, little is done, even in Catholic cemeteries, to brighten up the graves (Goody, 1993). Anthropologist Jack Goody (1993) counted the graves of those buried within the past 50 years and found that the percentage with flowers ranged between 0 and 25 percent in cemeteries in selected northeastern and western states but that graves in selected cemeteries in southern Europe had 100 percent flowers on them (primarily fresh-cut or plants). Thus, behavior and attitudes toward death vary within the United States and between the United States and other countries.

On November 1 families in Mexico celebrate the Day of the Dead, which coincides with All Saints Day in the United States (Caistor, 1994). According to Mexican beliefs, on the night of November 1, the spirits of the dead come back to visit this world, and Mexicans everywhere are determined to meet them. They take a picnic to the cemetery where relatives are buried and spend the night there, eating, drinking, and singing. The deceased's favorite food is brought, and his or her favorite songs are sung.

The continuity between the living and the dead is elaborated in ideas of reincarnation and in other ways in non–Western as well as in Western societies. For

Decoration Day: Celebrating Kin in the Blue Ridge Mountains

Deep in the balsam groves of the Blue Ridge Mountains, time moves reluctantly. Old folk customs linger like the thick mists that creep in at twilight and huddle in the coves until the rising sun nudges them over the horizon.

TV dishes may scar the hillsides and unpicturesque mobile homes line up next to the chestnut bark cottages of another generation, but even in the midst of 20th-century clatter some hardy mountain people continue to live their traditions, celebrations, and superstitions in much the same way they always have. Old ways and rituals are still important to the life of family and community. A keen example of this is the survival of the family graveyard decoration day.

There is hardly a summer Sunday in any area that is not some family's decoration day. Perhaps this tradition has its roots in the outdoor communions and field preachings of 17th-century Scotland; no one knows for sure. Whatever its beginnings, decoration day has survived as a time to renew ties of kinship and friendship, share a meal, and honor the dead.

Each festival day falls on its own established Sunday—the first Sunday of June, for instance, or the last Sunday of July—and is referred to by its ancestral name. There is a Houston Decoration Day, a Pitman Decoration Day, and as many decorations as there are descendants of the pioneer families. These are family graveyards and not churchyards, so there may or may not be a church nearby. On decoration day the preacher and singers situate themselves in a visible spot and begin to preach and sing as people arrive with baskets of fresh flowers and food. The graves are soon heaped with a blaze of color, and care is taken that no grave is slighted.

A long row of tables is set up adjacent to the graveyard. Family members, no matter how extended, are expected to come bearing food and flowers. Friends bring flowers but no food. Both friends and family arriving from a distance are greeted so enthusiastically the preacher may have to shout to be heard. Each family has developed its own liturgy over the years, and each decoration day has a personality of its own.

When I was a child, my favorite decoration fell in early September when chinquapins were ripe and the late summer days were fading into harvest. We were always invited to the Woody family decoration. I remember this last decoration of summer as a mournful celebration in which laughter and handshakes were often punctuated by the sudden onset of tears, especially if the conversation moved into the past.

But the Woody decoration had a beautiful ritual built into the day's structure that was unique. Just as the preacher concluded his remarks for the

(continued)

(continued from previous page)

day and just before the women left the graveyard to set out the stacks of fruit pies and platters of chicken, the family patriarch stood to speak.

"Now, dear friends, we are going to have our living decoration. Tell someone you love them, what they mean to you, while they can still hear you. Tell them today!"

The singers started to sing again, and everyone joined in the minor wails of "Give Me My Roses While I Live." Old men, young men, women and children milled among the tombstones pinning blossoms on one another's lapels and collars. At the singers' discretion the singing stopped. Tears dried as abruptly as they had begun and we all went to lunch.

"Decoration Day: Celebrating Kin in the Blue Ridge Mountains," by D. W. Boulton, September–October 1991, *Utne Reader*, pp. 81–82.

example, many Japanese today think that a person's spirit belongs to the same family and the same local community before and after death (Nagamine, 1988, p. 67). A person's spirit gradually fades away from its family as time goes on. The Japanese do not clearly distinguish the dead from the living and seem to recognize the continuity between life and death. Especially in rural Japan, the dead remain an integral part of life and offer constant solace to the living (Kristof, 1996).

The Japanese are not alone in believing that the dead remain a vital part of their lives. For instance, in some parts of southern India, where many Hindus spend 13 days of mourning, each person serves part of a meal on a banana leaf to provide for the needs of the dead person's soul (Tully, 1994). The meal is laid out in the open and, if the crows eat it, that means that the offering has been accepted.

The Hopi Indians viewed life and death as phases of a cycle (Oswalt, 1986, p. 174). Death was an important change in individual status because it represented an altered state for the person involved. The Hopi believed that a duality of being existed in each person—a soul and a body expressed as a "breath-body." A person dying on earth literally was reborn in the afterworld. Corpses were washed and given new names before burial. The breath-body's pattern of existence would supposedly be the same in the domain of the dead as it had been on earth—when it died in the afterworld, it would be reborn on earth.

During their elaborate ceremonies, the Hopi performed specific rites for making the desires of the living known to the dead, notes W. H. Oswalt. Thus, the living solicited the active aid of the dead. The dead returned symbolically to earth at given times through **kachina performers** (masked and costumed individuals who impersonated spirits of the dead).

The Igbo in Nigeria (Uchendu, 1965) believe that death is important for joining the ancestors. Without death, there would be no population increase in the ancestral households and thus no change in social status for the living Igbo. The lineage system is continued among the dead. Thus, the world of the "dead" is a world full of activities.

The Ulithi of Micronesia are not morbid or defeated by death, according to William A. Lessa (1966). Their rituals afford them some victories, and their mythol-

The traditional funeral for the Igbo of Nigeria includes males dancing to celebrate the life of the deceased.

ogy provides a hope for a happy life in another realm. Though their gods are some-what distant, these gods assure that the world has an enduring structure, and their an-cestral ghosts stand by to give more immediate aid when merited. Thus, after the Ulithi express their bereavement, rather than retreat, they spring back into their nor-mal work and enjoyment of life.

For the Dunsun of northern Borneo, few events focus on the beliefs and acts concerned with the nonnatural world more than the death of a family member (Williams, 1965, p. 39). Death is considered a difficult topic of which everyone is fear-ful of talking, yet it must be prepared for because it causes great changes.

The Abkhasians on the coast of the Black Sea (Benet, 1974) view death as irra-tional and unjust. The one occasion when outbursts of feeling are permitted is at a funeral—wailing and scratching at one's flesh are permitted.

Thus, attitudes toward death vary significantly among societies around the world—from seeing death as a continuation of life to the end of everything. Next, we will look at death customs among various cultures.

Customs at Death

As will be discussed in chapter 12, a professional is called upon in the United States to prepare the body for final disposition because we are a very specialized society with a high division of labor. The funeral director takes the body away and returns it later for viewing. The kin and friends in the United States normally play no significant role in handling the corpse. Compared with most societies, we are unique in the level of professional specialization relative to the preparation of the corpse and the actual disposition of the body. Most of the cultures discussed in this section encourage families and friends to become very involved in preparing the corpse for its final disposition.

NORMS PRIOR TO DEATH

Some societies have specific norms just prior to the death. It is important in many societies, including the United States, that one be with the dying person at the time of death. So often it is said, "If only I had gotten there a few minutes earlier . . . " A visit prior to death allows one to say goodbye. Among the Dunsun of northern Borneo (Williams, 1965), relatives come to witness the death. The dying person is propped up and held from behind. When the body grows cold, the social fact of death is recognized by announcing "he exists no more" or "someone has gone far away."

The Salish Indians of the northwestern United States (Habenstein & Lamers, 1974) leave the dying person alone with an aged man who neither receives pay nor is expected to have any special qualifications for the task. One who is near death must confess his or her misdeeds to this man. The confession is to prevent the ghost from roaming the places that were frequented in life by the dying person.

The Ik of Uganda (Turnbull, 1972) place the dying person in the fetal position because death for them represents a "celestial rebirth." The Magars of Nepal (Hitchcock, 1966) purify a dying person by giving him or her water that has been touched with gold.

The Maori of New Zealand (Mead, 1991, p. 49) have a ceremony just before the person dies to send the spirit of the dying away while the person is still alive and conscious of what is happening. After the spirit is gone, the individual may be medically dead, but, in a Maori sense, is not wholly dead yet. Now that the person is a corpse, ceremonies begin and a space is set aside in the meeting house for the corpse to lie in an open coffin.

Having a cultural framework prescribing proper behavior at the time of death provides an established order and perhaps gives comfort to the bereaved. These behavioral norms give survivors something to do during the dying process and immediately thereafter, thus facilitating the coping abilities of the bereaved.

HANDLING THE CORPSE

Cleaning the Body

Family members' preparation of the body for final disposition, especially cleaning the body, is very evident in some societies. Anthropologist Linda Connor (1995) notes that corpse washing in Bali is a pivotal point in the process of grieving for relatives.

For the Bornu of Nigeria (Cohen, 1967) family members are required to wash the body, wrap it in a white cloth, place it onto a **bier,** and take it to the burial ground. Similarly, the Semai in Malaya (Dentan, 1968) have the housemates bathe the corpse and sprinkle it with perfume or sweet-smelling herbs to mask the odor of decay. They then wrap the body in swaddling. A Hindu's body in India is washed by members of the family, then laid out decently clad with the face open for all to see until the time comes for the procession to the cremation ground (Tully, 1994).

The Mapuche Indians of Chile (Faron, 1968) sometimes smoke the body, then wash and dress it in the person's best clothes, lay it out on a bier in the house, and place the body into a pine coffin. Among some groups in southern Thailand (Fraser, 1966), the body is held and bathed with water specifically purified with herbs and clay. The corpse is then rinsed and dried and all orifices plugged with cotton.

In the French West Indies (Horowitz, 1967) the neighbors wash the body with rum and force a liter or more of strong rum down the throat as a temporary preservative before dressing the body and placing it onto a bed. Rather than use a strong drink like rum, the Zinacantecos of Mexico (Vogt, 1970) pour water into the mouth of the deceased about every half hour "to relieve thirst" while the grave is being dug.

Other Customs Regarding the Corpse

In addition to cleaning the corpse, many groups spend time decorating the body. For example, the Tiwi of Australia (Hart & Pilling, 1960) wrap the body in bark. The Qemant of Ethiopia (Gamst, 1969) wrap the body in a piece of white cloth and cover it with a mat of woven grass. Tewa Indians in Arizona (Dozier, 1966) bury a woman in her wedding outfit and wrap a man in a blanket for burial. The Hopi Indians wrap a man in buckskin and a woman in her wedding blanket, bury them in the clothes that they were wearing at the time of death, and do not wash or prepare the body other than to wash and tie back the hair (Cox & Fundis, 1992). After cleaning the body, the Ulithi in Micronesia (Lessa, 1966) cover it with a tuberous plant and decorate the head and hands with flower garlands. The Navajo in the southwestern United States (Cox & Fundis, 1992) bathe the corpse, then dress it in fine clothes and put the right moccasin onto the left foot and the left moccasin onto the right foot.

Not all groups are interested in decorating the corpse. For example, the custom of Anglo-Canadians in and around Toronto, Canada, and in suburban London, England (Ramsden, 1991, p. 38), is to remove the corpse from the company of the living immediately following death. The corpse is never to be seen by them again. It is disposed of as quickly as is practical in a way that precludes any suggestion of further involvement by the deceased. The complete avoidance of the corpse also precludes any opportunity to note changes in the individual following death, thus reinforcing the perception of the Anglo-Canadians that death is a static state. They wish to get across the idea that the dead are physically and socially immediately gone. From the moment of death, the physical condition of the body is of no consequence with the exception that it must be permanently removed from the world of the living just as the dead person must be banished from social relations. The event of death is perceived as an instantaneous occurrence and marks a distinct boundary between a state of being alive and a state of being dead.

Funeral Home Proposed for Special Rituals of Indians

The strange odyssey of Steve Perion, the man who wants to open a funeral home in Minneapolis for American Indians, has already taken him to the State Capitol posing for pictures with Gov. Rudy Perpich and to City Hall looking for money.

He has impressed politicians with his business acumen and collected a stack of letters praising his sensitivity from people he hardly knows. "His particular expertise in and commitment to serving the funeral needs of the American (Indian) community here would fill a desperate need," says Minneapolis Democratic Farm Labor (DFL) Party member Rep. Karen Clark, who acknowledges she barely knows him.

Perion has huddled with financial analysts and come away with a polished business plan for success based on death—60 indigent Indian deaths a year will mean $15,600 in gross profits.

So goes the balancing act for Perion, a Chippewa Indian who admits he has no money of his own. Entering an arena where many Indian families can't afford even the simplest of funerals, he is trying not to be viewed as an opportunist. But Perion, who claims his will be the first funeral home for Indians in urban America, is quickly enlisting support by promising the city's large Indian community a perspective other funeral homes can't match and promising financiers a steady cash flow from county welfare payments for indigent deaths.

"The issue is sensitivity," said the Rev. James Notebaart, director of the Catholic Indian Ministries in south Minneapolis. "It's really a clash of cultures—the urban economic life and culture and the (Indian) tradition of living off the land and living without dollars. . . . The business of burying the dead costs money and there's often a clash there."

As Perion moves to bridge the two worlds using a yellow Ford station wagon as a hearse, the task also can be tiring. That point was driven home only last week as Perion coordinated a wake for a 38-year-old Sioux woman who died in Duluth. Between Tuesday and Friday, Perion had gone to Duluth to get the body; used a Richfield funeral home to prepare it for burial and then had overseen a 24-hour wake at the American Indian Center on Franklin Avenue in Minneapolis.

Then there was a 10-hour drive with the coffin to Belcourt, N.D., for another wake and burial. In between, there was the haggling by phone with a North Dakota funeral home that wanted a consulting fee of nearly $400. And finally, there were arrangements with the family to place a hatchet in the coffin—an Indian custom to ward off evil spirits—and to put tobacco between the body's fingers to feed the spirits.

(continued)

(continued from previous page)

Perion's fee, excluding the price of the poplar wood coffin: $927. "It's really amazing. When I get through with a funeral, I'm exhausted," he said.

It is that commitment that has won Perion friends. "I see a pretty big need," said Philip Gleason, coowner of Gleason Mortuary in Richfield where Perion uses space for embalming. "The white man does not understand the Indian and his traditions . . . (Perion's) all set to go, you might say, if he can come up with a building."

Perion's financial plan, written with the help of economic development experts, lists start-up costs of $100,245—more than half of which would go to buy a four-wheel-drive funeral coach and two new Buicks. Regarding the size of the building he'll need, Perion said: "The square footage is based on how many Indians will die in the first year—how many will die in Minneapolis and St. Paul, and how many calls I'll get out of that."

But he also stresses the sensitivity he will bring to the role. He advertises his familiarity with the water drum ceremony, during which an Indian elder wraps an animal hide around a canister of water that symbolizes the purification of the spiritual world. Perion talks also of the star quilt burial rite, in which a large quilt with a star in the middle hangs behind the casket during the wake and is often then used to wrap the body before burial.

And he talks of the pain of burying his own people.

His most heart-wrenching Indian funeral? That, says Perion, might be the time the family of an Indian infant who had died wanted to wrap the body in a blanket just before the casket was closed. But when the family began wailing and wouldn't let the body go, Perion finally found himself having to pry the body from them. "I'll never do that again," he said.

Others agree the uniqueness of Indian burials can make them challenging. "They have evening wakes that last the entire (night)," said Les Rosecke, a funeral director at Albin Funeral Chapel in south Minneapolis. The funeral home, which Rosecke said handles an estimated 35 Indian burials a year, is considered to have the largest number of Indian funerals locally. Of a funeral home for Indians, he said: "We certainly would cooperate with them."

As Perion searches for money and a funeral home, the supports continue to roll in. "I tell ya', I think it would be a marvelous idea if it works," said Mary Williams, a funeral director in Duluth who once worked with Perion. "It's a culture that's very unique to itself—different rituals, different time considerations. (Steve's) very much involved in tribal activities."

M. Kaszuba, *Minneapolis Star and Tribune,* October 9, 1989. Reprinted with permission of the *Star and Tribune.*

The Huicholes of Mexico (Weigand & Weigand, 1991, p. 62) handle the corpse with a great deal of respect and care. A singer/curer who is usually closely related to the deceased supervises the preparation of the corpse for burial or placement into a cave: Clothing is changed, personal items are arranged to accompany the body, and the individual's hands and face are washed with water. Most adults aid in the preparation unless "emotional collapse prevents such activity." However, most people are rather calm during these preparations.

The Konyak Nagar in India (Furer-Haimendorf, 1969) place the corpse onto a bier. Six days after the funeral, the head is removed from the body, and the skull is placed into an urn hollowed from a block of sandstone. For three years the skull is given portions of food and beer whenever the kinsmen celebrate a feast.

Bronislaw Malinowski (1929) reported that the Trobriand Islanders continually handle the remains throughout the death ritual. The body is **exhumed** (removed from its grave or tomb) twice and cut up. Some of the bones are peeled out of the carcass, handled, and given to different individuals.

Among the Yanomamo Indians of Venezuela and Brazil (Chagnon, 1992), the body of one dying in an epidemic is placed onto a tree platform and allowed to decay. After several months, an elderly man is appointed to strip the remaining decayed flesh from the bones, which are then cremated. Under normal circumstances, the body of a deceased Yanomamo is burned, and the ashes are mixed with boiled plantain soup and are eaten at a feast. This **endocannibalism** is supposed to put the warriors into an appropriate frame of rage prior to going out to kill the enemy. Such behavior is considered a supreme form of displaying friendship and solidarity for the Yanomamo.

It seems significant in most societies that the body be cleaned and steps taken to assure a tolerable odor prior to final disposition. A reverence for the body also seems prevalent. As in the United States, it is important in many other societies that the deceased "look good" to the mourners.

The body is not exhumed to take various parts home in the United States, but some individuals have been known to keep the **cremains** (remains from cremation) in a vase in the home or to carry them around in their purse. Others take photographs (see Chapter 1) of the deceased or collect important reminders to be placed into scrapbooks or albums. According to Judy Tatelbaum (1980), keepsakes like photographs, clippings, and stories about the deceased can provide a satisfying memorial later on. Fearing that we will be unable to remember the deceased distinctly enough, we desire a "piece" of the person we loved.

Burial Rites

As noted in chapter 5, Bronislaw Malinowski (1948) stressed religion and magic as means of reducing death anxiety and fears. A. R. Radcliffe-Brown (1965) argued for a different interpretation, suggesting that rites may contribute to death anxiety and insecurity. These are simply different explanations for the same rites. Conrad Kottak (1993) states that for one raised within the tradition of a particular culture, performance of the rites does relieve anxiety—it is the socially approved means of doing so. On the other hand, anxiety may result *because* the rites exist. A common stress may

The Yanomamo

Approximately 12,000 Yanomamo Indians live in Venezuela and Brazil in villages ranging in size from 40 to 250 inhabitants. Being horticulturalists, the Yanomamo grow 85 percent of their food. They occasionally enjoy the delicacies of caterpillars, roasted spiders, and armadillos.

The Yanomamo are a very aggressive and fierce people living in a state of chronic warfare and believing it is the "nature of men to fight." Because they define themselves as fierce, they act accordingly. The "fierceness" of the Yanomamo is exemplified by their gruesome methods of infanticide and abortion, their raiding parties where men are killed and women raped and captured as wives, their games of chest pounding, side slapping, club pounding and ax fights played at village feasts, their chopping on their wives with machetes to "show their love," and 24 percent of adult males dying in warfare.

Women's status among the Yanomamo is not high. They perform the bulk of the garden work, while men do the initial heavier ground-breaking duties with their digging sticks. Almost daily, the men lie in their hammocks getting high on hallucinogenic drugs. The drugs are taken from the bark of the ebene tree and shot into their nostrils in a powdery form. Though side effects of the drug are vomiting, runny nose, and watery eyes, the men have contact with the deceased ancestors while under the drug's influence. Husbands beat their wives, and brothers will trade their sisters to other groups of brothers for wives for themselves.

Competition and aggressiveness are certainly prevalent in the United States, especially among the middle class. We too are a somewhat fierce people. We have a reputation of high crime and violence and of cutthroat economics. While not like the Yanomamo, the United States would likely fall closer to the Yanomamo on a continuum with aggressive behavior at one end and passive behavior at the other.

Adapted from *Yanomamo: The Fierce People* (4th ed.), by N. A. Chagnon, 1992, New York: Holt, Rinehart and Winston.

be produced by participation in the rites, thus enhancing the social solidarity of the participants.

FUNCTIONS

The term *function* refers to the extent to which some part or process of a social system contributes to the maintenance of that system. *Function* means the extent to which an activity promotes or interferes with the maintenance of a system (Cuzzort & King, 1995, p. 250). Robert Merton (1957) distinguished between two forms of social function. **Manifest functions** are objective consequences for the person, subgroup, or social system that contribute to its adjustment and were so intended. **Latent**

Burial Rites of Russian Immigrants in Oregon

Members of the Russian Old Believer community which settled in Oregon since 1964 represent an eminently traditional group with ancient Slavic roots. Their way of life is fashioned after a mid-17th century religious ethic of the Old Orthodox Russian Church. Death is a "village" affair, and all turn their attention to it, when it happens. They rather rapidly do what they consider necessary to lay the body to rest, rarely taking more than 24 hours.

When death occurs, the body is washed and dressed in a white, loosely based cloth. The body is then placed inside the casket with the arms crossed on the chest and the hands formed into the sign of the cross in the old style: the first two fingers are extended and the thumb is joined with the third and fourth fingers. The service occurs in the living room of the home, where the casket has been placed.

Another service is held at the grave site. In addition to final prayers, the grave is circled three times in a clockwise direction. The immediate kin give their final farewell as they take their last look and sometimes give a kiss to the deceased. After the lid is placed on the casket, it is lowered into the ground. The grave is then filled by the closest kin, followed by distant kin, and then others, all of whom throw three handfuls of dirt onto the casket.

The graves are lined up in an easterly direction. At the foot of each grave stands an eight-ended Orthodox cross, thus, at sunrise, the shadow of the cross is cast onto the grave, superimposed on the deceased in proper perspective. At the Second Coming, when the dead are called from the grave, the deceased will simply rise up to stand next to their crosses and face the East, from whence they believe Christ will come. After the burial, those in attendance return to the home of the deceased for a dinner which has been set to commemorate the dead.

Taken from "Po Starykovsky (The Old People's Way): End of Life Attitudes and Customs in Two Traditional Russian Communities" (pp. 91–112), by R. A. Morris, 1991. In D. R. Counts and D. A. Counts (Eds.), *Coping With the Final Tragedy: Cultural Variation in Dying and Grieving*, Amityville, NY: Baywood Publishing.

functions are consequences that contribute to adjustment but were not so intended. Manifest functions are the official explanations of a given action (such as going to a funeral to pay respects to the deceased and to let the survivors know that you care). Latent functions are the sociological explanations (for instance, a funeral really becomes a family reunion). Ronald Barrett (1992) observes that African American funerals are indeed "a primary ritual and a focal occasion with a big social gathering after the funeral and the closest thing to a family reunion that might ever take place."

Rather than leave all corpses to environmental elements, an event like a burial rite obviously has some positive consequences for the survivors of the deceased. Burial rite functions can be enumerated as follows. First, burial rites are the reaffirmation of group structure and social cohesiveness of the individuals suffering loss. Second, they give meaning and sanction to the separation of the dead person from the living. Third, burial rites help effect the transition of the soul to another, otherworldly realm.

Fourth, they assist in the incorporation of the spirit into its new existence. Fifth, according to Melvin Williams (1981), for the middle class in Pittsburgh, Pennsylvania, a funeral may establish, validate, and reinforce social status, whereas for the lower class, funerals tend to be rites of intensification and solidarity as people put aside feuds and squabbles for the moment.

To assure that the spirit will be reborn, some societies go to great lengths. For example, the Dunsun of northern Borneo (Williams, 1965) kill animals to accompany the deceased on the trip to the land of the dead. The Ulithi in Micronesia (Lessa, 1966) place a loincloth and a gingerlike plant in the right arm of the deceased so that gifts can be presented to the custodian at the entrance of the other world. For the Zinacantecos of Mexico (Vogt, 1970), a chicken head is put into a bowl of broth beside the head of the corpse. The chicken allegedly leads the "inner soul" of the deceased. A black dog then carries the "soul" across the river.

Though not the common practice, in 1987 an 18-year-old woman in India rested the head of her dead husband on her lap, sat on his funeral pyre, and was burned alive (Salamat, 1987). No one could stop her from committing **sati,** the most noble act of loyalty that a widow can perform for her husband, who, in the Hindu religion, is supposed to be considered a god by his wife. A widow cannot remarry and is treated as an evil omen and an economic liability. If she chooses to live, she has to remain barefoot, sleep on the floor, and can never go out of the house because she would be slandered if seen talking to a man. Some would argue that she is better off dead. Prior to this widow's act, however, sati had not been performed in that community since early in the 20th century.

As with the Zinacantecos of Mexico, a chicken is used in the burial rites of the Yoruba in southwestern Nigeria (Bascom, 1969). A man with a live chicken precedes the carrier of the corpse, plucking out feathers and leaving them along the trail for the soul of the deceased to follow back to town. Upon reaching the town gate, the chicken is killed by striking its head against the ground. The blood and feathers are then placed into the grave so that others will not die. A second chicken is killed, and its blood put into the grave so that the soul of the deceased will not bother the surviving relatives.

Soul houses are built in some parts of America's Appalachia (Gaines, 1981) to provide protection for the deceased from evil spirits, wild animals, grave robbers, and other unwelcome visitors. These little houses are placed directly over the grave. Some have flat tops, are box-shaped and concrete, whereas others have rooftop structures. The most elaborate of the soul houses are miniature homes with actual tin roofs, gutters, drainpipes, carpets, furniture, and various objects dear to the deceased. Most of the soul houses (sometimes called *grave houses*) constructed in the 19th and 20th centuries have decayed and disappeared or have been torn down (Crissman, 1994, p. 132). Concrete and metal vaults, along with the growing popularity of mausoleums, have tended to make these houses obsolete, notes Crissman (1994). However, soul houses can also be found in other parts of the country: Kevin Ladd (1997), for example, writes about an east Texas cemetery with "ten grave houses built of stacked rocks in a style roughly similar to the family's ancestral graves in Dundee, Scotland."

For the Cree in Quebec, Canada (Preston & Preston, 1991, pp. 143–144), it is important not to delay the burial. Delay may interfere with the forthcoming journey of the deceased and result in intense expression of grief for the bereaved. Thus, the Cree respond quickly in preparing the body for burial.

In summary, burial rites serve the functions of maintaining relations with ancestral spirits, reaffirming social solidarity, and restoring group structures dismembered by
death. As Gerry Cox and Ronald Fundis (1992) sum up so well in their discussion of
Native American burial practices, "If nothing else is known, it is that tribal groups did
not abandon their dead. They provided them with ceremony and disposal." Indeed, a
lot of ceremony and a way of disposing of the dead tend to go hand in hand with
death among different cultures. These burial rites not only reaffirm group structure,
but also enhance social cohesiveness. Even with the death of pets, a way of disposing
of the remains is important, as is shown in the following reading about the Japanese.

VARIATIONS

Just as expressions of mourning vary among cultures, so do burial rites. The depth of
the grave, the place of disposal, and the importance of the status of the deceased are
examined here.

In the old days of the Wild West in the United States, one was buried "six feet
under with his boots on." It is true that graves were six feet deep in earlier periods of
United States history, but today graves are less than six feet deep—typically around
four and a half feet with 18 inches of dirt above the top of the casket/vault. With
sealed, heavier caskets today—often placed within a steel or concrete vault—it is not

---

A Good Friend Up in Smoke
Tom Torok

The death of a pet can be especially devastating for most Japanese. Most
don't have a garden where they can lay the departed critters to rest. A
cemetery plot could cost more than a Toyota. So typically when Fido passes
on, folks just wait for trash night, stuff him in the can and bid him a fond
farewell.

"A pet is a member of the family," Hideki Arasawa said. "You shouldn't
just throw them in the rubbish—you should treat them like a human being."

Arasawa's firm has an alternative to trash night. The company man-
ufactures a mobile pet crematorium that lets owners give their cats, dogs and
birds a fitting send-off—right in front of their homes.

One firm using the vans charges $275 to cremate a 15- to 17-pound dog.
Cats, rabbits and birds, which use less fuel, cost $196. The firm, The Dog's
Friend, conducts funerals that closely mimic human send-offs. As an added
bonus, the temperature of the furnace is closely controlled, to leave the
bones intact.

"If people just send their pet off somewhere for cremation they're left
with an unsettled feeling," said Takayuki Sato, who runs the Tokyo branch.
"If they can actually see it with their own eyes and then put the bones in a
jar, they feel extremely satisfied."

Adapted from T. Torok, *Philadelphia Inquirer,* June 28, 1992, p. 3A.

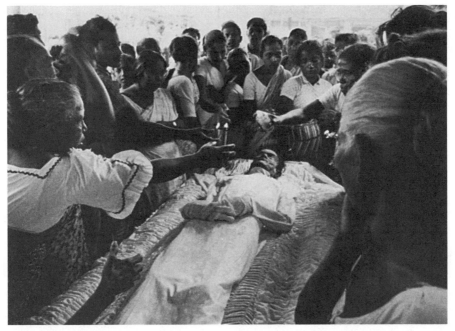

This Buddhist funeral in Ceylon demonstrates the communal nature of the special care taken in preparing the body for final disposition.

necessary to place the body so deep in the ground, as was the case with an unsealed pine box of an earlier period.

The Kalingas of the Philippines (Dozier, 1967) bury adults in graves six feet deep and three feet wide. The Mardudjara aborigines of Australia (Tonkinson, 1978) dig a rectangular hole about three feet deep, line the bottom with leafy bushes and small logs, then place the body inside. Similarly, the Semai of Malaya (Dentan, 1968) dig the grave two to three feet deep.

In death as in life, gender differences exist: Among the Abkhasians near the Black Sea (Benet, 1974), women are buried 10 centimeters deeper than men. In examining men's and women's 18th- and 19th-century gravestone epitaphs in cemeteries in the northeastern United States, Tarah Somers (1995) revealed major differences in the social expectations of men and women. Women were described in more passive and private terms ("meek and affectionate" and "joyfully departed life"), whereas men were often memorialized with active and public terms ("skillful and valiant in truth" and "triumphant at the approach of death").

Some societies keep the corpses in or near the home of the deceased. The Yoruba of Nigeria (Bascom, 1969), for example, dig the grave in the room of the deceased. An adult man among the Lugbara of Uganda (Middleton, 1965) is buried inside his first wife's hut in the center of the floor. The Swazi of Africa (Kuper, 1963) bury a woman on the outskirts of her husband's home.

A deceased person's rank or status in the community or village may determine how the corpse is treated or its final disposition. For example, a deceased Buddhist common person in Thailand (Leming & Premchit, 1992) will be cleaned, dressed, and placed into a casket. A high-status Buddhist individual, however, will be embalmed, then bathed and dressed with new clothes. The face will be covered with gold leaves prior to the body being placed into the casket. Cremation follows in the Buddhist tradition as the form of final disposition. The Barabaig of Tanzania (Klima, 1970) place the bodies of women and children out into the surrounding bush, where they are consumed by hyenas. Only certain male and female elders will receive a burial. In Greece (Brabant, 1994) the majority of individuals cannot afford "permanent" burial, thus they rent a grave for 3 years, then the remains are exhumed and the bones placed into the "bone room." The more prosperous individuals in Greece can afford to pay to have their remains stay buried permanently. The following reading about the Kapauku Papuans further details the fact that one's position in the community determines how and where burial or final disposition will occur.

Thus, in death as in life, one's social status determines how one is treated. Whether one is buried or left to the elements is often determined by gender, age,

---

Burial Rites Among the Kapauku Papuans

Among the Kapauku Papuans of West New Guinea, burial rites are determined by the deceased's status and cause of the death. The simplest burial is given to a drowned man, whose body is laid flat on the bank of the river and protected by a fence erected around it. The body is then abandoned to the elements. Very young children and individuals not particularly liked and considered unimportant are completely interred. Children, women, and the elderly who were unimportant but loved are tied with vines into a squatting position and semi-interred with the head above ground. A dome-shaped structure of branches and soil is then constructed to protect the head.

A respected and loved adult male among the Kapauku Papuans receives a tree burial. Tied in a squatting position, the corpse is placed in a tree house with a small window in front. Corpses of important individuals, who are feared by their relatives, and of women who died in childbirth require a special type of burial. Their bodies are placed in the squatting position on a special raised scaffold constructed in the house where death occurred. The house is then sealed and abandoned.

The most elaborate burial among the Kapauku Papuans is given to a rich headman. A special hut is built on high stilts, the body is tied in a squatting position, and a pointed pole is driven through the rectum, abdomen, chest cavity and neck with its pointed end supporting the base of the skull. The body is then placed in the dead house with the face appearing in the front window of the structure. The body is pierced several times with arrows to allow the body fluids to drain away. Years later, the skull of the respected man may be cleaned and awarded a second honor of being placed on a pole driven into the ground near the house of the surviving relatives.

Taken from *The Kapauku Papuans of West New Guinea*, by L. Pospisil, 1963, New York: Holt, Rinehart and Winston.

standing in the community, and cause of death. If one is buried in the ground, even the depth of burial may vary by one's social position.

Conclusion

As discussed in chapter 2, dying is more than a biological process. One does not die in a vacuum but rather in a social milieu. The act of dying has an influence on others because it is a shared experience. The sharing mechanism is death-related meanings composed of symbols.

Because death meanings are socially constructed, patterns of "correct" or "incorrect" behavior related to dying and death will largely be determined within the social setting in which they occur. Death-related behavior of the dying person and of those relating to him or her is in response to meaning relative to the audience and the situation. As noted, death-related behavior is shared, symboled, and situated.

Because death generally disrupts established interaction networks, shared "scripts" aid in providing socially acceptable behavior for the bereaved. Such "scripts" are essential because they prevent societal breakdowns while providing social continuity. Burial rituals are important in assuring social cohesion at the time of family dismemberment through death. Because death is a family crisis (see Dickinson & Fritz, 1981), appropriate networks for coping must be culturally well grounded.

Death-related meanings are socially created and transmitted. Through participant observation, small children learn from others how to respond to death. If children are sheltered from such situations, their socialization will be thwarted. As noted in this chapter, family involvement plays an important role in most societies as individuals prepare for death, as they prepare the corpse for final disposition, and as burial rituals that follow are performed. Therefore, whether death rituals involve killing a chicken, scraping the meat from the bones of the corpse, crying quietly, wailing loudly, mutilating one's own body, or burning or burying the corpse, all bereavement behavior has three interconnected characteristics—it is shared, symboled, and situated.

Summary

1. Customs for caring for the dying prior to death assist both the dying individual and the survivors in coping with the impending death.
2. For some, death is viewed as the end, whereas for others it is viewed as a continuation of life in a different form.
3. Although mourning rituals tend to be commonplace in different cultures, the prescribed behavior is affected by the social status and gender of the individuals involved.
4. Some social groups mourn for a few hours after death, whereas others mourn for months or years.
5. The depth of burial often varies by the gender and socioeconomic status of the deceased.
6. Burial rituals serve the functions of appeasing the ancestral spirits and the soul of the deceased, bringing the kin together, reinforcing social status, and restoring the social structure.

7. In most societies the body of the deceased is cleaned and prepared for burial. Some groups even keep parts of the body for ornamental or special purposes.
8. Anthropologists are interested in the meanings that different events, such as death, have for different cultures.
9. Being familiar with cross-cultural death customs should help one to better understand the American concept of death.

Discussion Questions

1. Why is it important to learn about bereavement patterns in other cultures?
2. Cite as many death custom similarities between other cultures and the United States as you can. Cite death custom differences between other cultures and the United States.
3. What is your own concept of "soul"? How is your concept of soul similar to and different than some other cultures' concept of "soul"? How does a concept of "soul" relate to death?
4. Drawing upon your own knowledge, discuss any U.S. behavior patterns for the dying just prior to death. How do these customs compare with those cited in this chapter?
5. Describe mourning rituals commonly found in the United States. Mourning rituals may differ by region of the country or ethnicity. Discuss these differences.
6. It is suggested that an explanation for crying when someone dies may be rather complex. Discuss the reasons for crying over a death.
7. A professional generally prepares the corpse for final disposition in the United States, but this is not universally true. Discuss the importance of the family being involved in preparing the body for final disposition.
8. In death as in life, gender discrimination occurs. Discuss with a local funeral director the differences in funerals for males and females. Do you notice differences in graves (such as size of the headstone and length of epitaphs) between males and females?
9. Unlike in many societies where squatting childbirth occurs, in the United States we basically give birth and bury in a horizontal position. Why do you suppose the United States has a "laid-back" approach from the womb to the tomb? Can you cite advantages and disadvantages to horizontal burials?
10. What are some of the functions of burial rites discussed in this chapter?

Glossary

Bier: A framework upon which the corpse and/or casket is placed for viewing and/or carrying.

Cremains: That which is left after cremation.

Endocannibalism: The Yanomamo Indian practice of eating the ashes of the deceased in order to charge up a warrior prior to going into battle and to display friendship and solidarity.

Ethnocentrism: Literally means "culture-centeredness." The belief that one's own culture is superior to the culture of others.

Ethnography: The systematic description of a culture based on firsthand observation.

Exhume: To remove a corpse from its place of burial.

Kachina Performer: A masked and costumed individual who impersonates spirits of the dead.

Latent Function: Consequences of behavior that were not intended (for example, a funeral brings the family together, usually in an amiable way).

Levirate: A marriage rule whereby a widow marries her deceased husband's brother.

Lineage: A group of relatives who trace their descent unilineally from a common ancestor.

Manifest Function: Consequences of behavior that are intended and overt (such as going to a funeral to pay respects to the deceased).

Pyre: A combustible pile (usually of wood) for burning a corpse at a funeral rite.

Rites of Passage: Ceremonies centering around transitions in life from one status to another (including baptism, marriage ceremony, and the funeral).

Ritual: The symbolic affirmation of values by means of culturally standardized utterances and actions.

Sati: A controversial practice rarely exercised in some areas of India in which the widow throws herself onto the funeral pyre of her deceased husband. This "most noble act of loyalty" makes her a goddess who is worshipped at her cremation site.

References

Barrett, R. K. (1992). Psychocultural influences on African American attitudes toward death, dying and funeral rites. In J. Morgan (Ed.), *Personal care in an impersonal world.* Amityville, NY: Baywood Publishing.

Bascom, W. (1969). *The Yoruba of southwestern Nigeria.* New York: Holt, Rinehart and Winston.

Bendann, E. (1930). *Death customs: An analytical study of burial rites.* New York: Alfred A. Knopf.

Benet, S. (1974). *Abkhasians: The long-living people of Caucasus.* New York: Holt, Rinehart and Winston.

Bloch, M., & Parry, J. (1982). *Death and the regeneration of life.* Cambridge: Cambridge University Press.

Brabant, M. (1994, September). The high price of everlasting peace. In *Worldwide report: Death.* London: BBC Worldwide.

Caistor, N. (1994, September). Having a wail of a time at the wake. In *Worldwide report: Death.* London: BBC Worldwide.

Chagnon, N. A. (1992). *Yanomamo: The fierce people* (4th ed.). New York: Holt, Rinehart and Winston.

Cohen, R. (1967). *The Kanuri of Bornu.* New York: Holt, Rinehart and Winston.

Connor, L. H. (1995, September). The action of the body on society: Washing a corpse in Bali. *Journal of the Royal Anthropological Institute, 1,* 537–560.

Cowell, D. D. (1986). Funerals, family, and forefathers: A view of Italian-American funeral practices. *Omega, 16,* 69–86.

Cox, G. R., & Fundis, R. J. (1992). Native American burial practices. In J. Morgan (Ed.), *Personal care in an impersonal world.* Amityville, NY: Baywood Publishing.

Crissman, J. K. (1994). *Death and dying in central Appalachia.* Urbana, IL: University of Illinois Press.

Cuzzort, R. P., & King, E. W. (1995). *Twentieth century social thought* (5th ed.). New York: Holt, Rinehart and Winston.

Deng, F. M. (1972). *The Dinka of the Sudan.* New York: Holt, Rinehart and Winston.

Dentan, R. K. (1968). *The Semai: A non-violent people of Malaya.* New York: Holt, Rinehart and Winston.

Dickinson, G. E., & Fritz, J. L. (1981, September 2). Death in the family. *Journal of Family Issues,* 379–384.

Dozier, E. P. (1966). *Hano: A Tewa Indian community in Arizona.* New York: Holt, Rinehart and Winston.

Durkheim, E. (1915/1954). *Elementary forms of the religious life.* New York: The Free Press.

Enright, L. (1994, September). Keeping the corpse company with a whiskey. In *World-wide report: Death.* London: BBC World-wide.

Faron, L. C. (1968). *The Mapuche Indians of Chile.* New York: Holt, Rinehart and Winston.

Feldman, D. A. (1990). *Culture and AIDS.* New York: Praeger.

Fraser, T. M., Jr. (1966). *Fishermen of south Thailand: The Malay villagers.* New York: Holt, Rinehart and Winston.

Furer-Haimendorf, C.V. (1969). *The Konyak Nagar: An Indian frontier tribe.* New York: Holt, Rinehart and Winston.

Gaines, J. (1981, November 1). Appalachia comes alive in studying tombstones. *Louisville Courier Journal,* p. 5.

Gamst, F. C. (1969). *The Qemant: A pagan-Hebraic peasantry of Ethiopia.* New York: Holt, Rinehart and Winston.

Goldman, I. (1979). *The Cubeo: Indians of the northwest Amazon.* Urbana, IL: University of Illinois Press.

Goody, J. (1993). *The culture of flowers.* Cambridge: Cambridge University Press.

Habenstein, R. W., & Lamers, W. M. (1974). *Funeral customs the world over* (Rev. ed.). Milwaukee: Bulfin Printers.

Hallenbeck, J. M., Goldstein, K., & Mebane, E. W. (1996, May). Cultural considerations of death and dying in the United States. *Clinical Geriatric Medicine, 12,* 393–406.

Harris, M. (1974). *Cows, pigs, wars and witches.* New York: Vintage Books.

Hart, C. W. M., & Pilling, A. R. (1960). *The Tiwi of north Australia.* New York: Holt, Rinehart and Winston.

Haviland, W. A. (1991). *Anthropology* (6th ed.). Fort Worth, TX: Holt, Rinehart and Winston.

Heider, K. (1991). *Grand Valley Dani: Peaceful warriors* (2nd ed.). Fort Worth, TX: Holt, Rinehart and Winston.

Helman, C. (1985). *Culture, health, and illness.* Bristol, England: Wright.

Hitchcock, J. T. (1966). *The Magars of Manyan Hill.* New York: Holt, Rinehart and Winston.

Hoebel, E. A. (1960). *The Cheyennes: Indians of the Great Plains.* New York: Holt, Rinehart and Winston.

Horowitz, M. M. (1967). *Morne-Paysan: Peasant village in Martinique.* New York: Holt, Rinehart and Winston.

Huntington, R., & Metcalf, P. (1992). *Celebrations of death: The anthropology of mortuary ritual* (2nd ed.). Cambridge: Cambridge University Press.

Kellehear, A. (1990). *Dying of cancer: The final year of life.* Chur, Switzerland: Harwood Academic Publishers.

Klima, G. J. (1970). *The Barabaig: East African cattle-herders.* New York: Holt, Rinehart and Winston.

Kottak, C. P. (1993). *Cultural anthropology* (6th ed.). New York: Random House.

Kozak, D. L. (1991). Dying badly: Violent death and religious change among the Tohono O'Odham. *Omega, 23,* 207–216.

Kristof, N. D. (1996). For rural Japanese, death doesn't break family ties. *New York Times,* p. 10.

Kuper, H. (1963). *The Swazi: A south African kingdom.* New York: Holt, Rinehart and Winston.

Ladd, K. (1997, Summer–Fall). The Sturrock family cemetery in Tyler County, Texas. *Association for Gravestone Studies Quarterly 20,* 4.

Leming, M. R., & Premchit, S. (1992). Funeral customs in Thailand. In J. Morgan (Ed.), *Personal care in an impersonal world.* Amityville, NY: Baywood Publishing.

Lessa, W. A. (1966). *Ulithi: A Micronesian design for living.* New York: Holt, Rinehart and Winston.

Malinowski, B. (1929). *The sexual life of savages.* New York: Harcourt, Brace and World.

Malinowski, B. (1948). *Magic, science and religion, and other essays.* Boston: Beacon Press.

Mandelbaum, D. (1959). Social uses of funeral rites. In H. Feifel (Ed.), *The meaning of death.* New York: McGraw-Hill.

Marcus, F. F. (1988, November 1). An invitation to become the life of the cemetery. *New York Times,* p. 8.

Mead, H. M. (1991). Sleep, sleep, sleep; farewell, farewell, farewell. Maori ideas about death. In D. R. Counts & D. A. Counts (Eds.), *Coping with the final tragedy: Cultural variation in dying and grieving* (pp. 43–51). Amityville, NY: Baywood Publishing.

Merton, R. K. (1957). *Social theory and social structure* (Rev. ed.). New York: The Free Press.

Middleton, J. (1965). *The Lugbara of Uganda.* New York: Holt, Rinehart and Winston.

Morris, R. A. (1991). Po starykovsky (the old people's way): End of life attitudes and customs in two traditional Russian communities. In D. R. Counts & D. A. Counts (Eds.), *Coping with the final tragedy: Cultural variation in dying and grieving* (pp. 91–112). Amityville, NY: Baywood Publishing.

Nagamine, T. (1988). Attitudes toward death in rural areas of Japan. *Death Studies, 12,* 61–68.

Oswalt, W. H. (1986). *Life cycles and lifeways.* Palo Alto, CA: Mayfield Publishing.

Palgi, P., & Abramovitch, H. (1984). Death: A cross-cultural perspective. *Annual Review of Anthropology, 13,* 385–417.

Pospisil, L. (1963). *The Kapauku Papuans of west New Guinea.* New York: Holt, Rinehart and Winston.

Preston, R. J., & Preston, S. C. (1991). Death and grieving among northern forest hunters: An East Cree example. In D. R. Counts &

D. A. Counts (Eds.), *Coping with the final tragedy: Cultural variation in dying and grieving* (pp. 135–155). Amityville, NY: Baywood Publishing.

Radcliffe-Brown, A. R. (1964). *The Andaman Islanders.* New York: The Free Press.

Radcliffe-Brown, A. R. (1965). *Structure and function in primitive society.* New York: The Free Press.

Ramsden, P. G. (1991). Alice in the afterlife: A glimpse in the mirror. In D. R. Counts & D. A Counts (Eds.), *Coping with the final tragedy: Cultural variation in dying and grieving* (pp. 27–41). Amityville, NY: Baywood Publishing.

Rappaport, R. A. (1974). Obvious aspects of ritual. *Cambridge Anthropology, 2,* 2–60.

Rosenblatt, P. C., Walsh, R., & Jackson, A. (1976). *Grief and mourning in cross cultural perspective.* New Haven: Human Relations Area Files Press.

Salamat, A. (1987). A young widow burns in her bridal clothes. *Far Eastern Economic Review, 138,* 54–55.

Somers, T. S. (1995, June 22–25). *Relict, consort, wife: The use of Connecticut Valley gravestones to understand concepts of gender in the late eighteenth and early nineteenth centuries.* Unpublished paper presented at the Annual Meeting of the Association for Gravestone Studies, Westfield, MA.

Sweeting, H. N., & Gilhooly, M. L. M. (1992). Doctor, am I dead? A review of social death in modern societies. *Omega, 24,* 251–269.

Tatelbaum, J. (1980). *The courage to grieve.* New York: Lippincott and Crowell Publishers.

Taylor, R. B. (1988). *Cultural ways* (3rd ed.). Boston: Allyn and Bacon.

Tonkinson, R. (1978). *The Mardudjara aborigines.* New York: Holt, Rinehart and Winston.

Tully, M. (1994, September). When body and soul go their separate ways. *Worldwide report: Death.* London: BBC Worldwide.

Turnbull, C. M. (1972). *The mountain people.* New York: Simon and Schuster.

Tylor, E. B. (1873). *Primitive culture.* London: John Murray.

Uchendu, V. C. (1965). *The Igbo of southeast Nigeria.* New York: Holt, Rinehart and Winston.

Van Gennep, A. (1960). *The rites of passage* (M. B. Vizedom & G. L. Caffee, Trans.). Chicago: University of Chicago Press. (Original work published 1909)

Vogt, E. Z. (1970). *The Zinacantecos of Mexico: A modern Maya way of life.* New York: Holt, Rinehart and Winston.

Weigand, C. G., & Weigand, P. C. (1991). Death and mourning among the Huicholes of western Mexico. In D. R. Counts & D. A. Counts (Eds.), *Coping with the final tragedy: Cultural variation in dying and grieving* (pp. 53–68). Amityville, NY: Baywood Publishing.

Williams, M. D. (1981). *On the street where I lived.* New York: Holt, Rinehart and Winston.

Williams, T. R. (1965). *The Dunsun: A north Borneo society.* New York: Holt, Rinehart and Winston.

Suggested Readings

Barber, P. (1988). *Vampires, burial, and death: Folklore and fealty.* New Haven, CT: Yale University Press. This book is about how people in preindustrial cultures look at the processes and phenomena associated with death and the dissolution of the body.

Bendann, E. (1930). *Death customs: An analytical study of burial rites.* New York: Alfred A. Knopf. A thorough anthropological analysis of death customs, including an analysis of burial rites, causes of death, attitudes toward the corpse, mourning, and beliefs in the afterlife.

Bloch, M., & Parry, J. (1982). *Death and the regeneration of life.* Cambridge: Cambridge University Press. This anthology focuses on the significance of symbols of fertility and rebirth in funeral rituals from China, India, New Guinea, Latin America, and Africa.

Bond, G. C., Kreniske, J., Susser, I., & Vincent, J. (1997). *AIDS in Africa and the Caribbean.* Boulder, CO: Westview. This book offers detailed ethnographic studies to explain AIDS in a global and comparative third-world context.

Counts, D. R., & Counts, D. A. (Eds.). (1991). *Coping with the final tragedy: Cultural variation in dying and grieving.* Amityville, NY: Baywood Publishing. An anthology that discusses death and grieving in various parts of the world.

Crissman, J. K. (1994). *Death and dying in central Appalachia: Changing attitudes and practices.* Urbana, IL: University of Illinois Press. An exploration of cultural traits related to dying and death in Appalachia, showing how they have changed since the 1600s.

Dettwyler, K. A. (1994). *Dancing skeletons.* Prospect Heights, IL: Waveland Press. A biocultural anthropologist reports from her fieldwork on living and dying in west Africa.

Habenstein, R. W., & Lamers, W. M. (1974). *Funeral customs the world over* (Rev. ed.). Milwaukee: Bulfin Printers. A review of the cultures of the world especially significant in cross-cultural study of the various practices of funerals in all cultures.

Huntington, R., & Metcalf, P. (1992). *Celebrations of death: The anthropology of mortuary ritual* (2nd ed.). Cambridge: Cambridge University Press. An anthropological analysis of dying and death, including universals and culture, death as transition, and the royal corpse and the body politic.

Irish, D. P., Lundquist, K. F., & Nelson, V. J. (1993). *Ethnic variations in dying, death and grief.* Washington, DC: Taylor and Francis. An anthology that discusses dying, death, and grief in the following groups: African Americans, Mexican Americans, Hmong, Native Americans, Jews, Buddhists, Islamics, Quakers, and Unitarians.

McGuire, R. H. (1992). *Death, society, and ideology in a Hohokam community.* Boulder, CO: Westview Press. An archaeologist explores the nature of Hohokam social organization in the prehistory of southern Arizona.

Narasimhan, S. (1990). *Sati: Widow burning in India.* New York: Doubleday Anchor Books. A noted Indian journalist outlines the reasons why women choose to become, or are forced to become, sati and what this reveals about the society as a whole.

Parry, J. K., & Ryan, A. S. (1995). *A cross-cultural look at death, dying, and religion.* Chicago: Nelson-Hall Publishers. This book is about dying, death, and religion and how these subjects are integrated into the belief systems of various cultures: African Americans, Buddhists, Roman Catholics and other Christians, Chinese, Dominicans, Filipinos, Muslims, Jews, Koreans, and Mexican Americans.

Stannard, D. E. (1977). *The Puritan way of death.* New York: Oxford University Press. A portrayal of death in the Western tradition, including discussions of death, childhood, and burial.

Strocchia, S. T. (1992). *Death and ritual in Renaissance Florence. Baltimore: Johns Hopkins University Press.* An historian shows how death rites in Renaissance Florence reflected Florence's quick rise to commercial wealth in the 14th century and steady progress toward power in the 15th and 16th centuries.

Subedi, J., & Gallagher, E. B. (1996). *Society, health, and disease: Transcultural perspectives.* Upper Saddle River, NJ: Prentice-Hall. Discusses the sociocultural context of health and disease, sociopolitical constraints in health and health care, the psychology of health and well-being, the threat of AIDS, and emerging areas in international health.

Related Web Sites

http://www.lsds.com/death/   Thanatolinks contains links to some of the best Internet sites related to dying and death.

http://www.emanon.net/~kcabell/death.html   Contains many World Wide Web links to resources on death and bereavement.

http://WWW.Trinity.Edu/~mkearl/death-1.html#cu   An article about death written by Michael Kearl provides a multicultural perspective.

http://coombs.anu.edu.au/ResFacilities/DemographyPage.html
The Internet Guide to Demography and Population Studies.

http://members.aol.com/kmedeke/tod.htm   *Optima philosophia et sapientia est meditatio mortis* is an index of worldwide cemeteries by location (national and international). The cemetery links might be of historic, genealogical, or just touristic interest and contain pictures, lists of surnames, and historic information.

http://www.umanitoba.ca/anthropology/courses/122/module1/dimensions.html This article discusses method and theory in the field of cultural anthropology.

http://www.orci.com/personal/jim/grave/alphabet.html Find a Grave is a Web site that will enable you to locate (and, in some cases, view) the final resting places of many famous people.

http://Axis.LLX.COM:80/~bardo/ Bardo of Death Studies is an eclectic collection site for questions and answers from all cultures and backgrounds about dying and death and their integration with living and life. The site's purpose is to be of service to those who have curiosities or comments on the subjects of dying and death, as well as to serve as an Internet memorial for those who have gone before us into this journey called death.

http://www2.hawaii.edu/uhpress/Journals/BC/BCArts.html The home page of the *Journal of Buddhist-Christian Sights.*

http://www.vt.edu:1002/org/islam_sa/death.txt A Web site concerned with Islamic views of dying and death.

http://www.eas.asu.edu/~voegele/bioarchy/said.html An article on death and burial in Islamic societies.

http://www.sisfotel.net.id/htm/dsi/ngaben.htm A Web site dedicated to the celebration of Day of the Dead *(Dia de los Muertos).*

http://uts.cc.utexas.edu/~gwynneth/main.html This Web site is concerned with the interaction of culture, death, and literature.

http://www.vmedia.com/shannon/voodoo/death.html Web site dedicated to the topics of voodoo and death.

http://www.realtime.net/~rlp/dwp/mystic/Buddhist/Sogyal/book.html Web site dedicated to the *Tibetan Book of Living and Dying.*

http://www.tiac.net/users/smurungu/shona_religion.html Shona religion and beliefs with an article about an African tribal religion.

http://www.nua.ie/dagda/Fermanagh/Roslea/story/funeralBeliefs.html A Web site dealing with the cultural practices of the Irish wake.

http://www.latino.com/heal912.html "Immigrants' Views on Death" features a Latino perspective on death.

http://uscj.org/michigan/s-fielcs/bergde.html A very comprehensive bereavement guide for Judaism.

http://hyperlink.com/weaver/95/25_5/newcon/sikh/death/sikhdeth.htm Death from the point of view of the Sikh religion.

http://www.cmcc.muse.digital.ca/cmc/cmceng/ghhileng.html A Box of Souls presents the northwest Native American viewpoint.

http://mission.inter.net.th/princess/mother/ Funeral ceremonies for Her Royal Highness, the Princess Mother of the King of Thailand.

Chapter 11

The History of Bereavement and Burial Practices in American Culture

As long as the cemetery is being filled with a fresh stream of the recently dead, it stays symbolically a live and vital emblem, telling the living of the meaning of life and death.

—W. LLOYD WARNER, *THE LIVING AND THE DEAD*

This chapter traces the development of bereavement practices in America from the Puritans to the present. As death bereaves family members, friends, and more distant relatives, the survivors generally follow established rituals to care for the corpse, to reaffirm the solidarity of important groups, to create a new status for the dead person, and to comfort each other in such a way that they can eventually resume their roles in society. These rituals were established in time and come to us from the past. Therefore, we need a historical explanation to fully understand them.

We deal with historical explanations every day, but we seldom consider what constitutes a historical explanation. Historians mainly determine chronology and context in order to demonstrate causation and coincidence in human affairs. We begin with chronology in order to determine the order in which events or processes occurred. This in itself has a certain explanatory value; for example, it is useful to know that discovery of the germ theory of disease preceded the widespread use of embalming in America. Too often, however, history begins and ends with chronology, and students are stuck with memorizing names and dates. History also explores the context of events to help explain them. For example, it is easier to understand the development of the funeral parlor if we see it in the context of developments in the domestic parlor.

Sometimes, historians can use chronology and context to determine causation. Knowing, for example, that rural cemeteries preceded the public parks movement in America, we might conclude that cemetery reforms caused the parks movement. More frequently, however, chronology and context allow us to identify only coincidences (events or processes that occurred during the same period of time).

Especially in social and cultural history, this chronicle of coincidences is crucial because people think analogically as much as they think logically. They do not isolate problems or ideas when they are faced with them; instead their whole range of prior experience affects their decisions. In evaluating embalming, for example, few people treated the preservation of the corpse as a discrete issue. Instead, it coincided with other issues such as the importance of appearances in a consumer culture, the sanitary movement, the germ theory of disease, the privacy of the home, a stress on the "natural," a respect for surgery and surgeons, and the need to delay many funerals so that distant relatives could return home.

Likewise, history shows that bereavement is but one part of a social construction of reality that changes through time. Bereavement practices are virtually inseparable from prescriptions for dying and descriptions of death, just as the whole American way of death is inseparable from the American way of life. Therefore, this chapter explains how changes in the American way of life brought changes in the American way of death and bereavement. It traces the historical roots of our bereavement practices so that we can better predict the routes of future change.

Living Death, 1600–1830

Between 1600 and 1830, death was a living part of the American experience. Most people in this primarily agricultural period were well acquainted with death. In New England towns, for example, if people escaped death in their own homes, they still heard the toll of the funeral bell, encountered the funeral procession winding through the streets, or saw the stark *memento mori* of the graveyard. Even more, death was highlighted by the intellectual and emotional framework of the Reformed Tradition.

THE REFORMED TRADITION

The Reformed Tradition was the one part of the Protestant Reformation that most influenced colonial Americans. Although most colonists followed the beliefs of the Reformers, the New England Puritans made the most convincing synthesis of their ideas and attitudes. In their view, a sovereign God ruled over an earth inhabited by depraved people. God displayed his sovereignty in "special providences" in which he intervened in the natural or social world. One such providence was death.

Because of original sin and their own sinfulness, Puritans knew that they deserved death and damnation. They also celebrated, however, the fact that God freely elected a select few for salvation. Therefore, they approached death with an amazing ambivalence. They believed that "the last Enemy was Death; and God had made that

When death was viewed as a part of life, the body of the deceased was laid out in the home for friends of the bereaved to offer their condolences.

a friend too" (Sewall, 1973, pp. 1, 599). Death was an enemy for several reasons: It was painful, a punishment for sin, a possible prelude to everlasting hellfire, and brought separation from loved ones. Death was a friend, however, because it ended the pain and the earthly pilgrimage of the deceased, served as a "sanctified affliction" (Geddes, 1981, p. 31)—either confirming a saint's faith or converting a sinner—and could open the gates to heaven. Indeed, it was both a friendly enemy and a fearful friend.

Unlike modern thanatologists, the Puritans encouraged each other to fear death. They increasingly used that strong human emotion to rouse people from their psychological and spiritual security. Puritans knew that they would die, but not *when* they would die, or if they were among the elect. Therefore, they admonished themselves and each other to be constantly prepared for death. "It will do you no hurt. You will Dy not One Minute the sooner for it," argued Cotton Mather, "and being fit to Dy, you will be the more Fit to Live" (Geddes, 1981, pp. 64–65). Over and over again they prayed, "Lord, help me to redeem the time!" Like modern thanatologists, they felt that an awareness of death could improve the quality of their lives and that they had a role to play in the work of God's redemption. Indeed, for them, dying, death, and bereavement were opportunities to glorify God by demonstrating human dependence on divine providence.

The deathbed was the final place of preparation. Dying Puritans received visitors who wanted to help provide "a lift toward heaven." Unlike Catholics, who relied on the sacramental rite of Extreme Unction, the Puritans focused on the state of the dying person's soul and mind. They prayed together, read the Bible, and urged active acceptance of the will of God.

In the same way, "the funeral was another opportunity for the bereaved to turn affliction into spiritual growth through resignation to, and joyful acceptance of, the will of God" (Geddes, 1981, p. 104). Most Puritan deaths occurred at home. The family sent out for midwife-nurses to care for the corpse, ordered a coffin, and notified friends and relatives not already present. Puritans considered the corpse a mere shell of the soul. They simply washed it, wrapped it in a shroud, and placed it into the coffin. They embalmed bodies only to transport them to other towns for burial or to prevent an offensive stench in hot weather.

Friends and relatives visited the home to console and congratulate the bereaved. They brought gifts of food to allow the survivors an opportunity to mourn and to prepare the funeral. In this way, as in their own participation in the funeral, they reaffirmed the solidarity of the covenanted community. The funeral itself usually took place within a few days of death, and it followed the simple guidelines of the 1644 Westminster Confession: "When any person departeth this life, let the dead body, upon the day of Buriall, be decently attended from the house to the place appointed for publique Buriall, and there immediately interred, without any ceremony" (Geddes, 1981, pp. 110–124).

Pallbearers, ministers, and civil officials were commonly invited to a funeral with a gift of gloves. Wealthier families might also bestow scarves and/or memorial rings and give gloves to anyone who marched in the procession. These items were the common symbols of mourning in a colonial society, but more elaborate mourning apparel was also available. The tolling of the town bell announced the onset of a funeral, and participants gathered at the home for prayer and the procession.

Puritans prayed not for the soul of the deceased but rather for the comfort and instruction of the living. They believed that judgment occurs at death and that the dead are beyond human aid, so they prayed to reaffirm their faith and to glorify their God. For example, upon the death of his 2-year-old daughter, Samuel Sewall had his surviving children read passages from the Bible. John read Ecclesiastes 3 on the acceptance of the seasons of life, Elizabeth read Revelation 22 on the theme of hope, Hannah read Psalm 38 on the mercy of God, and young Samuel asked for God's comfort in Psalm 102 (Sewall, 1973, pp. 1, 364). In addition to prayers, Puritans might also read an **elegy,** which generally depicted the dead person as a saint freed from the world and entering eternal bliss. Such elegies confirmed the new, separate status of the deceased, helping to bring grief under control, and provided a good example for structuring life after bereavement. Sometimes a copy of the elegy was pinned to the coffin or hearse for the funeral procession (Geddes, 1981, pp. 130–131).

The mourners walked from the home to the graveyard, where the men of the family, or the **sexton,** had opened a grave. They carried the coffin on a bier, covered with a black cloth "pall"—both of which were the property of the town instead of the church, as was the custom in England. During the procession, mourners were supposed to "apply themselves to meditations and conferences suitable to the occasion." At the grave site, the pallbearers lowered the coffin into the earth, and the grave was refilled (Geddes, 1981, pp. 111, 133–135).

After the burial, the mourners returned home, where they shared food, drink, prayers, and comforting words. The family members thanked the pallbearers and participants and sometimes gave additional presents. They might also ask the minister to deliver a funeral sermon, which would occur not on the day of burial, but rather at the next regular meeting of the congregation. Sometimes families had such sermons and/or the elegies published and distributed to friends as *memento mori*. At a later date, the family might also erect a marker over the grave to proclaim the imminence of death or God's promise of salvation. Such markers near the much-frequented meetinghouse were another way of maintaining the vitality of death in early American culture (Geddes, 1981, pp. 139–140; Ludwig, 1966).

The Puritan funeral was the primary social institution for channeling the grief of survivors. It provided for the disposition of the body and the acknowledgment of the absence of the deceased. It drew the community members together for mutual comfort, and it allowed mourners to honor the dead, to express their sorrow at separation, and to demonstrate their acceptance of God's will. After the funeral, Puritans expected mourners to return to their calling and to resume their life's work. They did not approve elaborate or extended mourning of the sort that became customary in the 19th century because it undermined the cheerful resignation to God's will that was essential to the Puritan experience.

REFORMING THE REFORMED TRADITION

In 1802 Nathaniel Emmons delivered a magnificent funeral sermon entitled "Death Without Order." In it, he reviewed the Puritan orthodoxy of death, observing that "in relation to God, death is perfectly regular; but this regularity he has seen proper to conceal from the view of men." Emmons saw the uncertainty of death as a demonstration of God's sovereignty and human dependence and as a way of teaching people "the importance and propriety of being constantly prepared for it." However, he also saw that, despite the fact of death's disorder, multitudes of Americans had resolved "to observe order in preparing to meet it" (Emmons, 1842, pp. 3, 29–38). Between the 1730s and the 1830s, such orderly Americans were influenced by the Enlightenment, the American Revolution, Unitarianism, and Evangelicalism—and all of these were influenced by an underlying market revolution. These movements slowly but surely reformed the Reformed Tradition and gave Americans an eclectic tradition from which to fashion new beliefs and behavior about dying, death, and bereavement.

The Enlightenment replaced the Puritans' providential God with a First Cause who designed the universe to operate by orderly and observable natural laws, and it replaced depraved dependent Puritans with enlightened, rational people. Enlightened people, therefore, viewed death not as a time of judgment, but rather as a natural occurrence. They looked for a serene and stoic death and a simple, emotionally controlled funeral. Because enlightened ideas were exchanged almost entirely among the educated classes of the eastern seaboard, they had little immediate impact on overall American bereavement practices. In conjunction with the social forces of the American Revolution, however, the Enlightenment eventually affected American society.

In most areas of America, a basically Puritan way of death persisted until the 19th century, especially in rural areas where religion remained the focus of life. The increasing specialization and commercialization of life, however, eventually shaped death customs, too. During the 18th century, economic, geographic, and population growth began to produce cities, social stratification and diversity, political dissent, and cultural controversy. Anxiety over the ideology of opportunistic individualism that produced many of these internal conflicts combined with extended imperial control to produce

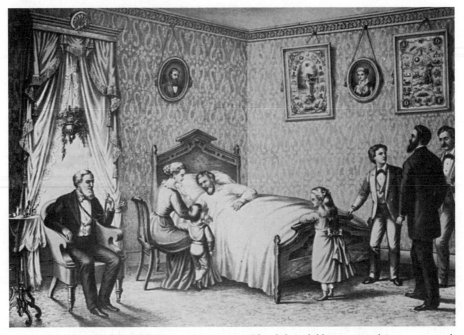

During the early part of the 19th century, Americans socialized their children to view dying as a natural process to be accepted by all members of the family.

a revolution that reinforced Enlightenment ideas of rationality and activity. The American revolution "acted as an inspirational model of human beings' power to alter their own lives, to think new thoughts, to act on the best ideas of humanity, to liberate themselves from the dead weight of the past" (Gross, 1976, p. 191). As a newly independent people pursued life, liberty, and happiness, they no longer depended on God's will; instead they made their own plans—plans that did not include death as a fact of life.

In religious developments, both Unitarianism and Evangelicalism accepted the enhanced view of human nature and human agency. The Unitarian gospel of "capitalism, theism, liberalism, and optimism" appealed especially to the commercial and professional classes of Boston—America's cultural capital in the 19th century (Howe, 1970, p. 21). The Unitarians, however, were influential far beyond their numbers. Many people in other denominations accepted their progressive optimism—which derived from conceptions of a beneficent God. Unitarians were viewed by others as being basically good people whose lives were the best evidence of their religiosity, and they were admired for their rational approach to religion. Almost all Americans accepted the mid-19th-century rural cemetery reform that began in Brahmin Boston.

Outside of Boston, more Americans were affected by revivalistic Evangelicalism than by Unitarianism. The Second Great Awakening of American Evangelicalism began in the 1790s as a response to the Enlightenment and grew throughout the 19th century. Evangelicals stressed the Bible, a conversion experience, and a Christian life (and death). They preached God's persuasiveness more than his arbitrary power, his moral government more than the ideas of predestination and election, and the concept of willful sinfulness more than that of innate depravity. Therefore, although

Evangelicals generally approached death from a Puritan position, they believed that God offers salvation and that people can take it if they will. Consequently, Evangelicalism offered assurance to the saved, even as it heightened the anxiety of the unregenerate. With the idealization of home and family, this could account for the abundant literature on the death of children, as parents agonized over an ailing child, hoping all the while that death would terminate the suffering, yet fearing that something worse would be the result. After 1850, however, the romanticization of childhood overcame ideas of infant damnation, provided more assurance to worried parents, and tipped the delicate balance of evangelical belief from anxiety to assurance. By that time, however, Evangelicalism had begun to be affected by sentimentalism, scientific naturalism, and liberal theology, as well as by the social and institutional developments of the dying of death.

The Dying of Death, 1830–1945

Between 1830 and 1945, the ideas and institutions with which Americans approached death changed in a process that an English author of 1899 called "the dying of death." This process brought "the practical disappearance of the thought of death as an influence bearing upon practical life" ("The Dying of Death," 1899) and the tactical appearance of funeral institutions designed to keep death out of sight and out of mind.

THE RISE OF THE MIDDLE CLASS

Both ideas and institutions were the product of a new American middle class—a group of people trying to distinguish themselves from the European aristocracy and from the American common people. Alexis de Tocqueville saw the middle class as "an innumerable multitude of men almost alike, who, without being exactly rich or poor, possess sufficient property to desire the maintenance of order" (de Tocqueville, 1835/1945, pp. 2, 145); historians today see them as substantial property owners, professionals, businessmen and merchants, shopkeepers and skilled artisans, commercial farmers, and their families. They possessed property, but their property (and the hope of increasing it) also possessed them, intensifying their fear of death. For the acquisitive member of the middle class, "the recollection of death is a constant spur. . . . Besides the good things that he possesses, he every instant fancies a thousand others that death will prevent him from trying if he does not try them soon." Therefore, the middle class wanted death with order.

One strategy for achieving death with order was the ideology of separate spheres. In the course of the 19th century, middle-class people separated management from labor, men's work from the home, and women's work from men's. They also tried to separate death from life, both intellectually and institutionally. Increasingly, specialists (either medical or clerical or academic) revised ideas of death, while other specialists segregated the funeral from the home, and the cemetery from the city.

Both separation and specialization were strategies of control, an increasingly important idea in Victorian society. Nineteenth-century Americans worked for self-control, social control, and control over nature. They saw self-control as the key to character and sexual control as the key to marriage. In separating their homes from their shops, they tried to control both spheres of their lives. The home would be a controlled environment for reproduction and socialization, while the workplace would be a controlled environment for increased production and time discipline. Schools served as a transition from one controlled environment to another, while asylums provided controlled environments for societal deviants. Science and technology attempted to make the whole continent a controlled environment. Therefore, it should not surprise us that the same class that practiced birth control should also devise forms of death control (Hale, 1971, p. 25; Howe, 1970, p. 304; Rosenberg, 1973, p. 137).

INTELLECTUAL INFLUENCES

In the process of the dying of death, the most important intellectual influences were Romanticism, sentimentalism, scientific naturalism, and liberal religion.

Romanticism

Romanticism was an intellectual response to the rationality and uniformity of the Enlightenment. Romantics discarded the Enlightenment idea of God as First Cause of a mechanistic universe operating according to predictable natural cycles. Instead, they emphasized the emotional and intuitive communion with the Oversoul (or Cosmos) in a mysteriously organic nature. Asher B. Durand depicted the essential correspondence of God, nature, and humanity in his painting *Kindred Spirits* (1849). It shows painter Thomas Cole and poet William Cullen Bryant in a beautiful natural setting, kindred to each other, to nature, and to the spirit that informed them all.

Such Romantic naturalism converted death from an untimely, unnatural event into a natural, conclusive communion with nature. In Romantic poetry, such as Bryant's "Thanatopsis" or "A Forest Hymn," death was swallowed up in the teeming life of the landscape. Such soothing conceptions of natural death encouraged people to accept their demise. At the same time, such Romantic ideas influenced the inception of rural cemeteries, which institutionalized Romantic naturalism even as they provided the consolations of Mother Nature to mourners.

Sentimentalism

The Romantic emphasis on emotions led to simple sentimentalism, which was "part of the self-evasion of a society committed to laissez-faire industrial expansion and disturbed by its consequences" (Douglas, 1977). As Americans began to experience the hardheaded rationalism of the Industrial Revolution, they began to create counterpoints to the "railroad principle" of American life. These counterpoints included the conventions of romantic love, the cult of true womanhood, the idealization of childhood, the home as "haven in a heartless world," residential suburbs, and an "emotional revolution" that bound family members with ties of intimacy. Domestic intimacy heightened the sense of loss upon the death of a "loved one" and required public outlets for the expression of private grief (Douglas, 1977, pp. 12–13, 200–226).

For most of the 19th century, the main outlet for the grief of sentimentalism was the ritual of mourning, including the funeral but also extending beyond it. This ritual differed markedly from the simple Puritan rite as mourners immersed themselves in grief to become, through their expressive (and often excessive) emotions, the central feature of the ritual. It allowed many members of the middle class (especially the women, who were supposed to be creatures of the "heart") to indulge in grief as "therapeutic self-indulgence." Like other forms of sentimentality, the sentimental mourning ritual counterpointed "the real world" because it forced all mourners to consider the power of personal connections in their lives. It turned people from life to death, from the practical to the ceremonial, from the ordinary to the extraordinary, and from the banal to the beautiful (Taylor, 1980, pp. 39–48).

Belief in the beauty of death and the funeral was new to the 19th century as the middle class used its aesthetic awareness to beautify corpses, door badges, caskets, casket backdrops, hearses, horses, funeral music, cemeteries, monuments, mourning costumes, and death itself. In the process, they made death so artistic that it almost became artificial, and, therefore, less fearful. At the same time, concerned with an etiquette of proper social relations, people used the beauty of the funeral to preserve appearances among their middle-class peers. Finally, the middle class called for "taste" and "refinement" in funerals as mourning rituals served to distinguish the middle class from the common folk (Farrell, 1980, pp. 110–111).

Especially around the mid-1800s, the tastefully refined middle-class funeral was a dark and formal affair. After death, which still generally occurred in the home, the family members either cleaned and dressed the corpse, or, if possible, hired an undertaker to care for the corpse. If they had secured an undertaker, he would place a black badge over the doorbell or door knocker to indicate the presence of mourning and to isolate the family from the unwanted intrusions of everyday life. The family members would also close window shades and drapes. Sometimes they draped black crepe over pictures, mirrors, and other places throughout the house (Habenstein & Lamers, 1962, pp. 389–444).

By the time of the funeral, family members had swathed themselves in black mourning garb that symbolized their intimacy of relationship to the deceased and their depth of grief. After the funeral, custom encouraged the continued expression of grief, as widows were expected to spend a year in "deep" mourning and a year in "second" mourning. For the 1st year, a bereaved woman wore dull black clothes, matched by appropriately somber accessories. In the 2nd year, she gradually lightened her appearance by using a variety of materials in somewhat varying colors. Widowers and children were supposed to follow a similar regimen, but in practice, women bore the burden of 19th-century mourning. Social contact and correspondence followed similar rules, with widened social participation or narrowed black borders on stationery as indicators of different stages of mourning.

The funeral ceremony itself reflected and affected the somber atmosphere in which it occurred. In the mid-1800s people were invited to funerals with hand-delivered printed cards. By the end of the century the **obituary** began to serve as a funeral notice, and the telephone allowed people to deliver their own invitations without leaving the house of mourning. After they were invited, people generally came to the house, offered condolences to the bereaved family, viewed the corpse, and sat in chairs arranged in the parlor by the undertaker. Sometimes, however, the funeral took place in a church, in which case people would particpate in a procession from the home to the church. In either place, services were generally extended affairs in which ministers counterbalanced fears of death, decay, and damnation with hopes of regeneration and resurrection. Funerals might include music and hymns, but the central feature of the ceremony was the sermon, which combined an elegy with exhortations for repentance and renewal. This gloomy funeral was not, however, the only

During the latter part of the 19th century, mourners were expected to dress the part. In this picture, pallbearers wear mourning clothes, black sashes, badges, and dark hats.

type of sentimental funeral. As the 19th century proceeded, a more hopeful sentimentality entered funeral services as middle-class religious liberalism began to domesticate death (Habenstein & Lamers, 1962, pp. 389–444; Hillerman, 1980, p. 101; Stannard, 1980, p. 26).

After the funeral, the procession continued to the cemetery, which was, as we shall see, beautified in order to belie the presence of death. There, the body was interred, and people returned home, not like the Puritans to resume their life's work, but rather like Victorians to extend their emotional expressions of grief. Mourning garb was one symbol of such grief, but mourning portraits and consolation literature were other ways to prolong the period of grief.

In the early 19th century, embroidered or painted mourning pictures flourished as a form of memorialization. These pictures often showed stylized graveyard scenes, including such standard features as the weeping willow, the gravestone and **epitaph** (tombstone inscription) of the deceased, the mourners, and a *memento mori*. These remained popular until the 1830s, when printed memorials with spaces for names and dates came into vogue. During the middle third of the century, posthumous mourning portraiture also flourished, depicting the deceased with conventional symbols of mortality like the broken shaft or roses held with blooms downward. These paintings were drawn from the corpse, and they expressed "the desire for the restoration of the dead through art." All of these forms of mourning art provided icons for the bereaved to contemplate as a part of the extended mourning ritual (Lloyd, 1980, pp. 71–89).

A Walk Through a Cemetery
George E. Dickinson

When one goes to a cemetery, the purpose is usually to attend a burial service. At such times the individual reflects on the life of the recently deceased person and pays little attention to the surrounding gravestones. Try visiting a cemetery, especially an old one, under less stressful circumstances to examine the gravestones.

If you are fortunate enough to have access to gravestones dating back to the early 18th century, you may see some markers with crossbones and a skull, pointing out the stark reality of death—after death, muscle and skin deteriorate, and the skeleton remains. Other markers may have a "soul face," usually a smiley, portraitlike face, often with wings. Unlike the crossbones and skull, the soul face with wings symbolizes the idea of an afterlife. Some markers in the early 1700s may have a bust of the deceased engraved on the stone. These busts are usually reserved for someone of prominence, such as a minister. Eighteenth-century markers are typically made of slate or sandstone.

Walking on through the cemetery, the student of history might see various symbolisms of the passing of life and of death on the gravestones: an hourglass ("like sands in the hourglass, so are the days of our lives"), babies and women weeping (rarely see men weeping), Greek and Roman urns (the open urn symbolic of the separation of the soul from the body), broken columns (not whole and complete but broken), weeping willow trees (not just any willow tree), fallen trees (thus, will die), broken limbs (severed from life), the eternal flame (life continues), the Grim Reaper ("cometh" in the night to "take one away"), and a lamb on children's markers (innocence and gentleness).

The idea that we do not die in the United States, but simply go to sleep, is evident in a cemetery. The word cemetery itself derives from Greek and means "sleeping place." "R.I.P." ("rest in peace") is sometimes seen on a gravestone. Bed-shaped markers, complete with headboard, footboard, and sideboards surrounding the grave, are symbolic of "resting." Double beds, single beds, and "cribs" for children can be found. One 19th-century marker in Columbia, South Carolina, gives the birth date of the deceased, yet rather than say "died" says "went to sleep" on a certain date.

The stroll through an older cemetery might also reveal "tabletop" markers with four "legs" and a top. These markers served a function during the Civil War in that they were used as operating tables in some southern cemeteries. With a limited number of

(continued)

(continued from previous page)

hospitals available and with a need for surgical facilities, these were available and about the right height. There are also false crypts that are "enclosed tables" with sides filled in between the "legs." False crypts are part of the English table tombs, the preferred burial style of socially prominent people.

Epitaphs (inscriptions) on the markers were often rather lengthy in the 18th and 19th centuries and gave a brief history and personal traits of the persons buried there. Though worn by the passing of time, many of these gravestones are still very legible. The viewer can sometimes note historically when various plagues or diseases occurred from the numerous members of a family who died within days of each other. One of my favorite inscriptions is on a marker in Charleston, South Carolina, for a sea captain, age 37, who went down with his ship in 1754. A reclining, smiling skeleton is displayed with its head resting on a winged hourglass. Above the smiling figure of death is the inscription: "Yesterday for me, today for thee."

In contrast to the earlier U.S. cemeteries, modern cemeteries are more uniform, less personalized, and have limited gravestone variation in size and shape. Contemporary markers, typically made of granite or marble, basically have the name of the deceased and the birth and death dates. Rarely does a marker today have an epitaph other than perhaps an occasional quotation.

Thus, a walk through a cemetery, especially an older one, could prove to be a peaceful and enlightening experience for the observer. In a place for the dead, the cemetery seems to have life with all the flowers and trees. The venture can be like walking through a history book. In a *memento mori* field that reminds the individual of mortality, one is surrounded by immortality.

Consolation literature allowed people to share their grief without sharing it with people they knew. It showed mourners that they were not alone in the house of sorrow, and it showed them the emotional and moral benefits of their sorrow. Consolation literature included obituary poems and memoirs, mourner's manuals, prayer guidebooks, hymns, and books about heaven. Such writings inflated the importance of dying and the dead by every possible means; they sponsored elaborate methods of burial and commemoration, communication with the next world, and microscopic viewings of a sentimentalized afterlife. Books like *Agnes and the Key of Her Little Coffin* (1857) or *Stepping Heavenward* (1869) or *The Empty Crib: The Memorial of Little Georgie* (1873) all featured and championed the ideal of "the sensitized mourner" (Douglas, 1977, pp. 240–249).

To the modern mind, these sentimental expressions of grief may seem forced, overdone, or even false. Such attitudes, however, tell more about us than about our

Greek and Roman columns, false crypts, and tabletop markers are prominent in Charleston, South Carolina, where the oldest gravestone dates back to the 1690s.

Victorian ancestors. Nineteenth-century Americans "mourned well" because they gave themselves symbols, rituals, and time in which to work out their feelings. We do not understand this because of important intervening historical forces, one of which was scientific naturalism.

Scientific Naturalism

If sentimentality was one way of controlling the hard fact of death, scientific naturalism was another. Although it systemized the hardheaded rationalism that sentimentalism tried to smother, it contributed to the dying of death as the middle class used the "laws" of science as it used the "customs" of etiquette to legitimize its cultural values.

"What strikes the historian," writes Burton J. Bledstein, "is the totality of the mid-Victorian impulse to contain the life experiences of the individual from life to death by isolating them as science." Another instance of the ideology of separate spheres, the rise of science in the last half of the 19th century allowed Americans to invoke authority for "those scientific plausibilities which fitted most conveniently into their social needs and presuppositions" (Bledstein, 1976, p. 55). An integral part of the social construction of reality, science isolated the mystery of death as "a matter of fact" and interpreted that fact in order to reduce the impact of death on practical life.

Scientific naturalists insisted first that death is "natural, a product of natural causes, the same as any other natural phenomenon, and that these causes are bound to the fixed, and as we believe beneficent, laws of the universe" (Johnson, 1896, p. 77). Their insistence on the "natural" quality of death complemented the natural death of

Romanticism, but the scientific fact of death eliminated providential intervention and the possibility of death as punishment.

Consequently, scientific naturalists insisted that death is painless and that all people can eventually attain an "easy," natural death at an advanced age. Pain, which (like fear) was an important part of the Puritan world, lost its cultural relevance in the 19th century. With the discovery of ether in the 1840s and the coining of the word *painkiller* in the 1850s, Americans applied physical and mental anesthetics to kill the pain of death. Magazine articles constantly stressed "the modern belief that the dying process is easy," as easy and "as painless as falling asleep" ("The Fear of Death," 1912). In so doing, they eliminated a major reason for people to think seriously about death.

Other scientific and medical innovations persuaded many Americans that death might be postponed or prevented. Even before the demographic transition, death began to be treated as an occurrence of old age, an idea that encouraged people to postpone or preempt preparation for death. In addition, some prominent medical researchers asserted that even old age is a curable congenital disease and asked, "Why not live forever?" Indeed, when Elie Metchnikoff, the head of the Pasteur Institute in Paris, claimed that cultured milk products could combat the "autointoxication" of old age, Americans immediately began to buy yogurt and buttermilk. Especially between 1900 and 1920, the prestige of science convinced many Americans that individual physical immortality might be imminent (Farrell, 1980, pp. 60–61).

Other scientific naturalists admitted individual mortality but promoted a species immortality whereby "we are immortal if we but form a sturdy link in the great chain of life." Influenced by Darwin's idea of natural selection, these scientists viewed death as "an inevitable corollary to the advancement of the species" (Hutchinson, 1893, p. 637). Therefore, they advised Americans not to take death personally, but rather to accept it as part of human progress. This species perspective did not prevent individuals from dying, but it did turn their attention from death and the deceased to survivors and posterity. As we shall see, this species perspective of death and immortality was institutionalized in "life" insurance.

By itself, scientific naturalism had almost no impact on American bereavement practices. However, in conjunction with religious liberalism and the culture of professionalism, scientific naturalism did effect changes in funeral service.

Liberal Religion

Religious liberals tried to reconcile new scientific knowledge with traditional religious interpretations of death. Between 1850 and 1930, liberals like Henry Ward Beecher and Phillips Brooks enunciated "the attitudes and values of a new urban middle-class" (Clark, 1978, p. 3). They combined scientific naturalism, higher biblical criticism, Romantic idealism, and sentimentality in order to show the place of evolution in God's plan, the place of death in evolution, and the progress of life through death to an exalted immortality. In addition, changing ideas of death and immortality brought these men and women into the arena of funeral reform.

Henry Ward Beecher was the most popular and influential liberal clergyman of his day. His pulpit at the Plymouth Congregational Church of Brooklyn Heights in New York gave him opportunities for public speaking and publication, and he became a "symbol for a middle-class America" (Clark, 1978). He rejected the Evangelicalism of his youth and preached instead a gospel of divine immanence, natural law, and human hope. He accepted scientific naturalism and wrote an article for the first issue of *Popular Science Monthly.* He believed that God acts primarily in the world through natural laws and that people respond naturally to God by electing their own salvation. Eventually, he rejected even the doctrine of everlasting punishment in hell.

Beecher viewed death as the first step up toward heaven, as God's call to "come home!" "I would not, for the world, bring up a child to have that horror of death which hung over my own childhood," claimed Beecher, because "the thought of death was to me awful beyond description" (Beecher, 1859, pp. 194–195). Instead, he wanted people to see that "a funeral is the nearest place to heaven" and that sorrow is inappropriate. He suggested:

> When friends have gone out from us joyously, we should go with them to the grave, not singing mournful psalms, but scattering flowers. Christians are wrong to walk in black, and sprinkle the ground with tears, at the very time when they should walk in white, and illumine the way by smiles and radiant hope. The disciples found angels at the grave of Him they loved; and we should always find them too, but that our eyes are too full of tears for seeing. (Beecher, 1858, p. 189)

At his own funeral in 1887, Beecher's family reversed the somber formality of the Victorian funeral by making sure that "no emblem of parting or sorrow was there, but the symbols of love, and faith, and hope, the glad tokens of eternal reward, such as befitted his life, his death, and his fame" (Handford, 1887, pp. 47–49). On a practical, pastoral level, other ministers counseled people to follow Beecher's example. They celebrated death as a passage to eternal life, not as a moment of judgment. They tried to soothe survivors instead of promoting self-examination or preparation for death. They worked with funeral directors to effect funeral reforms. In 1913 Lyman Abbott recalled the achievements of liberal funeral reform:

> We have done much to Christianize our farewells to those who have gone before us into the next stages of life. We no longer darken the rooms that now more than ever need the light and warmth of the sun; we no longer close the windows as if to shut out Nature at the moment when we are about to give back to Mother Earth all that was mortal in the earthly career now finished; we no longer shroud the house in black, we make it sweet with flowers; for the hymns of grief we are fast substituting the hymns of victory; for words charged with a sense of loss we listen to words that hold wide the door of hope and faith; and on the memorials which we place where they lie who have vanished from our sight we no longer carve the skull and cross-bones, the hourglass and the scythe—we recall some trait or quality of achievement that survives the body and commemorates the spirit.

Such changes, thought Abbott, help people "to think of life as one and indivisible, of immortality as our possession, here and now, of death as normal change in an eternal process of growth" (Abbott, 1913).

By defining death as part of evolutionary progress propelled by an immanent and merciful God, liberals allowed bereaved Americans to approach death optimistically. This new definition of death derived from ideas of Romanticism, scientific naturalism, and religious liberalism. Together with the institutional innovations of cemetery superintendents, life insurance agents, and funeral directors, these ideas caused the dying of death in America.

INSTITUTIONAL INFLUENCES

Like religious liberalism, cemetery reform derived from Romantic naturalism, middle-class family sentimentality, and scientific concerns. In 1895 a writer in *American Gardening* wrote that "the modern garden cemetery like the modern religious impulse seeks to assuage the cheerlessness and the sternness of life and to substitute the free and gracious charity of One who came to rob death of its hideousness" ("Extracts," 1895). By the 1830s many physicians had begun to worry about the possible health hazards of city graveyards. By the same time, commercial development had raised the price of land on which graveyards were located, and Romantic ideas of landscape architecture had begun to affect the aesthetically oriented members of the middle class. Also, space limitations of city graveyards prevented the possibility of family plots, and many of the burial places had become overcrowded, unkempt, and unsightly.

Rural Cemeteries

The solution to these problems was the rural cemetery—a landscaped garden in a suburban setting. In 1831 Mount Auburn Cemetery was founded four miles west of Boston, and its success stimulated the spread of such cemeteries all over the country. In rural cemeteries, family plots averaging 300 square feet were nestled among trees and shrubs upon the slopes of soft hills or on the shores of little lakes. Paths curled throughout the grounds, passing lots enclosed by stone coping or wrought iron fences and surmounted by a monument of some sort. Such cemeteries were invented to bury bodies; to ease the grief of survivors; to bring people into communion with God, with nature, and with deceased family and friends; to teach them important lessons of life; to surround bereavement with beauty and to divert the attention of survivors from death to the setting of burial; to display "taste" and "refinement"; and to reinforce the class stratification of the status quo (Bender, 1973, pp. 196–211; French, 1975, pp. 69–91; Rotundo, 1973, pp. 231-242).

The founders of Mount Auburn were liberal Unitarian reformers—progressive professionals and businesspeople who considered the cemetery in the context of social developments of their day. They equated the family with the garden and imagined both as a counterpoint to a society of accumulation. In the same way that upper-middle-class families moved to suburbs where curved roads and greenery contrasted to the grid-block plan of the cities and offered space to raise a family, they moved from the "cities of the dead" to rural cemeteries that offered space to "plant" a family.

This was also the period of "the discovery of the asylum," when social deviants were located in restorative rural settings that would rehabilitate people away from the contaminating influence of urban life. Many reformers saw the cemetery, like the insane asylum, the orphanage, and the penitentiary, as an "asylum" from urban ills. In the cemetery, "the weary and worn citizen" was also rehabilitated. Cleaveland (1847, pp. 13–14, 26) noted:

> Ever since he entered these greenwood shades, he has sensibly been getting farther and farther from strife, from business, and care. . . . A short half-hour ago, he was in the midst of a discordant Babel; he was one of the hurrying, jostling crowd; he was encompassed by the whirl and fever of artificial life. Now he stands alone in Nature's inner court—in her silent, solemn sanctuary. Her holiest influences are all around him.

The rehabilitation of the rural cemetery paralleled the philosophy of education found in the common school. Like the new compulsory schools, rural cemeteries responded to middle-class fears of mobilization of the masses in the Age of Jackson. Educational reformers like Horace Mann both reflected and affected cemetery proponents in their belief that "sentiment is the great conservative principle of society" and that "instincts of patriotism, local attachment, family affection, human sympathy, reverence for truth, age, valor, and wisdom . . . constitute the latent force of civil society" (Tuckerman, 1856, pp. 338–342).

Like these other reforms of antebellum society, rural cemeteries "took the public mind by storm." Cities throughout the United States established rural cemeteries, and people flocked to visit them. In New York, Baltimore, and Philadelphia, Andrew Jackson Downing estimated that over 30,000 people a year toured the rural cemeteries. Consequently, he wondered whether they might not also visit landscaped gardens without graves. In articles like "Public Cemeteries and Public Gardens" and "The New York Park," Downing (1921, pp. 28–40, 374) advanced the idea that would result in New York's Central Park and a new direction for cemetery development.

The new direction was the lawn-park cemetery emphasizing a new aesthetic—efficiency—and the absence of death. By the end of the century, members of the Association of American Cemetery Superintendents routinely wrote in journals like *Park and Cemetery* that "a cemetery should be a beautiful park. While there are still some who say 'a cemetery should be a cemetery,' . . . the great majority have come to believe in the idea of beauty" (Simonds, 1919, p. 59). This new aesthetic emphasized the open meadows of the beautiful style over the irregular hill-and-dale outcroppings of the picturesque style and the irregular outcroppings of obelisks and monuments in the unregulated rural cemetery. This aesthetic coincided with considerations of efficiency as the uncluttered landscape required less upkeep than the enclosures and elaborate monuments of the rural cemetery. Finally, this aesthetic buried death beneath the beauty of the design. Andrew Jackson Downing (1921, p. 59) had said that "the development of the beautiful is the end and aim of all other fine arts. . . . And we attain it by the removal or concealment of everything uncouth or discordant." The cemetery superintendents practiced what Downing preached. "Today cemetery making is an art," said one superintendent in 1910, "and gradually all things that suggest death, sorrow, or pain are being eliminated" (Hare, 1910, p. 41).

Cemetery superintendents eliminated suggestions of death by banning lot enclosures and grave mounds and by encouraging fewer gravestones and fewer inscriptions. They banned lot enclosures (fencing or stone coping) because these broke up the unified landscape, blocked the path of the lawn mower, and signified a "selfish and exclusive," possessive individualism. While grave mounds obstructed the view and the lawn mower, they also reminded people of death. Without them, a cemetery lot would evoke "none of the gruesomeness which is invariably associated with cemetery lots . . . *No grave mounds are used, so save the headstones, there is nothing to suggest the presence of Death*" (Smith, 1910, p. 539).

Some superintendents did not want to save the headstones either, proposing instead "a cemetery where there is no monument, only landscape" (*Association,* 1889, p. 59). Most superintendents favored sunken stones at the site of the grave. Howard Evarts Weed (1912, p. 94), author of the influential *Modern Park Cemeteries,* argued that "with the headstones showing above the surface we have the old graveyard scene, but buried in the ground they do not appear in the landscape picture and we then have a park-like effect." Some superintendents zoned the cemetery to permit monuments only on large "monument lots." This allowed the superintendent, like a real estate agent, to charge premium prices for such lots and for prime locations for corner lots or hillside or lakeside property. This **social stratification** of the cemetery allowed for the social mobility of the dead as ambitious dead people moved to better "neighbor-

---

Grave Remarks

I'll Write My Own Epitaph Before I Leave, Thank You

Epitaphs are footnotes chiseled on tombstones.

They are parting shots taken at or by the deceased. They can be patriotic, poetic, profound, or pathetic. They can be wise, witty, or just weird. They can glorify, be grievous, or gruesome.

Few of them have summed up a person's attitude toward life as well as one found in a Georgia cemetery:

I told you I was sick!

Perhaps the most famous epitaph is one credited to W. C. Fields, written for himself:

On the whole I'd rather be in Philadelphia.

But Fields's epitaph was not used, and his tombstone in Glendale, California, contains only his vital statistics. Here are some others.
Epitaph from Kilmurry Churchyard, Ireland:

This stone was raised to Sarah Ford.
    Not Sarah's virtues to record,
    For they're well known to all the town,
    No Lord, it was raised to keep her down.

From Streatham Churchyard, England:

Here lies Elizabeth, my wife for 47 years,
    and this is the first damn thing she ever
    did to oblige me.

Epitaph on one of three tombstones in a family burial plot in Niagara Falls, Ontario:

(continued)

hoods" as their survivors saw fit. Where superintendents could not ban or limit the number of monuments, they tried to make them as unobtrusive as possible, preferring horizontal monuments to the earlier upright markers and preferring inexpressive epitaphs to the poetic epitaphs of earlier times. They wanted to replace the *memento mori* of earlier stones with "forgetfulness" as they buried death with the dead (Farrell, 1980, pp. 122–127).

(continued from previous page)

Here I lie between two of the best women
in the world; my wives. But I have requested
my relatives to tip me a little toward Tille.

In a Falkirk, England, cemetery:

At rest beneath this slab of stone
Lies stingy Jimmy Wyatt;
He died one morning just at ten,
And saved a dinner by it.

Here's one from Boot Hill, Dodge City, Kansas, that reflects a popular epitaph theme:

Here lies the body of Mannie,
They put him here to stay;
He lived the life of Riley
While Riley was away.

From Burlington Churchyard, Massachusetts,

Sacred to the memory of Anthony Drake
Who died for peace and quietness sake,
His wife was constantly scolding and scoffin',
So he sought repose in a twelve-dollar coffin.

Railroad conductor Charles B. Gunn's tombstone in Colorado Springs, Colorado, contains these words:

Papa—Did you wind your watch?

And in a Moultrie, Georgia, cemetery:

Here lies the father of twenty-nine
He would have had more but he didn't have time.   *(continued)*

(continued from previous page)

From Burlington, Massachusetts, again:

Here lies the body of Susan Lowder
Who burst while drinking Seidlitz powder;
Called from the world to her heavenly rest
She should have waited til it effervesced.

On the tombstone of a hanged sheep-stealer from Bletchley, Bucks, England:

Here lies the body of Thomas Kemp
Who lived by wool and died by hemp.

Abraham Newland, a lonely London banker, wrote his own epitaph:

Beneath this stone old Abraham lies;
Nobody laughs, and nobody cries.
Where he has gone, and how he fares,
Nobody knows and nobody cares.

In a Thurmont, Maryland, cemetery:

Here lies an atheist—All dressed up
and no place to go.

And in a Stowe, Vermont, cemetery:

I was somebody. Who is no business of yours.

An infant's epitaph in a Plymouth, Massachusetts, cemetery:

Since I have been so quickly done for
I wonder what I was begun for.

In a Uniontown, Pennsylvania, cemetery:

Here lies the body of Jonathan Blake;
Stepped on the gas instead of the brake.

Written by a widow on her adulterous husband's tombstone in an Atlanta, Georgia, cemetery:

Gone. But not forgiven.

(continued)

(continued from previous page)

Similarly, a Middlesex, England, widow put this on the gravestone of her wandering husband:

At last I know where he is at night!

An "old maid's" epitaph in Scranton, Pennsylvania:

No hits, no runs, no heirs.

At Cripple Creek, Colorado, an epitaph to a man who died by accident:

Within this grave there lies poor Andy;
   Bit by a snake no whiskey handy.

Another one from Cripple Creek:

Here lies the bones of a man named Zeke,
   Second-fastest draw in Cripple Creek.

Near Atlanta, Georgia, a cemetery hosts this unique epitaph:

Due to lack of ground in this cemetery,
   two bodies are buried in this one plot.
   One of them was a politician, the other
   was an honest man.

An English epitaph over the grave of Sir John Strange, a lawyer:

Here lies an honest lawyer, and that is Strange.

Epitaph to Joseph Crump, a musician:

Once ruddy, and plump
   But now a pale lump
   Beneath this same hump
   Lies honest Joe Crump
   What, tho' by Death's thump
   He's laid on his rump
   Yet up he shall jump
   When he hears the last triumph.

An 1890 epitaph of Arthur C. Hormans of Cleveland, Ohio, puts things into startlingly clear perspective:

Once I wasn't. Then I was.
   Now I ain't again.

Epitaphs from *The People's Almanac* (pp. 1312–1320), by D. Wallechinsky and I. Wallace, 1975, Garden City, NY: Doubleday, and *Lexington Herald,* September 21, 1979, p. D5.

Superintendents tried to structure cemetery services "to mitigate the harshness and cruelty of death and its attendant details and ceremonies" (Seavoy, 1906, p. 488) and to provide a sort of grief therapy for bereaved individuals. They encouraged private, family funerals, and they tried to remove or conceal the uncouth and discordant aspects of interment. They carted the dirt away from the grave, or they hid it beneath cloth, flowers, or evergreens. They lined the grave with cloth to make it look like a little room. They suggested changes in religious services, and they escorted mourners away from the grave before filling it in order to shield them from the finality of death. In all of these services, "everything that tends to remove the gloomy thoughts is done. . . . The friends cannot but leave the sacred spot with better, nobler thoughts, freed from the gloom and terror that otherwise would possess them" (Hay, 1900, p. 46).

Life Insurance

A second institutional innovation, life insurance, tried to exorcise the anxiety and financial insecurity that would otherwise possess people contemplating death. Established about the same time as rural cemeteries, life insurance flourished after 1850. In

---

Forest Lawn

Song by Tom Paxton

Oh, lay me down in Forest Lawn in a silver casket,
　　Put golden flowers over my head in a silver basket.
　　Let the drum and bugle corps blow taps while cannons roar,
　　Let sixteen liveried employees pass out souvenirs from the funeral store.
　　I want to go simply when I go, and they'll give me a simple fun'ral there, I know.
　　With a casket lined in fleece,
　　And fireworks spelling out "rest in peace."
　　Oh, take me when I'm gone to Forest Lawn.

Oh, lay me down in Forest Lawn—they understand there.
　　They have a heavenly choir and a military band there.
　　Just put me in their care, and I'll find my comfort there,
　　—with sixteen planes in last salute, dropping a cross in a parachute.
　　I want to go simply when I go, they'll give me a simple fun'ral there, I know.
　　With a hundred strolling strings.
　　And topless dancers in golden wings,
　　Oh, take me when I'm gone to Forest Lawn.

(continued)

1850, 48 companies held policies valued at $97 million; by 1920, 335 companies held 65 million policies worth $40 billion. Life insurance contributed to "the practical disappearance of the thought of death as an influence bearing upon practical life," and thus it contributed to the dying of death (U.S. Bureau of the Census, 1975, pp. 1050–1059).

Life insurance emerged from the same historical context as did rural cemeteries and funeral reform; it assumed the uniformity and continuity of death as natural occurrences. Life insurance depended on the science of statistics and on a species perspective of death and immortality that focused attention not on the life of the individual policyholder, but rather on the lives of beneficiaries. Like the rural cemetery, it was praised for its educational benefits as it taught lessons of self-reliance, forethought, thrift, discipline, and (very) delayed gratification. For these reasons, clergymen like Henry Ward Beecher endorsed the system of life insurance, responding to critics that in effect, God helps those who help themselves. Also, life insurance accentuated the importance of the family, as did Romantic sentimentalism and the family plot of the rural cemetery. Finally, life insurance provided families with money to pay for elaborate funerals, a fact that affected both the development of funeral service and the history of bereavement.

(continued from previous page)

Oh come, come, come, come,
  Come to the church in the wildwood,
  Kindly leave a contribution in the pail.
  Be as simple and as trusting as a child would
  And we'll sell you a church in the dale.

To find a simple resting place is my desire,
  To lay me down with a smiling face comes a little bit higher.
  My likeness done in brass will stand in plastic grass,
  And weights and hidden springs will tip its hat to the mourners filing
  past.
  I want to go simply when I go.
  And they'll give me a simple fun'ral there, I know.
  I'll sleep beneath the sand, with piped in tapes of Billy Graham.
  Oh, take me when I'm gone to Forest Lawn.
  Rock of Ages, cleft for me, for a slightly higher fee.
  Oh, take me when I'm gone to Forest Lawn.

Life Insurance

The middle-class American value of planning ahead for the future is exemplified by the fact that the majority of Americans have life insurance. Life insurance is to protect one's dependents and to give the insured a feeling of security in knowing that his or her dependents will have some coverage in the event of death.

The amount of life insurance needed is related to the number of dependents one has. For example, if one is the primary provider in a family consisting of three small children, he or she would have a greater need for life insurance than a single person with no dependents. If the primary provider were to die, these dependents would have some financial coverage at least for the time being. At the time of death, the added burden of the loss of income is not needed.

If one's only purpose for life insurance is to provide for one's dependents, **term life insurance** is probably the best choice. Term life insurance tends to have the lowest premiums for the greatest amount of coverage. Group policies, such as those provided by one's place of employment, tend to have lower premiums than policies obtained outside of a group. Term life insurance is for a specific number of years, such as 5 or 10, with premiums going up as one ages. "My suggestion is to start with term,

(continued)

Funeral Services

Like burial service, funeral service also changed between 1850 and 1920. Because "the growing wealth and prosperity of our country has caused people to demand something more in accordance with their surroundings" (Benjamin, 1882, p. 3) and because funeral directors cultivated a "steadily advancing appreciation of the aesthetics of society" ("Funeral Directors," 1883), the new funeral would be, like the 19th-century cemetery, a work of art. As cemetery superintendents used their art to hide the uncouth and discordant aspects of death, so did funeral directors use "the varied improvements in (their) art . . . to conceal much that is forbidding in (their) calling" ("Funeral Directors," 1883). As cemetery superintendents institutionalized "the modern religious impulse" to "assuage the cheerlessness and sternness of life," funeral directors worked to "adopt some philosophy or some new customs and ideals that will make death less of a tragedy" ("The Ideas of a Plain Country Woman," 1913).

The demand for a new funeral service came from the American middle class, but it was created and supplied by casket manufacturers and funeral directors. The National Funeral Directors Association was founded in 1882 in Rochester, New York, the home of the Stein Casket Manufacturing Company. The association's official journal was *The Casket,* founded and funded for several years by the Stein Company. As this suggests, the first widespread innovation in funeral service was the casket, a stylish container for the corpse. Before 1850, most Americans were laid to rest in a coffin, a six-sided box that was constructed to order by the local cabinetmaker. By

(continued from previous page)
but if there is a permanent insurance need, convert to a good universal life policy," says Andrew Gross, a financial planner in Washington, DC (Smith, 1988, p. 154).

Today, however, life insurance for many individuals is more than security for one's dependents. Some policies are a form of tax-deferred investment from which one can also borrow. Thus, one can have coverage in the event of death and can have the opportunity to build cash assets at the same time. These insurance policies are called **whole life policies,** from which, for a set premium, one receives life insurance and a savings fund. A common type of whole life policy is called **Universal life insurance** which is more flexible, has investment opportunities, and allows one to raise or reduce premiums and the amount of coverage on one's life. Another type, **Variable life insurance,** does not allow for the premium or minimum coverage on one's life to change, but one can switch the savings from among money markets or various forms of stock.

It is advisable to shop around and compare the benefits of the different insurance programs. Premiums vary considerably for the same coverage. Be cautious of high-powered salespersons trying to sell coverage not needed. Become informed about life insurance by talking with knowledgeable consumers and by reading consumer magazines before purchasing any life insurance. Comparison shopping should pay off.

1927 "the old wedge-shaped coffin (was) obsolete. A great variety of styles and grades of caskets (were) available in the trade, ranging from a cheap, cloth-covered pine box to the expensive cast-bronze sarcophagus" (Gebhart, 1927, p. 8). The rectangular shape of the new caskets complemented the artwork in concealing the uncouth corpse. In applying for a casket patent in 1849, A. C. Barstow explained:

> The burial cases formerly used were adapted in shape nearly to the form of the human body, that is they tapered from the shoulders to the head, and from the shoulders to the feet. Presently, in order to obviate in some degree the disagreeable sensations produced by a coffin on many minds, the casket, or square form has been adopted. (Habenstein & Lamers, 1962, pp. 270, 251–310)

The adoption of the word *casket* also accelerated the dying of death, as the word had previously denoted a container for something precious, like jewels.

Accepting the associated idea of the preciousness of the body, Americans decided that a dead-looking corpse looked out of place in an elaborate silk-lined casket. Rather than remove the casket, they decided to stylize the body. Originally a way of preserving bodies for shipment home from Civil War battlefields or western cities, embalming soon became a way of preserving appearances. Responding to the germ theory of disease and the public health movement, funeral directors attempted to gain professional status by emphasizing the disinfectant qualities of embalming. Most funeral directors, however, wanted simply "to retain and improve the complexion" so that the corpse would look "as natural as though it were alive" (Hohenschuh, 1921,

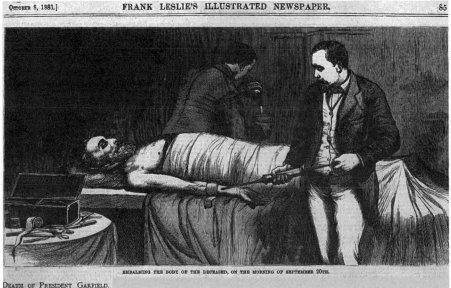

[OCTOBER 8, 1881.]   FRANK LESLIE'S ILLUSTRATED NEWSPAPER,   85

EMBALMING THE BODY OF THE DECEASED, ON THE MORNING OF SEPTEMBER 20TH.

DEATH OF PRESIDENT GARFIELD.
THE NATION'S GREAT AFFLICTION.

An artist's sketch of the embalming of the body of President Garfield on the morning of September 20, 1881, in preparation for the train ride from Elberon, New Jersey, to Washington, DC. Though originally a way of preserving bodies for shipment home from Civil War battlefields, embalming soon became a way of preserving appearances.

pp. 82, 88). To do this, they began to cosmetize the corpse and to clothe and position the body naturally. They replaced the traditional shroud with street clothes, and they tried "to lay out the body so that there will be as little suggestion of death as possible." By 1920, they succeeded so well that a Boston undertaker supposedly advertised (Dowd, 1921, p. 53):

For composing the features $1
For giving the features a look of quiet resignation $2
For giving the features the appearance of Christian hope and contentment $5

Bereavement practices were affected by the change from coffin to casket and by the "restorative art" of the embalmer; they were also affected by the movement of the funeral from the domestic parlor to the funeral parlor. As people began banishing death from their homes to hospitals, they started moving the funeral from the family parlor to a specialized funeral parlor. After the Civil War, middle-class Americans began to exclude the formal parlor from their homes and to replace it with a "living room." At the same time, funeral directors wanted full control of the corpse and the funeral. The ease and efficiency of directing funerals in a funeral home made them more profitable. In spite of these benefits, the transition to the funeral parlor was slow, extending well into the 20th century (Farrell, 1980, pp. 172–177).

Both in the domestic parlor and in the funeral parlor, the procedure of the turn-of-the-century funeral changed. In conjunction with the reform forces of religious liberalism, funeral directors began to redirect funerals to be shorter, more secular, and more soothing. They shortened the service by trying to revise the long sermon with its exhortations of repentance and renewal. Although some clerics resisted, funeral directors wanted the sermon redirected from theology to psychology, from preaching to grief therapy, and from the state of survivors' souls to the state of their emotions. The funeral director took care of all of the details of the funeral and performed as much as a stage manager as a mortician. "Really it is much the same," wrote one director, "I work for effect—for consoling and soothing effect" ("The Man Nobody Envies," 1914).

After 1880, funeral directors used their arts and the culture of professionalism to effect a massive change in the American way of bereavement. Professionalism was part of the middle-class strategy of specialization. It required education in an area of expertise and an ethic or service, and it provided autonomy and income for its practitioners. The American undertaker sought professional status because it would help him to become "enough of an *authority* to convince his clients, without offense, that there are better methods than are prescribed by custom" (Hohenschuh, 1921, p. 9). Etiquette books reinforced this culture of professionalism by advising readers that "the arrangements for the funeral are usually left to the undertaker, who best knows how to proceed" (Wells, 1887, p. 303). To the middle-class people who feared death anyway, this established a situation in which the public passively accepted changes in funeral service suggested by funeral directors (Hohenschuh, 1921, p. 9; Wells, 1887, p. 303).

Indeed, *restraint* and *passivity* became the watchwords of 20th-century bereavement. If the funeral director was a stage manager, then the family was the audience, responding to the drama in prescribed ways in the hopes of achieving a catharsis of death. Instead of the expressive grief of the sentimental funeral, family members were expected to contain and control their emotions and to meet death stoically. At the turn of the century, some religious liberals saw grief as lack of faith in the imminence of immortality. Others reacted to the central place of the mourners in the mournful Victorian funeral and charged that "over-much grief would seem mere selfishness" (Mayo, 1916, p. 6). Over and over again, writers proclaimed that "the deepest grief is the quiet kind" (Sargent, 1888, p. 51). An 1890s etiquette book suggested that "we can better show our affection to the dead by fulfilling our duties to the living, than by giving ourselves up to uncontrolled grief" (Pike & Armstrong, 1980, p. 125). Portraying grief as a selfish ploy to stop the ongoing business of life, these reformers called for controlled and private grief. In the long run, they predicted the modern practice of grief therapy in which grief is seen as a disorder by people who still want death with order (Mayo, 1916, p. 6; Pike & Armstrong, 1980, p. 125; Sargent, 1888, p. 51).

With this new ideal of grief, Americans reduced their symbolic expressions of grief—mourning wear, for example, which declined after World War I—because extended grief offended others who preferred to live for life. In concealing mourning, Americans reversed the 19th-century tradition that required good mourning. Like cemetery superintendents and funeral directors, Americans in general began to conceal the uncouth and discordant emotion of grief. Thus, modern grief isolates the mourners and forces them to discover their own private mourning ritual. It dictates the appearance of control and the dying of death (Hillerman, 1980, pp. 104–105; Oxley, 1887, pp. 608–614).

The Display of the Dead

Truly, we need to do away with some of the false ideas of Death which are shown in so many gruesome ways at funerals, and strive to give the young a different and truer idea of what the passing away of a soul means. The awfulness of some funerals is nothing short of criminal, especially as it affects the minds of the young. If there is work cut out for the minister of today, it is the enlightenment of his people on the subject of death and the funeral. But the minister must, first of all, imbibe a wholesome lesson of self-restraint for himself, and abolish the fulsome and tiresome eulogy which is the bane of so many funerals. He must learn for himself, and teach to his people, the beauty and solemnity of the brief service as prescribed by his church and attempt nothing more, and he must also relentlessly oppose the tendency which exists to turn the modern funeral, especially in the country, into a picnic. The present outpouring of a heterogeneous mass of folk from every point of the countryside is a farce that cannot be too soon abolished. A funeral is essentially a time for the meeting of the family and relatives and the closest friends, and the fewer the number of outsiders present the better. Nor is there anything quite

(continued)

The modern bereavement practices described proceeded from a simple desire to make death as painless for survivors as for the deceased. It came from a widespread cultural attempt "not to mention trouble or grief or sickness or sin, but to treat them as if they do not exist, and speak only of the sweet and pleasant things of life" ("The Ideas of a Plain Country Woman," 1913). This dying of death came from the desire of the middle class for control—of self, society, and the environment. It ended exactly where de Tocqueville (1835/1945, pp. 2, 4) predicted:

> As they perceive that they succeed in resolving without resistance all the little difficulties their practical life presents, (the Americans) readily conclude that everything in the world can be explained, and that nothing in it transcends the limits of the understanding. Thus they fall to denying what they cannot comprehend.

Denying and disguising death, middle-class Americans achieved, on the surface at least, the dying of death.

The Resurrection of Death, 1945 to the Present

Although Americans sought a death sentence for death, the judge granted only life imprisonment. Consequently, although death had disappeared from the streets,

(continued from previous page)

so barbarous as the present custom at so many funerals of "viewing the remains" by a motley collection of folk, many of whom never even knew the dead in life, or, if they did, never thought enough of him to come and see him. The vulgar curiosity that prompts "a last look" at a loved one cannot be too severely denounced. Only second to it is the pretentious line of vehicles that "escorts the remains to the grave" and the mental calibre of a community that bases the popularity of a man on the number of carriages that follow him to the grave!

If there is a crying need of the gospel of simplicity it is in connection with funerals. It seems inconceivable that Death should be made the occasion for display, and yet this is true of scores of funerals. The flowers, including those fearful conceptions of the ignorant florist, such as "Gates Ajar"; the quality of casket and even of the raiment of the dead, the "crowd" at the "obsequies," the number of carriages in the "cortege"—oh, oh, "what fools these mortals be," to say naught of the wicked and wanton waste of much-needed money. It is difficult to conceive that a national love of display should have become so deep-rooted as to lead to the very edge of the grave!

Ladies Home Journal, September 1903.

Americans worried that this hardened killer might escape. After World War II, some Americans suggested instead that death had been rehabilitated, and like 19th-century "resurrectionists," they began to resurrect death. Presently Americans are deciding between the dying of death and "living with dying."

THE ATOMIC AGE

On August 6, 1945, the United States dropped a single atomic bomb on the Japanese city of Hiroshima. It exploded in the air, with a heat flash that inflamed clothing within a half-mile radius and trees up to a mile and a half. The shock wave followed soon after, rupturing internal organs. Finally, the blast blew bodies at 500 to 1,000 miles per hour through the flaming, rubble-filled air. The bomb destroyed everything within 8,000 feet, killed at least 70,000 people, and destroyed or damaged 98 percent of Hiroshima's buildings. The effects of atomic radiation have disfigured or killed thousands more, and the whole world bears the psychological scars of the blast.

President Truman announced the explosion:

It is an atomic bomb. It is a harnessing of the basic power of the universe. . . . What has been done is the greatest achievement of organized science in history.

"Wouldn't you know it! Now the Hendersons have the bomb."

One scientist, Albert Einstein, responded, "Ach! The world is not ready for it." Within a year, Einstein argued that "the unleashed power of the atom has changed everything save our modes of thinking, and we thus drift toward unparalleled catastrophe."

The atomic bomb and the arms race did, however, begin to change our mode of thinking about death. In a prescient 1947 article on the social effects of the bomb, Lewis Mumford had this to say about the Atomic Age:

> Life is now reduced to purely existentialist terms: existence towards death. The classic other worldly religions undergo a revival; but even more quack religions and astrology, with pretensions to scientific certainty, flourish; so do new cults. The young who grow up in this world are completely demoralized: they characterize themselves as the generation that drew a blank. The belief in continuity, the sense of a future that holds promises, disappears; the certainty of sudden obliteration cuts across every long-term plan, and every activity is more or less reduced to the life-span of a single day, on the assumption that it may be the last day. . . . Suicide becomes more frequent . . . and the taking of drugs to produce either exhilaration or sleep becomes practically universal. . . .
>
> These conditions—as unfamiliar to the experience of the race as the atom bomb itself—must lead to grave psychological disruptions. We can posit the familiar forms of these regressive actions: escape in fantasy would be one; purposeless sexual promiscuity would be another; narcotic indulgence would be a third.

Late Night Thoughts on Listening to Mahler's Ninth Symphony

Lewis Thomas

I cannot listen to Mahler's *Ninth Symphony* with anything like the old melancholy mixed with the high pleasure I used to take from this music. There was a time, not long ago, when what I heard, especially in the final movement, was an open acknowledgment of death and at the same time a quiet celebration of the tranquillity connected to the process. I took this music as a metaphor for reassurance, confirming my own strong hunch that the dying of every living creature, the most natural of all experiences, has to be a peaceful experience. I rely on nature. The long passages on all the strings at the end, as close as music can come to expressing silence itself, I used to hear as Mahler's idea of leave-taking at its best. But always, I have heard this music as a solitary, private listener, thinking about death.

Now I hear it differently. I cannot listen to the last movement of the Mahler *Ninth* without the door-smashing intrusion of a huge new thought: death everywhere, the dying of everything, the end of humanity. The easy sadness expressed with such gentleness and delicacy by that repeated phrase on faded strings, over and over again, no longer comes to me as old, familiar news of the cycle of living and dying. All through the last notes my mind swarms with images of a world in which the thermonuclear bombs have begun to explode, in New York and San Francisco, in Moscow and Leningrad, in Paris, in Paris, in Paris. In Oxford and Cambridge, in Edinburgh. I cannot push away the thought of a cloud of radioactivity drifting along the Engadin, from the Moloja Pass to Ftan, killing off the part of the Earth I love more than any other part.

I am old enough by this time to be used to the notion of dying, saddened by the glimpse when it has occurred but only transiently knocked down, able to regain my feet quickly at the thought of continuity, any day. I have acquired and held in affection until very recently another sideline of an idea which serves me well at dark times: the life of the Earth is the same as the life of an organism: the great round being possesses a mind: the mind contains an infinite number of thoughts and memories: when I reach my time I may find myself still hanging around in some sort of midair, one of those small thoughts, drawn back into the memory of the Earth: in that peculiar sense I will be alive.

Now all that has changed. I cannot think that way anymore. Not while those things are still in place, aimed everywhere, ready for launching.

This is a bad enough thing for the people in my generation. We can put up with it, I suppose, since we must. We are moving along anyway, like it or not. I can even set aside my private fancy about hanging around, in midair.

What I cannot imagine, what I cannot put up with, the thought that keeps grinding its way into my mind, making the Mahler into a hideous

(continued)

(continued from previous page)

noise close to killing me, is what it would be like to be young. How do the young stand it? How can they keep their sanity? If I were very young, sixteen or seventeen years old, I think I would begin, perhaps very slowly and imperceptibly, to go crazy.

There is a short passage near the very end of the Mahler in which the almost vanishing violins, all engaged in a sustained backward glance, are edged aside for a few bars by the cellos. Those lower notes pick up fragments from the first movement, as though prepared to begin everything all over again, and then the cellos subside and disappear, like an exhalation. I used to hear this as a wonderful few seconds of encouragement: we'll be back, we're still here, keep going, keep going.

Now, with a pamphlet in front of me on a corner of my desk, published by the Congressional Office of Technology Assessment, entitled "MX Bashing," an analysis of all the alternative strategies for placement and protection of hundreds of these missiles, each capable of creating artificial suns to vaporize a hundred Hiroshimas, collectively capable of destroying the life of any continent, I cannot hear the same Mahler. Now, those cellos sound in my mind like the opening of all the hatches and the instant before ignition.

If I were sixteen or seventeen years old, I would not feel the cracking of my own brain, but I would know for sure that the whole world was coming unhinged. I can remember with some clarity what is was like to be sixteen. I had discovered the Brahms symphonies. I knew that there was something going on in the late Beethoven quartets that I would have to figure out, and I knew that there was plenty of time ahead for all the figuring I would ever have to do. I had never heard of Mahler. I was in no hurry. I was a college sophomore and had decided that Wallace Stevens and I possessed a comprehensive understanding of everything needed for a life. The years stretched away forever ahead, forever. My great-great-grandfather had come from Wales, leaving his signature in the family Bible on the same page that carried, a century later, my father's signature. It never crossed my mind to wonder about the 21st century; it was just there, given, somewhere in the sure distance.

The man on television, Sunday midday, middle-aged and solid, nice-looking chap, all the facts at his fingertips, more dependable looking than most high-school principals, is talking about civilian defense, his responsibility in Washington. It can make an enormous difference, he is saying. Instead of the outright death of eighty million American citizens in twenty minutes, he says, we can, by careful planning and practice, get that number down to only forty million, maybe even twenty. The thing to do, he says, is to evacuate the cities quickly and have everyone get under shelter in the countryside. That way we can recover, and meanwhile we will have retaliated, incinerating all of Soviet society, he says. What about radioactive fallout, he is asked. Well, he says. Anyway, he says, if the Russians know they

(continued)

(continued from previous page)
can only destroy forty million, this will deter them. Of course, he adds, they have the capacity to kill all two-hundred and twenty million of us if they were to try real hard, but they know we can do the same to them. If the figure is only forty million, this will deter them, not worth the trouble, not worth the risk. Eighty million would be another matter, we should guard ourselves against losing that many all at once, he says.

If I were sixteen or seventeen years old and had to listen to that, or read things like that, I would want to give up listening and reading. I would begin thinking up new kinds of sounds, different from any music heard before, and I would be twisting and turning to rid myself of human language.

From *Late Night Thoughts on Listening to Mahler's Ninth Symphony,* by L. Thomas. Copyright 1982 by Lewis Thomas. Reprinted by permission of Viking Penguin, a division of Penguin Books USA.

Not a single life will yet have been lost in atomic warfare; nevertheless death has spread everywhere in the cold violence of anticipation. (Mumford, 1947, pp. 9–20, 29–30)

"For the first time in six centuries," wrote Edwin Shneidman (1973, p. 189), "a generation has been born and raised in a thanatological context, concerned with the imminent possibility of the death of the person, the death of humanity, the death of the universe, and, by necessary extension, the death of God." "The bomb," said philosopher William Barrett (1958, p. 65), "reveals the dreadful and total contingency of human existence. Existentialism is the philosophy of the atomic age." Indeed, the Bomb did lead many postwar people to the philosophy of existentialism, which began with the reality of death, worked through anxiety and alienation, and culminated with individuals condemned to the freedom to undertake responsible action in the world. Like the "God is dead" theology of the 1960s, atomic existentialism returned Americans to the basic fact of death.

The threat of "megadeath" has also taken the traditional future away from young people. Twenty-eight percent of high school seniors from 1975 to 1978 believed that "nuclear or biological annihilation will probably be the fate of all mankind in my lifetime." Even younger children are aware of the Bomb, and many are pessimistic about the possibilities of preventing a nuclear war. "Others report deep despair, a sense of living totally for today, anger at adults for appearing impotent to do anything, and varying degrees of ability to commit to a future or to invest in their own personal capacity to do anything about one" (Greenwald & Zeitlin, 1987). This affects not only the way that children live their lives, but also the way that they deal with death. "What happens to the child's concept of death and capacity to cope with death in a rational way," asks one researcher, "when death ceases becoming an end state of the growth process, or an incidental accidental happening, but rather becomes a catastrophic threat for all humans by our own doing?" (Greenwald & Zeitlin, 1987, pp. 21, 30–31).

The apocalyptic possibility of nuclear megadeath reminded many people of the fragility of life and the uncertainty of existence—ideas that the Puritans could surely appreciate. Because the historical context was different, however—now people could plan their own extinction—the effects were different. Instead of experiencing death in life as an incentive for righteousness, people experience the "death in life" that comes from psychic numbing. By psychic numbing, we block our capacity to feel as strongly about other aspects of everyday life. In extreme cases, we become emotionally dead; in most cases, we are merely schizophrenic, ignoring the threat of the Bomb and consequently ignorant of the ways that we might try to reduce the threat (Lifton & Falk, 1982, pp. 103–106).

The threat of the end of the world had taken away some of the traditional consolations of the dying and bereaved, including three cultural conceptions of immortality: biosocial (immortality through reproduction); natural (immortality through the continuity of nature); and creative (immortality through creative endeavors). It has forced people to reconsider their faith in the future or to place their faith fully in spiritual immortality, a choice that is difficult in a secular society (Fulton & Gottesman, 1981).

At a Country Funeral
Wendell Berry

Now the old ways that have brought us
farther than we remember sink out of sight
as under the treading of many strangers
ignorant of landmarks. Only once in a while
they are cast clear again upon the mind
as at a country funeral where, amid the soft
lights and hothouse flowers, the expensive
solemnity of experts, notes of a polite musician,
persist the usages of old neighborhood.
Friends and kinsmen come and stand and speak,
knowing the extremity they have come to,
one of their own bearing to the earth the last
of his light, his darkness the sun's definitive mark.
They stand and think as they stood and thought
when even the gods were different.
And the organ music, though decorous
as for somebody else's grief, has its source
in the outcry of pain and hope in log churches,
and on naked hillsides by the open grave,
eastward in mountain passes, in tidelands,

(continued)

(continued from previous page)

and across the sea. How long a time?
Rock of Ages, cleft for me, let me hide my
self in Thee. They came, once in time,
in simple loyalty to their dead, and returned
to the world. The fields and the work
remained to be returned to. Now the entrance
of one of the old ones into the Rock
too often means a lifework perished from the land
without inheritor, and the field goes wild
and the house sits and stares. Or it passes
at cash value into the hands of strangers.
Now the old dead wait in the open coffin
for the blood kin to gather, come home
for one last time, to hear old men
whose tongues bear an essential topography
speak memories doomed to die.
But our memory of ourselves, hard earned,
is one of the land's seeds, as a seed
is the memory of the life of its kind in its place,
to pass on into life the knowledge
of what has died. What we owe the future is not a
new start, for we can only begin
with what has happened. We owe the future
the past, the long knowledge
that is the potency of time to come.
That makes of a man's grave a rich furrow.
The community of knowing in common is the seed
of our life in this place. There is not only
no better possibility, there is no
other, except for chaos and darkness,
the terrible ground of the only possible
new start. And so as the old die and the young
depart, where shall a man go who keeps
the memories of the dead, except home
again, as one would go back after a burial,
faithful to the fields, lest the dead die
a second and more final death.

Conclusion

This historical approach to attitudes toward death has gone full circle from living death, to the dying of death, to the resurrection of death. This change of attitude has taken place over a 400-year period. One of the real assets of history is its ability to demonstrate causation and coincidence in human affairs by determining chronology and context.

In this chapter we have discussed the development of bereavement and burial practices in the United States from the early beginnings of European settlement. Although European influences were obviously present in this development, a "breaking away" from the European aristocracy is evidenced by middle-class Americans in the 1830s. Certainly various "*isms*" played significant roles in the shaping of American bereavement and burial practices. A historical perspective blends the various influences on the development of American death customs as we know them today.

With the developing of cemeteries, the building of funeral homes, and the establishing of life insurance companies, certain needs of Americans have been fulfilled. Security comes from the sheer orderliness and structure of these "institutions." One should know what to "expect" from these services, and payment turns the responsibility over to the professionals. We Americans differ significantly from nonliterate societies where such functions are completed within the kin network. However, paying someone else to perform a service fits middle-class Americans' specialization and division of labor.

It is important that the consumer stay well informed about burial practices and insurance in our society by staying abreast of various funeral home regulations and various life insurance offerings. It is also important with the threat of nuclear war that the public be well informed and actively involved in seeking peace and avoiding such a war. Perhaps this recent "resurrection of death" in the Atomic Age will be history behind us that will not continue into the future.

Summary

1. Historians mainly determine chronology and context in order to demonstrate causation and coincidence in human affairs.
2. Rural Americans between 1600 and 1930 were well acquainted with death; it was commonplace.
3. The Reformed Tradition of the Protestant Reformation stressed that death and damnation were deserved but God had elected a select few for salvation. Thus, death was approached with ambivalence.
4. Death was feared by the Puritans, who prayed not for the soul of the deceased but rather for the comfort and instruction of the living. The funeral was the main social institution for channeling the grief of Puritan survivors.
5. The Enlightenment replaced depraved, dependent Puritans with rational people who viewed death as a natural occurrence rather than a time of judgment. Unitarianism and Evangelicalism accepted this view of human nature.

6. Between 1830 and 1945, as a middle-class America emerged, "the dying of death" occurred as funeral institutions designed to keep death out of sight and mind appeared.

7. Important intellectual influences on "the dying of death" were Romanticism, sentimentalism, scientific naturalism, and liberal religion.

8. At the middle of the 19th century, the rural cemetery evolved—a landscaped garden in a suburban setting. Life insurance was established at this time to remove anxiety and financial insecurity.

9. Death was resurrected after 1945 with the advent of the Atomic Age.

Discussion Questions

1. Describe and discuss the Puritan view of death. Describe the procedures and atmosphere surrounding the typical Puritan funeral.

2. How did the Enlightenment affect the Reformed Tradition concerning funerals and view of death?

3. Discuss influences of the following on the "dying of death": Romanticism, sentimentalism, scientific naturalism, and liberal religion.

4. What are the influences of the following occupations upon the "dying of death": life insurance agents, cemetery superintendents, and funeral directors?

5. Describe and explain the reforms that have taken place over the years in the construction and maintenance of the cemetery.

6. What effect has the dropping of the atom bomb had on American death conceptions?

7. Describe the changes that have taken place with regard to the role of the family in the funeral process.

Glossary

Elegy: A song or poem expressing sorrow, especially for one who is dead.

Epitaph: An inscription, often on a tombstone, in memory of a deceased person.

Obituary: Notice of a death, usually with a brief biography.

Sexton: A church custodian charged with the upkeep of the church and parish buildings and grounds.

Social Stratification: A ranking of social status (position) in groups; upper, middle, and lower classes are basically distinguished in the U.S. social class system, for example, whereas India's stratification is a caste system.

Term Life Insurance: A type of insurance policy covering the insured for a fixed period of time (5, 10, 20, or so years). Premiums are usually lower for a greater amount of coverage than with other types of life insurance.

Universal Life Insurance: A type of insurance policy that is flexible and allows one to raise or reduce premiums and the amount of coverage on one's life.

Variable Life Insurance: A type of insurance policy that does not allow for the premium or minimum coverage on one's life to change but allows one to switch the savings from among money markets or various forms of stock.

Whole Life Insurance: A type of insurance policy in which, for a set annual premium, one receives life insurance coverage and, at the same time, invests one's money.

References

Abbott, L. (1913, August 30). There are no dead. *Outlook, 104,* 979–980.

Association of American Cemetery Superintendents, (1889). *3,* 59.

Barrett, W. (1958). *Irrational man: A study in existential philosophy.* New York: Doubleday.

Beecher, H. W. (1858). *Life thoughts.* Boston: Phillips, Sampson.

Beecher, H. W. (1859). *Notes from Plymouth pulpit.* New York: Derby and Jackson.

Bender, T. (1973, June). The "rural cemetery" movement. *New England Quarterly, 47,* 196–211.

Benjamin, C. L. (1882, February). Essay. *The Casket, 7,* 2.

Bledstein, B. J. (1976). *The culture of professionalism: The middle class and the development of higher education in America.* New York: Norton.

Clark, C. E., Jr. (1978). *Henry Ward Beecher: Spokesman for a middle-class America.* Urbana, IL: University of Illinois Press.

Cleaveland, N. (1847). *Green-wood illustrated.* New York: R. Martin.

de Tocqueville, A. (1945). *Democracy in America* New York: Vintage Books. (Original work published 1835).

Douglas, A. (1977). *The feminization of American culture.* New York: Knopf.

Dowd, Q. L. (1921). *Funeral management and costs: A world survey of burial and cremation.* Chicago: University of Chicago Press.

Downing, A. J. (1921). *Landscape gardening* (10th ed.). New York: Wiley.

The dying of death. (1899, September). *Review of Reviews, 20,* 364-365.

Emmons, N. (1842). Death without order. In J. Ide (Ed.), *The works of Nathaniel Emmons* (Vol. 3). Boston: Crocker and Brewster.

Extracts. (1895, August). *Park and Cemetery, 5,* 108.

Farrell, J. J. (1980). *Inventing the American way of death, 1830–1920.* Philadelphia: Temple University Press.

The fear of death. (1912, October 5). *Harper's Weekly, 56,* 21.

French, S. (1975). The establishment of Mount Auburn and the "rural cemetery" movement. In *Death in America.* Philadelphia: University of Pennsylvania Press.

Fulton, R., & Gottesman, D. J. (1981). Loss, social change and the prospect of mourning. Unpublished paper.

Funeral directors. (1883, June). *The Casket, 8.*

Gebhart, J. C. (1927). The reasons for present-day funeral costs. Unpublished article.

Geddes, G. (1981). *Welcome joy: Death in Puritan New England.* Ann Arbor, MI: U.M.I. Research Press.

Greenwald, D. S., & Zeitlin, S. J. (1987). *No reason to talk about it: Families confront the nuclear taboo.* New York: W. W. Norton.

Gross, R. A. (1976). *The Minutemen and their world.* New York: Hill and Wang.

Habenstein, R. W., & Lamers, W. M. (1962). The pattern of late 19th century funerals. In *The history of American funeral directing.* Milwaukee: Bulfin.

Hale, N. G. (1971). *The origin and foundations of the psychoanalytic movement in the*

United States, 1876-1918. New York: Oxford University Press.

Handford, T. W. (Ed.). (1887). *Beecher: Christian philosopher, pulpit orator, patriot and philanthropist.* Chicago: Donahue, Henneberry.

Hare, S. J. (1910). The cemetery beautiful. *Association of American Cemetery Superintendents, 24,* 41.

Hay, E. E. (1900). Influence of our surroundings. *Association of American Cemetery Superintendents, 14,* 46.

Hillerman, B. (1980). Chrysalis of gloom: Nineteenth century mourning costume. In M. V. Pike & J. G. Armstrong (Eds.), *A time to mourn: Expressions of grief in nineteenth century America.* Stony Brook, NY: The Museums at Stony Brook.

Hohenschuh, W. P. (1921). *The modern funeral: Its management.* Chicago: Trade Periodical Company.

Howe, D. W. (1970). *The Unitarian conscience: Harvard University Press, 1805–1861.* Cambridge: Harvard University Press.

Hutchinson, W. (1893, May). Death as a factor in progress. *North American Review, 156,* 637.

The ideas of a plain country woman. (1913, April). *Ladies Home Journal, 30,* 42.

Johnson, J. B. (1896). A more rational view of death. *Proceedings of the Association of American Cemetery Superintendents, 10,* 77.

Lifton, R. J., & Falk, R. (1982). *Indefensible weapons: The political and psychological case against nuclearism.* New York: Harper and Row.

Lloyd, P. (1980). Posthumous mourning portraiture. In M. V. Pike & J. G. Armstrong (Eds.), *A time to mourn: Expressions of grief in nineteenth century America.* Stony Brook, NY: The Museums at Stony Brook.

Ludwig, A. (1966). *Graven images: New England stonecarving and its symbols.* Middletown, CT: Wesleyan University Press.

The man nobody envies: An account of the experiences of an undertaker. (1914, June). *American Magazine, 77,* 68-71.

Mayo, W. R. (1916). Address. *Association of American Cemetery Superintendents, 2,* 51.

Mumford, L. (1947, March). Atom bomb: Social effects. *Air Affairs, 1,* 370–382. Reprinted as: Mumford, L. (1954). Assumptions and predictions. *In the Name of Sanity* (pp. 10–33). New York: Norton.

Oxley, J. M. (1887, February). The reproach of mourning. *Forum, 2,* 608–614.

Pike, M. V., & Armstrong, J. G. (Eds.). (1980). *A time to mourn: Expressions of grief in nineteenth century America.* Stony Brook, NY: The Museums at Stony Brook.

Rosenberg, C. E. (1973, May). Sexuality, class, and role in nineteenth century America. *American Quarterly, 25,* 137.

Rotundo, B. (1973, July). The rural cemetery movement. *Essex Institute Historical Collections, 109,* 231–242.

Sargent, A. H. (1888). Country cemeteries. *Association of American Cemetery Superintendents, 2,* 51.

Seavoy, Mr. (1906, February). Twentieth century methods. *Park and Cemetery, 15,* 488.

Sewall, S. (1973). In M. H. Thomas (Ed.), *The diary of Samuel Sewall* (2 vols.). New York: Farrar, Straus and Giroux.

Shneidman, E. (1973). Megadeath: Children of the nuclear family. In *Deaths of man.* Baltimore: Penguin Books.

Simonds, O. C. (1919). Review of progress in cemetery design and development with suggestions for the future. *Association of American Cemetery Superintendents, 24,* 41.

Smith, B. (1910, March). An outdoor room on a cemetery lot. *Country Life in America, 17,* 539.

Smith, M. T. (1988, December). Why you might go for a cash-value policy. *Money,* 153–161.

Stannard, D. E. (1980). Where all our steps are tending: Death in the American context. In M. V. Pike & J. G. Armstrong (Eds.), *A time to mourn: Expressions of grief in nineteenth century America.* Stony Brook, NY: The Museums at Stony Brook.

Taylor, L. (1980). Symbolic death: An anthropological view of mourning ritual in the nineteenth century. In M.V. Pike & J. G. Armstrong (Eds.), *A time to mourn: Expressions of grief in nineteenth century America*. Stony Brook, NY: The Museums at Stony Brook.

Tuckerman, H. (1856, November). The law of burial and the sentiment of death. *Christian Examiner, 61,* 338-342.

U.S. Bureau of the Census. (1975). *Historical statistics of the United States, colonial times to 1970* (pp. 1050–1059). Washington, DC: Department of Commerce, Bureau of the Census.

Warner, W. L. (1959). *The living and the dead*. New Haven: Yale University Press.

Weed, H. E. (1912). *Modern park cemeteries*. Chicago: R. J. Haight.

Wells, R. A. (1887). *Decorum: A practical treatise on etiquette and dress of the best American society*. Springfield, MA: King, Richardson.

Suggested Readings

Bailey, B. (1987). *Churchyards of England and Wales*. Bristol, England: WBC Printers. Discusses the origin and history of churchyards, legends surrounding them, and traditions and rituals. Includes over 100 photographs and drawings.

Farrell, J. (1980). *Inventing the American way of death, 1830–1920*. Philadelphia: Temple University Press. Examines the transformation from the Puritan way of death to the American way of death. Includes intellectual and institutional changes and concludes with a case study of how such changes affected a single county.

Geddes, G. (1981). *Welcome joy: Death in Puritan New England*. Ann Arbor, MI: U.M.I. Research Press. Good descriptive study, rich in detail. Particularly good on the Puritan funeral and bereavement.

Habenstein, R., & Lamers, W. (1962). *The history of American funeral directing*. Milwaukee: Bulfin. Prepared for the National Funeral Directors Association, this detailed study is a good history of the development of the profession.

Jackson, C. O. (Ed.). (1977). *Passing: The vision of death in America*. Westport, CT: Greenwood Press. A collection of classic essays on death in America, a few of which have been superseded by more recent work in the area.

Meyer, R. E. (Ed.). (1993). *Ethnicity and the American cemetery*. Bowling Green, OH: Bowling Green State University Popular Press. This anthology of eight essays explores the manner in which representative ethnic groups in America have made their cemeteries. The book has an interdisciplinary focus from folklore, cultural history, historical archaeology, landscape architecture, and philosophy.

Pike, M., & Armstrong, J. G. (Eds.). (1980). *A time to mourn: Expressions of grief in nineteenth century America*. Stony Brook, NY: The Museums at Stony Brook. A beautifully illustrated collection of excellent essays, a must for anyone who wants to see and feel the grief of 19th-century America.

Sloane, D. C. (1991). *The last great necessity: Cemeteries in American history*. Baltimore: Johns Hopkins University Press. Explores changing attitudes about cemeteries as well as changing landscapes. Describes many of America's most famous cemeteries.

Stannard, D. (Ed.). (1975). *Death in America*. Philadelphia: University of Pennsylvania Press. The December 1974 special issue of *American Quarterly*, with an added essay on the cemetery as a cultural institution by Stanley French.

Related Web Sites

http://web.gmu.edu/chnm/aha/index.html   The home page of the American Historical Association.

http://www.lsds.com/death/   Thanatolinks contains links to some of the best Internet sites about dying and death.

http://home.intranet.org/~polygon/cemeteries.html   Links to many Web sites and resources on cemetery history and preservation.

http://www.uh.edu/~cleimer/   The Tombstone Traveler's Guide explores American cemeteries and funeral practices.

http://www.funeral.net/info/notices.html   Funeral Net's intention is to help people gain a basic understanding of the funeral and grief process so that they may be better equipped, emotionally, psychologically and mentally, to deal with the closure of significant relationships in their lives.

http://funeral.netm.com/   Home page of the National Academy of Mortuary Science.

http://www.csn.net/~mhand/Presidents/   Web site on the graves of dead presidents.

http://www.orci.com/personal/jim/grave/alphabet.html   Find a Grave is a Web site that will enable you to locate (and in some cases view) the final resting places of many famous people.

http://www.primenet.com/~trix/gyard.htm   A Web site with many humorous epitaphs.

http://www.best.com/~gazissax/city.html   City of the Silent Web site contains many resources regarding cemeteries.

http://www.best.com/~gazissax/silence/altfunin.html   The Post-Mortem Page and Paths to Other Grave Sites contains many resources regarding cemeteries.

http://members.aol.com/kmedeke/tod.htm   *Optima philosophia et sapientia est meditatio mortis* is an index of worldwide cemeteries by location (national and international). The cemetery links might be of historical, genealogical, or just of touristic interest and contain pictures, lists of surnames, and historical information.

http://www.forest-lawn.com/   The Web site of America's most famous cemetery.

http://www.csi.ad.jp:8080/ABOMB/index.html   The A-Bomb WWW Museum.

Chapter 12

The Funeral:
Expression of Contemporary American Bereavement

You must express your grief at the loss of a loved one and then you must go on. The eyes of the dead must be gently closed and the eyes of the living must be gently opened.

—JAN BRUGLER, INDIAN LAKE, OHIO, HIGH SCHOOL STUDENT

Most anthropologists agree that all civilizations have, in some form, given social recognition of death through a process involving activities, rites, and rituals associated with the final disposition of the deceased's body. This process varies greatly from culture to culture, but the basic elements of the recognition of the death—a rite or ritual and the final disposition of the body—have their counterparts in every culture. As we concluded in chapter 10, funeral rituals allow individuals of every culture to maintain relations with ancestors while uniting family members, reinforcing social status, fostering group cohesiveness, and restoring the social structure of the society.

Social and Cultural Roots of American Funeral Traditions

In contemporary American culture, the process of final disposition of the body should be studied within its cultural and historical context. As we discovered in

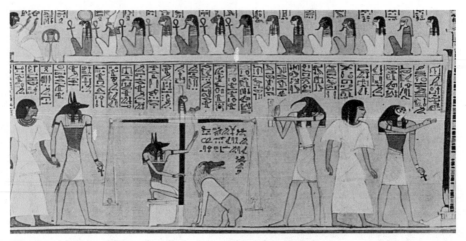

The most elaborate and famous burial customs were those of the Egyptians.

chapter 10, it is wrong to believe that the funeral is either unique to Western culture or has been invented or created by it. To bury the dead is a common social practice. The methods to accomplish burial, and the meanings associated with it, are culturally determined.

This burial process requires the involvement of a functionary, who may be a professional, tradesperson, religious leader, servant, or even a member of the family. The functionary in each society is closely associated with the folkways and mores of the society and its philosophical approach to life and death.

The Hebrew scripture reveals in Genesis 50:2 that physicians embalmed the body of Jacob, the father of Joseph. This description is followed by a detailed description of the funeral and burial. The historian Herodotus records embalming preparation as early as circa 484 B.C. These two sources and archaeological discoveries of earlier cultures give evidence of the disposition of the dead.

It is often stated that ancient Egypt had a secret process for the preservation of the dead. The Egyptian embalming process, however, is fully described in several sources. Perhaps no other ancient culture provides more evidence of its burial procedures than does Egypt with its great number of mummies available for study.

The ancient Egyptians believed that the soul makes a journey following death. According to their beliefs, this journey lasts approximately 3,000 years, followed by the soul's returning to the body that it had left. This belief required the preservation of the body so that the soul, upon its return, would have a final destination. In addition to the embalming procedures, the Egyptians attempted to exclude air and moisture from the body by the liberal use of wrappings, oils, and gums. They also practiced elaborate encasement and burial of the remains. Such attempts at body preservation were obviously effective as evidenced by the many specimens still in existence.

In many cultures the religious beliefs of the people influence their funeral and burial practices. Such was the case in Europe during the medieval period of the feudal estates. Each landholder or lord was responsible for the people who worked for

Death in Ancient Egypt

The earliest burials known in Egypt date to a period well before 3000 B.C. and display evidence, through funerary gifts in the graves, of a belief of continued existence after death. The earliest graves were very simple affairs consisting of shallow circular or oval pits in the ground where the body was placed in a fetal position. The introduction of methods to protect the body from the filling of the pit was motivated by a desire to improve the conditions for the dead.

During the middle and late Predynastic Period (before 3100 B.C.) the practice of wrapping the body in animal skins gradually gave way to other forms of protection, particularly the use of basket trays upon which the body was laid out. Wooden coffins, made of rough planks joined by dowels, became common by the end of the Predynastic Period (circa 3000 B.C.). By the beginning of the Fourth Dynasty (2613 B.C.), a significant number of burials occurred in which the body was placed in a coffin in a fully extended position.

The main advance in Predynastic tomb design (before 3100 B.C.) was the gradual introduction of wood-roofed graves, thus creating an underground chamber within which the coffin could be placed and separated from the sand. The pits were often lined with mud-plaster or wood therefore providing an additional barrier between the body and the ground. An important consequence of the added separation between the body and the filling of the grave, however, was the loss of the natural preservative effects of direct contact with the dry sand which served to preserve some of the soft tissues through rapid drying.

Wrapped bodies of the first three dynasties were not truly mummified, since no treatment other than the use of linen bandages and resin was employed. By the Fourth Dynasty, however, evidence was found of deliberate attempts to inhibit decomposition by removal of the soft internal organs from the body—accomplished by means of an incision in the side of the abdomen. Removal of the liver, intestines, and stomach improved the chances of securing good preservation because the emptied body-cavity could be dried more rapidly. The removed organs were deposited in a safe place in the tomb in order for the body of the deceased to be complete once more in the netherworld.

Bandages soaked in resin were carefully molded to the shape of the body in order to reproduce the features, particularly in the face and the genital organs. As the resin dried, it consolidated the linen wrapping in position, preserving the appearance of the body for as long as it remained undisturbed. The corpse itself decomposed very rapidly within this linen shell, leaving the innermost wrappings in close contact with the skeleton.

(continued)

(continued from previous page)

An important factor in the development of the Egyptian tomb was the necessity to provide storage space for the items of funerary equipment considered essential for continued use by the deceased in the hereafter. A significant part of the material provided for the dead took the form of actual offerings of food and drink—required for the "very survival" of the deceased before enjoying all the other possessions in the tomb. Because of the need to provide offerings of food at the tomb, the tomb had to combine the function of a burial-place with that of a mortuary chapel in which the priests could officiate.

The Egyptians believed there were two main spiritual forms of the deceased. The Ka was supposed to dwell in the tomb in the mummified body. The Ba was usually represented as a human-headed bird, which left the body at the time of death, and was free to travel in the tomb during the daytime but returned to dwell in the mummy at night. The Predynastic cultures may have believed that continued existence after death resembled earthly life, also a popular belief in later times.

From *Death in Ancient Egypt*, by A. J. Spencer, 1982, New York: Penguin Books.

him and who were members of his extended family. These lords had a chaplain or religious person as a part of their staff, and these persons became responsible for the care and burial of the dead.

In the structure of the Christian church, priests were assigned to certain duties during specified hours. It is suggested that our use of the word sexton today comes from the practice of assigning to the priest in charge of the 6th hour (in Latin, *sex*) the burial of the dead and the supervision of the churchyard or cemetery.

As Western civilization developed, there is evidence that many of the functionaries were anatomists, doctors, or artists. Each profession wanted to preserve the human body to further its own interests and offered to do so in return for the availability of bodies for study and research. Still in existence are anatomical plates that Leonardo daVinci drew from his observations of human specimens.

With the discovery of the circulatory system of the body, circa 1600, and the possibility of diffusion of preserving chemicals through that system, more sophisticated methods of embalming the body were developed. Dr. Hunter of England and Dr. Gannal of France, independently of each other, furthered the process in the early 1600s. In France, this work coincided with the advent of the bubonic plague. During this period of time, extensive attempts were made to preserve the bodies of the dead to protect the health of those who survived the plague.

Early American Funeral Practices

There is early evidence of the care and burial of the dead during the colonization of America. There is, however, no evidence of any attempt at body preservation, even

Historically, through a considerable period of time, the pattern of mortuary behavior in any society is subject to change, although basic death beliefs remain fundamentally unchanged. The roots of American funeral behavior extend back in a direct line several thousand years to early Judeo-Christian beliefs as to the nature of God, man, and the hereafter, and, in turn, these beliefs and practices were influenced to some extent by even earlier beliefs and practices.

From *The History of American Funeral Directing*, by R. W. Habenstein and W. M. Lamers, 1962, Milwaukee: Bulfin.

though the body was bathed and dressed prior to burial. This was usually done by nurses, midwives, or members of the family. It was not until the time of the Civil War that embalming was promoted to temporarily preserve the bodies of soldiers for return to their hometowns. Some reports credit this practice to a military doctor by the name of Thomas Holmes. It was not until the late 1800s and early 1900s that states began to promote the practice of embalming to protect the public's health. With the advent of the practice of embalming, laws were soon passed to regulate both the practice and the practitioner.

The current practitioner of the funeral profession evolved from the artisan or cabinetmaker (invariably a man who built the casket as part of his trade) and the livery owner (who provided the special vehicles needed for the funeral—particularly the hearse and special buggies for the family). As the public came to expect the services associated with the casket and transportation, persons began to specialize in providing these services, and the funeral functionary of today evolved as a provider of these services.

With the development of contemporary funeral services over the past 90 years, it is interesting to observe the kind of facilities that have evolved to provide these services. It was not customary to hold funerals in the church in colonial America. The Puritans gave little importance to the funeral and seemed to demand only proper and reverent disposition of the dead by burial. Almost without exception, death occurred in the home. It was, therefore, expected that the dead would be bathed, dressed, put into a casket, and laid out (viewed) in the home. The funeral rite was either in the home or at the grave site. When the first practitioners began to specialize in the burial of the dead, they continued to use the home for this purpose. They often would acquire a large house in the community and convert it to use as a "funeral home." It should be noted that the word home was associated with this facility and today is still the most commonly used term to describe funeral facilities.

It was only natural that with specialization, special facilities would be developed for the funeral ceremony. The influence of the family and the church is readily seen in that most facilities try to provide both a homelike atmosphere for the gathering of the community and a chapellike atmosphere for the funeral service. If the family chooses not to use a church for the funeral service, the funeral home provides a similar setting. Approximately 50 percent of funerals are currently held in churches, and the remaining 50 percent are held in funeral homes or cemetery chapels (National Funeral Directors Association, 1986). The United States Department of Health and

New Funeral Option for Those In a Rush

The convenience and high technology of drive-through banks and hamburger places have come to the funeral world. A Chicago funeral home has set up a drive-through service with cameras and a sound system that let on-the-go visitors pay their respects, sign the funeral register and view the remains of the loved one round the clock without ever leaving the car.

Carloads of working people pressed for time, as well as bus loads of senior citizens confined to wheelchairs, have paraded through the drive-in at Gatling's Funeral Home on the city's South Side to see the images of embalmed friends and relatives on a television screen covered by a white canopy that is lit up at night.

The owner, Lafayette Gatling, a former construction worker who says he used to feel uncomfortable himself paying his respects in soiled work clothes, added the drive-through service two years ago. "The working person doesn't have time to come in," Mr. Gatling said. "They want to see the body but they don't want to have to wait. I always thought there should be some way they could see the body any time they want."

The procedure goes something like this: Visitors, cautioned to drive through slowly, ride to a speakerphone and push a button for service. An attendant in a control room asks whom they wish to see. "I would like to view the remains of John Doe," the visitor says into the speakerphone. "You may proceed," the attendant says, using controls to turn on the lights and cameras over the body of the deceased lying in one of the rooms.

The motorist then signs the register, conveniently tucked underneath the speakerphone, and drives a couple of feet to the viewing area where a head shot of the loved one in a coffin instantly appears on a 25-inch screen. The picture lasts three seconds, but visitors can push a button to request to see the loved one over and over again, and some stare at the

(continued)

Human Services estimates that approximately 22,153 funeral homes serve the families of the approximately 2.3 million people who die annually (National Funeral Directors Association, 1997).

The Contemporary American Funeral

Most people use the words *death, grief,* and *bereavement* imprecisely, which can lead to difficulty in communication. The words are closely interrelated, but each has a specific content or meaning. As discussed in chapter 1, death is that point in time when life ceases to exist. *Death* is an event. It can be attached to a certain day, hour, and minute. *Grief* is an emotion, a very powerful emotion. It is triggered or stimulated by

(continued from previous page)

screen for half an hour. When the car moves on, the next in line takes its place.

The feature has been a hit with visitors, who are used to ordering hamburgers and fries from a drive-through, a comparison that Mr. Gatling finds insulting. "We're dealing with remains here—I wouldn't compare that with food," Mr. Gatling said. "The only thing similar is the speaker system."

Drive-up windows displaying a single coffin came on the scene briefly several years ago at a few funeral homes in Florida and California, but there have been none using the complex system of relays, switches and timers needed to accommodate requests to see as many as a dozen bodies as the Gatling Funeral Home allows.

Mr. Gatling is now seeking a patent for the system. And he is planning bigger and better things for his funeral home, which already sells flowers and sympathy cards for mourners who forgot theirs and holds weddings in the main chapel on off-days. In addition to adding more chapels and parlors, he plans to make videotapes of the remains and the funeral services, which he hopes to sell to the bereaved.

Others worry about what all this convenience could do to the funeral business. "You could have the curious going through and checking out who happens to be laid out today," said W. Timothy Simms, president-elect of the Illinois Funeral Directors Association. "It lends a circus atmosphere to the services. It seems we're in a changing world."

Bernard Beck, an associate professor of sociology at Northwestern University, agreed, saying: "There seems to be no end to the need to save time. There has been a loosening of our communal ties. Still this is a way of putting in an appearance."

I. Wilkerson, February 23, 1989, *New York Times,* p. 10. Copyright © 1989 by the New York Times Company. Reprinted by permission.

death. Although one can have anticipatory grief prior to the death of a significant other, grief is an emotional response to death. *Bereavement* is the state of having lost a significant other to death. Alternative processes—such as denial, avoidance, and defiance—have been shown by psychologists and psychiatrists to be only aberrations of the grief process and, as such, are not viable means of grief resolution.

The decisions about ultimate method of final disposition of the body should be determined by the persons in bereavement. Those charged with these decisions will be guided by their personal values and by the norms of the culture in which they live.

With over three fourths of American deaths occurring in hospitals or other institutions for the care of the sick and infirm, the contemporary process of body disposition begins at the time of death when the body is removed from the institutional

The Decline of Mourning

A decade ago, anthropologist Geoffrey Gorer wrote a much reprinted article on "the pornography of death." Gorer's point, also made by German theologian Helmuth Thielicke, is that death is coming to have the same position in modern life and literature that sex had in Victorian times. Some support for the theory is provided by the popular movie *The Loved One,* which turns death into a slapstick dirty joke.

Is grief going underground? People want briefer funeral services, says Dr. Quentin Hand, an ordained Methodist minister who teaches at the theological school of Georgia's Emory University. "No one wants a eulogy any more—they often ask me not to even mention Mother or Father." Even those much scolded death-deniers, the undertakers, seem to sense that something is missing. Dean Robert Lehr of the Gupton Jones College of Mortuary Science in Dallas says that whereas students used to study only embalming, they now go in heavily for "grief psychology and grief counseling." Explains Lehr: "There are only 16 quarter hours in embalming now and 76 in other areas. We're in a transition period."

The outward signs of mourning—veils and widow's weeds, black hat and armbands, crepe-hung doorways—are going the way of the hearse pulled by plumed horses. There is almost no social censure against remarrying a few months after bereavement in what one psychiatrist calls "the Elizabeth Taylorish way" (referring to her statement six months after husband Mike Todd was killed in a plane crash: "Mike is dead now, and I am alive"). Many psychologists who have no quarrel with the life-must-continue attitude are dubious about the decline in expression of grief. Psychology Professor Harry W. Martin of Texas Southwestern Medical School deplores the "slick, smooth operation of easing the corpse out, but saying no to weeping and wailing and expressing grief and loneliness. What effect does this have on us psychologically? It may mean that we have to mourn covertly, by subterfuge—perhaps in various degrees of depression, perhaps in mad flights of activity, perhaps in booze." In his book, *Death, Grief and Mourning,* anthropologist Gorer warns that abandonment of the traditional forms of mourning results in "callousness, irrational preoccupation with and fear of death, and vandalism."

(continued)

setting. Most frequently the body is taken to a funeral home. There, the body is bathed, embalmed, and dressed. It is then placed into a casket selected by the family. Typically, arrangements are made for the ceremony, assuming that a ceremony is to follow. The funeral director, in consultation with the family, will determine the type,

(continued from previous page)

Whether or not such conclusions are justified, the take-it-in-stride attitude can make things difficult. Gorer cites his brother's widow, a New Englander, whose emotional reticence, combined with that of her British friends, led her to eschew any outward signs of mourning. As a result, "she let herself be, almost literally, eaten up with grief, sinking into a deep and long-lasting depression." Many a widow invited to a party "to take her mind off things" has embarrassed herself and her hostess by a flood of tears at the height of the festivities. On occasion, Gorer himself "refused invitations to cocktail parties, explaining that I was mourning; people responded to this statement with shocked embarrassment, as if I had voiced some appalling obscenity."

Funerals seem ever harder to get to in a high-pressure, computerized way of life. But the social repression of grief goes against the experience of the human race. Mourning is one of the traditional "rites of passage" through which families and tribes can rid themselves of their dead and return to normal living. Black funeral parades, Greek klama (ritual weeping), Irish wakes each in their own way fulfills this function. Orthodox Jewish families are supposed to "sit shiv'ah"; for seven days after the burial they stay home, wearing some symbol of a "shredded garment," such as a piece of torn cloth, and keeping an unkempt appearance. Friends bring food as a symbol of the inability of the bereaved to concern themselves with practical affairs. For eleven months sons are enjoined to say the prayers for the dead in the synagogue twice a day.

By no means all observers agree that the decline of such demanding customs is a bad thing. The old rituals, while a comfort and release for some, could be a burden to others. And grief expressed in private can be more meaningful than the external forms. London psychiatrist Dr. David Stafford-Clark thinks that the new attitude toward death should be considered in the context of "the way the whole structure of life has changed since World War II, particularly the very different attitude toward the future which has arisen. It is a much more expectant attitude-an uncertain one, but not necessarily a more negative one."

time, place, and day of the ceremony. In most instances, the ceremony will have a religious content (Pine, 1971). The procedure just described is followed in approximately 75 percent of funerals. Alternatives to this procedure will be examined later in this chapter.

Following this ceremony, final **disposition** of the body is made by either earth burial (79 percent) or cremation (21 percent). (These percentages are approximate national averages and will vary by region.) The bereavement process will then be followed by a period of postfuneral adjustment for the family.

How the Funeral Meets the Needs of the Bereaved

Paul Irion (1956) has described the following needs of the bereaved: reality, expression of grief, social support, and meaningful context for the death. For Irion, the

Memorial on the Net
David Colker

Ana Durarte-Coiner's home page doesn't look, at first glance, much different than that of any other 12-year-old, Net-savvy kid. There's a picture of her practicing the piano and one at her computer, with a U.S. map and jam-packed bulletin board visible on the nearby wall. And there are plenty of links to friends and messages that mention her many interests, including choral singing, reading, softball, and ballet.

But Ana did not create this site. It was put together by her online friends—none of whom she ever met in person—as a tribute and a memorial. Ana and her mother, who lived in Binghamton, New York, were among the passengers on their way to Paris on TWA Flight 800 when it exploded and crashed off Long Island, New York, in July. "I just know that I have to do it—write as much as I can, remember as much as I can, so I can try to make sense of what happened," wrote Andrea Norstad, 15, in an essay about her friend posted on the Web site.

Andrea was one of the regulars on the newsgroup, alt.kids-Talk, where Ana met most of her online friends. Ana's peers belong to the first generation to look upon computers as a comfortable, everyday form of communication. It is therefore no surprise that in addition to trading information, gossiping, flirting and arguing online, it's also where they go to mourn. Their

(continued)

funeral is an experience of significant personal value insofar as it meets the religious, social, and psychological needs of the mourners. Each of these must be met for bereaved individuals to return to everyday living and, in the process, resolve their grief.

The *psychological* focus of the funeral is based on the fact that grief is an emotion. Edgar Jackson (1963) has indicated that grief is the other side of the coin of love. He contends that if a person has never loved the deceased—never had an emotional investment of some type and degree—he or she will not grieve upon death. Evidence of this can easily be demonstrated by the number of deaths that we hear, see, or read about daily that do not have an impact on us unless we have some kind of emotional involvement with those deceased persons. We can read of 78 deaths in a plane crash and not grieve over any of them unless we personally knew the individuals killed. Exceptions to the preceding might include the death of a celebrity or other public figure, when people experience a sense of grief even though there has never been any personal contact.

In his original work on the symptomatology of grief, Erich Lindemann (1944) stressed this concept of grief and its importance as a step in the resolution of grief. He defines how the emotion of grief must support the reality and finality of death. As long as the finality of death is avoided, Lindemann believes, grief resolution is impeded. For this reason, he strongly recommends that the bereaved persons view the dead. When the living confront the dead, all of the intellectualization and avoidance

---

(continued from previous page)

remembrances (the Web site is http://www.Capital.net/users/mfree) portray a girl who was extremely bright (and knew it), gushingly enthusiastic, protective of her online buddies and endlessly curious. The site offers much more than the heartfelt remembrances. There are links to news about the Flight 800 investigation, to other pages created in tribute to crash victims, and to information about scholarship funds set up in honor of Ana and her mother.

But perhaps the most affecting section contains Ana's own words. There you can find the more than 300 messages—some only a few words long—that Ana wrote during the time she was online. Her combined words are a kind of diary, but not that of someone in extraordinary conditions, such as Anne Frank or an explorer. The power of her words are in their ordinariness. Ana was someone who had her whole life before her. There are several references to her upcoming vacation to Europe and how excited she was about it. And even though she usually tried to act mature, sometimes the little girl came through strong. "I talked to, like, a really really really famous person on national TV!" she gushed after getting through to talk show guest Coolio, the rapper. "And he talked back! And Tom Snyder commented about me!!!"

It was her last posting to alt.kids-Talk.

D. Colker, January 23, 1997, *Minneapolis Star and Tribune,* pp. E1, E3.

techniques break down. When we can say, "He or she is dead, I am alone, and from this day forward my life will be forever different," we have broken through the devices of denial and avoidance and have accepted the reality of death. It is only at this point that we can begin to withdraw the emotional capital that we have invested in the deceased and seek to create new relationships with the living.

On the other hand, viewing the corpse can be very traumatic for some. Most people are not accustomed to seeing a cold body and a significant other stretched out with eyes closed. Indeed, for some this scene may remain in their memories for a lifetime. Thus, they remember the cold corpse, not the warm, responsive person. Whether or not to view the body is not a cut-and-dried decision. Many factors should be taken into account when this decision is made.

Grief resolution is especially important for family members, but others are affected also—the neighbors, the business community in some instances, the religious community in most instances, the health care community, and the circle of friends and associates (many of whom may be unknown to the family). All of these groups will grieve to some extent the death of their relationship with the deceased. Thus, many people are affected by the death. These affected persons will seek not only a means of expressing their grief over the death, but also a network of support to help cope with their grief.

Sociologically, the funeral is a social event that brings the chief mourners and the members of society into a confrontation with death. The funeral becomes a vehicle to bring persons of all walks of life and degrees of relationship to the deceased together for expression and support. It is for this reason that in our contemporary culture the funeral becomes an occasion to which no one is invited but to which all may come. This was not always the case, and some cultures make the funeral ceremony an "invitation only" experience. It is perhaps for this reason that private funerals (restricted to the family or a special list of persons) have all but disappeared in our culture. (The possible exception to this statement is a funeral for a celebrity—where participation by the public is limited to media coverage.)

At a time when emotions are strong, it is important that human interaction and social support become high priorities. A funeral can provide this atmosphere. To grieve alone can be devastating because it becomes necessary for that lone person to

An Extraordinary Support Group

Lest we forget, funerals really are the social event, consider the February 1990 funeral of publisher Malcolm Forbes. The mourners included ex-President Richard Nixon, actress Elizabeth Taylor (who sat in front pew with the ex-President), Chrysler Chairman Lee Iacocca, Hell's Angels cyclists, Barbara Walters, Joan Rivers, David Rockefeller, Ann Landers, Mrs. Douglas MacArthur, former New York City mayor Edward Koch, and 1,700 others. What other social occasion can bring together such a collection of individuals?

Source: Web site http://www.trinity.edu/~mkearl/death-6.html#funerals

absorb all of the feelings into himself or herself. It has often been said that "joy shared is joy increased"; surely grief shared is grief diminished. People need each other at times when they have intense emotional experiences.

A funeral is in essence a onetime kind of "support group" to undergird and support those grieving persons. A funeral provides a conducive social environment for mourning. We may go to the funeral home either to visit with the bereaved or to work through our own grief. Most of us have had the experience of finding it difficult to discuss a death with a member of the family. We seek the proper atmosphere, time, and place. It is during the funeral, the wake, the shivah, or the visitation with the bereaved that we are provided with the opportunity to express our condolences and sympathy comfortably.

Anger and guilt are often deeply felt at the time of death and will surface in words and actions. They are permitted within the funeral atmosphere as honest and candid expressions of grief, whereas at other times they might bring criticism and reprimand. The funeral atmosphere says in essence, "You are okay, I am okay; we have some strong feelings, and now is the time to express and share them for the benefit of all." Silence, talking, feeling, touching, and all means of sharing can be expressed without the fear of their being inappropriate.

Another function of the funeral is to provide a *theological* or *philosophical* perspective to facilitate grieving and to provide a context of meaning in which to place one of life's most significant experiences. For the majority of Americans, the funeral is a religious rite or ceremony (Pine, 1971). Those grievers who do not possess a religious creed or orientation will define or express death in the context of the values that the deceased and the grievers find important. Theologically or philosophically, the funeral functions as an attempt to bring meaning to the death and life of the deceased individual. For the religiously oriented person, the belief system will perhaps bring an understanding of the afterlife. Others may see only the end of biological life and the beginning of symbolic immortality created by the effects of one's life on the lives of others. The funeral should be planned to give meaning to whichever value context is significant for the bereaved.

"Why?" is one of the most often asked questions upon the moment of death or upon being told that someone we know has died. Though the funeral cannot provide the final answer to this question, it can place death within a context of meaning that is significant to those who mourn. If it is religious in context, the theology, creed, and articles of faith confessed by the mourners will give them comfort and assurance as to the meaning of death. Others who have developed a personally meaningful philosophy of life and death will seek to place the death in that philosophical context.

Cultural expectations typically require that we dispose of the dead with ceremony and dignity. The funeral can also ascribe importance to the remains of the dead.

THE NEEDS OF CHILDREN AND THEIR ATTENDANCE AT FUNERALS

For children, as well as for their elders, the funeral ceremony can be an experience of value and significance. At a very early age, children are interested in any type of family reunion, party, or celebration. To be excluded from the funeral may create questions and doubts in the minds of children as to why they are not permitted to be a part of an important family activity.

Another question to be considered when denying the child an opportunity to participate in postdeath activities is what goes through the child's mind when such participation is denied. Children deal with other difficult situations in life, and when denied this opportunity, many will fantasize. Research suggests that these fantasies may be negative, destructive, and at times more traumatic than the situation from which the children are excluded.

Children also should not be excluded from activities prior to the funeral service. They should be permitted to attend the visitation, wake, or shivah. (In some situations it would be wise to permit children to confront the deceased prior to the public visitation.) It is obvious that children should not be forced into this type of confrontation, but, by the same token, children who are curious and desire to be involved should not be denied the opportunity.

Children will react at their own emotional levels, and the questions that they ask will usually be asked at their level of comprehension. Two important rules to follow: Never lie to the child, and do not overanswer the child's question.

At the time of the funeral, parents have two concerns about their child's behavior at funerals. The first concern is that the child will have difficulty observing the grief of others—particularly if the child has never seen an adult loved one cry. The second concern is that parents themselves become confused when the child's emotional reactions may be different than their own. If the child is told of a death and responds by saying, "Oh, can I go out and play?" the parents may interpret this as denial or as a suppressed negative reaction to the death. Such a reaction can increase emotional concern by the parents. However, if the child's response is viewed as only a first reaction, and if the child is provided with loving, caring, and supportive attention, the child will ordinarily progress into an emotional resolution of the death.

The final reasons for involving children in postdeath activities are related to the strength and support that children give other grievers. They often provide positive evidence of the fact that life goes on. In other instances, because they have been an important part of the life of the deceased, their presence is symbolic testimony to the immortality of the deceased. Furthermore, it is not at all unusual for children to change the atmosphere surrounding bereavement from one of depression and sadness to one of laughter, verbalization, and celebration. Many times children do this by their normal behavior, without any understanding of the kind of contribution being made.

The American Practice of Funeral Service

EDUCATION AND LICENSURE

Earlier in this chapter we noted that with the evolution of the funeral there likewise has been an evolution of a funeral functionary. Our contemporary American culture refers to that functionary as a funeral director. A hundred years ago this functionary was a "layer out of the dead," often a member of the family who physically and emotionally could perform the necessary tasks of bathing the body, closing the eyes and

Children and Funerals

Before the visit to the funeral home children should be told that they will have a chance to see grandma, if they desire. They should be told that she is no longer breathing, that she is not just "asleep"; that she is no longer alive. They might be told that she does not look exactly the way she used to, but that this is all right; that it is easier to say "goodbye" if it is possible to see the person and be certain that they appear calm and at peace. They should be told that they may have questions, some of which will be hard to answer.

Children, depending on their age, will react differently to viewing the deceased. Children between five and ten years of age seem to ask many questions; they tend to be more open than adolescents. Older children usually experience and express stronger emotions than younger children. They need assurance that this, too, is all right. Children need assurance that they may have questions even after this last "goodbye" visit and that every attempt will be made to help find the answers.

The same sort of approach is indicated when preparing a child for attendance at a funeral or for a visit to the cemetery. In general, it is easier to include children in the entire course of the funeral than to exclude them from part or all of the activities and then try to deal with their subsequent inability to understand what happened at the funeral.

In order to be most supportive of their children when a friend or family member has died, parents should be told that it is natural for children to want to be included in funeral activities. They should be advised that advance preparations, some explanation and time for questions will provide children with the support and understanding needed for respectful involvement. Parents should be told that children are welcome to come to the funeral home, that staff will be pleased to assist the parents in this work, and that children should be invited to attend and even participate in funeral service activities.

Parents should be told to invite and encourage children to be part of the funeral service—but not to force them or coerce them into participating. If the parents are having a difficult time because of the death, the children can be brought to services in the care of a close friend or relative with whom they are comfortable. If there is some concern that the children might have a difficult time at the funeral, it is best to encourage attendance and, at the same time, see that supportive people are available to them.

"Helping the Child to Grieve" (pp. 105–120), by W. Lamers , 1986. In G. H. Paterson (Ed.), *Children and Death, London,* Ontario: King's College Press.

mouth, and dressing the body. It was not unusual for a midwife or other person who provided nursinglike services in the community to be called on to assist the family. Early advertisements indicate that nurses did offer such services.

The advent of the cabinetmaker and the livery person has been discussed, and out of this transition evolved the funeral director. As early as the 1890s, various states began to enact legislation to protect the public's health by licensing embalmers. Early licensing agencies directed their attention to the embalming process, and it was not until the 1920s and 1930s that licensing agencies began to regulate other aspects of the funeral and the operation of funeral homes.

> Lawyer Clarence Darrow, discussing an ancestor reported to have been an undertaker, said: "One could imagine a more pleasant means of livelihood, but almost any trade is bearable if the customers are sure."

The rationale for this licensure was based upon the need to protect the public, primarily in the financial area. However, regulations also addressed the conduct of the funeral when the cause of death was contagious disease. Another issue of public health protection was the transportation of the dead from the place of death to the location of final disposition. Public health authorities claim that regulating the treatment of the dead has significantly contributed to the advanced standard of health of our country.

Based on these concepts, the licensing agencies most often charged with responsibility to regulate the funeral industry have been the various state boards of health. In some states, special boards were established to implement regulation and enforcement procedures.

Licensure has been reserved for the individual states and includes 3 basic licenses. A license as an *embalmer* permits a person to legally remove the dead from the place of death and prepare the body through the process of embalming for viewing and funeralization. All states (with the exception of Colorado) require persons who perform these functions to be licensed. A second license, to practice as a *funeral director,* permits the holder to arrange the legal details of the funeral, including preparing the death certificate and counseling with the family to arrange and implement the kind of funeral desired for the deceased. A third license is one that permits the holder to practice *mortuary science*—an all-inclusive specialty that covers the practices of both embalming and funeral directing.

A few states issue a funeral director license, which may be held by only one person in each firm (usually the owner or manager) that serves to give the licensing agency control over all of the practitioners within that firm. A greater number of states have created a *funeral home* license or permit that is required for each funeral home and permits the state to close the funeral home by withdrawing the license without taking action against the licensees employed by that firm. In addition to requiring embalmers to be licensed, with the exception of Colorado, all states and the District of Columbia require embalming practitioners to also be licensed as funeral directors. The exact number of states requiring funeral home licenses or permits is difficult to determine because some are required by law, some by regulation, and some by local ordinance. Approximately 25 states have some requirement that governs the operation of the funeral homes located in them.

The qualifications for licensure chiefly concern age, citizenship, and specific education. As of 1995 (with the exception of Colorado, which currently has no basic licensure requirement), all states require a high school education and some post-secondary education in mortuary science. Fourteen states require 2 years of college, including the 1-year major in funeral service or mortuary science, 16 states require 3 years of college, including the 1-year funeral service program, and 1 state requires the bachelor's degree for licensure in funeral service. The typical funeral service student graduates with an associate degree in funeral service or mortuary science.

> "There is a major misconception about how much money funeral directors make," says John Everly. "When I was at mortuary school, a teacher asked how many of us thought funeral directors made a lot of money. Several raised their hands. Then he told us how much funeral directors actually made. Two weeks later, about half those people were gone."
> H. Cox, December 30, 1996, *Insight*, p. 42.

Following academic preparation, and in some cases before, all states require applicants to serve an apprenticeship that varies from 1 to 3 years, depending on individual state regulations. Upon the completion of academic and internship or apprenticeship requirements, applicants for licensure are required by all states to pass a qualifying examination prior to the issuance of the license to practice (Bigelow, 1997).

As of 1997, 28 states mandate continuing education in order to renew the license to practice. The Academy of Professional Funeral Service Practice certifies and approves all continuing education programs and courses. The average number of hours per year required by states for relicensure is 8, but it varies from 1 hour per year required by West Virginia to 12 hours per year required by Illinois and Iowa (National Funeral Directors Association, 1997).

According to the *National Director of Morticians/The Red Book* (National Funeral Directors Association, 1997), there are 22,153 funeral homes in the United States with 45,000 licensed personnel and 89,000 funeral service and crematory personnel. Approximately 5 percent of the licensees in the United States are women (Goldman, 1993). However, in the last decade, the number of women entering colleges of funeral service education and becoming licensed has greatly increased. In 1996, the latest year for which statistics are available, 32 percent of the 2,168 graduates from the 48 accredited schools of mortuary science in the United States were women. In 1976 only 8 percent of graduates were women (Bigelow, 1997).

In a recent survey of funeral homes by the Federated Funeral Directors of America (1997), it was determined that in 1995 the average salaries for full-time, licensed personnel ranged from $33,200 per year in communities of 10,000 to 30,000 population to $35,000 in communities with more than 100,000 population.

THE ROLE OF THE FUNERAL DIRECTOR

Rabbi Earl Grollman (1972) describes the role of the funeral director as that of a caretaker, caregiver, and gatekeeper. He indicates that the etymology of the word

Biography of Violet Guymer, Western Canada's First Woman Mortician

In the autumn and early winter of 1918, the war was almost over, but there was another deadly killer of young men: Spanish Influenza. This epidemic killed more healthy young men than did the war itself, although history has almost forgotten it.

Violet Guymer was the young widow of one of the flu's victims. She was the owner of a busy transportation operation and was also the undertaker in a town in northern Manitoba; a growing, vibrant community serving the prospectors, railwaymen, trappers and families north of the fifty-third parallel. The Guymers had immigrated from England in 1909, pioneering the establishment of this newly incorporated town in the expanded province of Manitoba. She was prevailed upon by the town council to continue in her husband's footsteps, even though it was almost unheard of for a woman with five children to work outside the home. But to work as an undertaker? That was inconceivable in 1918!

Violet was hesitant at first; she knew nothing about her husband's business. She had been completely occupied in the home with her five children who were only eleven months to twelve years old. She was also responsible for providing board and room for railwaymen and teamsters, and looking after the horses, pigs and chickens. How could she add the responsibilities of bookkeeping, hiring and firing employees and bidding on contracts, as well as the myriad of duties associated with being a Funeral Director?

Through the encouragement of friends who also provided care for the children, she traveled to Winnipeg to take the embalming course at Bardal Funeral Home. She obtained her diploma in 1919 and was licensed by the

(continued)

undertaker is based upon the activities of the early undertaker who "undertook" to do for people at the time of death those things that were crucial in meeting their bereavement needs. The funeral director, from the perspective of the community, was viewed as a secular gatekeeper between the living and the dead.

John Brantner (1973), elaborating upon the caregiver role, emphasizes that the funeral director is a crisis intervenor. This idea can be documented in the vast amount of literature on the counseling role of crisis intervenors, who are not clinical practitioners by training but to whom the public turns in crisis.

The funeral director serves families by determining their needs and responding to them (Raether & Slater, 1974). This service includes, but is not limited to, the funeral (or its alternative) that the director and the family plan and implement together. As a licensee of the state, the funeral director handles the details that require the death to be properly recorded and files permits for transportation and final disposition of the body. The funeral director serves as a liaison with other professionals, working

(continued from previous page)

Manitoba Government the same year. She was the first woman to receive such a license in Western Canada, and held that record for twenty years. It is believed she was the first woman in all of Canada to hold a license as a Funeral Director.

Violet served as a member of the Board for the Manitoba Funeral Directors Association for several years beginning in 1924. This was at a time when women were fighting for the vote; fighting to be declared "persons." The Funeral Director's Association was a very progressive organization indeed! She also served on the Chautauqua Committee, another position usually reserved for men. Violet was a member of the Order of the Eastern Star, reaching the position of Worthy Grand Matron in 1936. Violet had a decade of prosperity and success in the twenties. It looked like she would be able to fulfill her husband's dream of having a business to pass down to their boys. But she suffered adversity at the hands of competitors and was forced out of business in the late thirties. Some of her own employees set up transportation companies in direct competition with her while still in her employ. The funeral home was sold to the competition for a fraction of its true value.

Although Violet was encouraged to continue in her husband's business in 1918 by men who believed she could do it, in the end it was men who believed she shouldn't be doing it, who forced her out. One "gentleman" had unsuccessfully tried to buy her out earlier. His words to her when she refused was, "I'll run you out of town!"

A book chronicling her life is currently in production. It is titled: "Quite an Undertaking" and can be ordered directly from the publisher, Nip & Tuck Publishing, 3335 Packers Court, Kelowna, B.C. V1W 2W3. The price is 16.95 (US) 19.95 (CAN).

Source: Web site http://www.funeral.net/info/ladyfd.html.

with the family medical personnel, clergy, lawyers, cemetery personnel, and, when necessary, law enforcement officials.

According to the National Funeral Directors Association (NFDA) (National Funeral Directors Association, (1997), 85 percent of funeral homes are family-owned and average 63 years in operation in the same community. According to a 1996 survey by the NFDA, the average funeral home arranges 148 funerals a year and has 1.6 locations; 46 percent of these funeral homes are located in small towns or rural areas, and 21 percent are in large or moderate-size cities (National Funeral Directors Association, 1997).

BODY PREPARATION

Whereas the ancient Egyptian process of embalming required 70 days to perform, body preparation today is completed within a few hours and is more effective and

---

Should Funeral Directors Professionalize?
Raymond DeVries

Like many other occupations, funeral directors would like to be thought of as professionals. Should we as consumers support the attempts of funeral directors to become more professional?

Our first response to this question is, "Yes, of course." But let's not be so hasty. We must first consider what it is that makes an ordinary job a "profession." How do we distinguish a profession from a regular job? One way is to list the features or traits of occupations commonly accepted as professions. If asked which occupations are professions, most of us would answer: Physician, lawyer, minister. What sets these occupations apart? They are characterized by:

1. A specialized body of knowledge
2. A long period of training
3. An orientation toward service rather than profit
4. A commonly accepted code of ethics
5. Legal recognition (most often through licensure)
6. A professional association

Implicit in this definition is the assumption that professionals have the best interest of the public in mind. After all, they submit to a long period of training, look forward to serving others, abide by a code of ethics, and police

(continued)

---

acceptable. Body preparation may be as simple as bathing the body, closing the eyes and mouth, and dressing the body for final disposition. This procedure, infrequently selected, is utilized by families who wish direct disposition, which we will discuss later in this chapter as a procedure that may be an acceptable and logical choice.

Nationally, it is estimated that four out of five bodies are embalmed before final disposition. **Embalming,** by definition, is the replacement of normal body fluids with preserving chemicals. This process is accomplished by using the vascular system of the body to both remove the body fluids and to suffuse the body with preserving chemicals. The arterial system is used to introduce the chemicals into the body, and the venous system is used to remove the body fluids. This intravascular exchange is accomplished by using an embalming machine. The machine can best be described as an artificial heart outside of the body that produces the pressure necessary to accomplish the exchange of fluids. This, together with the filling of the chest and abdominal cavities with embalming fluid, constitutes the embalming procedure.

In addition to embalming and thorough bathing of the body, cosmetic procedures are used to restore a more normal color to the face and hands. When death occurs,

---

(continued from previous page)

themselves through their professional associations. All occupations should become professions!

But this is not the only way to define a profession. Others look more cynically on the role of professions in society. George Bernard Shaw said, "Professions are a conspiracy against the laity." What did he mean? Shaw's comment hints at an alternative definition of the professions, a definition that suggests that there is just one distinguishing characteristic of the professions: power. Professions are those occupations that have accumulated enough power to control the definition and substance of their work. For example, this view contends that physicians are professionals by virtue of their complete control of matters of health. Through their associations they control the number and training of doctors, they limit the practices of competitors (e.g., chiropractors, nurse-practitioners), they set rates of reimbursement for health care. Adherents to this view point out that professionals in fact incapacitate us: they limit our choices, make us feel unable to help ourselves, encourage dependency.

Should funeral directors become more professional? Not all would agree. Funeral directors subscribe to the first definition and assert that professionals can better attend to the needs of the public. Followers of the second definition conclude that the move toward professionalization would limit competition, drive prices up, and, by promoting dependency, make us less able to deal with death.

R. DeVries, associate professor, St. Olaf College, Northfield, MN.

---

the pigments of the skin, which give the body its normal tone and color, no longer function. Creams, liquids, and/or sprays are used to give the appearance of normal skin coloration.

The question "But why embalm or cosmetize the dead body?" is based on the assumption that one of the needs of the family is the reality of death; thus the body should be left in its most deathlike appearance. Those who have seen a person die (especially if the dying process was painful, prolonged, and emaciating) know that the condition of the body at the time of death can be very repulsive. Many people cannot accept this condition. This is why contemporary funeral directors embalm and cosmetize the body.

Another reason for embalming is the mobility of the American population. Viewing, which is practiced in over 75 percent of the funerals today that involve earth burial and 22 percent of cremation services (Dawson et al., 1990), often requires more than a bathing and dressing of the body. Embalming is necessary to accomplish a temporary preservation of the body to allow time for the family to gather—as many as 2 or 3 days may be needed. If the body were to remain unembalmed for this length of time, the distasteful effects of decomposition would create a significant problem for grievers.

Though arguments favoring embalming have been presented, it may not always be necessary or desired. Embalming is not required in all states. In many states, for example, if the body is disposed of within 72 hours, is not transported on a common carrier or across state lines, and/or the person did not die of a contagious disease, embalming is not required. If a body is to be cremated and no public viewing is held, embalming would not be necessary. Many consumers just assume that embalming should or must occur.

A frequently asked question is, "If a body is embalmed, how long will it last?" There is no simple answer to this question. This is why funeral directors talk in terms of temporary preservation. Most families are interested in a preservation that will permit them to view the body, have a visitation, and allow the body to be present for the funeral. Beyond that, they are not concerned with the lasting effects of embalming.

FINAL DISPOSITION

Earlier in this chapter we discussed two primary forms of final disposition and their approximated utilization. According to a study by Randall Cottrell and associates (1984), persons choosing earth burial are more likely to do so for religious reasons and for family considerations or social acceptability, whereas persons choosing cremation do so for economic, simplicity, or altruistic considerations.

Earth burial as a method of final disposition is by far the most widely used in the United States. It is used in approximately 79 percent of the 2.3 million American deaths annually. Almost without exception, earth burial takes place within established cemeteries. In some instances, earth burial can take place outside of a cemetery if the landowner where the interment is to be made and the health officer of jurisdiction grant their permission. In 1997 Bill Cosby acquired permission from local authorities to bury his son Ennis on the grounds of his estate. By law, cemeteries have the right to establish reasonable rules and regulations to be observed by those arranging for burial in them. A person does not purchase property within a cemetery, but rather purchases the "right to interment" in a specific location within that cemetery. Most cemeteries require that the casket be placed into some kind of outer receptacle or burial vault. The cemetery will also control how the grave can be marked with monuments or grave markers.

Entombment, occurring in less than 5 percent of all final dispositions, might be considered as a special form of earth burial. It consists of placing the body (contained within a casket) into a building designed for this purpose. Cemeteries offer large buildings **(mausoleums)** as an alternative to earth burial or cremation. In some instances, families may purchase the right to interment in a cemetery, and on the designated space build a private or family mausoleum that will hold as few as 1 or 2 bodies or as many as 12 to 16. Both types of mausoleums must be designed and constructed to provide lasting disposition for the body. Most states and/or cemeteries regulate the specifications and construction of the mausoleum.

Cremation is the other method of final disposition. In the last decade the number of cremations has nearly doubled. In 1995 21 percent of deaths in the United States involved cremation. Hawaii leads the nation with 56 cremations per 100 deaths, followed by Alaska and Nevada with 54 percent, and Washington state with more than 52 percent. States with the fewest cremations are Mississippi and Al-

---

Father Keeps Son's Memory Alive With Corpse in Home

William Sneed's son died November 8 of injuries suffered in an auto accident. He won't be buried. Instead, Sneed said, the body will remain in a casket with a clear plastic top in a room off the family kitchen.

"There are three especially painful moments one goes through at the death of a loved one," Sneed said. "The first is at the news of the death, the second when you see the body in the casket at the funeral home, and the third and most difficult is when you have to turn away from the grave site and know you'll never see that person again. We simply decided not to go through that last step."

Sneed obtained a burial permit naming himself custodian of the body of his son, William B. Sneed III, 29. The permit names the place of entombment as the Sneed Family Mausoleum—the room off the kitchen.

There is no law in Louisville, Kentucky that requires burial below ground. Sneed said the decision to keep the body of his son at home really began eight years ago.

"At first, it was like a joke, just between the three of us (himself, his daughter and his son)," he said. "But after talking about it for a while, it got serious. We decided then—I don't remember how long ago it was—that whichever one of us was the first to go, the other two would take care of everything like this."

Sneed said he plans to remodel the interior of his home to accommodate a small chapel at the rear, and the body will be placed there.

Adapted from the *Minneapolis Tribune,* November 20, 1975.

---

abama (3.9 percent), and Kentucky (4.6 percent). In Canada 36 percent of all deaths involve cremation (eastern and western province percentages are 31 and 49 percent, respectively).

In a 1992 study of 1,000 Americans conducted by the Funeral and Memorial Information Council (1992, p. 8), it was discovered that 37 percent of respondents over the age of 30 said that they would choose cremation for themselves, whereas 32 percent said they would choose it for a loved one (Associated Press, 1989). The Cremation Association of North America predicts that in the year 2010, 40 percent of all deaths in the United States will involve cremation and that in the state of Alaska cremation will be selected 86 percent of the time (Cremation Association of North America, 1997).

Asked why they were likely to choose cremation for themselves or a loved one, the respondents in the study conducted by the Funeral and Memorial Information Council (1992) gave the following explanations:

19 percent said it saves land

18 percent said it saves money

13 percent said they did not like to think of the body in the earth

8 percent said it is "convenient"

The columbarium provides families with an additional option for body disposition. For approximately 17 percent of the 2.2 million annual deaths in the United States, cremation is used as the method of final disposition.

Until recently, the **crematory** was generally located within the cemetery. With the increase of cremation as an option for final disposition, however, many funeral homes have now installed crematories, and there is a trend in the industry to change the name of the establishment from "funeral home" to "funeral and cremation services." In 1995 there were 1,155 crematories in the United States performing nearly a half million cremations annually. For Canada the respective numbers are 132 and 76,000 (Cremation Association of North America, 1997) .

Crematories generally require containment of the body in an appropriate casket or other acceptably rigid container. The containerized body is not removed or disturbed after it arrives at the crematory and is placed into a furnace or retort. Cremation is accomplished by the use of either extreme heat or direct flame. In either instance, reducing the casket (or alternative container) and the body to "ashes" takes 2 to 3 hours. Cremated remains do not have the appearance or chemical properties of ashes; they are primarily bone fragments. Some crematories process cremated remains

---

A True Die-Hard Fan: He'll Attend Game in Urn

Les Boatwright's death won't keep him from going to the Super Bowl today. He'll be there in a small brass urn. Boatwright, 75, died of a heart attack Monday, clutching two Super Bowl tickets as he prepared to place a bet with his bookie, said Boatwright's widow, Midge.

His two sons will take the urn carrying the ashes of the San Jose, California, resident to the Big Game between the San Francisco 49ers and the Cincinnati Bengals, Mrs. Boatwright said. "I told the boys, 'Do it for your daddy,'" she said. Boatwright's 33-year-old son Todd flew to south Florida with his father's ashes early yesterday. His brother Marc, 37, arrived earlier.

From the *Arizona Daily Star,* January 22, 1989, p. E3.

---

to reduce the overall volume; others do not. Depending on the size of the body, cremation results in three to nine pounds of remains (National Funeral Directors Association, 1997).

After the cremation, the remains are collected, put into an **urn** or box, and then disposed of according to the wishes of the family. The cremains may be buried in a family plot or cemetery, placed into a **niche** in a **columbarium** (a special room in a cemetery), or kept in another place of personal significance, such as the home or church crypt. Subject to some restrictions, cremated remains can be scattered by air, over the ground or over water. Some cemeteries provide areas for scattering and may provide a space where families can place a commemorative plaque or other memorial.

Many people choose to memorialize the site of disposition because they find consolation in knowing that there is a specific place to visit when they wish to remember and feel close to the person they have lost, regardless of whether the deceased person's remains are actually located at that place. Families should always choose an option that best fits their emotional needs.

One might assume that cremation would be the least expensive form of final disposition because the typical cost of a simple "no-frills" cremation is approximately 40 percent of the cost of the traditional funeral service with burial (Lino, 1990). However, a cremation service may be as simple or as elaborate as family members wish. Some people are surprised to learn that cremation does not preclude a funeral with all of the traditional aspects of the ceremony. Visitation and viewing with a funeral ceremony and church or memorial services are options to be considered. In some states, funeral homes are permitted to rent caskets for viewing and services (National Funeral Directors Association, 1997). It is entirely possible to spend *more* money on a funeral involving cremation if plans include a "traditional funeral" that includes viewing a casketed body and placing the cremated remains into an urn in a niche in a columbarium.

Alternatives to the Funeral

People often ask if there are alternatives to the traditional funeral. There are three alternatives: immediate disposition of the body of the deceased, the bequest of the body by the deceased to a medical institution for anatomical study and research, and the memorial service.

Immediate disposition occurs when the deceased is removed from the place of death to the place of cremation or earth burial without any ceremony; proper certificates are filed and permits received in the interim. In these instances, the family is not present, usually does not view the deceased after death, and is not concerned with any further type of memorialization. Disposition is immediate in that it is accomplished as quickly after death as is possible. In this situation the body will not likely be embalmed, and the only preparation will consist of bathing and washing. The 1985 National Funeral Directors Association survey of members found that approximately 5 percent of all deaths involved immediate disposition. The frequency of this alternative differs by region of the country—it is performed most in the south central part of the United States (approximately 7 percent of cases) and least in New England and the mountain states (less than 1 percent of cases).

Body-bequest programs have become better known in the last 4 decades and permit the deceased (prior to the death) or the family (after the death) to the body to a medical institution. A compendium of body donation information (National Funeral Directors Association, 1981) indicates that, when the family desires, 75 percent of the donee institutions permit a funeral to be held prior to the delivery of the body to the institutions for study or research. Some medical schools will pay the cost of transporting the body to the medical schools, others will not. This is the least expensive way of final disposition, especially if a memorial service is conducted without the body present. The compendium also indicates that in almost every instance the family may request that either the residue of the body or the cremated remains be returned when they are of no further benefit to the donee. In those instances when the family does not desire to have the body or the cremated remains returned, the donee institution will arrange for cremation and/or earth burial—oftentimes with an appropriate ceremony. People who are considering donating their bodies should be aware of the fact that at the time of death the donee institution may not have the need of a body. If this does happen, the family will have to find another institution or make other arrangements for the disposition of the body. The 1985 NFDA survey found that anatomical gifts are made in less than 1 percent of all deaths.

To some, body donation may not appear to be an alternative to the funeral (especially when a ceremony is held prior to the delivery of the bequested body), but inasmuch as the procedure is different than the most common methods of disposition, it may be considered as an alternative. According to the NFDA, approximately 7,000 such donations are made out of 2,300,000 deaths each year.

The *memorial service* is defined as a service without the body present. It is true that every funeral is a memorial service—inasmuch as it is in memory of someone—but a memorial service, by our definition, is an alternative to the typical funeral. It may be conducted on the day of the death, within 2 or 3 days of the death, or sometimes as much as weeks or months following the death. Those who wish to have a viewing can do so on the evening prior to the day of the memorial service. The memorial service typically places little or no emphasis on the death. Instead, it often is a service of acclamation of philosophical concepts. Religious or nonreligious in content, such a service can meet the needs of the bereaved.

Organizations called **memorial societies** exist for consumers. An example is in Ithaca, New York. The bylaws of this particular nonprofit and nonsectarian organization establish the following as purposes of this society:

1. To promote the dignity, simplicity, and spiritual values of funeral rites and memorial services
2. To facilitate simple disposal of deceased persons at reasonable costs, but with adequate allowances to funeral directors for high-quality services
3. To increase the opportunity for each person to determine the type of funeral or memorial service that he or she desires
4. To aid its members and promote their interests in achieving the foregoing

Livening Up the Funeral Industry

With upbeat marketing and personalized services, Jim Bradshaw wants to change perceptions of the funeral business.

Hanging on the pea-green fleur-de-lis wallpaper in the lobby of the Bradshaw funeral home on Rice Street in St. Paul is a photograph of a coffin being pulled in an elegant horse-drawn carriage with a top-hatted driver at the reins. The white dome of the state capitol is visible in the background. "This is a good example of what we're about," CEO Jim Bradshaw says, pointing at the photo. "You might think this happened a long time ago. But it was 1992. See?" And he picks out the tiny modern cars parked near the capitol.

The Bradshaw Group, Inc., funeral homes depart from convention by offering services that reflect the personalities and interests of the deceased. For example, a woman who had driven her husband everywhere was allowed to drive the hearse to his burial; a motorcycle fanatic's Harley-Davidson was rolled into the funeral home and displayed by his casket during the funeral; and when a family requested a horse-drawn carriage, Bradshaw's people said yes first and then found the carriage and horses.

Bradshaw's funeral directors also arrange for food and beverages, loudspeakers, closed-circuit TV, and other amenities to ensure that the funeral services are as comfortable and inviting as possible. "These are things we give no second thought to; it's just done," Bradshaw says with a shrug. "I don't think what we do is all that unusual."

Perhaps not. But add Bradshaw's upbeat marketing plan, flat management structure, and mission to change funeral and cremation services from somber and impersonal to celebratory and individualized, and the result is a truly lively approach to the business.

(continued)

(continued from previous page)

Bradshaw steers clear of the word *funeral* to describe his business. Although the sign on his first facility still bears the words *Funeral and Cremation Services* his advertisements and other signage read only, "*Bradshaw—Creating Meaningful Events that Celebrate Life.*" "The focus has been to bury the dead, but . . . has not been as focused on caring for the living," he says. "I have a mission in life to create a new conversation about funeral homes in our country."

Bradshaw, 52, has been fostering that mission since he was 15, when he decided he wanted to be a funeral director because he thought it was a good way to take care of people. At 17 he left home to live and work in a mortuary. In 1964 he received a degree in mortuary science from the University of Minnesota and went to work in various funeral homes until 1972, when Larry Hauge, who owned several funeral homes in the Twin Cities, offered to sell him one of his homes for $1,000. Hauge even lent Bradshaw the money to buy it.

After 10 years, Bradshaw bought the building his business was in and then began to accept offers to buy additional funeral homes from Hauge and other funeral directors leaving the business. Today, Bradshaw and his wife, vice president Jane Bradshaw, run a $4 million business employing about 50 people at six funeral homes—four in St. Paul, one in Minneapolis, and one in Stillwater. Next spring, the Stillwater facility is where Bradshaw is

(continued)

Thus, such a memorial society would help educate consumers regarding death prior to the actual death of a significant other and present options for final disposition of the body. Likewise, many funeral directors today serve as valuable resource persons by sharing information regarding death with various community groups.

Funeral, Final Disposition, and Related Expenses

Charges made by a funeral home ordinarily are for the services of the professional staff, the use of the funeral home facilities and equipment, transportation, and the casket or other container. In addition, most funeral homes provide burial vaults or other types of outer enclosures for the casket and ancillary items that may be purchased from the funeral director—clothing, register books, acknowledgment cards, and stars of David, crucifixes, or crosses.

The other major cost of the funeral is the cemetery charges—either for the purchase of cemetery property for the right to interment therein, for mausoleum space, or for an urn for the cremated remains (in some instances, there will be a charge for providing a space in a columbarium for the urn). Most families will also select, in one

(continued from previous page)

planning to take his celebratory bent on the funeral business one step further. Nestled on 23 acres, the new funeral home will have large gathering halls and an outdoor memorial garden. With multimedia capabilities, the facility will accommodate creative presentations at funerals, Bradshaw says, as well as make the location a suitable place for conventions, lunches, dances, art shows, and weddings.

There was a time, Bradshaw says, when his business had lost its way. "About 11 years ago . . . I was not happy with what I had created," he says, "We were very focused on our debt," and he was neglecting the very reason he'd gotten into the funeral business: to care for the living.

Bradshaw hired a consultant to provide new direction and a psychologist to help the disgruntled staff adjust. "And then I began what I consider the hardest work I've ever done, and that was changing the culture of the company," he says. Together, he and his staff created a new mission statement, philosophy, and culture. He now considers his role to care for the staff so they can spend their time caring for the bereaved.

While the number of funeral services in the Twin Cities has dropped over the past 10 years, Bradshaw's volume has stayed steady and the company is third in Twin Cities market share. Bradshaw is happy: "The goal is to try to create something meaningful," he says, "to handle the living side."

B. Waller, October 1996, *Twin Cities Business Monthly*.

form or another, a monument or marker to identify the grave or other place of final disposition.

A final category of expenses incurred by the family is money that the funeral home sometimes advances, at the request of the family, to other people involved in the final disposition. Such cash advances typically pay for the following: charges for opening and closing the grave, crematory costs, honoraria for clergy and musicians, obituary notices, flowers, and transportation costs in addition to the transportation ordinarily furnished by the funeral home.

In a survey by the Federated Funeral Directors of America of more than 200,000 funerals conducted in 1995, it was determined that the average cost for an adult funeral in the United States was $4,149.86. This cost did not include grave or cremation expenses, the cost of a vault, clothing, or extra service requirements, nor cash advances (including to minister, florist, and musicians). In 1995 the operating expenses for a regular adult funeral were $3,048.31, the average casket cost was $711.78, and profit reported was $389.77—9.39 percent of sales. In 1981 the typical funeral home's profit was 13.17 percent; thus in 14 years profits in the funeral industry have declined by more than one fourth. In 1995 (Federated Funeral Directors of America, 1997) the average cost of $4,149.86 for an adult funeral were broken down in the following

In addition to providing a service to families in bereavement, funeral directors sell burial merchandise to their customers. Typically, the cost of such merchandise comprises approximately 25 percent of the total amount of revenue collected by funeral directors.

manner (these figures do not include cemetery charges and cash advances to ministers, florists, and musicians):

Personnel (owner salary, employee salaries, retirement plan, payroll taxes, insurance, professional services)	$1,454.47
Cost of facilities (rent allowance/rent, depreciation, heat, water, electricity, insurance/general maintenance and repairs, taxes, telephone, leased music, interest expense)	$892.23
Automotive equipment (depreciation and insurance, automotive expenses, livery expense, leased autos)	$245.29
Promotion (advertising, business contributions, convention/meeting, organization dues, subscriptions, business promotion, meals/entertainment)	$167.28
Supplies (preparation room supplies, miscellaneous funeral supplies)	$89.64
Business services (legal services, postage, office supplies, consultants, accounting)	$103.23
Casket cost	$711.78
After-sale expenses (bad debts and discounts)	$84.97
Sundry (tips and gratuities, laundry and cleaning, freight, travel)	$11.20
Profit	$389.77
Total cost of average adult funeral	$4,149.86

A 1996 survey of National Funeral Directors Association members (1996, p. 4) determined that nationally, for every dollar taken in by affiliated funeral homes, money was distributed in the following manner:

29 cents for salaries and benefits

26 cents for other operating expenses

21 cents for merchandise (caskets, vaults, etc.)

13 cents for facilities

11 cents for before-tax profits

The 1996 and 1986 NFDA financial surveys provide us with a number of other important findings. First, the data suggest that funeral service is a competitive industry. When the costs of average funerals are compared, the difference between the highest and the lowest prices charged varies less than $600 regardless of demographic category (region of the country, number of families served, number of facilities operated, or metro/rural location) (National Funeral Directors Association, 1986, p. 1).

Second, approximately 64 percent of firms operate only one funeral home facility, and 23 percent operate two facilities (National Funeral Directors Association, 1997, p. 1). Third, on average, 56 percent of all funeral home assets are owned by the funeral home—funeral directors appear to be more willing to leave their assets within the company than do other service professionals (National Funeral Directors Association, 1986, p. 4).

Finally, the average funeral service firm's actual return on net worth is 11.3 percent (before taxes). This relatively low return on equity makes funeral service (like other capital-intensive industries) a very difficult one to enter as a new entrepreneur. For the entrant, the price of land and buildings would result in higher operating expenses to perform the same service as a more established funeral home (National Funeral Directors Association, 1997).

Until 1984 a funeral home charged for its services and merchandise in basically three ways. The first was the unit method of pricing. In this method, all of the costs involved with the funeral home (including for the staff, the facilities, the automotive equipment, and the casket) were included in a single charge. In making a selection under this method, the family looked at a "bottom line" figure to which only other charges paid by the funeral home (such as a vault, additional burial merchandise, cash advances) might be added.

The second method was the biunit or triunit pricing systems. The biunit system made separate charges for professional services and the casket, and the triunit system made separate charges for professional services, the use of facilities, and the casket selected. This method enabled families to understand the charges for the three basic components making up funeral costs.

A third method of presenting costs was referred to as either functional, multiunit, or **itemization.** In this method, each and every item of service, facility, and transportation was shown as a separate item together with its cost. In this method usually a minimum of 8 to 10 items was listed, and the family decided in each instance whether or not that item would become a part of the funeral service. In 1984 the Federal Trade Commission (FTC) mandated that all American funeral homes

President Franklin D. Roosevelt left detailed instructions for his funeral and burial, should he die while in office. He directed that the funeral service be simple, that the casket be plain and made of wood, that there be no embalming of the body or sealing of the casket and that his grave have no lining.

These instructions were found in a private safe days after his burial, too late to be considered. Consequently, Franklin D. Roosevelt's remains were embalmed, sealed in a copper coffin and placed in a cement vault.

Consumer Survival Kit: The Last Rights: Funerals, Owings Mills, MD: Maryland Center for Public Broadcasting, 1977.

itemize their fees and that consumers have access to pricing information over the phone.

A major advantage of itemization is that family members have greater flexibility in arranging a funeral and controlling costs. The family members should have the freedom to decline those items that they do not want, and a proper allowance should be made for such items that are not used. For example, one may ask to see "the pine box"—usually a cloth-covered casket of wood or pressed wood. These caskets are relatively inexpensive and may or may not be in the display room. If the body is to be transported a great distance to the grave site or crematorium, perhaps the funeral director's van or station wagon could be used rather than the expensive hearse. Similarly, the consumer should have the right to choose among types of **vault liners.** The greatest advantage of itemization is that one can look carefully at the itemized services and obtain the most adequate services at the best price.

There are two major disadvantages of the FTC policy requiring funeral homes to give prices over the phone and to itemize funeral expenses. The first is that when consumers receive prices over the phone it is difficult to make accurate price comparisons. One firm can say that it sells an oak casket for $1,800, and another will price a different oak casket at $3,800. It is entirely possible that the price-quality ratio is better for the more expensive casket. A helpful analogy might be to imagine calling two import automobile dealerships, Yugo and Mercedes, to ask each, "How much do cars cost in your dealership?" The only way that one can make accurate price comparisons is to personally inspect both products. The same is true for the funeral industry. Families are better served when they can make careful comparisons between the costs of services provided by funeral firms prior to the death of a significant other. Most people do not wait until the car breaks down before they shop for a new one. Furthermore, if they did find themselves in this situation, they would not purchase a car over the telephone.

The disadvantage of the FTC ruling requiring itemization of funeral expenses is that itemization did not uniformly result in decreasing expenses to families. Prior to the 1984 ruling, many funeral firms included some merchandise and services as part of the standard funeral. With itemization, funeral directors could provide justification to raise the cost for funeral services. The analogy of restaurant pricing may be appropriate at this point—it is often less expensive to order a complete meal than to order food a la carte.

While the Grim Reaper Toils, Corporations Reap Big Profits
Hank Cox

Consolidation driven by expansionist corporations is sweeping the country. Three companies in particular—Service Corp. International, or SCI, based in Houston; Stewart Enterprises Inc., located in New Orleans; and the Loewen Group of Canada—are gobbling up independent funeral homes from coast to coast. SCI alone boasts 29,000 employees and $1.7 billion in annual revenues; the company (which also owns shares in competing chains) handled 230,000 funerals, or one in 10, in the United States in 1996. The mega-mortuary would like to take over the Loewen Group, creating a worldwide conglomerate of more than 3,750 funeral homes and 600 cemeteries. "I would say SCI has a better than 50-50 chance of acquiring Loewen," Steven Saltzman, an industry analyst, tells *Insight*, adding that SCI has completed hostile takeovers of three publicly traded European funeral companies during the last two years. "When they set their minds to something, they're likely to see it through to fruition."

According to Saltzman, overall revenues from funeral homes, cemeteries, crematoria and suppliers range between $13 billion to $15 billion a year, and the big corporations are cornering a major chunk of that money. "Right now, the seven largest consolidators own about 13 percent of the rooftops in the industry and probably account for twice that percentage of revenue." He says, "This trend has a long way to go. There are no other major firms in this industry outside North America. There is nothing to stop them from expanding throughout the world."

Funeral directors are considering offers by big consolidators. "People sell out for many reasons," says Joe Everly of the Everly Funeral Homes in Virginia, which were bought by Stewart in 1990. "One is government regulation. With all these new regulatory laws, it got expensive to be in the funeral business real quick. The Americans with Disabilities Act, in particular, requires expensive reconstruction for the handicapped. Doors must be widened, entry ramps must be built. It costs a lot of money. Many smaller operations simply cannot afford it."

But the primary reason many independents sell out is simple economics. Rising property values have put the purchase of funeral homes out of reach for most local investors, leaving the field to large consolidators. Based upon NFDA industry averages, a typical funeral home commands a price of $1.8 million or more depending on the market and potential for growth. "I had the opportunity to buy this business when the owner retired," says Don Stottlemeyer of the Stein Funeral Home in Washington. "He offered it to me. I had been here for years, but I could never afford to pay what they (the consolidators) could."

Unfortunately for the bereaved, takeovers often translate into higher prices. In 1995, the average service charge levied by chain-owned homes was

(continued)

> *(continued from previous page)*
>
> 17 percent higher than that of independents, according to *Funeral Service Insider,* a trade journal.
>
> In 1990 *Forbes* magazine reported that Robert Waltrip, SCI's chief executive officer, and other members of his family earned $5 million, or 8 percent of SCI's profits, though they own only 3 percent of SCI stock. According to industry-watchdog Graef Crystal, Waltrip is the 12th most overpaid executive in the country.
>
> H. Cox, December 30, 1996, *Insight*, p. 42.

New Trends in Funeral Service

The newest trend in funeral service is to cultivate new business by courting the living with special services. Included in these services are working with the public in preneed funeral planning, providing aftercare for survivors, and assisting community and religious organizations in providing death education for the public. All of these efforts can be thought of as an extension of past efforts at marketing and advertising, but the funeral industry has made concerted efforts to make these efforts effective in a very competitive industry where, in the past 15 years, no-frills cremation services have increased significantly and corporate profits have declined by more than one fourth—as a percent of sales, from 13.17 percent in 1981 to 9.39 percent in 1995 (Federated Funeral Directors of America, 1997).

PRENEED FUNERALS: A "NEW" TREND IN PLANNING FUNERALS

One of the more controversial issues today in funeral service is the trend toward **preneed funerals. Prearranging** is the process of arranging funerals in advance of need. This process can include selecting merchandise, planning the service, determining method of viewing and final disposition, and selecting persons to be involved in the funeral. In addition to prearranging, **prefunding,** or making the legal commitment of money to pay for the funeral service, is also common. This is usually accomplished through *insurance* or a *trust*. Preneed is a generic term that refers to both processes of prearranging and prefunding (Hocker, 1987, pp. 1–2).

According to a 1983 national survey conducted by the National Research and Information Center (Will, 1988, p. 366), 9.2 percent of Americans have made prearrangements for their funerals, and 62 percent feel that they should make funeral prearrangements with a funeral director. Presently, approximately 1 million people a year prearrange their funerals, compared with 22,000 in 1960 (Anderson, 1997). A 1995 survey of its members conducted by the American Association of Retired Persons (AARP) determined that 7 million people had prearranged their funerals for a total cost exceeding $15 billion (American Association of Retired Persons, cited by National Funeral Directors Association, 1997).

Now Your Loved One Can Be a TV Star
James Anderson

Videotaped tributes to the dead are increasingly popular. For up to $125, National Music Service of Spokane, Washington, guarantees shipment of a Video Tribute with photographs of the deceased, natural scenery and songs from a 3,000-song playlist within 48 hours.

A typical six-minute tribute opens with a sunrise and features pictures of the deceased, places he or she lived and liked to visit, and closes with a sunset. Quotations from favorite authors or religious works can be screened.

Company president Merrill Womach, who sings on many of the tracks, said his firm has prepared 50,000 such tributes.

"It's what a funeral service should be all about," Womach said. "When you take pictures and put them to beautiful music you can tell what that person's life was about."

Womach acknowledged many people aren't comfortable with the idea. "There is resistance to having a television set at a funeral chapel. People look at it and say, 'I don't know,'" he said. But many like it so much they order their own tributes ahead of time.

Wulff Family Mortuaries in St. Paul reports that of the 525 funerals held at its funeral homes last year, nearly two-thirds of the families ordered videotapes. "It makes it very personal for the family," says owner Greg Wulff (Scott and Dolan, 1991).

"Funeral Industry, Seeking New Business, Courts the Living With Special Services," by J. Anderson, Associated Press, *New York Times*, May 27, 1991, p. B1.

According to James Will (1988, p. 367) and William Hocker (1987, pp. 4–11), consumers prearrange and/or prefund funerals for these reasons:

1. To provide a forum for death-related discussions that is not profoundly affected by the grief that naturally accompanies death
2. To make one's funeral preferences known to one's survivors, thus assuring that survivors will not select a type of funeral that differs from the one desired
3. To provide an opportunity to personalize the funeral
4. To provide the dying with peace of mind—planning one's funeral can be one of the last pieces of unfinished business that one can accomplish for one's survivors
5. To give individuals an opportunity to get the most for their money through comparison shopping at a time when they are not faced with urgent need or overwhelmed by grief
6. To unburden loved ones of the obligation of planning and paying for a funeral
7. To protect an estate from funeral expenses in the future
8. To assure that funds are available in the future for the type of funeral that is desired

The disadvantage of preneed funerals from the perspective of consumers and funeral service professionals is the potential for consumer fraud. Some consumers have paid unethical funeral salespersons (some licensed and others not) for funerals and later found at the time of death that either the firm was no longer in business, the money had not been put into a trust account, and/or the deceased had moved to a location not served by the firm. For these reasons Thomas D. Bischoff (cited by Kelly, 1987, p. 32), senior vice president of the Prearranged Funeral Division of Service Corporation International (the largest chain of funeral homes in the world), has made the following recommendation:

> We, as funeral service professionals, must encourage that everything be done to minimize these eventualities. We would again suggest that an insurance-funded prearranged funeral program is the best safeguard that the funeral director and the consumer have. Insurance companies are very tightly and closely regulated and are required to maintain sufficient funds on hand to meet requirements. An insurance-funded prearranged funeral program has very little potential for mismanagement or fraud and as such should become the standard for the industry.

Ultimately, consumers must protect themselves against fraudulent entrepreneurs and dishonest "get-rich-quick" salespersons. Insurance-funded prearranged funeral programs are important potential safeguards, but the words of Robert W. Ninker (cited by Kelly, 1987, p. 32), executive director of the Illinois Funeral Directors Association, should also be heeded:

> The best protection a buyer can have is to purchase from a funeral director with a long history of success, after asking and understanding that this person is licensed and, in fact, trusts his funeral funds. . . . The buyer should also check references with acquaintances. That is about as much certainty as there is in life. Of course, if the buyer responds to door-to-door sellers or boiler room operations, he is his own victim! No one can protect someone from his own fool-like actions.

AFTERCARE: THE FUTURE BUSINESS IS TO BE FOUND IN TODAY'S CUSTOMERS

The funeral industry has always known that 80 percent of its business is with families served in the past. However, aftercare is one method to increase the likelihood of getting repeat business. The newest trend in funeral service is to provide extensive aftercare services and products for widows and widowers. Among these services and products are grief therapy, bereavement support groups, video tributes, and even greeting cards sent to survivors to mark the anniversary of death or the deceased's birthday (Scott & Dolan, 1991).

In 1984 Accord Aftercare Services began providing bereavement support materials to funeral homes, public and private organizations, hospices, hospitals, support groups, counselors, and individuals. Through its professional development seminars and grief programs, Accord offers training in the areas of grief counseling, communications skills, and aftercare for funeral service personnel and the families they serve. Accord designs materials, such as a self-study grief workbook, a quarterly magazine, the videotape *The Positive Power of Grief,* and brochures for "forgotten grievers," that can be redistributed by local funeral homes to maintain contact with families after the funeral service. Accord serves 50,000 bereaved families annually through its products, programs, and seminars.

An example of such aftercare efforts can be found at Bradshaw Funeral and Cremation Services in the Twin Cities (Minnesota) and in the work of Paul Johnson. Johnson taught classes in sociology and dying and death at Bethel College (St. Paul) for 10 years until he resigned in 1985 to become the bereavement services director at the Twin Cities chain of seven funeral homes. Johnson's work requires that he be involved in service plans of all deaths where problematic grieving is likely—the death of a child, accidental death, homicide, suicide, and death from AIDS. Johnson also contacts the surviving spouse or other family members a few weeks after the funeral to "hear their concerns about their own particular situation." Johnson recommends grief support groups and provides families with information about the grieving process. Johnson also conducts bereavement workshops for the public, sponsored by the funeral home, and recently he created a special self-help support group of widowers that meets monthly with six to eight men in attendance.

For many years Johnson has edited *Caregivers Quarterly*—a newsletter that is produced by Bradshaw Funeral and Cremation Services and distributed without charge to 1,200 clergy and caregivers in the Twin Cities area. In the near future Johnson plans to distribute a set of four pamphlets to newly bereaved persons at prescribed time intervals after the death anniversary (3 months, 6 months, 9 months, and 1 year). The purpose of these pamphlets is to empower the bereaved in their grief work.

Many other funeral homes in the United States are now offering grief counseling and support groups for their clients. In the 1970s the Carbon Funeral Home in Windsor Locks, Connecticut, created a support group called Begin Again. Begin Again meets weekly and sponsors seminars on a wide range of topics, including financial management, car maintenance, and occupational reentry. Begin Again even has meetings whose primary function is entertainment—featuring magicians and ventriloquists (Anderson, 1997).

Other funeral establishments are sponsoring tree-planting ceremonies and annual memorial observances as a service to the families of the deceased. In Chicago, the Blake-Lamb Funeral Home even provides free limousine services for weddings in the family of the deceased (Scott & Dolan, 1991). An optional service sponsored by the Fitzgerald and Son Funeral Home of Rockford, Illinois, is the annual Walk to Remember for families mourning stillbirths, miscarriages, and early infant death. During the walk, participants plant a tree in a public park, write their babies' names on paper, and put them next to the tree (Anderson, 1997).

And a new professional association is emerging for funeral service personnel who are involved in bereavement counseling and aftercare. With 150 members and a 15-member board of directors, the National Association of Bereavement Support Providers in Funeral Service has met four times in 1996 and 1997 at the annual meetings of the National Funeral Directors Association and the Association for Death Education and Counseling in order to create an organization to support the funeral industry in providing aftercare as a vital part of the funeral services that it offers.

Conclusion

Grief is the emotional working through of a significant loss. The funeral is a part of the grief process in contemporary America.

In our discussion, we have described funerals and their alternatives within a cultural and historical perspective. In the United States an evolutionary, not a revolutionary, process has occurred. Americans did not invent the funeral or the funeral functionary. However, contemporary Americans have found an expression for their bereavement.

Summary

1. To understand contemporary funerals conducted in the United States, one must understand the American cultural and historical context.
2. Embalming, a process as old as 484 B.C., was introduced in France and England in the 1600s and in the United States during the Civil War. Presently four out of five American bodies are embalmed.
3. The contemporary role of funeral director has evolved from the occupations of cabinetmaker and livery owner.
4. Presently there are approximately 23,500 funeral homes in the United States serving the families of the approximately 2.3 million persons who die annually. Associated with the contemporary funeral in the United States, final disposition of the body is made by either earth burial (79 percent) or cremation (21 percent). These percentages are approximate national averages and vary by region of the country. The funeral is designed to meet the psychological, sociological, and theological or philosophical needs of bereaved persons.
5. A person does not purchase property within a cemetery, but rather purchases the right to interment in a specific location within that cemetery.
6. Alternatives to funerals include immediate disposition, body donation, and memorial services.
7. Funeral bills have been presented to customers utilizing the following pricing systems: unit pricing, biunit or triunit pricing, and itemization. The latter is mandated in all states by the Federal Trade Commission. In 1995 the cost of the average adult funeral was $4,149.86.
8. Children should not be excluded from participating in funerals. To do so might have adverse effects on the children's emotional well-being and impede their bereavement.

Discussion Questions

1. Describe and compare each of the following processes: burial, cremation, and entombment.
2. Based on Irion's concept of psychological needs of the bereaved, explain how funerals can meet various needs of grievers.
3. Discuss the factors affecting postdeath costs and the expenses related to funerals and final disposition.
4. Discuss the psychological, sociological, and theological or philosophical aspects of the funeral process. How do each of these aspects facilitate the resolution of grief?
5. What would you include in your own obituary if you were to write it?
6. What would be your choice of final disposition of your body? Why would you choose this method, and what effects might this choice have upon your survivors? Describe how the funeral process can assist in coping with grief and facilitate the bereavement process.
7. Distinguish among grief, bereavement, and the funeral process.
8. What is the difference among preneed, prefunded, and prearranged funerals? What are the advantages and disadvantages of preneed funeral arrangements?

Glossary

Cremation: The reduction of a human body by means of heat or direct flame. The cremated remains are called *cremains* or ashes and weigh between 3 and 9 pounds. "Ashes" is a very poor description of the cremated remains because they are actually processed bone fragments and calcium residue that have the appearance of crushed rock or pumice.

Crematory: An establishment in which cremation takes place.

Columbarium: A building or wall for above-ground accommodation of cremated remains.

Disposition: Final placement or disposal of a dead person.

Embalming: A process that temporarily preserves the deceased by means of displacing body fluids with preserving chemicals.

Entombment: Opening and closing of a crypt, including placing and sealing of a casket within.

Itemization: A method of pricing a funeral in which every item of service, facility, and transportation is listed with its related cost. This is a service mandated by the Federal Trade Commission.

Mausoleum: A building or wall for above-ground accommodation of a casket.

Memorial Society: A group of people joined to obtain dignity, simplicity, and economy in funeral arrangements through planning.

Niche: A chamber in a columbarium into which an urn is placed.

Prearranging: Arranging funerals in advance of need. This process can include selecting merchandise, planning the service, determining method of viewing and final disposition, and selecting persons to be involved in the funeral.

Prefunding: Legally committing money to pay for the funeral service.

Preneed Funerals: A generic term that refers to both prearranged and prefunded funerals.

Urn: A container for cremated remains.

Vault or Grave Liner: A concrete or metal container into which a casket or urn is placed for ground burial. Its function is to prevent the ground from settling.

References

Anderson, James. 1991. Associated Press. Percentage of cremations increases in Palmetto State. (1989, May 26). Charleston, SC, *Post and Courier,* p. B6.

Anderson, James. 1997. "Funeral Industry, Seeking New Business, Courts the Living with Special Services." Associated Press, *New York Times,* May 27, page B1.

Bigelow, G. (1997, January 29). Letter from Dr. Gordon Bigelow, executive director of the American Board of Funeral Service Education, Brunswick, ME.

Brantner, J. P. (1973, January). Crisis intervenor. Paper presented at the Ninth Annual Funeral Service Management Seminar, National Funeral Directors Association, Scottsdale, AZ.

Cottrell, R. R., Eddy, J. M., Alles, W. F., & St. Pierre, R. W. (1984). An analysis of college students' attitudes and beliefs concerning body disposal. *Death Education, 8,* 113–122.

Cremation Association of North America, Milwaukee, WI. (1997). Fact sheet 1997.

Dawson, G. D., Santos, J. F., & Burdick, D. C. (1990). Differences in final arrangements between burial and cremation as the method of body disposition. *Omega, 21*(2), 129–46.

Federated Funeral Directors of America. (1997). *1995 facts on funeral costs.* Springfield, IL: Author.

Funeral and Memorial Information Council. (1992, March). The Funeral and Memorial Information Council conduct study. *Canadian Funeral Director, 8.*

Goldman, A. L. (1993, February 15). Increasingly, funeral business gets female touch. *New York Times,* p. A8.

Grollman, E. A. (1972, May). Commencement address. Department of Mortuary Science, University of Minnesota, Minneapolis, MN.

Hocker, W. V. (1987). Financial and psychosocial aspects of planning and funding funeral services in advance as related to estate planning and life-threatening illness. Unpublished article distributed by the National Funeral Directors Association.

Irion, P. E. (1956). *The funeral: An experience of value.* Milwaukee: National Funeral Directors Association.

Jackson, E. N. (1963). *For the living.* Des Moines, IA: Channel Press.

Kelly, T. E. (1987, February). Predict preneed vital to financial future. *The American Funeral Director,* 31–69.

Lindemann, E. (1944, September). Symptomatology and management of acute grief. *American Journal of Psychiatry, 101,* 141–148.

Lino, M. (1990, July). The $3,800 farewell. *American Demographics,* 8.

National Funeral Directors Association. (1981). *Body donation: A compendium of facts compiled as an interprofessional source book.* Produced by the College of Health Sciences (University of Minnesota) and the National Funeral Directors Association.

National Funeral Directors Association. (1986). *Financial operations survey for fiscal 1985.* Milwaukee: Author.

National Funeral Directors Association. (1992). *Fact sheet for 1991*. Milwaukee: Author.

National Funeral Directors Association. (1997). *Fact sheet for 1996*. Milwaukee: Author.

Pine, V. R. (1971, June). *Findings of the professional census*. Milwaukee: National Funeral Directors Association.

Raether, H. C., & Slater, R. C. (1974). *Facing death as an experience of life*. Milwaukee: National Funeral Directors Association.

Scott, C. R., & Dolan, C. (1991, April 11). Funeral homes hope to attract business by offering services after the service. *Wall Street Journal*, p. B1.

Will, J. (1988). Preneed: The trend toward prearranged funerals. In H. Raether (Ed.), *The funeral director's practice management handbook*. Englewood Cliffs, NJ: Prentice-Hall.

Suggested Readings

American Association of Retired Persons. (1996). *AARP Product Report: Funeral Goods and Services, 2*(3). American Association of Retired Persons. (1992). *AARP Product Report: Pre-Paying Your Funeral? 2*(2). Two reports by the American Association of Retired Persons for consumers on prepaying and preplanning conventional funerals, burials, and alternatives, including cremation, direct burial, and body donation.

Carlson, L. (1997). *Final act of love: Caring for your own dead*. Hinesburg, VT: Upper Access Book Publishers. Morgan, E. (1990). *Dealing creatively with death: A manual of death education and simple burial* (12th ed.). Bayside, NY: Barclay House Books. Two consumer resources that assist the bereaved in bypassing the funeral director and arranging everything themselves, including burial at home, where it is feasible and permitted.

Habenstein, R. W., & Lamers, W. M. (1962). *The history of American funeral directing*. Milwaukee: Bulfin. An excellent source for the study, review, and analysis of the history of funeral directing in the American culture from its introduction in colonial times to 1962.

Raether, H. C. (Ed.). (1988). *The funeral director's practice management handbook*. Englewood Cliffs, NJ: Prentice-Hall. A valuable resource on the internal workings of funeral service in America.

Related Web Sites

http://www.trinity.edu/~mkearl/death-6.html#funerals Web site has many resources regarding funeral guides and planning.

http://meded.com.uci.edu:80/~anatomy/willed_body/wbpe1.htm The University of California at Irvine's introduction to medical school embalming.

http://www.com.uci.edu/~anatomy/willed_body/ The Willed Body Program is a universal program in which people can donate their bodies for medical science after death. The program is a division of the Department of Anatomy and Neurobiology at the University of California at Irvine's College of Medicine.

http://www.com.uci.edu/~anatomy/willed_body/schools.htm A list of colleges of mortuary science and some Internet links.

http://www.cwo.com/~skip/index.html Funeral Industry Consulting Services provides assistance to funeral professionals.

http://www.vaxxine.com/info/fnhinet.html Funeral homes on the Internet.

http://www.webcom.com/~lewrose/brochures/funerals.html "Funerals: A Consumer Guide" is an article produced by the Federal Trade Commission.

http://www.funeral.net/info/notices.html Funeral Net's goal is to help people gain a basic understanding of the funeral and grief process so that they may be better equipped emotionally, psychologically, and mentally to deal with the closure of significant relationships.

http://www.funeral.net/info/ladyfd.html Biography of Violet Guymer, western Canada's first woman mortician.

http://www.cremation.org/ The Internet Cremation Society Web site has statistics on cremations and links to funeral industry resources.

http://www5.electriciti.com/crem8me/index.html The *Cremation Consultant Guidebook* provides information to families who are interested in cremation and memorial services.

http://funeral.netm.com/ Home page of the National Academy of Mortuary Science.

http://www.alcor.org/ Web site of Alcor, the world's largest cryonics organization.

http://www.cryocare.org/cryocare/ A Web site dealing with cryonics.

http://www.xroads.com/%7Efunerals/ A Web site that is very critical of the funeral industry and specializes in exposing funeral home financial fraud.

http://www.monitor.net/monitor/decca/death.html An Internet resource that provides a critical perspective on the funeral industry in America.

http://www.ilhawaii.net/dovetail/ Resources for the Family Funeral assists families who want to conduct a "do it yourself" funeral that is legal, uncomplicated, dignified, and inexpensive without professional help.

http://www.funeral.com/links/newlinks.html Funeral Service Center Automated Link Page with 51 sections.

http://www.uio.no/~mostarke/forens_ent/afterdeath.html Forensic Entomology home page provides information about the process of body decomposition.

http://pages.prodigy.com/caregiving/ *Grief and Healing Caregiving* newsletter each month contains useful information about a topic pertinent to your lifestyle: setting and keeping priorities, hiring home health help, purchasing home medical equipment supplies, and finding time for your own interests and hobbies.

http://ube.ubalt.edu/www/bereavement/ Bereavement and Hospice Support Netline is an on-line national directory of bereavement support groups and services and hospice bereavement programs that provides information to help you or those you care about find support to cope with loss and grief.

http://www.growthhouse.org/ Growth House, Inc., is a nonprofit organization working with grief, bereavement, hospice, and end-of-life issues.

http://www.readersndex.com/admpub/ National Directory of Bereavement Support Groups. The death of a loved one is an emotionally devastating time for survivors. But not knowing what to expect can often lead to unnecessary additional pain. This Web site has resources and answers to help people to clear up some of the confusion, to begin to examine the many issues that are often hard to discuss, and to find all the help that bereaved individuals need as they begin this journey.

http://www.inforamp.net/~bfo/index.html   The Web site of Bereaved Families of Ontario Support Center has a bereavement self-help resources guide that indexes resources of the center along with over 300 listings of other resources and information.

http://www.funeral.net/info/notices.html   Death Notices provides a placement of death notices for information purposes.

Chapter 13

The Bereavement Process

Only people who avoid love can avoid grief. The point is to learn from it and re-main vulnerable to love.

—JOHN BRANTNER
FROM J. WILLIAM WORDEN, *GRIEF COUNSELING AND GRIEF THERAPY*

If at the conclusion of the funeral service grief work were finished, the process of reintegration of the bereaved into society would be completed. The funeral service and the final disposition of the dead, however, mark only the end of public mourning; private mourning continues for some time.

The Bereavement Role

In earlier chapters we discussed bereavement behavior within historical and cross-cultural perspectives. We have given a general description of the norms and cultural patterns that prescribe proper conduct for the bereaved within American society. When we apply these bereavement norms to particular persons occupying statuses within a group or social situation, we are talking about the **bereavement role.**

In discussing the adaptation to the crisis of becoming ill, Talcott Parsons (1951, pp. 426–437) describes the sick role as being composed of two rights and two obligations. The first right of the sick person is to be exempted from "normal" social responsibilities. The extent to which one is exempted is contingent upon the nature and severity of the illness. The second right is to be taken care of and to become dependent on others as one attempts to return to normal social functioning. In exchange for these rights, the sick person must express a desire to "want to get better" and must seek technically competent help.

J. D. Robson (1977) suggests that behavior related to the death of a significant other (spouse, parent, etc.) is similar to illness behavior patterns. At the onset of death, the bereaved are exempted from their normal social responsibilities. Depending on the nature and the degree of relationship with the deceased, the bereaved are awarded time away from employment in much the same way that they are given sick leave—spouses and children may be given a week, whereas close friends and relatives may be given time only to attend the funeral.

The bereaved are also allowed to become dependent on others for social and emotional support and for assistance with tasks related to the requirements of normal, daily living. In offering this type of support, neighbors and friends call on survivors with gifts of food, flowers, and other expressions of sympathy. This custom led Robert Kavanaugh's younger brother to ask if "dead people ate meatloaf and chocolate cake" (Kavanaugh, 1972, p. 32).

In exchange for these privileges created by the death of a loved one, those adopting the bereavement role not only are required to seek technically competent help from funeral directors and clergy members, but also are expected to return as soon as possible to normal social responsibilities. The bereavement role is considered a temporary one, and it is imperative that all role occupants do whatever necessary to relinquish it within a reasonable period of time. Time extensions are usually granted to spouse and children, but there is a general American value judgment that normal grieving should be completed by the first anniversary of the death.

American folk wisdom would contend that "time heals"—with the intensity of the grief experienced diminishing over time. According to Paul Rosenblatt (1983), however, a more accurate notion of mourning is that the time intervals between intense experiences of grief increase with the passing of time. Furthermore, in analyzing 19th-century diaries, Rosenblatt discovered that it was quite common to experience periods of mourning for losses that occurred many years earlier. What is abnormal behavior, from the perspective of the American bereavement role, is being preoccupied with the death of the loved one and refusing to make attempts to return to normal social functioning. Examples of deviant behavior of this type would include the following:

1. Malingering in the bereavement role and memorializing the deceased by refusing to dispose of articles of clothing and personal effects and living as if one expected the dead to reappear

2. Rejecting attempts from others who offer social and emotional support, refusing to seek professional counseling, and taking up permanent residence in "Pity City"

3. Rejecting public funeral rituals and requesting that the funeral functionaries merely pick up the body and dispose of it through cremation without any public acknowledgment of the death

4. Engaging in aberrant behavior such as heavy drug or alcohol usage
5. Rushing into major life changes such as hastily remarrying or moving to a new home

Behaviors such as these may be sanctioned by others through social avoidance, ostracism, and criticism. As a consequence, most people are not only encouraged but also forced to move through the grieving process.

A Wednesday Afternoon
Jane Soli

The hot, humid air of August enveloped us in the crowded car. Sig drove. The Air Force had flown him home from Tahiti. Behind him sat Karen, her arm around Johanna. Peter sat on the other side looking vacantly out the window. Tina sat between Sig and me. The handle of my black purse felt as moist as my sweaty palms. My dress stuck to the skin of my back. How lucky it was that Harmar's Fashion Shop had a black linen dress, size 12. The yellow dotted Swiss I sewed for summer best would not be appropriate today.

The procession crept down Division Street. The neon sign at the Rock County Bank flashed 94 degrees and 3:06. Behind the plate glass of The River Inn, businessmen shook dice for their afternoon coffee. Lois Palmer came out of Hanson's Variety Store carrying a lamp shade.

We turned the corner at the lumberyard, crossed the wagon bridge, then, over the tracks and up the hill. Once in the country the long line of cars moved a little faster. After the turn at Benson's farm the gravel road narrowed. I could see the cemetery.

Why did you die, Dan? Did you have to die when the children were so young? You were lean and fit, physically active, no apparent health problems. You were fine when you went to bed, but I heard your death rattle; a small cough, I thought. You were dead when I came to bed five minutes later.

Is there any money? Will Karen be able to finish her last year of college? How about Peter—he's only seventeen. And then Johanna and Tina, thirteen and eleven. At least Sig is out of school. Such problems. Such a loss. How will I ever manage?

Two things came back to me during those early days of worry, fear, and grief. I recalled twenty years of bridge games with Judy and Elmer and the late-night discussions of death and funerals as we ate brownies and drank coffee. We spoke of our own deaths and our personal wishes. Dan, always the most vocal, stated again and again, "Don't spend any money on me when I am dead," and "Give me a military funeral." There was not a man in the USA more proud to be a Marine than Dan Soli. To hear him tell it, the Marines fought World War II single-handedly. Though he was 33 and the others in boot camp were 18, he was a member of the United States Marine Corps and never mind if the recruits called him "Grandpa."

(continued)

(continued from previous page)

With Dan's wishes uppermost in my mind, the children and I had the gruesome task of selecting a casket at the Anderson Brothers Mortuary. A basement room displayed a dozen or more for my choice. Mr. Anderson, ever solicitous, hovered over me giving the cost in a hushed voice—$2500, $3000, or, if we wanted the best, it would be $5000. Together we returned to the main floor for my decision. I asked, "What is your cheapest casket?"

"We have a pine box for county paupers at $50," he answered.

"What is your next price?"

"There is a casket we use for servicemen. It is made of wood and covered with grey velour. The flag would go over it. That sells for $100."

"I'll take it," I said quickly. In my mind I was doing rapid arithmetic. Twenty-five hundred dollars would pay for Karen's last year of college.

The entire tenor of our meeting changed. The solicitousness ended. The Anderson brothers conferred in the hallway and practically rushed us out of there.

Dan's wish was fulfilled in that regard; we would spend minimum money. A call to the Veterans of Foreign Wars would insure the military funeral.

The hearse turned into the City Cemetery; we followed. Behind our blue Chevy were twenty more vehicles. To the right I saw the Erickson family plot with remnants of Memorial Day decorations: white plastic crosses with letters in gold—"Mother," "Father," "Sister." We passed the graves of my grandparents, my infant brother, my father.

About one hundred yards into the cemetery the procession came to a stop. I saw the fake grass surrounding the open grave over by the fence. Close by stood the caretaker's tool shed with a barrel for refuse in front. Someone had lettered a crude sign above the barrel. It said, "RUBBAGE." The grave diggers stood behind the tool shed waiting to complete their job.

(continued)

Disenfranchised Grief

Like other aspects of death-related behavior, grief is socially constructed—people grieve only when they feel it appropriate. Social scripts are provided for grievers, and social support is given to those who are recognized as having experienced loss and who act in accordance with the norms. However, not all loss is openly acknowledged, socially sanctioned, and publicly shared. Kenneth Doka (1989) uses the term **disenfranchised grief** when referring to phenomena of this type.

According to Doka (1989) four types of situations lead to disenfranchised grief. The first situation is one in which *the relationship to the deceased is not socially recognized.* Examples of this type of disenfranchised grief include nontraditional relationships—

(continued from previous page)

As the casket moved from the hearse to the waiting pallbearers, the honor guard, smart in their black uniforms, aligned themselves on either side of the men carrying the casket and accompanied them to the gravesite.

The children and I left the car to follow. Tina cried, "I'm too young to be without a father," and clung to me. I had vowed to remain dry-eyed. My silly little purse held a lawn hanky—no Kleenex, no billfold, no lipstick. I would not open that purse.

Friends and relatives surrounded the grave as Pastor Jensen gave the committal service. Somehow the next part took me by surprise. Two of the honor guards stepped forward and together removed the American flag from the casket. With ceremony they folded it in the traditional way and presented it to me—the widow.

The two uniformed men rejoined the honor guard and they all stepped back from the mourners. At the command of the captain they fired a twenty-one gun salute.

At that point Peter moved away from the family, raised his trumpet and blew Taps for his dad. Sweet, melancholy notes rose plaintively over the gathered crowd. From the other side of the hill came the faraway echo. My heart ached with the pain of that moment.

The worst of the day was over. Everyone returned to the basement of the Lutheran Church for sandwiches, cake, and coffee. The Ladies Aid was famous for their "funeral sandwiches," made from ground pork and beef, and each lady brought her special cake. The choices of cake on the plate seemed endless. People sat around the tables, enjoying the food and visiting. Many expressed their condolences to me. My food remained untouched.

As we were leaving, Alice Overbeck came over to me, reached for my hand and said, "Too bad your husband died, but you'll get over it."

She was wrong; I didn't get over it.

I cry when I hear Taps.

Jane Soli is the retired secretary to the academic dean of Saint Olaf College, Northfield, MN.

such as extramarital affairs, heterosexual cohabitations, and homosexual relationships (Doka, 1987; Thornton et al., 1991, p. 356). If outsiders are unaware that a relationship exists and the bereaved are unable to publicly acknowledge their loss, they will not receive social support for their grief, and their bereavement will be problematic.

A second type of disenfranchised grief occurs when *the loss is not acknowledged by others* as being a genuine loss. An abortion or miscarriage is often deemed to be of lesser significance because the mother never had the opportunity to develop a face-to-face relationship with the child (Thornton et al., 1991). In the case of abortion, it is assumed that because the pregnancy was unwanted, grieving is unnecessary. According to Idell Kesselman (1990, p. 241), whatever one's position on abortion, "we must acknowledge that at least one death occurs—in addition to the fetus, there is

often the death of youth, of innocence, of dreams, and of illusion." Kesselman maintains that women who have had an abortion need to express "unresolved feelings of loss" and to deal with "issues of 'death, loss and separation.'" Kesselman concludes that grief therapy is a necessary part of abortion counseling.

Two examples of unacknowledged losses are the death of a pet companion and the death of a former spouse. According to Avery Weisman (1990–1991, p. 241), the loss of a pet companion is often accompanied by intense grief and mourning but is seldom recognized by others as an important and authentic occasion for bereavement. Likewise, the death of a former spouse is rarely thought of as a legitimate loss because most people believe that grief work should be completed shortly after the divorce.

Related to the unacknowledged loss is the third type of disenfranchised grief, in which *the grievers are unrecognized*. The grief over the death of an adolescent peer or friend is rarely openly acknowledged and socially sanctioned. One of the reasons why wakes and visitation services often attract larger audiences than do funerals is that employers are increasingly unwilling to provide employees with time from work to attend a funeral of a person who is not a family member (Sklar & Hartley, 1990). Other unrecognized grievers are young children, the mentally incompetent and/or retarded, and elderly adults. In each of these cases the bereavement needs of individuals are also often ignored by most social audiences (Sklar & Hartley, 1990; Kloeppel & Hollins, 1989).

The final type of disenfranchised grief occurs when *the death is not socially sanctioned,* as in the case of a death occurring in the act of a crime, or when death is caused by suicide, or autoerotic asphyxia (Thornton et al., 1989; Ness & Pheffer, 1990; Murphy & Perry, 1988). When people feel ambivalent, awkward, and/or uncomfortable about the cause of the death, they are generally unable or unwilling to provide the social support needed by the bereaved.

According to Kenneth Doka (1989), whenever disenfranchised grief occurs, the experience of grief is intensified and the normal sources of social support are lacking. Disenfranchised grievers are usually barred from contact with the deceased during the dying process. They are also frequently excluded from funeral rituals as well as from care and support systems that may assist them in their bereavement. Finally, they may often experience many practical and legal difficulties after the death of their loved one. All of these circumstances intensify the problematic nature of bereavement for disenfranchised grievers.

Three Questions That Deserve Attention in Transforming Grief

Paul V. Johnson

Anytime we experience a loss, especially a loss as significant as the death of a loved one, it changes us. In most cases, we do not have control over the loss we have experienced. We do, however, have some control over the ways in which we respond to that loss. Some people grow through a grief experience while others seem to get stuck. How are such opposite results possible?

The answer to this question is closely related to how individuals grieve following their loss. Individuals who shut themselves off from the grief process also shut themselves off from the transformative experience which can result.

The transformative nature of the grief focuses not only on the process of "getting through" a time of sadness and loneliness immediately following the loss, but also on reconstructing one's life following the loss.

The transformative process which grief encourages includes three components that can best be understood by responding to the following three questions: What have I lost?, What do I have left?, and What may be possible for me? Honestly answering these questions in response to your situation may help facilitate a grieving process that shifts from limits to opportunities.

What have I lost? This question seeks to discover how extensive our loss is; that is, to clearly identify what has been lost. The grief process cannot begin or progress to completion until the loss, and secondary losses which accompany it, have been identified. Once the losses have been identified, and we believe we can go on, the healing process of grief has begun.

What do I have left? In responding to this question we allow the meaningful aspects of what remains in our lives to be recognized, remembered, and valued.

Initially, and often depending upon our loss, it is possible to wonder if enough remains to even make our life worthwhile. No matter how small what is left may seem, it is enough to build upon.

What may be possible for me? Once we have determined what is left, we are able to move on and begin to determine what is possible, in spite of the significant loss that has occurred. Success in responding to this question is based on our perspective. Rather than looking at our limitations, our opportunities are viewed instead. By focusing on what is possible we allow ourselves to discover new ways to relate, understand, create, and commit to an on-going process of renewal and discovery.

The process of transformation takes time, and each question mentioned above deserves attention. Honestly answering each of them is a significant step toward a healthy grief experience.

"Creating Meaningful Events That Celebrate Life," by P. V. Johnson, April 1997, Bradshaw Quarterly.

The Grieving Process

In chapter 12 we defined grief as a very powerful emotion that is often triggered or stimulated by death. Thomas Attig makes an important distinction between grief and the grieving process. Although grief is an emotion that engenders feelings of help-lessness and passivity, the process of grieving is a more complex coping process that presents challenges and opportunities for the griever and requires energy to be invested, tasks to be undertaken, and choices to be made (Attig, 1991, p. 387).

Most people believe that grieving is a diseaselike and debilitating process that renders the individual passive and helpless. According to Attig (1991, p. 389):

Grief Tips—Help for Those Who Mourn
James E. Miller

Following are many ideas to help people who are mourning a loved one's death. Treat this list for what it is: a gathering of assorted suggestions that various people have tried with success. Perhaps what helped them through their grief will help you. The emphasis here is upon specific, practical ideas.

Talk regularly with a friend—Talking with another about what you think and feel is one of the best things you can do for yourself.

Walk—Go for walks outside every day if you can. If you like, walk with another.

Visit the grave—Not all people prefer to do this. But if it feels right to you, then do so. Don't let others convince you this is a morbid thing to do. Spend whatever time feels right there.

Create a memory book—Compile photographs which document your loved one's life. Arrange them into some sort of order so they tell a story. Go through it and reminisce as you do so.

Light a candle at mealtime—Especially if you eat alone, but even if you don't, consider lighting a taper at the table in memory of your loved one. Pause to remember them as you light it.

Carry or wear a linking object—Carry something in your pocket or purse that reminds you of the one who died.

Create a memory area at home—In a space that feels appropriate, arrange a small table that honors the person: a framed photograph or two, perhaps a prized possession or award, or something they created, or something they loved.

Plant something living as a memorial—Plant a flower, a bush, or a tree in memory of the one who died. If you do this planting where you live, you can watch it grow and change day by day, season by season. You can even make it a part of special times of remembrance in the future.

(continued)

It is misleading and dangerous to mistake grief for the whole of the experience of the bereaved. It is misleading because the experience is far more complex, entailing diverse emotional, physical, intellectual, spiritual, and social impacts. It is dangerous because it is precisely this aspect of the experience of the bereaved that is potentially the most frustrating and debilitating.

Death ascribes to the griever a passive social position in the bereavement role. Grief is an emotion over which the individual has no control. However, understanding that grieving is an active coping process can restore to the griever a sense of autonomy in which the process is permeated with choice and there are many areas over which the griever does have some control. James Miller provides several options for grievers involved in active coping. See the box that begins on page 476.

(continued from previous page)

Purchase something soft to sleep with—A teddy bear is a favorite choice for some. Select something that feels warm and cuddly. Then, whatever your age, cuddle it.

If you're alone, and if you like animals, get a pet—The attention and affection a pet provides may help you adapt to the loss of the attention and affection you're experiencing after this significant person has died.

Invite someone to be your telephone buddy—If your grief and sadness hit you especially hard at times and you have no one nearby to turn to, ask someone you trust to be your telephone buddy. Ask their permission for you to call them whenever you feel you're at loose ends, day or night.

Tell people what helps you and what doesn't—People around you may not understand what you need. So tell them. People can't read your mind, so you'll have to speak it.

Avoid certain people if you must—No one likes to be unfriendly or cold. But if there are people in your life who make it very difficult for you to do your grieving, then do what you can to stay out of their way.

Change some things—As soon as it seems right, alter some things in your home to make clear this significant change that has occurred. This does not mean to remove all signs of the one who died. It does mean not treating your home or your loved one's room as a shrine which cannot be altered in any way.

Plan ahead for special days—Birthdays, anniversaries, holidays, and other special events can be difficult times, especially for the first year or two. Give thought beforehand to how you will handle those days. Do things a little differently than you used to, as a way of acknowledging this change in your life. But also be sure to invoke that person's presence and memory somehow during the day.

Donate their possessions meaningfully—Whether you give your loved one's personal possessions to someone you know or to a stranger, find ways to pass these things along so that others might benefit from them.

(continued)

(continued from previous page)

Family members or friends might like to receive keepsakes. Some wish to do this quickly following the death, while others wish to wait awhile.

Allow yourself to laugh—Sometimes something funny will happen to you, just like it used to. You won't be desecrating your loved one's memory. You'll be consecrating their love of life, and your own, too.

Allow yourself to cry—Crying goes naturally with grief. It may feel awkward to you, but this is not unusual for a person in your situation. A good rule of thumb is this: if you feel like crying, then cry. If not, then don't.

Plan at least one thing you'll do each day—Even if your grief is very painful and your energy very low, plan to complete at least one thing each day, even if it's a small thing. Then follow through with your plan, day after day.

Journal—Write out your thoughts and feelings. Do this whenever you feel the urge, but do it at least several times a week, if not several times a day.

Write the person who died—Write letters or other messages to your loved one, thoughts you wish you could express if they were present.

Rest—Grieving is hard work. Give yourself plenty of permission to take things easy.

Consider a support group—Spending time with a small group of people who have undergone a similar life experience can be very therapeutic. You can discover how natural your feelings are.

Speak to a clergyperson—If you're searching for answers to the larger questions about life and death, religion and spirituality, consider talking with a representative of your faith, or even another's faith.

(continued)

Coping With Grief

The grieving process, like the dying process, is essentially a series of behaviors and attitudes related to coping with the stressful situation of changing the status of a relationship. As discussed in chapter 6, many have attempted to understand coping with dying as a series of universal, mutually exclusive, and linear stages. However, because most will acknowledge that not all people will progress through the stages in the same manner, we will list a number of coping strategies used as people attempt to resolve the pain caused by the loss of a significant relationship.

Robert Kavanaugh (1972) identifies the following seven behaviors and feelings as part of the coping process: shock and denial, disorganization, volatile emotions, guilt, loss and loneliness, relief, and reestablishment. It is not difficult to see similarities between these behaviors and Kübler-Ross's five stages (denial, anger, bargaining, depression, and acceptance) of the dying process. According to Kavanaugh (1972, p. 23), "these seven stages do not subscribe to the logic of the head as much as to the irrational tugs of the heart—the logic of need and permission."

(continued from previous page)

Connect on the Internet—If you're computer savvy, search the Internet. You'll find many resources for people in grief, as well as the opportunity to chat with fellow grievers.

Read how others have responded to a loved one's death—You may feel that your own grief is all you can handle. But if you'd like to look at the ways others have done it, try C. S. Lewis's *A Grief Observed,* Lynn Caine's *Widow,* John Bramblett's *When Good-Bye Is Forever,* or Nicholas Wolterstorff's *Lament for a Son.* There are many others. Check with a counselor or a librarian.

Learn about your loved one from others—Listen to the stories others have to tell about the one who died, both stories you're familiar with and those you've never heard before. Celebrate your time together.

Vent your anger rather than hold it in—You may feel awkward being angry when you're grieving, but anger is a common reaction. Even if you feel a bit ashamed as you do it, find ways to get it out of your system. Yell, even if it's in an empty house. Cry. Hit something soft. Resist the temptation to be proper.

Give thanks every day—Whatever has happened to you, you still have things to be thankful for. Perhaps it's your memories, your remaining family, your support, your work, your own health—all sorts of things.

Source: James E. Miller, http://www.opn.com/willowgreen/gtips.html.

SHOCK AND DENIAL

Even when a significant other is expected to die, at the time of death there is often a sense in which the death is not real. For most of us our first response is, "No, this can't be true." With time our experience of shock diminishes, but we find new ways to deny the reality of death.

Some believe that denial is dysfunctional behavior for those in bereavement. However, denial not only is a common experience among the newly bereaved, but also serves positive functions in the process of adaptation. The main function of denial is to provide the bereaved with a "temporary safe place" from the ugly realities of a social world that offers only loneliness and pain.

With time the meaning of loss tends to expand, and it may be impossible for one to deal with all of the social meanings of death at once. For example, if my wife dies, not only do I lose my spouse, but also I lose my best friend, my sexual partner, the mother of my children, a source of income, the person who writes the Christmas cards, and so on. Denial can protect me from some of the magnitude of this social loss, which may be unbearable at one point in time. With denial, I can work through different aspects of my loss over time.

DISORGANIZATION

Disorganization is that stage in the bereavement process in which one may feel totally out of touch with the reality of everyday life. Some go through the 3-day time period just prior to the funeral as if on "automatic pilot" or "in a daze." Nothing normal "makes sense," and they may feel that life has no inherent meaning. For some, death is perceived as preferable to life, which appears to be devoid of meaning.

This emotional response is also a normal experience for the newly bereaved. Confusion is normal for those whose social world has been disorganized through death. When my father died, my mother lost not only all of those things that one loses with a death of a spouse, but also her caregiving role—a social role and master status that had defined her identity in the 5 years that my father lived with cancer. It is only natural to experience confusion and social disorganization when one's social identity has been destroyed.

VOLATILE REACTIONS

Whenever one's identity and social order face the possibility of destruction, there is a natural tendency to feel angry, frustrated, helpless, and/or hurt. The volatile reactions of terror, hatred, resentment, and jealousy are often experienced as emotional manifestations of these feelings. Grieving humans are sometimes more successful at masking their feelings in socially acceptable behaviors than other animals, whose instincts cause them to go into a fit of rage when their order is threatened by external forces. However apparently dissimilar, the internal emotional experience is similar.

In working with bereaved persons over the past 15 years, I have observed that the following become objects of volatile grief reactions: God, medical personnel, funeral directors, other family members, in-laws, friends who have not experienced death in their families, and/or even the person who has died. I have always found it interesting to watch mild-mannered individuals transformed into raging and resentful persons when grieving. Some of these people have experienced physical symptoms such as migraine headaches, ulcers, neuropathy, and colitis as a result of living with these intense emotions.

GUILT

Guilt is similar to the emotional reactions discussed earlier. Guilt is anger and resentment turned in on oneself and often results in self-deprecation and depression. It typically manifests itself in statements like "If only I had . . . ," "I should have . . . ," "I could have done it differently . . . ," and "Maybe I did the wrong thing." Guilt is a normal part of the bereavement process.

From a sociological perspective, guilt can become a social mechanism to resolve the **dissonance** that people feel when unable to explain why someone else's loved one has died. Rather than view death as something that can happen at any time to any one, people can **blame the victim** of bereavement and believe that the victim of bereavement was in some way responsible for the death—"If he had been a better parent, the child might not have been hit by the car," or "If I had been married to him I might also have committed suicide," or "No wonder he died of a heart attack, her

Anger as a Path to Grief
Tom Golden

The expression of anger seems more natural for men than expressing other feelings. When expressing anger, we need to take a stand, to define our ground. This is quite different from the mechanics of sadness, which require a more open and vulnerable stance. It is important to note that men in our culture will sometimes find their other feelings of grief through their anger. Many times in working with men I have found that while a man is expressing anger (and I mean really expressing it . . . loudly, with movement of the body, etc.), he suddenly will be moved to tears. It is almost as if touching on that profound and deep feeling of anger has brought him in touch with his other feelings. This process is reversed with women. Many times a woman would be in tears, crying and crying. I might ask what her tears are about, and she often would state plainly and many times loudly "I'm angry."

A person's anger during grief can range from being angry with the person who died to being angry with God, and all points in between. My mentor, Father William Wendt, once told me a story about anger and grief. It seems that Bill had been visiting a widow and working with her on her grief. He noticed that many times when he arrived she was driving her car up and down the driveway. One day he asked her what she was doing. She proceeded to tell him that she had a ritual she used in dealing with her grief. She would come home, go to the living room, and get her recently deceased husband's ashes out of the urn on the mantle. She would take a very small amount and place them on the driveway. She then told Bill that, "It helps me to run over the son of a bitch every day." Bill concluded the story by saying, "Now that is good grief."

Bill thought it was "good" grief because it was this woman's way of connecting to and expressing the anger component of her grief.

From *Swallowed by a Snake,* by T. Golden, published on Web site
http://www.webhealing.com/3anger.html.

cooking would give anyone high cholesterol." Therefore, bereaved persons are sometimes encouraged to feel guilt because they are subtly sanctioned by others' reactions.

LOSS AND LONELINESS

As we discussed earlier, loss and loneliness are the other side of denial. Their full sense never becomes obvious at once; rather, each day without the deceased helps us to recognize how much we needed and depended upon those persons. Social situations in which we expected them always to be present seem different now that they are gone. Holiday celebrations are also diminished by their absence. In fact, for some, most of life takes on a "something's missing" feeling. This feeling was captured in the 1960s love song "End of the World."

Of all the emotions related to the bereavement process, feelings of grief, loss, and loneliness are generally the most intensely experienced.

Why does the world go on turning?
Why must the sea rush to shore?
Don't they know it's the end of the world
'Cause you don't love me anymore?

Loss and loneliness are often transformed into depression and sadness fed by feelings of self-pity. According to Kavanaugh (1972, p. 118), this effect is magnified by the fact that the dead loved one grows out of focus in memory—"an elf becomes a giant, a sinner becomes a saint because the grieving heart needs giants and saints to fill an expanding void." Even a formerly undesirable spouse, such as an alcoholic, is missed in a way that few can understand unless their own hearts are involved. This is a time in the grieving process when anybody is better than nobody, and being alone only adds to the curse of loss and loneliness (Kavanaugh, 1972, p. 118).

Those who try to escape this experience will either turn to denial in an attempt to reject their feelings of loss or try to find surrogates—new friends at a bar, a quick remarriage, or a new pet. This escape can never be permanent, however, because loss and loneliness are a necessary part of the bereavement experience. According to Kavanaugh (1972, p. 119), the "ultimate goal in conquering loneliness" is to build a new independence or to find a new and equally viable relationship.

RELIEF

The experience of relief in the midst of the bereavement process may seem odd for some and add to their feelings of guilt. My mother found relief in the fact that my father's battle with cancer had ended, even though this end provided her with new problems. I have observed a friend's relief 6 months after her husband died. This older friend of mine was the wife of a minister, and her whole life before he died was his ministry. With time, as she built a new world of social involvements and relationships of which he was not a part, she discovered a new independent person in herself whom she perceived was a better person than she had ever been.

Although relief can give rise to feelings of guilt, like denial, it can also be experienced as a "safe place" from the pain, loss, and loneliness that are endured when one is grieving. According to Kavanaugh (1972, p. 121):

> The feeling of relief does not imply any criticism for the love we lost. Instead, it is a reflection of our need for ever deeper love, our quest for someone or something always better, our search for the infinite, that best and perfect love religious people name as God.

REESTABLISHMENT

As one moves toward reestablishment of a life without the deceased, it is obvious that the process involves extensive adjustment and time, especially if the relationship was meaningful. It is likely that one may have feelings of loneliness, guilt, and disorganization at the same time and that just when one may experience a sense of relief, something will happen to trigger a denial of the death. What facilitates bereavement and adjustment is fully experiencing each of these feelings as normal

Don't Reduce My Grief to Something Logical and Universal

Grief discriminates against no one. It kills. Maims. And cripples. It is the ashes from which the phoenix rises, and the mettle of rebirth. It returns life to the living dead. It teaches that there is nothing absolutely true, or untrue. It assures the living that we know nothing for certain. It humbles. It shrouds. It blackens. It enlightens.

Grief will make a new person out of you, if it doesn't kill you in the making. People say "How are you?" and they have that look in their faces again. And I look at them like they're crazy. I think, how do you think I am? I'm not strong enough for talk. A woman said to me, in a comforting tone of conspiracy, "My mother had breast cancer and lost her right breast. . . ." "Oh," I say, "that's awful . . ." and wonder if that is supposed to be some sort of comparison. A tit, a husband—same thing? Strange how people want to join you in your intensity, your epiphany, by trying to relate—grabbing at straws of a so-called "like" experience while simultaneously they are repulsed by the agony. They see you on the street, driving by and pretending they don't see you. Shit, we all have our stuff to deal with. I suppose it's hard enough dealing with your own.

I can't tell them to shut up, not because I'm not rude by nature (it takes too much energy to be polite) but because I am afraid they'll go away. One more abandonment. "I lost my father two years ago . . ." and I think, schmuck, that's supposed to happen, it's a natural part of becoming adult—children are supposed to outlive their parents. Did you lose the only other person in the world who would love your child the way you do? Did you lose the person you held all night, who slept next to you, warmed your bed so much you didn't need an extra blanket in the winter? Do you know how many blankets it takes to replace a husband? Did you lose the person who would worry about bills with you? Screw in a light bulb when you were busy with the baby? Don't reduce this experience to something logical, universal. Even if it is, I walk alone amongst the dead, it's my death, my pain. Don't pretend you know it, like you know batting averages. Don't sacrilege all over my crucifixion.

"The Agony of Grief," by S. Ericsson, September–October 1991, *Utne Reader,* 75–78.

and realizing that it is hope (holding the grieving person together in fantasy at first) that will provide the promise of a new life filled with order, purpose, and meaning.

Reestablishment never occurs all at once. Rather, it is a goal that one realizes has been achieved long after it has occurred. In some ways it is similar to Dorothy's realization at the end of *The Wizard of Oz*—she had always possessed the magic that could return her to Kansas. And, like Dorothy, we have to experience our loss before we really appreciate the joy of investing our lives again in new relationships.

The Four Tasks of Mourning

In 1982 J. William Worden published *Grief Counseling and Grief Therapy*, which summarized the research conclusions of a National Institutes of Health study called the Omega Project (occasionally referred to as the Harvard Bereavement Study). Two of the more significant findings of this research, displaying the active nature of the grieving process, are that mourning is necessary for all persons who have experienced a loss through death and that four tasks of mourning must be accomplished before mourning can be completed and reestablishment can take place.

According to Worden (1982, p. 10), unfinished grief tasks can impair further growth and development of the individual. Furthermore, the necessity of these tasks suggests that those in bereavement must attend to "grief work" because successful grief resolution is not automatic, as Kavanaugh's (1972) stages might imply. Each bereaved person must accomplish four necessary tasks: (a) accept the reality of the loss, (b) experience the pain of grief, (c) adjust to an environment in which the deceased is missing, and (d) withdraw emotional energy and reinvest it in another relationship (Worden, 1982).

ACCEPT THE REALITY OF THE LOSS

Especially in situations when death is unexpected and/or the deceased lived far away, it is difficult to conceptualize the reality of the loss. The first task of mourning is to overcome the natural denial response and realize that the person is dead and will not return.

Bereaved persons can facilitate the actualization of death in many ways. The traditional ways are to view the body, attend the funeral and committal services, and visit the place of final disposition. The following is a partial list of additional activities that can assist in making death real for grieving persons.

1. View the body at the place of death before preparation by the funeral director.
2. Talk about the deceased and the circumstances surrounding the death.
3. View photographs and personal effects of the deceased.
4. Distribute the possessions of the deceased among relatives and friends.

EXPERIENCE THE PAIN OF GRIEF

Part of coming to grips with the reality of death is experiencing the emotional and physical pain caused by the loss. Many people in the denial stage of grieving attempt to avoid pain by choosing to reject the emotions and feelings that they are experiencing. Some do this by avoiding places and circumstances that remind them of the deceased. I know of one widow who quit playing golf and quit eating at a particular restaurant because these were activities that she had enjoyed with her husband. Another widow found it extremely painful to be with her dead husband's twin, even though he and her sister-in-law were her most supportive friends.

J. William Worden (1982, pp. 13–14) cites the following case study to illustrate the performance of this task of mourning:

Prince Philip (former father-in-law), Prince William (son), Earl Spencer (brother), Prince Harry (son), and Prince Charles (former husband) walking in the funeral procession for Diana, Princess of Wales. In the bereavement process, the meaning of a lost relationship is changed to varying degrees, depending on the nature of the relationship. There are qualitatively different needs and types of grief experienced by survivors. Consider the above photo and your reaction to the differences in grief experienced by Diana's former father-in-law, brother, ex-spouse, and children.

One young woman minimized her loss by believing her brother was out of his dark place and into a better place after his suicide. This might have been true, but it kept her from feeling her intense anger at him for leaving her. In treatment, when she first allowed herself to feel anger, she said, "I'm angry with his behavior and not him!" Finally she was able to acknowledge this anger directly.

The problem with the avoidance strategy is that people cannot escape the pain associated with mourning. According to Bowlby (cited by Worden, 1982, p. 14), "Sooner or later, some of those who avoid all conscious grieving, break down—usually with some form of depression." Tears can afford cleansing for wounds created by loss, and fully experiencing the pain ultimately provides wonderful relief to those who suffer while eliminating long-term chronic grief.

ADJUST TO AN ENVIRONMENT IN WHICH THE DECEASED IS MISSING

The third task, practical in nature, requires the griever to take on some of the social roles performed by the deceased, or to find others who will. According to Worden (1982, p. 15), to abort this task is to become helpless by refusing to develop the skills necessary in daily living and by ultimately withdrawing from life.

I knew a woman who refused to adjust to the social environment in which she found herself after the death of her husband. He was her business partner, as well as her best and only friend. After 30 years of marriage, they had no children, and she had no close relatives. She had never learned to drive a car. Her entire social world had been controlled by her former husband. Three weeks after his funeral she went into the basement and committed suicide.

The alternative to withdrawing is assuming new social roles by taking on additional responsibilities. Extended families who always gathered at Grandma's house for Thanksgiving will be tempted to have a number of small Thanksgiving dinners after her death. The members of this family may believe that "no one can take Grandma's place." Although this may be true, members of the extended family will grieve better if someone else is willing to do Grandma's work, enabling the entire family to come together for Thanksgiving. Not to do so will cause double pain—the family will not gather, and Grandma will still be missed.

The final task of mourning is a difficult one for many because they feel disloyal or unfaithful in withdrawing emotional energy from their dead loved one. One of my family members once said that she could never love another man after her husband died. My twice-widowed aunt responded, "I once felt like that, but I now consider myself to be fortunate to have been married to two of the best men in the world."

Other people find themselves unable to reinvest in new relationships because they are unwilling to experience again the pain caused by loss. The quotation from John Brantner at the beginning of this chapter provides perspective on this problem: "Only people who avoid love can avoid grief. The point is to learn from it and remain vulnerable to love."

However, those who are able to withdraw emotional energy and reinvest it in other relationships find the possibility of a newly established social life. Kavanaugh (1972, pp. 122–123) depicts this situation well with the following description.

> At this point fantasies fade into constructive efforts to reach out and build anew. The phone is answered more quickly, the door as well, and meetings seem important, invitations are treasured and any social gathering becomes an opportunity rather than a curse. Mementos of the past are put away for occasional family gatherings. New clothes and new places promise dreams instead of only fears. Old friends are important for encouragement and permission to rebuild one's life. New friends can offer realistic opportunities for coming out from under the grieving mantle. With newly acquired friends, one is not a widow, widower, or survivor—just a person. Life begins again at the point of new friendships. All the rest is of yesterday, buried, unimportant to the now and tomorrow.

Assisting the Bereaved

In his book *Bereavement: Studies of Grief in Adult Life,* Colin Parkes (1972, p. 161) notes that the funeral often precedes the "peak of the pangs" of grief that tends to be reached in the second week of bereavement. The face put on for the funeral can no longer be maintained, and the bereaved has a need to be freed to grieve. The most valued person at this time is the one making few demands on the bereaved, quietly completing household tasks, and accepting the bereaved person's vented anguish and anger—some of which may be directed against the helper.

It is important to recognize that the bereaved person has painful and difficult tasks to perform that cannot be avoided or rushed. The best assistance that one can offer to those in grieving is to encourage them to attend to the four tasks of mourning described earlier.

One can help the bereaved come to grips with the reality of the death by talking about the deceased and encouraging the bereaved to conceptualize the loss. Parkes observes that it is often reassuring to the bereaved person when others show that they are not afraid to express feelings of sadness. Such expressions make the bereaved person feel understood and reduce a sense of isolation. How people grieve will vary; the important thing is for feelings to emerge into consciousness. How they appear on the surface may be of secondary importance.

It is not uncommon for one approaching a newly bereaved person to be unsure how to react. Parkes suggests that although a conventional expression of sympathy can probably not be avoided, pity is the last thing that the bereaved person wants. Pity makes one into an object—the bereaved person somehow becomes pitiful. Pity puts the bereaved person at a distance from, and in an inferior position to, the intended

The Art of Condolence

Based upon their study of thousands of condolence letters and analysis of their structure, Leonard and Hillary Zunin (1991) share seven components that provide the writer with a practical, simple, and clear outline for sharing his or her thoughts. Though all seven components need not be included in every letter of condolence, keeping them in mind will provide an effective guide for sharing thoughts in such a letter. The components include:

1. Acknowledge the loss. Mention the deceased by name and indicate how you learned about the death. It is very acceptable to relate personal shock and dismay at hearing such news and such an acknowledgement sets the tone for your letter.

2. Express your sympathy. Share your sorrow in an honest and sincere fashion. In so doing you are showing that you care and relate in some way to the difficult situation they are facing. Do not hesitate to use the words *died* or *death* in your comments.

3. Note special qualities of the deceased. As you reflect upon the individual who has died, think about those characteristics you valued most in that person and share them in your letter. These may be specific attributes, personality characteristics, or other qualities. Sharing these with the bereaved help them realize that their loved one was appreciated by others.

4. Recount a memory about the deceased. At the time of a death, memories we have of the deceased person are a most valued

(continued)

comforter. Parkes maintains that it is best to get conventional verbal expressions of sympathy over as soon as possible and to speak from the heart or not at all. There is not a proper thing to say at this time; a trite formula serves only to widen the gap between the two persons.

The encounter between the bereaved and the helper may not seem satisfactory because the helper cannot bring back the deceased and the bereaved person cannot gratify the helper by seeming to be helped. Bereaved people do, however, appreciate the visits and expressions of sympathy paid by others. These tributes to the dead confirm to the bereaved the belief that the deceased is worth all of the pain. The bereaved are also reassured that they are not alone and feel less insecure.

The Hallmark Card Company sells its products with the slogan, "When you care enough to send the very best, send a Hallmark." Although sending a card is one way to validate the loss of the bereaved and to assist them in their grieving, if you really care enough to send the very best, a personal visit or a handwritten letter is better. On the other hand, if you find it impossible to communicate a personal expression of sympathy, sending a card is preferable to doing nothing. In "The Art of Condolence," 7 suggestions are given for expressing condolence.

(continued from previous page)

possession and something which can never be in too great a supply. Because the bereaved often have difficulty keeping those memories in the forefront of their thoughts, your sharing of memories will be very gratefully received. Feel free to recall humorous incidents as they can be very beneficial at this time.

5. Note special qualities of the bereaved. Grieving people also need to be reminded of their personal strengths and other positive qualities—those characteristics which will help them through this difficult time. By reminding them of the qualities you have observed in them, you will be encouraging them to use these qualities to their advantage at this time.

6. Offer assistance. Offering help need not be part of a condolence letter, but if help is offered, it should be for a specific thing. An open-ended offer of help places the burden for determining what that help will be on the bereaved and they have enough burdens already. Making an offer to do something specific and then doing it is a most welcome extension of yourself.

7. Close with a thoughtful word or phrase. The finals words in your letter of condolence are especially important and should reflect your true feelings. Flowery or elaborate phrases do not help. Honest expressions of your thoughts and feelings communicate best.

From "Book Review of *The Art of Condolence*," by P.V. Johnson, Fall 1991. In *Caregivers Quarterly*, 6(3), 3–4.

Although many bereaved people are frightened and surprised by the intensity of their emotions, reassurance that they are not going mad and that this is a perfectly natural behavior can be an important contribution of the helper (Parkes, 1972, pp. 164–165). On the other hand, absence of grief in a situation where expected, excessive guilt feelings or anger, or lasting physical symptoms should be taken as signs that not all is going well. These persons may require special help, and the caregiver should not hesitate to advise the bereaved to get additional help if the caregiver is uncertain about the course of events.

Support Groups for the Bereaved

Support groups empower persons to cope with social crisis and loss in a dealienating environment. According to Louis LaGrand (1991, p. 212), the power of support groups lies in the "introduction of new ways of looking at one's problems and the development of belief systems that enhance the twin attributes of self-determination and interdependence, all of this accruing in a socially secure setting."

The grieving process often socially isolates the bereaved by marginalizing them from normal patterns of social interaction. Bereavement self-help groups, by their very nature, challenge the assumption that grievers are unique by confronting them with caring people who understand their experience of loss and are willing to practice patterns of coping that reduce feelings of despair and depression (LaGrand, 1991, p. 212).

Some national support groups for grievers are Compassionate Friends, Candle-lighters, Empty Arms, Begin Again, Widow to Widow Program, the Omega Project, Parents Without Partners, and various hospice programs and/or hospital grief therapy groups. Another resource is the Internet or World Wide Web. There are chat rooms for grievers, and one can do grief work by creating memorial tributes to the person who has died. The end of this chapter provides a number of Internet resources for grievers. A good place to start is GriefNet (http://rivendell.org/), which provides insights into the bereavement process, resources for grievers, and information concerning grief support groups.

Grieving Parents and the Loss of an Infant

Adapting to the death of a loved one is always difficult. However, the death of a child is typically regarded as the most difficult of all deaths. As we discussed in chapter 3, the death of a child goes against the natural order—parents are supposed to die before their child. Furthermore, the death of a child symbolically threatens the family's hope for a future.

In order to conceptualize the nature of loss involved in the death of a child, we should remember that the relationship of a parent with a child begins long before birth (Raphael, 1983, pp. 230–231). For each parent, from the time of conception, the child becomes a source of fantasy—the imagined child whom he or she will become. These hoped-for extensions of self are very common among expectant parents. As the pregnancy progresses, the fantasy relationship with this imagined child intensifies with the selection of the name for the baby, the rehearsal for parenting, the fantasies

The AIDS memorial quilt is the largest on-going community arts project in the world. Each of the over 41,000 colorful panels that make up the enormous quilt was made to remember the life of a person lost to AIDS. Panels are 3 feet by 6 feet—the size of a human grave. As the epidemic claims more lives, the quilt continues to grow with over 50 new memorial panels added each week. The quilt stands as a remembrance of the thousands of names sewn into the fabric. It stands, as well, for the sorrow, anger, and hope of those who make the panels.

shared with others, and finally the birth of the child. With the death of a newborn or a stillbirth, the bubble of one's fantasy world is suddenly burst.

The death of an infant places severe strains on parents and members of the family—a sense of loss that will likely persist over a number of years. Studies show (Nicol, Tompkins, Campbell, & Syme, 1986) that up to one third of mothers experience a marked deterioration in their health and well-being after the loss of an infant. The death of a child also has dysfunctional consequences for family systems. J. William Worden (1982, p. 101) reports the results of a study at Stanford University Hospital in which 70 percent of the parents whose children had died of leukemia were divorced within 2 years following the death. Another study by Nixon and Pearn (1977) reported that 7 of 29 couples separated following the deaths of their children. In a more recent study by Reiko Schwab (1992) of the effects of a child's death on the marital relationship, it was discovered that there is an increase in general irritability between spouses and a loss of communication and sexual intimacy following the death of a child.

Longitudinal studies of grieving parents demonstrate that the experience of grief does not go away with time, rather its focus changes. According to McClowry, Davies, May, Kulenkamp, and Martinson (1987), even after 9 years, parents are still experiencing significant pain and loss—which the researchers refer to as "an empty space." This "empty space" feeling takes on three recurring patterns of grieving. The first is "getting over it." In this pattern the grievers do what they can to get back to life as usual and accept death matter-of-factly.

The second pattern of dealing with the empty space is to "fill the emptiness" by keeping busy. Some parents attend grief groups, others immerse themselves in work, become more religious. increase their food or alcohol intake, or become involved as volunteers in organizations such as Candlelighters (a support group for parents of children with cancer), Compassionate Friends or Empty Arms (two support groups for bereaved parents). Other parents attempt to replace the dead child with another by getting pregnant or by adopting.

The third pattern of dealing with the empty space is described as "keeping the connection." In this pattern of grieving, parents attempt to integrate this pain and loss into their lives (McClowry et al., 1987):

> Although most of the grievers who were "keeping the connection" expressed satisfaction with their present lives, they continue to reserve a small part of themselves for the loss of a special relationship which they view as irreplaceable.

Mourning the death of a fetus or newborn baby differs from mourning the death of another loved one (Furman, 1978). Mourning is a process of detachment from the loved one that is moderated by identification. The bereaved parents take into themselves aspects of the deceased, but because a fetus or newborn has not lived long enough as a separate person, the parents have little of their baby to take into themselves. Thus, they suffer detachment without identification. Parents must readjust their self-image with the knowledge that the baby will never again be part of them.

SUPPORT FROM HEALTH CARE PROFESSIONALS

In order for parents to make their adjustment, they need support from those around them. In a study of 130 parents who had experienced a **perinatal death,** Judith Murray and Victor Callan (1988, p. 242) discovered that a consistent predictor of better adjustment was the parents' level of satisfaction with the comfort and support provided by physicians, nurses, and other hospital staff. Parents who were pleased with the level of support that they received from medical personnel were also less depressed and had higher levels of self-esteem and psychological well-being. Furthermore, emotional support from the other parent, family, and hospital staff was linked to fewer grief reactions and better overall adjustment. Therefore, support from others can go a long way to facilitate parental bereavement at the death of a child.

Hospital-based intervention is especially necessary and helpful to parents who are experiencing the death of a newborn or a stillbirth, and medical personnel are in a unique position to assist parents in their grief (Davis, Stewart, & Harmon, 1988, p. 242). However, although the majority (70 percent) of bereaved parents wish to discuss their concerns with their physician (Clyman et al., 1979), 50 percent of parents received no physician follow-up, and many others had no contact with their physicians until a regularly scheduled postpartum check (Rowe et al., 1978). Thus, although parents seem to desire medical personnel to acknowledge their feelings of shock, guilt, and grief, such desires do not seem to be fulfilled in many instances.

Part of the emotional support needed by parents involves encouraging them to accept the reality of death and to express their feelings of loss and then validating these feelings. Communication and understanding by the medical staff will be great sources of support and comfort. By being available, medical personnel can help to reduce the isolation that parents often feel at this difficult time. Because grief is a necessary process, whenever bereavement is facilitated, the parents become subject to a lower risk for psychological and physical disturbances.

Table 13.1 identifies various ways in which professionals can contribute to the adjustment of grieving parents.

PARENTAL INVOLVEMENT WITH PROFESSIONAL HELPERS: PERINATAL DEATHS

The death of a fetus or a newborn infant is stressful not only for parents and siblings, but also for all people who are involved with the child. Increasingly, parents are being included in the direct care of critically ill children until the time of death and following. Familiarity with the types of procedures and decisions that parents may face at the death of their child is essential. Most bereaved parents will learn about hospital procedures and how to share in decision making only when they are faced with such a situation.

The nursing procedures are fairly clear, and nurses are instructed to respond in ways that can help in the socioemotional adjustments. Nurses notify a nursing-social

Table 13.1

Behaviors of Professionals Identified As Helpful by Grieving Parents

Helpful Behaviors	Primary Responsibility For This Behavior
1. Informs the parents immediately of the condition of the baby	Doctor
2. Expresses feeling over the baby's death with consoling words to parents	Doctor/Nurse
3. Provides as much factual information surrounding the baby's death as is available	Doctor/Nurse
4. Describes the appearance of the baby in factual and tender terms before bringing the baby to them	Doctor/Nurse
5. Encourages parents to see and hold the baby and stays with them while they initially examine the baby	Doctor/Nurse
6. Touches parents affectionately and appropriately; words are not always necessary	Doctor/Nurse
7. Encourages parents to grieve openly	Doctor/Nurse
8. Acknowledges the baby's death at first contact with parents and daily thereafter; does not act like death has not occurred	Doctor/Nurse
9. Spends extra time with the parents to provide time to review the events surrounding the baby's death	Doctor/Nurse

P. Estok and A. Lehman, Perinatal Death: Grief Support for Families." *Birth* (March 1983) 10:1, p.19. By permission of Blackwell Scientific Publications, Inc.

worker counselor at the time of admission concerning the fetal death or infant trauma. Even baptism is offered by some hospitals, where it may be done by anyone in the absence of a chaplain. The pastoral care department of a hospital is notified, as is the communications department, so that accurate information is available to others.

In the case of stillbirths, fetal deaths, and infant deaths, the parents may be given the option to see and hold their infant, to learn the infant's gender, and to decide on an autopsy and funeral arrangements. The medical staff explains what the parents can expect the infant to look like. Believing that the age of siblings is the major factor in determining their involvement in these settings, Furman (1978, p. 217) notes:

> Adolescents should decide for themselves. Elementary grade children are helped by attending a service but not helped by seeing a malformed dead body. Children under school age are particularly not helped by seeing their dead brother or sister, but they are sometimes helped by being in the company of the parents at the time of the funeral.

The extent of individual involvement depends upon the preference of individual family members.

The nurses' responsibilities include attaching identification bands to wrist and ankle, measuring the weight, length, and head circumference, taking footprints and possibly a handprint, and completing standard forms. These forms might include a fetal death certificate, an authorization for autopsy, and a record of the death for the receptionist. Medical photographs may be taken by the medical photographer of a full front and back view, as well as close-ups of any abnormalities. These are used by physicians to describe the infant's medical condition. Nurses are also encouraged to take nonmedical photographs that include the infant unclothed in a blanket, a close-up of the face, and the parents holding the child if they so desire. These photos are given to the counselor and later to the parents.

The dead infant is wrapped in a blanket, labeled, and taken to the morgue. In the case of a fetus, the body is sent to the pathology department with a surgical pathology lab slip. The physician may request that the placenta be included in the case of spontaneous abortions or fetal deaths. Genetic studies may also be requested; these might include a cord blood sample, a placenta sample, fresh tissue such as gonadal tissue or connective tissue around the kidneys, skin sample, and a complete genetic study that is sent to the state laboratory. A nurse then completes a checklist for assisting parents who are experiencing perinatal deaths, and she or he may, if procedure calls for it, place an identifier by the name tag at the entrance to the mother's room.

Hospitals with a special program to help the survivors of fetal and infant deaths provide nursing, medical, social work, and/or pastoral counselors who may assist the surviving parents and siblings. Time is taken to explain and help in the following matters: (a) autopsies and hospital procedures after death; (b) funeral or cremation options (arrangements for the disposition of the body are required in most states if the fetus was at least 20 weeks); (c) the nature and expression of grief and mourning; (d) coping with the reactions of friends and relatives; (e) helping siblings to deal with the death of their brother or sister; and (f) decisions regarding another pregnancy. Monthly meetings of bereaved parents can be established to provide a setting for sharing and learning about grief. These experiences of sharing with other parents allow for reality-based comparisons and for active support of other parents whose loss is also great.

Although this list of hospital procedures is by no means complete, it does outline what parents who are grieving over spontaneous abortion, stillbirth, fetal death, or neonatal death may encounter. The attitudes and responses of physicians, nurses, and others may vary greatly. At times, for example, the helpers are in need of socioemotional support along with parents and siblings. Many hospitals, on the other hand, have not dealt with the special needs of families experiencing perinatal deaths. Although these practices are becoming more common around the country, one should not be surprised if a nurse or physician appears stunned at the request of parents to spend some time with the body of their dead child. We can only hope that the human values of medical care will prevail over bureaucratic values as the welfare of the whole person is taken into account in the medical arena. This can be accomplished most effectively if parents are provided with accurate information, encouraged to ask questions, given plenty of time to make decisions, and given opportunities to share their experience in parental bereavement with others.

The Death of Pets: A Special Kind of Grieving

According to Jack Kamerman (1988, p. 112), the death of pets represents an opportunity to study attitudes and behaviors toward human death. Such a loss often represents a child's first experience with death, and the stance taken by parents influences a child's attitude toward human death encountered later on. For example, in a study of college students recalling their first childhood experience with death (Dickinson, 1992, p. 171), a pet was involved for 28 percent of the students—birds, cats, chickens, cows, dogs, fish, mice, toads, rabbits, pigs, hamsters, gerbils, and turtles.

Examining the death of pets clarifies sociological issues, such as the process by which human traits are attributed to animals. For many individuals, a pet is a significant member of the family. People talk to pets and care for them as if they were their children. Pets often live with a family as many years as children live at home prior to leaving for college or emancipation. Pets can make people feel needed, can relieve loneliness, and can serve as friends and companions. Such a death is a traumatic experience for family members. As would occur for any other member of the family, the resulting dismemberment leaves a big void.

Unlike the person who loses a friend or relative and receives outpourings of sympathy and support, one who loses a pet often receives ridicule for overreacting, for being foolishly emotional, and for expressing grief over the death of an animal (Brody, 1985). There has not traditionally been a funeral or an acceptable time of mourning or standard words of comfort for friends to speak on the death of a pet. This leads to the problem of disenfranchised grief as discussed earlier in the chapter.

Grief, however, is a natural response to the loss of any significant object, person, or circumstance. Such attachments can be made to any pet—a rat, a guinea pig, a bird, a fish—providing that the pet provides emotional gratification. To a child, for whom a pet offers the most secure and certain acceptance, the loss can be especially painful.

Many individuals go through an agonizing separation when they lose a pet. Their symptoms are very similar to those experienced within the process of bereavement for a significant other. As when a person dies, when a pet dies suddenly, as in an accident, guilt is a common reaction. Putting an animal to sleep may also leave one with a feeling of guilt.

In discussing bereavement counseling for persons who had lost companion animals, Avery Weisman (1990–1991) discovered that clients were reluctant to tell others of their bereavement, but within the therapy group they spoke freely and with relief when they received acceptance and respect for their bereavement. According to Weisman (1990–1991, pp. 243–244):

> Clients felt that their grief was both exceptionally strong and abnormally tenacious, and they wept accordingly, as if confessing something unmentionable. Most people apologized for crying. One client hesitantly said, "I've actually mourned more than I did for my father."

Discussion of pet bereavement enables individuals to share their feelings of grief, fear, and loss. Weisman's (1990–1991) work with bereaved pet owners suggests that there were many similarities between grieving for a pet and grieving for a human—preoccupation was common, people reported mistaking shadows and sounds for their dead pet, guilt and ambivalence were experienced, and there were also corresponding feelings of loneliness and emptiness in the grieving process.

HAVING A PET "PUT TO SLEEP"

Like other professionals dealing with issues related to dying and death, veterinarians are concerned about discussing euthanasia and giving bad news to pet owners (Edney, 1988). Fears and anxieties experienced by the veterinarian who wants to succeed in curing the pet's illness make it difficult for the veterinarian to break the bad news. A prime fear is that the owner will blame the veterinarian for the animal's illness. If veterinarians can understand that blaming the professional is a normal grief reaction, they can learn to depersonalize this reaction.

When having a pet put to sleep is being contemplated, Herbert Nieburg and Arlene Fischer (1982) suggest asking the owner whether the pet can do the things that it once enjoyed, whether there is more pain or more pleasure in its life, whether the pet has become bad-tempered and snappish as a result of old age or illness, whether it has lost control of its bodily functions, and whether one can afford the expense and time involved in keeping a sick pet alive. Whatever the final decision, this is not an easy choice for an individual to make.

For those who do make the decision to euthanize their pet, at first there is a feeling of regret for having given permission for euthanasia, despite illness, invalidism, or senescence (Weisman, 1990–1991). According to Weisman this regret should not be interpreted as an indictment of euthanasia but rather as an expression of how guilty owners feel about invoking their power of life and death over their beloved companion.

DISPOSAL OF PETS AFTER DEATH

When a pet dies, many people arrange for disposal through their veterinarians or the local sanitation department. Though many people today may not choose to bury their pets, there are about 500 pet cemeteries in the United States, used by 2 percent of pet

The grave of a pet indicates the meaningful relationship that existed between the pet and its owner.

owners ("Pet's Death," 1987). The choice of pet caskets runs the gamut from simple fiberglass caskets ranging from $45 to $150, depending on size, to an actual child's casket. Casket, plot, and perpetual care average $300, but a body bag and temporary marker can be purchased for about half that amount (Langley, 1987). Markers for grave sites come in bronze and granite. In addition to the pet's name and dates of birth and death, markers often bear an affectionate word from the owner, an engraving of the pet's face, or a photo of the pet embedded in the bronze or granite. The following reading, however, shows that the cost of pet burials for the military is bothering certain officials.

Cremation is another alternative for disposal of one's deceased pet, whether by *communal cremation* or *separate cremation*. Communal cremation is less expensive and involves cremation in groups, with ashes distributed according to the law. Separate cremation allows the remains to be placed into an urn. Costs of communal cremation by a pet cremation service in South Carolina, for example, range from $40 to $75 depending on the size of the pet, and separate cremation costs range from $60 to $125.

The final disposition of pets is of such concern that the following was proposed to the American Animal Hospital Association by the Professional Animal Disposal Advisory Council (Cooke, 1988):

The recognition of the importance of the human/companion-animal bond as it relates to the veterinary profession has mandated changes in methods of disposing of pet animal carcasses. Recent legal decisions make it especially important to provide pet owners with a complete description of their options. In view of the fact pet owners view the final disposition of their pets in terms of human reference, it is important the attending veterinarian avoid the responsibility of providing the disposal options whenever possible. Pet disposal services should be turned over to outside contractors whenever possible, in order to avoid implications that veterinarians are purveyors of these services.

Suggestions by the Professional Animal Disposal Advisory Council include:

1. Acceptable methods of pet disposition, such as burial or cremation when available, or the use of landfills
2. Outline of suggested disposition procedures and a full-disclosure consent form, signed by the client and used in all hospitals to relieve the veterinarian of future legal ramifications
3. Sealing of the body in a sturdy plastic bag sufficient in size and strength to contain the entire pet and its body fluids
4. Proper identification of the body and storage in a freezer
5. Identification of pets known to have diseases contagious to human beings and/or other pets

Conclusion

In this chapter we have discussed the grieving process, bereavement roles, normal adaptations to experiences of loss, the four tasks of mourning, and special grieving issues related to the loss of children and pets. We have attempted to demonstrate that the bereaved must attend to grief work because successful grief resolution is not automatic. This grief work refers to Worden's (1982) four necessary tasks of bereavement: accepting the reality of the loss, experiencing the pain of grief, adjusting to an environment in which the deceased is missing, and withdrawing emotional energy and reinvesting it in other relationships.

Grievers need support and assistance in the bereavement process. One can help grievers come to grips with the reality of the death by talking about the deceased and encouraging them to conceptualize the loss that they are experiencing. It is often reassuring to the bereaved when others show that they are not afraid to express feelings of sadness. Such expressions make the bereaved feel understood and reduce their sense of isolation. Many well-meaning friends find it difficult to find proper words to say. Unfortunately, their discomfort often causes them to do nothing. Even trite words are better than no words at all. A well-known card company slogan says, "When you care enough to send the very best, send a Hallmark." When comforting bereaved friends, however, a better personal slogan might be, "When you care enough to send the very best, send yourself." At this time, the very best that we have to offer is our own caring presence.

Summary

1. The bereavement role is a temporary role that gives one the right to be exempted from normal social responsibilities and to become dependent upon others.

2. Abnormal bereavement behavior includes preoccupation with the death of the loved one and refusal to attempt to return to normal social functioning.

3. Disenfranchised grief involves loss that cannot be openly acknowledged, socially sanctioned, and publicly shared. There are four circumstances that lead to disenfranchised grief: (a) when the relationship to the deceased is not socially recognized; (b) when the loss is not acknowledged by others as being genuine loss; (c) when the grievers are unrecognized; and (d) when the death is not socially sanctioned.

4. The grieving process is similar to the dying process in that it is a series of behaviors and attitudes related to coping with the stressful situation of changing the status of a relationship. The grieving process need not be passive because the bereaved can make a number of decisions as they attempt to cope with their loss.

5. It is important in grieving to let feelings emerge into consciousness and not be afraid to express sadness.

6. It is not uncommon to be unsure of how to act around a newly bereaved person.

7. Rather than suggest that "time heals," an accurate description of the mourning process suggests that the time intervals between intense experiences of grief increase with the passing of time.

8. Seven behaviors and feelings are part of the normal bereavement process: shock and denial, disorganization, volatile emotions, guilt, loss and loneliness, relief, and reestablishment.

9. All persons who have experienced a loss through death will need to attend to the four necessary tasks of grief work before mourning can be completed and reestablishment can take place. These tasks involve accepting the reality of the loss, experiencing the pain of grief, adjusting to an environment in which the deceased is missing, and withdrawing emotional energy and reinvesting it in other relationships.

10. Mourning the death of a fetus or newborn baby differs from mourning the death of another loved one because parents must suffer detachment without identification.

11. The death of a pet often represents a child's first experience with death, and the stance taken by parents influences a child's attitude toward human death encountered later on.

12. Many individuals go through an agonizing separation when they lose a pet. Their symptoms are very similar to those experienced when people lose a significant other. However, unlike those who lose a significant other and receive outpourings of sympathy and support, those who lose a pet often receive ridicule for overreacting, for being foolishly emotional, and for expressing grief over the death of an animal.

Discussion Questions

1. How can one avoid "deviant" or "abnormal" behavior regarding the bereavement role? What are some functions of defining bereavement roles as "deviant" or "abnormal"?
2. What is the relation between time and the feelings of grief experienced within the bereavement process?
3. Discuss how the seven stages of grieving over a death can also be applied to losses suffered through going through a divorce, moving from one place to another, or having an arm or a leg amputated.
4. If grief is a feeling that is imposed upon the individual through loss, how can grieving be conceived of as being an active process?
5. What are the unique problems faced by those whose grief is disenfranchised? What are the different types of disenfranchised grief?
6. Describe the four necessary tasks of mourning. What are some of the practical steps that one can take to accomplish each of these tasks?
7. What does Parkes mean by "The funeral often precedes the 'peak of the pangs'"? How can one assist friends in bereavement?
8. What are the special problems encountered in the death of a child and in a perinatal death?
9. Explain how suggestions related to medical procedures involved in perinatal deaths might better help parents cope with the death of children.
10. What are some of the signs of aberrant bereavement? What could you do to assist people experiencing abnormal grief symptoms?
11. In what ways are the deaths of pets and the deaths of significant others similar with regard to the bereavement process? What are some special problems related to the death of a pet?

Glossary

Bereavement Role: Behavioral expectations for the bereaved that are structured around specific rights and duties.

Blaming the Victim: A strategy asserted by individuals to relieve the dissonance experienced when innocent people suffer loss.

Disenfranchised Grief: Grief that cannot be openly acknowledged, socially sanctioned, and publicly shared.

Dissonance: An inconsistency in beliefs and values—relative to a particular social situation—that causes personal discomfort or tension for the individuals involved.

Perinatal Death: The death of a child during or surrounding the event of its birth.

References

Akiyama, H., Holtzman, J. M., & Britz, W. E. (1986–1987). Pet ownership and health status during bereavement. *Omega, 17*(2), 187–193.

Attig, T. (1991). The importance of conceiving of grief as an active process. *Death Studies, 15,* 385–393.

Brody, J. E. (1985, October 27). Loss of a pet often agonizing for owners. Charleston, SC, *News and Courier,* p. 14E.

Clyman, R. I., Green, C., Mikkelsen, C., Rowe, J., & Ataide, L. (1979). Do parents utilize physician follow-up after the death of their newborn? *Pediatrics, 64,* 655–667.

Cooke, D. C. (1988). Animal disposal: Fact and fiction. In W. J. Kay et al. (Eds.), *Euthanasia of the companion animal.* Philadelphia: The Charles Press.

Davis, D. L., Stewart, M., & Harmon, R. J. (1988, December). Perinatal loss: Providing emotional support for bereaved parents. *Birth, 14,* 242–246.

Dickinson, G. E. (1992). First childhood death experiences. *Omega, 25*(2), 169–182.

Doka, K. J. (1987). Silent sorrow: Grief and the loss of significant others. *Death Studies, 11,* 441–449.

Doka, K. J. (1989). *Disenfranchised grief.* Lexington, MA: Lexington Books.

Edney, A. T. B. (1988). Breaking the news: The problems and some answers. In W. J. Kay et al. (Eds.), *Euthanasia of the companion animal.* Philadelphia: The Charles Press.

Furman, E. (1978). The death of a newborn: Care of the parents. *Birth Family Journal, 5,* 214.

Kamerman, J. B. (1988). *Death in the midst of life.* Englewood Cliffs, NJ: Prentice-Hall.

Kavanaugh, R. E. (1972). *Facing death.* Baltimore: Penguin Books.

Kesselman, I. (1990). Grief and loss: Issues for abortion. *Omega, 21*(3), 241–247.

Kloeppel, D. A., & Hollins, S. (1989). Double handicap: Mental retardation and death in the family. *Death Studies, 13,* 31–38.

LaGrand, L. E. (1991). United we cope: Support groups for the dying and bereaved. *Death Studies, 15,* 207–230.

Langley, L. (1987, September 13). Pet cemeteries first stop on way to hound dog heaven. Charleston, SC, *News and Courier,* p. 1D.

McClowry, S. G., Davies, E. B., May, K. A., Kulenkamp, E. J., & Martinson, I. M. (1987). The empty space phenomenon: The process of grief in the bereaved family. *Death Studies, 11,* 361–374.

Murphy, P., & Perry, K. (1988). Hidden grievers. *Death Studies, 12,* 451–462.

Murray, J., & Callan, V. J. (1988). Predicting adjustment to perinatal death. *British Journal of Medical Psychology, 61,* 237–244.

Ness, D. E., & Pheffer, C. R. (1990, March). Sequelae of bereavement resulting from suicide. *American Journal of Psychiatry, 147*(3), 279–285.

Nicol, M. T., Tompkins, J. R., Campbell, N. A., & Syme, G. J. (1986). Maternal grieving response after perinatal death. *The Medical Journal of Australia, 144,* 287–289.

Nieburg, H. A., & Fischer, A. (1982). Pet loss. New York: Harper and Row.

Nixon, J., & Pearn, J. (1977). Emotional sequelae of parents and sibs following the drowning or near-drowning of a child. *Australian and New Zealand Journal of Psychiatry, 11,* 265–269.

Parkes, C. M. (1972). *Bereavement: Studies of grief in adult life.* New York: International Universities Press.

Parsons, T. (1951). *The social system.* Glencoe, IL: Free Press.

Pet's death can be as grievous as person's. (1987, March). Charleston, SC, *News and Courier,* p. 7A.

Raphael, B. (1983). *The anatomy of bereavement.* New York: Basic Books.

Robson, J. D. (1977). Sick role and bereavement role: Toward a theoretical synthesis of two ideal types. In G. M. Vernon (Ed.), *A time to die.* Washington, DC: University Press of America.

Rosenblatt, P. (1983). *Bitter, bitter tears.* Minneapolis: University of Minnesota Press.

Rowe, J., Clyman, R., Green, C., Mikkelsen, C., Haight, J., & Ataide, L. (1978). Follow-up of families who experience a perinatal death. *Pediatrics, 62,* 166–170.

Savishinsky, J. S. (1988). The meanings of loss: Human and pet death in the lives of the elderly. In W. J. Kay et al. (Eds.), *Euthanasia of the companion animal.* Philadelphia: The Charles Press.

Schwab, R. (1992). Effects of a child's death on the marital relationship: A preliminary study. *Death Studies, 16*(2), 141–154.

Sklar, F., & Hartley, S. F. (1990). Close friends and survivors: Bereavement patterns in a "hidden" population. *Omega, 21*(2), 103–112.

Thornton, G., Robertson, D. U., & Mlecko, M. L. (1991). Disenfranchised grief and evaluations of social support by college students. *Death Studies, 15,* 355–362.

Thornton, G., Wittemore, K. D., & Robertson, D. U. (1989). Evaluation of people bereaved by suicide. *Death Studies, 13,* 119–126.

Weisman, A. D. (1990-1991). Bereavement and companion animals. *Omega, 22*(4), 241–248.

Worden, J. W. (1982). *Grief counseling and grief therapy: A handbook for the mental health practitioner.* New York: Springer Publishing.

Zunin, L. M., & Zunin, H. S. (1991). *The art of condolence.* New York: HarperCollins.

Suggested Readings

Attig, T. (1991). The importance of conceiving of grief as an active process. *Death Studies, 15,* 385–393. A very helpful article in assisting the bereaved to become active agents in their grieving process.

Davies, B. (1997). *Shadows in the sun: the experience of sibling bereavement in childhood.* Briston, PA: Taylor & Francis. The book brings together current informaton on sibling bereavement and explores the history of the study of sibling bereavement.

Doka, K. J. (1989). *Disenfranchised grief.* Lexington, MA: Lexington Books. A very helpful book for identifying "hidden" grievers and for expanding one's understanding of the grieving process.

Doka, K. J. (Ed.). (1995). *Children mourning, mourning children.* Washington, DC: Hospice Foundation of America. This anthology, consisting of 12 essays, covers these topics: the child's perspective of death, the child's response to life-threatening illness, grief of children and parents, and the worlds of dying children and their well siblings.

Grollman, E. (1982). *What helped me when my loved one died.* Boston: Beacon Press. A collection of personal stories of parents, wives, husbands, children, and friends.

Kay, W. J., Cohen, S. P., Nieburg, H. A., Fudin, C. E., Grey, R. E., Kutscher, A. H., & Osman, M. M. (Eds.). (1988). *Euthanasia of the companion animal.* Philadelphia: The Charles Press. An anthology of recent studies on relating to the death of pets and the effect of dying and death of pets on humans.

Lattanzi-Licht, M. E., Kirschling, J. M., & Flemming, S. (1990). *Bereavement care: A new look at hospice and community based services.* Binghamton, NY: Haworth Press. This book addresses the importance of delivery of bereavement care and services in a hospice setting. The book examines the grieving process and distinguishes between grief and clinical depression. The book is helpful for mental health professionals, social workers, chaplains, nursing personnel, and volunteers who work with the bereaved.

Manning, D. (1984). *Don't take my grief away from me.* Hereford, TX: In-Sight Books. Assistance for the bereaved in how to respond to "unhelpful friends."

Rando, T. A. (1993). *Treatment of complicated mourning.* Champaign, IL: Research Press. A comprehensive coverage of loss and grief written by a noted clinical psychologist.

Raphael, B. (1983). *The anatomy of bereavement.* New York: Basic Books. An encyclopedialike reference book on human grief and bereavement.

Schneider, J. (1994). *Finding my way: Healing and transformation through loss and grief.* Traverse City, MI: Seasons Press. An empowering book for grievers that helps to answer the following questions: "What have I lost?" "What do I have left?" and "What might be possible for me?"

Waszak, E. L. (1997). Grief: *Difficult times—simple steps.* Bristol, PA: Taylor & Francis. Practical information about what to do and what not to do for a person suffering from the death of a significant other.

Worden, J. W. (1991). *Grief counseling and grief therapy: A handbook for the mental health practitioner* (2nd ed.). New York: Springer Publishing. A very practical reference guide for the professional and lay grief counselor.

Zunin, L. M., & Zunin, H. S. (1991). *The art of condolence.* New York: HarperCollins. A book that will provide the reader with concrete skills in assisting the bereaved.

Related Web Sites

http://www.lsds.com/death/ Thanatolinks contains links to some of the best Internet sites on dying and death.

http://www.emanon.net/~kcabell/death.html Contains many World Wide Web links to resources on death and bereavement.

http://ube.ubalt.edu/www/bereavement/californ.htm Bereavement and Hospice Support Netline support groups are listed by type of bereavement loss and by group membership. Bereavement services offered by hospice programs are cross-listed under the bereavement type and the hospice heading.

http://www.growthhouse.org/ Growth House is a nonprofit organization working with grief, bereavement, hospice, and end-of-life issues.

http://www.indiana.edu/~hperf558/res_prac.html Practical Grief Resources: Grief in a Family Context.

http://www.readersndex.com/admpub/ National Directory of Bereavement Support Groups. The death of a loved one is an emotionally devastating time for survivors. But not knowing what to expect can often lead to unnecessary additional pain. This Web site offers help in alleviating some of the confusion, beginning to examine the many issues that are often hard to discuss, and finding all of the help that bereaved individuals need as they begin this journey.

http://www.inforamp.net/~bfo/index.html Bereaved Families of Ontario Support Center has an expanding information section that includes highlights from the center's newsletter as well as a monthly column. A bereavement self-help resources guide indexes the center's resources along with over 300 listings of other resources and information.

http://rivendell.org/ GriefNet provides many World Wide Web links on the bereavement process, resources for grievers, and information concerning grief support groups. Includes a link for those who have lost a pet.

http://www.equip.ac.uk/maag17/bereavement.htm The Child Bereavement Trust provides resources for families bereaved over miscarriage, stillbirth, neonatal death, and termination for abnormality.

http://gladstone.uoregon.edu/~dvb/perrylos.htm Provides core principles for helping grieving children.

http://pages.prodigy.com/CA/lycq97a/lycq97tcf.html Compassionate Friends is a self-help organization for bereaved parents and siblings. There are hundreds of chapters worldwide.

http://www.psych.med.umich.edu/web/aacap/factsFam/grief.htm The American Academy of Child and Adolescent Psychiatry provides this important information as a public service to assist parents and families in their most important roles. An article, "Children and Grief," is one such resource. Written in English, Spanish, and French.

http://www.aidskids.org/   Children With Aids Project is an organization whose role is to provide a fuller understanding of children with, and at risk of, AIDS, including the medical, psychosocial, legal, and financial issues. The mission of the organization is to develop local and national adoptive, foster, and family-centered care programs that are both effective and compassionate.

http://info-sys.home.vix.com/menmag/daddie.html   *MenWeb—M.E.N.* magazine posts an article, "Rites of Passage: Our Fathers Die," written by Bert H. Hoff (Copyright © 1993).

http://www.win.bright.net/~cnelson/Motherloss.htm   Motherloss is a group started to help with the grieving issues of adult children whose mothers have died.

http://www.fortnet.org/~goshorn/WidowNet/   Widow Net is an information and self-help resource for, and by, widows and widowers. Topics covered include grief, bereavement, recovery, and other information helpful to people of all ages, religious backgrounds, and sexual orientations who have suffered the death of a spouse or life partner.

http://www2.dgsys.com/~tgolden/honor.html   Tom Golden of the Crisis, Grief, and Healing Page offers a place to honor grief. This is a Web site where people write concerning the grief that they are experiencing at the death of a loved one.

http://members.aol.com/departed/index.html   Dearly Departed is a free service, dedicated to the memory of those who have passed away from this life but not from our hearts—a virtual World Wide Web mausoleum.

Copyrights and Acknowledgments

Literary Credits

"After Sixty Years of Marriage." *Minneapolis Star and Tribune*. 4 Oct. 1983. Copyright © 1983 Associated Press. Reprinted by permission.

Anderson, James. "Funeral Industry, Seeking New Business, Courts the Living with Special Services." Copyright © 1997 Associated Press. Reprinted by permission.

Armbruster, W.A. "Words and Meanings." *Bag of Noodles*. Copyright © 1973 Wally A. Armbruster. Reprinted by permission.

Attig, Thomas. "Death Themes in Adolescent Music." *Adolescence and Death*. Eds. C. A. Corr and J. N. McNeil. Copyright © 1986 Springer Publishing Company, Inc., New York 10012. Used by permission.

"Baby Without Brain Dies: Organs No Longer Fit to Transplant." *St. Paul Pioneer Press*. 31 Mar. 1992. Copyright © 1992 Tribune Media Services. Reprinted by permission.

Barrett, Ronald. "Psychocultural Influences on African-American Attitudes Toward Death, Dying, and Funeral Rights." *Personal Care in an Impersonal World*. Ed. John Morgan. Copyright © 1992 Baywood Publishing Company. Reprinted by permission.

Berry, Wendell. "At a Country Funeral." *The Country of Marriage*. Copyright © 1971 by Wendell Berry, reprinted by permission of Harcourt Brace & Company.

"Biography of Violet Guymer, Western Canada's First Female Licensed Funeral Director." *Quite an Undertaking*. Printed as it appeared on the World Wide Web in FuneralNet. Copyright © 1997 Nip & Tuck Publishing. Reprinted by permission.

Bishop, Katherine. "Chilling Answers to Life After Death." *New York Times*. 20 January 1989. Copyright © 1989 by The New York Times Co. Reprinted by permission.

Boulton, Doris W. "Decoration Day." *Festivals*. Sept./Oct. 1991. Copyright © 1991 ABC Consumer Magazine.

Charmaz, Kathy. "The Announcement of Death by the Coroner's Deputy." *Urban Life*. Copyright © 1975 McGraw Hill Publishing Company. Reprinted by permission.

Colker, David. "Memorial on the Net." *Minneapolis Star and Tribune*. 23 Jan. 1997. Copyright © 1997 Minneapolis Star and Tribune.

Corr, C.A. and McNeil, J. N., eds. "Talking About Death." *Adolescence and Death*. Copyright © 1986 Springer Publishing Company, Inc., New York 10012. Used by permission.

Cox, Hank. Insight. 30 Dec. 1990. Copyright © 1990 Insight Magazine.

"Cruzan v. Director, Missouri Department of Health." *The Economist*. 20 July 1991. Copyright © 1991 The Economist Newspaper Group, Inc.

DeVries, Raymond. "Bioethicists and the Medical System." Copyright © Raymond DeVries. Reprinted by permission.

DeVries, Raymond. "Should Funeral Directors Professionalize?" Copyright © Raymond DeVries. Reprinted by permission.

"Display of the Dead." *Ladies Home Journal*. Sept. 1903. Copyright © 1903 Ladies Home Journal. Reprinted by permission.

Donovan, Marilee and Sandra Pierce. "The Dying Person's Bill of Rights." *Cancer Care Nursing*. Copyright © 1976 Appleton-Century-Crofts. Reprinted by permission.

Egan, Timothy. "Creating a Pleasant Stop on the Journey to Death." *New York Times*. 8 Jan. 1992. Copyright © 1992 by The New York Times Co. Reprinted by permission.

Ericsson, Stephanie. "The Agony of Grief." *Companion Through the Darkness*. Copyright © 1993 by Stephanie Ericsson.

Faison, Seth. "Donation of Organs Is Unusual in China." *New York Times International*. 24 Feb. 1997. Copyright © 1997 by The New York Times Co. Reprinted by permission.

"Father Keeps Son's Corpse in the House." *Minneapolis Star and Tribune*. 20 Nov. 1975. Copyright © 1975 Associated Press. Reprinted by permission.

"A Few Words on Suicide: Don't Try It!" *Boston Globe*. 7 June 1981. Copyright © 1981 Boston Globe. Reprinted by permission.

Gibson, Richard. "Mother Goose, Teacher of Death." *Minneapolis Star and Tribune*. 11 April 1973. Copyright © 1973 Minneapolis Star and Tribune. Reprinted by permission.

Golden, Tom. "Anger as a Path to Grief." *Swallowed by a Snake: The Gift of the Masculine Side of Healing* by Thomas Golden LCSW. Published and excerpted through Crisis Grief and Healing <http://www.webhealing.com> at http://www.webhealing.com/3anger.html. Copyright © 1996 Tom Golden. Reprinted by permission.

Gordon, A. "The Tattered Cloak of Immortality." *Adolescence and Death*. Eds. C. A. Corr and J. N. McNeil. Copyright © 1986 Springer Publishing Company, Inc., New York 10012. Used by permission.

Greer, William R. "Putting a Price on Human Life Is Being Questioned." *The New York Times*. 30 June 1985. Copyright © 1985 by the New York Times Co. Reprinted by permission.

Grollman, Earl A. "Talking About Death." Copyright © 1970 Beacon Press. Reprinted by permission.

Hedges, Chris. "Egypt's Doctors Impose Kidney Transplant Curbs." *New York Times International*. 23 Jan. 1992. Copyright © 1992 The New York Times Co. Reprinted by permission.

Holden, Constance. "A Few Reservations Concerning the Hospice Movement." *Science*. Copyright © 1976 Science Magazine. Reprinted by permission.

"Jewish Group Buries Its Own." *Rocky Mountain News*. 25 June 1982. Copyright © 1982 Associated Press. Reprinted by permission.

Johnson, Paul V. "Book Review of The Art of Condolence by Leonard M. Zunin and Hilary Stanton Zunin." *Caregivers Quarterly*. Fall 1991. Copyright © 1991 Paul V. Johnson. Reprinted by permission.

Johnson, Paul V. "Creating Meaningful Events that Celebrate Life." *Bradshaw Quarterly*. April 1997. Copyright © Paul V. Johnson. Reprinted by permission.

Joseph, Jenny. "Warning" from *When I Am an Old Woman I Shall Wear Purple*. From SELECTED POEMS, Bloodaxe Books Ltd. Copyright © 1987 Jenny Joseph. (U.S. distributors: Dufours.) Reprinted by permission.

Kaszuba, Mike. "Funeral Home Proposed for Special Rituals of Indians." *Minneapolis Star and Tribune*. 19 Oct. 1989. Copyright © 1989 Minneapolis Star and Tribune. Reprinted by permission.

Kavanaugh, Robert E. "Religion and Dying." *Facing Death*. Copyright © 1972 Penguin Books. Reprinted by permission.

Kavanaugh, Robert E. "Religious and Secular Orientations." *Facing Death*. Copyright © 1972 Penguin Books. Reprinted by permission.

Kelly, Orville. "How to Live With a Life-Threatening Illness." *Make Each Day Count Newsletter*. Copyright © Orville Kelly. Reprinted by permission.

Klagsbrun, F. "How You Can Help in a Suicidal Crisis." *Youth and Suicide*. Copyright © 1976 Houghton Mifflin.

Lack, Sylvia A. "Hospice: A Concept of Care in the Final Stage of Life." *Connecticut Medicine*, 43(6). Copyright © 1979 Connecticut Medicine. Reprinted by permission.

Lamers, William. "Helping the Child to Grieve." *Children and Death*. Copyright © 1986 King's College Press. Reprinted by permission.

Leming, Michael R. and Sommai Premchit. "Funeral Customs in Thailand." *Personal Care in an Impersonal World*. Ed. John D. Morgan. Copyright © 1993 Baywood Publishing Company. Reprinted by permission.

"Man Revived After Obituary Published." *The News and Courier*. 28 Sept. 1985. Copyright © The News and Courier, Charleston, S.C. Reprinted by permission.

Martin, Douglas. "A Burden in Burying the Babies." *The New York Times.* 28 Mar. 1990. Copyright © 1990 by The New York Times Co. Reprinted by permission.

Maxwell, Elizabeth. "An Autopsy Observed and Experienced." Copyright © Elizabeth Maxwell. Reprinted by permission of author.

Metress, Eileen. "The American Wake of Ireland." *Omega.* Vol. 21 1990. Copyright © 1990 Baywood Publishing Company. Reprinted by permission.

Miller, James E. "Grief Tips—Help for Those Who Mourn." Copyright © 1997 James E. Miller, Willowgreen Publishing, Fort Wayne, Indiana. Reprinted by permission.

Moody Jr., Raymond A. "Life after Life." *Life after Life: The Investigation of a Phenomenon—Survival of Bodily Death.* Copyright © LAL, Inc. Reprinted by permission.

Morris, R.A. "Po Starykovsky (The Old People's Way)." *Coping With the Final Tragedy: Cultural Variation in Dying and Grieving.* Eds. D.R. Counts and D.A. Counts . Copyright © 1991 Baywood Publishing Company. Reprinted by permission.

Nordby, Ann. "With End in Sight: Daniel Rasmussen Chose How to Die." As it appeared in *Northfield [Minnesota] News,* Nov. 27, 1992. Copyright © 1992 Northfield News. Reprinted by permission.

Nygren, Rose. Letter. 26 Oct. 1994. Copyright © 1994 Rose Nygren. Reprinted by permission.

"On Death as a Constant Companion." *Time Magazine.* 12 Nov. 1965. Copyright © 1965 Time, Inc.

Paxton, Tom. "Forest Lawn." Copyright © 1969 c/o EMI UNART CATALOG INC. World print rights controlled and administered by CPP/BELWIN, INC., Miami, FL. All rights reserved.

Phipps, William E. "Individual Life Expectancy." Reproduced *from Death: Confronting the Reality* by William E. Phipps. Copyright ©1987 John Knox Press. Used by permission of Westminster John Knox Press.

Pieters, A. Stephen. "Home at the Hospice." Column carried at *The Body,* http://www.thebody.com, an AIDS and HIV information resource. Copyright © 1996 A. Stephen Pieters. Reprinted by permission.

Pospisil, Leopold. "Kapauku Papuans." *The Kapauku Papuans of West New Guinea.* Copyright © 1963 Holt, Rinehart, & Winston. Reprinted by permission.

Rahman, Fazlur. "Why Pound Life into the Dying." *New York Times.* 22 Feb. 1989. Copyright © 1989 The New York Times Co. Reprinted by permission.

Rambachan, Anant. "Understanding Death in Hinduism." Copyright © A. Rambachan. Reprinted by permission.

Richter, Elizabeth. "Did I Really Love My Brother?" *U. S. News and World Report.* 4 Aug. 1986. Copyright © 1986 U. S. News and World Report. Reprinted by permission.

Rigney, Ernest G. "Heaven's Gate: An Example of Mass Suicide." Copyright © 1997 Ernest G. Rigney. Reprinted by permission.

"The Ritual Solution." *Newsweek.* 22 Sept. 1997. Copyright © 1997, Newsweek, Inc. All rights reserved. Reprinted by permission.

Quill, Timothy E. "My Patient's Suicide." *New England Journal of Medicine.* 7 March 1991, Vol. 284. Copyright © 1991 New England Journal of Medicine. Reprinted by permission.

Salaam, J.K. "Cutting the Body Loose." *UTNE Reader* Sept./Oct. 1991. Copyright © 1991 K. Salaam. Reprinted by permission.

"Signs of Approaching Death and What to Do to Add Comfort." Copyright © Visiting Nurses Association of Los Angeles, Hospice in the Home Program. Reprinted by permission.

Smith, JoAnn Kelley. *The Free Fall.* Copyright © 1975 JoAnn Kelley Smith. Reprinted by permission.

Soli, Jane. "A Wednesday Afternoon." Copyright © Jane Soli. Reprinted by permission.

Spencer, A.J. *Death in Ancient Egypt.* Copyright © 1982 A.J. Spencer. Reproduced by permission of Penguin Books Ltd.

Swerdlow, Joel L. "The Recycled Man." *Washington Post.* 25 June 1989. Excerpted from *Matching Needs, Saving Lives* published by The Annenberg Washington Program in Communication Policy Studies of Northwestern University. Copyright © 1989 Joel L. Swedlow. Reprinted by permission.

Thomas, Lewis. *Late Night Thoughts on Listening to Mahler's Ninth Symphony.* Copyright © 1982 by Lewis Thomas. Reprinted by permission of Viking Penguin, a division of Penguin Books USA.

Titus, Sandra L., Paul C. Rosenblatt, and Roxanne M. Anderson. "Family Conflict over Inheritance of Property." *The Family Coordinator.* July 1979. Copyright © 1979 by the National Council on Family Relations. Reprinted by permission.

Torok, Tom. "A Good Friend Goes Up in Smoke." *Philadelphia Inquirer.* 28 June 1992. Copyright © 1992 Philadelphia Inquirer. Reprinted by permission.

"A True Die-Hard Fan: He'll Attend Game in Urn." *Arizona Daily Star.* 22 Jan. 1989. Copyright © 1989 Associated Press. Reprinted by permission.

Van Eys, Jan. "In My Opinion." *Children's Health Care.* Summer 1988. Copyright © 1988 Children's Health Care, ACCH. Reprinted by permission.

Vernon, Glenn M. "What Caregivers Should Not Assume about the Dying." Copyright © Glenn M. Vernon. Reprinted by permission.

Wallechinsky, D. and I. Wallace. "Grave Remarks." *The People's Almanac.* Copyright © 1975 Doubleday & Company. Reprinted by permission.

Waller, B. "Livening Up the Funeral Industry." *Twin Cities Business Monthly.* Oct. 1996. Copyright © 1996 Twin Cities Business Monthly.

Ward, Joe. "When Death Takes Your Child." *The Louisville Courier Journal,* 27 July 1980. Copyright © 1980 Louisville Courier Journal. Reprinted by permission.

White, Janet. "Sharing the Journey: A Ministry in Hospice." *The Lutheran Journal,* 60(3). Copyright © 1992 The Lutheran Journal, Minneapolis, MN. Reprinted by permission.

Wilkerson, Isabel. "New Funeral Option for Those in a Rush." *New York Times.* 23 Feb. 1989. Copyright © 1989 by The New York Times Co. Reprinted by permission.

"Woman Sends 'Love Letters' to 465 Seriously Ill Children." *The News and Courier.* 30 July 1988. Copyright © 1988 News and Courier. Reprinted by permission.

Cartoon Credits / Photo Credits

2 © Ed Simpson/Tony Stone Images. 12 © Tennessee Tech University Department of Archives. Used by permission. 17 © Robert Harbison. 28 United Nations/Jeffrey J. Foxx. 38 AP/World Wide Photos. 41 AP/World Wide Photos. 42 George Dickinson. 51 George Dickinson. 70 Reproduced form the collections of the Library of Congress. 87 © Robert Harbison. 91 © Joel Gordon. 108 © Skeeter Hagler. 111 © Skeeter Hagler. 127 © Joel Gordon. 132 © Spencer Grant/Photo Researchers. 140 © Abraham Menashe. 143 © Ed Lettau/Photo Researchers. 154 Michael Leming. 158 UPI/Corbis-Bettman. 165 Michael Leming. 171 AP/World Wide Photos 176 TV Guide, November 11, 1978. Used by permission of Henry Martin. 186 © Abraham Menashe. 191 George Dickinson. 196 © Skeeter Hagler. 209 Reprinted with special permission of King Features Syndicate. 212 © John Louthan. 217 © Spencer Grant/Photo Researchers. 230 © Joel Gordon. 237 © Joel Gordon. 239 © Joel Gordon. 250 © Joel Gordon. 252 George Dickinson. 274 © Joel Gordon. 288 Reuters/Corbis-Bettman. 298 © Mike Vogl. 306 © Abraham Menashe. 314 © Stanley J. Foreman/Boston World-American. 318 © Jack Pottle 1980/Design Conceptions. 330 STEVE BENSON, reprinted by permission of United Feature Syndicate, Inc. 346 © Skeeter Hagler. 355 © Bernard Pierre Wolff/Photo Researchers. 360 © Victor Englebert/Photo Researchers. 363 Peter Buckley/Photo Researchers. 373 © Bernard Pierre Wolff/Photo Researchers. 382 Corbis-Bettmann. 385 Reproduced from the collections of the Library of Congress. 388 Reproduced from the collections of the Library of Congress. 392 Michael Leming. 395 George Dickinson. 424 © Joel Gordon. 426 Reproduced by courtesy of the British Museum. 448 Mike Leming. 454 National Foundation of Funeral Directors. 468 © Abraham Menashe. 482 © Joel Gordon 1978. 486 AP/World Wide Photos. 491 The NAMES Project, Fort Worth/Tarrant County. 497 Frost Publishing Group/Bill Powers.

Index